D1594957

WASHINGTON CONFERENCE ON HOLOCAUST-ERA ASSETS
November 30-December 3, 1998

PROCEEDINGS

Hosted by the United States Department of State
and
The United States Holocaust Memorial Museum

Stuart E. Eizenstat, Under Secretary of State for Economic, Business and Agricultural Affairs
Miles Lerman, Chairman, United States Holocaust Memorial Council

The Honorable Abner J. Mikva
Conference Chairman

D
810
$.C8$
$W37$
1999

Edited by
J.D. Bindenagel
Conference Director
U.S. Department of State

For sale by the U.S. Government Printing Office
Superintendent of Documents, Mail Stop: SSOP, Washington, DC 20402-9328
ISBN 0-16-049949-6

ISBN 0-16-049949-6

9 780160 499494

90000

MESSAGE FROM THE EDITOR

These are the Proceedings of the Washington Conference on Holocaust-Era Assets, held November 30 – December 3, 1998 in Washington, D.C. The Conference, co-hosted by the U.S. Department of State and the United States Holocaust Memorial Museum, was a government-organized, international meeting of forty-four governments and thirteen non-governmental organizations (NGOs). Participants sought to address the issue of assets confiscated by the Nazis during the Holocaust (1933-45), specifically art and insurance, as well as communal property, archives and books, and to conclude any remaining gold issues. In addition, the Conference dealt with the role of historical commissions and Holocaust education, remembrance and research. The agenda for the Conference (see Appendix E, pages 931-948) consisted of plenary sessions where all asset classes were discussed, followed by "break-out" sessions in which each topic was discussed in greater detail. The daylong session on Holocaust education, remembrance and research was also an integral element of the Washington Conference.

The Proceedings of the Washington Conference include the following: formal statements made by presenters during the Conference; "delegation statements" submitted during or after the Conference; "position papers" provided by delegations as part of the official record; interventions made from the floor during free discussion periods that were submitted in writing for purposes of publication; and related documents that are included for the historical record.

The papers published in this report are reproduced from text provided by participants in the Conference. Some spelling and layout changes have been made, but content and word usage has not been altered. Authors of individual statements – not the publisher – are responsible for the use of italics, bold print or underlining for purposes of emphasis. The U.S. Department of State does not endorse the views expressed in individual statements.

The following people deserve recognition for their outstanding contributions to the compilation and production of these proceedings: Richard A. Smith, Jr., Jody Manning, Holly Waeger, Ananta Hans and Derrick Holmes. The publication of these documents would not have been possible without their efforts and steadfast dedication.

J.D. Bindenagel
February 19, 1999

Department of State Publication 10603
Bureau of European Affairs

Released April 1999

Washington Conference on Holocaust-Era Assets
PROCEEDINGS

TABLE OF CONTENTS

OPENING STATEMENTS

CONCLUDING STATEMENTS

DELEGATION STATEMENTS

NAZI-CONFISCATED ART ISSUES

Plenary Session

Break-out Session

HOLOCAUST-ERA INSURANCE CLAIMS

Plenary Session

Break-out Session

COMMUNAL PROPERTY

Plenary Session

Break-out Session

ARCHIVES, BOOKS AND THE
ROLE OF HISTORICAL COMMISSIONS

Plenary Session

Break-out Session

HOLOCAUST EDUCATION, REMEMBRANCE AND RESEARCH

APPENDICES

Opening Statements

Opening Ceremony Remarks at the United States Holocaust Memorial Museum Mr. Miles Lerman

CHAIRMAN, UNITED STATES HOLOCAUST
MEMORIAL COUNCIL
UNITED STATES

It is proper and most fitting that this conference began with a symbolic ceremony of silent contemplation in the Hall of Remembrance of the Holocaust Memorial Museum where we invoked memory and paid tribute to those who were consumed in the Nazi inferno.

Now let me welcome you to the Washington Conference on Holocaust-Era Assets. The United States Holocaust Memorial Museum is pleased to co-chair with the State Department this historic event.

For the next three days representatives of 44 countries will have the opportunity to explore a just and orderly return of confiscated assets to their rightful owners.

It took over 50 years for the world to come to grips with the fact that the biggest murder of the century; it was also, as my friend Ben Meed reminds us, the biggest robbery in history.

This fact is not limited to one country only. What really shocked the conscience of the world was the discovery that even after the war, some countries tried to gain materially from this cataclysm by refusing to return to the rightful owners what was justly theirs. The refusal to respond to these rightful claims was a great injustice, a moral wrong which can not be ignored.

And this is what brings us together today.

We are here to make sure that these wrongs are corrected in a just and proper manner.

Under Secretary Eizenstat and Edgar Bronfman deserve our gratitude for their unrelenting efforts to bring about full accountability for all wrongs that must be made right.

Among us are countries that on their own volition began this process. These countries are to be complimented for setting the right examples.

The issue of Nazi-era assets is very complex. It will require a thorough research of archival data of the countries involved. Some of these archival repositories are still inaccessible. This is a major obstacle to the discovery process, which we must overcome.

We, at the Holocaust Museum, have made strides in the area. We have gained access to many archival repositories and we hope to be helpful in the discovery process. However, we as a group must use our collective influence to obtain unrestricted access to all archival repositories of this period.

Only then will we be able to resolve the outstanding issues judiciously.

A lot of progress has been made. The agreement which the World Jewish Congress has negotiated with Swiss banks is a step in the right direction.

It is clear that survivors can never be compensated for their decimated families and destroyed lives. They are, however, entitled to a full accounting of all the assets that were confiscated from them or their families. For this, they must be fully compensated.

However, as imperative as the financial settlements are, it is important to bear in mind that the last word on the Holocaust cannot be gold or bank accounts.

The final objective must be remembrance. The lessons of the Holocaust must continue to serve as a reminder and a warning to you, to me and to future generations that will follow.

This is why this conference has decided to deal with ongoing Holocaust education extensively.

Some countries have begun various educational programs and we applaud them for there efforts. However, we must aim to create a global network of Holocaust education that would be both general and country specific.

We at the Holocaust Museum have substantial experience in this field. We work annually with 30,000 teachers on all levels, representing many disciplines. Should this conference endorse an international Holocaust education initiative, we at the Holocaust Museum stand ready to assist you in any necessary form to make sure that such efforts are fruitful and productive.

I am sure that Yad Vashem, who has vast experience in this field, would be ready to do the same.

Secretary Eizenstat, Judge Abner Mikva, the chairman of this conference, and I are looking forward to working with you to make sure that the next 3 days move us ahead with our goals and objectives and we return to our respective homes with a sense of tangible accomplishments. The memory of the victims demands no less.

Thank you very much.

And now I have the honor to introduce to you a man who has made an enormous effort to make this conference happen.

Ladies and gentlemen, please welcome the Under Secretary of State for Economic, Business and Agricultural Affairs, Stuart Eizenstat.

Opening Ceremony Remarks at the United States Holocaust Memorial Museum
Stuart E. Eizenstat

UNDER SECRETARY OF STATE FOR ECONOMIC, BUSINESS AND AGRICULTURAL AFFAIRS
UNITED STATES

Chairman Lerman, Members of Congress, Elie Wiesel, national delegations, ladies and gentleman: It is a great honor and privilege to address you this evening, here at this American national treasure – the U.S. Holocaust Memorial Museum.

More than five and a half years ago, when President Clinton dedicated this living memorial, he said: "This museum is not for the dead alone, nor even for the survivors who have been so beautifully represented; it is perhaps most of all for those of us who were not there at all, to learn the lessons, to deepen our memories and our humanity, and to transmit those lessons from generation to generation."

As we join together this evening, those eloquent words echo throughout this solemn space. Before I continue, let me pay tribute to my old and dear friend Miles Lerman for both his tireless leadership of this institution and for his willingness to join with me as the co-Chairman of the Washington Conference on Holocaust-era Assets.

In addition, it is a particular honor to be standing with another friend, Nobel Prize winner Elie Wiesel. His remarkable bearing of personal witness to the seemingly unimaginable horror of the Holocaust has shed eternal light on the darkness of that unique tragedy, By doing so, he has brought its enduring lessons to a worldwide audience and through his literature has ensured that his witness is an enduring gift to humanity.

The Washington Conference, like the London Nazi Gold Conference, of one year ago, promises to be a landmark event. It may well represent the last full opportunity for the international community to gather and write the final chapter in the unfinished business of perhaps the greatest human tragedy of this or any other century. It is yet another of this century's innumerable and seemingly endless tragedies that for nearly fifty years the fate of assets seized during the Holocaust remained largely undiscovered and uninvestigated.

For those who suffered at the hands of the Nazis; for those who lost entire families; for those who survived the Holocaust only to then fall under the iron fist of Communism; for those who have endured years of poverty and misery because of the world's neglect Slid failure; for those whose lives and deaths are poignantly memorialized in this museum: Our efforts to bring justice are done with a heavy heart and the knowledge that in so many ways, our work comes too late.

For those who, against unimaginable odds, are still alive today, our work must be guided by an urgent resolve to ensure that those who survived the tragedy of the Holocaust will not continue to suffer in poverty and fear.

For those who perished, our efforts must be galvanized by an unrelenting aspiration to uncover the truth and to seek justice for both the living and the dead.

Only then can we provide a last – albeit inadequate – measure of justice for those who died. As painful as it may sometimes be, we must not sweep these issues under the rug of embarrassment, silence and indifference.

The often traumatic efforts over the past several years of so many countries and institutions to come to terms with their conduct during World War II – however overdue – is nonetheless inspiring. The international community, at last, shares a common interest in the quest for justice and the search for truth.

Through our effort, we are together building lasting bridges between yesterday and today; between brutality and humanity; between searing history and enduring memory; between tragedy and rebirth; between darkness and light.

While turning the page on this black chapter of history, we must take from the lessons of yesterday a renewed commitment to usher in a new and brighter century. Our words must provide enduring lessons from this awful experience, guiding all our countries to act with a greater sensitivity to present and future crimes against humanity, even if on a different scale.

Only then will we know if our efforts have had a practical impact. Teaching future generations about the Holocaust and, the theft of

Opening Ceremony Remarks at the United States Holocaust Memorial Museum
Elie Wiesel

FOUNDING CHAIRMAN, UNITED STATES
HOLOCAUST MEMORIAL COUNCIL
AND NOBEL LAUREATE

Judge Mikva, Stuart Eizenstat, Chairman Lerman, distinguished members of Congress, my good friends.

As you are about to begin a three-day introspection of your national psyche, may I first ask a few questions. Why so late? Why only now? Why this sudden concern for stolen money and fortunes? Why has it taken so long in fulfilling the biblical command that stolen property must be returned to its owners? Why is it that it took an Edgar Bronfman, Stu Eizenstat, Israel Singer, Elan Steinberg? The group is so small. Why is it that all of a sudden things became apparent, thanks to these few people? Where were the others?

Permit me to express my hope that we have not come here to speak about money. We have come here to speak about conscience, morality and memory. Usually, anti-Semites say about us Jews that we speak about lofty things, but we mean money. Just the opposite. Here, we speak about money, but we think of other things. The man who speaks to you belongs to a traumatized generation which is still oscillating between anger and gratitude. Gratitude for what we owe our friends, and anger at those, who, in our times of distress and solitude, have withdrawn into comfortable indifference.

Inspired by moral rather than financial concerns, this conference in this place which is so particular, so important, so essential to our national survival as human beings everywhere, this conference is important because it illustrates and perhaps embodies an irresistible quest for both justice, as Stuart said, and compassion, as you have said.

But why now? Why is it taking place at such a late date under the moral pressure of public opinion? These questions face us when we deal with the issues that motivated these meetings. You know that.

More than fifty-odd years have elapsed since the Allied victory over Nazism and Fascism uncovered the horrors of Auschwitz, Majdanek and Treblinka. Innumerable testimonies have been published, witnesses interrogated, widely-publicized trials held, criminals prosecuted, and in some cases, punished.

Political scientists, psychologists, philosophers, essayists, psychiatrists and theologians have done much research on what happened in those years of malediction, in the darkest of all kingdoms.

Here and there, people wanted to know everything about all aspects of what we so poorly call the Holocaust. Yet, somehow, its simple economic aspect seems to have been utterly neglected.

Why? Is it that we all felt the memory of the tragedy to be so sacred that we preferred not to talk about its concrete, financial and material implications? Or is it that the task of protecting that memory was so noble, so painful, but so urgent that we simply felt it undignified to think of anything else – and surely not of bank accounts? In truth, we feel reticent to talk about it even now.

Is it that intellectually and morally we could not accept the possibility that the Holocaust was for the killers a combination of both perverse, hate-filled idealism and convenient, cheap robbery?

There may have been another reason as well. In those years, survivors had more urgent problems to solve than to demand restitution. They had to adjust to freedom, life and death – normal death. Their tragedy did not end with the end of the war. It continued long after. On ruins, and haunted by invisible cemeteries, they had to rebuild hope and faith. Those who wanted to go to Palestine could not get British certificates and had to go there illegally. Some returned to their homes and were met by open hostility.

My sister Beatrice went back to Sighet hoping to find me there. Our house was occupied by strangers. In certain cities and villages, local people greeted their former Jewish neighbors with scorn, "What, you are not dead?" and chased them away. So, many left everything behind and went to stay in D.P. camps in Germany and Austria, where they were treated with no special consideration.

Listen to excerpts from a report by The New York Times, dated September 30th, 1945.

"President Truman has directed General Eisenhower to clean up alleged shocking conditions in the treatment of displaced Jews in Germany outside the Russian Zone and in Austria." The report declared that "displaced Jews were held behind barbed wire in camps guarded by our men, camps in which frequently, conditions were unsanitary and the food poor and insufficient. With our military more concerned with other matters, some of the displaced Jews were sick and without adequate medicine," the report stated, "and many had to wear prison garb, or to their chagrin, German SS uniforms. All were wondering," it was added, "if they had been liberated after all, and were despairing of help while worrying about the fate of relatives."

They were, in many cases, the report said, "behind barbed wire in camps formerly used by the Germans for their prisoners, including the notorious Bergen-Belsen camp. Nearly all had lost hope," he stated. "The Germans in rural areas whom the Jews look out upon from the camps were better fed, better clothed, and better housed than the" quote, 'liberated' unquote, Jews, the report declared.

And the report noted – remember, a few months after liberation – "As matters now stand, we appear to be treating the Jews as the Nazis treated them except that we do not exterminate them. They are in concentration camps, in large numbers under our own military guard instead of S.S. troops. One wonders whether the German people, seeing this, are not supposing that we are following or at least condoning the Nazi policy."

And you would expect these refugees, uprooted human beings, to organize immensely complex legal mechanisms capable of obtaining from banks, museums and governments the restitution of what had been theirs? They were treated everywhere as poor cousins, at best. They were not even asked to play a role in the early negotiations with Germany in 1953.

In truth, the search for the missing monies, apartments and collections of art should have been initiated long ago and more elegantly, with a greater measure of grace – by banks and governments themselves. And I speak of neutral countries, as well as of countries which had been occupied by the Germans.

Now we know that some did that, some were gracious – but for the wrong reasons. More precisely, for the benefit of the wrong people. Almost under duress, efforts were being made to ask for the restitution of what had been stolen. In some places, because Jews had asked for the restitution, a new wave of anti-Semitism swept the country. The prophet's outcry to the king, *"Haraz-tachta vegam yarashta,"* "You have committed murder and now you wish to inherit the victim's fortune as well" reverberated in our ears and in our wounded hearts for many years. In Romania, Poland, Lithuania, the Ukraine and elsewhere in the Communist empire, Jewish cultural centers and synagogues, libraries and museums, hospitals and children's homes had been confiscated, demolished, or transformed into storage rooms, stables, shops or offices. And nobody cared. People in high places chose to forget that the "final solution" targeted both collectivities and individuals.

So, how can one not speak with anger?

Oh, yes. What they have done after the war to those who survived – a few of them – it had a double effect on the victims, surely, but also on those whom they have left behind. For a long, very long time, both were forgotten or humiliated.

This conference constitutes proof that there exists now, thanks to a few people that I mentioned – but then it became contagious – there exists a desire to correct the injustices. The fact is that you are here, and that proves that of course, you were not responsible for what happened years ago. But it proves also that you now are committed to this noble, magnificent effort.

I say injustices, but I mean some injustices. The true injustice, the one dealing with the murder of six million Jewish men, women and children, can never and will never be corrected. For them it is too late. For some of their heirs it is not.

It is up to you to provide all needy survivors with comprehensive health insurance and old age homes. Why don't you create a special publishing house to print their testimonies, give the survivors a feeling that their memories are important, that their experience is not lost? What they have to say, no one can say. No one ever will.

Thus, it is really a matter not of money but of moral demand and of commitment to conscience and memory. Memory is our shield. Memory is our fortune, our only fortune. So, let us remember not only the big fortunes, palaces and art treasures. Let us remember also the less wealthy families: the small merchants, the cobblers, the peddlers, the school teachers, the water carriers, the beggars. The enemy robbed them of their poverty.

Even if we could receive, as a gesture of compensation or an act of repentance, all the money in the world, it would not diminish the pain we feel for the death of one Jewish child in Birkenau.

We are here because we remember. And that, in itself, is sufficient to enable us to replace justifiable anger with impossible hope, especially since we must admit that there were good people, too. There were good people in all of those places, good men and women with kind hearts, good officials with compassionate attitudes. And we are eternally grateful to them, as we are always, on a different level. We say *lehavdil* always to the state of Israel, simply because the state of Israel is here as a home, as a dream that continues to be a dream even in reality.

Now, you are about to begin your discussions. May I tell you that personally I was not and am not involved in this phase of remembrance. We were not rich at home. Romania's former president wanted to make my house into a new museum, but I preferred it to be inhabited by homeless families. My books, those I bought with my pocket money in my childhood are lying in dust somewhere; I don't even know where. Who can give them back to me? Who will give back the prayerbooks, the *tallith* and the *tefilin* my father and I had in our bags when we left for a place named Auschwitz? Who will give back what we have lost as individual Jews and as communities?

I remember – I shall always remember – a little girl, a child with golden hair and blue eyes, so heartbreakingly innocent. She had taken a beautiful scarf with her, a scarf which she had received as a present for Passover. She had no golden earrings, no bracelet, no watch, no jewelry, nothing expensive, nothing special, nothing but that scarf. That was her most cherished possession. You tell me: Are there enough funds in all your banks to compensate her brother for her beautiful scarf and for her golden hair? It is of them that you must think, today and tomorrow, the day after tomorrow, and the day after and the year after when you discuss money.

Thank you.

Opening Remarks
Mr. Miles Lerman

CHAIRMAN, UNITED STATES HOLOCAUST
MEMORIAL COUNCIL
UNITED STATES

Distinguished Dignitaries, Members of the Diplomatic Corps, Conference Delegates, Ladies and Gentlemen:

Last night at the opening ceremony of the Washington Conference on Holocaust Era-Assets, which was held in the Hall of Remembrance of the United States Holocaust Memorial Museum, we invoked memory and paid tribute to the victims of the Nazi inferno.

We remembered the six million Jews who were murdered for one reason only because they were born Jewish. We paid tribute to the millions of others who perished at the hands of the Nazis.

In our personal introspection, we remembered the fact that the Holocaust did not begin with the mass killings in Eastern Europe. The Holocaust began when Nazi mobs burned and desecrated synagogues throughout Germany and Austria, looted Jewish stores, and humiliated and incarcerated their owners while neighbors and friends remained silent and looked the other way.

The Holocaust began when Germany's social and legal institutions supported a political regime that openly professed total disregard for the sanctity of human life.

These are facts that we must always bear in mind.

Within the next three days, the representatives of 44 Nations will engage in personal soul searching in an effort to undertake a financial and moral audit of their own Nation's conduct in those dreadful days.

We are here to acknowledge and bring to the attention of the world the fact that the Holocaust was not limited to mass murder.

With the Holocaust also came the greatest theft in human history – the theft of money, art, gold, precious manuscripts, insurance policies, and a host of other victims' assets.

It was not merely about murder and theft; it was also about the destruction of a way of life. Indeed, the collective culture of the Jewish people of Europe was devastated. Communal Jewish life in Eastern Europe was totally shattered and irreparably eviscerated.

For decades, some in this room and many others around the world have worked hard to preserve the memory of those who perished in the Holocaust. These guardians of memory deserve our sincere admiration for ensuring that the flame of remembrance will burn brightly into the next century.

But you are looking at a man and a generation that understand that the process of passing the torch must begin. It is only a matter of time before the last Holocaust survivor and witness passes on.

We are fortunate that the children of survivors and their children understand the imperative of continuing the legacy of remembrance.

For the sake of their future, our responsibility in the coming days is to further a process that began in London to bring some justice to the victims, their heirs, and to surviving remnant communities.

We must ask ourselves, how will history judges us? We must ask, was there enough done to save lives, to stop the robbery, to fight the evil that descended across Europe?

Our responsibility must be to examine the conduct of our own respective nations. We must look at our own governments, our own population. And most importantly, we must ask ourselves, is there enough being done today in our respective countries to teach our citizens about this tragic period in history? Are we bearing witness to both – to the noble and the hideous?

Do we have the courage to acknowledge the black spots on our national history?

Are we teaching our children the horrible lessons of the Holocaust? And are we using these stories as a lesson and a warning?

Some of these themes will be covered at the State Department, but especially at the Holocaust education sessions on Wednesday at the United States Holocaust Memorial Museum. On that day, delegates from around the world will explore and share ideas of how best to implement a global network of Holocaust educational and remembrance programs, as well as, research projects.

These are the programs that will be a true measure of the success of this conference, since Holocaust education will impact generations to come long after all outstanding financial claims will be accounted for.

As we begin our deliberations and as we begin to involve ourselves in the minutia of one asset category or another – let us resolve to not forget why we are here and what history expects of us.

Among those special people who fully understand and the magnitude and importance of this Washington Conference is its Chairman, whom I have the pleasure of introducing at this time.

We are fortunate that Judge Abner Mikva was chosen to chair this Conference. He is a man of great intelligence, broad public service, and has a deep and heartfelt appreciation of the Holocaust and its consequences.

Judge Mikva served as White House Counsel to President Clinton, and for many years served with distinction as Chief Judge of the U.S. Court of appeal for the District of Columbia.

Before coming to the bench, he ably represented his Chicago district in the U.S. House of Representatives for 10 years.

Ladies and Gentlemen please welcome Judge Abner Mikva.

Chairman's Opening Statement
The Honorable Abner J. Mikva

CONFERENCE CHAIRMAN

INTRODUCTION

Secretary Albright, Under Secretary Eizenstat, Mr. Lerman, distinguished delegates and friends: I am deeply honored to serve as Chairman of this remarkable conference, and I am grateful for the confidence you have placed in me. I have a great admiration and respect for the groundbreaking work initiated at the London Nazi Gold Conference exactly one year ago. I have particular respect for Lord Mackay's skillful and impartial chairmanship of that Conference -- a standard that I will strive to meet.

The London Conference was a significant milestone in documenting the historical record of Nazi-era confiscation of gold and monetary assets. Out of that conference emerged an international consensus that remaining issues needed to be addressed quickly and compassionately. Thanks to your work then and since, which we will review briefly later this morning, we all have a better understanding of the terrible human price exacted during this tragic period. I am honored to participate in this process – itself historic – of completing some of the unfinished business of the Holocaust and the Second World War.

GOALS OF THE CONFERENCE

Our goal this week is to build on the positive momentum generated by the London Conference as we turn to other categories of assets: art and insurance in particular, as well as communal property. First, we need to complete the international historical record in this area so that we can gain a better understanding of the events and issues that have shaped where we stand today. Second, with this historical context as our basis, we can then turn to current efforts for handling these issues fairly and openly. Countries have already made important progress in developing broad principles and specific processes for dealing with these issues. Finally, I look forward to hearing the reports and discussions of the presenters and delegations and expect we will be able to draw on these shared initiatives and experiences to forge consensus on principles and practices that we can use to resolve remaining issues. This is the central concept underpinning our agenda and I hope that it will frame the legacy of the Washington Conference.

The basic framework for the plenaries and break-out sessions will be to review and add to the historical record, identify the issues involved, discuss past and present restitution efforts and consider how the international community can agree on effective ways to move forward on finding solutions in the art, insurance and communal property areas in particular—as well as highlighting the importance of opening archives, considering the fate of looted books and not least important, promoting Holocaust education and remembrance.

As you can see, the agenda for this Conference is exceedingly challenging, even for the three days allotted. The issues with which we will be dealing are both extremely complex and highly charged. We have over 80 presenters providing expertise and opinion. We also have 60 delegations. As a result, some delegations may not have an opportunity to make interventions from the floor, or will want to make more detailed interventions than the time available. As Chairman of the Conference, I – and the Chairmen of the various break-out sessions – will seek to maximize the time available for interventions and to recognize as wide a body of comment as possible. If, in the end, this proves insufficient, I want to remind delegations that they may submit position papers that will become part of the official record of this Conference. Instructions for this have already been provided to delegations.

In the field of Nazi-confiscated art, we are honored to have as presenters several scholars who have studied the historical record to identify what the Nazis did with art and why they did it. We know that thousands of works were taken from victims of the Holocaust, some by expropriation, some by forced sale, some after house-to-house searches by agents of the Nazi regime. Many were parts of important collections; all were precious to those who owned them.

In recent years there has been a growing awareness of the problem and greater efforts to identify confiscated art. Resolving ownership claims presents questions for governments, as well as for museums, galleries, dealers and collectors. We hope, in this Conference, to explore what happened to art during the War and its aftermath, to hear how various countries are addressing the issue today, to gain an understanding of the practical problems involved in identifying this art and finding its pre-War owners, and to encourage a candid discussion of the problems and the equities involved. As we continue to work to find missing art works and missing owners or heirs, we must establish creative, constructive guidelines for the often complex and emotional cases of confiscated art that remain.

As a judge, I know that justice is often in the eye of the beholder. One such example of a creative solution involved a contested art work that was resolved by one party receiving compensation for half of the value of the work, while the other party donated its half of the work to a museum where it will be available for viewing by the public. That happened in my own city of Chicago.

Much work has already been done on both sides of the Atlantic by a number of governments and private entities alike to identify guidelines for use in resolving these issues. I hope the Conference can agree on a group of principles that can be followed in resolving these questions, so that justice can be done, and the purchase and sale and display of works of art can proceed, free of the impediment of history. Indeed, the Conference organizers circulated a discussion paper comprising eleven general principles relating to Nazi-confiscated art during consultations for this Conference. We have put another copy of this paper in each delegation's box. I urge you to consider these principles and hope that we can reach consensus on them during the Conference.

On insurance, another immensely complex and sensitive issue, we will also examine the historical record and consider the particular efforts of governments to provide compensation. We will also focus on current solutions to this half-century old problem—including the recent establishment of the International Commission (IC) made up of regulators, companies, survivor organizations, and Jewish groups. The IC will adjudicate claims and pay claimants even if they cannot establish a claim. It can also provide relief to survivors in need. I hope that the Conference will consider whether this particular process is a promising way forward to resolve these very difficult issues.

The issue of communal property encompasses property seized by the Nazis and other authoritarian regimes from religious groups. In addition to real estate, this property also includes religious artifacts including torahs. The circumstances of each property vary considerably, as do the legal situations in each country where the property is located. Our presenters will describe the wartime, post-war, and post-Cold War history as well as efforts on the part of countries, including those in Central and Eastern Europe, to identify procedures that are realistic and practical. I hope we can identify a procedure in each country, which is equitable, transparent, non-discriminatory and expeditious. While that is a tall order, nothing less will assure that justice is finally done in this area.

The Conference will also address two other important sets of issues, which, while not categorized as assets, are no less tangible or essential to our entire enterprise. First, we will consider the issue of archives both in terms of their progressive opening in recent years and their role as the basis for the work of the many national historical commissions that are with us at the Conference.

Second, we will also focus on the importance of Holocaust education and remembrance activities. We will highlight the work of the International Task Force on Holocaust Education, Remembrance and Research—an unprecedented and innovative effort on the part of Sweden, the United Kingdom, the United States, Germany and Israel to promote international cooperation in these areas of enduring importance. By identifying common projects that countries can undertake in the area of education, we have the opportunity to make a long-lasting contribution to widespread understanding and acknowledgement of this tragic period in the world's history.

CONCLUSION

I am enthusiastic and excited about the opportunity this Conference has to clarify the historical record, increase the world's awareness of the many layers of complexity at work during the Holocaust era, and to establish common approaches to the problems remaining from that time. We are all affected by and held responsible for the consequences of our history. In striving to remember the past honestly, we show our respect for the unprecedented human suffering that occurred and our commitment to reconciliation. By remembering, by providing a measure of justice, we can accept the past and build a more equitable future.

By our actions we are setting an example for following generations of integrity. We need to seek solutions for difficult circumstances that express our inner sense of justice. The fact that we have assembled 56 delegations made up of government officials, historians, art experts and NGOs from 43 countries is a tribute to the international community's involvement in working together to find common approaches to these important issues. While we are not here to make government decisions on specific course of action on each set of issues, we do have the opportunity to reach a consensus where we can. I hope to use my concluding statement to highlight some of these specific ways where our countries are moving forward to resolve, finally, these issues still lingering from the past.

I want to thank you all for coming together at this historic Conference; your active participation in this process has already contributed to the international search for truth and the quest for justice. It is a privilege for us to work together to face these difficult issues and find solutions. Our efforts here this week can go far towards restoring trust and faith in the rule of law and accountability for acts regardless of historical constraints.

Keynote Address
Madeleine K. Albright

SECRETARY OF STATE
UNITED STATES OF AMERICA

Thank you, Stu, very much, for that introduction. On behalf of President Clinton and the American people, I'm pleased to join in welcoming all of you to the Washington Conference on Holocaust-Era Assets. I want to begin by thanking Miles Lerman and the US Holocaust Memorial Museum for co-hosting this event and for their unceasing efforts to keep before us the memory and lessons of history's most monstrous crime.

I also want to thank one of our nation's most accomplished public servants, Judge Abner Mikva, for accepting the role of Conference chairman. And I want to express appreciation to each of you who are participating in our sessions, and especially to those who will chair them, including New York Federal Reserve Bank Chairman Bill McDonough, a good friend; Ambassador Louis Amigues of France; US Representative Ben Gilman; and Congressman Jim Leach; and US Ambassador to Sweden, Lyndon Olson.

We're here to chart a course for finishing the job of returning or providing compensation for stolen Holocaust assets to survivors and the families of Holocaust victims. This mission began more than five decades ago, even before the war was over, when Nazi looting was condemned by the London Declaration of 1943.

In the early post-war period, the allies made good faith but incomplete, efforts at restitution. For decades thereafter, the job lingered unfinished, with vital questions unanswered, important documents unexamined and critical issues unresolved.

Then, in just the past few years, as Holocaust survivors aged and the century began drawing to a close, the quest for answers received a fresh burst of energy; and for that, the credit must be widely shared. Certainly, the eyes of the world would have remained averted from this issue if not for the remarkable work of the World Jewish Congress and other Jewish and public interest groups. In the face of daunting obstacles, they've been tireless, creative and very effective.

We are indebted as well to the many governments represented here that have come forward to address this issue with generosity and zeal. I mention particularly Foreign Secretary Robin Cook and the British Government for their insightful publications and statements and for convening last year's landmark conference in London on Nazi gold. And I am very, very proud of Under Secretary of State Stu Eizenstat and his team for setting out the historical record with rigorous objectivity and exhaustive detail in two US Government reports. Stu, I think we all owe you an incredible debt.

All this is important work and hard. It requires that painful memories be revisited, easy evasions confronted and inconvenient questions asked and answered. Above all, it demands that we be relentless in our search for truth, despite the fact that in dealing with the Holocaust, the truth is terrible beyond comprehension.

In recent years, the world has done much to retrieve facts from obscurity concerning the secretive handling and pernicious use of Nazi looted gold. No fewer than 17 historical commissions are studying the subject from the perspective of their own countries. The Tripartite Gold Commission has closed out its work; and almost $60 million has been pledged to the relief fund for the victims of Nazi persecution that was launched at the Conference in London.

We hope that the progress on gold will serve as a catalyst for similar progress in the categories of assets we will focus on this week, which are insurance and art as well as communal property. In each of these areas, the world's experts are here - from governments and non-governmental organizations, corporate boardrooms and university classrooms. We're here to compare views and share knowledge, frame the issues and achieve consensus on ways to move forward as rapidly, thoroughly and fairly as possible.

The historical and legal challenges vary from issue to issue, but whether we're seeking the payment of life insurance to families of those who perished in the camps, researching artwork from the walls of a museum in Warsaw, or weighing compensation for a synagogue reduced to ashes in Czechoslovakia, the moral imperative is the same. I hope, therefore, that we will be able to work together constructively in an atmosphere free from threats to develop specific principles and identify best practices for art, insurance and other topics.

I hope, as well, that our work will be driven by certain overarching imperatives. The first is that our goal must be justice, even though justice in this searing context is a highly relative term. We know well our inability to provide true justice to Holocaust victims. We cannot restore life nor rewrite history. But we can make the ledger slightly less out of balance by devoting our time, energy and resources to the search for answers, the return of property and the payment of just claims.

Our second imperative must be openness. Because the sands of time have obscured so much, we must dig to find the truth. This means that researchers must have access to old archives; and by that, I don't mean partial, sporadic or eventual access - I mean access in full, everywhere, now.

Our third imperative is to understand that the obligation to seek truth and act on it is not the burden of some, but of all; it is universal. As the United States has recognized by declassifying documents and creating its own presidential advisory commission on Holocaust assets, every nation, every business, every organization and every person able to contribute to the full telling of the story is obliged to do so. In this arena, none of us are mere spectators, none are neutral; for better or worse, we are all actors on history's stage.

The fourth imperative that propels our work is urgency. Remaining Holocaust survivors have reached an advanced stage in life. More than five decades have passed since the Nazis perpetrated their thefts and murders. As records are lost and memories fade, effective restitution becomes more difficult. So let us each vow that by the dawn of the new century, we have done all things possible to conclude the unfinished business of the old.

Finally, we must remember that our efforts here serve a twin purpose. Part one is to forge a common approach to the issues still surrounding Holocaust assets. Part two is to advance Holocaust education, remembrance and research. This is a task that knows no end. It must be renewed as the human race is renewed, generation by generation, so that the reality of the Holocaust is always before us and never ceases to disturb us.

It is encouraging that in the months preceding this conference, we have seen significant strides forward. The American Association of Art Museum Directors has formulated principles and guidelines to govern the handling of tabled Holocaust-Era art. An international commission led by former Secretary of State, Larry Eagleburger, has been formed to resolve unpaid insurance claims. Companies participating in that commission have agreed to establish a $90 million humanitarian fund and to audit their books to identify unpaid Holocaust-Era claims. And at Sweden's initiative, an unprecedented inter-governmental [effort] to promote Holocaust education around the world is underway. We hope that every country will participate in that effort.

The struggle to reveal and deal with the full truth surrounding the handling of Holocaust-Era assets is wrenching, but also cathartic. Only by knowing and being honest about the past can we gain peace in the present and confidence in the future. That is true for nations and for institutions, and it's true as well for people.

I cannot conclude this statement without addressing briefly a subject for which I have not yet found - and will never find - exactly the right words; and that concerns my grandparents, whom I learned recently were Jewish and died along with aunts, uncles and cousins in the Holocaust.

When I was young, I didn't often think about grandparents; I just knew I didn't have any. I was an infant when I separated from them. Now I, too, have become a grandparent, and I look at my children's children and the love and pride literally overflows. I am sure now that I was once the object of such affection not only from my parents, but from those who gave them life. And as I think of my life now in my 62nd year, I think also of my grandparents' lives in those final years, months and days.

I think of the faces at the Holocaust Museum and Yad Vashem and the long list of names on the wall of the Pynkas Synagogue in Prague; among them those of my grandparents, Olga and Arnost Korbel and Ruzene Spieglova. I think of the blood that is in my family veins. Does it matter what kind of blood it is? It shouldn't; it is just blood that does its job. But it mattered to Hitler and that matters to us all; because that is why 6 million Jews died. And that is why this obscenity of suffering was visited on so many innocent, irreplaceable people - people who loved and enriched life with their warmth, their smiles and the embrace of their arms; people whose lives ended horribly and far too soon; people whose lives and suffering we must never forget or allow to diminish, even if we must, from time to time, intentionally shock our collective memory.

The peoples of the world differ in language, culture, history and choices of worship. Such differences make life interesting and rich. But as the Holocaust cries out to us, we must never allow these distinctions to obscure the common humanity that binds us all as people. We must never allow pride in us to curdle into hatred of them.

Remembering that lesson is what this effort at research and restitution of Holocaust-Era assets is really all about. For it is about much more than gold and art and insurance; it's about remembering that no one's blood is less or more precious than our own.

There are those who say that we're all prisoners of history and that humankind is doomed to repeat its worst mistakes over and over again. There are those who view the Holocaust as the freakish consequence of a sole demented mind - an accident of history whose repetition we need not fear. Still others point to the passing decades and ask whether it's not time to forget and move on and leave remaining questions unasked and the rest of the truth unknown. And yes, there are still a few who deny the reality that it happened at all.

In reply, we must admit that we're not given perfect wisdom, nor the power to change human character, nor the gift of prophecy. But we do have the power of memory, and can make certain that the dead shall never be forgotten from our hearts. We have the power of reason and can separate right from wrong. We have the power of hope and can pray, in the words of the Psalms, for a time when "truth shall spring out of the Earth and righteousness shall look down from Heaven."

And we have the power to choose. We can contemplate the Holocaust in despair, or we can consider the Holocaust and vow never again to allow complacency or fear or despair to excuse inaction.

We gather here this week not to achieve miracles, but rather to do everything in our power to replace dark with light, injustice with fairness, contention with consensus and falsehood with truth. That is the most we can do. That is the least we must do. It is what we owe to the past; it is our hope for the future; and in the largest sense, it is the hope of the world.

Let me welcome you again to this conference, and may our shared efforts prosper. Thank you all very, very much.

Message from Robin Cook,
Foreign Secretary
United Kingdom

DELIVERED BY MR. ANTHONY LAYDEN
HEAD OF DELEGATION
UNITED KINGDOM

Secretary of State, Chairman, distinguished delegates,

When I opened the London Conference on Nazi Gold almost exactly a year ago, I said that the group of 41 countries and 6 non-governmental organizations taking part had come together to "clarify one of the darkest episodes in human history", and to "shine a light in corners which have stayed dark too long".

The London Conference undoubtedly accomplished that: the papers presented there, later published in book form and distributed to delegates, represent the largest and most diverse body of information on the subject of Nazi Gold yet assembled.

But the London Conference did more than that. It also addressed the question of compensation for those whose gold the Nazis had seized, both countries and individuals. It looked backwards at what had already been done, and forwards at the case for further help to victims of Nazi persecution, especially those in greatest need, and for whom least had been done until then.

The Chairman of the London Conference, Lord Mackay of Clashfern, noted in his Conclusions that "all present were agreed that the international community must look urgently and imaginatively for ways to bring relief to such people". The International Fund for Needy Victims of Nazi Persecution, whose establishment I announced in London on 2 December last year, aims to do exactly this. It has met a ready response from the countries receiving shares of the Tripartite Gold Commission's monetary gold pool, and from a number of other countries as well.

Your Conference will shortly hear reports from the French and United Kingdom Delegations on progress made since the London Conference in winding up the Tripartite Commission, releasing its archives, and making the Fund a reality. In my view this process has been an extremely imaginative and successful piece of modern diplomacy, of which all the participants can feel justly proud.

Much has been done since this group of countries and organizations met in London a year ago. The United Kingdom, as chairman of the Tripartite Commission and as Account Holder for the Fund account, has played an important role in this. More needs to be done in the future. I hope your Conference will provide a stimulus for this; and I pledge that the UK will continue to play its part as the Fund's Account Holder with energy and diligence.

This Conference in Washington goes on to address a wider group of issues than we dealt with in London: art, insurance, property, archives and education. All are important aspects of the search for clarity about the tragic events of half a century ago. I am sure your proceedings will be imbued with the same spirit of ready, practical co-operation between governments and nongovernmental organizations which we saw in London.

Perhaps the most valuable part of your agenda for its long-term effect is Holocaust education, commemoration and research. In the UK, we have been active in this area for many years. When our National Curriculum for Education was introduced seven years ago, the Holocaust was included as a compulsory component of the modern history curriculum for students aged 13 to 14. There is close cooperation between Government and the relevant nongovernmental organizations. Five of these organizations are represented in the UK Delegation to this Conference, including the Holocaust Educational Trust, of which Lord Janner, who first suggested that the London Conference be held, is Chairman.

It is vital that future generations worldwide should learn about the Holocaust. We must heed this warning about what can happen if discrimination and intolerance are allowed to grow unchecked. We have also found in the UK that learning about the Holocaust can help considerably in reducing social, racial and other tensions in schools. Schools have described the effect in this area of visits by Holocaust survivors as "near-miraculous".

The UK has been an enthusiastic participant in the International Task Force on Holocaust Education, which will be reporting to your Conference on 3 December, since it was suggested to Prime Minister Tony Blair and President Bill Clinton by the Swedish Prime Minister, Goran Persson, earlier this year. We have agreed to take on the Chairmanship of this group, which now includes also Germany and

Israel, after the Washington Conference, and shall continue to do all we can to advance its work.

Secretary of State, Chairman, and distinguished Delegates, I wish you every success in your endeavors.

Opening Remarks
Ambassador Stuart E. Eizenstat

UNDER SECRETARY OF STATE FOR ECONOMIC,
BUSINESS AND AGRICULTURAL AFFAIRS
UNITED STATES
HEAD OF DELEGATION

Mr. Chairman, delegates, ladies and gentlemen: Let me begin by saying what a privilege it is to head the United States delegation for this landmark event. I want to first take a moment to thank Judge Abner Mikva for agreeing to be the Chairman of the Washington Conference on Holocaust-Era Assets. His probity and integrity will give this Conference the leadership that will be essential to its success.

It is also a pleasure to follow my friend Anthony Layden of the United Kingdom. Anthony's diplomatic and organizational abilities brought the London Conference to life, exactly one year ago, and his leadership, along with that of our French colleagues has helped bring the Tripartite Gold Commission to an honorable close.

Finally, I want to say a special word about British Foreign Secretary Robin Cook, whose leadership in convening the London Conference helped capture the world's attention and galvanize action toward the cause of justice. I will have something to say later in the Conference about another person from the United Kingdom, Lord Janner.

Opening the London Conference, Foreign Secretary Cook spoke of our dual responsibilities to the victims of the Nazis. "To those who are still alive, we must ensure that the unbearable tragedy of living through the Holocaust is not compounded by an old age marked by the fear and sadness of poverty.... To those who died, we have a different duty – to document the facts, to gather the evidence, to locate the truth."

We also have a further responsibility – to heed the lessons of these tragic events by renewing our commitment to usher in a new and brighter century, marked by freedom and respect for the fundamental dignity of each individual. We, who have listened to the stories of the survivors and have tried to absorb the memory of the unimaginable horror inflicted on the victims, now have a solemn responsibility: To be the trustees of their memory and their advocates for justice.

It is this responsibility that must serve as our guiding beacon while we seek to illuminate the tragedies of the past and provide enduring lessons for future generations.

Our overarching responsibilities and priorities are clear – to complete the historical record, however complex, while providing some measure of justice, however belated, for the survivors,

We must review our current efforts while developing a clear and realistic consensus on how to sustain, and where possible to accelerate the momentum generated by the London Conference so that we can complete our tasks by the end of this century – December 31, 1999.

A year ago at the London Conference the international community addressed the issue of Nazi-looted gold. On the final day of the Conference, we broadened the scope of our discussion to encompass other categories of assets confiscated by the Nazis. In light of the importance, complexity, and urgency of these issues, the United States recognized the need to hold a second conference, which would primarily focus on looted art and insurance policies, as well as communal property and other assets.

As the host of the Washington Conference, the United States has attempted to construct a Conference that reflects the widest possible points of view compromising all 44 governments and 13 NGOs represented here. Through continuing consultations with you and an organizing seminar held this past June, we have refined the agenda and the goals that we hope the delegations assembled here can constructively pursue this week. We are very pleased that so many countries have joined with us in moving the process forward. In particular, I want to thank the British government for the advice and strong support it has given our Conference. Also, I extend my appreciation to the French government for playing such a critical leadership role on the issues of art, insurance and archives. Let me say a few words about each of the major issues comprising the Conference agenda, and the view of the United States on how they might best be approached.

The subject of looted art is significant to the heritage and culture of all peoples – well beyond its value in monetary terms. One-fifth of all the art in Europe was uprooted during World War II and today there are countless survivors and families who still do not know the whereabouts of their priceless artworks. Today, a growing number of nations and institutions are acknowledging these claims and are demonstrating a new willingness to locate missing artworks, publicize their existence, determine their provenance and come to a just and fair resolution of ownership questions. A number of European countries are addressing these issues in a constructive manner, none more so than Austria, which recently passed a law allowing claims to be made on Nazi-looted artworks found in the nation's federal museums. This is the first time a European government has taken such a far-reaching step and it is our hope that Austria's actions will serve as an example for other nations to emulate.

Based on our consultations over the last several months, I am hopeful that the Conference can achieve consensus on ways to bring about a speedier and far less confrontational resolution to the problem of looted art. Tomorrow I shall suggest a set of principles based closely on existing practices drawn from both sides of the Atlantic. They will call for new efforts to find missing art, including the use of new technologies in searching for evidence and matching art with claims as well as new methods of dispute resolution for deciding these claims. I urge your consideration for establishing a consensus around these principles. What we do here can go a long way toward reconciling the very real sensitivities and needs of current owners and those who lost art during the war.

The international art market must be open, stable, and free of uncertainty that it might be trading in works that are tainted by Nazi looting. The exchange of art is essential to our understanding and recognition of different cultures, and the resolution of Nazi-confiscated art issues will be critical for ensuring that this age-old process of cultural exchange continues for future generations. But, it is equally critical that families from whom art was looted by the Nazis have the full opportunity to find and reclaim their artworks.

Regarding the issue of insurance, our goals are twofold: First, we must review the historical evidence relating to the loss of insurance assets during the Holocaust era. Second, we must examine subsequent efforts by governments and companies to provide compensation. From these reviews, we need to understand the post-war programs for compensation and examine the steps we can take today to continue redressing past injustices.

The establishment of the new international Commission on Holocaust-Era Insurance Claims – inspired by leaders of the National Association of Insurance Commissioners like Neil Levin of New York and Glenn Pomeroy of North Dakota and chaired by former Secretary of State Lawrence Eagleburger – is a particularly encouraging development because it offers an efficient and effective means of advancing the swift and just resolution of these issues. By bringing together key actors such as insurance regulators, insurance companies and Jewish groups, we are helping ensure that the goals and purposes of the Commission will be met.

I look forward to hearing from the Commission about their very encouraging efforts to resolve these difficult issues. For those who have perished, we must ensure that their policies are finally paid. For Holocaust survivors – many of whom are in their later years – it is absolutely imperative that we act now.

In this regard, I want to express my great appreciation for the strong interest that the former Communist countries of Central and Eastern Europe have begun to show in resolving Holocaust insurance and communal property issues. After the enormous destruction and despair of World War II, these nations lived under the iron fist of Communist dictatorship and economic deprivation, which prevented them from addressing these issues in a just manner, They, as well as Holocaust survivors, have been the double victims of World War II, having suffered under both Nazism and Communism. To be sure, it was not only Jewish, but also Catholic and Protestant communal property that was confiscated. And today the region's democratic governments are taking concrete steps to rectify these injustices. It is now time to build on these encouraging examples and shape an international consensus on principles for moving forward so that we can advance the cause of justice and strengthen democratic institutions in adherence to the rule of law.

At the same time, the return of Jewish communal property, such as synagogues, cemeteries, day schools, and community centers, is absolutely essential to the reemergence and rebirth of Jewish communal life in Central and Eastern Europe. During my travels as the State Department's Special Envoy on Property Restitution, I have seen firsthand how many of these communities are impoverished and in need have outside support if they are to survive and prosper into the next millennium.

Of course, if we are to truly make a better world for the future, then all nations must be willing to take a long-delayed and serious examination of the events of the past. After nearly five decades of silence, there has been an explosion in scholarship and research by various national governments, international institutions and independent scholars about the events surrounding the Holocaust. In fact, the U.S. government has made more than 15 million pages of documents available for researchers. Having recently returned from South America and meetings with the Commission for the Clarification of Nazi Activities in Argentina and the Special Commission for Investigation of Nazi Property in Brazil, I can attest to the fact that many nations around the world are demonstrating great courage and determination in coming to grips with their actions during the Nazi quest for global domination.

Much work, however, remains to be done in setting the record straight and more steps should be taken to ensure that the fullest possible openness and accessibility of archives on the fate of Nazi looted assets is provided by the end of 1999. Only by opening these archives can we fully illuminate the long-hidden issues of Holocaust-era assets, and gain a complete and unvarnished view of the events surrounding the Holocaust.

Over the past five decades, many nations have undertaken the often painful steps of educating their citizens about their behavior during the Nazi era. Nowhere has this been more evident than in Germany, which has taken notable and commendable steps to come to grips with its past conduct. Another positive example is Sweden, which has not only strengthened its own Holocaust education efforts at home, but has launched the International Task Force on Cooperation on Holocaust Education, Remembrance and Research. The Task Force report, which I will be presenting tomorrow on behalf of the United States, Sweden, the United Kingdom, Germany and Israel, includes a declaration calling on all countries represented at the Washington Conference to join us in strengthening their Holocaust educational activities.

A commitment to strengthening Holocaust education, remembrance and research must be a fundamental goal of each of our nations. Such remembrance is the most appropriate means of taking from the dark lessons of the past a renewed vigor in ensuring that similar horrors are never repeated again. As we prepare to enter a new century, it must be our continuing determination to ensure that we fulfill our responsibilities by educating future generations on the horrors of the past-century. We must keep in mind the ancient Jewish saying that "The only truly dead are those who have been forgotten."

To be sure, our gathering today is not a decision-making body. Nonetheless, it is the hope of the United States that issue by issue and session by session we strive to craft a strong and durable consensus on the complex and sensitive issues before us this week.

As we prepare to begin our deliberations, we must be guided by this simple proposition: We can only usher in a freer and more dignified next century by penning the final chapter on the most horrific and soul-searching event of the past century.

Our efforts this week will bring a greater determination, a greater understanding and a greater resolve to continue and complete in the months ahead the process of pursuing the truth, uncovering the facts, providing restitution, achieving closure, educating future generations, righting the wrongs of the past and finally seeking justice.

These efforts are critical not just to the survivors and to the deceased, but in fact to all humanity and to the simple proposition of a better world firmly anchored in truth, justice and the fundamental dignity of each human being. Thank you.

Opening Remarks
Mr. Avraham Hirchson

MEMBER OF KNESSET
ISRAEL
HEAD OF DELEGATION

Perla Danziger from Lodz, killed in Auschwitz, 2 years old.

Shmuel Davner from Lodz, killed in Treblinka, 6 years old.

Feya Damchzek from Riga, killed in Riga, 8 years old.

Lenny Davids from Holland, killed in Sobibor, 9 years old.

Renya Federgreen from Krakow, killed in Bergen-Belsen, 12 years old.

Rosa Danzon from Paris, killed in Auschwitz, 16 years old.

Gittel Dantos from Warsaw, killed in Treblinka, 13 years old.

Yosef Danziger from Sosnovitz, killed in Birkenau, 16 years old.

Daniel Danielek from Warsaw, killed in Treblinka, 16 years old.

Motel Danishevsky from Poltowa, killed in Treblinka, 16 years old.

Ladies and gentlemen,
        These are just a few names from a list – a very, very long list – a list which should never have existed; a list of victims of the Jewish people in the Holocaust period.

If I were to read out the names of the entire six million people on this list, taking just one second to read each name, each individual person, each human being – it would take me more than two months.

In the time available today, I cannot share with you even the names of the million and half Jewish children who were exterminated in the Holocaust.

Today, I am addressing you as a representative of the State of Israel, which was founded for the Jewish people. I am speaking to you on behalf of each mother and daughter, each father and son, each and every one of those six million Jews who can no longer speak for themselves and who did not have the privilege of seeing the renaissance of the Jewish people in its historical homeland.

Today, at this Conference, we can look with pride at what we have achieved so far on the issue of restitution of Jewish property but we must also recognize the challenges still to come.

From the very beginning, all of us involved in this issue set ourselves no boundaries – neither the geographical boundaries of any particular state nor any particular area (such as insurance, banking or art). As things unfolded, we found that we were dealing with the restitution of goods stolen in the greatest robbery ever carried out in the history of the world, let alone in Jewish history. The extent of this robbery is so great that no one dares put a figure on its real magnitude, and only a few people are willing to confront the broad, almost unlimited range of countries and bodies which took part in it, whether actively, passively or by simply closing their eyes.

Today, we know for certain that Jews throughout the whole of Europe were stripped utterly bare on their way to the crematoria. They were robbed not only of the clothes on their backs, but also of any sign or distinguishing sign of their human image.

Therefore, we should also look into the moral aspect of our activity. We are not involved in vengeance, but rather a sacred duty. Vengeance is driven by instinct. Duty is driven by the feeling of mission.

We are the emissaries of those people – the elderly and the children, the men and women – who were condemned to suffer such torments on their way to physical destruction, torments which were intended to strip them of absolutely everything – their entire social or cultural worth, their total humanity. There is no other explanation for taking away clothes and glasses, for burning books, plundering works of art, destroying all cultural symbols, denying all religious freedom. Not only did the Nazi oppressors and their allies rob us of our parents and fellow Jews; they also tried to strip us of the symbols of our culture and history. They were not satisfied with our physical extermination; on the way to the death pits and the smoking crematoria they also stripped their victims of every single personal object.

Therefore, the struggle which we are waging is not only the determination of the Jewish people to recover its looted property – it is also a struggle for the very image and character of the world and its moral system.

The fact that this conference is taking place does not mean that our work is completed. The struggle has begun. It is not over. We know that the despicable robbery was not only carried out by the German Nazi oppressor and his collaborators in the offensive against free Europe, but there were also partners from various nations. Even the neutral countries were unconcerned that they were making handsome profits from trading in goods and works of art expropriated from their rightful owners. Even the Allies contributed, in certain ways, albeit unwittingly, to this greatest robbery of all time.

Some of the wrongs have been redressed. Norway has shown sensitivity and responsibility. Its Government has set up a Commission which is in the final stages of compensating its Jewish citizens and its Jewish community for the property stolen from them by the Germans and those Norwegians who saw fit to identify with them. Other countries should follow a similar path and act as bravely and honestly as Norway has done.

Some of them have already seen fit to open their archives and make their findings available to all those bodies, organizations and individuals interested in examining them. Some of the countries are adamantly refusing to do so and I believe, Ladies and gentlemen, that one of the resolutions of this Conference should be an unmistakable call to all those countries and bodies still refusing to open their archives – to do so sooner rather than later.

The arrangement reached with the Swiss banks after a long drawn-out struggle was a first step in the right direction for all matters involving private institutions and companies. If they have not yet done so, the insurance companies, other banks and institutions must follow the correct path which has already been taken by other institutions. This means examining their records and the information in their possession and reaching an appropriate arrangement on the basis of their findings.

It is my pleasant duty now to refer to the United States, the world's greatest democracy, under whose auspices this Conference is taking place. This is not the first time that the United States has been involved in and contributed to the struggle for the return of Jewish assets.

With President Clinton's blessing and under the leadership of Under Secretary of State, Stuart Eizenstat, the United States has undertaken not only to contribute to the struggle on one front together with us, but also to examine the documents and the archives in the United States itself – a thorough, in-depth, responsible and honest examination, even if less pleasant aspects of its past are exposed by some of its findings. In this way, the United States has also set an appropriate and correct model for all other countries. The wrongs of the past cannot be redressed, but there must be an honest, penetrating look at the past. This is the only way to ensure that a change has, indeed, taken place in the post-war period.

There are those of us who always knew that the accounts might be dormant but the memories were not; who always believed that the money might have vanished from sight but that justice would emerge; that we were right to risk the world's favor in order to ensure that the entire world would respect us and relate to us as equals, and admire those who have already chosen to take the correct path, and encourage those who are still hesitating to tread that path with us.

We will, without a doubt, have to continue our efforts to make sure that the last chapter of the Second World War be written clearly and fairly, in order to restore Jewish honor and Jewish pride to our people, who have suffered so terribly. We are just at the beginning of the path and there is much to be done in order to complete our task in the many countries and different areas concerned.

All of us who are involved in this task have vowed to remember and not forget, to remember and to remind.

I hope that by the end of this millennium we will be able to close this chapter in the history books and open a new chapter in the relationship between the Jewish people and the countries of the free world.

Opening Remarks
Dr. Rajko Djuric

INTERNATIONAL ROMANI UNION
HEAD OF DELEGATION

Ladies and gentlemen,

The International Romani Union is most grateful for the invitation to participate in this conference. We are grateful above all to the government and the people of the United States of America who have made it possible for the historical truth of the around 12 million Romanies be heard, the truth of a people which the Nazis planned to completely exterminate, as too they planned to eliminate the Jews. Receiving the opportunity to participate in this conference also moves us to express our gratitude to our brothers and sisters to whom we are linked by historical fate, the Jews, whose systematic study of the Holocaust has contributed to keeping alive the memory of our people's Holocaust.

In contrast to the Enlightenment, whose most learned representatives, Denis Diderot and Jean d'Alambert, gave humanity the encyclopedia, a compendium of all the scholarship, social and artistic experience of the time, our Age has seen the creation of an "Encyclopedia of the Holocaust!" The sufferings and the anguish of my people, the Romanies, and the half a million Romanies murdered in Auschwitz, Auschwitz-Birkenau, Treblinka, Belzec, Buchenwald, Dachau, Mauthausen, Ravensbrück, Jasenovac etc., occupy significantly more space in this encyclopedia, an encyclopedia of death, than do the entries in contemporary general encyclopedias on my people's history, social life and culture from our origins through until today. My people's entire history and current way of life are literally overshadowed by our better documented and more comprehensively researched "way of death." This trail of death and suffering began in Dachau in 1934 and led via Marzahn near Berlin (where in 1936 during the Berlin Olympics [!] a camp with the cynical name "resting Place" was set up specially for Sinti and Romanies) all the way to Auschwitz-Birkenau and the so-called "Gypsy Camp" B IIe. Christian Bernadac describes in his book "Vergessener Holocaust" (Forgotten Holocaust) how 4,000 Sinti and

Romanies were sent to Crematorium no. 1 there in just one night, from the 2nd to the 3rd of August 1944.

On the 3rd of August 1994 the 50th anniversary of the beginning of the Romanies' extermination was marked in Auschwitz. Assembled there at the place of our mothers' and fathers' suffering, we received letters from the then President of Poland, Lech Walesa, from the President of the Czech Republic, Václav Havel, and also from Pope John Paul II. The message from the Pope read as follows:

> *"Together with all the participants of the commemoration in Auschwitz I kneel down, deeply moved and in deference, at the place which holds the ashes of the Nazis' genocide. In particular I remember the tragic fate of the Gypsies, our sisters and brothers, who were interned in the concentration camp in Auschwitz-Birkenau. I have done this many times as Metropolitan Bishop of Kraków, and today I do it as Pope."*

Ladies and gentlemen,

When I contemplate the history of my people an image of Simon Luis appears before me. Simon Luis was a Romanie from France interned in the concentration camp in Buchenwald. Simon was tattooed over much of his body – on his fingers, his back, his arms and hands. When the Commandant noticed this he ordered that Simon be flayed alive. The English Holocaust researchers, the Romanies Donald Kenrick and Grattan Puxon, describe how Simon's skin was removed from his body, treated, and then used to cover the Commandant's desk. When I try to imagine the tattooed signs and symbols on that poor man's skin I always arrive at the conclusion that the history of my people is in fact like the skin of that martyr.

To respect the historical truth I also must mention another incident from the long series of sufferings and sorrow of my people. In a group of people who Dr. Mengele was conducting experiments on were two Sinti children, the Mechau brothers. These children were selected out to suffer for the simple "reason" that, following an interplay of the laws of genetics, each had one blue aye and one dark eye - a case of so-called heterochromia. It is told that Dr. Mengele pulled out the children's eyes *and* then killed them single-handedly. The eyes of these martyrs, which will remain open as long as we exist on this planet, and which I feel are also watching us here at this conference, were sent to the laboratory of the Ophthalmological Clinic in Berlin.

Ladies and gentlemen,

There is no scale on which to measure the eyes and the screams of children! Never will there be scales to weigh human skin with tattooed signs and symbols. There is no gauge for the ashes and the blood of Auschwitz.

Truth and justice are the only measure of things.

For my people, however, truth and justice have passed us by.

My people did not suffer only under the Nazi Regime – in various countries Communist dictatorships also took a terrible toll: Romanies were murdered in the Stalin era in the former USSR; in Romania under Ceausescu they were brutally persecuted; in former Czechoslovakia Romani women were forcibly sterilized...A new, dark chapter in the history of the Romanies began in 1989: there were anti-Romani pogroms in Romania; in the Czech Republic and in Slovakia Romanies were beaten up and killed; in former Yugoslavia there was suffering on a massive scale, particularly in Bosnia. My people have gone down in history for their suffering, and only as such. Is survival, its naked physical existence, bears the imprint of death, suffering and anguish much more indelibly than it shows any signs of progressive legislations, social justice or democracy. The historical knowledge about my people's past and the facts of its current life stir in me the words of the Spanish poet Antonio Machado y Ruiz: *"Sing him a song, dear brother/the Gypsy Jesus is still waiting/to have the blood washed from his hands, to be taken from the cross!"*

If it is true that all those who suffer and die for their truth are united with God and humanity, that they become a cornerstone of the future building of humanity which after all the anguish and blunders will finally be erected on earth in keeping with principles of humanity, that would at least be a consolation to us. We expect of this conference that it open our people the door to justice. What our people deserves, in keeping with the laws of historical truth and justice, must be utilized to serve its progressive activity and social development.

Only those who know the history of the Romanies, who have studied the Romani community, and who recognize the current economic, political and social conditions and circumstances which the Romanies live under in various countries of the world – particularly in Europe, where the Romanies' Holocaust and that of the Jews began – can contribute to this process. Whoever neglects these facts and circumstances could cause unforeseeable damage to the Romanies and our community, which in itself is segmentary and is still based on organic solidarity. A redistribution must therefore be carried out in harmony with historical awareness and real needs, and must be as fair as possible. Priority should be given to investments in the Romanies' future, above all in the schooling and education of the younger generation; furthermore, it has to serve the construction of ethnic and cultural institutions which will guarantee the preservation of the Romanies' identity but also contribute to our development. Institutions which will enable us to effectively combat racism in the contemporary world will also be of significance. Parallel to this, the economic and social problems of the many Romani families have to be resolved.

Ladies and gentlemen,

Today our people is faced with grave dangers, beginning with the armed injustice in the former Yugoslavia and Bosnia, the violence and the threats of the neo-Nazis, and including the fact that it is forced to live in ghettos, without enough daily bread, which is a negation of every purposeful existence in this world. Thus for us Romanies the future has not yet been freed from the past, nor has the past been resolved on the scale of a humane future; our people has still seen neither victory nor defeat – we are living proof of the fact that in the countries of both the victors and the vanquished of the Second World War people are still tormented and humiliated. Like no other people in the world we have been left with the burdens of life – all that is hard, meager and cheerless. Even our children are born, so to speak, with pre-determined dark fates. Those who deprive our children of the right to a future commit a crime against our people.

Myself and the members of the International Romani Union's delegation – *Mr. Victor Famulson, Deputy Chair; Dr. Emil Scuka, General Secretary; Dr. Marcel Cortiade, Secretary; Fredi Hoffmann, Committee member; the writer Jovan Nikolic, Deputy Chairman of the Romani PEN-Center; Mr. Böhmer and Mr. Jörg Böcken, representatives of the Sinti and Romanies in Germany; Ms. Rosa Martl from Austria; Mr. Robert Huber from Switzerland; Mr. Milorad Vujicic from Yugoslavia; Mr. Alija Mestic from Croatia; Mr. Stefan Palison from Sweden; Mr. Zoran Dimov from Macedonia; Mr. Velko Georgiev from Bulgaria; Mr. Sean Nazareli from the Czech Republic; Mr. Bobu Nicloae, lawyer, Romania; and our lawyer Mr. Barry Fisher* – appeal to this high and respected conference and request that, in the spirit of historical truth and justice and in accordance with the word and the notion "holocaust", it make a contribution towards resolving these problems, which will allow our dead to rest in peace and will give a sign of hope to the living, especially our children. Those who feel the sufferings and misfortune of our people and who sympathize with its pain will be able to set up standards of justice and fair redistribution simply and easily. Those, on the other hand, who neither know of nor understand the Holocaust of our people, who do not *want* to hear of the Romanies' misfortune, will be prepared to walk all over these principles, our dead, and the future of our people.

Together with the delegates of the International Romani Union I hope – and am even deeply convinced – that this high and eminent conference will effectively hinder and repulse any potential attempt of this kind, whichever quarters it comes from.

In the hope that the memory of the victims of the Holocaust will live eternally and the hope of the living will never falter, I sincerely thank you for all your attention.

Opening Statement
Ambassador Alexander Philon

GREECE

HEAD OF DELEGATION

As Under Secretary Eizenstat stated in the First Conference on Holocaust Era Assets, held here in Washington, it is dispiriting that for nearly half a century the fate of Holocaust-Era Assets remained largely obscured, but at the same time it is encouraging that over the last several years, these issues have come to command the world's attention and touch the conscience of humanity.

As Head of the Greek Delegation to the London Conference on Nazi Gold last year, I wish to stress the importance of these forums in achieving a just solution to these problems. I certainly hope that the Washington Conference will produce similar results in the form of a consensus among governments and that it will inform those involved internationally on the size of the problem and the best ways to deal with its many different aspects.

We now have the opportunity to see clearly and establish the facts in an effort to obtain justice.

The Washington Conference is not a forum for government decision-making. It is a forum in which we will try to identify the injustices committed in the fields of art, insurance, archives and other assets during the Nazi occupation.

In this spirit, Greece fully understands and shares the Jewish drama, especially the one that took place during World War II, when my country suffered not only loss of innumerable human lives but also immeasurable economic devastation.

The Nazi occupation resulted in a decrease of about 10% of Greece's population. It also wrecked the monetary and financial mechanisms of the country and caused the disintegration of the administrative system.

In this respect, please allow me to bring to the attention of the delegates a particular issue concerning Greece.

During the occupation years, the Axis exacted from Greece contributions of huge sums of money. In addition to direct monetary contributions, the Axis also demanded large credits from the Bank of Greece.

The first "forced loan" protocol was signed in March 1942 and it was subsequently amended several times during the occupation. In this protocol, high-ranking officials of the German and Italian Ministries of Foreign Affairs had undertaken to pay back the loan to the Athens government and began doing so in 1943, thus recognizing liability to repay a debt.

We would like to focus upon the fact that the "forced loan" extracted from Greece was not a part of "regular" occupation costs and that the claim for repayment of that loan is therefore different in nature from reparations claims.

With one exception, the Bonn government responded to all war claims placed and substantiated by countries, after German unification. These responses constituted either some kind of material compensation or at least a beginning of negotiations on the claims.

The only exception is Greece.

The full Greek argumentation and documentation on the subject is contained in a memorandum which is available and which deserves, I believe and I hope, your attention.

Furthermore, I would like to inform you that on the issues of education, archives, art and communal assets, members of the Greek Delegation will intervene in the respective panels.

Stuart E. Eizenstat

UNDER SECRETARY OF STATE FOR ECONOMIC, BUSINESS AND
AGRICULTURAL AFFAIRS
UNITED STATES

Review of Gold Issues, Research and Resolution

Plenary Session: Review of Gold Issues, Research and Resolution

I want to take this opportunity to thank Bill McDonough for taking part in this Conference and to acknowledge the critical role of the Federal Reserve Bank of New York over the past 50 years in dealing with the restitution of monetary gold looted by Nazi Germany. The New York Fed was there from the beginning of the process established by the Allies in 1946 to receive monetary gold on behalf of the Tripartite Gold Commission and to be the caretaker for this unique "Gold Pool" until the conflicting claims to the looted gold could be carefully adjudicated. With the closing down of the Commission in September of this year, the New York Fed's remarkable custodianship came to a satisfying conclusion. Bill McDonough is personally responsible for the extraordinary contribution the New York Federal Reserve has made over the last two years to our own country's explanation of the facts behind the Nazi gold issue – and I salute him and his colleagues.

The surge of interest over the last several years in the fate of monetary gold looted by the Nazis in World War II has reopened the long-neglected record of tragic events of half a century ago and has thrown new light on its long-hidden dimensions and long-neglected victims. This recent research has allowed a new, clear understanding of the origins of looted gold and the uses to which it was applied during the War. It has also shown the general inability of the international community to fully grasp or acknowledge until very recently the full extent of the looting of gold and its horrible misapplication in the support of the Nazi war effort.

This unprecedented effort of discovery and rediscovery owes much of its impetus to the original leadership and initiative of the World Jewish Congress. In the United States President Clinton and a bipartisan group in the U.S. Congress, led by Senator D'Amato and Congressman Leach, urged and insisted on establishing and publishing the facts. The massive U.S. Government interagency project for reviewing the U.S. official record and publishing the results in two historical reports, followed the lead set by the British Government whose Foreign and Commonwealth Ministry's chief historian Gill Bennett took the first step with a path-finding study released in September 1996.

In the course of 1996 and 1997, other governments, those of nations who were occupied during the War as well as those who remained neutral or non-belligerent, joined the international effort at discovery and disclosure. Now there are 17 national commissions, and other nations are using other approaches to sort through their records.

The redrawn and refocused historical picture of the scale and nature of Nazi looting of gold is emerging from this enormous body of recent work. Not all of the Commissions and other national historical investigations around the world have examined the origins and fate of the Nazi regime's gold. Research into the fate of Holocaust victims' assets in bank accounts, insurance, real property, art, and other cultural collections and possessions is still going forward even as we approach a more complete understanding of the monetary gold question. The painful and complicated record of Nazi looting of the monetary gold of occupied Europe was placed before the Tripartite Gold Commission by the United States, Britain, and France more than 40 years ago.

Let me underline the importance of the opening of the TGC archives at the French Foreign Ministry in France at the same time as the U.S., Britain, and France closed out this body. While we do not expect any surprising revelations from the TGC archives, they will now be available in their entirety to researchers, historians, and the public at large. Full transparency and openness when dealing with such historical records is a responsibility that we must not just accept but welcome.

The extensive wartime gold transactions that sustained the German war effort until 1945 involving the neutral nations have only become broadly understood as a result of the hard and dispassionate work of historians and other experts on the national commissions of these neutrals. The report of Switzerland's Independent Commission of Experts in May 1998 made extensive use of the records of the Swiss National Bank as well as those of other nations to develop its detailed and comprehensive picture of the intersection of German gold, however acquired, and the financing of the wartime commerce of the other neutral nations. The accounts of the wartime banking of their countries by the Spanish, Portuguese, and Swedish historical commissions, and of the acquisition of German monetary gold directly from Germany or more likely through Switzerland, complement the authoritative Swiss report.

The hard and urgent research in the last two years on the part of the various national historical commissions on wartime gold transactions has provided a truly international analysis and description. The Portuguese Commission had provided a full and careful accounting of the movement of gold through their official agencies during the war. The Spanish Commission tracked the movement of gold and placed it in a broad, objective context of Spanish official policy-making. The Swedish Commission provided a comprehensive account and analysis of Swedish gold transactions during the War and the efforts through 1955 to resolve the difficult issues that delayed the final restitution of nearly $20 million to the TGC. And the remarkable interim report of the Swiss Independent Commission released last May not only reviewed in great and careful detail the full range of Swiss gold transactions during the War with the Axis, the Allies, and the neutrals, but it courageously confronted the awareness of the government, the Swiss National Bank, and the public as a whole of the nature and significance of these dealings.

Turkish Commission experts have conducted extensive research in their own records and those of other governments in order to address their serious concerns about the accuracy of the historical account in the U.S. reports. In particular, exhaustive examination of Central Bank of Turkey records accounted in minute detail for all of the monetary gold acquired by the Bank during the War, without finding any evidence of looted gold. Research by the Turkish Foreign Ministry has also fully documented the conviction of Turkish officials at the time of what they considered the necessity of Turkey's exports of chromium to Nazi Germany in 1943 and early 1944, especially after Britain forfeited its opportunity in 1940 to acquire all of Turkey's chromium supplies. Foreign Ministry research also reviewed Turkey's orderly settlement of German wartime assets issues directly with the Federal Republic of Germany in the 1950s.

The impressive research of these commissions, together with the concurrent and converging work done by our two U.S. interagency reports of May 1997 and June 1998 as well as the pioneering British reports, demonstrate both the complexity of the unfinished task of 50 years ago and also the great results that come from working together toward a common and deserved goal. I will not claim that all research on the fate of looted gold is finished. Not every conceivable question was asked by the researchers, and differences among the various national reports indicate other areas for further careful study in order, as Foreign Secretary Cook put it last year, to "recreate the jigsaw." I think we can all agree, however, on many of the major areas of consensus established by the recent work of so many of the commissions represented here today.

First, there is now general understanding and agreement on the scale of the Nazi looting of gold from occupied Europe, both from central banks and from individual victims. Moreover, our commissions have cumulatively demonstrated that the Nazi regime used this loot deliberately and ruthlessly to finance its acquisition of supplies essential to its capacity to wage war. The research of the various commissions and the review of our U.S. records have confirmed the nature and scale of German looted gold in financing this crucial wartime trade. The Swiss Independent Commission put the total amount of looted gold transferred to or through Switzerland during the War at around $444 million (almost $4 billion in today's values). The Commission's report also estimated that about $82 million of the total Reichsbank gold holdings during the War was taken from individuals, some $700 million in today's values, including $2.9 million ($25 million today), from Nazi victims.

Second, in the light of the results of this research – not least of all by the Swiss Independent Commission but also by the work of the Portuguese, Spanish, Swedish, as well as the U.S. and British reports – the central role of Swiss institutions, especially the Swiss National Bank, in managing the financing and facilitating wartime commerce in Europe by receiving Nazi-looted gold and converting it to hard currencies is now fully established and accepted. As Dr. Berger, in his preface to the Swiss Independent Commission report, expressed it best: "Switzerland lay at the heart of the gold transactions."

Third, the considerable evidence in the U.S. reports and the comprehensive review of victim gold in the report of the Swiss Independent Commission leave no doubt of the considerable scale and the barbarous nature of the Nazi theft of gold stolen from concentration camp victims and its addition to the gold reserves that the Reichsbank used to finance the Nazi war effort. The full amount of stolen victim gold that was incorporated into the Reichsbank holdings – from the Swiss Independent Commission estimate of $2.9 million ($25 million in today's values) to the U.S. estimate of $4.6 million ($40.5 million in today's values) – may never be known. Despite a thorough search in both German and U.S. archives, the records of the Precious Metals

Department at the Reichsbank have not been found, making it impossible to document completely the extent and disposition of the infamous Melmer account at the Reichsbank, into which the SS put the gold they stole from their victims, largely Jewish as well as many Romani, including dental fillings. A recent effort by the German Government was unable to locate records of the Melmer account, which were either destroyed or lost at some point after the conclusion of World War II.

Fourth, after the War, the Allied nations, especially the three major powers – the U.S., Britain, and France – fully intended to regain as much of the looted gold as possible and restitute it to the liberated nations of Europe. But it has become painfully clear that the Allies fell far short of recovering from the neutral states all the looted gold they were able to identify. Of the more than $550 million of looted gold that the neutral nations of Europe, including Switzerland, received, only $78 million was turned over to the monetary gold pool at the Tripartite Gold Commission. Likewise, of the estimated $722 million in German external assets located in Switzerland, Spain, Portugal, and Sweden at the end of the War, only about $128 million was liquidated for the benefit of the Allies and the reconstruction of war-torn Europe. This resulted from a combination of the change of priorities on the part of the Allies as they concentrated on the new threats imposed by the onset of the Cold War, as well as the intransigent negotiating positions taken by the wartime neutrals.

Fifth, despite the Allies' shortcomings in recovering looted gold, they worked through the Tripartite Gold Commission in one of the more determined and selfless actions of the postwar period. By 1959, more than 336 tons of gold was assembled, and the Tripartite Gold Commission was able to meet 64 percent of the validated claims of the countries from which the gold was taken, restoring the gold to its rightful owners without benefit to the Allies. In addition, agreement was ultimately reached in 1998 to apply the great bulk of the approximately 6 tons of remaining undistributed gold to the unmet needs of the dwindling number of surviving victims of the Nazis. This was based on moral grounds and on the factual determination in the 1997 U.S. Government report, demonstrating that some portion of the looted Nazi gold inadvertently included victim gold, which was swept up with monetary gold and returned to the claimant countries by the TGC.

These contributions funded the Nazi Persecutee Relief Fund, created by the U.S., France, and Britain at the 1997 London Conference to provide resources for the relief of needy victims of Nazi persecution who to date have received very little or no compensation. It is immensely satisfying to report that so far 15 nations – 10 TGC claimant countries and 5 non-claimant countries – have pledged $58.5 million to the Fund. Most of the TGC recipient countries have also pledged to contribute all or a part of their final shares to the Fund, with the remainder going to victim relief within their own countries. I am especially proud to be able to say that the United States has now contributed $4 million and has pledged an additional $21 million over the next three years.

CONCLUSION

I close these remarks by paying tribute to the magnificent efforts of France and Britain, our TGC partners, in working to close out the Commission's work after half a century of effort to bring its efforts to a just conclusion and in establishing the Nazi Persecutee Relief Fund. I look forward to hearing their reports during the balance of this session.

Ambassador Louis Amigues

DIRECTOR OF ARCHIVES AND DOCUMENTATION, MINISTRY OF FOREIGN
AFFAIRS
FRANCE

The Closing of the Tripartite Commission for the Restitution of Monetary Gold

Plenary Session: Review of Gold Issues, Research and Resolution

On September 9, the three governments charged with administering the Tripartite Commission for the restitution of monetary gold officially announced their dissolution in Paris, thus legally and symbolically ending a complex historic process begun after the Second World War.

The Paris Accords of January 14, 1946 on reparations assigned the American, British and French governments to return to the countries the despoiled monetary gold that was put in their Central Banks by the Nazi regime. Accordingly, on September 27, 1946, these three governments created in Brussels the Tripartite Commission for the restitution of monetary gold.

Its task was to compile petitions from despoiled countries, give these claims a ruling, and proceed to the distribution of monetary gold, based on a collective amount gathered before the Commission was created. This amount reached 336.5 tons.

The Tripartite Commission defined the monetary gold as follows:

"Any gold, which at the time of despoiling or illegitimate transfer, belonged to the petitioning country's monetary reserve, whether in the accounts of the petitioning country itself, or in the accounts of the petitioning country's Central Bank, or any other financial institution within or outside its borders."

Eleven countries filed petitions with the Tripartite Commission: Albania, Austria, Belgium, Czechoslovakia, Greece, Italy, Luxembourg, the Netherlands, Poland, and Yugoslavia. The petitions validated by the Tripartite Commission claimed about 514 tons of gold.

To answer the eligible countries urgent reconstruction needs, a preliminary distribution was effectuated between 1947 and 1950. About 80% of the gold available was distributed during that period, and the Commission displayed a remarkable speed, given the complexity of such a procedure.

After that, the restitution process continued at a more regular pace. A second distribution, described as "quasi-final," took place between 1958 and 1959 for the majority of eligible countries, however some of them did not receive their share until legal issues had been settled: The Netherlands in 1973, Poland in 1976, Czechoslovakia in 1982, and Albania in October 1996. At that time, only 5.5 tons of gold remained for distribution.

In the fall of 1996, a few representative organizations questioned this mechanism, and in parallel, offered for the victims of the nazi regime to be compensated.

Keeping this in mind while continuing to work on the mandate of the Paris Accords, the member governments of the Tripartite Commission decided to temporarily defer the distribution of the remaining gold, and began a historic research. This was notably the case for the United States (resulting in the "Eizenstat" report, released in April 97) and Great Britain (resulting in the Foreign Office Historic Notes, released at the same time). These countries had kept documentation from the years of war. Investigations revealed that an undisclosed, but not significant, amount of non-monetary gold could have been included in the amount of gold entrusted to the Tripartite Commission.

On June 27, 1997, in an effort of transparency and truth, the three governments decided to notify the eligible countries of this situation. To materialize these steps and help with considerations, two diplomatic notes were sent to the concerned countries:

- The first, signed by the Tripartite Commission, informed them that distribution of the remaining gold was to take place;
- The second, signed by the three governments, disclosed previously mentioned issues, inviting all eligible countries to draw the practical consequences from it. This verbal note listed various possibilities for making a contribution, inspired by the duty of equity and memory.

Among the options contemplated, it was suggested that an International Fund for compensating the victims of Nazi persecution should be financed. This Fund was implemented at the London Conference in December 1997. Open to the contributions from countries aspiring to join an action of justice and international solidarity, it gathered over the course of a year numerous and large contributions. My British colleague will tell you about the generous collections in this Fund.

For its part, the French government has decided to contribute as much as FF 20 million (about $3.5 million) to express the international solidarity of France toward the victims of this tragic period.

This amount was included in the 1999 budget plan, and approved by the Parliament on November 18. It will be available as early as January 1, 1999.

One of the initial objectives of this Fund was to help the "double victims" of Nazi persecutions who, up until now, have been deprived from any compensation. In addition, the first results of an investigation made by the "Study Mission of the despoiling against the Jews of France" remind that, before the war, France had welcomed many refugees from Central and Eastern Europe, who were the first victims of the persecution and despoiling perpetrated by the Nazis during the occupation.

It is under these circumstances that, in the allocation of its contribution, the French government wished to aid the international Non-Governmental Organizations leading indisputable activities in Central and Eastern European countries. The sums contributed in this framework should, inasmuch as possible, first be used to rescue the members of communities that are faced with the greatest material hardships.

The Tripartite Commission thus completed its duties in a general consensus. During the first half of 1998, the eligible countries received the 5.5 tons of remaining gold owed to them, except for the countries that belonged to the Former Yugoslavia, whose part remains frozen until a treaty of State succession is signed.

The Tripartite Commission fulfilled its mission, and ended its work on September 9 in Paris. It submitted its final report to the three governments. This report was also presented on that same day to the representatives of the eligible countries. At this occasion, France, the United Kingdom and the United States released two joint statements: the first concerns the dissolution of the Tripartite Commission, and the second pertains to the conservation and the transmission of its archives.

Indeed, in accordance with the commitment made and reaffirmed in the London Conference, the complete archives of the Tripartite Commission are now stored at the Foreign Ministry in Paris, and were made available to the public and to researchers.

This desire for transparency is in keeping with two efforts: historic truth and the duty of memory. As far as the French government is concerned, it will continue to abide by these two obligations.

Mr. Anthony Layden

HEAD, WESTERN EUROPEAN DEPARTMENT, FOREIGN AND
COMMONWEALTH OFFICE
UNITED KINGDOM

The International Fund for Needy Victims of Nazi Persecution

Plenary Session: Review of Gold Issues, History and Research

ESTABLISHMENT OF THE FUND

Chairman, distinguished Delegates

1. In his message to this Conference, the Foreign Secretary, Robin Cook, recalled his announcement at the London Conference a year ago that a new International Fund had been set up to assist needy surviving victims of Nazi persecution, and to fund related educational projects. This followed earlier discussions between the member countries of the Tripartite Gold Commission and the countries due to receive shares of the remaining gold in its monetary gold pool. The three Commission member countries - France, the United Kingdom and the United States - had invited the recipient countries to contribute all or part of the value of the gold they were to receive to this Fund. The Fund was also open to contributions from other countries.

2. The Fund was set up in such a way as to minimize bureaucratic procedures. It takes the form of an Agreement between the Federal Reserve Bank of New York, where the Fund's account is located, and the British Government as Account Holder. Briefly, donor governments pay their contributions directly into the Fund Account, and specify to which non-governmental organizations they wish to allocate the money, on the basis of proposals made directly to them by the organizations. The Bank then transfers the money to the specified organizations.

3.   In the course of these transactions, donor governments and recipient organizations signal their acceptance of the Fund's Terms of Reference, which describe in a general way the purposes for which contributions are to be used. There is no central auditing mechanism: it is left to donors to satisfy themselves that their contributions are used for the purposes they intend. Thanks to the agreement of the Federal Reserve Bank not to levy charges for operating the Account, no running costs of any kind are incurred in the working of the Fund. There are no legal or accountants' fees. All of the money contributed by donor governments goes to the NGOs, and through them to the victims.

CONTRIBUTIONS PROMISED UP TO 19 NOVEMBER 1998

4.   During the London Conference, seven delegations announced that their governments intended to contribute to the Fund, subject, in some cases, to legal or other procedures. These were Argentina, Austria, Croatia, Greece, Luxembourg, the United Kingdom and the United States. Three further delegations - those of France, the Netherlands and Poland - said contributions by their governments might be considered.
5.   Since the end of the London Conference, contributions by France, the Netherlands and Poland have been confirmed, and five further governments have announced their intention to contribute: Belgium, the Czech Republic, Italy, the Slovak Republic and Sweden. This means that with only two exceptions, all of the countries sharing in the final distribution of the Tripartite Commission's gold pool have responded positively to the suggestion by the Commission member countries that they contribute to the Fund. Five other countries have also decided to do so, and I am aware of three others who are actively considering contributions.
6.   The two exceptions mentioned above are Albania and the former Yugoslavia. The Albanian Government has from the outset given strong and welcome support to the Fund process, but made it clear that the serious economic situation in Albania was likely to prevent them from making a contribution. The successor states of the former Yugoslavia have not yet agreed on the division between them of assets of that country. Therefore, when the Tripartite Commission was wound up, the gold due to Yugoslavia was retained in its existing account at the Bank of England. One successor state, Croatia, undertook as soon as the Fund was launched to contribute to it its share of the gold pool, whatever

that might be. It has been suggested to the other successor states that if they were all to make similar undertakings, the value of this gold could be made available to the Fund in advance of agreement on the wider question of dividing Yugoslav assets. We await responses. This morning we have been told by Ambassador Rupel, the leader of the Slovenian delegation that Slovenia has also decided to contribute its share of the remaining TGC gold to the Fund. We welcome this decision.

7.   Not all donor governments have yet specified the amounts they will contribute, but the amounts specified up to the 19th of November, when a review meeting of donor countries was held in London, total $59.6 million - almost exactly the value of the gold which was in the Tripartite Commission's pool at the time the Fund was launched. It is already clear that the final total will considerably exceed this sum.

PAYMENTS MADE TO THE FUND ACCOUNT

8.   Up to the 19th of November, five donor countries had made payments into the Fund Account at the Federal Reserve Bank, as follows:

27 March 1998	United Kingdom $1,647,000
23 June	Sweden $1,014,055
10 & 17 July, 13 October	Poland $366,615
24 September	Czech Republic $162,012
23 October	United States $4,000,000

ALLOCATIONS FROM THE FUND ACCOUNT

9.   The Federal Reserve Bank made the first disbursements from the Fund Account on the 22nd of July 1998, in accordance with an Allocation Instruction from the United Kingdom. Two payments each of $139,750 were made. One was to the Board of Deputies of British Jews; the other was paid into an account opened for the purpose by the World Jewish Restitution Organization, from which it was transferred to the American Jewish Joint Distribution Committee. A further disbursement of $431,505 was made on the 24th of August 1998, in accordance with an Accelerated Allocation Instruction from the United Kingdom, again to the Board of Deputies of British Jews.

10.   The balance of principal and interest in the Fund Account on the 16th of November 1998 was $6,595,667.

SELECTION OF RECIPIENT NON-GOVERNMENTAL ORGANIZATIONS

11.   The British Government began consultations with NGOs about the allocation of its contribution of 1 million pounds announced by the Foreign Secretary at the London Conference, immediately after that event. We decided to allocate one-third of the amount to the Board of Deputies of British Jews, who had made a proposal to form a committee of a number of separate organizations working with surviving victims in the UK, and make cash grants to victims with particular needs.

12.   The remaining two-thirds of the UK contribution was allocated to the American Jewish Joint Distribution Committee (AJJDC), who proposed to use it for medicines and medical equipment, to be provided to victims in Belarus, Moldova, Russia and Ukraine through community organizations (hesedim) in that region. After presentations from the World Jewish Restitution Organization (WJRO) and the Conference on Jewish Material Claims, who wished to be associated with this activity, it was agreed that this portion of the UK contribution would be paid into an account opened for the purpose by the WJRO, from which it would be transferred immediately to an AJJDC account. This arrangement, for which the Fund Agreement provides, has worked satisfactorily.

13.   It is understood that an Austrian contribution of about $8.6 million is likely to be paid into the Fund Account soon, and will probably be allocated to the Austrian National Fund for Victims of National Socialism. The Czech Republic contribution mentioned earlier will be allocated to two NGOs in the Republic, the Union of Freedom Fighters and the Union of Forced Laborers. An Italian contribution of about $7.2 million is likely to be paid into the Account soon, and to be allocated to the Union of Italian Jewish Committees. The Swedish contribution mentioned earlier is to be allocated in equal shares to the European Jewish Congress, the Jewish Central Committee of Sweden, and the Swedish Red Cross (for Romani victims). A total of 17 NGOs have so far been designated by donors as Fund recipients.

14.   A number of countries are ready to make contributions or allocations, but are awaiting detailed proposals from the NGOs they have selected. Indeed, it emerged at the London review meeting

mentioned earlier that up to the present, there has always been more money available in the Fund Account than there were proposals from NGOs for its use. NGOs represented at this Conference are therefore urged to respond as quickly as possible when invited by donor governments to submit proposals for Fund allocations.

15. In a few cases, the British Government as Account Holder has had difficulty in contacting NGOs selected by donors as recipients of allocations, and in obtaining from them their written agreement to the Fund Terms of Reference, as required by the Agreement. Again, NGOs are urged to respond quickly when asked by us to sign and return copies of the Terms of Reference. We shall be glad to offer help or advice about the operation of the Fund to anyone who needs it.

HELP SO FAR GIVEN TO VICTIMS

16. The Board of Deputies of British Jews has made payments of 400 pounds each to 600 Jewish and non-Jewish applicants in the UK who applied up to June 1998. The Board is now arranging payments in respect of 166 applications received between July and September. It has approved 100 applications received since then, and estimate that the total may approach 1000 by the end of the year, when a cut-off date has been set.

17. The American Jewish Joint Distribution Committee has informed us in a preliminary report that between July and September this year it deployed the portion of their allocation disbursed on 22 July to supply medicines to more than 14,500 elderly Nazi victims in 55 cities and towns in Belarus, Moldova, Russia and Ukraine, and to provide 4,120 items of medical rehabilitative equipment to recipients in 106 cities and towns in the same region. The program continues.

CONCLUSION

18. Chairman and distinguished delegates, I am conscious as I come to the end of this presentation that a great deal more remains to be done to discharge effectively the duty Robin Cook suggested in London last year that the international community owed to surviving victims of Nazi persecution. He said: "...we must ensure that the unbearable tragedy of living through the Holocaust is not compounded by an old age marked by the fear and sadness of poverty." We are still a long way from

ensuring that.   But a start has been made.   The machinery of the International Fund is in place. Help has begun to flow to those who need it most. And the pace of that flow will accelerate rapidly from now on.

19.   Chairman, I wish to pay tribute to all those who have worked together in this enterprise. When we began it the difficulties seemed immense. The legal and moral obligation on the Tripartite partners to convey the remaining gold to the designated recipient countries was clear. It was also clear that somehow in the process of ending our long stewardship of the monetary gold pool we must find a way of helping needy individual survivors. As always happens in such cases, each country - and we are a diverse group - responded to the challenge in its own way. Each was subject to different pressures and influences. And many different approaches to the situation were put forward. NGOs too had many different ideas about what should be done.

20.   Throughout the complicated discussions that took place in Brussels, Paris, Washington and other capitals all participants showed consistent flexibility, goodwill, and a shared determination not to let differences of perception and approach prevent us from meeting a need that we all saw as both highly important and extremely urgent. The International Fund was the outcome: together we have made it work and together we shall ensure that it completes the job we designed it to do. Robin Cook described this as "an imaginative and successful piece of modern diplomacy," and so of course it is. For me, it has also been one of the most worthwhile and rewarding tasks I have been engaged in. I am grateful to the Foreign Secretary for entrusting me with it. And I am grateful to my colleagues, diplomatic and non-governmental, in France, the United States and the other countries present here, for their unfailing co-operation and friendship.

Thank you all very much.

Mr. Edgar Bronfman

PRESIDENT
WORLD JEWISH CONGRESS/WORLD JEWISH
RESTITUTION ORGANIZATION

Address at the Conference

History, in its own cruel fashion, has imposed a heavy burden on all of us gathered here. It is this realization that must guide our deliberations and actions during the period of the Conference. A burden can weigh you down, or it can challenge you to rise to the demands that it imposes. From this understanding comes the stark comprehension that we are not here to talk about money or art or insurance policies; we have come together to express the moral imperative that justice must prevail, that truth must be expounded, and that we have committed ourselves to the higher values of integrity – to preserve the memory of those who were victims of unspeakable crimes.

The cliché that we should learn the lessons of history and not repeat the mistakes is particularly apt here. Conferences are all too often a cheap substitute for coming to grips with the substantive nature of the issues they were called to deal with. When the Jewish people were faced with annihilation during the Second World War, the United States and Britain convened the 1943 Bermuda conference, ostensibly to find a solution for wartime refugees. In fact that conference was a sham and actually was an effort to thwart the rescue of European Jewry. This conference must be different or the judgment of history will harshly condemn us.

On innumerable occasions I have sought to describe the goals we are seeking to achieve as being "moral and material restitution."

Clearly in the last several years, and indeed since our last international conference in London, marked progress has been made. There have been notable achievements in the effort to secure material restitution: the fund established in London arising from the remaining gold in the TGC; the settlements with Swiss banks and the earlier commitment by Swiss banks and industry, which created an important humanitarian fund; expansion of benefits to Holocaust survivors within the context of ongoing German reparation payments – particularly as they apply to Eastern European victims; an agreement by major

European insurance companies to resolve unpaid claims through the mechanism of the International Commission established for that purpose.

One particularly shining example should be cited, that of Norway. The government not only established an historical commission of inquiry and approved monies for compensation, but even more movingly sought to underline the moral dimensions of the issue by adopting the minority position of the commission that it had established; the Norwegian example is a lesson for all – combining the twin principles of moral and material restitution.

In so far as material restitution is concerned, I appeal to those governments and institutions and experts that are gathered here; do not allow this to become a Bermuda conference. We must come away from this meeting with practical and immediate proposals to secure justified financial compensation for those who have been so long denied, and we must establish an ongoing mechanism to verify that governments and institutions are taking these practical steps. This effort must not end with this conference.

In some ways the struggle for moral restitution may be more difficult. It involves what we call in Hebrew "heshbon nefesh" – searching of the soul. This is not a challenge only to the neutral countries; this is a challenge which must be confronted by the Allies, the former Axis states, the bystanders, the churches, industrial concerns, bankers and Jewish people.

Our inescapable obligation is to set forth the record of events as they happened, without embellishment, without self-serving alteration, and with brutal honesty. We owe this first and most of all to the memory of the victims, because that is what we are striving to achieve – the preservation of memory and the power of its piercing truthfulness.

For those nations and those peoples, or those institutions for which the critical examination of this historic period will give rise to dark moments of unpleasant realities, the answer is – there is no choice. We cannot know where to go or where we are going, unless we know where we have come from. And foundations built on gossamer evasions cannot support the pressing weight of historical accuracy.

But as painful as the process may be, the other lesson that history has taught us is that the struggle to honestly come to terms with the past makes us stronger – spiritually and intellectually – in the long run.

This then is the ultimate irony. The process that causes us so much pain also provides us with purification and the strength of conscience to face our children and future generations.

I appeal to you therefore to act – and not merely to deliberate – in a manner which measures up to the historical task before us. If we fail to do so in this, the last minute of this dying century, we will be reproached not only by the victims of the crime but by our own children. Let us therefore dedicate ourselves to overcome whatever obstacle to reach that level of action and honesty that will allow the peoples of the 42 nations represented here – and more importantly their children – to say the struggle for memory was validated here.

Ms. Nili Arad

DIRECTOR-GENERAL, MINISTRY OF JUSTICE
ISRAEL

Address at the National Archives

Thank you, Mr. Carlin.
Distinguished fellow delegates, Ladies and Gentlemen:

"Almost a Love Poem"

> **"If my parents and your parents
> hadn't migrated to Eretz Yisrael in 1936,
> we would have met in 1944**
>
> **there on the platform at Auschwitz.
> I at twenty,
> and you, at five.**
>
> **Where's Mammele?
> Where's Tattele?**
>
> **What's your name?
> Hannale."**

written by Yehuda Amichai,
an outstanding Israeli poet.

That is how we have grown up in Israel since the Holocaust, where the shadow of our extinguished families has become part of our personal history. Striving to build a safe haven for Jews all over the world, we took the pledge *Never to Forget; Always to remember*.

In the past two days, we have felt that this promise has touched each of you. It has become the goal of us all, representatives of different countries, non-govern mental organizations, insurance companies, private agencies, Jews and non-Jews alike.

The holistic understanding and agreement on which we are all focussing here is not about material possessions – but about historical Justice. Justice long due to the families, to real people who were stripped of their human dignity, robbed of their pride, dispossessed of their property, uprooted from their homes and finally systematically murdered by the most brutal methods.

We are not seeking justice for crimes of war, nor the restitution of the improperly acquired spoils of war. Rather, we are talking about the Holocaust – the Nazi's program of unspeakable human suffering and physical devastation inflicted upon the Jewish people and unmatched in history.

Now, we are building an *international consensus for justice* that goes far beyond the question of identifying stolen assets and returning them to their rightful owners.

We today must reach a higher moral ground, to ensure the memory of those who perished, the acknowledgement and preservation of the history of their fate, the culture and public institutions of the devastated Jewish communities of Europe, endeavoring to ensure that the survivors of these great communities live in comfort and dignity.

Indeed the result of our deliberations is the recognition of an urgent need to proceed with the efforts to give life to the mute pages in archives; to reveal the identities of the unknown people in yet unpublished lists. To ensure free access to all knowledge and information essential to the establishment of justice. In the words of the esteemed Supreme Court Justice Louis Brandeis:

> *"Sunlight is said to be the best disinfectant,*
> *electric light the most efficient policeman."*

We leave this Conference heartened and encouraged, convinced that we are, indeed, part of a worldwide consensus dedicated to the relentless pursuit of justice in the various areas where justice was denied.

Throughout the intensive and enlightening discussions of the last two days, we have been moved – and very much aware – of the great historical nature and significance of this gathering.

At the closing of the twentieth century, on the threshold of a new era, let all people of goodwill join together in pursuit of the noble goals which we have set for ourselves.

Together we spoke of them in London; we speak of them again here in Washington. Let us vow to continue our united effort to strengthen the hands of those who dedicate themselves to the achievement of justice, and to those who strive to further the principles of human dignity and the freedom of mankind. Thank you.

Concluding
Statements

Concluding Statement

Mr. Miles Lerman
CHAIRMAN,
UNITED STATES HOLOCAUST MEMORIAL COUNCIL

Thank you. Ambassadors, Delegates, Ladies and Gentlemen:

We are nearing the end of this extraordinary conference on Holocaust-Era Assets. We have heard many speakers; we have listened to impassioned pleas; we have been moved; we have been called to action. Indeed, much has been accomplished – yet so much more remains to be done.

As I stated before, the success of this conference will ultimately be judged by the manner in which every nation here will assume its own obligation towards an ongoing, intensive program of Holocaust Education.

History will judge all of our nations by the demonstrated degree of willingness to confront the truth about our own past. We will be judged on how diligently we will pursue efforts to make our archives available for scholarly research. Without these archival records, the full story of the Holocaust and all related issues cannot be told.

The story we will convey to future generations must be factual and fully documented. Otherwise, it will not withstand the test of history.

But there are other critical issues that I want to address this morning.

I believe all of us should be concerned with the recent phenomenon that is arising as a result of increased attention to Holocaust assets. I am referring to the rise of anti-Semitism in certain European countries. So far the drummers of hate are still somewhat subdued. They seem to come in the form of a whisper campaign. But remembrance teaches us that we cannot ignore or take lightly early signs of anti-Semitism.

One manifestation of this phenomenon appears to be taking place in Switzerland.

On November 5, 1998, Switzerland's Federal Commission Against Racism reported that, "Latent anti-Semitism is again being increasingly expressed in public word and deed." The Commission reports that, "Comments from Swiss politicians helped make anti-Semitism socially acceptable." Again this fact is highly disturbing.

This resurgence of anti-Semitic sentiments seemed to be explained as a reaction to the negotiated financial compensation with some of the Swiss banks.

Should this phenomenon continue, we should keep in mind that such retaliatory anti-Semitism will only compound the problems that this conference is trying to address.

Let it come forward from here to all concerned that the days when Jews were afraid to speak up to defend their rights are gone and will never return again.

It is essential that we recognize that the debate, in which we are now engaged, is not only about assets, but it is about what is right and what is wrong and what is just and what is unjust.

The moral aspect of this debate is perhaps more important than the material consequences.

There is another matter that I must bring to your attention. It is eloquently expressed in the letter that appears in your packet that was written by David Harris, the Director of the American Jewish Committee, regarding the identification and preservation of the places of martyrdom throughout Europe.

Some countries are dedicated to the task to preserve these sites; in others, little or no effort is made.

In some countries, legislation exists to protect these sites; in others, there is no protection whatsoever.

It is imperative to prevail upon the nations that have failed to preserve and protect their sacred sites, that they must ensure that these places remain as reminders of the horrible crimes of a half century ago. If we are to pursue an intensive program of Holocaust education and remembrance, these sites must be preserved and they must become our eternal witnesses to a horrid past.

As you can see, Ladies and Gentlemen, we are ending our conference with great accomplishments – but even greater challenges, much in the way of education, research and preservation remains to be done, but I feel hopeful that with goodwill and true understanding of what is at stake for future generations, we will succeed in our efforts.

Thank you.

Concluding Statement
AMERICAN GATHERING OF JEWISH HOLOCAUST SURVIVORS

By Mr. Benjamin Meed
HEAD OF DELEGATION

Mr. Chairman Abner Mikva, thank you for your kind introduction.

As we are about to conclude this historic conference, I would like, on behalf of the survivor community, to express our appreciation especially to Stuart Eizenstat and Miles Lerman for bringing together such a distinguished international gathering.

In the last four days much good will was expressed and we are grateful. There were many highlights, many expressions of solidarity with the victims. The aim of the conference was to unite us for future activities and we hope this was achieved. A better understanding of what the Holocaust did to our people.

Although this conference dealt mostly with pragmatic issues, Holocaust survivors must never allow to forget the enormity of the catastrophe which befell especially our Jewish people and remember the murder of six million European Jews. We realize that we will never learn the enormity of our losses, but we must demand that justice and morality be the guidelines in future deliberations.

I am here together with my fellow officers of the American Gathering of Jewish Holocaust Survivors. As Americans we feel proud that under the seal of the United States, under the leadership of America, this conference was organized and this work will continue. We are working very closely with the Israeli delegation, with whom we have special bonds. In the field of education we work very closely with Yad Vashem in Jerusalem and Lochamei Hageta'ot in Nahariya.

We were inspired by many people, but personally, for me were the remarks by our Secretary of State Madeleine Albright. While she spoke and summoned us to remember, I could not help but think of my own family murdered in the Holocaust, and about so many Jewish children never given a chance of growing up and doing so much for society and humanity.

The aims of the Holocaust survivors in all their years after liberation can be summed up in three objectives: our responsibility to **commemorate, document and educate**. To the end of our lives we will continue to bear witness.

As we rebuilt our lives in this country, in the State of Israel and countries throughout the world, survivors took upon themselves the responsibility of not letting the world forget. In the last fifteen years the American Gathering created, under the leadership of Vladka Meed, the acclaimed program of education of the Holocaust and Resistance. Six hundred seventeen alumni from throughout the country are today teaching nationwide about Holocaust and Resistance.

We are pleased that the flame of education, which we survivors ignited and which we would like to instill in our future generations, has today become the most important theme. The Conference and assets also had to become the platform of remembrance, this time, not only by survivors, but by countries worldwide. We are grateful to the State Department, under the leadership of Under Secretary Stuart Eizenstat, and Miles Lerman, the chairman of the United States Holocaust Memorial Museum, as well as all representatives of Yad Vashem of the State of Israel and we are commending their goals.

Naturally, those who lived through that period have a special sensitivity and passion, and are bound by Remembrance. Most important to us survivors is the subject of Remembrance. What should be remembered is that truth and morality must be our guide.

We are grateful that today, the Days of Remembrance is officially observed in the United States as a full week of remembrance. Hundreds of thousands of people annually remember the Holocaust through these observances.

Many institutions in the United States did help in documenting the Holocaust through eyewitnesses and we are grateful to them. But the official documentation of Holocaust survivors in the United States is the National Registry of Jewish Holocaust Survivors, which was, and is being, compiled jointly by the American Gathering and the United States Holocaust Memorial Museum.

Our records and data base today already represent more than 120,000 Holocaust survivors and their families. This work is of the utmost importance and we must continue with it. Our goal is that every living survivor, as well as those who passed away, in the United States should have his or her record, including the family, recorded. History will need this documentation. Although it is work we are doing for more than twenty years, we hope it will continue as a major priority of our activities. We need, for all this, cooperation from Holocaust survivors and their descendants.

We hope that education will become now the tool of erasing ignorance and preparing new generations free of hatred and bigotry.

Concluding Statement
BELARUS

By Vladimir Adamushko
HEAD OF DELEGATION

Mr. Chairman, Ladies and Gentlemen,

On behalf of the delegation of the Republic of Belarus allow me to thank the Conference hosts for their invitation to participate in it, for their hospitality, good organization and conditions of our work.

The problems viewed at this conference are of great importance for the mankind. The cooperation and mutual understanding of nations depend greatly on how fairly they are going to be resolved.

Speaking at the opening of our conference Secretary of State Madeleine Albright precisely defined the Holocaust as history's most monstrous crime. This 'monster" cost more than 2.5 mln. lives to my small country in the center of Europe. Nearly 800 thousand of the victims were Jews, which accounts for 1/7 of the total Holocaust victims.

Regrettably, the problems of the Holocaust to the east of Poland have been hardly touched upon at this Conference.

Immediately after the London Conference we in Belarus came back to the problem of Nazi gold: we thoroughly studied documents in our national archives, as well as in those of Germany and Russia.

Our research resulted in the collection of documents "Nazi Gold from Belarus" published in September, 1998, which had included 46 documents containing data on gold, silver and other jewelry confiscated by the Nazis from the population of Belarus and sent to the Reich.

Out of the book's 410 pages, 185 pages are devoted to the documented lists of persons whose jewelry had been confiscated by the Nazis. They are Belarusians and Jews, Russians and Poles, Ukrainians and Tartars, and people of other nationalities.

But these lists of looted valuables have one discrepancy. Jews make up only 5 percent in them, though Belarus was a major center of Jewish pale in the former Soviet Union. The fact is that only few Jews could get into these lists. The Holocaust victims were in another list.

Nearly 800 thousand Jews were killed in more than 200 ghettos in Belarus, among them almost 50 thousand Jews from various European countries. Jews were killed "wholesale'. All at once. They were robbed of anything: documents, valuables, personal belongings, gold, silver and the most dear thing - the life itself. The archival documents prove it.

It's worth noting that the research included documents and materials dealing mainly with the central part of Belarus (during the Nazi occupation it formed the General Region of Byelorussia incorporated into the Ostland Reichkommissariat) which accounts for a quarter of today's territory of the country. The remaining part of the Belarusian territory was under the authority of the military occupation administration of the Center Army Group Rear and the General Regions of Bialostok and Lithuania. Therefore, the real number of citizens whose jewelry was confiscated by the Nazis is much larger.

And the documentary database was far from being complete. A part of archives on this problem was either destroyed or sometimes inaccessible for researchers on other reasons. We present here only the documents which our researchers could find by fragments and which apply to non-monetary gold, or to be more exact, the gold confiscated from the Belarusian citizens.

Distinguished Delegates,

Today, due to economic reasons, my country cannot become a donor to the International Fund for Needy Victims of Nazi Persecution. Unfortunately, it needs assistance itself due to various reasons, the Chernobyl disaster among them, with its consequences continuing to affect nearly half the country's territory for many years to come.

We propose to make within the International Fund for Needy Victims of Nazi Persecution a special list of states that suffered most during the Holocaust era and cannot become the Fund's donors yet but whose Holocaust victims could be assisted through this Fund. Belarus is among the European countries which suffered the heaviest losses from Nazism. Its people, Nazi victims, both Jews and non-Jews, hope that their country will be included into the group states which are to be compensated for their confiscated assets.

There are more than 400 persons among them whose names had been or are about to be commemorated in Jerusalem's Avenue of the Righteous Amongst the Nations.

We believe and hope that our research will be taken into account as well when sealing the final fate of Nazi non-monetary gold.

We hope for a just solution of this problem. Thank you.

Concluding Statement
BULGARIA

By Ambassador Philip Dimitrov
HEAD OF DELEGATION

Mr. Chairman, Ladies and Gentlemen,

I would like first to thank, on the behalf of the Bulgarian delegation, all who worked hard to make this conference possible. Permit me to thank personally Secretary Eizenstat for his efforts and for his efficiency.

Restitution is not merely an economic but mainly a moral issue. It is generally accepted that crime and violence should not and will not be tolerated to benefit anyone. Restitution is a – if not *the* – practical way to make this perfectly clear.

I cannot agree with people who think that what has been said and done about the Holocaust until now is enough. We need to protect our world from the possibility of any new outburst of totalitarian savagery, and memory is one of the most important factors in this respect. The memory of the Holocaust should be kept alive. The sufferings of the Jewish people who were systematically tortured and industrially slaughtered represent the most blatant and terrifying example of what tyranny and teaching of hatred brought to people in the twentieth century. And it is not surprising that quite a few issues directly deriving from the Holocaust could be raised only now when the other poisonous social structure – communism – fell.

The need to recall and discuss the Holocaust is not a matter of fashion, but of an intrinsic human necessity which should be respected, supported and encouraged not only in memory of the past but for the sake of the future as well.

For obvious reasons, the contribution of my delegation to the work of this Conference is very modest. Fortunately, Bulgaria does not face most of the problems that are being discussed here. The Bulgarians, like the Danes, took a firm stand in support of their Jewish compatriots during the war. Bulgaria was the only country in Hitler-dominated wartime Europe which emerged from the war with more Jews living in it than before the war, and managed to save fifty thousand human beings from deportation to the death camps. This was only achieved due to the combined and sustained efforts of the State Institutions (Parliament and King), the Church, the intellectuals of different trends of thought and the common people who went out into the streets. It is true that the Bulgarian nation could not save the Jews from Trace and Macedonia, and this is painful indeed. But the Jews in Bulgaria, even when they suffered the humiliation of yellow stars and labor camps, knew that this was the only way to save them from deportation and that when the Nazi pressure was over, their position would be restored. Most of the Bulgarian Jews later chose to leave post-war Bulgaria and it was then that a good part of their property was robbed by the communist regime.

However, one thing that gives me courage for the future of my nation is the awareness that even now there are thousands of Bulgarian-born Jews living in the State of Israel and elsewhere, who keep on mentioning Bulgaria in their prayers.

In fact, my country has considerable experience with restitution of Jewish (as well as every other) property robbed by the communist regime and we are ready to share this experience with respect to problems that can occur in such complicated procedures.

Weekend Jewish schools in Bulgaria were started soon after the fall of the Berlin wall and last fall a full-time Jewish school was established in Sofia with the generous assistance of the Lauder Foundation.

The University of Sofia has already introduced Jewish Studies into its curriculum, and steps are being taken to increase the amount of data on the Holocaust in the curriculum of the public high schools. Naturally, I would like to use the opportunity of this Conference to express our openness to exchange of experience in these matters as well.

I would also like to express the support of my delegation to the proposal for measures aimed at the full preservation of sites of the Holocaust. These ugly monuments of despicable inhumanity should not be destroyed. Their existence is a weapon in the fight for human memory, i.e., for human conscience. We should not deprive ourselves of this weapon as long as there are still voices saying that the story of the Holocaust is a bit exaggerated.

Concluding Statement
CANADA

By Mr. Howard Strauss
HEAD OF DELEGATION

Mr. Chairman, hosts, fellow delegates:

As the Conference draws to a close, we join others who have spoken to congratulate the U.S. authorities on their initiative in convening this Conference. It was a success by any standard.

Mr. Chairman, the ratio of the holocaust survivor community in Canada to the Canadian Jewish population is higher than that of any other country in the world, except Israel. The Conference has, therefore, a special importance for us.

Canada has opened its holocaust-era national archives to the public. Canadian insurance companies are in the process of reviewing their holocaust-era files. Bank of Canada records have been reviewed both internally and by outside experts. The Canadian Art Museums Directors Organization fully supports the principle of return of Holocaust Era Assets, and is working on guidelines similar to the ones discussed here.

Our education facilities provide cutting edge holocaust education programs: a chair has been dedicated to holocaust studies at a major university, courses are offered at all levels, holocaust memorial museums have been established in Montreal, Toronto, Winnipeg and Vancouver. An international symposium on hate on the Internet took place in Canada in 1997. A follow-up international conference will take place in Canada in March of next year.

Through our written contributions and oral participation, we have sought to provide others attending this Conference with the benefit of our experience. And we, in turn, have benefited from the insights offered by colleagues.

We will complete the work begun in Canada. We will also continue to contribute what we can at the international level.

It is too late for the many who have died, but we can provide a small measure of justice to their memory and to the survivors. And, we can, through education, try to save our children from reliving their horrors.

We should do it because it is the right thing to do. Thank you.

Concluding Statement
CZECH REPUBLIC

By Mr. Jiri Sitler
HEAD OF DELEGATION

Ladies and gentlemen,

This conference has not been summoned to account for successes; it was intended to stimulate a deeper international debate on Holocaust era assets.

In our country, we take part in the debate, and support the creation of diverse committees, task forces, and funds for victims. Nevertheless, I have a feeling that the overflow of memorandums, committees, and press declarations in the last years and months was sometimes self-purposed. I will tell you why I believe so.

We sometimes ask our citizens who have survived the horrors of the Holocaust about their opinion on international foundations that are being announced in the headlines of the world press. Usually they answer politely that they welcome the current discussion, nevertheless, none of the Czech Jews or Roma has ever received a dollar from these funds. I am sure it will happen soon, but still, more agility would not hurt.

Victims who survived and stayed in Czechoslovakia or other countries of the Central and Eastern Europe were de facto excluded from the compensation remedies arranged between the Allies and the German government. We actually do not know the reason for this. The argument that they lived in a communist country is not clear – it meant that they needed the money even more. Moreover, no arguments ever prevented retirement payments to ex-members of the Nazi army. Well, be it as it may, the lost decades are not to come back. But it is the reason why international community should focus much more on the real situation of the Nazi victims in Central and Eastern Europe, not on the virtual world of statements, memorandums, moralizing, and press conferences.

Of course, there is a lot to do in my own country too. That is why the Czech Republic established a governmental committee chaired by the Deputy Prime Minister. We know that the results of its work will be more important than the intentions and plans.

However, you could allow me to share with you some of our good experiences. As waiting for a compensation or humanitarian aid from abroad seemed to take too long, in 1994 the Czech Parliament adopted an act providing financial aid to the Nazi victims. By this day, 55 million dollars were distributed from a Czech government agency, without any request for its operating budget increase.

In December 1997, the so-called 'Czech-German Fund for the Future' was established. The Czech share is 17 million dollars while the German one is 93 million dollars. 53 million dollars out of this amount is to be handed directly to the victims. Both the Czech and the German members of the board of administrators and of the supervisory board of the Czech-German Fund fulfill their job for free.

We are proud that funds in which Czech side is participating are running smoothly and inexpensively and I hope that you will forgive me mentioning this so much. After all, this is the only aid that the Czech victims of Nazism have ever seen. They rightly hope that it was not the last one. We can show to all the attorneys, members of boards and others involved in this issue how things worked out so swiftly and without any expensive salaries and fees. Of course, only if they would like to see something so strange.

Much more important issue is to make everybody see what the victims of Nazism from Central and Eastern European countries think. It is no surprise that we can find representatives of Roma and Jews among the Czech delegates. We do not want them to function only as a matter of the debate. We wish them to be involved in solving the problems concerning them most, not only in our country, but also in appropriate international councils. It is still not that way. Therefore, I highly appreciate the speech given yesterday by the representative of the American Jewish Committee who addressed this problem.

The Washington conference gave us the opportunity to discuss all these issues in an open and frank manner. I would like to thank all the organizers who made it possible, especially Judge Abner Mikva, Undersecretary Stuart Eizenstat and Miles Lerman, Chairman of the United States Holocaust Memorial Council.

Several decades ago we were united in the battle against Nazism. Now we should become allies in fighting its consequences. We can sure teach each other a lot in that. Thank you very much for your interest and patience.

Concluding Statement
FRANCE

By Ambassador Louis Amigues
HEAD OF DELEGATION

Ladies and Gentlemen,

First of all, I would like to join my colleagues in thanking the organizers of this conference. These three days were full of exchanges on the tragic subject of the looting of assets during the Holocaust. They have allowed all the participants, I hope, to better understand what happened during that period and to take the necessary steps toward fulfilling our duty to remember.

This final speech gives me an opportunity to reaffirm the desire of the highest authorities of my country to shed all possible light on this painful aspect of our history.

In 1995, President Chirac indicated his concern for seeing France fulfill its duties of remembrance and history through the recognition of the horror and tragedy that struck the Jews of France in the form of the Holocaust ordained by the Nazi occupier and implemented by the Vichy government. Just a few days ago, on November 28, the Prime Minister reaffirmed this determination before the Representative Council of Jewish Institutions of France.

I want to quote the following passage from his speech:

"The test of truth is always delicate. Nevertheless it remains indispensable. A nation always benefits from a clear-minded look at its past, including its darker pages. That is why, after approving without reservations the declarations of the President of the Republic with regard to the anti-Semitic crimes of the Vichy regime, I myself expressed the same sentiment." And: *"You have legitimately stressed the concerns of the Jews of France regarding the question of looted assets. Such expectations are well founded. It is normal for those who*

*were the victims of this unprecedented tragedy – the
Shoah – to demand rights that are indeed theirs."*

There cannot be the slightest doubt as to France's will.

Indeed, it has resulted in the establishment of the Commission
headed by Mr. Jean Mattéoli, Chairman of the Economic and Social
Council. Several of its members are part of our delegation, notably its
Vice President, Professor Steg, who is also president of the Universal
Israelite Alliance. They had an opportunity to talk about their work so I
will not go back into the details, but I do want to underscore the
following points:

The work being accomplished is considerable, exceptionally
wide-ranging, and is mobilizing all the administrations and bodies
concerned to investigate all possible sources. It is being carried out with
determination and total independence on the part of Commissioners.

The government has taken the necessary measures, both in
financial terms and in terms of staff, to complete this enormous task by
the end of 1999. If necessary, its resources will be increased in order to
meet this goal.

The results of this investigation will be accompanied by
proposals regarding the nature and modalities of reparations that seem
justified. The government will then make the decisions it deems
necessary.

As you can see, France's approach is thus extremely ambitious. It
is also specific, given that France – and first and foremost its Jewish
community – was a victim of Nazi looting. As soon as the legitimate
Republic was re-established, our country systematically began making
restitutions in all areas: financial assets, works of art, real estate,
industrial and commercial assets and so on. The work under way will
make it possible to very precisely identify the extent of the sizable
restitutions that have already been made and to determine those that were
unable to be made.

Finally, this approach is directed first and foremost toward
France's Jewish community. We favor the concept of individual
restitution, despite the considerable work it entails. This legal concept,
which differs from the collective and communitarian treatment that may
be current elsewhere, allows us to respond specifically to the claims
made by our fellow citizens. To this end, the Prime Minister has just
approved the creation of a body responsible for examining individual
claims by the victims of anti-Semitic measures and their heirs.

That does not prevent us from taking part in the duty to pursue remembrance and education at the international level, as shown by our contribution of some 20 million francs to the activities of the international fund assisting the victims of Nazi persecution.

Thank you for your attention.

Concluding Statement
GERMANY

By Ambassador Professor Tono Eitel
HEAD OF DELEGATION

Mr. Chairman, Excellencies, Ladies and Gentlemen:

Thank you, Mr. Chairman, Judge Mikva, for the understanding and impartiality with which you have conducted the conference over the past days. We are sure that your balanced judgment will also be brought to bear in your summary, which will contain your findings about our work. We shall study it with the greatest interest and with the greatest respect and sympathy for you personally, Mr. Chairman, and for the cause of the conference.

I thank the State Department, Ambassador Eizenstat, and the Holocaust Memorial Museum, Mr. Lerman, for their hospitality.

Ladies and Gentlemen,

The subjects with which we have been dealing over these days are very difficult for everyone in this room. They are and they will remain a source of shame for Germans. The liberation of Auschwitz on January 27, 1945, is a day of remembrance in Germany. We also commemorate Kristallnacht, the night of the pogrom on November 9, 1938, when synagogues were burned. This was a turning point in the history of the persecution and plundering of German Jews. On the sixtieth anniversary of that event, Federal President Roman Herzog, said in a Berlin synagogue:

> *The night of November 9 to 10, 1938, was one of the most terrible and disgraceful moments in German history. It was a slap in the face of humanity and civilization.*

Ladies and Gentlemen,

Immediately after the end of the war, it was clear to everybody that there could never be complete compensation for the immense suffering, both human and material, which the Hitler regime had brought upon the world. Germany nevertheless endeavored to do what it could at the time. Nazi victims included Jews, politically and religiously persecuted persons, and also Sinti and Roma, whose terrible suffering was so vividly brought to life by the remarkable intervention of the President of the International Romani Union.

Today, Germany can look back on nearly fifty years of compensation totaling more than 100 billion German marks, and annual payments of 1.7 billion German marks continue to be made. This corresponds to more than 60 billion dollars plus continuing annual payments of 1 billion dollars.

In Germany, the restitution of assets belonging to Nazi victims began immediately after the war. Prior to the foundation of the Federal Republic of Germany in 1949, the victorious powers had already done a considerable amount of work to right the wrongs and give back to the victims what belonged to them. The Federal Republic of Germany carried on where the Allies had left off. Movables and immovables that could be identified as having belonged to victims of Nazi persecution were returned to survivors, to their heirs, or to successor organizations. Compensation was paid for material assets that could no longer be restituted. This compensation also covered cases where there was no successor. These assets were dealt with in global agreements with the Jewish Claims Conference. Our policy of restitution and compensation has been developed over the years in constant dialogue with the Allies, with the successor organizations set up by survivors and trusted by everyone involved, and also with the State of Israel.

Ladies and Gentlemen,

Allow me to make a few comments on the main subjects of our conference.

On the issue of Nazi gold, we regret to admit that the Reichsbank files concerning the victims' gold were, based on the documents available, divided up according to the then prevailing standards and ultimately lost 25 years ago. It seems their political and historical significance was not properly understood. Documentation is available to you on this regrettable loss.

The German Government welcomes and supports efforts by German and other European insurance companies to pursue in the International Commission the question of insurance policies held by Nazi victims that were not paid out. I would like to emphasize at this point that it was the declared intention of the Hitler regime to channel all

Jewish assets to the state or one of its organizations. That policy also applied to insurance claims. If the victims did not collect on such policies, their surrender value was confiscated by the Reich Treasury, that is, by the tax offices. After the war, these insurance policies became part of German compensation payments. The International Commission should therefore be concerned only with insurance claims which, for whatever reason, were not stolen by the Nazis, or, in rare cases, for which no compensation was paid.

As far as works of art are concerned, the German Government's position is clear, and I am sure that this can be confirmed by representatives of the Conference on Jewish Claims against Germany. Any work of art that belonged to a victim of the Nazis and may be still in the possession of the German Government, will be returned to the survivors or given to their successors. If neither victims nor successors can be traced, the work will be handed over to the Jewish Claims Conference. I can assure you that this policy will also apply to any works of art taken out of Germany as individual or collective war booty which will be returned to my country in the future. We expect that binding and unequivocal treaty obligations will be honored. We very much welcome efforts by European museums and other bodies to track down works of art whose provenance is in doubt and to find their former owners.

That is the policy the German Government applies not only in cases of art works but also in the area of libraries and archival documents belonging to Nazi victims.

Please allow me a word on the land formerly owned by Jewish communities and the victims of the Nazis. After reunification in 1990, the Government took over responsibility for handling open claims in the same manner as had been practiced to date, i.e., with a clear preference for returning such assets. Of course, fifty years after the end of the war, it is much more difficult to resolve those kinds of questions when possession has changed several times. We are confident that this work can soon be brought to a satisfactory conclusion in close and trustful cooperation with the Claims Conference.

The subject of Holocaust remembrance also looks ahead to our common future. In Germany, knowledge of the Third Reich and its crimes is an established part of all school curricula. We have acquainted you with our wide-ranging educational materials. Teaching tolerance and historical awareness also includes visits to memorial sites, especially to former concentration camps. When visiting a former concentration camp in Germany, one always encounters young Germans.

We believe that international cooperation on Holocaust remembrance is essential to strengthening a common international attitude towards crimes such as racism and anti-Semitism. It is in this spirit that we welcome the Swiss Government's proposal to host a governmental conference on the fight against the use of the Internet for racist, anti-Semitic or hate purposes.

We consider it important and useful to make available our experience and wide range of German teaching materials to other countries for use in their curricular development.

Allow me to close by again quoting President Herzog:

No community, no society, and no state can live without remembrance. Living without remembrance means living without identity and orientation. Remembrance must be passed on, for the sake of the victims, but also for our own sake. Anyone who wants to be honest must face up to his entire history, history which, in both its good and its evil aspects, makes up the identity of our people.

Remembrance - when we talk of remembrance in the context of the Nazi era, we mean, above all, remembrance of the victims. But it also signifies remembrance of the crimes and the criminals. It is our responsibility to refute anyone who claims that being a human depends on race or origin, convictions or beliefs, health or ability.

Thank you very much.

Concluding Statement
ISRAEL

By Mr. Yaakov Levy
DEPUTY DIRECTOR GENERAL,
MINISTRY OF FOREIGN AFFAIRS

On behalf of the Israeli Delegation, I wish to express appreciation to all of you who have participated in this Conference; special appreciation is due to the United States, under whose auspices we are convening, in particular to Under-Secretary of State Stuart Eizenstat and his dedicated staff, who worked diligently in preparing and implementing the Conference.

Mr. Chairman: Not all the victims were Jews, but all Jews were victims. Following the defeat of the Nazis, a majority of Holocaust survivors immigrated to Israel, where they and their families built their lives anew. The State of Israel sees itself as the central representative of the survivors and their offspring and is dedicated to achieving justice on their behalf and to the remembrance of the Shoah.

The matter of Jewish assets is not merely a material issue; it is a moral imperative. "Thou shalt not steal" appears in the same Decalogue with the injunction against murder. There is no adequate compensation for the loss of life, but justice must be sought for the Jewish communities and individuals that were despoiled.

Compensation must also be sought for the men and women turned into slave laborers, whose bodies were violated for profit. All civilized nations outlaw slavery and whomever exploits slave labor must provide reparations for this heinous crime.

We support the adoption of a universal principle of restitution of communal property. The obligation of restituting private property to its rightful owners or to their descendents is of paramount importance. If restitution is not possible, adequate compensation should be made.

Individuals and institutions who acquired looted property should pay restitution. Financial institutions such as banks and insurance companies should accept responsibility for their Holocaust era clients. This also applies to those who acquired art works and ritual objects looted from Jewish homes and synagogues. The original owners have an indisputable claim to what is rightfully theirs, even though these items may have passed through a number of hands.

We welcome the openness and the cooperation of the countries researching the facts regarding property looted during the Holocaust. We note with satisfaction that many countries have established commissions to investigate their own past. We urge all countries, groups, financial institutions and individuals to allow immediate and unrestricted access to all archival and state archive materials relevant to the period.

We welcome the establishment of the International Commission on Holocaust Era Claims and look forward to its equitable resolution of all outstanding Holocaust era claims.

The World Jewish Restitution Organization (WJRO) is the umbrella organization representing the Jewish people, in close coordination with the State of Israel, in matters of restitution.

It is imperative that the International Task Force on Holocaust Education, Research and Remembrance succeed in promoting worldwide awareness of the horrors of the Holocaust and help combat racism, anti-Semitism, Holocaust denial and ethnic hatred.

The State of Israel, together with Yad Vashem, in cooperation with Jewish communities worldwide and all other relevant institutions, will work to effect the widest dissemination of knowledge about the Holocaust, its prelude, its aftermath and its lessons for all humanity.

Many of the Speakers were cognizant of the need to focus on the high moral ground of maintaining the memory of the Holocaust and to promote educational projects. The need to put a face and a name on every victim, as well as to impart the universal lessons of the Shoah, will forever remain a primary goal for us all. At the same time, it is vital that we focus on the plight of the survivors among us, and of their descendants. The need for expeditious material compensation is of paramount importance during the survivors' lifetime. The swift implementation of all legitimate claims of the survivors is the very basis for maintaining a high moral ground struck during these days.

This Conference is not the conclusion of the process. The issue of Jewish assets will remain on the Worlds agenda until just solutions are found.

To this end, we urge further gatherings and consultations in the months and year to come.

The State of Israel commits itself to full cooperation with all governments and non-governmental organizations in an effort to uncover the truth, promote humanitarian solidarity and accord justice to the victims of the Holocaust and their heirs.

"Tzedek Tzedek Tirdof"

"Justice, justice, thou shall seek....."

Concluding Statement
REPUBLIC OF MACEDONIA

By Mr. Vladimir Naumovski
HEAD OF DELEGATION

Ladies and Gentlemen,

There are documents on the presence of Jews in Macedonia from the 6th century B.C., who came here from Persia. Those comprise the first Jewish settlements in Europe. The Diaspora brought masses of other Jews (during Alexander the Great, and the Roman Empire), who are known as Romaniots. Many known families remained in Macedonia until the Holocaust. The most numerous population and the culture came from Spain and Portugal (1492 and 1498 respectively), bringing the highest level of civilization and culture in these territories. We always stress the fact that in Macedonia, the Jews brought with themselves the Bible, Judaism, Christianity, the alphabet and part of the Jewish fate. All of the Judaism in Macedonia has gone with the Holocaust. The last 7148 Macedonian Jews, were arrested and gathered by the Bulgarian Army on March 11, 1943, and deported to Treblinka, where they were exterminated. This number comprise 98% of the Jewish population at that time, which rate is incomparable with any other, except maybe in Northern Greece (Aegean Macedonia) and Trakia. Very few survivors have joined the Resistance movement, but also many of them have lost their lives on the battles. Documents about the history of the Macedonian Holocaust are collected by the Macedonian Academy of Sciences and Arts and the Macedonian Archives. As the SS Nazi troops stormed through former Yugoslavia (April 6, 1941) to invade Greece, they delivered most of the Macedonian territories to the Bulgarian occupation forces who remained in those territories until the end of the World War II 1945. A few months just before the occupation, the Bulgarian government issued the "Law for Protection of the Nation" signed by the King Boris III on January 21, 1941, and it was immediately operative in Macedonia.

On this occasion I would like to point out that according to the claim of Riebbentrop (Nazi-German Minister of Foreign Affairs), King Boris III approved initial deportation of 20,000 Jews to the Nazi -

concentration camps, mainly persons from the occupied territories, communists or socialists. On March 11, 1943 all Jews from Macedonia were gathered on the temporary concentration camp "Monopol" in Skopje. The conditions of living there were horrible, including minimal food and water, with no bathroom and toilette, with no heating in an exceptionally severe winter. Towards the end of March and the beginning of April 1943, three convoys with Jews were deported to Treblinka. In each carriage without windows there were around 80 persons, in standing position. Not a single person came back from Treblinka. In Bulgaria, although many of the Jews were arrested and 5000 died during the arrest and in the labor camps, were spared from deportation and extermination, thanks mainly to the organized protests of the Bulgarian people and ethnic Macedonians, the Orthodox Church and some MPs. Many ethnic Macedonians took the first initiative and had the crucial part in the organization and participation of the protests (as stated by the Bulgarian writers Harry Nisimov and Aaron Assa):..."For hundreds of years the Macedonian and Jewish peoples have lived together as brothers in misfortunes, suffering and destiny. We have the same enemies. Therefore our struggle against them should be identical (The Macedonian Liberation Front, end of 1942) ... There is indisputable evidence that several prominent members of the Macedonian movement in Bulgaria, in the town of Kjustendil to be precise, played a decisive role in saving Bulgarian Jews from extermination in Poland... "(Aaron Assa). The anti-Semitism and anti-Macedonism are practiced in the certain countries for centuries. The very basic principles of moral and social ecology are treaded constantly mainly in the same European countries. We do believe in the hope of U.S. Sen. Daniel Inouye (D--Hawaii), "The Chief Rabbi" in U.S. Senate and Congress, that the concentration camps and Holocaust will not happened again; to have this security "the vigilance is not enough, we need active participation", said the U.S. Sen. Daniel Inouye.

Ladies and Gentlemen,

For more than two and a half millennia, Jews and Macedonians have a life of tolerance, peace, mutual help, friendship and understanding. During many centuries both Jews and Macedonians are under vitriolic pressure of assimilation and prosecution of Babylonians, Persians, Romans, Byzantinians. Many rulers of European empires were seeking to obliterate the Jewish and Macedonian identity of the People and the Land. For example the name of the Jewish Land was changed by Romans to Palestina, after the long-vanished Philistines, an Aegean people, the name of Jerusalem was changed to Aelia Capitolina. For some of our neighbors, the name and the identity of Macedonians are questionable even now! The name of Macedonia was changed several times in the last two and a half millennia. And in spite of all possible forms of intolerance, hatred, prosecution, suppression and Holocaust the moral and spiritual identity of Jewish and Macedonian People survived the falls of many "eternal" empires! The main goal was to annihilate the ethical and spiritual identity of Jewish and Macedonian People! The annihilators were ready to assimilate these peoples, but not their ethical and spiritual nature. But it was not possible to kill the ideas of their ethics and spirit. There was and always will be an Israel and a Macedonia, a Jewish Spirit and a Macedonian Spirit! A Spirit of Justice, Tolerance and Peace Promotion! The Jews and Macedonians love all nations. They have never promoted or conducted any ethnic cleansing. The existence of Jewish and Macedonian people is a terrible but glorious history of death, sorrow, remembrance and hope. A transcendental surmountableness of the "European Justice" and "The borders of Auschwitz"! A permanent extermination and pillage of these, two peoples and their material and spiritual culture! In the memory of Macedonian Jews perished in the concentration camps, in Skopje, in Macedonia, the President of the Republic of Macedonia Mr. Kiro Gligorov, in 1996 laid the foundation stone of Macedonian Holocaust Memorial Center. The center will be finished at the end of 1999. There is also a commitment for supporting the construction of this Holocaust Memorial Center in Skopje.

The possibility for study stay of an independent world expert aimed at examine the participation of Nazi-Bulgaria at the period in the deportation of Jews, is being considered and its scholarship is approved by the Government of the Republic of Macedonia. The financial claims of Macedonian Jews if they are return, will be given in that case, to the Jewish Community of the Republic of Macedonia.

The Jews in Macedonia identified themselves as Macedonian Jews all over the Balkan. After 1912 and the Balkan Wars, when Macedonia was territorially divided by her neighbors in the Almanac of Macedonian emigrants, published 1931 in Sophia, Bulgaria, is written: "Macedonian Jews were always the best friends of Macedonians in their struggle for independence."

Dear participants, I would like to mention the considerations in the Republic of Macedonia are divided in two parts, as follows:

1. The Nazi laws, with brief description of the discriminative and humiliating measures in order to demonstrate the mode of violation of the human rights in occupied Macedonia, and

2. Documents on the confiscated properties. Nazi laws, after the occupation, the Bulgarian Nazi Army has imposed series of restrictive and discriminative laws and regulations.

We will stress only few illustrative examples.

The "Law for the Protection of the Nation" was issued on January 21, 1941, for whole Bulgaria and the occupied territories. This law contained five parts on the origins, general restrictions, places of living restricted for Jews, on the Jewish properties, on the professional and economical activities of the Jews.

On February 17, 1941, additional regulative act entitled "Principles for the Application of the Law for the Protection of the Nation" was issued as integrative part of the Law.

On July 13, 1941 the Ministry of Internal Affairs and Public Health was applied "The Law for the special single Tax payable on all Jewish Real and Personal Estate".

The Department of Jewish Affairs at the same ministry, issued the "Decree No 32" on December 29, 1942, with detailed instructions for wearing special badge, with six pointed, bright yellow star, on all clothes, for all Jews older than 10 years.

"Decree No 5" of the same Department on September 8, 1942 was forbidding all Jews to keep cash and valuable items (gold, jewels, Chinese vases,' silverware, archeological items, historical items, paintings, collections, stamps, etc), and they should be deposited on the bank. Confiscation of all Jewish properties continued on the beginning of 1943, and continued until the deportation and final solution on March 11, 1943 Before deportation, the Jews were gathered in labor groups ("trudovi druzini"), along with other minorities, distributed in labor camps in Bulgaria (Naroden glas No. 6 1942).

The second part of our view is addressed on documents of the confiscated assets. This presentation uses documents from the Archives of Macedonia (Skopje, Bitola and Stip). Although abundant documentation is kept in the Archives of Sofia, Belgrade and Salonika, the experts of the Republic of Macedonia still do not have access to those documents. Minimal part of these documents is previously published and kept in the Macedonian Academy of Sciences and Arts, and the Jewish Community in Skopje: Archive in Skopje has 1001 archive units with documents written on 10358 pages. All archive documents are copied and sent to The United States Holocaust Memorial Museum. The values of confiscated Jewish assets and the details from the laws and regulations are given in separate listings of the prepared information, which we estimate that will contribute to the final documents and conclusions of this important Conference, in which Macedonian representatives participate for the first time.

Ladies and Gentlemen,

The deportation of the Jews from Eastern Aegean Macedonia, Western Trakia and Vardar Macedonia (Republic of Macedonia) was ordered on the base of a Decision of Bulgarian Ministerial Council from March 2, 1943 and it was an Agreement between Bulgarian and German representatives based on this decision. The appropriation of Jewish assets (real and personal estate, money, deposits, insurance, gold, and other valuable belongings) was done by Bulgarian authorities. The experts of National Bank of Republic of Macedonia estimate (only for Jews from Skopje, Vardar Macedonia) on the basis of available, but not complete documents the total amount of Jewish assets to be 16,498,383.95 US dollars and 6,310,909.43 US dollars is the value of the assets without the value of real estate.

On behalf of the delegation of Republic of Macedonia, I hope that on this conference, the commission for claims and returning of the Jewish estate will be formed, covering the Jewish communities in the world, including the Jewish Community in the Republic of Macedonia.

Thank you for your attention.

Concluding Statement
THE NETHERLANDS

By Ambassador Jan d'Ansembourg
HEAD OF DELEGATION

My delegation is very grateful to the organizers of this conference to have given us the opportunity to exchange views on the way governments and NGO's deal with the many injustices which form part of the legacy of the Holocaust.

It has been an extraordinary occasion to explain what has been done in the past, what is currently being done and what will be done in this respect in the future. As far as my delegation is concerned we are happy to have been able, mostly in the break-out sessions, to inform you about what has been done in the Netherlands and what we intend to do.

As a concluding contribution to this conference let me briefly give you an overview of where we stand on the past, present and future of the subjects we have discussed during the last three days.

As far as the past is concerned I will not exhaust you with an enumeration of all the regulations and measures that were devised to give material and immaterial support to the victims of the war. Let me just mention that the drafting and promulgation of measures designed to remedy, wherever possible, the action taken by the Germans against Dutch Jews and other population groups, were undertaken by the Netherlands Government in exile already before the liberation of our country. After the war these measures grew into an extensive corpus of legislation and legal protection in the field of the restoration of legal rights. In retrospect these measures may not always have been successful in taking away the feelings of injustice inflicted by the Nazis on our Jewish population.

Over the years a unique system of legislation was created to meet the needs of different categories of Dutch war victims. It has led, inter alia, to the Victims of Persecution Benefits Act, which awards payments and grants, a total of 4 billion dollars, also to victims who no longer live in the Netherlands, like, for example to some 1,400 people in the U.S.A. In addition to material assistance the Dutch Government funds a number of organizations that specialize in non-material assistance to war victims.

In the field of art, guidelines for restitution were set in 1947 by the Council of the Netherlands Art Property Foundation which recovered many thousands of items and returned a substantial part of them to their rightful owners. Nevertheless, of all the works of art stolen from the Netherlands during the war more than 8,000 paintings alone are still missing.

As far as Jewish life insurance policies is concerned a situation evolved which led to case law under which insurance policies were generally restored and a large number of amicable settlements were concluded between insurance companies and policy holders. Between 1948 and 1950 some 12,000 amicable settlements were dealt with in this manner. In 1954 nearly all life insurance companies and the Dutch State concluded an agreement for the amicable restitution of legal rights with regard to life insurance and annuity policies of people who had died.

The recent surge in interest in and concern with the fate of the victims of World War II has led, in the Netherlands to the appointment of a ministerial committee chaired by the Prime Minister that oversees the activities of 5 investigative committees. They deal, respectively with Art, Nazi Gold, Financial assets, other tangible assets, and assets seized by the Japanese in the former Dutch East Indies. Some first results of the activities of these committees are starting to come in but the final reports are expected at different moments between later this month and the middle of next year. Apart from this the Jewish community has set up a claims center funded by the Government, where Jewish victims and their heirs can claim stolen property. More than 1,500 substantiated claims have already been received. In 30 cases, mostly insurance policies the claims were honored. More settlements are to be expected.

In the field of restitution of art I want to mention the fact that, after a pilot study, we are going to research the provenance of all state owned works of art that were returned after World War II. Of many of these we know that they are rightfully in the State collection because they were sold voluntarily to the Germans. But since we have found out that in a limited number of cases serious doubts were raised, we want to investigate the total collection.

The example of the Government collections is being followed by the Dutch museums. The details of these investigations and their timetables have been set forth by a member of my delegation during yesterday's break-out session on Nazi Confiscated Art. In the execution of its restitution policy the Netherlands has applied principles which correspond with the eleven principles proposed by the US delegation.

Many injustices of the Holocaust cannot be rectified because loss of life is irreplaceable and suffering cannot be undone. What can in any case be done though, is to redress unjust situations in the material field which, for whatever reason, have not yet been dealt with until now. While, in the Netherlands war victims have generally benefited from our legislation in the field of restitution, compensation or non-material support, those in Eastern Europe have, until recently, remained deprived of this kind of benefits. For that reason the Dutch Government has decided to allot half of its voluntary contribution to the Nazi Persecutee Relief Fund established at the London Conference to projects in Central and Eastern Europe. Apart from that I should recall that the proceeds of the sale of the last share of the Dutch Nazi gold has been almost totally allotted to the Dutch Jewish community for the support and reinforcement of that community.

As I have mentioned before the reports of the several commissions which dealt with Holocaust-era assets in our country are scheduled to be published in the months to come. The Government is determined to remedy defects in government policy in this area if and where this policy is shown to be deficient.

Other actions that have been undertaken in the Netherlands concern a 364 page archival finding aid, a catalogue of actors involved in the looting of assets, their recuperation, restoration of legal rights and restitution and compensation which will be published next week. This will facilitate research into our archives to which any claimant has free access.

Another current activity that should be mentioned is the request, by the Dutch Government addressed to a foundation to carry out a study of the circumstances in which war victims returned to Dutch society and the way in which they were received and treated in the early postwar years. Next Monday a seminar organized by this foundation will take place in the Netherlands on the way the different groups of returnees have been received back in the Netherlands after the war. This will make it possible for returnees to give expression to their feelings about that period. This meets a general feeling in our country that people in the Netherlands after the war were generally busy with getting their own existence back in order and therefore had insufficient understanding and empathy for their compatriots who felt they did not get the attention they needed.

In one of the break-out sessions in the Holocaust Museum a member of our delegation has pointed out that the focus of Government efforts in the non-material field is aimed at informing and educating young people about the Second World War in an effort to avoid a similar catastrophe in the future. The Government will contribute to the work of the Task Force for International Cooperation on Holocaust Remembrance, Education and Research. We hope this conference is a start for more international cooperation especially to inform our youngsters.

Concluding Statement
POLAND

By Mrs. Agnieszka Magdziak-Miszewska
ADVISOR TO THE PRIME MINISTER

Ladies and Gentlemen,

On the 8th of November, the 60th anniversary of "Kristallnacht", participating in the ceremony of the rededication of the Wrocław synagogue recovered by the local Jewish community, the Prime Minister of Poland, Jerzy Buzek said: "Sixty years ago it was decided that the Jews of Wrocław, as well as German, Polish and European Jews; and their temples will be erased from history, whose new chapters would henceforth be written solely by the racially pure hands of Aryans.

This satanic idea failed. For over fifty years, you Jews and we Christians have been recording the horrible history of he enormous atrocity committed by the Nazis in the heart of Europe. For over fifty years we have been asking in horror: How it was possible? And, as the years go by, we realize more and more that we must not shun an answer to that question, for the future of our continent depends on that answer.

The Wrocław synagogue is rising from the ruins. The Jewish community of this city is returning from oblivion. I believe that a new chapter of Christian-Jewish and Polish-Jewish dialogue has opened. I believe that in spite of all difficulties, obstacles and mutual prejudices, our common dealings will once again be imbued with trust, cooperation and ordinary human friendship. I believe that the current renaissance of the culture of Polish Jews will once again become an integral part of he culture of Poland, as it had been for eight hundred years.

What I wish from the bottom of my heart I wish it to you, to Wrocław, and all of Poland."

Ladies and Gentlemen,

Poland regained its independence a few years ago. After a long period of communist regime, Poland has started the process of regaining of its own history. An integral part of this history is a history of Polish

Jews. The Polish society started the process of regaining its memory. The Holocaust is an integral part of this memory.

It will be a long and painful process also – for Poles but, thinking about our future as a future of the free, democratic country, we must be ready to confront our past in a full truth. This is why we are ready, and will be very, proud to become a part of Task Force for International Cooperation on Holocaust Education, Remembrance and Research. This is not only our moral obligation, but we feel that our experience on that field – the experience of the Educational Center of the Auschwitz State Museum and our archives can well serve in that task.

Ladies and Gentlemen,

Let me, in the name of the Polish delegation, and especially in the name of the head of this delegation – Polish Minister of Culture, Mrs. Joanna Wnuk-Nazarowa – to say "thank you" to Miles Lerman and to the Under Secretary of State, Stuart E. Eizenstat, for this conference which starts the international dialogue about the past which should never be forgotten, and about future which is expected to establish the truth and justice. Let me assure you that Poland is ready to participate in it with a good will and openness. We are proud to participate in this great and noble undertaking. We are proud to participate in implementing the moral values to international policy.

Thank you.

Concluding Statement
SWITZERLAND

By Ambassador Thomas G. Borer
HEAD OF DELEGATION

Mr. Chairman, Honorable Delegates:

We are nearing the end of a century that has produced more victims on battlefields and in towns and villages, witnessed more crimes against humankind, more atrocities against minorities and political dissidents, has lead to greater waves of refugees - has, in short, seen more human suffering than our minds will ever be able to grasp. Within this sad record, the Nazi crimes against humanity are unparalleled. They remain the symbol of the most complete denial of Humanity. As such, they stand before us as a constant warning never to let history repeat itself.

Everyone here will agree that the Holocaust and its unspeakable atrocities must never be forgotten. It is indeed important to develop ways and means of remembrance and sensitivity, and we welcome the opportunity that was given to us here to discuss Holocaust remembrance and education. In remembering the past, we build an important basis for promoting tolerance for the future.

Mr. Chairman, Dear Delegates:

It is in this spirit that I would like to raise an important issue which, I hope, will be of particular interest for the Governments and NGOs gathered here in Washington:

- As you know, the rapid development of racist and anti-Semitic propaganda on the Internet has become a matter of concern for many countries. The Swiss Federal police, for instance, identified 700 such websites in 1997. Not one was based in Switzerland, as the dissemination of racist and anti-Semitic propaganda is strictly forbidden in our country. However, as the Internet has no borders, prohibition in specific countries is not an adequate solution, for hate propaganda can be disseminated via foreign providers and anonymizers. The need for international cooperation in this field is obvious. Moreover, the development of Internet as a platform for racist, anti-Semitic, and revisionist activists, many of which disseminate the "Auschwitz lie", is all the more worrying as the web appeals to and is used by younger generations. As such, it is a critical task for every nation to contain the spread of hate propaganda on the web. **The Washington Conference carries a huge moral weight. It could thus, in our opinion, send an important signal: A signal showing that its participants are committed to fighting anti-Semitism and racial hatred. A signal that they will not allow the use of new technologies to deny a past that must never be repeated.**

This is why the Swiss delegation would like to inform the various delegations that the Swiss government would be ready, if so wished, to host a governmental conference on the fight against the use of the Internet for racist, anti-Semitic or hate purposes, and to propose concrete remedial steps.

The signal we will send will undoubtedly contribute to the concrete objective of the present conference, which represents one of the great tasks and challenges for the next century: To prevent denial and oblivion of the horrors of this century, as well as their recurrence. Switzerland is committed to this effort towards the future.

Before concluding, Mr. Chairman, let me say a few words about the other topics dealt with during this conference.

On the insurance question, Switzerland welcomes the constructive participation of the three Swiss insurance companies in the "International Commission", and supports the cooperative approach the Commission chose. However, in our view the on-going class action suits are not compatible with this cooperative spirit, and we expect that an intensive dialogue, involving especially the American participants in the said Commission, will soon bring an end to this confrontational element.

Regarding the looted art issue, Switzerland welcomes the on-going discussion on this complex subject. My country has taken important measures in this matter, and welcomes the proposal submitted by the American delegation.

The request for the complete opening of the archives has long been met at the Federal level in Switzerland. Furthermore, the Bergier

Commission has special rights guaranteeing complete access even to private archives.

In concluding, Mr. Chairman, I would like to thank the US Department of State, as well as the Holocaust Memorial Museum, for the perfect organization of this important and fruitful conference. Finally, I would not fail to express my appreciation of the very skilled and able Chairmanship of Judge Mikva.

Thank you very much.

Concluding Statement
UNITED STATES

By Under Secretary Stuart E. Eizenstat
HEAD OF DELEGATION

It has been a great honor for me and for the State Department to have co-hosted the Washington Conference on Holocaust-Era Assets. It is a particular privilege to have had as our partner the U.S. Holocaust Memorial Museum, which is doing so much to ensure that the memory and the lessons of the Holocaust endure for future generations.

A year ago, at the London Nazi Gold Conference, we established a goal to complete by the end of this century the unfinished business of the middle of the century: the completion of the long-hidden historical record on Holocaust-era assets and the provision of some measure of justice -- however belated -- to the victims and survivors of that unparalleled tragedy. Now with the conclusion of this conference approaching, we have made great strides toward achieving that historic goal.

As a result of the inspiring seriousness of purpose and spirit of dedication, openness, cooperation, and commitment you -- the 57 delegations, 44 countries, 13 NGOs, and scores of presenters -- have demonstrated, we can genuinely call the Washington Conference a great success. Indeed, we have surpassed our highest expectations and together accomplished more over the past several days than any of us could have possibly imagined when we began our preparations many months ago or even when we began these proceedings this week.

To all those who have participated and contributed, I offer my heartfelt gratitude and appreciation. Most of all, I want offer my thanks to Judge Abner Mikva, whose guiding hand has been critical to the success of this Conference. I also want to commend the Conference Director, J.D. Bindenagel, and our entire team for bringing such a complex undertaking to life and helping ensure its success.

While we must acknowledge our failure to address these issues earlier, we must also acknowledge the work of individuals and organizations who heard the pleas, who understood that justice must be completed, and who in the face of apathy worked so hard to uncover the truth and to come to the aid of survivors and their families. You refused to let the world forever turn its back to the truth, and to you we owe our enduring appreciation.

Building on those efforts, both governments and NGOs have achieved remarkable progress, particularly in our efforts to shape principles and processes that can guide our efforts to complete the historical record and to seek justice. I would like to briefly address some of those important achievements and focus on our remaining challenges.

First, we can be encouraged that our efforts last year at the London Conference continue to motivate countries to contribute to the Nazi Persecutee Relief Fund. Pledges to the fund -- augmented by Spain at this conference -- which will be used to assist the neediest survivors of the Holocaust, now total $60 million. We also appreciate Slovenia joining Croatia in pledging their share.

Second, the issue of Holocaust-era insurance claims was one of the more complex and difficult challenges facing this conference. This week's presentations systematically walked us through the historical record of Nazi confiscation. They painted a vivid picture of the well-intended but inadequate compensation efforts after the war, and they updated us on recent actions by insurance regulators and companies to address these issues.

I am pleased that so many delegations have supported the International Commission as the best mechanism for adjudicating claims. The U.S. Government strongly supported the creation of the commission and will work intensively with it. The commission brings together the key actors on both sides of the Atlantic, and we firmly believe that it represents the most appropriate mechanism for promptly resolving unpaid insurance claims from the Holocaust era in a swift, just, and cooperative manner. We urge other companies to join this process.

The commission will help us avoid the trans-Atlantic tensions that at times have been apparent on other Holocaust-era issues. In addition, the commission will seek to expedite a fair settlement of heirless claims so that those funds can be used to urgently help the aging survivors in need.

Resolution of the insurance issue is also being pursued on three separate tracks: through the courts, through legislation, and through regulation. It is our hope that the credibility and effectiveness of the commission's work will convince all the actors pursuing resolution of this issue, including those pursuing litigation, to merge with the IC process as the best means for quickly and equitably resolving these claims.

Third, art, without a doubt, represents the most complex set of issues we have faced at this conference. Yet I am pleased to note that we have achieved a breakthrough far exceeding our most ambitious expectations. As Philippe de Montebello told us, "The genie is out of the bottle." The art world will never be the same in the way it deals with Nazi-confiscated art. From now on, the sale, purchase, exchange, and display of art from this period will be addressed with greater sensitivity and a higher international standard of responsibility. This is a major achievement which will reverberate through our museums, galleries, auction houses, and in the homes and hearts of those families who may now have the chance to have returned what is rightfully theirs. This will also lead to the removal of uncertainty in the world art market and facilitate commercial and cultural exchange.

We have reached a remarkable degree of consensus on a set of substantive principles, which while not legally binding represent a moral commitment among nations which all in the art world will have to take into account. These principles are the result of intensive consultations with art experts, cultural institutions, and countries before and during the conference. We have listened and incorporated many of your suggestions in order to achieve consensus, and we are very pleased by the explicit support given by so many countries directly to the principles. These principles encourage research into the provenance and identification of art, they call for these findings to be publicized and for the establishment of a central digital registry which will link all Holocaust-era art-loss databases, and they encourage alternative dispute-resolution strategies.

I am pleased to note that several countries have already taken courageous steps to address these issues. For example, Austria, Switzerland, and the Netherlands are researching the provenance of works in their national collections; the French Government has established a web site to display a portion of the some 2,000 pieces of art restituted after the war still unclaimed; and Austria has passed a law to allow restitution notwithstanding such legal obstacles as the statute of limitations. In addition, we are particularly pleased by the announcement of the Russian delegation that they will actively cooperate in resolving outstanding issues related to Holocaust-era art. The actions of these nations could provide useful models for other countries. Indeed, the Austrian law is a model for all countries to follow.

To be sure, it is not enough to identify art that was stolen. We must also establish a system to resolve issues of ownership and compensation. In that spirit, I urge each national delegation to commit itself to the task of faithfully implementing these principles.

Fourth, this conference is the first time that international attention has been focused so sharply -- with genuine debate -- on the issue of communal property restitution. It was an important opportunity to review both the progress that has been made and the very real obstacles that remain. We also were reminded that restitution is essential to the revitalization of religious and other pluralistic communities as well as to democratic institutions and the rule of law.

We have worked to encourage the new democracies of the region to provide restitution and/or compensation for property wrongfully confiscated -- and to do so in an equitable, transparent, non-discriminatory, and expeditious manner. While most countries in the region recognize their obligation to return confiscated property, there remains in some countries a lukewarm commitment to completing quickly the work at hand.

There is a compelling reason to finish this task as urgently as possible. I have met with Holocaust survivor communities throughout Central and Eastern Europe. Cut off from freedom, their relatives, and the compensation that was available to survivors in the West, many of these elderly survivors are living out their remaining years in poverty and fear. They are truly the double victims of the 20th century -- first of the Nazi Holocaust and then more than 4 decades of communist repression. They deserve to see the return of their communal properties within their lifetimes so their communities can rebuild their shattered existence.

Precisely because restitution of communal property is a difficult process, it requires the urgent, cooperative, and steadfast support of both governments and non-governmental organizations.

We certainly recognize that there are many practical difficulties in resolving these issues, and that circumstances vary among countries. That is why the U.S. has proposed some general principles to address the difficulties faced by all communities. We are urging governments to return secular as well as religious communal properties, to take necessary steps to ensure that restitution policies established at the national level are implemented at the regional and local levels, and to make the legal procedures for filing claims clear and straightforward. At the same time, restitution procedures must take into account the legitimate interests of the current occupants.

On the other hand, we recognize that in some countries local communities are not always able to bear the full cost of restitution. That is why we also urge the establishment of foundations where needed to help local communities organize their restitution claims as well as involve other groups in assisting local communities with research, legal counsel, and funding for rebuilding. Above all, communal properties should be returned at a much faster rate than they have been so far. This may require more resources from governments and from non-governmental organizations. Even more important, it will require renewed energy and commitment by all concerned. The U.S. Government hopes that in 1999 we can see an intensification of efforts on these issues -- and concrete progress as a result.

We were pleased to hear that Poland has expressed tentative interest in hosting a conference on communal property restitution. This is encouraging, and we would urge other countries in the region to support the idea.

Fifth, a key to success in all the areas this conference has addressed -- and in all aspects of Holocaust-era assets -- is the openness and accessibility of archives. We are concerned that in some countries, archives are still accessible on only a limited basis and others unfortunately appear destined to remain closed. The U.S. vigorously supports the archival openness declaration of the Task Force for International Cooperation on Holocaust Education, Remembrance and Research. That declaration urges that all Holocaust-relevant archives, both public and private, be made widely accessible and that all documentation bearing on the Holocaust be made available to researchers by December 31, 1999.

The work of the 17 historical commissions has been the centerpiece of an amazing outpouring of scholarship on the Holocaust. And a consensus has emerged on the need to use the Internet in making their reports and other related information available. At the planning seminar for this conference in June 1998, we agreed to establish, on the Internet, an international guide to archival sources on gold and other assets looted by the Nazis. I am pleased to report that this guide is up and running. Valuable archival information from the U.K., France, Croatia, and the Bank for International Settlements is linked through a central site hosted by the Holocaust Museum, and more countries are preparing their contributions.

This experience has convinced us to further expand our use of the Internet and institute what we might call a "Mega Web Site" to link the sites of all commissions, governments, and institutions. A "Mega Web Site" is fully possible using current technology. Its users will be able to share all currently available reports and documents on Holocaust-era assets. This "Mega Web Site" will become even more useful as new participants add their Internet sites and new materials are published.

As a contribution to Holocaust education, research, and remembrance, we plan to include the proceedings of this conference on the website. Although we will publish a volume of the proceedings of this conference in January 1999, we intend to keep the record open until the end of 1999 so that researchers and delegations can contribute the results of work completed subsequent to this conference -- and move toward completing the historical record on the wide range of issues we have addressed this week.

I would like to take note of the fact that Greece, one of the first countries in post-war Europe to restitute property to Holocaust survivors and their heirs, has undertaken another crucial aspect of uncovering history. The Greek Government is funding the publication of a collection of Greek Foreign Ministry documents, which shed new light not only on the history of Thessaloniki, the largest Sephardic community in Europe, but also on the creation of the state of Israel. I would also like to take note of the contribution made by Belarus on developing a book on Holocaust-era assets in their country. We appreciate the spirit in which the Swiss Government has made its proposal on Internet racism and anti-Semitism.

Sixth, our greatest, most solemn and enduring responsibility is to memorialize the lives of the victims by committing ourselves to educating future generations on the full dimensions of the Holocaust. That is why I am so encouraged by the groundbreaking work launched by Sweden to create the Task Force for International Cooperation on Holocaust Education, Remembrance and Research, which has forged the first intergovernmental effort to promote Holocaust education. The U.S. wants to urge the representatives of each country present here to endorse the Task Force declaration on Holocaust education and its call to "undertake with renewed vigor and attention Holocaust education, remembrance and research, with a special focus on our own countries' histories." We are also pleased by the interest on the part of France and the Netherlands to join the task force, which will meet later today to discuss, among other things, how to reach out to include more countries in its work. The U.S. strongly supports the proposal by Sweden to host a conference on Holocaust Education and Remembrance in late 1999 or early 2000.

The Washington Conference comes to a close today, but the process of resolving the outstanding issues of Holocaust-era assets must not. We must use the historical record established, the information shared, and the consensus reached in the past 3 days to galvanize our efforts in all areas. As a result of our work this week, we can point to principles in some cases, processes in others, and initiatives in still others that will continue to focus our attention and accelerate our progress toward justice. A number of countries have come forward to suggest follow-up efforts by the international community on many of the issues we have discussed here, and these should be seriously considered.

Let me close with a proposed roadmap for fulfilling the call of the London Conference -- and now the Washington Conference as well -- to complete our work for justice before the end of this millennium.

- On insurance, we look to the International Commission to fulfill its mandate and reach a swift and just solution. We recognize the need to merge the IC process with litigation, and the U.S. will support any such efforts.
- On art, the consensus achieved on principles should be translated into action, databases should be linked, and provenance research expedited – all leading to the resolution of claims and the restoration of confidence in the world art market.
- On communal property, we urge the governments to embrace the principles we have proposed and make substantial progress in 1999. I encourage the countries in the region to support the proposal for a follow-up conference to focus further attention on this issue.
- On archives, we urge all the delegations to implement the declaration on opening all public and private archives pertaining to the Holocaust, including assets, by the end of next year.
- On Holocaust education and remembrance, we encourage countries to strengthen their efforts and support the International Task Force and the Stockholm Conference.

It is also important to mention briefly two related issues that were not on the conference agenda:

- Private property restitution was omitted from the conference agenda because of the complexities of the issue, not to indicate that it was unimportant. Countries in the family of democracies should move swiftly to conclusively address the unjust confiscations that took place during the war and after.

- The landmark settlement by the Swiss banks must be finalized, and the distribution called for in the settlement should be made swiftly so that it can benefit needy Holocaust survivors.

As representatives of our nations and as representatives of humanity, we must never forget that the commitment and resolve we are demonstrating today comes more than 50 years late. Each and every one of us has a solemn and awesome responsibility to see that some small measure of justice for the victims of the Holocaust can be achieved. By doing so, we will rededicate ourselves not only to the work at hand, but also to ensuring that the millions of individual victims will not be forgotten and indeed will guide our efforts in the weeks and months to come.

We appreciate the statements by the Ukrainian and Russian delegations on non-Jewish survivors of the concentration camps and their needs as aging survivors. This merits our serious consideration. As Elie Wiesel has said, "All Jews were victims, but not all victims were Jews." To those who perished in the gas chambers; to those who lost families, homes, property, even their communities and homelands; to the double victims who suffered not only the unimaginable horror of the Holocaust but also 40 years of communist repression; to the survivors, whose cries for justice and restitution were ignored; to the victims' families, to their children, grandchildren, and great grandchildren whose pain and sense of loss will never disappear -- it is to their individual memories that we must continue to commit ourselves.

As we pen the final chapter in the unfinished business of the 20th century, we ask that each delegate remember that our efforts at this conference, in some small way, are helping restore that sense of individual dignity and personal humanity for those who amazingly survived and those who tragically perished. May that solemn goal guide us as we tackle the great challenges that lie ahead.

Thank you very much.

Chairman's Concluding Statement
The Honorable Abner J. Mikva

CONFERENCE CHAIRMAN

INTRODUCTION

We have just completed a series of fascinating and challenging discussions over the past 3 days. I believe that the work of this conference has been a landmark event in fulfilling the international community's long-overdue commitment to focus on Holocaust-era assets. It has been a personal privilege to chair proceedings that may well be considered to have made a historic contribution to justice.

I want to thank the delegations from Europe, the United States, Canada, South America, Australia, and the international Jewish and Romani Union communities that have brought a diversity of perspectives and views, but also a common commitment to address candidly these immensely complex and sensitive issues. Our presenters, ranging from historians to insurance regulators, from government officials to museum directors, together with the delegates' responses, have made rich contributions to our substantive agenda.

I also want to express my gratitude to the chairs of our plenary sessions: New York Federal Reserve President McDonough on gold; Ambassador Olson on insurance; Congressman Leach on art; Congressman Gilman on communal property; and French Ambassador Amigues on archives, books, and historical commissions.

Finally, of course, I want to thank Stuart Eizenstat and the State Department, together with Miles Lerman and the U.S. Holocaust Memorial Museum, for so ably hosting the Conference. I also want to commend J.D. Bindenagel, the Conference Director, and his entire team for their skillful management of this week's sessions and their painstaking preparations over many months.

In her remarkable keynote address on Tuesday morning Secretary Albright displayed a frankness and openness that set the tone for the entire Conference. She called on our nations "to chart a course for finishing the job of returning or providing compensation for stolen Holocaust assets to survivors and the families of Holocaust victims." I believe that together we have risen to the challenge.

We have made important advances in developing principles and processes for addressing the complex issues relating to restitution for confiscated insurance, art, and communal property assets in particular. We have also made significant strides in identifying the specific problems that must be surmounted in order to achieve the widest possible openness and accessibility of relevant archives. We have also emphasized the enduring importance of Holocaust education and remembrance for future generations. I would like to add the personal observation that throughout our deliberations, Conference delegates have displayed a willingness to examine the historical record and to consider the case for justice.

My purpose in this statement is two-fold: first, to summarize highlights of the many presentations and discussions; and second, to crystallize major areas of consensus around principles and processes which I believe have been reached. Let me be clear: Consistent with the terms of reference of the conference, these are areas of general consensus, not formal agreement or binding commitment. I invite each delegation to add any supplementary material to the conference record by mid-January. The conference proceedings will be published in the spring of 1999 and a second volume will be issued at the end of 1999 documenting further research and progress. Moreover, I believe that we have achieved a basis for sustaining and accelerating the international community's willingness to act.

Let me now turn to each of the substantive sections of the agenda we have completed, proceeding in the order in which they were addressed in plenary sessions.

LOOTED GOLD AND THE TRIPARTITE GOLD COMMISSION

The brief plenary session held on looted gold may be the final large-scale discussion on the part of so many countries on this set of issues. From the head of the U.S. delegation we heard an overview of the major research completed on wartime gold transactions over the last year since the London Conference by national historical commissions in Switzerland, Portugal, Spain, Sweden, and Turkey, as well as by the United States. Drawing on these and other previous reports, elements of an historical consensus have now been established on looted gold.

France reported on its completion, together with Britain and the United States, of their governments' collective responsibility as custodians of the Tripartite Gold Commission over five decades. With the opening of its archive and the actions of many countries in dealing with remaining claims on gold, its mission has been completed with dignity and justice.

The United Kingdom presented an encouraging report on the progress of the Nazi Persecutee Relief Fund, a laudable effort by which Tripartite Gold Commission claimant countries and others have now pledged over $60 million to assist the neediest survivors of the Holocaust. The mechanisms through which donations can be made and projects implemented were described. A number of delegations -- including Italy, the Netherlands, and Belgium -- shared details about their previous pledges or contributions. We also heard from Spain that it would channel its previously announced contribution through the Nazi Persecutee Relief Fund. Slovenia and Croatia indicated their intention to pledge to the Fund.

INSURANCE

I believe that this Conference has brought unprecedented international focus on the wrenching history of Holocaust insurance claims. We have learned that, through direct and indirect means, the Nazi regime deliberately sought to confiscate the insurance assets of Jewish victims. In recognition of this massive loss and injustice, the postwar West German Government made an effort to compensate the victims. According to the German delegation, after the war and as of January 1998, the German Government had paid out 102 billion deutsche marks in compensation to victims of Nazi persecution. Over the next several years, the German compensation program is expected to pay out another 24 billion deutsche marks (about $14 billion), including for the first time direct payments to central and eastern European survivors.

Other delegates indicated that there is also a need to address claims arising from assets and liabilities that were nationalized by former communist regimes in central and eastern Europe.

By bringing together key parties on both sides of the Atlantic, the International Commission offers the most effective vehicle for resolving these issues swiftly and justly. The insurance firms Allianz and Generali noted their commitment to pay all valid claims against their companies and to participate fully in the Commission. The Commission also will help forge a positive, cooperative approach that can avoid transatlantic tensions of the kind that have at times arisen on other Holocaust-era issues.

Delegates representing survivor organizations and American insurance commissioners thanked those on the International Commission for addressing their concerns, noting that the Commission is a voluntary organization that includes, *inter alia*, six European insurers and two European insurance regulators. Many delegates called for other companies and countries to join the International Commission. The head of the Czech Delegation reported on the activities of the Czech Working Group on Holocaust Insurance and said that the Czech Government supports the proper representation of the survivor communities in the Czech Republic and other central and eastern European countries on the International Commission. The Hungarian delegation indicated its interest in cooperating with the International Commission.

The Chairman of the International Commission has assured us that he will move quickly to press for expanded membership, an audit to identify unpaid Holocaust-era insurance claims, and an expeditious adjudication of claims, using relaxed standards of proof.

Moreover, a view was often expressed that a humanitarian relief fund may provide swift means for compensating Holocaust survivors promptly. In this regard, many welcomed the $90 million contribution by insurance companies to the International Commission's fund for humanitarian relief.

ART

On the topic of art, the conference was presented with the history of how the Nazis confiscated art works of individuals as part of a deliberate and premeditated program to enrich their leaders, finance their military aggression, and exterminate an entire people. We were told how post-war restitution policies were generally successful, but fell short of restoring property to many individuals. We have reached a greater understanding of why restitution issues were dormant for so many years and why they have suddenly reappeared with renewed force, creating a challenge to legal frameworks, all sectors of the art world, and concepts of morality and justice.

Several delegations described what their countries are trying to do in order to balance the claims of pre-war owners against the rights and responsibilities of current owners, be they museums, galleries, or individual collectors. Representatives of several museums emphasized the challenges in establishing clear provenance of artworks caught in the dislocation of the War and its aftermath. Delegates were also briefed on the work being done with claimants to help them recall the nature and circumstances of their loss with the specificity needed to make a viable claim.

The work being done using new technologies to check claims against catalogues and inventories has also helped expedite the process. As we have heard, there is already a substantial effort to locate and publicize missing art works, determine their provenance, and come to an equitable resolution of ownership questions. The Russian delegation indicated its willingness to search for confiscated art works, to help create a database, and to entertain properly presented claims for the return of looted art.

My sense from these discussions is that the nations represented at this conference are willing to open their archives to facilitate research leading to the identification and location of art confiscated during the Holocaust. They welcome the development of computerized research tools designed to aid this search by matching identified art with claims. They look forward to the completion of central on-line repositories -- a "digital collecting point" as one participant called it -- that would include complete lists of missing and recovered art works and mechanisms for filing claims.

The delegates' discussions during the conference helped develop a set of principles to guide the international community toward a consensus on Nazi-confiscated art. All countries want to contribute toward a speedy resolution of all art claims, those of individuals as well as those of nations, so that stability can be restored to the art market and beneficial international cultural exchange will not be disrupted.

As Chairman, I am pleased to recognize one of the most important accomplishments coming out of the discussion of this conference: a consensus that, within the context of the national laws and national judicial processes of the participating nations, the 11 principles on art offer a means for addressing the major issues relating to Nazi-confiscated art. Although they are non-binding, they will be a moral force and guide for dealing with this issue.

COMMUNAL PROPERTY

Delegations discussed the varying and difficult circumstances surrounding restitution of communal property and artifacts. Much of this property is in run-down condition, owned by the government or currently inhabited. One delegate made the point that at the end of the War and during the communist period, the political and social environment for Jews in central and eastern Europe was inhospitable and that emigration was considered the main alternative. With new democratic governments, religious life is reviving throughout the region for Jewish, Catholic, and Protestant communities alike. Return of their property is essential.

Much has been done to return communal property, but historical differences and current political realities have led each country to proceed on restitution in its own way. The conference heard encouraging reports indicating that the countries of eastern and central Europe have perceived the need for communal property restitution and some have set up legal structures to provide restitution or compensation. However, obstacles remain, making the process of restitution very slow.

The Polish, Romanian, and Hungarian delegations shared their national experiences in handling communal property restitution in their countries, including the laws passed and the status of implementation. Two speakers described the relative success of property restitution in eastern Germany and expressed the hope that it would also be successful elsewhere. Almost all affected countries have taken action to return property or compensate religious groups for their confiscated property. We also heard the perspectives of international organizations on the progress and stumbling blocks to restitution, including the significance of return and care for religious artifacts and cemeteries.

The United States described a set of principles to make the process of restitution just and effective. To implement these principles, "best practices" include: clear restitution policies implemented at the national, regional and local levels and not limited to religious communal property; transparent and simple procedures for legal claims; and, where needed, establishment of foundations jointly managed by local communities and international groups to assist with claims and administration of restituted property. Lastly, governments should take into account legitimate needs of current occupants of restituted property. The Chair encourages governments to implement these principles.

ARCHIVES AND HISTORICAL COMMISSIONS

One of the central achievements of the London Conference was to highlight the importance and urgency of greater openness and accessibility of archives and records bearing on Holocaust-era assets. Since London, we have had the occasion to applaud the immense progress achieved on all Holocaust-era assets issues and to recognize that it has only been possible as a result of the opening in so many countries of the relevant historical archives. We have heard during this conference of the great outpouring of important Holocaust research undertaken in the last several years by 17 national historical commissions that have been established to compile an accurate and final historical accounting of Holocaust assets issues. These national commissions, with varying mandates but with a common goal of examining wartime experiences have done vital and courageous work examining the formerly hidden aspects of a terrible period of history.

We heard yesterday from a broad range of commissions and experts who described the current status of their individual projects and the progress they have made and the problems they have encountered in identifying and preserving records and making sense of them. The U.K. delegation described to us the research at the Foreign and Commonwealth Office on postwar British policies on reparations and restitution. The U.S. delegation reviewed the great success of the National Archives in Washington in quickly assembling more than 15 million pages of Holocaust-era records, devising a finding aid to those records that now approaches 1000 pages in length, and making the National Archives research room the center of international study of these issues.

The German delegation reminded the conference of the destructive impact of the Nazi German regime, the war, and the dislocations of the postwar period on the critical historical records in Germany, and pointed to the vital importance of accurate document "provenance," in order to assure a properly preserved historical record for any society. Finally, Switzerland gave us a summary of the wide-ranging mandate of the Swiss Independent Commission of Experts which has already reported in great detail on wartime gold transactions and is close now to publishing a final report on the treatment of refugees in Switzerland before and during the war.

Break-out sessions yesterday heard many reports on the problems and possibilities confronting archivists and commissions in many countries. I cannot summarize here all that was discussed, but it was important to hear of the issues facing the Netherlands as it established its Commission on Jewish assets and of the Holocaust-era archival projects undertaken by the Yad Vashem Institute, particularly the list of lists with its 18 million entries thus far. I believe we all took encouragement from the reports we heard about the diverse but critical research underway or recently completed by the historical commissions in Spain, Sweden, Turkey, and Argentina.

While we congratulate those countries that have worked to identify and make available archives and other sources of information on this period, many conference participants emphasized the importance of full archival openness. The Task Force on International Cooperation on Holocaust Education, Remembrance and Research presented a declaration encouraging all archives, both public and private, be made more widely accessible and that all documentation bearing on the Holocaust be available to researchers by a target date of December 31, 1999.

BOOKS

The conference was reminded of an issue thus far not fully grasped in our consideration of Holocaust-era assets. We heard reports from U.S. experts that will help define and deal with the despoliation of libraries and private collections of books in occupied Europe and the vital urgency of setting the book issue to rights. The delegate from the U.S. Justice Department detailed how the American occupation authorities in Germany rescued 3 million books looted from Jewish individuals and communities and was able to return 2.5 million of these books to their countries of origin or rightful owners by 1948. The remainder of the books were distributed to appropriate recipients by Jewish groups. Another delegate warned that a shortage of resources threatened preservation activities and access to many invaluable books and papers from the Holocaust era.

EDUCATION

A striking aspect of this conference, from the solemn ceremony and eloquent speeches made on Monday evening at the Holocaust Museum, to the statements we heard earlier in our closing plenary session this morning, is the emphasis placed so forcefully by so many on the importance of Holocaust education and remembrance. Speaker after speaker from country after country told us of their appreciation of the importance of teaching future generations about the unique tragedy and the lessons it can offer as this century comes to a close.

A remarkably rich series of break-out panels held yesterday at the Holocaust Museum featured leading Holocaust educators from both sides of the Atlantic, including both distinguished scholars and leaders of non-governmental organizations. A number of materials on Holocaust curricula and remembrance activities being undertaken by these organizations and others, as well as by governments, were on display and available for delegates.

The break-out sessions at the Museum and more briefly our plenary session earlier today highlighted the Task Force for International Cooperation on Holocaust Education, Remembrance, and Research. Initiated by Sweden, currently chaired by the United States, and also composed of the United Kingdom, Israel and Germany, the Task Force presented a report describing its specific efforts underway to promote international cooperation in these important areas. The Task Force report includes a declaration committing the Task Force countries and calling on others to strengthen or undertake new efforts on Holocaust education and remembrance. France and the Netherlands have already expressed a desire to participate in the Task Force, and it is likely that other countries will join them.

As the conference drew to a close, the delegates looked forward to other gatherings to continue the work of this historic meeting. The Swedish delegation announced its intention to convene an international conference on Holocaust education. The World Jewish Restitution Organization suggested on behalf of many of the non-governmental organizations that the important work of the conference should be continued next year in Jerusalem. The U.K. delegation spoke in favor of "satellite conferences" to address different issues. The head of the U.S. delegation urged conference countries to use the historical record established, the information shared, and the consensus reached in the past 3 days to galvanize our efforts in all areas.

CONCLUSION

Let me conclude by reaffirming my view that this conference has added substantially to the historical record on these events, so terrible and tragic for those involved, while strengthening the framework for countries to work together to act on the difficult and painful issues of restitution and justice.

The willingness of so many countries to confront the past is enormously encouraging, especially after so many decades. I urge us all to continue down this path, determined to meet our historic responsibilities to address the unparalleled wrongs of this century as the new millennium beckons.

Delegation
Statements

AMERICAN JEWISH COMMITTEE

Statement by
David A. Harris
EXECUTIVE DIRECTOR

To the Delegates to the Washington Conference on Holocaust-Era Assets:

As one of the non-governmental organizations privileged to be accredited to the Conference, we join in expressing our hope that this historic gathering will fulfill the ambitious and worthy goals set for it.

The effort to identify the compelling and complex issues of looted assets from the Second World War, and to consult on the most appropriate and expeditious means of addressing and resolving these issues, offers a beacon of light at the end of a very long and dark tunnel for Holocaust survivors, for the descendants of those who perished in the flames, for the vibrant Jewish communities which were destroyed, and for all who fell victim to the savagery and rapacity of those horrific times.

We are pleased as well that, in addition to discussion of these enormously important topics, the Conference will also take up the matter of Holocaust education, for, in the end, this can be our permanent legacy to future generations.

We hope that the Conference will reach a consensus on the need for enhanced international consultation, with the aim of encouraging more widespread teaching of the Holocaust in national school systems. Moreover, we commend those nations that have already taken impressive steps in this regard.

Not only can teaching of the Holocaust provide young people with a better insight into the darkest chapter in this century's history, but, ultimately, it can serve to strengthen their commitment to fundamental principles of human decency, mutual understanding and tolerance – all of which are so necessary if we are to have any chance of creating a brighter future.

When we speak of education, we must recognize that it cannot be limited to the classroom or the textbook, necessary though both are.

One element regarding both historical memory and education that deserves, in our view, greater attention from the international community is the identification, preservation and protection of sites of destruction and extermination connected to the Holocaust. Experience has taught us that visits to sites have a profound impact, not least on young people.

In some countries, considerable attention has been devoted to this matter; in others, regrettably, this has not been the case.

In some countries, great care has been taken to designate such sites, provide demarcation, ensure adequate security, and introduce pedagogical elements; in other countries, sites go unmarked, threatened by commercial or other development, and therefore destined for disappearance.

In some countries, comprehensive national legislation exists; in others, either there is no relevant legislation or responsibility lies with local rather than national governments, leading, sad to say, to an inconsistent and unreliable approach.

In some countries, ample funds have been earmarked to maintain the sites; in others, few, if any, resources have been committed.

In addition to our concern for strengthening Holocaust education, we raise this issue because it also serves other vital goals – seeking to preserve memory by reminding us all of what once was and what has been lost, and paying our respects to those who perished in the Final Solution, and to the vibrant civilization that was destroyed.

Many questions can surely be raised about specific aspects of our proposal – for example, issues of definition and jurisdiction. Our aim is precisely to raise these questions, leading, we would earnestly hope, to greater international consultation and coordination on guidelines and approaches among the distinguished nations and non-governmental organizations represented at this Conference.

Kindly be assured that the American Jewish Committee stands ready to assist in this effort in the months and years ahead.

We extend our best wishes and the expression of our highest esteem to all the delegates attending the Conference.

Respectfully submitted,

David A. Harris, Executive Director

ARGENTINA

Delegation Joint Statement

Argentina and its Commission of Enquiry into the Activities of Nazism (CEANA) wish to thank Under Secretary of State Stuart Eizenstat for his indefatigable efforts to organize this important conference on Holocaust-era assets. Our thanks are also extended to Ambassador Eizenstat's kind and often repeated expressions of support for CEANA's work, as most recently highlighted by the decision to postpone his departure from Buenos Aires in order to participate – together with Foreign Minister Guido Di Tella and Swedish Trade Minister Leif Pagrotsky – in the opening session of CEANA's plenary session in November 1998.

This conference's significance for Argentina not only stems from the need to take a joint approach to the wide gamut of issues that, sad to say, still await clarification more than half a century after the demise of the Third Reich, but also to do justice to its Jewish and other victims, as well as their descendants. Argentina's solidarity with the latter has led it to join the growing number of countries taking part in Ambassador Eizenstat's proposed relief fund, as was announced at the London conference an Nazi gold. Argentina's recent history suggests that this healing process is also a valuable way to consolidate our democracy, as well as to prevent the recurrence of the terrible episodes that the country witnessed during past decades.

The meeting is also important for CEANA's work. Created in 1997 and supported by the Argentine government as a sign of its commitment to try to eradicate the scourge of Nazism in the country and elsewhere, CEANA, nonetheless, is a non-governmental commission; its findings require certification by an array of Argentine and foreign personalities of different political and other affiliations. Owing to Argentina's recent past, CEANA's research agenda is somewhat broader then that of peer commissions, covering not only the subject of expoliated assets but also the issues of war criminals who found an Argentine refuge and the influence of Nazism in the country. Such a research agenda led CEANA's International Panel and Advisory

Committee to approve in November an extension of the Commission's life for another year, as well as to endorse the notion that the lessons arising from this self -introspective exercise should be made available to Argentine's student population, and to other sections of Argentine society as soon as possible.

Against this background, Argentina is keen to see that the recently established Task Force does not exclude Latin America in general and Argentina in particular, Clearly, permanent changes in public perceptions of Nazi era and other genocides can only be achieved through educational programs. Education also means familiarizing the public and honoring Argentines and others who took risks in order to save numbers of those whose lives were threatened by Nazism. Not surprisingly, therefore, CEANA's plenary coincided with the unveiling of a Buenos Aires monument of Raoul Wallenberg and issuing of a commemorative stamp (initiatives jointly sponsored by a CEANA international panelist, Sir Sigmund Sternberg; Argentina's Foreign Ministry; and the city of Buenos Aires autonomous government). Not well known in Argentina and elsewhere, Wallenberg's exertions to rescue countless Jews were partly assisted by a former employee of the Argentine consulate in Budapest inasmuch as Sweden represented Argentine interests in several European capitals after the country's belated severance of diplomatic relations with the Axis in January 1944.

Discussed at greater length in CEANA academic coordinator Ignacio Klich's presentation at the relevant panel, Commission work has fueled the opening of a number of Argentine archival repositories. Yet it is clear that all interested parties stand to benefit from the exchange of information afforded by this meeting. To this extent, CEANA reiterates its offer to share with others the fruits of its research at Argentine and other repositories, as well as acknowledges the important benefits derived from the seminar held here in June 1998 and from this conference, in particular by its research unit an art.

Such a unit has sought to confirm information arising from non-Argentine sources about the arrival of looted works of art, as well as the possible use of the country as a transit point for this trade. This has prompted the painstaking scouring of catalogues of Buenos Aires-based art galleries and analyzing the history of acquisitions by museums, as well as to recording individual art work losses in Europe by victims of Nazism who settled in Argentina and relaying such information to a U.S. database.

As previously mentioned, education is the way to avoid a sorry repetition of Nazi and other more recent genocides. While Argentina is only at the beginning of this road, before long its students will be exposed to such subjects as the implications of Hitler's rise to power and Argentina's performance during the Nazi era. Likewise, a Buenos Aires-based Holocaust museum, an initiative supported by the government's grant of the building to house such a museum and of monies to set it up, will be inaugurated in the near future. Not too far away is the day when Argentina will also join the nations that year in, year out commemorate the Nazi extermination of Jews.

All this is part of Argentina's wish to build a democratic and pluralist society, an indispensable ingredient to achieve this being learning from history. From this angle, the opening of archival sources, like the creation of CEANA, are only part of the tools that are meant to facilitate such learning. In the future, it is to be hoped that international events, like the London and Washington conferences, will contribute to further this process wherever necessary.

AUSTRIA

Delegation Statement

Executive Summary

Austria welcomes the holding of the Conference on Holocaust-Era Assets in Washington as an important step to complete knowledge of historical facts related to assets looted by the Nazis including art, insurance and other assets. We share the objectives of the conference, to strengthen the international commitment to open relevant national archives and other records for research on Nazi-looted assets and to examine steps taken to return looted assets as well as promoting broad consensus for further action. We are ready to assume our part in investigating those facts as far as they relate to our own country and to make every effort to shed complete light on all unresolved questions.

HISTORICAL BACKGROUND

Of the approximately 210,000 Jews who lived in Austria before World War II, approximately 110,000 were forced to emigrate. Some 65,000 Austrian Jews were murdered by the Nazis.

"ARYANIZATION" (THE TAKEOVER OF JEWISH PROPERTY BY NON-JEWS)

In preparation for the return of properties taken from the rightful owners by the Nazis, a law regarding the submission of claims was passed as early as 1945. The holders of Aryanized properties were requested under threat of penalty to register those assets and to refrain from any legal transactions regarding the property in question, except "regular administrative measures". Between 1946 and 1949 seven restitution laws were passed by the Austrian Parliament which provided for restitution in several phases. The immediate victims as well as direct descendants and siblings were eligible for restitution. In addition, four laws dealt with claims for restitution of property, for example to democratic institutions, including Jewish and non-Jewish religious institutions.

Not all aryanized and registered property was actually claimed and therefore could not be restored. A law on the collection of those assets was passed in 1957 and the „Collection Points A and B" created. Collection Point A received all unclaimed property of persons who in 1937 had belonged to the Jewish community, Collection Point B received other claims. After the disbursement of the proceeds to victims of persecution, the collection points were liquidated in 1972.

While the legal framework for the resolution of restitution cases (with the exception of leases which were not included) was generally accepted by the Allies and victims' organizations, questions concerning the practical implementation of the laws remain. There is no systematic overview of the files or any historical analysis on that subject. Of the 42,096 claims submitted, approximately one-fifth was granted, one-third was settled by agreement, one-third was rejected or the claim withdrawn. There exist no reliable data about the monetary value of restored property.

In order to gain comprehensive knowledge of historical facts related to assets looted by the Nazis and of restitution of property after the war, the Austrian Government recently established an independent **Commission of Historians** with international participation to study all aspects of Aryanization and the country's restitution efforts to victims of the Nazi era after the war. The mandate of the Commission ranges from "dispossession of property on the territory of the Republic" to "restoration and compensation" as well as economic and social efforts by Austria after 1945. The Commission had its inaugural session on 26 November 1998. It is required to submit an outline of its future work to the Federal Government within three months.

WORKS OF ART

By January 1949 over 13,000 art objects had been returned to their rightful owners or their legitimate heirs of the over 18,500 items which had been seized during the Nazi era or which had been voluntarily given up to air-raid shelters. Restitution of the remaining objects was spread out over the subsequent years. For this purpose, two specific laws pertaining to the settlement of claims regarding art and cultural heritage were passed in 1969 and 1986. The latter law was amended 1995 to allow for the so-called "Mauerbach Sale": in 1996 an auction of Nazi-confiscated works of art which could not be restituted to the former owners or their heirs was held to benefit Holocaust victims.

In 1998 Federal Minister for Education and Cultural Affairs, Elisabeth Gehrer, established a "Commission for Provenance Research" which was mandated to study available historical material relating to looted art in the Bundesdenkmalamt (Federal Authority for the Preservation of Monuments) and in the various federal museums and collections. The goal of this very extensive historic survey was to shed light on the looting by the Nazis during the period from 1938 to 1945 and to establish which questionable acquisitions may have been made by public collections during that time. Furthermore, the restitution procedures of the immediate post-war period were to be examined.

The findings of the Commission which has up to now completed a substantial part of its work, served as basis for a "Federal Law on the Restitution of Works of Art from Federal Museums and Collections" adopted by Parliament on 5/19 November 1998 and which is expected to enter into force shortly. The law provides the legal basis for restituting those works of art that fall under one of the categories mentioned in the Federal Law to the former owners or their legal heirs. An advisory board which will hold its inaugural session on 9 December 1998 will assist the Minister. National and international experts may be asked to participate in the Board's deliberations. In the course of the debate in Parliament, Minister Gehrer has promised to urge also non-federal museums and collections to follow suit and take similar action. A number of communities and municipalities had, however, already established similar commissions.

MONETARY GOLD

Austria is among those countries whose claims for restitution of official gold reserves looted by the Nazis were recognized by the Tripartite Gold Commission (TGC). The gold reserves of the Austrian Central Bank, amounting to 78,267 metric tons as of 17 March 1938, had to be transferred to the German Reichsbank immediately after the Anschluss in 1938. The TGC recognized the greater part of the Austrian claim after the war and 50,183 tons were returned in several installments. The remaining claim to the gold still held by the TGC amounted to some

27,000 troy ounces which have in the meantime been transferred to the account of the Austrian National Bank.

Austria was among the first countries to publicly express support for the proposal to put a substantial portion of its claim to the remainder of the Nazi gold into an international fund for the benefit of survivors of the Holocaust. To implement this political decision of principle, once the Nazi Persecutee Relief Fund had been set up, a Federal Law was passed by Parliament on 5/19 November 1998 which authorizes the National Bank to transfer the total Austrian share in the remaining gold (valued at AS 102 million, which is app. 8.5 million US Dollars) to the Nazi Persecutee Relief Fund. The law provides that the money should go mainly to those needy victims who up to now had received no or no adequate compensation. In addition, it will be possible to support projects designed to fight against anti-Semitism, racism, xenophobia and intolerance. The law furthermore stipulates that the distribution of the money must be made through the **"National Fund of the Republic of Austria for the Victims of National Socialism"**, established in 1995 to make contributions to Austrian Holocaust victims from funds provided by the national budget of Austria. The National Fund is one of the eligible NGOs mentioned in the Annex to the Fund Agreement through which national contributions to the International Relief Fund can be disbursed to individuals and projects

INSURANCE CLAIMS

In addition to the general restitution laws introduced in Austria immediately after the Second World War, a settlement of insurance claims could also be obtained on the basis of the Insurance Compensation Act of 1958. It referred to those cases in which insurance companies had already paid the benefits from the insurance contract in full but the benefits were confiscated according to applicable German laws. By the end of the fifties, such compensation payments, arising from insurance contracts that were part of the domestic portfolio of insurance companies registered in Austria, were made to the claimants.

The Austrian insurance companies have offered and still offer good-will payments to Holocaust victims or their heirs without any legal obligation in those individual cases where no payments had been up to now and the claims would fall under the statute of limitation.

The legal situation in Austria prevents the Insurance Supervisory Authority to oblige insurance companies to make payments on the basis of insurance contracts falling under the statute of limitation. However, the Insurance Supervisory Authority could already help in a number of individual cases to identify legal successors to the Austrian insurance companies and portfolio transfers, provided that such contracts were part of the domestic (i.e. Austrian) portfolios.

FEDERAL MINISTRY OF FINANCE
INSURANCE SUPERVISORY AUTHORITY

The Legal Situation in Regard to "Holocaust and Insurances" in Austria

1. THE FORFEITURE OF INSURANCES TO THE THIRD REICH

The "forfeiture" of insurance contracts to the Third Reich results from the 11th Ordinance concerning the Law on Reich Citizens (1935) of 25 November 1941 in conjunction with a circular of the Reich Supervisory Office (Reichsaufsichtsamt), reference no. R. 53/42.

Section 1, sentence 1 of the 11th Ordinance concerning the Law on Reich Citizens adopted in 1935 provides that "a Jew who has his ordinary residence abroad cannot be a German citizen". Section 3 of the Ordinance prescribes that "the loss of citizenship also entails the forfeiture of property to the Reich and that the forfeited property is to serve the aim of promoting all objectives relating to the solution of the question of the Jews".

Under Section 7 para. 1 of the above Ordinance, all persons - including insurance companies - had to report "objects belonging to forfeited property" in their possession to the Senior Finance President in Berlin within a period of six months from the day of forfeiture. Failure to comply with this reporting requirement was punishable by imprisonment or payment of a fine.

[At that time, the (Austrian) insurance supervisory authority was merely a "branch office" of the Reich Supervisory Office in Berlin. Except for information of a general nature such as laws, official publications and insurance reference books (so-called "*Assekuranzkompaesse*"), the insurance supervisory authority has no further records in this respect. The Austrian State Archives have hardly any files from that time in their possession.]

On the basis of this 11th Ordinance, a circular issued by the Reich Supervisory Office for Private Insurance in Berlin in 1942, reference no. 53/42, to the supervised insurance companies, provided, inter alia, for the following:

Endowment insurances of any kind with regular premium payments forfeited to the Reich in accordance with the Ordinance were regarded as being canceled as of 31 December 1941. The Reich was entitled to the surrender value (minus outstanding contributions) calculated for that date in accordance with the general operational plan. For the period from 1 January 1942 to the date of notification (cf. reporting requirement under Section 7 of the 11th Ordinance), the insurance companies had to pay the Reich interest payable on arrears.

In the case of annuity insurances of any kind where the General Standard Terms and Conditions made provision for surrender, the insurance companies also had to pay the Reich the surrender value calculated for 31 December 1941 in accordance with the general operational plan. As regards all sorts of annuity insurances where the General Standard Terms and Conditions provided no option for surrender, the Reich retained 75% of the premium reserve calculated for 31 December 1941 on the basis of the general operational plan plus the annuities due but still unpaid.

Property insurance contracts concerning the assets of "Jews" which had been forfeited to the Reich after the adoption of the 11th Ordinance still remained in force until the Reich decided to either transfer the insured object into its ownership or else to sell it. Any liability or accident insurance contracts of "Jews" who had lost their German citizenship under the terms of the 11th Ordinance, however, expired.

2. THE REESTABLISHMENT OF THE AUSTRIAN INSURANCE INDUSTRY

The development of the Austrian insurance industry has always been closely related to the economic situation. After years of inflation, monetary reform and international financial crises, there was a short period of economic recovery, followed by what became known as the Phoenix crash (*Phönix-Krach*). Repair measures ordered by the legislators in 1936, such as the creation of a fund designed to cover domestic Phoenix life insurance contracts, obliged the life insurance companies to render substantial benefits.

The explanatory remarks to the government's draft of the Insurance Re-establishment Act of 1955, Federal Law Gazette No. 185/1955 (*Versicherungswiederaufbaugesetz*) describe and summarize the postwar situation of the Austrian insurance industry as follows:

At the end of the war, insurance companies suffered losses because most of their covering funds consisted in securities which had to be bought in the era of the German Reich and became entirely worthless after it collapsed. Likewise, the value of houses and mortgages was severely affected. As a result of the currency reform, insurance companies lost around 60 percent of their deposits with banking institutions. Of all branches of the insurance industry, life insurance business was hardest hit by the losses occurring during and after the war. In order to be able to meet their hitherto limited liabilities, the insurance companies had to rely on public assistance.

3. PAYMENTS RENDERED BY THE REPUBLIC OF AUSTRIA

Article 26 para. 1 of the State Treaty of 15 May 1955 (Federal Law Gazette No. 152/1955) on the restoration of an independent and democratic Austria provides for Austria's obligation to restitute property confiscated by the German Reich and, where this is no longer possible, to grant compensation.

To implement the above provision, the "*Auffangorganisationsgesetz*" 1957, Federal Law Gazette No. 73/1957, (Absorption Organization Act) was adopted with five amendments (Federal Law Gazette Nos. 285/1958, 62 and 306/1959, 287/1960 and 1949/1966), under which collecting agencies (*Sammelstellen*) "A" and "B" were established through which heirless and unclaimed property that was liable to restitution was registered for use for the benefit of persecuted persons.

Collecting agency "A" was assigned all claims arising out of estates, legal titles and interests within the meaning of Art. 26 para. 2 of the Austrian State Treaty which were due to persons belonging the Israelite religious community on 31 December 1937. After the complete distribution of funds, both collecting agencies were dissolved.

Under the Ordinance of 26 April 1938, Reichs Gazette I Sec. 414, Jews (within the meaning of the Nuremberg Laws) had to report property held until 7 April 1938 no later than 30 June 1938. In this report, all assets exceeding 5,000 Reichsmark had to be reported. These property records also included numerous life insurance contracts. These were registered in the same manner as life insurance contracts resulting from the files of the Senior Finance President. Overall, there were 20,815 life insurance contracts in force in 1938.

a) Historical review of the former restitution laws

As from 1946, laws were passed in Austria the object of which was the restitution of confiscated and ownerless or heirless assets. Immediately after the war, the prewar legal situation was reestablished by the so-called restitution or repayment laws in order to remedy previous acts of injustice suffered with regard to property rights. Within the context of specific restitution or repayment laws, it was also possible to restore - along with other assets - insurance policies to the beneficiaries or their legal successors.

The following property categories were restored under the First and Second Restitution Acts: real estate, buildings, real estate earnings, insurance policies, securities, cash accounts, mortgage claims, business shares and undertakings as well as other movable assets (e.g., artworks, carpets, means of production).

First Restitution Act

Special mention must be made of the First Restitution Act, Federal Law Gazette No. 156/1946 on the basis of which property assets that were administrated by the Federation or by the *Länder* (regional governments) when the law entered into force in 1946 were given back to their owners.

Included in the scope of this law were mainly those emigrated or deported persons of Jewish denomination or descent whose property assets were confiscated by the Gestapo for being hostile to the people or the state and whose property assets had been declared forfeited for the benefit of the German Reich under the 11th Ordinance to the Reich Citizens Act of 25 November 1941, with the administration of these property assets being assigned to the Senior Finance Presidents.

Second Restitution Act

Similarly, the 2nd Restitution Act, Federal Law Gazette No. 53/1947, concerned confiscated property assets that were in the possession of the Republic of Austria as a result of forfeiture and that had to be restored to the original owners or their legal successors.

This law dealt with the restitution of assets which had been taken away from the lawful owners and subsequently gone into the possession of a natural or legal person which was distributed or dissolved after the liberation of Austria under the Nazi Prohibition Act and War Criminal Act and whose property was therefore forfeited for the benefit of the Republic of Austria.

Third Restitution Act

The 3rd Restitution Act, Federal Law Gazette No. 54/1947, regulates the restoration of assets which, during the German occupation of Austria, were taken away from their owners or legitimate holders in connection with the seizure of power by the Nazis either high-handedly or under some law or other regulation. It is currently unclear whether it was possible, in view of specific constellations of facts, for insurance policies to fall within the scope of this Act.

b) Insurance Compensation Act, Federal Law Gazette No. 130/1958 (*Versicherungsentschädigungsgesetz*): Federal law of 26 June 1958 concerning the regulations on life insurance claims contracts sequestrated by the German Reich

The Republic of Austria has under certain circumstances made payments in the private insurance sector in those cases where life insurance contracts were "sequestrated" by the German Reich before 1945.

Section 1 of the Insurance Compensation Act of 1958, Federal Law Gazette No. 130/1958, focuses on "sequestrated" or "forfeited" life insurance contracts that were part of the domestic portfolio of insurance companies registered in Austria and were fulfilled by payment to the Third Reich on the basis of Reich regulations rescinded in Austria (or administrative regulations based thereupon). - The question whether an insurance contract was part of the domestic portfolio of an insurance company had to be determined according to Articles I and II of the Insurance Reestablishment Act (Federal Law Gazette No. 185/1955).

Beneficiaries under the Insurance Compensation Act of 1958 had to raise their claims with the insurance company concerned in writing and within a year, viz. until June 30, 1959, in order to prevent their rights from lapsing ("preclusion").

The amount of compensation was subject to the determination of benefits as defined in the Insurance Reestablishment Act 1955, which provided that under explicit legal provisions it was admissible in many cases only to render 40% of contractual payments. The amounts thus disbursed were rather small, not least because of missing premiums or, occasionally, due to policy loans that had previously been paid out. Other reasons for poor benefits are related to the monetary reform of 1946 and to the amounts insured, which were rather low by present-day standards.

4. Functions and limits of Austrian insurance supervision within the Federal Ministry of Finance

In Article 18 para. 1 of the Federal Constitution Act, the principle of legality is laid down as a pillar of the Austrian Federal Constitution which provides that public administration must only be executed on the basis of the law. The Insurance Supervisory Authority is thus strictly obliged to observe legal limits in the discharge of its supervisory duties with regard to insurance companies.

Apart from the system of substantive executive supervision, the state also has to protect the interests of insured parties directly vis-à-vis the insurance company, and indirectly by preserving the different insurance enterprises and the insurance sector in its economic integrity.

The Insurance Supervisory Authority also deals with complaints and inquiries about insurance contracts submitted to it by insured persons. It is obliged to ensure that the insurers observe the applicable rules regulating the operation of insurance contracts and the generally accepted principles of proper business operation.

Even though it is considered desirable for insurers to offer adequate goodwill payments in connection with Holocaust policies, the Insurance Supervisory Authority has no legal means of coercing the insurance industry to make payments on accommodating terms arising from barred claims.

The Insurance Supervisory Authority may assist claimants in identifying Austrian legal successors of Austrian insurers in connection with "old policies" (e.g. in the case of name changes or asset transfers within Austria). -Immediately after having been informed about the New York class action in March/April 1998, the Insurance Supervisory Authority also examined the fate of "old" life insurance policies (assessment of the legal situation roughly starting in the 1930s, during the Nazi period and the cancellation of forfeitures/confiscations of insurance policies after the war in 1945; investigations in the State Archives and in the insurance industry, more specifically with the Association of Insurers as the interest group of the Austrian insurance industry, as well as among insurance companies known to be affected).

Austrian Restitution of Works of Art

Background Information

Within the limits of the restitution laws adopted after the end of WWII, the Republic of Austria returned, among other things, works of art which were unjustly seized to their rightful owners or their legitimate heirs. In certain unambiguous cases a formal restitution procedure was deemed unnecessary. With the two art and culture restitution laws of 1969 and 1986, as well as the amendment of 1995 (which established a legal foundation for the transfer of those works of art which could neither be returned to their rightful owners nor to their legitimate heirs to the Federation of Jewish Communities in Austria) the restitution legislation found its conclusion.

Due to the results of a review of archival materials concerning art restitution as well as concrete cases, which was begun in the 90's, it was ordered in January 1998 that the archives of the federal museums and collections as well as the Bundesdenkmalamt archives undergo a systematic review in order to gain insight into the occurrences of the period between 1938 and 1945, as well as into the restitution results after the end of WWII. Independently, surveys were also carried out in the collections of the „Bundesimmobilienverwaltung". Within the Federal Ministry for Education and Cultural Affairs, a "Commission for Provenance Research" was appointed which was entrusted with the assignment of systematically categorizing all of the acquired art objects during the time in question, in order to clear up all questions about their ownership during the National Socialist Rule and the immediate Post-War period.

The first results of the work of this Commission are now available. The following categories of art objects have been identified:

1) Art and cultural objects which were retained under the law prohibiting exportation of works of art and entered into the property of Austrian museums and collections labeled as "Gifts" or "Dedications". All works or art in this category have already been subject to restitution and were thus returned to their rightful owners. These cases are therefore thoroughly documented. In return for the granting of an export

allowance under the law prohibiting the exportation of art, it was agreed upon with the owners who sought exportation that some of these pieces should go to Austrian museums. From today's standpoint and based on the fact that both the art and cultural restitution laws were explicitly exempt from the application of the regulations of the statute prohibiting exportation, the course of action chosen at that time is unjustifiable.

2) Art and cultural objects which legally became property of the Federal Government, but were previously subject to a legal transaction which has been declared void under the regulations of the so-called "Nullity law" (Nichtigkeitsgesetz). After the war, several museum directors purchased art works in good faith from authorized dealers, whereas doubts to the origin of these works only emerged at a later time. Several such cases have been discovered in the course of the Provenance study.

3) Art and cultural objects which, despite restitution attempts, were unable to be returned to their rightful owner or legitimate heirs and thus became property of the Federal Government as ownerless goods.

With the present draft law, the legal foundation shall be laid in order to return these art objects to their original owners or legitimate heirs.

The law provides for an advisory board, which is assembled as follows:

A Representative of the Federal Ministry for Education
A Representative of the Federal Ministry for Economic Affairs
A Representative of the Federal Ministry for Justice
A Representative of the Federal Ministry for Defense
A Representative of the Finanzprokuratur (branch of the Ministry for Finance)
A historian and art historian nominated by the Conference of University Deans

It is the duty of the advisory board to give advice regarding the determination of all persons to whom works of art shall be restituted. The advisory board can invite additional experts to its meetings.

The statute prohibiting exportation does not apply to the law. For this law the regulations of grants are freed from all taxes and duties. The law applies to a period of 25 years.

Federal Minister Elisabeth Gehrer has stated during the parliamentary debate of the new law that she will contact the nine federal states, the various communities as well as other museums in Austria to put a comparable initiative in place.

A progress report will be given before the end of the regular session of parliament. Further reports will be given on a yearly basis.

3) Arguments and Facts:

a) Status of the review and order of magnitude of the objects in question:

Category 1 para. 1, subpara. 1: Due to archival information available to the Bundesdenkmalamt the dimension of this category can be determined quite precisely. The review of the various museum's archives is, at this point, almost complete. This category encompasses stock from 13 former collections, amounting altogether to approximately 405 catalog entries and approximately 500-600 object pieces (among them coins and dishes). Well known names of these collections are, among others; Rothschild, Lederer, Bloch-Bauer and Lanckoronski.

Category 2 para. 1, subpara. 2: This category deals with purchases of the federal museums during WWII and their acquisitions after the war. So far the provenance research brought to light a number of cases, which total under 20. The study under this category is the least advanced because research proves to be most difficult in these cases.

Category 3 para. 1, subpara. 3: Due to the recent and systematic archival review, additional art works and objects have been discovered, which belong under the category "Naziraubkunst" (artwork stolen by the Nazis). At this moment, this category contains up to 200 objects. None of them are „major pieces" of art but rather furnishings (decorations) and installation objects.

b) The law provides that ownerless goods or goods where no heirs can be found shall be transferred to the National Fund for the Victims of National Socialism. Concurrently with the adoption of the art restitution law, the law governing the National Fund has also been amended. Thereby the National Fund was authorized to transfer the proceeds from the sale of these art works to victims of National Socialism.

4) Additional questions:

Bloch-Bauer: There are claims from the family, which - given today's level of information - fall under category 1 of the law and are therefore governed by the new law. Further claims by the family must, however, be looked into by the advisory board to determine whether or not they fall under the restitution law.

Claims by the Mahler family: For these claims too, the advisory board must examine archival materials in order to determine whether the claims are legitimate according to the law.

Such cases which do not fall under any of the three categories of the law and therefore cannot be restituted, should be looked into by the Commission of Historians.

Leopold Museum (Leopold-Privatstiftung): Concerning the two Schiele paintings in New York, the Leopold Foundation has been advised (upon the initiative of Minister Gehrer) to propose to the New York District Attorney that - after the return of the paintings to Vienna - the Leopold Foundation will issue a legally binding waiver of its right to a plea concerning the statute of limitations in these cases.

The actual return of property under the law can begin as soon as the law enters into force (expected by the beginning of December 1998): Federal Minister Gehrer has already written to the above mentioned institutions and requested their nominations to the advisory board. The nine federal states and communities were likewise contacted by the Minister with the request to follow suit and take similar action. The inauguration of this advisory board will take place in a first meeting on 9 December.

Austrian Historical Commission

Handout for the Washington Conference

The Historical Commission was established jointly by the Austrian Federal Chancellor (i.e. Prime Minister), the Vice-Chancellor, the Speaker of the National Assembly and the Speaker of the Federal Council (i.e. the second chamber of the Austrian Parliament). The Commission will be their agent.

The Commission's mandate is to investigate and report on the whole complex of expropriations in Austria during the Nazi era and on restitution and/or compensation (including other financial or social benefits) after 1945 by the Republic of Austria (cf. the decision of the Austrian Cabinet of 1 October 1998).

MEMBERS OF THE COMMISSION

Prof. Clemens Jabloner, President of the Austrian Administrative Court, Chairman,
Dr. Brigitte Bailer-Galanda,
Dr. Avraham Barkai,
Prof. Lorenz Mikoletzky, Director-General of the Austrian State Archives,
Dr. Bertrand Perz,
Prof. Roman Sandgruber.

HOW THE MEMBERS WERE CHOSEN

One reputed foreign expert. The "Yad Vashem" Institute, Jerusalem, the Holocaust Memorial Museum, Washington DC, and Mr. Simon Wiesenthal, Vienna, were invited to draw up short list of three.

One Austrian economic and social historian. The heads of the Departments of Economic and Social History of the Universities of

Vienna, Linz, Innsbruck and Graz and of the Vienna University of Economics were invited to draw up a short list of two.

Two Austrian experts on contemporary history. The heads of the Departments of Contemporary History of the Universities of Vienna, Graz, Linz and Innsbruck, the head of the History Department of Salzburg University, the head of the Contemporary History Section of the History Department of the University of Klagenfurt and the head of the Boltzmann Institute for Research into the Consequences of the War, who also heads the Documentation Archive of Austrian (Anti-Nazi) Resistance, were invited to draw up a short list of four.

From the nominations submitted by these organizations, the Austrian Federal Chancellor, the Vice-Chancellor, the Speaker of the National Assembly and the Speaker of the Federal Council selected the members of the Commission. The Commission's Secretariat is at the Austrian State Archives (Österreichisches Staatsarchiv, 1030 Wien, Nottendorfer Gasse 2, phone +43 1 79540/180 or 181, fax +43 1 79540/186, e-mail hiskom@oesta.gv.at).

The constituent session of the Commission will take place on 26 November 1998. The agenda will include the following items: rules of procedure; should the Commission's sessions be public or private; outlines of the Commission's work program; suggestions on methods to be used; organizational requirements; time schedule; budget. As required by its mandate, the Commission will announce its general work program within 3 months of its constituent session.

The Commission's budget is part of the Austrian Parliament's Budget. The Commission will probably submit intermediate "Progress Reports" from time to time. In addition to the work of its members, the Commission will subcontract some research work to outside historians in order to speed up its work and make it more efficient.

As the Federal Chancellor said in the Cabinet on proposing the Commission, the object of the exercise is to make "another significant step towards an objective, transparent, independent and comprehensive coming to terms with one of the most painful chapters" of the history of the Republic of Austria.

BIOGRAPHIES OF THE MEMBERS OF THE COMMISSION

1. Clemens Jabloner

Born 28 November 1948, Vienna.

Studied law at Vienna University

June 1972	Graduated as Doctor of Law
1975	Assistant in public law, Vienna Economic University
1 January 1976	Assistant, Institute for Public and Administrative Law, Vienna University
1 March 1978	Seconded to Federal Chancellery, Department of Legal Advisers
1982	Appointed head of media subdivision of that Department
December 1989	Appointed head of the Civil Service Department, Federal Chancellery
1988	Habilitation as lecturer (*Dozent*) in constitutional law, Vienna University (under Prof. Walter)
1993	Chosen to be Second Executive Secretary of the Hans Kelsen Institute; received title of "Associate Professor" from Federal President
1 December 1991	Appointed Vice-President of the Administrative Court
1 April 1993	Appointed President of the Administrative Court
1 October 1998	Appointed Chairman of the Historical Commission

Dr. Jabloner continues to lecture at the university and to publish on law and legal philosophy.

Selected publications

* With R. Walter, *Hans Kelsen (1881-1973) - Leben-Werk-Wirkung* [on the life, work and echo of Hans Kelsen], in: Luther, Stiefel and Hoeflich (ed.), *Der Einfluß deutscher Emigranten auf die Rechtsentwicklung in den USA und in Deutschland* [The Influence of German Emigrés on Legal Developments in the USA and Germany] (1993), p. 521 (part IV);

* "Kelsen" in: Schlink and Jacobson (ed.), *Weimar: A Jurisprudence of Crisis* (in preparation);

* "Menschenbild und Friedenssicherung" [The Concept of Man and Action to Secure Peace], in: Walter and Jabloner (ed.), *Hans Kelsens Wege sozialphilosophischer Forschung* [on Kelsen's approach to social philosophy](1997), 57;

* "Der Bundesstaat und die Gerichtbarkeit des öffentlichen Rechts" [The Federal System of Government and Public Law Courts], in: Schambeck (ed.), *Bundesstaat und Bundesrat in Österreich* [on the federal system and the second chamber of parliament in Austria] (1997), 135;

* "Legal Techniques and Theory of Civilization - Remarks on Hans Kelsen and Carl Schmitt", in: Dinerand Stolleis, *Hans Kelsen and Carl Schmitt. A Conference in Legal History* (1998) (in preparation).

2. Brigitte Bailer-Galanda

Born 1952, Vienna

Studied social science, economics and history at Vienna University (Master of Social and Economic Science, Dr. phil.)

Since 1979   Staff member of Documentation Archive of Austrian Resistance

Since 1993-94   Instructor, Institute of Political Science, Vienna University

Dr. Bailer-Galanda has researched and published on the Nazi era in Austria, particularly on the resistance movement and Nazi persecution, and on racism and rightist extremism after 1945 with special emphasis on Nazi apologists and Holocaust deniers as well as the problems of compensation for Nazi victims and the Austrian response to the country's Nazi past in general.

Selected publications

Own publications or co-editor:

Wiedergutmachung - kein Thema. Österreich und die Opfer des Nationalsozialismus [Compensation - Not a Suitable Subject: Austria and the Victims of Nazism], Vienna 1993;

With Wolfgang Neugebauer, *"... ihrer Überzeugung treu geblieben". Rechtsextremisten, "Revisionisten" und Antisemiten in Österreich* [on the extreme right, revisionism and anti-Semitism in Austria], Stiftung Dokumentationsarchiv des österreichischen Widerstandes [Foundation for the Documentation Archive of Austrian Resistance] (ed.), Vienna 1996;

Co-editor and contributor with Wolfgang Benz and Wolfgang Neugebauer, *Wahrheit und "Auschwitzlüge". Zur Bekämpfung "revisionistischer" Propaganda* [Truth and "Auschwitz Lie". How to counter revisionist propaganda], Vienna 1995, expanded edition under licence in Germany;

Die Auschwitzleugner. "Revisionistische" Geschichtslüge und historische Wahrheit [Those Who Deny Auschwitz: "Revisionist" Historical Lies and Historical Truth], Berlin 1996 (co-editor and contributor).

Contributor:

* *Erzählte Geschichte. Berichte von Widerstandkämpfern und Verfolgern und Verfolgten*, Vol. 1: *Arbeiterbewegung* [Vol. 1 - dealing with the workers' movement - of an oral history collection featuring resistance fighters, persecutors and persecuted people], ed.

Stiftung Dokumentationsarchiv des österreichischen Widerstandes, Vienna 1985 (contributor and project director);

* *Jüdische Schicksale, Berichte von Verfolgten* [Jewish Stories: Reports by Persecuted Persons], ed. Stiftung Dokumentationsarchiv des österreichischen Widerstandes, Vienna 1992 (vol. 3 of *Erzählte Geschichte* [Oral History]), (contributor and project director);

* "Verfolgt und vergessen. Die Diskriminierung einzelner Opfergruppen durch die Opferfürsorgegesetzgebung" [on discrimination against certain categories of victims in Austrian legislation], in: Yearbook 1992, Dokumentationsarchiv des österreichischen Widerstandes, pp. 13-25, Vienna 1992;

* "'Ohne den Staat weiter damit zu belasten ...' Bemerkungen zur österreichischen Rückstellungsgesetzgebung" ["Without Creating Additional Burdens for the State": Notes on Austrian Restitution Legislation] in: *Zeitgeschichte* 11/12 (1993), pp. 367-381;

* "Gleiches Recht für alle? Die Behandlung von Opfern und Tätern des Nationalsozialismus durch die Republik Österreich" [Equal Rights for All? The Treatment of Nazi Victims and Nazi Perpetrators by the Republic of Austria], in: *Der Umgang mit dem Holocaust. Europa-USA-Israel* [Coming to Terms with the Holocaust: Europe-USA-Israel], ed. Rolf Steininger, pp. 183-197 Vienna, Cologne and Weimar 1994 (Publications of the Contemporary History Department of Innsbruck University and the Jewish Museum of Hohenems, Vol. 1);

* "Anschreiben gegen die Leugner, Neue Literatur zum Thema "Revisionismus'" [Writing against the Deniers: New Literature on the Subject of "Revisionism"], in: *Jahrbuch für Antisemitismusforschung* [Yearbook for Research on Anti-Semitism], ed. Wolfgang Benz for the Centre for Research on Anti-Semitism of the Berlin Technical University, pp. 287-300, Frankfurt and New York 1995;

* "Das Konzentrationslager Mauthausen" (Mauthausen Concentration Camp) in: Simon Wiesenthal, *Denn sie wußten, was sie tun. Zeichnungen und Aufzeichnungen aus dem KZ Mauthausen* [For

They Knew What They Were Doing: Drawings and Notes from Mauthausen Concentration Camp], pp. 11-13, Vienna 1995;

* "'Alle haben gleich gelitten?' Antisemitismus in der Auseinandersetzung um die sogenannte 'Wiedergutmachung'" [All Suffered to the Same Extent? Anti-Semitism in the Debate about So-Called 'Reparation'], in: *Die Macht der Bilder. Antisemitische Vorurteile und Mythen* [The Power of Images: Anti-Semitic Prejudices and Myths], ed. Jüdisches Museum der Stadt Wien [Jewish Museum of the City of Vienna], pp. 333-345, Vienna 1995;

* "Die sogenannte 'Auschwitz-Lüge' - neue Ausdruckform für althergebrachten Antisemitismus" [The So-Called 'Auschwitz Lie' - a New Expression of Traditional Anti-Semitism], in: *Die Macht der Bilder. Antisemitische Vorurteile und Mythen*, ed. Jüdisches Museum der Stadt Wien, pp. 360-365, Vienna 1995;

* "Alle waren Opfer. Der selektive Umgang mit den Folgen des Nationalsozialismus" [They Were All Victims: The Selective Treatment of the Consequences of Nazism], in: Wolfgang Kos and Georg Rigele (ed.) *Inventur 45/55. Österreich im ersten Jahrzehnt der Zweiten Republik* [Stocktaking 45-55: Austria in the First Decade of the Second Republic], pp. 181-200, Vienna 1996.

In English:

* "They Were All Victims: The Selective Treatment of the Consequences of National Socialism", in: Günter Bischof and Anton Pelinka (ed.), *Austrian Historical Memory and National Identity*, New Brunswick Austrian Contemporary Studies, Vol. 5), London 1996;

* "'Revisionism" in Germany and Austria: The Evolution of a Doctrine", in: *Anti-Semitism and Xenophobia in Germany after Unification*, ed. Hermann Kurthen, Rainer Erb and Werner Bergmann, New York and Oxford 1997.

3. Avraham Barkai

Born 1921, Berlin.

1938-1940	Emigrated to Palestine, student of agriculture at Mikveh, Israel
since 1941	Member of Kibbutz Lehaveth Habashan
1977	Ph.D., Tel Aviv University in History of Economics, since 1986 part-time assistant-professor at the Tel-Hai-College, Israel.

Visiting professor at Israeli and foreign universities

Member of the historical commission investigating the history of Deutsche Bank under the Nazis (report has been submitted)

Member of the Board of Directors(1994-1997 chairman), Leo Baeck Institute, Jerusalem

Currently Research Fellow at Yad Vashem's International Center for Holocaust Studies where he is researching the history of "Centralverein deutscher Staatsbürger jüdischen Glaubens", 1893-1938, the largest and most representative German-Jewish organization.

Selected publications

*   *Vom Boykott zur Entjudung. Der wirtschaftliche Existenzkampf der Juden im Dritten Reich 1933-1943*, 1988 [about the economic struggle for survival of Jews in Nazi Germany] ; Engl. ed. *From Boycott to Annihilation*, Hanover: Brandeis UP 1989;

*   *Das Wirtschaftssystem des Nationalsozialismus* (1st ed. 1977, 2nd enlarged ed. 1989, Engl. ed. *Nazi Economics. Ideology, Theory, Policy*, New Haven: Yale UP and Oxford, UK: Berg 1990);

*   *Jüdische Minderheit und Industrialisierung in Westdeutschland 1850-1914* [The Jewish Minority and Industrialization in West Germany, 1850-1914] (1988);

*   With Paul Mendes Flohr, *Deutsch-Jüdische Geschichte in der Neuzeit* [German-Jewish History in the Modern Age, Vol. IV, 1918-1945] (1997), Engl. edition New York: Columbia UP 1998;

*   Many essays and conference papers on German Jewish history, the ideology, economics and politics of Nazis, the Holocaust etc.

4. Lorenz Mikoletzky

Born 12 May 1945, Vienna.

1964-1969	Studied history and classical archaeology at Vienna University
1969	Graduated as Dr. phil., joined Austrian State Archives
1 February 1991	Appointed head of General Administrative Archive
1 July 1991	Promoted to *Hofrat* (Chief Archivist)
1 July 1994	Appointed Director-General of Austrian State Archives and Chairman of Central Archives Office
13 January 1993	Appointed Honorary Professor of Modern Austrian History, Faculty of Letters and Humanities, Vienna University

International Activities (inter alia):

Member, Executive Committee of the International Council on Archives, for Europe and North America

Austrian representative in CIBAL (Comité et Centre International d' information sur les sources de l'histoire balkanique et méditerranéenne).

Work in academic commissions and organizations:

Honorary member of the Historical Commission of the Grand Duchy of
    Luxembourg
Honorary member of the Association of Romanian Archivists
Executive Vice-President of the Union of Austrian Historians and
    Historical Associations
Member of the Board of the Commission for Austrian Modern History
    Member of the Board of Curators of the Documentation Archive of
    Austrian Resistance
Member of the Board of the Austro-Polish Society
Member of the Letters and Humanities Committee of the Austrian
    Commission for UNESCO

Selected publications

*   "The Independence of Economics and Politics. An Example from the
    Austro-Russian Alliance during the Napeolonic Wars", .in: *The
    Journal of European History*, 2/2, 1973, pp. 355-362;

*   "Le recensement des archives des firmes et des entreprises en
    Autriche: état actuel" [The Present State of the Inventorization of
    Business Archives in Austria], in: *Bulletin du Comité des Archives
    d'Entreprises* 3/1980, pp. 21-26;

*   "Josef Bürckels Dienststelle und die Steiermark 1938/39.
    Ausgewählte Materialien aus dem Amt des Reichskommissars für
    die Wiedervereinigung Österreichs mit dem Deutschen Reich" [Josef
    Bürckel's Office and Styria, 1938-39. Selected Materials from the
    Office of the Reich Commissioner for the Reunification of Austria
    with the German Reich] in: *Siedlung, Macht und Wirtschaft*
    [Settlement, Power and the Economy], 1981, pp. 281-291;

*   "Bibliographie zum 12. Februar 1934. Eine Auswahl" [Selected
    Bibliography on 12 February 1934] in: *Erwachsenenbildung in
    Österreich* [Adult Education in Austria] 4B/1983, pp. 11-13;

*   "Überblick über das österreichische Archivwesen seit dem Zweiten
    Weltkrieg" [Survey of Austrian Archival Work since World War II],
    in: *Archives et Bibliothèques de Belgique*, LV/1-4/1984, pp. 73-83;

* "Österreichische Parlaments- und Parteiarchive" [Austrian Parliamentary and Party Archives], in: *Archives et Bibliothèques de Belgique*, LX/3-4/1989, pp. 77-81;

* "Das Österreichische Staatsarchiv und das Problem der Massenaktenbewältigung" [The Austrian State Archives and the Problem of Handling Large Quantities of Files], in: *Scrinium* 44/45, 1991, pp. 206-210;

* "Austrian Archival Work - Yesterday, Today and Tomorrow", in: *Bulgarische Archivzeitschrift* 1-2/1995, pp. 77-87 (in Bulgarian);

* "Die österreichischen Archive und Europa - Das Österreichische Staatsarchiv" [Austria's Archives and Europe - The Austrian State Archives] in: *Scrinium* 49/1995, pp. 451-455;

* *Archives of the Holocaust. An International Collection of Selected Documents*, Vol. 21: *Allgemeines Verwaltungsarchiv, Archiv der Republik* [General Administrative Archive and Archive of the Republic], Vienna, New York and London 1995.

5. Bertrand Perz

Born 9 February 1958, Linz.

Studied history and for some semesters geology, philosophy and art history at Vienna University. In lieu of military service, served at the Documentation Archive of Austrian Resistance. Doctoral dissertation supervised by Karl Stuhlpfarrer (with Erika Weinzierl as second examiner) at Department of Contemporary History, Vienna University, subject: "Melk Concentration Camp: Expansion of the Armament Industry and Forced Labour by Concentration Camp Prisoners at the Steyr-Daimler-Puch AG Company". Graduated as Dr. phil., 1990.

Since 1981	Contributed to numerous research projects at the Contemporary History Department, University of Vienna, on subjects such as Nazi concentration camps and ghettos, forced labour, the Holocaust, the culture of remembrance and commemorative shrines at concentration camps

1982-1987	Member of the Commission for Research into Resistance and Persecution in Lower Austria in preparation of the publication of the same name
1991-1992	Expert for the Duisburg Regional Court (Germany) in the criminal trial of former member SS guards of Wiener Neudorf concentration camp
since the academic year 1991-92	Instructor, Contemporary History Department, Vienna University, conducting classes inter alia on Nazism and its impact on cultural history and the history of technology
1992	With Gottfried Fliedl planned and did the historical work for the permanent exhibit on the history of Melk concentration camp opened in Melk on 8 May 1992
1993-1995	Member and coordinator of the international commission of experts appointed by the Federal Minister of Education and Art for the Mauthausen commemorative shrine
1995-1996	Instructor, Contemporary History Department, Innsbruck University
since 1997	Staff member of the Independent Commission of Experts on Switzerland in World War II (Bergier Commission)

Secretary of Forschungsgemeinschaft zur Geschichte des Nationalsozialismus (organization of researchers working on the history of Nazism) |
| since 1 July 1998 | Holder of a fellowship from the Hamburg Foundation for the Encouragement of Science and Culture to enable him to work on his |

habilitation thesis the subject of which will be
the department run by Odilo Globocnik as SS
and police chief in Lublin (organization and
personnel).

Selected publications

Self-contained

* With Florian Freund, *Das KZ in der Serbenhalle. Zur
  Kriegsindustrie in Wiener Neustadt* [on a concentration camp
  connected with war industries in the town of Wiener Neustadt],
  Vienna 1988;

* *Projekt Quarz. Steyr-Daimler-Puch und das Konzentrationslager
  Melk* [The Quartz Project: Steyr-Daimler-Puch and Melk
  Concentration Camp], Vienna 1991;

* *Konzentrationslager Melk. Begleitbroschüre zur ständigen
  Ausstellung in der Gedenkstätte des ehemaligen
  Konzentrationslagers Melk* [Visitor's handbook for the
  commemorative shrine in Melk] (with a contribution by Gottfried
  Fliedl), Vienna 1992;

* *Il campo di concentramento di Melk. "Commando" di Mauthausen -
  Impianto sotteraneo "Quarz"*, Burolo (TO) 1993 (enlarged Italian
  version of the Melk brochure).

Essays

* With Hans Safrian, "Wege und Irrwege der Faschismusforschung"
  [Routes and Wrong Turnings of Research on Fascism], in:
  Zeitgeschichte, 11/12 (1980), pp. 437 ff;

* Joint editor with Hans Safrian and Karl Stuhlpfarrer of *Faschismus
  in Österreich und International* [Austrian and International Fascism].
  Yearbook 1980-81 of the Austrian Society for Contemporary
  History, Vienna 1982;

* With Werner Eichbauer and Florian Freund, Die Außenlager des KZ Mauthausen in Niederösterreich [The Sub-camps of the Mauthausen Concentration Camp in Lower Austria] in: *Widerstand und Verfolgung in Niederösterreich* [Resistance and Persecution in Lower Austria], Vol. 3, pp. 602-631, Vienna 1987;

* With Florian Freund, "Industrialisierung durch Zwangsarbeit" [Industrialization through Forced Labour] in: Emmerich Talos, Ernst Hanisch and Wolfgang Neugebauer (ed.), *NS-Herrschaft in Österreich 1938-1945* [Nazi Rule in Austria 1938-1945], pp. 95-114, Vienna 1988;

* "Die Errichtung eines Konzentrationslagers in Wiener Neudorf. Zum Zusammenhang von Rüstungsexpansion und Zwangsarbeit von KZ-Häftlingen" [The establishment of a Concentration Camp in Wiener Neudorf: the Connection between Armament Expansion and Forced Labour by Concentration Camp Prisoners], in: Dokumentationsarchiv des Österreichischen Widerstandes (ed.), *Jahrbuch 1988* [Yearbook], pp. 88-116, Vienna 1988;

* "Der Todesmarsch von Wiener Neudorf nach Mauthausen. Eine Dokumentation" [The Death March from Wiener Neudorf to Mauthausen: Documents], in: Dokumentationsarchiv des Österreichischen Widerstandes (ed.), *Jahrbuch 1988* [Yearbook], pp. 117-137, Vienna 1988;

* "Steyr-Münichholz, ein Konzentrationslager der Steyr-Daimler-Puch AG, Zur Genese der Zwangsarbeit in der Rüstungsindustrie" [Steyr-Münichholz, a Concentration Camp of Steyr-Daimler-Puch AG: Notes on the Genesis of Forced Labour in the Armament Industry], in: Dokumentationsarchiv des österreichischen Widerstandes (ed.), *Jahrbuch 1989*, pp. 57-61, Vienna 1989;

* With Florian Freund and Karl Stuhlpfarrer, "Das Getto in Litzmannstadt (Lodz)" [The Ghetto in Litzmannstadt, i.e. Lodz] in: *"Unser einziger Weg ist Arbeit." Das Getto in Lodz 1940-1944* ["Our Only Way Is Work. The Lodz Ghetto, 1940-1944], ed. Jewish Museum, Frankfurt am Main, pp. 17-31, Vienna 1990;

* With Florian Freund and Karl Stuhlpfarrer, "Bildergeschichten - Geschichtsbilder" [Pictorial Histories, Historical Pictures], in:

"Unser einziger Weg ist Arbeit". Das Getto in Lodz 1940-1944, ed. Jewish Museum, Frankfurt am Main, pp. 50-59, Vienna 1990;

* With Florian Freund and Karl Stuhlpfarrer, selection of colour slides from the archives of the German ghetto administration in Lodz (including quotes), in: *"Unser einziger Weg ist Arbeit". Das Getto in Lodz 1940-1944*, ed. Jewish Museum, Frankfurt am Main, pp. 50-59, Vienna 1990;

* With Florian Freund, "Fremdarbeiter und KZ-Häftlinge in der 'Ostmark'" (Foreign Workers and Concentration Camp Prisoners in Nazi-Occupied Austria), in: Ulrich Herbert (ed.), *Europa und der "Reichseinsatz". Ausländische Zivilarbeiter, Kriegsgefangene und KZ-Häftlinge in Deutschland 1938-1945* [Europe and "Assignment for the Reich": Foreign Civilian Workers, Prisoners of War and Concentration Camp Prisoners in Germany, 1938-1945], pp. 317-350, Essen 1991;

* With Florian Freund and Karl Stuhlpfarrer, "Farbdias aus dem Ghetto Lodz" [Colour Slides from Lodz Ghetto], in: *Zeitgeschichte* 18 (1990/91) No. 9/10, pp. 271-303;

* With Gottfried Fliedl, Florian Freund and Eduard Fuchs, "Den Toten zur Ehr - den Lebenden zur Lehr?" [To Honour the Dead and to Teach the Living a Lesson?] in: *Österreichische Zeitschrift für Geschichtswissenschaften* 2 (1991), No. 4;

* With Florian Freund and Karl Stuhlpfarrer, "Der Bau des Vernichtungslagers Auschwitz-Birkenau. Die Aktenmappe der Zentralbauleitung Auschwitz 'Vorhaben Kriegsgefangenenlager Auschwitz (Durchführung der Sonderbehandlung)' im Militärhistorischen Archiv Prag" [The Construction of Auschwitz-Birkenau Annihilation Camp: The Files of the Auschwitz Central Construction Management on "Project POW: Camp Auschwitz (Application of Special Treatment)"], in: *Zeitgeschichte* 20 (1993), No. 5/6, pp. 187-214);

* "Rüstungsindustrie in Wiener Neustadt 1938-1945" [Armament Industries in Wiener Neustadt, 1938-1945], in: Sylvia Hahn and Karl Flanner (ed.), *"Die Wienerische Neustadt", Handwerk, Handel und*

Militär in der Steinfeldstadt [Crafts, Trade and the Military in Wiener Neustadt], pp. 47-90, Wien, Cologne and Weimar 1994;

* "Perspektiven der österreichischen Forschung zu Zwangsarbeit und Arbeitsmigration im Nationalsozialismus" [Perspectives of Austrian Research on Forced Labour and Worker Migration under Nazism], in: *Österreichischer Zeitgeschichtetag Innsbruck 1993* [Proceedings of the 1993 Congress of Austrian Contemporary Historians], ed. Ingrid Böhler and Rolf Steininger, p. 209-215, Innsbruck and Vienna 1995;

* "Das Konzentrationslager Mauthausen in der historischen Forschung" [Mauthausen Concentration Camp as Reflected in Historical Research], in: *Nouvelles recherches sur l'univers concentrationnaire et d'extermination nazi. Revue d'Allemagne et des pays de langue allemande*, vol. 27, No. 2 - April/June 1995, pp. 265-274;

* "'Auf Wunsch des Führers ...'. Der Bau von Luftschutzstollen in Linz durch Häftlinge des Konzentrationslagers Linz II" ["It is the Führer's Wish" The Building of Air-Raid Dugouts by Prisoners rom Concentration Camp Linz II], in: *Zeitgeschichte*, 22nd Year, September/October 1995, No. 9/10, pp. 342-346;

* "Politisches Management im Wirtschaftskonzern. Georg Meindl und die Rolle des Staatskonzerns Steyr-Daimler-Puch bei der Verwirklichung der NS-Wirtschaftsziele in Österreich" [Political Management in a Business Concern: Georg Meindl and the Role of the State-Owned Steyr-Daimler-Puch Company in the Implementation of Nazi Economic Objectives in Austria], in: Hermann Kaienburg (ed.), *Konzentrationslager und deutsche Wirtschaft 1939-1945* [Concentration Camps and the German Economy, 1939-1945], pp. 95-112, Opladen 1996;

* "Das Ghetto in Lodz und die Errichtung des Vernichtungslagers Chelmno-Kulmhof" [The Ghetto in Lodz and the Construction of Chelmno-Kulmhof Annihilation Camp], in: *Österreichischer Zeitgeschichtetag Linz 1995, Österreich - 50 Jahre Zweite Republik* [Proceedings of the 1995 Congress of Austrian Contemporary Historians in Celebration of the Fiftieth Anniversary of the Second

Republic], Rudolf G. Ardelt und Christian Gerbel (ed.), pp. 220-224, Innsbruck 1996;

* As member of the historical staff, co-authored the report of the Swiss Commission on gold transactions in World War II (*Bericht der Unabhängigen Expertenkommission: Schweiz - Zweiter Weltkrieg: Goldtransaktionen im Zweiten Weltkrieg: Kommentierte statistische Übersicht. Ein Beitrag zur Goldkonferenz in London, 2.-4. Dezember 1997*), Berne 1997;

* "Der Arbeitseinsatz im KZ Mauthausen" [Work Assignments in Mauthausen Concentration Camp], in: *Die nationalsozialistischen Konzentrationslager - Entwicklung und Struktur* [The Nazi Concentration Camps - Development and Structure], Ulrich Herbert, Karin Orth and Christoph Dieckmann (ed.), pp. 533-557, Göttingen 1998;

* (In the press): "'Selbst die Sonne schien damals ganz anders ...'. Die Entstehung der KZ-Gedenkstätte Mauthausen 1945-1970" ["Even the Sun Shone Quite Differently Then..." The Genesis of the Camp Shrine in Mauthausen], in: *Steinernes Bewußtsein. Die öffentliche Repräsentation staatlicher und nationaler Identität Österreichs in seinen Denkmälern* [Remembrance in Stone: The Public Representation of Austria's Statehood and National Identity in Her Monuments], Vol. 2, Heidemarie Uhl (ed.), Vienna, Cologne and Weimar (to be published spring 1999).

6. Roman Sandgruber

Born 20 February 1947, Rohrbach, Upper Austria

1965-1971	Studied history, German literature and economics at Vienna University
1972-1988	Assistant, Department for Social and Economic History, University of Vienna (under Professors Alfred Hoffmann and Michael Mitterauer)
1982	Habilitation as lecturer (*Dozent*) in Economic and Social History, Vienna University

since 1982	Full Professor and Head of the Department of Economic and Social History, Linz University
since 1995	Corresponding Member of the Austrian Academy of Science
since 1996	Chairman of the Senate of Linz University
1998	Academic Director of the Upper Austrian Regional Exhibition 1998, "Land of Hammers - Iron Ore Land" and Chairman of the Academic Advisory Committee of the "Iron Road" regional association in Upper Austria Chairman, Economic History Section, Union of Austrian Historians and Historical Associations

Prof. Sandgruber has published a comprehensive account of the economic history of Austria from the Middle Ages to the present (*Ökonomie und Politik. Wirtschaftsgeschichte Österreichs vom Mittelalter bis zur Gegenwart*, Vienna 1995) in the ten-volume series *Österreichische Geschichte*. In this book, he deals *inter alia* with the question of confiscations of property, forced labour, restitution and various forms of compensation. He has also done research on the history of Austrian farming, the iron industry in the Alps, historical statistics, demand patterns in the age of industrialization, the history of everyday life, the changing environment and general Austrian economic and social history in the 20th century. He has published seven monographs and about 150 articles in academic journals and collections of essays (see below). He is a regular contributor to a number of daily papers and magazines.

In addition to numerous smaller awards, he has been honoured with the Sandoz Prize for distinguished research achievements (1987), the Karl von Vogelsang Prize from the Austrian government (1988) and the Economic Research Award of the state government of Upper Austria (1990).

Selected publications

Self-contained

* *Ökonomie und Politik, Österreichische Wirtschaftsgeschichte vom Mittelalter bis zur Gegenwart* (Vol, 10 of *Österreichische Geschichte*, a series of publications on Austrian history ed. by Herwig Wolfram), Vienna 1995 (see above);

Essays

* "Rollenverständnis in Bauern-, Heimarbeiter- und Industriearbeiterfamilien Österreichs im 18., 19. und 20. Jahrhundert" [Role Perception in Peasant, Homeworker and Industrial Worker Families in Austria in the 18th, 19th and 20th Centuries] in: Peter Borscheid and Hans J. Treuteberg (ed.), *Ehe, Liebe, Tod* [Marriage, Love and Death], pp. 135-149, Munich 1983;

* "Die Postsparkassensparer. Sozialstruktur und Alltagsleben im Lichte von Bankkunden" [The Postal Savings Bank Savers: Social Structure and Everyday Life in the Light of Bank Customers], in: Roland Löffler and Michael Wagner (ed.), *Stillstand ist Rückschritt. Der erste Postsparkassen-Gouverneur 1910* [Standstill Means Retrogression: The First Governor of the Postal Savings Bank, 1910], pp. 43-67, Vienna 1986;

* "Von der Ersten zur Dritten Republik. Stationen eines erstaunlichen Weges durch das 20. Jahrhundert" [From the First to the Third Republic: Stages of an Amazing Progress through the 20th Century], in: *Standort Österreich. Über Kultur, Wirtschaft und Politik im Wandel* [Location Austria: Culture, Economy and Politics in a Period of Change], ed. Gerd Bacher, Karl Schwarzenberg and Josef Taus, pp. 287-316, Graz 1990;

* "The Industrial Tradition in Lower Austria", in: John Komlos (ed.) *Economic Development in the Habsburg Monarchy and in the Successor States*, pp. 303-316, New York 1990;

* "Le cooperative in Austria: sviluppo storico e struttura attuale" [Cooperatives in Austria: History and Present Structure], in: *Cooperazione di credito. Rivista trimestale di cultura cooperativa*

[Italian journal of the Cooperative Movement], No. 126, 41st Year, pp. 413-422, 1989;

*   "Österreich 1650-1850" [Austria 1650-1850], in: *Handbuch der europäischen Wirtschafts- und Sozialgeschichte* [Handbook of European Economic and Social History], Vol. 4, ed. by Ilja Mieck, pp. 619-687, Stuttgart 1993;

*   With Vera Mühlpeck and Hannelore Woitek, "The Consumer Price Index from 1800 to 1914. A Calculation in Retrospective for Vienna and the Contemporary Territory of Austria", reprinted in: Herbert Matis (ed.), *The Economic Development of Austria since 1870*, pp. 199-229, Cambridge 1994;

*   "Der 'lange Schatten' der österreichischen Wirtschaftspolitik" [The "Long Shadow" of Austrian Economic Policy], in: *Information zur politischen Bildung* [Political Education Information Sheet] 1996, No. 11, pp. 43-56.

*   "Spiegel von Wirtschaftsrechnungen und Lebenserinnerungen" [Reflecting Mirror: Economic Accounts and Biographical Reminiscences], in: *Wiener Wege der Sozialgeschichte. Themen - Perspektiven - Vermittlungen. Michael Mitterauer zum 60. Geburtstag* [Festschrift to celebrate the 60th birthday of Prof, Michael Mitterauer], pp. 299-334, Vienna 1997.

Gold Transactions Carried out by the Oesterreichische Nationalbank during Austria's Occupation (1938-1945), and the History of the so-called Salzburg Gold

Summary of the preliminary report of Fritz Weber
(English translation of the German original)

On Austria's *Anschluss* to Nazi Germany, the Oesterreichische Nationalbank (OeNB) de facto lost its independence immediately; de iure its independence was taken away a few days later on March 17, 1938, through a decree which stipulated that the OeNB was to be liquidated and put under the Reichsbank's control. Another decree, dated April 23, 1938, declared the OeNB's right to issue banknotes null and void. All the OeNB's gold and foreign currency holdings – which at the time of the *Anschluss* exceeded the Reichsbank's holdings – became Reichsbank property. Moreover, the German Foreign Exchange Act, which as of March 23, 1938, superseded the Austrian regulations hitherto applicable, made it compulsory for all private holdings of gold bars to be registered with the Reichsbank. This obligation was subsequently extended to include gold coins through a decree dated July 16, 1938.

The body which purchased the gold assets delivered to the OeNB between March 17 and April 25, 1938, was *technically* still the OeNB under liquidation; as is evident from the OeNB's records, these assets were at a later stage credited to the OeNB's liquidation account by the Reichsbank. The assets in question had not been sold under duress; much rather it was the premium on the German gold price that was offered in Vienna which had spurred those deals (which also explains why there were gold coins among the assets bought).

Beyond those gold purchases, there is no evidence in the OeNB's archives of any other transactions with gold during the period 1938 to 1945 (with the sole exception of the Reichsbank's gold transports to the Balkans via Vienna – for this mission, gold shipped by train from Berlin was temporarily stored at the *Reichsbankhauptstelle*, or Vienna branch of the Reichsbank, before being transported onward by plane).

This evidence shows that the OeNB did not profit from the gold transactions carried out under the Nazi regime. Likewise the OeNB did not benefit illegally from the so-called Salzburg gold that was detected on Austrian territory in May and June 1945 and subsequently transferred to the OeNB by the U.S. occupation forces in 1947, because these gold assets were entered in the books as a down-payment for amounts that would in any case have been restituted to Austria by the Tripartite Commission.

BELARUS

Delegation Statement

The problems viewed at the conference are of great importance for the mankind. The cooperation and mutual understanding of nations depend greatly on how fairly these problems are going to be resolved.

Immediately after the London Conference Belarus came back to the problem of Nazi gold: documents in national archives, as well as in those of Germany and Russia were thoroughly studied.

This research resulted in the collection of documents "Nazi Gold from Belarus" published in September, 1998, which had included 46 documents containing data on gold, silver and other jewelry confiscated by the Nazis from the population of Belarus and sent to the Reich.

Out of the book's 410 pages, 185 pages are devoted to the documented lists of persons whose jewelry had been confiscated by the Nazis. They are Belarusians and Jews, Russians and Poles, Ukrainians and Tartars, and people of other nationalities. It's worth noting that the research included documents and materials dealing mainly with the central part of Belarus (during the Nazi occupation it formed the General Region of Byelorussia incorporated into the Ostland Reichkommissariat) which accounts for a quarter of today's territory of the country. The remaining part of the Belarusian territory was under the authority of the military occupation administration of the Center Army Group Rear and the General Regions of Bialostok and Lithuania. Therefore, the real number of citizens whose jewelry was confiscated by the Nazis is much larger.

Work on this collection of documents leads to the conclusion that citizens of Belarus have their full right to demand that their country be included into the group of states which will be compensated for the assets confiscated from them. We do hope that our research will be taken into account when deciding finally the fate of Nazi gold.

The second very important question viewed at this conference deals with the Nazi-confiscated works of art, property and documents of national archives and museums. This problem is very acute for Belarus, too, because it was among the most Nazi-stricken countries in Europe.

During the W.W.II a great number of the works of art, property of national museums, documents and publications of national archives and libraries were taken away from the country, the rest was completely or partially destroyed. Similar to Germany of the 30s where the Nazis burned books of Goethe, Schiller, Heine, they destroyed national masterpieces in Belarus of the 40s. Who and how will compensate these irretrievable losses?

The damage (far from being complete) inflicted only by the taking away to Germany of more than 11 thousand museum exhibits amounted to 163 mln. pre-war roubles or nearly the same value in US dollars. Only a part of them were returned back to Belarus.

There are documents on that score from German, Russian and Belarusian archives.

In 1997, Belarus hosted the UNESCO-sponsored Conference on the Restitution of Cultural Values which considered the legal, scientific and moral aspects of this problem. What is the Belarusian vision of its solution? We believe that the cultural values, in case of their misappropriation during or after the W.W.II, must be returned to their countries of origin or their private owners.

Further, we consider it necessary:

- to carry out the systematization of international legal acts on restitution and returning of cultural values to the countries of their origin and set up common international standards;
- to bring national legislations in conformity with international standards;
- to continue work on creating national databases of lost cultural values. With that end in view it is necessary in all countries to create favorable conditions for the experts to study migration of cultural values;
- to organize the exchange of information on this problem, through the Internet included.

When studying and solving this problem another question arises – what is to be done with the cultural values of arguable origin. In our opinion, such works of art, archive funds, book collections can and must be commonly researched, published, exhibited or deposited. Their description, publication, displaying are to some extent their return to their native land.

We believe in the future of inter-governmental and inter-regional projects aimed at returning the cultural values.

And one more: whatever good recommendations we may accept the above problems will not be resolved without a free access to the archive information. Belarus has made a certain step in this direction. In accordance with national legislation, the wartime documents kept in state archives are now accessible to all researchers except those dealing with personal privacy. On the eve of the Washington Conference the annotated reference book "The Documents on the History of the Great Patriotic War in the State Archives of the Republic of Belarus" was out of print. All the documents of that period have been declassified and opened to public.

How Much Did 800,000 Murdered Belarusian Jews Cost?

By
Leonid Levin

PRESIDENT, BELARUSIAN ASSOCIATION OF JEWISH ORGANIZATIONS AND COMMUNITIES

A STATEMENT REGARDING THE BOOK, "NAZI GOLD FROM BELARUS"

First of all, I don't separate the tragedy of Belarusian Jews during the wartime from the tragedy of all Belarusian people.

Let me stop on the Jewish issue.

Taking into account the available documents.

Victims.

Politics.

Documents.

The Nazi goal was to capture the "living space" through human death.

Jews, Gypsies, Slavs were in first lines.

Annihilation of Jews took place immediately after the capture of a town or village. It's easier to kill all together.

For this matter - ghetto.

Thus,

There were more than 200 ghettos on the territory of Belarus.

Nearly 800,000 Jews were murdered.

The year 1946.

The Conference on Nazi gold fate.

The international conference. 42 countries participating. 11 international organizations.

The issue is Nazi gold.

The list of 15 European countries which could claim to get Nazi gold was made.

Today.

All those who are entitled to solve this problem represent a new civilized world.

From today's viewpoint.

The fact that Belarus, Ukraine and Russia have not been included into the List looks like a mockery.

There is a formal reason:

Stalin refused from Nazi gold.

All that is in the past.

Europe became Europe.

The Soviet Union exists no more.

There is no Stalin.

An amazing book has been published in Belarus.

"Nazi Gold from Belarus."

The book is based on documents.

46 official Nazi orders, instructions, protocols of interrogations.

The second part of the book.

Lists of those whose jewels were confiscated.

But there are no Jews in the List.

They couldn't be there.

The Jews were annihilated all together.

All at once.

Their documents were taken away.

Their jewels, personal belongings, gold, silver, crockery, their lives were seized.

This "contribution" was packed in casks, boxes.

Out of 46 documents published in the book only a few do not deal with the Jewish issue.

All other documents:

- to put Jews into ghettos,
- to seize gold,
- to seize jewels,
- to seize clothes,
- to seize even metal beds,
- execution, execution, execution,
- evidences.

Official data:

January, 1947. The Belarusian Soviet Socialist Republic's Memorandum on the Peace Treaty with Germany.

Direct damage for the Republic - $ 15 bln.

Personal damage for citizens - $ 4,720 mln.

For the Jews this "damage" was their death 1/3 of the sum mentioned above.

Special Account No 34 in the Minsk German Credit Bank for money of the Jews and for their death.

The center of all looted - Riga.

The final destination point - Berlin.

1942. From: Glubokoye, Gebitskommissar Peterson.

To: Riga, Ostland Reichskommiissar Lose:

- valuables seized from Jews: 3,610 gold Rubles and 3,069 kg of gold, 20 gold Czar Rubles - 0.026 kg, 210 gold Dollars - 0,351 kg and a box of 4,267 gold items of various kinds. the box is marked "Fish".

1941. Borisov.

Burgmeister Stankevich's report. List of items seized from Jews and handed by Vasilyev and Meleshkevich.

1942. In the village of Glubokoye seized from Jews for Account No 34:

June 4, 1942 - DM 169,909.77.

July 6, 1942 - DM 115,247.11.

December, 1942. Grodno.

"I turn in gold, valuables, money, discovered in the ghetto. The list is enclosed."

February, 1943. Grodno.

"The list is enclosed - total DM 7,717.65."

Report of the Chief of the Gendarmery Office.

April, 1943. Grodno.

After the execution, DM 4,874.12 were turned in from six gendarmery posts and DM 7,424.58 more in April.

thousands of victims changed into Deutsche marks.

May, 1943. Vertilishki.

The last Jews were annihilated.

Total DM 808,32 received.

January, 1946. A trial in Minsk.

Defendant Skakun: "I counted 2,000 gold and silver items." Witness Yanshtob: On July 12, 1941, the German occupation authorities informed us that all Jewish citizens aged 15 to 60 are to gather in the synagogue. There all their documents were taken away and they were ordered to come here in the afternoon and bring various valuables, such as gold, silver, foreign currency. When everybody came the Nazis lead them out across the River Viliya and shot them dead by 7-8 p.m.

Facts, only facts.

There are plenty of them.

And what was going on in the biggest ghetto on the territory of Belarus - the Minsk Ghetto.

May, 1943. Minsk. The chief of the city prison reports to the General Kommissar of Belarus.

"In April, 1943, former German dentist Ernest Tischauer and his wife Elsa Tischauer testified that all German and Russian Jews had undergone an operation of pulling or breaking out their gold teeth and crowns. It took place 1-2 hours before the appropriate actions." Since April 13, 1943, 516 German and Russian Jews were killed with Hauptscharfurher Ruber in attendance who took the gold. It was determined that 50 percent of the Jews had gold teeth, bridges or fillings.

Here are only a few examples.

And how many of them in all ghettos, in entire Belarus.

An approximate calculation shows that the Jews of Belarus alone were robbed of several hundred kilograms of gold, hundreds of kilograms of silver, jewels of various kinds.

I am not mentioning the losses of the entire peaceful population of Belarus.

Ladies and Gentlemen,

The time has come.

The world has changed.

Each was held responsible for the crimes he had committed.

The history puts everything in its place.

Today the Belarusian Jewish community amounts to nearly 100 thousand people.

Today more than 10 million people live in Belarus.

All of us hope for a fair solution of this problem.

It is not Stalin's signature at the Potsdam Conference that is before us.

It is the world that changed.

It is thousands of graves of those killed.

It is your high and just solution.

Letter to the Conference Chairman

HE Judge Abner J. Mikva, Chairman
Washington Conference
on Holocaust-Era Assets

December 1, 1998
Washington, D.C.

Dear Sir,

The delegation of the Republic of Belarus would like to reiterate its appeal to include our country into the list of claimant states, rightfully seeking positive solution of their claims for Holocaust-Era Assets.

The looted Nazi gold should return to its rightful owners, people of Belarus, which suffered through all the tragedy of Holocaust, among them.

Numerous archival records are available now to support these claims.

Vladimir Adamushko
Head of the Delegation,
Deputy Chairman, Belarus State Committee on Archives

Valyantsin Gerasimau
Chairman, Mutual Understanding and Reconciliation Fund

Leonid Levin
President, Belarusian Association of Jewish Organizations
and Communities

Olga Nekhai
President, Belarusian Association of Former Nazi Prisoners

BELGIUM

MINISTRY OF ECONOMIC AFFAIRS

The Spoliation of Cultural Goods in Belgium during the Second World War

THE GERMAN ORGANIZATION

On May the 10th 1940, like its neighbors Netherlands, Luxembourg and France, Belgium was invaded and occupied by the German army. The first spoliations took place during the military conquest of Belgium, but were mostly of private nature.

In June 1940, a German Military Occupation Government (*Militärverwaltung*) was installed in Brussels with General A. von Falkenhausen at its head. Regarding cultural matters, this military government relied on the specialists of the *Kunst, Archiv* and *Bibiliothekschutz*.

Many German services took part to the plundering of Belgium, but the two most important for cultural matters were certainly the group of *Sicherheitspolizei-Sicherheitsdienst* (SIPO-SD), which was in charge of collecting the political archives and documentation of the enemies of national-socialism (mainly Jews, freemasons and socialists) and the *Einzatstab Reichsleiter Rosenberg* (ERR) which received the order to « savekeep » the cultural goods of these enemies of the Third Reich.

The organized looting began in the summer of 1940 with the plundering of the freemasons lodges, the Jewish organizations, the socialist organizations and of the artworks, archives and libraries of the persons who had fled Belgium before May 1940. Meanwhile, the *Archivschutz* was active in looking through the Belgian ministerial archives, with special interest for the archives of the Ministries of National Defense, Colonies, Foreign Affairs and Economic Affairs. The ERR reported that the first 340 crates were collected and partly sent to Berlin in November 1940.

The German services also focused on cultural goods they regarded as German considering that Belgium had received them after the first World War in compensation for the destructions (mainly the archives of Eupen-Malmédy, *The Mystic Lamb* of the Van Eyck brothers and *The Last Supper* of D. Bouts).

THE SPOLIATION OF THE BELGIAN JEWISH COMMUNITY

The persecutions against the Jewish community of Belgium (which counted about 65.000 people, of whom less than one tenth had the Belgian nationality. The rest was made up of immigrants from Germany and Central and Eastern Europe) started as soon as October 1940 with different nazi decrees aiming the complete isolation of the Jews in the Belgian society. In order to organize the economical spoliation of the Jewish community, the Militärverwaltung set up in Brussels, the *Brüsseler Treuhandgesellschaft*, to control and to liquidate « enemy property ». In June 1942, started the first razzia's in Brussels and Antwerp and the first convoy left from the Caserne Dossin in Malines to Auschwitz on the 4th of August 1942. Between August 1942 and July 1944, 25.257 Jews were deported from Belgium, of whom only 1.207 survived.

Meanwhile had started the *Möbelaktion*, the purpose of this operation was to liquidate the households of the houses where Jews lived. The buildings were sealed, transport firms brought the contents over to centralized depots where the selection was made: all interesting cultural objects were given to the ERR and sent to Germany or Paris and the normal furniture were sent to Germany for the victims of the allied bombings. In less than two years, more than 4.500 houses were emptied in Belgium alone.

THE ART MARKET

Aside these plunderings, some Belgian collectors and art-dealers seized the opportunity to sell their collections under or without any pressure. Large sums were paid by agents working, for example, for the Hitler's Linz Museum project, for H. Goering's collection or others. The most famous collection that has been sold is the Renders collection of twenty Flemish primitive paintings. From these twenty paintings, ten were recuperated after the war and the ten others are still missing.

BELGIAN RECUPERATION EFFORTS

Right after the end of the war started the first step of the Belgian recuperation with the especially created *Office de Récupération Economique* (ORE) which main task was the recuperation of economic goods such as trains, ships, coal, steel... Within the ORE, a small unit was formed to search the spoiled cultural goods in Germany and Austria. This essential step went on until 1952 and allowed Belgium to find back 492 artworks and 2.749 books; among them were masterpieces such as *The Mystic Lamb* of the Van Eyck brothers or the Michelangelo's *Madonna* from the Church of Our Lady in Bruges. Meanwhile, hundreds of goods found in Belgium were returned to their owners.

A second step started in 1950 in close contact with the West-German authorities and lasted until 1964 without any concrete result and in 1967 the ORE was dismantled and unfortunately its archives were not properly kept.

Besides the recuperated artworks, still 3.273 documented paintings, drawings, sculptures, tapestries, furniture... remain lost. One should be careful with these figures for several reasons: the looting is only partly documented, many figures come from German sources or from claims introduced after the war (who did not make a claim is not taken in account) and the ORE selected only identifiable artworks in its claims.

The recuperation effort started again in 1993 within the Ministry of Economic Affairs because of the opening of Eastern Europe and the conviction that only a part of the cultural goods were returned to their rightful owners. The major problem faced at that time was the lack of documentation, both the losses and the efforts for recuperation made after the war are poorly documented and the first task has been and is still the search for archives in order to make restitution possible.

Today, this effort continues on two levels. First, within the Ministry of Economic Affairs with the Mission Restitution Spoiled Goods which edited two catalogs documenting the losses of artworks belonging to the Belgian State and prepares three others catalogs that will document the private losses but also the spoiled libraries and archives.

Secondly, in July 1997, the Belgian government decided to establish a commission that is now investigating what has happened to the goods belonging to members of the Jewish community of Belgium during the German occupation. The commission which is part of the Prime Minister's services, is presided by Lucien Buysse, and the members of the commission are representatives of the different Ministries involved (namely Economic Affairs, Foreign Affairs, Justice and Public Health), historians and representatives of Jewish organizations. The first intermediary report was submitted to the government in July 1998. The commission is presently investigating various fields, including the bank sector, the insurance, the real estate and cultural goods.

Person to contact on this subject
Nicolas Vanhove (with the help of Jacques Lust's works)
Mission Restitution Spoiled goods
Ministry of Economic Affairs of Belgium
Tel +32 2 206 58 62
Fax +32 2 514 03 89

MINISTRY OF FOREIGN AFFAIRS

The Antwerp Diamond Sector during the Second World War

Although the Belgian commission studying the fate of the Jewish assets during WWII has still to conclude its findings concerning the diamond sector, the following note gives some first indications of how the Antwerp diamond sector survived World War II.

Diamonds are, as gold, luxury goods but where appreciated during the last war also for their industrial (the hardest ore known by that time) and the monetary ("valeur refuge") value and were therefore considered rightfully as strategic goods. During these years Belgium put the diamond as well as the uranium ore extracted in its former colony Congo at the disposal of the allied war effort.

Antwerp was for centuries an important diamond trading, carving and policing center and remains so today. Its recent history can be resumed as follows.

THE THIRTIES: THE ECONOMIC CRISIS

The slump of 1927 heralded the major economic crisis of 1929-1930. The diamond world survived these difficult times virtually unscathed, despite some heavy blows. Undeterred by these difficulties, in 1928-1929, the sector made an 800 million BF profit and employed 25.000 people.

In 1929, "Antwerpsche Diamantkring" (the Antwerp Diamond Circle) was founded, Antwerp's fifth diamond bourse at the time. At that time, several social improvements were introduced in the diamond trade, which were later adopted by other branches of industry, and acquired legal validity in Belgium.

The crisis of 1930 was the inevitable result of the Wall Street crash in November, which shook the economic foundations of the entire world; for, suddenly, there was an enormous discrepancy between consumption and production.

Its influence was felt after the 1930 world exhibition at which the Antwerp diamond sector participated predominantly.   Also the "Forminière", the company that exploited the diamond mines in (Belgian) Congo had a remarkable stand there.

Soon afterwards however consumption in important outlets like India, China, Egypt, Russia, Japan, Brazil and Argentina dropped sharply.

The Antwerp and Amsterdam diamond exchange houses decided therefore to limit production by 50 % during a limited period in order to prevent further overproduction, and because of a faltering market due to sundry financial crises elsewhere. As a result 25.000 people in Belgium, including the Jewish traders were affected to some extent by decreased working hours.

At the international level similar decision of the London Syndicate to temporally limit the sights for the manufacturers was respected by the entire sector, including the Kempen district.

This period of general economic regression contrasted sharply with the revival of the German economy, including its diamond sector.

THE SECOND WORLD WAR

The Second World War drastically hit the diamond sector and all people involved in it. The industry itself temporarily left the scene. Just before the war, though, the market had again become active. A sense of foreboding made people look for a safe investment in diamonds, because of its high and stable value, and because it was easy to hide and transport. With the outbreak of war, many took refuge in places where the conqueror could not set foot, in particular, the Jewish families who were well aware of the anti-Semitism of the German regime. Antwerp diamantairs surfaced in the USA, Portugal, Cuba and the then Palestine. Others took their stock across the Channel, to the United Kingdom, in the hope of taking up their activity in the vicinity of the London Syndicate. They got united into the "Refugees Branch", with over five hundred members, who managed to process a considerable amount of rough stones. They had to contend with persistent attempts, to organize a British diamond industry, in Brighton amongst other places, in place of the defunct industries of Antwerp and Amsterdam. In Antwerp, only clandestine work was possible. The Antwerp Jews, of whom 80 % were engaged in diamond activities in 1940, were robbed of their stocks without recourse to justice. The dire fate of the Jews in the hands of the Nazi's is well known. Of the many Jewish prisoners and deportees, only few returned.

In 1941, the German publications admitted that 90 % of the diamonds that were available in Antwerp before the invasion had been smuggled out of Belgium.

It was to the credit of the Antwerp mayor Camille Huysmans, together with two prescient diamantairs, Messrs. Romi Goldmuntz and Herman Schamisso, that they went to considerable pains to save as much as possible of the goods of the Antwerp dealers. Wartime conditions made this anything but easy. The British Navy, which closely policed the seas, had been given authority by the Admiralty to stop all ships anywhere and investigate their freight. Goods bound for hostile or occupied territories could be confiscated in exchange for a receipt; the owner could file a complaint with a special tribunal, which was assisted by technical experts when passing judgement.

The gentlemen mentioned above established the "Correspondence Office for Diamond Industry" (COFDI) to advise the court in the event of diamond consignments and thus entire fortunes were saved for the Antwerp diamond industry. Most of the goods were held for safekeeping in London, which allowed for a speedy recovery of the Antwerp diamond industry, even before the hostilities had completely ended. As soon as one felt the end of the war was approaching, the return to Belgium was prepared for, both materially and psychologically.

MINISTRY OF FOREIGN AFFAIRS

Belgian Jewish Museum of Deportation and Resistance

The Museum of the Deportation and Resistance of Jews in Belgium is housed in a wing of the former "Dossin de Saint Georges Barracks" at Mechelen. This historic site is also a place of remembrance, for it is here, halfway between Brussels and Antwerp, that the Nazis set up the "SS-Sammellager Mecheln", which served as the assembly point for Jews about to be deported from Belgium.

"SS-Sammellager Mecheln" was the first step on a journey from which only a handful returned. Between 1942 and 1944, 28 train convoys carried 25,257 prisoners from Mechelen to Auschwitz in Poland. Two-thirds of the deportees were gassed upon arrival. Only 1,207 were still alive when the camps were liberated. The Dossin barracks were nothing less than the antechamber of death.

Visitors to the Museum of the Deportation and Resistance of the Jews in Belgium can follow the history of the Endlösung or "Final Solution" and how it affected Belgium and Europe. Numerous aspects of the holocaust are considered in the Museum, including the help and support given to the SS, although only a relative small group, by Belgian institutions; the collaboration by ultra-right organizations; the extermination of almost half of Belgium's Jews; the resistance of those Jews who managed to elude deportation and the efforts of a broad section of Belgian society to foil the SS, which enabled numerous Jewish children to survive the occupation.

SOME HISTORICAL FACTS:

The Jews of Belgium
In 1940, there were 56,000 Jews living in Belgium.

Occupation

After the invasion of Belgium on March 10, 1940, the country was occupied by the German army and the Nazis stayed in Belgium until the complete liberation of the country in October 1944.

Persecution

April 14, 1941: the Antwerp pogrom.

May 27, 1941: an order is promulgated forcing Jews to wear a yellow star. "The Jew is known, registered, branded, confined to his home, ... ready for the "Final Solution".

Deportation

August 4, 1942 - July 31, 1944: 25,257 prisoners were deported from Mechelen to Auschwitz (Oswiecim).

Extermination

16,000 Jews deported from Mechelen were gassed on arrival in Auschwitz (Oswiecim).

Only 1,207 of the deportees survived.

Resistance

The Resisters were Jewish or non-Jewish, armed or not, who rose up against the Nazi torment and made some heroic actions, such as the famous "Attack of the 20th Convoy" who gave the opportunity to more than 230 Jews to escape.

The Righteous among the Nations

Despite the Nazi atrocities, there were many Belgians who risked their lives and those of their families to save their Jewish neighbors. After the war, they were recognized by the Yad Vashem and called the "Righteous among the Nations".

MINISTRY OF FOREIGN AFFAIRS

Belgium and the Relief Fund for Victims of Nazi Persecution

- Belgium recently adhered to the Nazi Persecutee Relief Fund.

- Belgium will contribute to the Fund for an amount of 1 million USD.

- The Belgian government will soon take a decision on the selection of NGOs and the projects' beneficiaries of this sum of 1 million USD.

CANADA

Statement on Insurance

SUMMARY

Our investigations indicate that no Canadian life insurance companies operated in continental Europe during the years from 1930 to 1945. This search did indicate that several Canadian life insurance companies operated in the United Kingdom during that period. These foreign operations of Canadian life insurance companies, as well as their Canadian operations, may have sold policies insuring persons who subsequently became victims of the Holocaust. We do not know, at this time, the extent to which such policies may have been sold; however, based on our preliminary investigations, the numbers are likely to be very small. In addition, there is no indication of life insurance policies relating to the events of this period that may not have been properly paid.

INTRODUCTION

The Office of the Superintendent of Financial Institutions (OSFI), a branch of the government of Canada, is responsible for the prudential regulation of Canadian banks, and federally chartered insurance and trust companies. OSFI has coordinated a preliminary investigation pertaining to Holocaust-Era insurance claims.

The Canadian financial institution regulatory system, like that in some countries, is a shared responsibility between two levels of government. Insurance companies may be incorporated at either the federal or provincial levels; however, market conduct matters (e.g., the registration of insurance sellers, and laws pertaining to disclosure and contracts) are solely a provincial responsibility. The implication of this shared responsibility is that investigating life insurance policies relating to the Holocaust requires coordination with Canadian provincial regulators, in addition to coordination with the industry.

INVESTIGATIONS

The former Department of Insurance, a predecessor organization to OSFI, was required to file an annual report to the Minister of Finance, outlining the progress of business and the condition of federal life insurance companies. Based on a review of these reports for each year from 1930 to 1945, and other inquiries, we have been able to conclude that no Canadian life insurance company operated in continental Europe during this period. These reports did indicate that several Canadian life insurance companies operated in the United Kingdom during this period, and it is conceivable that these companies, because of their close proximity to continental Europe, sold some policies to persons who subsequently became victims of the Holocaust. It is also conceivable, although less likely, that Canadian life insurance companies sold polices from their Canadian operations to persons who subsequently became victims of the Holocaust.

We do not know, at this time, the extent to which Canadian insurance companies might have sold polices to persons who subsequently became victims of the Holocaust. More work will be required to determine the extent of the issue. However, based on the finding that no Canadian life insurance company operated in continental Europe during this period, and other investigations we have made, it appears unlikely that anything more than a very small number of polices were sold to persons who became victims of the Holocaust.

Our investigations have also included OSFI's public affairs group, which is responsible for dealing with public inquires, contacting the Canadian Life and Health Insurance Association (CLHIA), which is the industry association for life insurance companies, contacting certain life insurance companies and contacting major provincial insurance regulators.

The purpose of these investigations was to determine if any of these organizations have any knowledge of, or have had any information brought to their attention, indicating that Canadian life insurance companies may have sold polices to persons who became victims of the Holocaust, and for which monies relating to these policies may not have been properly paid. Based on these preliminary investigations, there is no indication of this, although work will continue by the CLHIA and individual companies to determine if additional relevant information may be available.

OTHER ARRANGEMENTS

The CLHIA has established a toll free number, and provided training for its call center staff, to assist persons with any inquiries they may have about Canadian or non-Canadian life insurance companies in relation to Holocaust-Era insurance assets. This service will be well publicized within the Canadian Jewish community.

FURTHER INQUIRIES

Anyone with concerns regarding possible unclaimed proceeds of insurance policies purchased from Canadian and other life insurance companies before and during the Second World War, may contact the life and health insurance industry's Consumers Assistance Center either by telephone or by writing:

Inquiries in English:
Canadian Life and Health Insurance Association Inc.
1 Queen Street East
Toronto, Ontario
Canada
M5C 2X9
1-800-860-3413

Inquiries in French:
Association canadienne des compagnies d'assurances de personnes inc.
1001, boul. de Maisonneuve Ouest
Bureau 630
Montréal (Québec)
H3A 3C8
1-888-361-8070

Statement on Other Assets

SUMMARY

Canada used legislative devices to deny to the Axis powers any economic resources in which Canadian interests were involved. These controls were aimed at jurisdictions under the control of the enemy and did not differentiate between the enemy and those residing in enemy occupied territory or those resisting the enemy. At the end of the war the Custodian of Enemy Property was controlling bank deposits, securities, commercial equity, real properties, mortgages, pension funds, patents and copyrights and other assets which eventually totaled $1 billion Canadian. The disposal of these assets took place under the conditions set down in international negotiations. The records of all assets affected by the Government have been preserved at the National Archives of Canada.

HISTORICAL AND LEGISLATIVE BACKGROUND

On 2 September 1939 Canada enacted *Regulations Respecting Trading with the Enemy* (*RRTWE*), one of its principal legislative weapons for conducting economic warfare against the German Reich. These all-encompassing regulations were aimed at depriving the enemy of any financial assistance that could be controlled by the Canadian Government and, then, mobilizing these enemy external assets to support the Allied war effort. Responsibility for these regulations and the control of all enemy property was in the hands of the Custodian of Enemy Property, whose legal powers surpassed other Allied Custodians by virtue of the fact that he was a member of the Cabinet War Committee, being *ex officio* the Secretary of State. As a result, he could operate without recourse to courts or other bodies of government in seizing or vesting enemy property in his name and acted earlier than his counterparts in declaring countries overrun by the Axis powers as enemy territory.

The objective of thwarting Germany from exploiting the economic resources of those nations in her path was paramount and necessitated a policy whereby all bank deposits, securities, real properties, patents and copyrights were brought under the control of the Custodian. Consequently, the RRTWE provided the Canadian Custodian with a blunt instrument which did not allow for distinguishing between victims of Nazi persecution and genuine enemies. Relief agencies communicated to the Canadian Government that these actions were often hampering efforts of genuine refugees to flee, and prior to the US entry into the war, efforts were made to use neutral consular services to determine the status of those seeking relief from the RRTWE. By 1942, Axis control over Eastern Europe prevented even these attempts to assist.

Of the assets under the control of the Custodian, securities and other forms of commercial equity posed a particular problem. Securities were generally sold through brokerage houses in Europe and were in the form of bearer bonds and certificates; the actual bearer was often not known to the Custodian. The solution adopted was to block the securities at source; thus prohibiting liquidations or payment of interest or dividends to enemy and enemy occupied territory. This power was also used to block accounts in neutral countries where the status of the beneficial owner of the account was unknown.

At its peak the Custodian was controlling a billion Canadian dollars in assets. These assets were ultimately disposed of in one of three ways. Enemy external assets were disposed of according to the accounting principles set down by the Inter-Allied Reparations Agency, allowing for the restitution of property to the victims of persecution. The Custodian returned property belonging to nationals of former enemy occupied territory when the former owners or their heirs presented themselves. The remaining property was transferred to the Canadian War Claim Fund.

FURTHER RESEARCH

The records of the Office of the Custodian of Enemy Property have been transferred to the National Archives in Ottawa. The records consist of subject files, case files and ledgers and card indexes, allowing for a researcher to follow the handling of every individual account. Case files for all individuals and firms who were affected by the actions of the Custodian and RRTWE have been listed and will be available on line in the near future. These records are now available for research subject to the provisions of the *Access to Information and Privacy Acts*. Parties interested in individual accounts or further study in Canada's handling of Holocaust era assets should contact the following address:

Researcher Services Division
National Archives of Canada
395 Wellington
Ottawa, Ontario
K1A 0N3
613 -992 -3884
www.archives.ca

Due Diligence:
A Report on the Bank of Canada's Handling of Foreign Gold during World War II

By
Dr. Duncan McDowall
November, 1997

Complete report available on the Bank of Canada website
(http://www.bank-banque-canada.ca/)

SUMMARY FINDINGS

During World War II, Canada played a major role in the earmarking of foreign gold for safekeeping at the Bank of Canada. Between the first rumblings of war in 1938 and peace in 1945, foreign central banks deposited 2,586 tons of gold in Ottawa for safekeeping. For many nations that had fallen under German occupation, this of safe gold was the ultimate guarantee of national survival. In particular, the central banks of Belgium, the Netherlands, France, Norway and Poland availed themselves of this unique type of Canadian wartime hospitality. The Bank of England was also a frequent earmarker of gold in Ottawa and in the dark days of 1940 even made plans to create a "shadow" Bank of England in Ottawa that could draw upon Britain's gold cache in Canada. Such deposits involved no profit for Canada beyond small handling charges.

The flow of earmarked gold to the Bank of Canada was almost exclusively one-way. Large amounts of gold crossed the Atlantic in the early war period, especially from the Bank of England and the Banque de France. After 1941, virtually no more gold arrived from Europe, with the exception of a shipment of 525 bars from the Bank Polski in London in 1944. During the course of the war, virtually none of the gold stored in Ottawa was shipped back across the Atlantic, with the exception of two small shipments of gold coin returned to England in 1942. All the transactions in question in this report were paper transfers of gold ownership between one central bank account at the Bank of Canada and other central bank accounts. There is therefore no possibility that tainted gold – gold looted by Germany – ever found its way into the Canadian gold stream.

The 1942-43 transfer of Bank of England gold earmarked in Ottawa to the Ottawa earmark account of the Banque Nationale Suisse involved 56 tons of gold, a small fraction of the overall wartime deposit of foreign gold in Ottawa. This gold was swapped for Swiss francs delivered to the British in Switzerland. This swap was necessitated by Britain's desperate need for Swiss francs to maintain its trade and diplomatic relationship with Switzerland and was entered into reluctantly by the Swiss. Switzerland already had large quantities of gold stockpiled beyond its borders in London and New York, but this was blocked and of no wartime use to Switzerland. The Swiss accepted the deal only as a pro tem. measure in the hope of keeping stalled trade negotiations with the British alive.

To safeguard the gold that had passed from Allied hands to neutral hands under earmark in Ottawa, the Bank of Canada altered the minimal prewar arrangements for foreign gold deposited in Canada to reflect the exigencies of war. The primary concern was that the 56 tons of gold held by Switzerland in Ottawa might find its way back to Europe and ultimately be applied to the ends of the Axis. These conditions stipulated that the gold received by the Banque Nationale Suisse from the Bank of England might be physically exported only to other central banks in the Western Hemisphere or transferred on paper to central banks in the Western Hemisphere and to the central banks of European neutral countries, namely Portugal, Sweden and Spain. These conditions were to apply until the end of hostilities. The Swiss agreed to these conditions.

The Bank of Canada's willingness to facilitate such swaps was strongly conditioned by its relationship with the Bank of England. Canada was one of the last Western powers to create a central bank and, since its inauguration in 1935, the Bank of Canada had relied heavily on the guidance of the Bank of England. This relationship was epitomized by the close personal friendship of Bank of Canada Governor Graham Towers and Bank of England Governor Montagu Norman. The Bank of England was, for instance, the first foreign central bank to open — in 1936 — an earmarked gold account in Ottawa. Similarly, the Bank of Canada's first deputy governor was seconded from the Bank of England in 1935. While Towers was never oblivious to protecting Canada's interests, there was an almost filial inclination to respond to England's bidding. This would precondition the Bank of Canada's positive response to Britain's request to facilitate the gold-for-francs swap with Switzerland and other European gold exchanges involving Canada.

The 1942 gold-for-francs swap had been preceded by another request from the Bank of England in September 1940. Confronted with an influx of small holdings of gold deposited in English commercial banks by Europeans anxious for the safety of their wealth and well-being, the British asked the Bank of Canada to earmark these deposits of personal gold under the umbrella of its own Ottawa accounts. This was a departure from usual earmark procedure in that it allowed foreign individuals the prerogative of the security of an earmark account well beyond the fray in Europe. Control of the deposits remained in the hands of the Bank of England. A handling charge of 5% of each individual's gold was imposed by the Bank of England and the depositor had to sign an agreement acknowledging that the gold would not be released until after the war, except in extraordinary circumstances approved by the Bank of England. During the course of September 1940 to June 1941, 155 of these so-called "sundry persons" deposits of personal gold at the Bank of England were included in shipments to the Bank of Canada from London. The total deposit was the equivalent of 1,315 bars of gold. Many of the depositors appear — by name and testimonial — to have been European Jewish refugees who had fled their homelands in the early stages of the war. They were generally well-to-do and had left their homelands early enough to avoid the Holocaust. Other deposits appear to have been made by Swiss and other nationals. A small number of the depositors — 34 sundry persons — were able to convince the Bank of England to release their gold in Ottawa before the end of the war. The remaining deposits were all closed after the war without incident or complication. The last deposit was closed in 1955.

Almost as soon as the process of swapping English gold for Swiss francs had begun in the spring of 1942, the Banque Nationale Suisse [BNS] began seeking ways to apply the gold it was accumulating in Ottawa to its domestic needs at home, principally the building up of internal gold reserves as a check on Swiss inflation. This desire was limited by the conditions set on the earmark account by the Bank of Canada. An initial attempt to establish Swiss commercial bank accounts in Ottawa and thereby open the way for transfers between off-shore central bank and commercial bank accounts was blocked by vigilant officials at the Bank of Canada. In the wake of this decision, Governor Towers informed the general managers of Canada's chartered banks that it was the government's wish that they stop opening new gold safekeeping accounts for non-residents and to report any future requests for such services to Ottawa. Rebuffed in this direction, the BNS began negotiations with the Banco de Portugal, which had gold accounts with it in Switzerland. In two equal transactions in April and May 1942, the BNS subsequently traded four tons of its earmarked gold in Canada for a similar amount of gold held by the Portuguese earmarked in its vault in Switzerland. Thus, the Swiss succeeded in obtaining the free use of four tons of gold in Switzerland in return for surrendering four tons of assuredly clean gold in Canada. To achieve this swap, the BNS was obliged to pay a steep commission to the Banco de Portugal of 1 1/2% on the first swap and 2 1/2% on the second swap. These commissions reflected the fact that the gold Portugal was obtaining in Ottawa was blocked for the duration of the war. In the wake of these swaps, the BNS board of directors decided to abandon the tactic of offering gold in Ottawa for gold in Europe because the transaction costs were exorbitant. The crucial question of whether the Portuguese gold released to the Swiss was tainted gold of German origin is elucidated by reference to classified British wartime documents drawn from British intercept of cables between the Swiss and Portuguese central banks and from banking records recently released by the Banco de Portugal. These reveal that, while the Banco de Portugal did receive large amounts of Reichsbank gold into its BNS accounts, the gold transferred to the Swiss in 1942 was generally believed to be drawn from an account "thought to be without German taint." There is no absolute assurance that this swapped gold was beyond all possible taint, but this evidence and the complete absence of any indication of concern on the part of Allied bankers involved in the swap indicate that this was likely the case. Once again, national liquidity needs, not schemes to launder dirty German gold, seemed to drive the transaction.

In 1944, Portugal itself encountered liquidity problems in its trade with Switzerland and Sweden. Increasingly unable to trade in gold because of the tightening Allied injunctions on looted gold, Portugal was driven to finance its trade with hard currencies like the Swiss franc and the Swedish krona. By August, the value of the Portuguese escudo was plummeting against the franc and the krona. Both the Swiss and Swedish proved reluctant to accept Portuguese offers of gold-for-currency swaps. In desperation, the Banco de Portugal therefore offered the Sveriges Riksbank, Sweden's central bank, clean gold in Ottawa in exchange for kronor. This offer of a ton and a half of gold in September and October of 1944 was accepted by the Swedes on the condition that the Portuguese applied the resultant kronor to the process of Swedish-Portuguese trade alone. Subsequently, the Sveriges Riksbank and the Banco de Portugal agreed to ease Portugal's ongoing exchange needs by using the swapping of gold earmarked in Ottawa back and forth to provide kronor for Lisbon. By the end of this process in September 1945, the Sveriges Riksbank had accumulated two and a half tons of gold previously owned by the Banco de Portugal in Ottawa.

One last gold swap rounded out the Bank of Canada's role in gold transfers between neutral European central banks. In the midst of its swaps with the Sveriges Riksbank in September 1944, the Banco de Portugal swapped another two tons of its gold in gold holdings in Switzerland for Swiss gold held in Ottawa. As in 1942, the gold in Switzerland was taken from Portugal's untainted account. This time, Portugal received a smaller commission of only 3/8%, probably because it saw the advantage of topping up its Ottawa reserve of gold at a time when its newly made agreement with Sweden might have required more gold if the escudo's exchange value had continued to deteriorate.

With the lifting of all conditions restraining foreign gold on earmark in Ottawa after the war, there was no rush by neutral central banks to clear out their accounts in Ottawa. In fact, all parties to the wartime swaps maintained their Ottawa earmarks well into the peace, often increasing their balances.

Throughout all these transactions, officials at the Bank of Canada, usually in consultation with officials at the Department of Finance and the Bank of England, exhibited due diligence in handling these transfer requests from Europe. The context of the times must be borne in mind. These transactions took place at the height of the war, when the pressures of wartime decision-making bore heavily on Ottawa's mandarins. These gold swaps between friendly and neutral central banks constituted fleeting decisions in a myriad of wartime challenges and must be seen in this light. By and large, the decisions taken around Canada's custodianship of foreign gold earmarked in the Bank of Canada conform to the stereotype of the cautious, deliberate and well-balanced demeanor of the senior bureaucrats who have come to be known by history as the "Ottawa men." They never possessed the absolute knowledge or the power to eliminate any possibility that Ottawa might facilitate the movement of looted gold, but their instincts led them to policies that made that possibility remote. In this sense, Canadians can take justifiable pride in the efficient manner in which the rather prosaic service of earmarking of gold was turned to commendable Allied and, at times, humanitarian ends during the war.

CONFERENCE ON JEWISH MATERIAL CLAIMS AGAINST GERMANY

Delegation Statement

We welcome the opportunity – following the historic Washington Conference on Holocaust-Era Assets – to present the position of the Conference on Jewish Material Claims Against Germany (Claims Conference) on the major issues of concern to Holocaust survivors and the world Jewish community.

The Claims Conference was established in 1951 by 23 major Jewish national and international organizations to attain the following objectives:

- to gain indemnification for injuries inflicted upon individual victims of Nazi persecution;
- to secure restitution of assets confiscated by the Nazis;
- to obtain funds for the relief, rehabilitation and resettlement of Jewish victims of Nazi persecution;
- to aid in rebuilding Jewish communities which Nazi persecution had devastated;
- to foster commemoration, research, documentation and education of the Holocaust.

For nearly 50 years the Claims Conference has and continues to vigorously pursue these objectives, primarily in its negotiations with the German and Austrian governments. It was instrumental in securing major indemnification and restitution legislation. The Claims Conference is also directly involved in the administration of limited individual compensation programs, in the recovery of heirless and unclaimed private and communal Jewish assets, in the allocation of funds for social care of needy Holocaust survivors and for research, documentation and education of the Shoah.

The Claims Conference is painfully aware of the fact that the destruction of Jewish life during the Holocaust cannot be made whole. It is imperative, however, that:

- the survivors of the Holocaust who were not or are not adequately compensated receive acceptable indemnification for their injuries and losses;
- Jewish private and communal assets which have not as yet been restituted should be restituted or compensated for in lieu of restitution;
- needy aging survivors receive necessary individual and institutional services;
- the lessons of the Holocaust be fully documented and disseminated throughout the world.

These are the guiding principles which must be applied in dealing with the unresolved indemnification and restitution issues. The fact that 53 years after the liberation of the concentration camps, many issues are still unresolved, and most survivors are of advanced age, calls for very urgent action by all governments concerned.

The Washington Conference highlighted progress on some issues but others have not as yet been considered in this unique forum of governments and nongovernmental organizations.

In order to insure that the survivors receive long overdue justice, it is essential to intensify the efforts to achieve the above objectives. We suggest that:

(1) a follow-up conference be convened in 1999;
(2) the United States and the United Kingdom – as convenors of the London and Washington conferences – establish a secretariat to:
   (a) monitor the implementation of matters considered at the London and Washington conferences, and,
   (b) prepare the next conference.

Dr. Israel Miller, President
Saul Kagan Executive Vice President
Gideon Taylor, Executive Vice President-Designate

CROATIA

Delegation Statement

The Republic of Croatia welcomes the organization of the Conference in Washington which, in the same way as the Conference on Nazi Gold held last year in London (2-4 December 1997), aims to finally determine the objective, historical truth about monetary gold and other expropriated assets.

Whereas the emphasis of the Conference in London was placed upon investigation of the destiny of monetary gold, the intention of the participants of the upcoming Conference in Washington is to examine ways and means of extending this issue to other expropriated property, primarily expropriated works of art, archive materials, insurance policies, the property of religious communities and others.

Now, at the end of the second millennium, it is indeed high time that the historical truth about the Holocaust be determined, and to find ways of indemnifying victims of the Holocaust.

This is the reason why, based on its decision taken on 13 November 1997, the Government of the Republic of Croatia established a Commission to investigate the historical facts of the property of victims of Nazism. This Commission includes representatives from the Ministry of Justice, the Ministry of Foreign Affairs, the Ministry of Economy, the Ministry of Finance, the National Bank of Croatia, the Institute for Migrations and Nationalities, the Jewish Community of Zagreb, the Croatian Institute for History, and Croatian National Archives.

The Commission has been tasked to gather and analyze all available materials pertaining to the period of the Holocaust, and to propose to the Government of the Republic of Croatia the positions it should take and to reach appropriate decisions with regard to it.

Additionally, in November of 1997 the Government of the Republic of Croatia reached a Decision to waive its part of the remaining resources of the Tripartite Commission, which should belong to it on the basis of the succession of successor States of the former Yugoslavia, in favor of Jewish people and other victims of Nazi persecution. The Republic of Croatia is, therefore, one of the first States to have supported the establishment of the new Fund for the compensation of Holocaust victims, undertaking to pay a certain financial amount into the Fund. The sum that the Republic of Croatia has decided to pay into the Fund, taking into consideration the criteria laid down by the International Monetary Fund for the distribution of financial resources according to the succession principle, amounts to US$ 118,000.

The Republic of Croatia considers that distribution of the remaining part should not wait for a final solution to the succession issue, but rather that the shares of individual successors may be determined independently of the outcome of negotiations held to decide other succession issues. Thus, Holocaust victims would receive their funds earlier.

The World War II archive materials at the disposal of the Republic of Croatia are open and are available to everyone for viewing. Further, Croatian National Archives has signed an Agreement with the Holocaust Memorial Museum in Washington, on the basis of which the archive materials from these archives are microfilmed and sent to Washington Holocaust Museum.

Regrettably, however, the Republic of Croatia is denied access to the common archives of the former Yugoslavia, which are kept in Belgrade. Therefore, not all materials relating to the Holocaust are available to us.

The Government of the Republic of Croatia has passed an Act on Compensation for Property Expropriated during the Yugoslav Communist rule, which sets out the principles, conditions and procedure for the return of expropriated property. This Act is also applicable to the compensation of victims of property expropriation carried out during World War II.

It is worth mentioning here that apart from overcoming the consequences of, and eliminating the damage inflicted as a result of, World War II, after gaining its independence the Republic of Croatia was to face further consequences and damage resulting from more than 50 years of communist rule.

Hence, the issue of returning expropriated property was made especially difficult and sensitive, since it was frequently necessary to rectify twofold consequences – those of the Holocaust and those of communism.

I.   CULTURAL TREASURES

A significant status within property expropriated from victims of the Holocaust in World War II is held by works of art, libraries and other cultural and art treasures.

Expropriation of that form of valuable property was taking place during, as well as immediately after, the war on the basis of a range of regulations that were coercive in character, although it frequently occurred without any legal basis whatsoever.

The legal bases and regulations applied in various procedures concerning works of art on the territory of Croatia after World War II were as follows:

The Decision made in 1944 by AVNOJ, which assumed temporary control over abandoned property or of the property of owners whose abode was known, and similar.

The Decision on the protection and preservation of cultural monuments and antiquities (made by the National Committee of the Liberation of Yugoslavia) on 20 February 1945. On the basis of that Decision, the "Commission for the gathering and preservation of cultural monuments and antiquities" was operational from 1945.

The Order issued to the Minister of Education dated 28 June 1945, on the "training and education of the Commission for the gathering and preservation of cultural monuments".

The Law on managing property which owners had to abandon during the occupation, and property taken from them by the occupying forces and their collaborators, dated 24 May 1945 and 2 August 1946, which emphasizes that the said property should be returned to the rightful owners, or to those who were using it, and that such property must be managed as property in trust until the court rules that it shall be returned.

The Law on transfer to state ownership of enemy property and on sequestration of property of absent persons.

The Law on confiscation of property and the implementation of confiscation.

The General Law on protection of cultural monuments and natural rarities, dated 4 October 1946, which was also the basis for placing under the protection of the State movable cultural heritage from numerous collection centers of such items after World War II. Stipulations of that law indicate that all the objects in such centers were nationalized as monuments and had to be under the administrative control of Institute for Conservation of the Federal Republic of Croatia, Zagreb, or any institution to which the Institute transfers its right.

No specific data on the nationalization of confiscated works of art is available. The existing documentation, the collection of Acts issued by the "Commission for the gathering and protection of cultural monuments and antiquities" (KOMZA) within the former Institute for Conservation in Zagreb points to the conclusion that the confiscation of property had to be followed by a decision for nationalization. Such decisions were made by the City Committees of the People – departments for public property.

The mentioned collection of KOMZA Acts, retained in the archives of the Administration for the protection of cultural heritage at the Ministry of Culture of the Republic of Croatia, could prove to be the main source of data on the question of confiscated items of cultural and artistic value.

The Register of KOMZA minutes for the years 1945 and 1946 is an available source of a wealth of information on this subject.

After World War II numerous commissions worked in the Institute for Conservation in Zagreb. Their task was, among other things, to maintain records on war damage inflicted on cultural monuments and structures possessing monument properties; selection of items of artistic value among the mass of confiscated goods held in collection centers; selection of items of artistic value in deserted houses and flats; storage of such objects in KOMZA premises or elsewhere; division of items possessing monument properties (paintings, sculptures, furniture, objects of artistic craft and similar, among new owners (or users), museums, galleries, other institutions in the field of culture, administration and others.

The post-war Commissions working within the Institute for Conservation in Zagreb were:

"KOMRAT" – National Commission for establishing the extent of war damage to cultural and historical objects on the territory of Croatia – Zagreb (1945-1947)

"KOMZA" – Commission for the gathering and protection of cultural monuments and antiquities – Zagreb (1945-1954)

Commission for the inspection of objects – Ministry of Science and Culture of the government of FNR Yugoslavia – Zagreb (1947–1951)

The above listed Commissions were engaged in the collection and preservation of surviving cultural monuments, antiquities and libraries following the period of the Holocaust.

"KOMRAT" was founded on the initiative of the Ministry of Education of the People's Republic of Croatia, its first session being held on 7 June 1945. Its work was supported by documentation, as well as by a register of inventories.

"KOMZA" was founded on 26 June 1945 on the orders of the Minister of Education of Croatia and was based on the Decision dated 20 February 1945 on the protection and preservation of cultural monuments and antiquities, adopted by the National Committee for the Liberation of Yugoslavia. Its main task was to gather data on expropriated items possessing monument properties.

Precise records were maintained, containing lists of objects of artistic significance (records were linked to the name and family name of the former owner and to a registration number, under which the total volume of goods confiscated from the same owner was entered in an individual regional collection center). The objects of artistic value, set aside by the commission, were placed into the trust of KOMZA from were they were distributed to various locations. Records were kept of such distributions, with the origin of an object being denoted by the registration number of the confiscated goods. It is impossible to trace a certain number of items beyond that stage (there are, for instance, remarks such as "Handed over at the request of the Federal Executive Council", and similar). The work of KOMZA is also supported by documentation, i.e., a register of inventories.

In the period from the commencement of KOMZA's work (1945–1949) the Museum for Arts and Crafts in Zagreb, as well as other museums and galleries, were receiving works of art from collection centers into permanent ownership.

The path of each individual work of art can be traced from a collection center in Zagreb to its location in a museum (provided that key documents are not missing) on the basis of documents, but the distribution of moveable works of art among private individuals was not followed up by detailed records, that is to say, their path cannot always be traced.

In certain areas KOMZA and KOMRAT complemented each other; in other areas their activities overlapped, and the same can be said for the Commission for Restitution (KOMREST). More information will become available when the collection of documents is brought out of storage.

The selection of objects (movables) of cultural and artistic significance was undertaken exclusively by the Commission for the gathering and preservation of cultural monuments and antiquities, and its associated, separate section, the Commission for Libraries. The return of such moveable property to rightful owners was also defined, provided that the owners registered the loss of said property.

Abandoned property of unknown owners was immediately nationalized in 1945, and the implementation of confiscation procedure was followed by a decision on the transfer of the same property into the ownership of the State. Likewise, the property of absent persons was sequestered and nationalized. On the basis of the then existing legal framework it was possible to convey works of art into ownership only after the finalization of court proceedings.

The Compensation Law (*Official Gazette* No.92/96) also regards moveable heritage of works of art, including those from World War II, as nationalized property, as stipulated in Articles 3. and 48. of the said law.

According to Article 48., only movables of cultural, artistic or historical value are to be returned to their former owners. Such movables, which are regarded as cultural heritage and are, in accordance with the rules and regulations on the protection of cultural heritage, a constituent part of Croatian galleries and museums, are to be returned to the ownership of the former owner, although not into his possession. Owners are entitled to a special type of compensation to be defined by a separate decree issued by the government of the Republic of Croatia.

The fundamental standpoint of the Ministry of Culture of the Republic of Croatia, based on professional and scientific arguments presented by museum experts and relevant institutions, and one that has been integrated into all the legislation on museum activity and the preservation of museum material, is that museum collections, protected and registered as moveable monuments of culture, are under the special protection of the State, are indivisible, and as such are kept and displayed in their entirety, regardless of who owns them, or their individual items.

All the items comprising a certain collection in a museum are inventoried and entered into museum registers and other museum documents, forming what is known as museological documentation. The entire museological documentation of all the museums in the Republic of Croatia constitutes national cultural heritage, a national fund of moveable cultural goods. Any extraction of works of art which form an individual museum collection is, in principle, prohibited and is subject to a special procedure defined by the valid law (Law on museums, *Official Gazette* No. 142, dated 28 October1998) and pertaining by-laws. This, however, does not mean that certain exemptions, strictly professionally argued, are not possible in individual and particularly justifiable cases.

The question of the possible loan, or of presenting for temporary use, certain works of art which form a part of the holdings of Croatian museums and galleries, shall be dealt with through a separate procedure in which experts will play a decisive role, bearing in mind requests for the restitution of works of art – now forming a part of the holdings of the Museum of Slavonija-Osijek; the Museum of Arts and Crafts, Zagreb; the Croatian Museum of History, Zagreb; the Archeological Museum, Zagreb; the Gallery of Visual Arts, Osijek; Trakoš_an Castle, and others – already received from the former owners by the Ministry of Culture of the Republic of Croatia.

In parallel with the Compensation Law, beginning from 1990 and particularly since the adoption of its Constitution, the Republic of Croatia has, through the notification of succession, become party to numerous international agreements and conventions, some of which are related to the preservation of cultural and natural heritage. Since 1995, representatives of the Ministry of Culture of the Republic of Croatia have enjoyed observer-member status of the UNESCO inter-governmental body charged with aiding the return of cultural treasures to their lands of origin, or their restitution in the event of illegal acquisition, as well as being members of the Committee for amendments and changes to the UNESCO Hague Convention of the same year.

Additionally, Croatia, as one of the successor countries of the former Yugoslavia, is demanding the restitution of material removed from its territory in the period from 1918 to 1991 and which now constitute joint cultural heritage involving museum and gallery holdings from the territory of the former Yugoslavia. This action is being conducted within the framework of the program of succession, coordinated by the Office for the project of succession with the government of the Republic of Croatia. To that end, necessary documentary support has been prepared, based on a survey carried out toward the end of 1992, to accompany claims made by museums and galleries in the Republic of Croatia.

In the war waged against Croatia from 1991 to 1995 our cultural heritage has suffered almost immeasurable losses through extensive material damage, which was also inflicted on museums and galleries. Based on an assessment of war damage to museums and galleries it has been established that of 204 museums, galleries and museum collections, 66 museum buildings have either been damaged or destroyed; 45 museums and galleries have suffered damage to their holdings (6551 items of museum holdings are missing; 1430 items have been destroyed and 728 damaged). Here it must be pointed out that at the time of writing the assessment has not been finalized.

According to reports of foreign experts, in just the first seven months of war in Croatia more cultural treasures were destroyed than during the entire period of World War II throughout the whole of the former Yugoslavia.

Negotiations on the return of stolen cultural heritage, scheduled to take place between groups of experts from the Ministry of Culture of the Republic of Croatia and the Ministry of Culture of SR Yugoslavia, based on the existing assessment of war damage, numerous reports of investigation missions of the Council of Europe, of ICOM, UNESCO and others, covering the period between 1992 and 1996, have not yet been realized despite the agreements reached at a meeting of foreign ministers of the Republic of Croatia and SR Yugoslavia that took place in Zagreb on 18 August 1998, and which was related to the normalization of relations between the two countries.

Bearing all the above stated in mind, the holdings of Croatian museums and galleries are therefore partially incomplete, which means that the expert services of the Ministry of Culture of the Republic of Croatia are faced with the daunting task of realizing the project of succession, as well as the return of expropriated property, establishing a definitive picture of the holdings held by our own museums, and reconstructing the ownership of the part of works of art collected during and after the period of Holocaust.

The existence of documents, on the basis of which such reconstruction can be at least partially made, will be of great assistance to the creation of a more comprehensive picture of the fate of moveable art heritage.

II.   LIBRARIES

During the existence of the Independent State of Croatia, books and libraries were confiscated from individual Jewish persons and handed over to the National and University Library, but without any listing. The same practice seems to have been adopted by the communist authorities following World War II – private books and libraries were confiscated and also handed over to the National and University Library.

In 1959 the library belonging to Dr. Lavoslav Šik was returned to the Jewish Council in Zagreb, and in 1989 his private archives were also returned. Also in 1989, 7,000 books were returned to the same institution, accompanied by an agreement made between the Jewish Council in Zagreb and the National and University Library, dated 4 October 1990.

III.   ARCHIVE MATERIAL

Documentation about the Holocaust in Croatia can be divided into several different groups.

The first and the most important group consists of official documents laws, provisions and archives of the Ustasha administration of the government of the Independent State of Croatia. They are stored for the most part in the Croatian State Archive which is in charge of the documents of the central government institutions, as well as in regional archives. A part of these archives is also to be found outside Croatia - in Belgrade. This group, which is the largest, contains lists of the Jews, figures about camps and victims, treatment of the Jews in public life, lists of Jewish properties and confiscation of these properties.

The second group consists of documents on the activities of the Anti-Fascist Partisan Movement, especially the ZAVNOH Antifascist Council for the Liberation of Croatia. They provide details about the efforts of anti-Fascists in assisting the Jews.

The third group consists of documents which came out after 1944 as a result of the activities of the committees of the People's Republic of Croatia, whose task was to establish the facts about the crimes committed by the occupying forces and their supporters. These are stored in the State Committee File in the Croatian State Archive, as well as in district, community and city files in regional archives. All these contain detailed figures about victims and crimes committed in camps and various sites in Croatia.

The fourth group consists of documents produced after 1945 as a result of legal proceedings conducted by the State Security Office against those accused of crimes committed in World War II. This documentation which was received after 1990 by the Croatian State Archive, provides an account of the atrocities against the Jews.

Finally, the fifth group consists of various press-clippings, photos, memoirs, archives of the Jewish communities, and private archives.

The most significant part of the archival material is stored in the Croatian State Archive, and by its nature, summarizes the archival materials of other lower bodies kept in regional archives. However, the future research should go beyond what has already been done. The research on the Holocaust in Croatia has not expanded further than establishing the number of victims. In our opinion it is necessary to analyze the historical context of the Holocaust in each country, using source material, in order to get to the truth, to the "genesis of the crime", the crime itself and the consequences of the crime. Sources provide brand possibilities researching the Holocaust in all its complexity, and should be used more, in both analytical and synthetical research done by the historians.

In this respect, we should also take into consideration the other side of the coin when speaking of those horrible times. In addition to the ideology of evil-Fascism and racism we must also mention the generosity and courage of many individuals who risked their lives to help the Jews, sometimes becoming victims themselves as a result.

Yad Vashem bestowed the honorary title of "righteous among nations" to 60 Croats who risked their lives to help the Jews. After the capitulation of Italy, Croatian partisans evacuated 3,500 Jews from the island of Rab in the Adriatic to the free territory of ZAVNOH. Jewish children together with Croatian women and children, were taken to the refugees camp El-Shat in Egypt.

Finally, we would like to point out that it is necessary for every nation to research the Holocaust in its own country. There should be no attempts to justify the evil and crimes committed by one's own nation by accusing other nations of evil and crimes. An evil committed should be condemned, but one must know to forgive and ask for forgiveness. To place the blame on somebody else is to blame oneself.

This is one of the reasons why the HDA accepted an invitation from the U.S. Memorial Holocaust Museum in Washington to sign an Accord on May 22, 1995, on cooperation on Holocaust research in Croatia. As a sign of good will, at the beginning of September 1995, we gave to the ten rolls of microfilms to the Museum with data on the mentioned 6,573 Jews executed or killed in World War II in Croatia.

The Croatian State Archive will continue to do its best to give support to research aimed at uncovering the truth about the victims of World War II.

EUROPEAN JEWISH CONGRESS AND EUROPEAN COUNCIL OF JEWISH COMMUNITIES

Joint Delegation Statement

The **European Jewish Congress** (EJC) and the **European Council of Jewish Communities** (ECJC) were privileged to be invited to attend the Washington Conference on Holocaust Era-Assets which was an international landmark event in restoring dignity to a chapter of the darkest history of mankind.

As the two European non-governmental organizations representing an entire cross section of leading Jewish organizations, including those dealing with the welfare needs of the elderly and in particular of the needy Holocaust survivors, we wish to express our thanks for the invitation to attend the Washington Conference and at the same time to take advantage of the opportunity to present a unified European Jewish position paper.

We are particularly keen to voice European Jewry's concerns and heightened sensibilities regarding the issues of restitution and Holocaust education. As members of Jewish communities living today in the very territory in which the Nazi regime perpetrated its unique onslaught on the Jewish people and where Jewish life was almost extinct by the end of World War II we have pledged all our energies to contribute to the continuity of well functioning Jewish institutions and services in Europe.

Nowhere more than Europe has the Shoah left its most destructive and indelible traces. Nowhere more than Europe will allocations from restitution funds be able to improve the personal well being of needy Holocaust survivors and enhance the infra structure of Jewish communal life.

It is from this particular European vantage point that we wish to make a united submission from our two European Jewish umbrella organizations.

I. HOLOCAUST EDUCATION:

We wish to emphasize our particular interest in the field of education and promotion of a global curriculum in the teaching of the Shoah. The European Jewish Congress is preparing for 1999 an updated background document which will give a fair overview of all existing actions in the field of formal and informal education, including textbooks in European countries. This document will be our contribution to the International Conference on Holocaust Education, which Sweden has offered to hold in early 2000 and to which EJC/ECJC wish to be closely associates.

II. ACCESSIBILITY TO ARCHIVES:

We concur with Secretary's Eizenstat's urgent call to all governments and non-governmental organizations to open all public and private archives pertaining to the Holocaust by the end of the year, notably the Tripartite Gold Commission as well as all relevant archives including German Nazi archives still in possession by some allied countries.

In this respect we feel that the Vatican should reconsider its resistance to such appeals for disclosure. What possible justification could there be for the Vatican to remain the last bastion of secrecy with regard to the Holocaust period? We have noted the statement by the Holy See, referring to documents available to 1922, but reiterate the absolute requirement to open archives so as to reach a just resolution to outstanding matters in relation to the 1933 - 1945 era.

III. ALLOCATIONS FROM THE INTERNATIONAL FUND FOR NEEDY VICTIMS OF NAZI PERSECUTION:

We take note that this fund now totals about USD 60 million and we are grateful to all donor countries who have generously contributed to this amount.

While we cannot underestimate the importance of direct payments and services to individual needy victims of Nazi persecution, we wish to emphasize the need for commensurate allocations for a variety of networking programs geared to the improvement of delivering Jewish communal services for small communities and communities in Central and Eastern Europe. Both the EJC and ECJC have specialized capabilities in providing training and support consultations in the area of public policy and advocacy, Jewish informal and formal education, youth work, social services provisions, cultural and Jewish Heritage activities and leadership training to European Jewish communities. All these programs are geared to consolidating Jewish life as a component of the pluralistic democratic societies in which these communities exist.

We strongly recommend that the most serious consideration be given to allocations to such programs as part and parcel of the commitment to right the wrong of the past in a region which has suffered doubly under oppression and neglect.

IV. INSURANCE CLAIMS:

We endorse the newly created International Commission on Holocaust-Era Insurance Claims as the best mechanism for dealing with unpaid life and property insurance dating back to the Holocaust era.

At the same time we express our wish that many more European insurance companies join the Commission and demonstrate their good will by pledging appropriate sums into an escrow fund from which future claimants will be paid.

V. COMMUNAL PROPERTY:

We deplore the lack of consensus on how to expedite the process of settling claims to religious and other communal properties (schools, hospitals, community centers, welfare organizations, club houses etc.).

We are encouraged by the idea muted by the Polish delegation that it would consider a conference on communal property and would hope that this conference could address the situation in all former communist countries. We are aware of the attempt by the region's democratic governments to take steps to rectify the injustices of the past. However we must stress that the speedy return of such property or appropriate compensation is absolutely essential to the re-emergence and rebirth of Jewish communal life in Central and Eastern Europe.

We are mandated by our member organizations - the national Jewish representative bodies - in this region to emphatically stress the urgency of this endeavor. Most of these communities are impoverished and in need of outside support if they are to survive and prosper into the next millennium.

VI. LOOTED ART:

We applaud the trend demonstrated by various governments to show a new willingness to locate missing artworks, publicize their existence, determine their provenance and come to a just and speedy resolution of ownership questions.

We support the introduction of the set of non-binding principles intended as an operational framework for the resolution of the above objectives.

We support the suggestion of a specific conference devoted to the questions of looted art, to be held in Austria.

London / Paris 31 December 1998

Submitted jointly by
EUROPEAN JEWISH CONGRESS
CONGRES JUIF EUROPEEN
President: Ignatz Bubis (Germany); Secretary General: Serge Cwajgenbaum
78 avenue des Champs - Elysees - 75008 Paris
Tel. 01 43 59 94 63; Fax. 01 42 25 45 28; Email: jewcong@imaginet.fr

and

EUROPEAN COUNCIL OF JEWISH COMMUNITIES
CONSEIL EUROPEEN DES COMMUNAUTES JUIVES
President: David L Lewis; Chairperson: Ruth Zilkha; Executive Director: Michael May
74 Gloucester Place, London W1H 3HN, United Kingdom
Tel. 0171 224 3445; Fax. 0171 224 3446; Email: ecjc@ort.org

FINLAND

Statement by
Ambassador Esko Kiuru
MINISTRY FOR FOREIGN AFFAIRS

Mr. Chairman,

First of all I would like to thank the Government of the United States, as well the State Department for convening the Washington Conference on Holocaust-Era Assets. The timeliness of the Conference is a demonstration of the fact that the past cannot be escaped. Building the future requires that the wrongdoings of the past must be corrected and lessons must be learned.

The participation of so many countries and organizations in this important Conference is a clear indication that Governments are recognizing that the level of the moral of a state is increasingly demonstrated by how they deal with and settle the events of their recent history, including the restitution of wrong-doings. This conference deals with the events of the Nazi era. Similar painful processes on the settlement of the issues from the past lie ahead of individual countries and international community as a consequence of the recent collapse of the communist system in Eastern Europe. Restitution of stolen and confiscated property to their legal owners is one of the tasks which has to be accomplished in the former communist countries.

The participation of the Finnish Government in this Conference is a strong demonstration of support to the international endeavors to rectify the wrongdoings during the Nazi era towards the Jews and Jewish communities. We find that the broadest possible international support is required. This Conference also gives us an opportunity to clarify the open and serious consideration given by the Finnish authorities to the linked issues and events before, during and after the Second World War.

As most of you know, Finland was in a rather unique situation during the Second World War. First the Soviet Union attacked our country in 1939. After the Winter War a peace treaty was concluded in the spring of 1940. From June 1941 Finland was again at war with the

Soviet Union until September 1944. After the armistice, Finland waged war against the Nazi-German troops remaining in Lapland.

The democratic structures of Finland were maintained during all this time. In this connection it may be mentioned that free and fair elections were held in Finland in the spring of 1945 after we had managed to step out of the war but while the fighting still took place elsewhere in Europe. Finland was also one of the few European countries which were never occupied by foreign troops during or after the war.

Mr. Chairman,

The special situation and circumstances of Finland were reflected in how the Jewish population of Finland participated in the war. The Jewish minority is and has been an equal part of society, with the same rights and obligations as other Finnish citizens. The Jewish population in Finland has never been subjected to persecution. Nor has their property been confiscated or taken in some other illegal way.

During the Second World War members of the Jewish community in Finland participated in the Winter War and the Continuation War between Finland and the Soviet Union in the same way as other citizens. In that situation no difference was made between different religions. Finland and the Finnish citizens fought for their existence, irrespective of religion or cultural differences. The Winter War did not create any ideological problems for the Finnish Jews. All the Jewish conscripts, in total 260 persons, served in the army. Of these 200 served at the front. Fifteen Jews were killed in action, which was a relatively significant loss for them. It has often been estimated that the Winter War made the Jews feel that they really belonged to the Finnish society.

During the Continuation War (1941-1944) the situation was quite exceptional and interesting. Finland fought a war of its own against the Soviet Union. There were German troops in the northern part of the country and people were aware of the cruel policy of anti-Semitism applied by the Nazis, although the extent of the atrocities was still not known. Despite all this, the Finnish Jews served at the front, and in other duties on equal standing with other citizens, even in the Continuation War. The same applied to all national minorities. Several Jewish soldiers were rewarded, they were promoted in a normal manner and they served as commanders. This was probably a unique phenomenon.

It has often been asserted that the Nazis demanded the Finnish Jews be surrendered. None, of course, were handed over. However, there is no documentary evidence of this kind of demand. The Finnish Jews were not saved because the Nazis forgot they existed. The fact that Finnish Jews were Finns like other Finns was stated by the Prime Minister of Finland to Germans (Heinrich Himmler) in the summer of 1942 in the mention that there is no Jewish problem in Finland. It was also repeatedly announced that there is no cooperation with Nazi-Germans as regards the Finnish Jewish community.

However, during the war a sad episode took place as to some Jewish refugees. Before the war, some 500 Jewish refugees came to Finland from Central Europe. Of these refugees 350 moved on to other countries and 150 remained in Finland. The State Police in Finland extradited eight Jews, who were allegedly accused of criminal activity, to the Gestapo. Only one of these Jews stayed alive. Intervention by the President of the Republic, Mr. Ryti, Marshall Mannerheim and the Government prevented the extradition of other refugees when it became known that eight people had been handed over.

Mr. Chairman,

The question of Nazi-confiscated assets, appearing on the conference agenda, has been investigated in Finland for quite a while already. These investigations have proved the earlier information according to which no property of the Jews was confiscated or taken in some other illegal way during the holocaust era. This is due to the fact that the Jewish community in Finland was in an equal position with other members of society.

A few examples of the investigations carried out so far:

The Bank of Finland as the holder of the Finnish Governments official reserve assets has carried out a study to ascertain whether the Bank was in any way involved in gold confiscated from the Jews or in other property seized from them in Europe during the Nazi regime. This study was conducted on the Bank's gold transactions and holdings during the years 1939-45. On the basis of extensive studies of the archives no indication was established that the bank would have been involved in the receipt of German-origin gold or confiscation or safekeeping of other Jewish property.

As is well-known from a survey published in May 1997 by the Bank for International Settlement (BIS) that Bank mediated gold as payment for international bilateral postal payment transactions between the central banks, including the Bank of Finland, and the Reichsbank on behalf of national postal authorities. In terms of size, these BIS-accounts were insignificant as an investment outlet for gold. No physical transfer of gold was involved but the gold was used as an accounting unit. A summary of the findings of the study has been handed over to the organizers of this Conference.

In the spring of 1998 the Finnish banks launched an investigation, with a view to finding out whether there were any unused bank accounts, belonging to Jews in refuge. No such bank accounts were found.

As regards insurance, in the light of current information, there are no unclear insurance policies that would have belonged to Jews in refuge in Finland. This is probably because Finland was so far away and was not considered a safe country in the political situation of the 1930's and 1940's. Thus it was not a good idea to take insurance policies or deposit money in Finland. An investigation is being carried out in respect of eventual assets of one refugee (one of the eight handed over to Gestapo and who died in a concentration camp). This study has been carried out in cooperation with the Jewish associations in Finland.

As regards art-objects, no immovable or movable property belonging to individual Jews or Jewish communities have been confiscated in Finland. However, two paintings have turned up in the market, in respect of which the owners are being traced. The traces seem to lead abroad, to Vienna and Berlin.

Education in the events of the holocaust era, as regards comprehensive school, secondary education, universities and other educational institutions, is given in connection with history courses. The universities naturally have a research interest in the events of the holocaust era. The subject is dealt with by several scientists and publishers, which is demonstrated by the great number of studies, books, publications, articles and TV programs concentrating on that era. We hope that this conference provides inspiration even for a more systematic study and education in the events of the holocaust era.

Mr. Chairman,

The uniqueness of the Finnish situation as well as, in particular, of the situation of the Finnish Jewish population as described above, should not be overemphasized, considering the seriousness of the issues before this Conference affecting so many countries. What I try to explain is that, in spite of the dark moments in the western history, there have also been gleams of hope, although not very strong compared to what happened to the Jews and to their property, on the whole.

The effects of the dark moments in the Western history also to Finland, and the measures we have taken to overwhelm them, do not in any way mean that the Finnish society would not have already gone through the sometimes painful discussion about the events in the past. This process will be continued although the number of cases is not too extensive in my country. This Conference, its results and conclusions can contribute to that on-going discussion.

The Jews of Finland and World War II

By
Tapani Harviainen
Professor of Semitic Languages
University of Helsinki

In several respects the history of the Jews in Finland has no counterpart, either in the Scandinavian and Baltic countries or in Eastern Europe. In order to be able to tell what happened during the Second World War, I must explain how there came to be Jews in Finland in that period. As a consequence, this presentation consists of two parts: first, the rise of the Jewish community in Finland, and, second, the fate of the Jews in Finland during the Second World War.

In theory, there was no place for Jews in Finland. From the 12th-13th century until 1809 Finland was a province of Sweden. When Sweden was opened up to the Jews in 1782, residential rights were restricted to three, later four, cities on the Swedish mainland (Stockholm, Gothenburg, Norrköping; Karlskrona). Consequently, Jews were not allowed to settle in Finland. Nevertheless, visits were allowed and thus we know that the first Jews attested in Finland were the "Portuguese singers" *Josef Lazarus, Meijer Isaac and Pimo Zelig,* who together with the conjurer *Michel Marcus* were granted a license to present their skills in Helsinki in 1782. [1]

During the Swedish period some Jewish converts to Christianity also settled in Finland. *Isak Zebulon* of Lübeck, who had by baptismal received the name Christoffer, chose Oulu in Northern Finland as his new hometown. The mother of *Zacharias Topelius,* the well-known Finnish writer - who lived in the 19th century was descended from this Oulu citizen of Jewish descent. [2]

---

[1] Jews expelled from Portugal in the 16th century settled in the Dutch cities and in Hamburg. Their offspring and communities were for centuries called Portuguese. The word is here used in this sense.

[2] Another famous convert was Meyer Levin, who in 1799 was admitted to the Medical Faculty of the University of Turku. Later on, Levin worked at the

Along with other Swedish laws, the 1782 regulations concerning Jews remained in force, as Finland became a Grand Duchy within the Russian Empire in 1809. Because of the high esteem enjoyed by the traditional laws of Sweden, the Grand Duchy of Finland remained a country out of bounds to Jews.

However, there is an exception which proves the rule. A part of southeastern Finland, so-called Old Finland, was incorporated into Russia as early as the middle of the 18th century, and Swedish laws did not apply to that area until 1811. This made it possible for some Jewish families to move from Russia proper to Old Finland at the end of the 1790s; several families (Jacobsson, Kaspi, Veikkanen etc.) in Finland are descendents of these Jewish pioneers.

The Grand Duchy of Finland was a country out of bounds to Jews. However, when the Jews were granted civil rights in the independent Republic of Finland in 1918, 1,400 Jews were living in the country. How do we explain this miracle?

The regulations prohibiting the entry of Jews into the Grand Duchy of Finland did not prevent the Russian Army from entering the country. Ever since 1827, the Jews of Russia were liable for military service. With very few exceptions, Jews came to Finland as soldiers of the Czarist army. During the reign of Emperor Nicholas I, the duration of military service could well be 25 years - and even later it was six years. The conversion of non-Christian soldiers was one of the aims of the prolonged period of service. As one can imagine, the Jews in Russia did not consider the conscription to be a great honor, and thus the majority of Jewish recruits were sons of the poorest families, orphans and other of the underprivileged, many of them handed over to the army by the notorious *chapers,* i.e. kidnappers. After the long years of service, the soldiers, often having lost all contact with their birthplaces, were inclined to stay where they were.

This type of settlement caused a problem for Finnish autonomy. As a reaction, a Russian military ukase was issued in 1858 concerning soldiers discharged from the Russian army. According to this decree, a soldier in possession of a letter of retirement, a passport or a travel document had the right to settle and support himself in Finland. The same right applied to his family and children and also to his widow. As I have mentioned before, the decree was a Russian ukase, not a regulation promulgated by an initiative of the autonomous authorities in Finland.

University teaching German, and in 1815 he was given a permit to set up a printing plant.

The ukase did not make any distinction between Christian and non-Christian soldiers, and the right of settlement of Jews was only implied from the general wording dealing with all ex-soldiers. Similarly, Moslems veterans were allowed to stay in Finland after that. Later, by a Finnish decree of 1869 and a letter from the Finnish Senate in 1876, ex-soldiers and their families were entitled to earn a living by selling home-made handicrafts, bread, berries, cigarettes, second-hand clothes and other inexpensive textile products. This type of trading was in which the Jewish *narinkka* markets in Helsinki began.[3]

At the beginning of the 1870s, organizational reforms in the Russian army brought about a rapid increase in the number of Jews in Finland to about five hundred - such a high figure![4] As a consequence, in 1872 a debate on their legal status was initiated in the Finnish Diet.

The four estates of the Diet, as well as the political parties of the subsequent Parliament, Senate, were unable to provide a solution to the problem. General conservatism, national protectionism and the fear of a mass exodus of the Eastern European Jewish proletariat were the main arguments of the opponents. The constitutional conflict between the Finnish and Russian authorities which began in 1899 further complicated the handling of the question.[5]

It was only in 1918, in connection with Finnish independence, that full citizen's rights were granted to the Jews in Finland. In Europe, only Rumania acted more slowly than Finland in giving civil rights to the Jewish population. In Russia Jews were naturalized after the Revolution

---

[3] From Russian *na rynke* 'at the market-place'.

[4] In the earliest list of Jews in Helsinki of which I am aware, drawn up in 1868, 21 families with 83 family members were enumerated (National Archives, KKK 36/1686).

[5] In a letter of the Finnish Senate written in 1889, certain Jews whose names were particularly mentioned, together with their families, were given the right to remain in Finland until further notice, and to reside in localities assigned to them. From these towns Jews were allowed to move only to Helsinki or Vyborg within Finland. The residence permit applied to children only as long as they lived with their parents. As soon as they married or entered military service, they lost their residential right. New Jews were no longer admitted to Finland.

At first "residence tickets" were very strictly scrutinized, and because of the problem of marriage, many Jews moved away from Finland and others were expelled. In 1890, there were about one thousand Jews in Finland, but in five years their number decreased by one quarter. At the turn of the century the practice of examining and renewing residence permits was no longer observed, but the regulation remained officially in force until 1918.

in 1917, and in Sweden this was achieved as early as 1870. - In this context it is worth noting that the great majority of Jews living in Sweden and other Scandinavian countries have a German background; immigration from Poland has also taken place.

Because of the restrictions, extremely few Jews could move to Finland on their own initiative. On the basis of the Finnish police archives it is evident that, excluding the *intelligentsia,* which was very small in number (a rabbi, a teacher and a circumciser), the background of all Jews was in one way or another in the Russian Army. They had not just come to Finland, it was the Army which had sent them – by chance – to Finland and finally they had settled in the country. The decision was not their own; it was a part of the inexplicable wisdom of the Army which chose who would be Jews of Finland in the future. No parallel case of this sort of genesis of a Jewish community is known to me.

The Russian Army thus sent Jews to Finland. However, a very important exception from this rule must not be forgotten. While the Army sent boys to Finland, it did not take care of providing wives for them. Actually, we have no precise information as to the measures to which the poor lonely soldiers resorted. Family legends tell of veterans who established a joint *'isqa* venture, i.e. they collected money and wrote a letter to a rabbi in a *shtetl* in Lithuania asking him to dispatch so-and-so many marriageable Jewish women to Helsinki. Since trains were few in Russia, a consignment was transported by a cart. The ex-soldiers had plenty of time to spend waiting in the market place in Helsinki, and when the cart at last arrived, the strongest *khaveyrim* were ready to take the most beautiful *meydelakh* down from the wagon; the slimmer lads had to be happy with the rest. The story has given rise to a saying current among Jewish ladies in Finland: "I have not been taken down from a cart" - *de-haynu: "I* come from a better *mishpokhe.* "[6]

Be that as it may be, it is evident that other nationalities in Russia were attracted to Finland by its reputation in Russia as a country of order, a strong economy and greater intellectual freedom.[7] Obviously it was this reputation which assisted the Jewish soldiers in obtaining wives from Russia with such success that in 1898 the majority of Jews

---

[6] Helsingin Sanomat (A. Hurwitz), no. 316, 21.11.1929, s 4.

[7] This conclusion is confirmed by the article Eyn vokh in Finland by Shemarya Gorelik, who participated in the 1906 Russian Zionist Congress in Helsinki. The article was published in Dos yudishe folk in Vilna the same year, and it was almost comic in its praise of the Finns and conditions in Finland.

living in Helsinki were born in Finland; this genesis was due to the great number of children in their families.

From which parts of Russia were the Jewish soldiers sent to Helsinki? The Helsinki police archives offer a clear answer to this question. All Jews resident in Helsinki in 1898 had come from Russia which at that time included the greater part of Poland.[8] According to the archives the most important "home towns" or the localities and districts where the heads of the families had been registered before their arrival in Finland, were (1) Schlüsselburg (now Petrokrepost) east of St. Petersburg, above the River Neva, (2) the governments of Novgorod and Tver, and (3) Lithuania and the north-eastern parts of Poland. A surprising element in this information is that Schlüsselburg, Novgorod and Tver were all outside the Pale of Settlement where Jews were allowed to reside. Equally surprising is the almost total absence of Estonia and Latvia in the domicile registers.[9]

During the first decades of *independent Finland,* in the 1920s and 1930s, the Jewish population in Finland numbered nearly 2,000, more than at any other time. At the outset, Jews spoke either Yiddish or Russian. Linguistic assimilation led first in the direction of Swedish and then also in the direction of Finnish. Yiddish was discarded surprisingly quickly; a student of mine could find only three speakers of Yiddish for tape-recording for his M.A. thesis in Helsinki in 1995. In giving up the Jewish language, Yiddish, Finnish Jewry was left without a significant uniting factor, a factor which, for example, the Finnish Tatars have preserved.[10] Religion and consciousness of being Jewish remained, thereafter, the only uniting factors.

---

[8] Most of the soldiers had served in the regiments of the 23rd division then stationed in Finland (the regiments of Dvinsk, Petshora, Onega and Belomorsk), but quite a few also in different auxiliary units (military hospitals, local detachments, feeding depots etc.) Among them were also many bandmasters, members of military bands and drummers.

[9] In the 1880s and 1890s nearly all Helsinki Jews made their living by selling new and second-hand clothes and fruit at the narinkka market: the name of Simo (i.e. Simeon) Square still refers to the Jewish market. More than three-quarters of the Jewish population lived in the same district of Kamppi, where both the narinkka (from 1876) and later also the Synagogue (from 1906) were located. As late as 1860s most Jews still lived in the districts of Siltasaari and Kruununhaka, where the market was located at the time.

[10] These Tatars also derive their origin from Russian, from the region on Nizhni-Novgorod, east of Moscow. Although Tatars also served in the Russian army in Finland, they did not settle in the country as ex-soldiers; their forefathers came

In the 1920s and 1930s, genuine anti-Semitism also found expression in Finland in certain ultra-right-wing circles, but it never gained wider sympathies. The fact seems to remain that in the young Republic all minorities suffered from prejudice and xenophobia to some extent but evenly distributed. In this period, the Jews did, however, carry one burden which may have made its position more difficult than that of other minorities: a significant number of the Soviet leaders and well-known Bolsheviks were Jews, and this fact easily led people to the following conclusion: because he is a Jew he must be a Bolshevik, and as such an enemy of Finland.

WORLD WAR II[11]

In the years 1939-1944 two different wars against the Soviet Union were imposed upon Finland. During the Winter War of 1939-1940 Germany remained strictly neutral on the basis of the Molotov-Ribbentrop Pact; Great Britain and France planned intervention in favor of Finland.

When the second, so-called Continuation War broke out in the summer of 1941, Finland was a co-belligerent of Germany, and Great Britain declared war on Finland in December 1941. *De jure,* however, Finland was never an ally of Germany, and at the end of the War, in the winter 1944-45, the Finnish armed forces expelled the German troops from Lapland, which was devastated by the Germans during their retreat to Norway.

Military service was compulsory for each male citizen of Finland. In 1939 the Jewish population of Finland numbered 1,700. Of

---

to Finland as peddlers of clothes and furs. In 1925 they established a Moslem congregation in Helsinki. As in the case of the Jews, the members of the Tatar community have been able to adapt themselves to Finnish society without radical difficulties; both of these minorities are of the same size, viz. one thousand persons. Besides being a religious congregation, the Tatar Moslem community has stressed national aspects, retention of the Turkic Tatar language, traditional habits and close family ties. In spite of competition in a number of lines of business, relations between the Tatar and Jewish minorities have been good; a sign of the rapport between them is a friendly football match arranged by them each spring.

[11] For details of the wartime history, see Hannu Rautkallio, Suomen juutalaisten aseveljeys (The comradeship-in-arms of the Jews of Finland). Tammi, Helsinki-Jyväskylä 1989. 250 p., ill., English summary.

these, 260 men were called up and approximately 200 were sent to serve at the front during the Winter War. Fifteen men lost their lives. In comparison with other communities in the country, the Jewish losses (8 %) were conspicuously heavy. However, it is obvious that the Winter War did not involve ideological problems - neither for the Jews nor for other citizens of Finland. In this respect a statement made by a Jewish veteran seems to be characteristic: "The Winter War gave us a deeper consciousness of being Finnish and of belonging to Finland more than any earlier period in our history."

As I mentioned earlier, the Continuation War broke out in the summer of 1941. Now Finland was a co-belligerent of Germany, and there were Wehrmacht and Waffen-SS troops in the country. However, no *Einsatzgruppe* was sent to Finland.

The comradeship-in-arms with Germany during the Continuation War did not alter the status of Jews in Finland or in its army. Jewish citizens served in the Finnish army, in women's voluntary defense services and in other duties alongside other Finns. The same was true with regard to all the ethnic minorities, Tatars, Russians, Gypsies, Lapps, without differentiation.

In a quite unique photo, in a snowy forest there is a millboard tent with an iron heating stove, the chimney on the left-hand side - and a number of soldiers are posing outside the tent. The tent is a field synagogue, "Scholka's shul", set up for the Jewish soldiers at the front beside the River Svir in Eastern Karelia. A field synagogue with a Torah Scroll was, no doubt, a very exceptional event in an Army fighting on the German side during the War.

Several Jewish soldiers were cited for bravery in action; a number of them served as company commanders and one as a captain and battalion commander; Jewish army doctors were promoted to the same officer ranks as their colleagues, inclusive of ranks of major.

During the two wars, 23 Finnish Jews were killed in action. As a tribute to their memory, their names are published annually in the Jewish Calendar of the *Bicur Cholim* Society in Helsinki.

It has been supposed that the Germans demanded the liquidation of the Jewish communities in Finland too. However, there is no evidence in favor of these claims. On the other hand, the small Jewish population of Finland was not rescued because of a "lapse of memory" among the Nazis as has sometimes been maintained. An evident confutation of this hypothesis is the case of a handful of Jewish citizens from Finland who were living in the German-occupied countries: their successful return to

Finland resulted in intense diplomatic activity between Berlin and Helsinki in the spring and summer of 1943.

It was the public conviction that "we have no Jewish Question", and the Finnish Prime Minister *J. W. Rangell* expressed such an opinion to *Heinrich Himmler* in July 1942. Consistent messages of this kind may have warned the Germans not to endanger relations with their useful brother-in-arms over an insignificant matter of little advantage to them - after final victory there would be nowhere for the Jews to escape to.

The position of Finnish Jewish soldiers was very similar to the political reality: none of the Jewish citizens of Finland refused to enter military service on the grounds of pacifism or of being Jewish. On the other hand, no instance is known of German soldiers refusing to co-operate with Finnish Jewish officers. As a rule, the attitude of Germans to Jewish soldiers in the Finnish army has been described as an "astonished" but "correct" one. The usual answer to incredulous questions put by Germans was that "there is no difference between Jews and other soldiers in the Finnish army." A number of Jewish officers were awarded German Iron Crosses, but they refused them.

Jewish soldiers were not unaware of the general anti-Semitism of Hitler's Germany, and reports of atrocities and mass murders circulated among them and their families. However, the brutality of the Holocaust did not become evident until the end of the Continuation War in the autumn of 1944. The awareness of being Finnish soldiers gave the Jews an assurance of safety even in the vicinity of German troops. At the same time, quite a number of Jewish soldiers seem to have felt the need to display that they were at least as brave soldiers as their comrades.

The complexity of comradeship with the Germans became a serious problem only after the wars, when the extent of the Holocaust was revealed. First of all, the Norwegian Jews who had suffered most during the Nazi occupation questioned the policy of the Jews in Finland. I consider that two reactions to these questions illustrate the views of the Jews in Finland quite well. A former Jewish member of the women's voluntary defense services *(lotta)* told me: "We were very surprised because of these questions. We were proud that we were also accepted to join the other Finns." Another reaction was: an association called the *Jewish War Veterans in Finland* was founded in Helsinki in 1981 During the first year of the association's activity, 84 members, more than 10 per cent of the members present in the Community, joined the association. It is self-evident that this is a most valid piece of evidence in favor of the exceptional, independent nature of the war which Finland waged on the side of Germany.

This is a short account of the Jewish citizens of Finland during the War. Another story is that of the Jewish refugees.

The persecution of Jews, launched by the National Socialists in Germany and in other countries under their influence, also brought refugees to Finland, where, however, they were received in a rather reluctant manner. In all, about 500 refugees arrived, and of these, 350 had by the summer of 1941 continued their journey to a third country, mostly to Sweden or the United States.

In contrast to the Jewish citizens of Finland, the position of the refugees turned out to be very difficult during the Continuation War. Some of the refugees were German nationals, and others had escaped to Finland from countries allied with or conquered by Germany. When the Continuation War broke out in 1941 there were about 150 Jewish refugees in Finland. They were taken to two villages in the countryside, but 43 men were sent to work camps first in southern Lapland (Salla) and then to the Isle of Suursaari (Gogland) in the Finnish Gulf.

In the autumn of 1942, Norwegian Jewry was annihilated; more than half of them (altogether 757 people) lost their lives. Most of the survivors were among those who succeeded in escaping to Sweden. As I have mentioned before, it has been supposed that the Germans demanded the liquidation of the Jewish communities in Finland. However, there is no documentary evidence in favor of these claims, either concerning the Jewish citizens or the refugees.[12]

Nevertheless, the State Police in Finland had agreed with the leaders of the Gestapo that Finland was allowed to deport the undesirable refugees to the areas occupied by the Germans. In October 1942 nine Jewish men were sent by the Finnish State Police from the Suursaari camp to Helsinki and ten Jews were arrested elsewhere in Finland. However, one of the men escorted from the Suursaari camp succeeded in sending a postcard to Mr. Abraham Stiller, a member of the Jewish community and brother of the famous stage-manager Mauritz Stiller. Stiller as well as his friends, both Jews and other Finns, made contact with various governmental and administrative organs including President

---

[12] The fate of the Jewish refugees in Finland has been the subject of lively discussion, see Elina Suominen, Kuolemanlaiva S/S Hohenhörn ('Ship of Death S/S Hohenhörn', Porvoo 1979); Taimi Torvinen, Pakolaiset Suomessa Hitlerin valtakaudella ('Refugees in Finland during the rule of Hitler', Keuruu 1984); Hannu Rautkallio, Finland and the Holocaust, the Rescue of Finland's Jews (1987).

Risto Ryti and Marshal of Finland Mannerheim.   As a result the governmental and public discussions the extradition was prevented.

However, on the 6th of October 1942, the State Police had already had five Jewish men and three (or four?) members of their families deported to the Gestapo in occupied Estonia. Officially, the men were claimed to be guilty of espionage and other criminal activities; four of them had minor offences in police records. Nineteen other persons, most of them citizens of the Soviet Union, were deported on board the same boat. The Gestapo transported the Jews to Birkenau concentration camp. Only one of these people (Georg Kollman, a former citizen of Austria) survived; after the war he immigrated to Israel.

There is no need to try and wash away the shame, but it should also not be forgotten that in October 1942, Germany was at the height of its power. After Stalingrad, it was considerably easier to say no. When after the war the victor, the Soviet Union, issued the demand that the Finnish Ingrians and other refugees be handed over to the Soviet Union, it was influential enough to get what it wanted.

Of the other refugees, Finnish citizenship was granted to 110 persons in 1943-44; some of them left the country before that or later on.

On the Finnish Independence Day, the 6th of December, in 1944, President Mannerheim, Marshal of Finland, visited the synagogue in Helsinki where the memory of the Jewish soldiers killed in action was honored. When Mannerheim died in 1951, the Jewish community raised a large sum of money which was donated to the Mannerheim Fund of Child Welfare as an expression of gratitude for the defense of the equal rights of Jews in Finland.

FRANCE

Ambassador Louis Amigues
DIRECTOR, ARCHIVES AND RECORDS
MINISTRY OF FOREIGN AFFAIRS

*Statement translated from the original French by the
U.S. Department of State Office of Language Services, Translating Division*

Intervention during the Plenary Session: Overview of Nazi-
Confiscated Art Issues

<u>Response to Speaker Ronald Lauder</u>

The French delegation was surprised to hear one of the speakers state that the French Government knew the identity of the owners of the 2,000 works of art deposited with the Museums of France at the end of the restitution campaign that permitted the return of more than 45,000 of the 61,000 works of art recovered in Germany.

I hasten to add that this statement is at odds with what we know. We will discuss that tomorrow.

However, since we are here to exchange information, I would like to ask the speaker on what information he bases his belief, and, if possible, to provide us with that information. He may rest assured that we will make the best use of it.

Press Conference by the Mattéoli Mission:

Prof. Adolphe Steg

Deputy Chairman
Fact-Finding Mission on the Looting of Jewish Assets
(Mattéoli Mission)

Opening Statement on Art Works
(Washington, December 2, 1998)

Concerning this last question, I would like to explain the Mattéoli Mission's approach to the MNR.

For several years the genealogy of these assets has been scrupulously and deeply investigated, and the results of this study are already available on the Internet.

But now the time has come within the next five months, when – due to the mandate given to us by the Government – we shall have to make proposals to the Prime Minister.

May I express some principles which guide us:

1) The MNR assets are not integrated in the national patrimony.

2) When seeking a solution (and for us a general rule in all fields) we refer ourselves only to the interest of victims. Clearly we do not protect any institution, or organization or corporation, but only the victims.

3) Finally, our mission will now begin a reflection on the definitive statute of the MNR and we will make proposals on the destination of these works of art.

Let me be clear:

When an asset will not, incontestably, be proven as a non-spoiled object, then [there] has to be a high probability of [it] being a spoliation.

GREECE

Delegation Statement

Greece became involved in the Second World War on October 28, 1940, when fascist Italy launched an unprovoked invasion from Albania. The aggressors, however, were defeated by the Greek army and thrown back into Albania. This first setback for the Axis made inevitable the assault by Nazi Germany, who came to the rescue of its Italian ally in order to safeguard its rear, pending its invasion of the Soviet Union. The Wehrmacht invaded Greece through Bulgaria on April 6, 1941, and crushed the resistance by the exhausted defenders as well as a British (and Commonwealth) expeditionary Force. By the end of that month, German troops had overrun the mainland and in May, conquered Crete against fierce resistance offered by Commonwealth forces and the local population. The tripartite (German – Italian – Bulgarian) enemy occupation lasted for 3,1/2 years, during which the exploitation of the population and the country's resources as well as the suppression of every freedom stimulated the development of a strong resistance movement. In early November 1944, the Greek mainland was free again, while several islands remained under German Occupation up to May 1945.

Greece, having actively participated in all Conferences on Holocaust issues, demonstrates a particular and continuous concern in this matter. Along with other countries, she has offered a part of its gold share to the "International Fund for needy victims of Nazi persecution", hoping that this symbolic act will be appreciated by the survivors of the Holocaust and the families of the persons who lost their life.

In the Washington Conference on "Holocaust-Era Assets," Greece focused on the following particular issues:

- the forced loan exacted from Greece during the Occupation period,
- art, archives and education issues,
- the claims presented by the Greek – Jewish Organizations.

FORCED LOAN

While in most occupied countries the annual cost of occupation corresponded to their defense appropriations before the German invasion, the size of Greece's levy was extremely high and covered requirements in excess of the direct occupation costs, even though according to the Hague Convention, the contributions levied must be in proportion to the country's resources and occupation costs cannot be charged in order to meet general war expenses or for the enrichment of the occupier. In 1941/1942, the levy represented 113,7% of the country's national income.

In addition to direct monetary contributions, the Axis also exacted large credits from the Bank of Greece for "all expenses of the war waged within the occupied country or from this country". This included German operations in the Eastern Mediterranean, North Africa, as well as the occupation of Southern Albania, which was subordinate to the German high command in Greece. Of the costs within Greece, 50% or more of the Greek payments were used for fortifications and similar "construction projects". In contrast to public German assertions that these projects were mainly for the purpose of "Greek reconstruction", the final German report admitted that no more than 1.2% were "in common German and Greek interest". Even Hitler himself stressed the point that out of the Greek payments only "the smallest part was used for the costs of occupation" but the major part was used for construction projects which were "of decisive importance for the African War", i.e., in particular for the reinforcements and supplies for the German "Africa – Corps".

The first "Forced loan" Protocol was signed in March 1942 and was subsequently amended several times during the Occupation. It stipulated that Greece was to make a monthly part – payment of 1.5 billion drachmas for both the Italian and German armies. The Bank of Greece was also obliged to advance additional funds and to open an interest – free loan account for each occupation Power for this purpose.

In this Protocol, high-ranking officials of the German and Italian Ministries of Foreign Affairs, undertook to pay back the loan to the Greek government and began doing so in 1943, thus recognizing liability to repay a debt. Thus, there is no doubt that, the loan in question was different from normal occupation levies.

What is more, internal Germans communications constantly used terms such as 'credit' and "Reichsverschuldung" (debt of the Reich). In early April 1945, the economic experts of the Former German Embassy in Athens submitted their voluminous Final report on "Economic Administration in German-occupied Greece" to the Foreign Affairs Ministry in Berlin with the explicit indication "for future use". It this report, they made serious efforts to calculate the German "debt" to Greece which they estimated as equivalent to 476 million German marks.

Since then, Greek representatives have always stressed that the forced loan extracted from Greece was not part of "regular" occupation costs and that it had to be paid back. As a loan, it could not be part of war reparations.

In the postwar years subsequent Greek governments have defended the view that Axis commitment to pay back the remaining amounts of the wartime credits was legally binding. To date, there has been no change in this position. Foreign Affairs Minister Th. Pangalos recently stated that the forced loan is a bilateral issue which remains open and pending. The claim concerning the forced loan is not related and should not be confused with the amounts which Germany has provided to Greece either by contributing to the European Union projects in Greece or within the framework of bilateral loan agreements.

With one exception, the Bonn government responded to all war claims placed and substantiated by countries, after German unification. These responses constituted either some kind of material compensation or at least the beginning of negotiations on the claims.

The only exception is Greece.

ARCHIVES, ART, EDUCATION

The fundamental elements of a national heritage are preserved in three significant aspects of culture: archives, art and education.

The preservation and accessibility to the public archives of a state is a sign of respect to history. In recent years, tremendous efforts have been made throughout Europe to improve the condition of state depositories and equip the facilities with the proper tools. In a continuous effort to accommodate historical research, the Ministry of Foreign Affairs of Greece participates in numerous research and publication efforts with other nations in Europe and also with educational institutions both in Greece and abroad.

An agreement between the United States Holocaust Memorial Museum in Washington DC, and the Service of the Historical Archives of the Hellenic Ministry regarding the exchange of archival records is currently being negotiated. This agreement, as well as the recent publication of the Ministry of Foreign Affairs (Documents on the History of the Greek Jews), indicates the perseverance of the Greek State to seek historical truth.

In this context special attention should be paid to the continuing efforts of the Jewish Community of Thessaloniki seeking to repatriate the archival collection of the community which was violently transported by the Germans during the war, and found only recently in Russia. The records depict the communal history of the Jews of Thessaloniki from 1870 until 1942. It is an important heirloom for one of the oldest Jewish communities in Europe and should therefore be repatriated.

Art and architecture demonstrate the spirit and the philosophy of a nation. Both are visual indicators of a time past, and the cultural reminders of an "ethnos". The artifacts looted or destroyed during the Second World War by the occupying forces are too numerous to mention here. The occupation forces vandalized classical and Byzantine monuments, transporting parts or entire structures while looting icons, library collections and heirlooms. The losses are staggering. 19 large Byzantine churches, monasteries, museums and libraries were destroyed. 26 illegal archeological excavations were carried out by Italian and German archeologists. Artifacts from 42 museums were looted and transported abroad by the Germans, while their Italian counterparts looted 33 museums and the Bulgarians 9. The damages were staggering, while the scars of the destruction are still visible on the surviving monuments of Classical and Byzantine Greece.

The most important element of cultural preservation is the continuous effort to preserve history alive through education. Greece, the cradle of civilization, a country which witnessed the birth of contemporary sciences, supports today the advancement of research and education. On a regular basis, Greece signs new agreements and renews older protocols of bilateral educational programs with nations interested in the exchange of cultural information. Most recently Greece signed such an agreement with the State of Israel. This four-year program calls for a collaborative effort in the educational, scientific and cultural fields.

This initiative aims, among others, to disseminate knowledge and information regarding unknown aspects of both the Jewish and Greek history.

CLAIMS OF THE GREEK JEWISH ORGANIZATIONS

The Greek Jewish Organizations, through the Greek Ministry of Foreign Affairs, presented at the Washington Conference memoranda stating the losses caused to their property between 1941 and 1944 by the German Occupation Authorities, their claims for restitution of property found anywhere in the world and financial restitution for property that cannot be found anymore.

1.   The Jewish Community of Thessaloniki stated that the German Occupation Authorities completely destroyed the Jewish Cemetery of the city where graves were untouched since 1492, constituting a treasure of historical and archeological information. Thus the historical memory of generations of Jews, who lived and died in Thessaloniki, was forever lost. The value of the building materials (marble slabs, bricks etc.) contained in the cemetery was estimated at that time to one hundred thousand (100,000) gold English sovereigns, while the historical memory lost is beyond estimation.

2.   The Jewish Community of Thessaloniki claimed that the German Authorities, under the supervision of Dr. J. Pohl, Director of the Jewish Department of the Library of Frankfurt plundered systematically Communal libraries namely:

a.   The Library of the Religious Tribunal (Beth-Din), containing approximately 2,500 volumes of rare editions.

b.   The Library of the Community Schools' Teachers, with about 600 volumes of reference books, etc.

c.   The Library of the Monastirioton Synagogue, that included exclusively books of religious and hieronomic interest.

d.   The Library of the Religious Establishment Haimoutcho Kovo located on 8, Menexe st. and of its annex on 74, Queen Olga Avenue, to which the personal libraries of its founder, the Great Rabbi Haim Asher Kovo, and the precious library of Chief Rabbi Asher Kovo had been added.

e.   The 250 manuscripts of the Holy Jewish Law (Pentateuque) treasured in the city's Synagogue, many of which had been brought from Spain in 1492.

3.   The Jewish Community of Thessaloniki claimed that the German Occupation Authorities had confiscated its archives and transported them to Germany. These archives, considered lost for many years, surfaced in Moscow three years ago. The Jewish Community of Thessaloniki demands its archives back.

4. The Jewish Community of Thessaloniki finally claimed that it was obliged to pay to the German Occupation Authorities the sum of 150,000 gold French Francs, in order to ensure to exception from compulsory civilian work of 1,000 of its poorest members, who were not able to meet this amount, and the sum of 1,900,000,000 Drachmas (DM 50,000,000) in order to liberate the rest of its members from compulsory civilian work. The Jews excepted from compulsory civilian work were, nevertheless, transported to the extermination camps in Poland and Germany and were exterminated in gas chambers.

5. The Central Board of Jewish Communities in Greece claimed that the sum of 1,700,000 gold English Sovereigns has been plundered from Greek Jews and that this sum must be restituted to its legal owners or their inheritors.

HUNGARY

Delegation Statement

I. HOLOCAUST-ERA ART ISSUES IN HUNGARY

Hungary took part in World War II as an ally of Germany. From March 19, 1944, however, the country was occupied by the Nazis. In October the Hungarian government attempted to achieve a cease-fire and so withdraw from the war, but these efforts were hampered by a pro-German fascist puppet government that came to power. Persecution of Jews proliferated and the confiscation of Jewish property took place only from March 1944 to April 1945. A Government Commission for the Registration and Safeguarding of Art Works taken from Jews was rapidly set up, whose activity was a cover-up for the sequestration of the art treasures of Hungarian Jews. These treasures were then - with a few exception - transported to Germany. There was a so-called Hungarian gold train with two trucks at the end of World War II, full with gold, jewelry, precious stones and a large amount of artifacts looted from Jews, and which were never returned to Hungary. We do not know anything about their fate.

It should be mentioned that after January 20, 1945 a Hungarian democratic government was established and Hungarian armed forces, allied with the Soviet troops, fought against the Nazis. After the war a body of specialists was established called Ministerial Commission for Art Works Taken from Private and Public Collections, which collected data on art assets with the aim of their restitution. The control over the country was later fully overtaken by communists with the support of the Soviet Union. The communist dictatorship was broken for a very short time by the 1956 revolution, a new democratic era started with the system change of 1989. The free elections of a new government paved the way to the genuine examination of World War II losses and reparations together with compensations for communist era injustices.

A significant portion of all cultural property found was returned to Holocaust survivors. However, a vast number of cultural assets are still missing: pieces of the Hatvani Collection. An important fraction of the looted objects – consisting of 152 works of art – have been identified in Moscow, the Hungarian origin of which was also acknowledged by the Russian authorities. Among them we can find invaluable paintings from collections of Hungarian Holocaust victims. The return of these objects is blocked by the Russian attitude of indifference towards international norms on restitution and also by the uncertain situation of their restitution law.

In the early 1990s the Hungarian government initiated a scientific research program, which has already resulted in a database containing over 60,000 items of art treasures lost during World War II and in its immediate aftermath. A publication containing the data and – if available – the picture of the 1000 most important pieces under the title: Sacco di Budapest, 1938-1949 - Depredation of Hungary, 1938-1949 has been put out recently.

The situation of how restitution was handled in Hungary under the Communist Era and after the political change during the past 50 years can be illustrated by the statements of two prominent U.S. personalities:

In 1996 at a hearing before the COMMISSION ON SECURITY AND COOPERATION IN EUROPE the Honorable Christopher Smith, presiding Chairman of the Commission characterized the approach of the Communist Government as follows:

> "In some places, such as Hungary, the government was required by the 1947 Paris Peace Treaty to restitute Jewish property, but the Communists ignored this obligation. Not only was justice denied for Holocaust survivors, but Communist regimes perpetrated their own brand of injustice and, in fact, were infamous for their complete disregard for private property..."

Under Secretary of State, The Honorable STUART E. EIZENSTAT, formulated at the same hearing as follows:

Hungary "is a good example of what a government can do when it puts its mind to it. The Hungarian Government has been very forward-thinking in its restitution program, and I have been impressed by their determination to resolve both communal and private property issues. It has accepted its obligations under the 1947 Paris Peace Treaty, and a 1993 Constitutional Court decision to provide fair compensation for those who lost their property in the Holocaust and afterwards is being honored."

And now, in the Sunday Times about restitution funds:

"The model here is Hungary, it established a special foundation with accountability and management" of the properties in question.

Still, certain criticism has been formulated by Hungarian and foreign observers about the Hungarian museums' approach towards some of their acquisitions during the early years of the Communist Era. Museums keep works of art – among others former property of Holocaust victims – the provenance of which is poorly documented. Some of these cultural objects are registered as unclear deposits, some others as part of the basic collection of the museum. In fact, it is one of the museum's most important missions to safeguard its holdings from being sold or alienated until unlawful ownership has not been proved incontestably.

In order to clarify what happened with some obscure acquisitions in Hungary, as a first step the Minister for Cultural Heritage has sent out a letter to museums and their authorities, in which he instructs – or if not entitled, he requests – museum directors to conduct a review of their inventory books and list out ambiguous items. As a next step a research team will examine the circumstances under which these cultural objects were placed to the museum.

The Hungarian government is fully committed to the restitution or compensation of Holocaust victims concerning cultural assets. For managing this complex task - which includes scholarly research, political decision making, bill drafting, and negotiations with representatives of foreign states, contacts with Holocaust survivors, etc. – a state commissioner will be designated.

II. EDUCATION

There is almost no family in Hungary which was not affected by the Holocaust either as victim or as witness or helper. Everyone knows what did what made Raoul Wallenberg, who saved thousands of Jews in the most dangerous times. The Jewish Institution and documentation centers have been working hard on revealing darkness about the horror of the Holocaust.

After World War II, there were made some scientific researches on Holocaust, but soon the Communists came to power, this scientific researched banned by them. István Bibó must be mentioned, who published several papers about the roots of the anti-Semitism and the democratic movements in Hungary. As the revolutionary changes came in 1989, serious historical research was started about the Holocaust. A thorough investigation could be made in the archives. Now the Hungarian archives are open to carry out such a research, and the newly-signed agreement enables Israel to get admission into these archives under organized circumstances. There is another successful historical research in Hungary, which can be demonstrated by many new volumes of selected documents and memoirs. More films were made in the last few years, than had been made during the proceeding decades. We should mention the document film, 'The Message of Elie Wiesel" made in 1996, Hungary's participation at the Baltimore Jewish Film Festival ("The Memoirs of a River") or at the Washington Jewish Film Festival, both held this year. The above-mentioned film of Judit Elek, "The Memoirs of a River" demonstrates not only the ultimate victory of Truth and Justice, but also the internal harmony and peaceful coexistence of Jews and Christians in Hungary.

Hungary has surely much to do for the better knowledge of the Holocaust Era in the field of education; Hungary is ready to do it. We have to emphasize that the Holocaust was part of the basic knowledge of the history taught in the Hungarian schools during the last 50 years, as it is now. The National Curriculum mentions the Holocaust several times, and it is implied in our schoolbooks. The high school history books consistently deal with the subject of the Hungarian anti-Semitism, including the special laws against Jews. There are several writers and poets of Jewish origin who became victims of the Holocaust and now their achievement is also part of the education. On the basis of an agreement with the Yad Vashem Institute every year 30 teachers can take part in a course in Jerusalem to study the best methods of Holocaust education.

Definite steps are to be taken in the frame of human rights, at the same time regarding the recent ethnical and historical challenges. The Department of Judaism at the Budapest University and the Department of Romology at the Pécs University are of great importance for both research and education. The Hungarian exposition in Auschwitz will be renewed in 1999.

To demonstrate its deep conviction regarding Holocaust education and remembrance, the Hungarian Government has adopted a resolution on establishing the Public Foundation of the Holocaust Research and Documentation Center. This Foundation together with one or more similar institutions will move to the oldest synagogue in Budapest to achieve their purposes more effectively. The execution of this and other resolution will testify the government's concern for Holocaust victims.

ISRAEL

Delegation Statement

Following the defeat of the Nazis, a majority of Holocaust survivors immigrated to Israel, where they and their families account for one-sixth of the Jewish population. The State of Israel, the Jewish State, sees itself as the central representative of the survivors and their offspring and is dedicated to achieving justice on their behalf and to the remembrance of the Holocaust.

Israel's delegation to this Conference welcomes efforts by other governments to obtain such justice. In particular, we would like to acknowledge the role of Great Britain and the United States, the initiators and chairs of the London and Washington Conferences on Holocaust Era Assets. The Government of Israel also wishes to express its appreciation to the Swedish Government for initiating an international effort to promote worldwide education about the Holocaust in cooperation with the United States, United Kingdom, Germany and Israel. We welcome the agreements reached so far regarding the settlement of claims from the Holocaust period, and we look forward to achieving similar agreements with other parties.

The matter of Jewish assets is not merely a material issue; it is a moral imperative. "Thou shalt not steal" appears in the same Decalogue with the injunction against murder. There is no adequate compensation for the loss of life, but justice must be sought for the Jewish communities and individuals that were despoiled.

Compensation must also be sought for the men and women turned into slave laborers, whose bodies were violated for profit. All civilized nations outlaw slavery and whomever exploits slave labor must provide reparations for this heinous crime.

People or institutions who knowingly acquired looted property should pay restitution. We appeal to financial institutions such as banks and insurance companies to accept responsibility for their Holocaust era clients. This also applies to those who acquired art works and ritual objects looted from homes and houses of worship. Though these items may have passed through a number of hands, the original owners have an indisputable claim to what is rightfully theirs.

We welcome the openness and the cooperation of the countries researching the facts regarding property seized during the Holocaust. We note with satisfaction that many countries have established commissions to investigate their own past. We join the initiative to persuade all countries, groups and individuals to allow immediate and unrestricted access to all archival and state archive materials relevant to the period. This applies especially to church records and archives of private concerns, corporations and individuals, as well as documentation not stored in archives. Any entity that withholds information from public access compounds the indifference and crimes of the past.

We sincerely hope that the International Task Force on Holocaust Education, Research and Remembrance will succeed in promoting worldwide awareness of the horrors of the Holocaust and help combat racism, anti-Semitism, Holocaust denial and ethnic hatred.

Israel supports and recognizes the World Jewish Restitution Organization (WJRO) as the umbrella organization which works in close cooperation with the State of Israel, to represent the Jewish people in matters of restitution.

The Israeli delegation wishes to express its support for the Roma to receive material compensation for they, too, were victims of the hatred and murder which occurred during the Holocaust.

The Israeli delegation commits itself to full cooperation with all governments and non-governmental organization in an effort to uncover the truth, promote humanitarian solidarity and accord justice to the victims of the Holocaust and their heirs. Together with Yad Vashem, (the central institution of Remembrance, Education, and Research on the Holocaust) and with others, Israel will work to effect the widest dissemination of knowledge about the Holocaust, its prelude, its aftermath and its lessons for all humanity.

ITALY

Monetary Gold and Italian Participation in the International Fund for Needy Victims of Nazi Persecution

Statement by
Minister Franco Tempesta
HEAD OF DELEGATION

Following the conclusion of the Tripartite Committee's work, which enabled Italy to receive one last quota of monetary gold, the Italian authorities began the procedures to participate in the Fund established at the Federal Reserve Bank aimed at offering financial support to needy victims of Nazi persecution.

The contribution made available by the Italian Government is a value almost equivalent to the monetary gold withdrawn on the eve of the conclusion of the Tripartite Committee's mandate. The amount in Italian Lire is 12 million (approximately 7.2 million dollars).

Another goal pursued by the Italian Government was to identify a non-governmental organization able to distribute the sum according to the rules contained in the founding statute of the Fund for needy victims of Nazi persecution. The "Unione delle Comunita' ebraiche italiane" (Union of the Italian Jewish Community) was chosen because they offered to carry out the task for those entitled to benefits.

In order to allocate said sum for the aforementioned Fund the Italian Government approved an ad hoc Bill for the appropriation of the indicated amount.

The proposed Bill is now being considered by Parliament where no specific difficulties are expected for its passage.

In compliance with the rules of the Fund I would like to provide the British Government and account holder the information pertaining to the aforementioned NGO, in order to obtain its inclusion in the list of Organizations:

> Unione Comunita' ebraiche italiane
> Presidente Professor Amos Luzzatto
> Lungotever Sanzio, 9 – 00153 ROMA
> Telephone: ++39 06 5803667
>   ++39 06 5803670
> Telefax: ++39 06 589969

Research Issues

Statement by
Minister Franco Tempesta
HEAD OF DELEGATION

I understand there will not be time for discussion.

I would just like to inform that the Italian Prime Minister yesterday officially formalized the creation of our national Commission for research on the economic and financial aspects of racial persecutions.

In this Commission the following will be represented:

> Office of the Prime Minister
> Ministry of Foreign Affairs
> Ministry of the Interior, on which depends the
State Archives
> Association of Italian Banks
> The Union of Italian Jewish Communities
> The Jewish Documentation Center
> A number of historians
> Other entities and/or NGO will bed invited, if
necessary

The Commission will work in close cooperation with similar bodies from other countries.

Education

Statement by
Minister Franco Tempesta
HEAD OF DELEGATION

Break-out Session on Holocaust Education, Remembrance and
Research

Since 1996 the Italian Ministry for Education has started to update the history teaching in High Schools in order to offer a deeper knowledge of the historical period between the two World Wars and the last fifty years.

In particular, teachers and students are now following together an historical itinerary named "The XX Century: The Young Generations and Memory" which includes works and research on racism, persecutions, deportations, and fascist racial laws.

To financially support this program, the budget of the Ministry of Education has been granted an amount of 3,5 billion liras (approximately 2 million dollars) by the Government to train teachers, and a further amount of 1 billion liras (approximately 600,000 dollars) to finance partially or totally visits by high school students attending the last year (generally young people 17 – 18 years of age) to the sites of the Holocaust.

Within this program – thanks to State financing – 300 students from various Rome High Schools traveled last October to Auschwitz, accompanied by their history teachers and by survivors belonging to the Italian Association of Deportees.

A number of similar trips are currently being organized. I understand there will not be time for discussion.

LATVIA

Delegation Statement

Latvia positively evaluates the Conference on Nazi Gold that took place in London in December 1997 and during which an announcement was made on the establishment of a special compensation fund for Holocaust survivors. To assist victims of Nazi persecution, Latvia fully supports the establishment of this fund and has taken a decision to contribute to the fund.

To promote awareness of the historic truth, in November of this year a commission of historians was established in Latvia. The main goal of the Commission is to carry out research in respect of the tragic events in Latvian history from 1939 through 1991. The Commission will encourage and promote research about deportations that were carried out in Latvia during the Nazi and Soviet occupations. It will address and highlight issues associated with the terrible legacy of the Holocaust in Latvia and the fate of Latvian Jews in the wake of those tragic years.

Regarding the issue of restitution of Jewish property, Latvia is convinced that return of property to its lawful owners is one of the most important aspects of a democratic society. Latvia considers that the issue of restitution of the Jewish property confiscated during World War 11 is of particular importance. The laws adopted in Latvia that regulate the process of property restitution are among the most liberal in the countries of Central and Eastern Europe, and ensure the restitution of property to lawful owners or their heirs regardless of their present place of residence or citizenship.

Latvia consistently carries out return of the property confiscated from Jews to its former owners and to date property rights on most pieces of property have been restituted. Latvia is aware of the unquestionable ties of Jewish organizations with religion and the Latvian government will continue the process of property restitution in accordance with the already existing state legislation. Presently arrangements are being made to establish the Council on Jewish Communities and Parishes of Latvia which could become the coordinating institution in respect of Jewish property restitution. In an effort to collect data on pieces of property that were confiscated from Latvian Jews, the Latvian State History Archive has informed the Latvian Ministry of Foreign Affairs that the archive has more than 3000 files related to the Holocaust and properties confiscated from Jews.

Latvia is aware of the need to give particular attention to Holocaust education and the necessity of teaching about the Holocaust at schools. To this end, the curricula that have been worked out in Latvia contain the subject of the Holocaust and books and other schooling materials about the Holocaust are being composed and published in Latvia.

Latvia recognizes the importance of the issues discussed during the 1997 London conference on Nazi Gold and during the preparatory seminar that was held in June 1998 in Washington and is ready to take active participation to address and solve issues related to contributions to the Holocaust survivors' fund, property restitution, the work of the historical commission, Holocaust education as well as lend assistance to solve issues relating to art, insurance and other assets.

Maintaining good relations among the various ethnic minorities in Latvia has always been of prime importance for Latvian government. Ever since the restoration of Latvia's independence, the government of Latvia has provided assistance to the Jewish community in Latvia to help them solve issues related to the Holocaust legacy. By doing so the Latvian government has committed itself to bolster the existing friendly relations with the Latvian Jewry.

LUXEMBOURG

Delegation Statement

GERMAN MEASURES TAKEN AGAINST JEWS AND EMIGRANTS

When German troops invaded Luxembourg on the morning of May 10th, 1940, some 3700 Jews are believed to have stayed in Luxembourg. About 1000 of them were of Luxembourg nationality. Some 2000 were refugees from Germany and other countries occupied by Germany after 1937. Most of the 700 remaining Jews were immigrants from Eastern Europe and stateless.

The night before the invasion a certain number of Jews had been informed that the invasion was imminent and so they were able to leave the country ahead of the German troops. 50000 Luxembourgers were evacuated to the south of France as their towns and villages were situated just in front of the Maginot-Line which the Germans prepared to attack. Some 1500 Jews left Luxembourg with these evacuees. In the following months under military administration some 600 Jews were able to emigrate from Luxembourg. So some 1700 to 2000 Jews were still living in Luxembourg when Gauleiter Gustav Simon was appointed Head of civil administration (*Chef der Zivilverwaltung, CdZ*) and hand in hand with the Gestapo started his anti-Semitic policy.

The German decrees taken against the Jews at the beginning of September 1940[1] brought into force the « Nuremberg Laws » as well as the discriminatory economic measures of 1938. The situation of the Luxembourg Jews was then identical to that of Jews in Germany.

The decree dated September 5th, 1940[2] concerning Jewish fortunes required every Jew living in Luxembourg to make a detailed declaration of his fortune[3]. Jews of foreign nationality had to give

---

[1] VOBl. 1940, Nr.2, pp.10-11: Verordnung über Maßnahmen auf dem Gebiet des Judenrechts.
[2] VOBl. 1940, Nr.2, pp.11-13: Verordnung über das jüdische Vermögen.
[3] Archives nationales, Luxembourg (ANLux): Consistoire israélite: Files 76-81: Déclarations de fortune.

indications on their fortune situated in Luxembourg only. All shares, coupons and bonds were to be deposited at a bank. All Jews had to inform their banks of their « being Jewish ». The banks were to provide lists of all Jewish accounts for the German administration. Nearly every economic activity where a Jew was involved was liable to a special authorization. Jews could be forced to sell their firms if the Germans decided so. Paragraph 7 forbade Jews of Luxembourg or German nationality to buy, to give as a security or to sell objects in gold, platinum or silver, precious stones and pearls as well as any work of art worth more than 1000 RM.

For the period pertaining from September 1940 to December 1940 the Germans in charge of recording and administrating Jewish assets apparently showed incapable of avoiding corruption and looting by Party members and other German officials active in Luxembourg. So in order to have the organized robbing of Jewish assets being implemented in an orderly way, *Gauleiter* Simon had to reorganize this section of his administration in December 1940.

On December 12th, 1940 he announced the creation of a new section in his administration (*Abteilung IVa*), « *Verwaltung des jüdischen und Emigranten- Vermögens* » (administration of Jewish and emigrants' fortune). A party member, *Gauinspekteur* Josef Ackermann, was put in charge of this section[4]. The same day an announcement obliged everyone in Luxembourg to inform section IVa of all acquisitions or donations they had received from Jews since May 10th.

By his decree dated February 7th, 1941[5] the CdZ put under German administration all the property of Jews and other emigrants from the day of their (forced) emigration. Furthermore he reserved the right to confiscate this property. The decree was applicable retroactively to May 10th, 1940. Thus, as soon as Jews left Luxembourg, taking with them an allowed maximum of 50 kg of luggage, their property fell into the hands of the Germans. Two months later the property of Jewish people still living in Luxembourg was also confiscated by the CdZ[6]. Section Iva

---

[4] Luxemburger Zeitung, 12/12/1940.

[5] VOBl. 1941, Nr. 12, p.90: Verordnung über Maßnahmen betreffend das Emigranten- und Judenvermögen.

[6] VOBl. 1941, Nr.31, p.208: Durchführungsverordnung zur Verordnung über Maßnahmen betreffend das Emigranten-und Judenvermögen vom 7.Februar 1941.

confiscated all Jewish property, but no report mentions expressly the gold confiscated from the Jews[7].

The property belonging to Jewish associations and communities was confiscated and administered by the « *Stillhaltekommissar* », a party authority. The synagogues in the cities of Luxembourg and Esch/Alzette were demolished and the ground transferred to the municipalities.

On October 1st, 1940 all Jewish bank accounts were blocked and the account holder was allowed to withdraw a maximum of 250 RM. per month. As many Jews were no longer permitted to have a regular income, they were forced to sell their furniture and other belongings in order to prepare for emigration or to buy some food. This situation got worse the longer the Jews stayed in Luxembourg under these circumstances. Those who were deported in 1942 and 1943 were in fact already robbed of all their belongings.

From October 15th, 1941, when the first train of deportation to Lodz left Luxembourg, the Gestapo began to confiscate systematically certain objects from the Jews: bicycles, cameras, films, magnifying glasses, binoculars, typewriters, fur coats, skis and ski boots, gramophones, electrical devices such as heating stoves, hotplates, Hoovers, hairdryers, etc. Radios had been confiscated already in October 1940.

All these things were sold and the money transferred to the German administration in Luxembourg.

The furniture was mainly sold to Germans who had it shipped to Germany, very often giving false names on the sales contracts.

ARYANIZATION OF THE ECONOMY

The aryanization of the Luxembourg economy had come to an end by 1943. At this time not only had all the Jews been deported, but the proceedings to exclude Jewish influence from Luxembourg economy had been concluded. 350 businesses engaged in industry, crafts or trade had been traced in September 1940. 1380 houses and buildings as well as 150 ha of land had been registered as Jewish property.

In the summer of 1941 more than 75% of the businesses had been or were on the point of being liquidated, i.e. wound up by a

---

[7] ANLux: Consistoire israélite: Files 7, 11:Receipts for confiscated jewellery, silver cutlery and savings bank-books.

provisional administrator, who had sold off assets, paid off liabilities and had the company removed from the company register.

31 businesses had been aryanized and 52 were left under provisional administration. The aryanization proved to be rather difficult as Luxembourgers were not ready to buy Jewish property. Some who did so, did it to preserve the best interest of the victims and returned the business to its rightful owner after the war.

Finally the German administration got some 20 millions of RM out of the liquidation and aryanization.

The same procedures were applied to Luxembourgers who were considered as enemies of the Reich. From January 1944 to August 1944 for instance some 380 procedures of dispossession were brought to conclusion.

INSURANCE COMPANIES

In the thirties some 34 insurance companies were active in Luxembourg, mainly as subsidiaries of larger Western European companies (French or Belgian, but also some Swiss and British). Their policies were sold by Luxembourg insurance agents. Three of the companies were local insurance companies, created after World War I. (*Le Foyer, La Luxembourgeoise, Terra*). After W.W.I the German economic influence in Luxembourg diminished and so there were nearly no German insurance companies active in Luxembourg.

They covered all the risks usual at that time, mainly: life insurance, fire insurance, insurance against theft, third party insurance, comprehensive insurance, car insurance, etc.

After the occupation of Luxembourg the Germans tried to gain control over the insurance business as well as other economic sectors. In a first step the main goal was to eliminate all French, Belgian or British, later also American, influence on Luxembourg economy. So when the Germans decided to reorganize the insurance business, they first decreed[8], that all authorizations that had been granted the insurance companies by the Luxembourg government were withdrawn retroactively to May 10th, 1940. An exception was made for the three local companies. Any new company wishing to write out insurance policies in Luxembourg needed a special authorization by the *Chef der*

---

[8]   VOBl. 1941, p.197: Verordnung über die Regelung des Individualversicherungswesens in Luxemburg vom 5.April 1941.

Zivilverwaltung. This did not put an end to any individual insurance policy. The portfolios of those companies whose authorizations had been withdrawn were managed by companies selected by the CdZ. In fact this meant that German insurance companies managed the portfolios of the French, Belgian and British companies. Two Swiss companies *Zürich* and *Basler* were also authorized to manage policies from other companies as well as to continue their own business.

By another decree dated November 8th, 1941[9], the CdZ created a "Public   Life   insurance   company"   (*Öffentliche Lebensversicherungsanstalt*) and a "Public insurance company" (*Öffentliche Sachversicherungsanstalt*) that took over all the Belgian, French and British insurance policies. From December 1st, 1941 the three Luxembourg insurance companies lost their authorization and their portfolios went over to the newly created Public insurance companies[10]. Some 30 German companies and three Swiss companies (*La Fédérale, Zürich* and *Basler*) were authorized to take up or continue their business in Luxembourg.

In fact, except for the three Swiss companies, the whole insurance business in Luxembourg was thus transferred into German hands.

With regard to life insurance policies of Jewish citizens the situation in Luxembourg was identical to the situation in Germany. The policies were confiscated by the German authorities who got the money out of them.

ART

When the German administration took over Jewish and emigrant property they found a certain number of works of art they were interested in. All these works of art had to be sent to the *Aussenstelle des Gaupropagandaamtes in Luxemburg* which took care of these objects. Unfortunately little is still known about these transactions and there are no lists of works of art taken from private homes. Our information

---

[9] VOBL. 1941, p.471: Verordnung über die Errichtung einer Oeffentlichen Lebensversicherungsanstalt in Luxemburg vom 8.November 1941. Verordnung über die Errichtung einer Oeffentlichen Sachversicherungsanstalt in Luxemburg vom 8.November 1941.
[10] VOBl. 1941, p.475: 3. Verordnung über die Regelung des Individualversicherungswesens in Luxemburg vom 8.November 1941.

indicates that art dealers in Luxembourg and in the Rhineland sold these works of art, but we lack clear evidence.

As for public collections the situation is somewhat different. First as Luxembourg was meant to become a part of Greater Germany there was no need to loot art and take it to German museums. Second the Luxembourg national Museum did not have in its collections works of art of the class that could be of great interest to the Germans. There was one notable exception, the « Reiffers collection » from which the Germans « bought » some paintings for the *Führer*-collection in Linz.

The collections of the Grand Ducal Family were confiscated in the same way and transferred to Germany. Joseph Bech, the Minister of Foreign affairs, saw his paintings and a very important library disappear somewhere in Germany.

A certain number of files were confiscated in the offices of the Ministry of Foreign Affairs and sent to Berlin.

RESTITUTION AFTER THE WAR

When Luxembourg was liberated on September 10th, 1944, the Government in exile had already had enough information on plundering and looting and consequently they had taken measures to grant restitution of plundered property to the rightful owners.

A decree of April 22, 1941[11] declared forced sales null and void. Buyers should report their purchases. All confiscations were likewise declared null and void.

After the Government returned to Luxembourg the *Office des Séquestres* put under sequestration all the property owned by Germans and Italians as well as that of collaborators. Together with the *Office des Dommages de guerre* they were responsible for all restitution questions. All claims were to be sent to these authorities.

In insurance business this meant that according to a decree of September 1944 the *Office des Séquestres* returned the insurance portfolios to the former owners, the Luxembourg and foreign (Belgian, French and British) insurance companies. If any money was claimed by insurance companies, the *Office des Séquestres* paid out the lost sums. The German companies were liquidated by the same authority, and no

---

[11] Mémorial, Journal officiel du Grand-Duché de Luxembourg (Montréal), 1941, N°2, p.5.

German company was given an authorization to resume its activity in Luxembourg until 1959.

Bank accounts that had been confiscated were reconstituted at the expense of the *Office des Dommages de guerre* if there was such a claim.

The 1950 compensation law[12] restricted any compensation to Luxembourg nationals who had been victims of nazi persecution for patriotic reasons. This excluded all those who had been victims of nazi persecution for racial, religious or political reasons: Communists, Jews, homosexuals, witnesses of Jehovah etc. When Germany paid some 12 million DM in 1959 to the Luxembourg Government to compensate nazi victims, this money was used to compensate people that had been excluded on the terms of the 1950 law.

Communal and private property that had been confiscated by Germany was returned to their rightful owners. The synagogues in Luxembourg-city and Esch/Alzette were rebuilt.

Luxembourg was not able to send specialists to Germany to identify the works of art that had been taken from the country. So the Belgian *Mission de Récupération* included the missing works of art in its own lists and managed to bring back to Luxembourg some 50% of what was missing. Neither private libraries, nor any archival material were returned to Luxembourg at that time.

Luxembourg is ready to join the international efforts for truth and justice.

Therefore we will work to open the archives in order to document plunder and looting as well as restitution and compensation.

Luxembourg is aware of the need to pay particular attention to Holocaust education.

Efforts should be made to teach about the Holocaust especially young people, but also those immigrants from countries not involved in World War II.

Luxembourg is committed to fighting anti-Semitism and racial hatred, especially against the misuse of the Internet for these purposes.

---

[12] Mémorial, Journal officiel du Grand-Duché de Luxembourg, 1950, p.509: Loi concernant l'indemnisation des dommages de guerre.

MACEDONIA

The Last Jews of Macedonia: Extermination and Pillage

By
Ivan Dejanov and Samuel Sadikario
MACEDONIAN ACADEMY OF SCIENCES AND ARTS
SKOPJE, REPUBLIC OF MACEDONIA

There are documents on the presence of Jews in Macedonia from the 6th century, B.C. (Rosanes), who came here from Persia. Those comprise the first Jewish settlements in Europe. The diaspora brought masses of other Jews (during Alexander the Great, and the Roman Empire), who are known as Romaniots, and many known families remained in Macedonia until the Holocaust. The most numerous population and the culture came from Spain and Portugal (1492 and 1498 respectively), bringing the highest level of civilization and culture in these territories. We always stress the fact that in Macedonia and other Slavophonic countries, the Jews brought with themselves the Bible, Judaism, Christianity, the alphabet and part of the Jewish fate.

All of the Judaism in Macedonia has gone with the Holocaust. The last 7,148 Macedonian Jews were arrested and gathered by the Bulgarian Army on March 11, 1943, and transported to Treblinka, where they were exterminated. This number comprises 98% of the Jewish population at that time, which rate is incomparable with any other, except maybe in Northern Greece and Trakia. Very few survivors have joined the Resistance movement, but also many of them have lost their lives in the battles. Documents about the history of the Macedonian Holocaust are collected by the Macedonian Academy of Sciences and Arts and the Macedonian Archives. They are published by Zamila Kolonomos and Vera Vangeli (Macedonian Academy of Sciences and Arts, including a detailed list of those deported in Treblinka, performed by the German administration), and some historical data are published by Alexander Matkovski in Macedonia, some Jewish authors from Bulgaria

(Aaron Assa, Harry Nisimov) and former Yugoslavia (Zeni Lebl) in Israel.

As the SS Nazi troops stormed through former Yugoslavia (April 6th, 1941) to invade Greece, they delivered most of the Macedonian territories to the Bulgarian occupation forces who remained in those territories until the end of the World War II in 1945. A few months just before the occupation, the Bulgarian government issued the "Law for Protection of the Nation" signed by the King Boris III on January 21, 1941, and it was immediately operative in Macedonia. Escalation of the restrictive measures and chauvinism was introduced through successive series of additional restrictive laws. According to the claim of Riebbentrop (Nazi-German minister of foreign affairs), King Boris III approved initial deportation of 20,000 Jews to the Nazi concentration camps, mainly persons from the occupied territories and communists or socialists.

On March 11, 1943 all Jews from Macedonia were gathered on the temporary concentration camp "Monopol" in Skopje. The conditions of living were horrible, including minimal food and water, with no bathroom and toilette, with no heating (the winter was exceptionally severe that year). Towards the end of March and the beginning of April 1943, three convoys with Jews were sent to Treblinka. In each carriage there were around 80 persons, in standing positions, some of them without windows. Not a single person came back from Treblinka. In Bulgaria, although many of the Jews were arrested (some 5,000 died during that act, and in the labor camps), some were spared from deportation and extermination, thanks mainly to the organized protests of the Bulgarian people and ethnic Macedonians, the Orthodox Church and some MP's. Many ethnic Macedonians took the first initiative and had the crucial part in the organization and participation of the protests (as stated by the Bulgarian writer Harry Nisimov and Aaron Assa):

"For hundreds of years the Macedonian and Jewish peoples have lived together as brothers in misfortunes, suffering and destiny. We have the same enemies. Therefore our struggle against them should be identical /The Macedonian Liberation Front, end of 1942/....There is indisputable evidence that several prominent members of the Macedonian movement in Bulgaria, in the town of Kjustendil to be precise, played a decisive role in saving Bulgarian Jews from extermination in Poland" (Aaron Assa).

Anti-Semitism and anti-Macedonism have been practiced in certain countries for centuries. The very basic principles of moral and social ecology are treated constantly, mainly in the same European countries. We do believe in the hope of U.S. Sen. Daniel Inouye (D-Hawaii), "The Chief Rabbi" in the U.S. Senate and Congress, that the concentration camps and Holocaust will not happen again; to have this security, "the vigilance is not enough, we need active participation" (U.S. Sen. Daniel Inouye). (U.S. Sen. Daniel Inouye was confined in a concentration camp himself and was in the unit of the American Army that first came in contact with a concentration camp and liberated it /Dahau/).

For more than two and a half millennia, Jews and Macedonians have lived a life of tolerance, peace, mutual help, friendship and understanding. During many centuries both Jews and Macedonians were under the vitriolic pressure of assimilation and prosecution: Babylonians, Persians, Romans, Byzantinians and many rulers of European empires were seeking to obliterate the Jewish and Macedonian identity of the People and the Land (e.g., the name of the Jewish Land was changed by Romans to Palestina, after the long-vanished Philistines, an Aegean people, the name of Jerusalem was changed to Aelia Capitolina). For some of our neighbors, the name and the identity of Macedonians are questionable even now! The name of Macedonia was changed several times in the last two and a half millennia. And in spite of all possible forms of intolerance, hatred, prosecution, suppression and the Holocaust, the moral and spiritual identity of Jewish and Macedonian People survived the falls of many "eternal" empires!

The main goal was to annihilate the ethical and spiritual identity of the Jewish and Macedonian People! The annihilators were ready to assimilate these peoples, but not their ethical and spiritual nature. It was not possible to kill the ideas of their ethics and spirit; and there was and always will be an Israel and a Macedonia, a Jewish Spirit and a Macedonian Spirit! A Spirit of Justice, Tolerance and Peace Promotion! The Jews and Macedonians love all nations. They have never promoted or conducted any ethnic cleansing. The existence of Jewish and Macedonian people is a terrible but glorious history of death, sorrow, remembrance and hope. A transcendental surmountableness of the "European Justice" and "The borders of Auschwitz!" In the memory of Macedonian Jews perished in the concentration camps, in Skopje, in Macedonia, the President of the Republic of Macedonia Mr. Kiro Gligorov, in 1996 laid the foundation stone of Macedonian Holocaust Memorial Center. The center will be finished at the end of next year.

The Jews in Macedonia identified themselves as Macedonian Jews all over the Balkans, even after 1912, after the Balkan Wars, when Macedonia was divided by her neighbors; in the Almanac of Macedonian emigrants, published 1931 in Sophia, Bulgaria, it is written, "Macedonian Jews were best friends of Macedonians in their struggle for independence."

Today, a memorial forest is erected in Israel for praising the Bulgarian people, and a monument for memorializing King Boris III is being proclaimed. In the name of the few survivors of the Macedonian Holocaust, and the dead in Treblinka, we praise what the Bulgarian people have done, and we approve that appreciation. On the other hand, glorification of King Boris III (who signed the Law for Protection of the Nation, and gave approval for deportation of 20,000 Jews from Macedonia, Bulgaria, Serbia and Greece) by Jews and others who consider themselves as free men and women is considered as a disgrace for all Jews.

Our article is divided in two parts:

1. The Nazi laws, with brief descriptions of the discriminative and humiliating measures in order to demonstrate the mode of violation of the human rights in occupied Macedonia, and

2. Documents on the confiscated properties. Nazi laws, after the occupation, the Bulgarian Nazi Army imposed a series of restrictive and discriminative laws and regulations, as listed on table 1. We will stress only a few illustrative examples from those laws and regulations.

LAWS

The "LAW FOR THE PROTECTION OF THE NATION" was issued on January 21, 1941, for whole Bulgaria and the occupied territories. This law contained five parts: 1. On the origins; 2. General restrictions; 3. Places of living restricted for Jews; 4. On the Jewish properties; 6. On the professional and economical activities of the Jews.

1. Jews are those who have at least one parent Jew. Declaration of Jewish origin at the communal authorities should be performed within one month, otherwise the penalty is imprisonment with fines up to 100,000 levs. Jews should not

change their names and surnames from the birth certificate, and in case of mixed marriages (previous) and conversion to Christianity. Jews are not allowed to have surnames with endings of "ov", "ev", "ic" and similar (suggesting non-Jewish origins). Adoption of Bulgarian children is not allowed to Jews.

2. Persons of Jewish origins are forbidden the following:
    - to take Bulgarian citizenship;
    - to elect or to be elected in any institutions or non-Jewish organizations;
    - to participate in any political or state functions, or public organizations;
    - to work as commercial representatives, managers, or to be representatives of any state, regional and autonomous institutions; such functions should be abandoned within one month;
    - to participate in the army, except for special physical works; those who are disabled should pay a special military tax;
    - to participate in any organizations sponsored by the Ministry of War;
    - to have marital or non-marital relationships with Bulgarian citizens; mixed marriages, after issuing of this law are outlawed;
    - to have any kind of servants or related services from persons of Bulgarian origin;
    - to be inscribed in schools of non-Jewish origin, except if permitted by the Minister of Popular Education with special decree;

3. Jews are not allowed to change the place of living without the permission of the Police Headquarters. The Ministerial Council with the Ministry of Internal Affairs can decide the places where Jews will be allowed to live.

4. Jews are not allowed ownership or management of "uncovered" properties (land, forest etc), and also "covered" properties (houses) in villages, except for their personal living. They should offer for sale the "uncovered" properties

to the Ministry of Agriculture within 3 months. The "covered" properties should be given out to Bulgarian citizens or organizations. In the contrary, the properties will be confiscated.

5. Further restrictions specified only for Jews include the following:

    • forbidden trade and work in industries (except the quota which is specified by the Government);
    • forbidden or restricted investment of Jewish capital to Bulgarian industries, trade etc. (as specified by the Ministry of Labor);
    • the Jews are obliged to declare all properties (real estate and personal properties) to the Popular Bank of Bulgaria; those who leave the country should depose the money from the sold property to the local bank; in the opposite, the properties are confiscated;
    • further, the Jews are forbidden: to owe stocks and bonds on educational, informative or entertaining companies (schools, journals, cinemas, theatres, gramophone-disk distributors, hotels, publishers, etc.);
    • to be managers of the same institutions; to be expert-accountants; to trade with state properties or gold and silver; to participate to any managerial council; to owe pharmacies or any sanitary services; in mixed capital companies, Jews should not surpass the capital and the number of Bulgarians;
    • transfer of Jewish capital to non-Jews; to owe concessions on any public company or institution.

On February 17, 1941, additional regulative act entitled "PRINCIPLES FOR THE APPLICATION OF THE LAW FOR THE PROTECTION OF THE NATION" was issued as integrative part of the Law. Examples of restrictions upon Jews include:
    • Jews are considered even those from christened parents if the mother is non-Bulgarian; Christian religions are considered: east-orthodox, roman-catholic, evangelicals (Lutherans, Baptists, Methodists) and Armenian-Gregorians; if the person has been converted after 1934, the Ministry of

Interior will review the case on separate session in the presence of the priest and the godfather.

On July 13, 1941 the Ministry of Interior in Sofia issued "THE LAW FOR THE SPECIAL SINGLE TAX PAYABLE ON ALL JEWISH REAL AND PERSONAL ESTATE". Among else, the regulations include:

- tax should be paid on any kind of property of Jews; the tax is single and independent of other taxes, and should be paid to the state treasury; Jews are defined by the Law for Protection of the Nation, and both Bulgarian and non-Bulgarian citizens are included;
- the tax is 20% of the total property, if it is bellow 3,000,000 levs, and 25% if it is over 3,000,000 levs;
- taxable real estate include: houses, flats, shops, buildings, factories, houses for rest, land (any kind), forests, pastures, vineyards, any kind of mines and mining stores;
- taxable personal properties include: money (cash, check, golden liras) - Bulgarian or foreign, bank accounts (Bulgarian and non-Bulgarian), gold in any form (money, pieces, sticks, jewelry, statues, watches, forks and knives etc); valuable stones (diamonds, rubies, pearls, etc); loans (Bulgarian or foreign); stocks and bonds; furniture (chairs, tables, bedroom furniture, kitchen, piano, radio-operator, bed etc); fur and valuable tissues; rags (all kinds - Persian, foreign etc); all vehicles (car, truck, bicycle, motorcycle, horse-carriage, boats, canoes, trains etc); machines (in factories, homes etc); all kind of goods (in factories, magazines, stores etc); operators and installations; non-anticipated (i.e. insurances, etc.);
- taxable inheritances: all properties, jewelry, stocks and bonds;
- applications, obligations and demands: in Bulgaria (landings, any property documents etc); in foreign countries; in other companies (confidential accounts etc);
- insurances (of Jewish insurance Co), credit accounts are declared; investments of Jews using non-Jewish capital (transfer of mixed stocks and bonds by Jews is forbidden);
- all Jews are obliged to fill a the special tax form on the period of one month, and issued to the National Bank;

non-declared properties up to the determined date are confiscated; Jewish properties of mixed companies (with Aryans) are also taxable;
- valorization of the properties is based on "market value" (not the price of purchase, or sale) on Dec.31.1940;
- the penalty for undeclared properties is: confiscation of the undeclared property, taxation of the other properties, up to 5 year jail and fine of 3,000,000 levs;
- since the lowest level of tax is 40,000 levs, the taxation is conducted by official commission, and instead of Jewish members, Aryans of orthodox confession should take their place (in a control commission); in case of higher estimated than declared taxes, 25% of the estimated difference (property value) is paid separate from the 25% of the tax itself-, half of the tax should be paid within one month, and the rest within three months, and the Jews can not leave the Kingdom of Bulgaria until the payment of the whole tax; undeclared properties are confiscated and the unpaid tax is tripled.

The Department of Jewish Affairs, at the Ministry of Internal Affairs and Public Health, issued the "DECREE NO. 32" on December 29, 1942, with detailed instructions for wearing special badges, with specifications: six pointed, bright yellow, on the left sleeve in all clothes, for all Jews above 10 years of age. "DECREE NO. 5" of the Department of Jewish Affairs (September 8, 1942) forbids all Jews to keep cash and valuable items (gold, jewels, Chinese vases, silverware, archeological items, historical items, paintings, collections, stamps, paintings etc), and they should be deposited in the bank. "DECREE NO. 8" stated that non-Jewish tenants should not pay rent to Jews. "ORDER OF THE CABINET" (Oct. 17. 1942) stated that larger Jewish houses should be occupied by several families, or abandoned by the Jews (all Jews in Biota came to live in the left bank of river Dragger in a ghetto). All businesses should be closed up to the date of February 23, 1943, and all employees of Jewish origin should be dismissed. Confiscations of all Jewish properties continued on the beginning of 1943, and continued until the deportation and final solution on March 11, 1943 (AS KEP, box 9, arch. No. 7, March 1943, quoted from Kolonomos et al.).

Before deportation, the Jews were taken in labor groups ("trudovi druzini"), along with other minorities, distributed in labor camps in Bulgaria (Naroden glas No. 6 1942).

During and after the deportation of the Jews in Treblinka, massive requests for the left Jewish properties (houses, books, furniture) were sent to the Department of Jewish Affairs, by individuals, libraries, humanitarian organizations and officials, as evidenced by large corpus of left documents.

DOCUMENTS ON THE CONFISCATED ASSETS

This article uses documents from the Archives in Macedonia (Skopje, Bitola and Stip). Although abundant documentation is kept in the Archives of Sofia, Belgrade and Salonika, we still do not have access to those documents, except few which have been previously published and kept by the Macedonian Academy of Sciences and Arts, and the Jewish Community in Skopje. The Archive in Skopje only has 1,001 archive units with 10,358 pages. All archived documents are copied and sent to The United States Holocaust Memorial Museum. The values of confiscated Jewish assets and the details from the laws and regulations are given in separate listings.

The deportation of the Jews from Eastern Aegean Macedonia, Western Trakia and Vardar Macedonia (Republic of Macedonia) was ordered by a Decision of Bulgarian Council of Ministers on March 2, 1943 and an Agreement between Bulgarian and German officials based on the ministerial decision from March 2, 1943.

The appropriation of Jewish assets (real and personal estate, money, deposits, insurance, gold, and other valuable belongings) was done by Bulgarian authorities. The experts of National Bank of Republic of Macedonia estimate (only for Jews of Vardar Macedonia) on the basis of available, but not complete, documents (some of them are in Archives in Bulgaria, some in Republic of Yugoslavia) the total amount of Jewish assets to be 16,498,383.95 USA dollars and 6,310909.43 USA dollars is the value of the assets without the value of real estate.

TABLE 1: A list of restrictive and discriminative Nazi laws issued by the Bulgarian government (1941-1943), as provided by the Macedonian Archives and the Macedonian Academy of Sciences and Arts (from Z. Kolonomos et al, and the Archives in Skopje).

DOCUMENT, ORIGINS	PLACE/DATE OF ISSUING
1. Law for Protection of the Nation	Sofia, Jan. 21, 1941
2. Principles for application of the Law for protection of the Nation	Sofia, Feb. 17, 1941
3. Decree with instructions for application of the Law for Protection of the Nation	Sofia, Jun. 21, 1941
4. The Law for the Special Single Tax on all real and personal estate	Sofia, Jul. 1941
5. Order issued by S. Simeonov (District Chief of Police) - on labor groups	Skopje, Aug. 7, 1941
6. Decree No.113 (Bulgarian Cabinet) concerning services of the army of the Jews	Sofia, Aug. 12, 1941
7. Directions for mortgages and applications of the Law for the Special Single Tax	Sofia, Aug. 15, 1941
8. Order of the War Minister of Bulgaria (order in the prohibited zone)	Sofia Mar. 17, 1942
9. Instructions for the Jewish Councils for complete loyalty	Sofia, Mar 17, 1942
10. Order, concerning the Law for Urgent solution of Pressing Problems in the Newly Liberated Territories (by the Ministry of Justice)	Sofia Jun. 5, 1942
11. Decree No. 5, on item 6 of the Law for the Special Single Tax (by King Boris 111)	Sofia Jul. 3, 1942
12. Decree No 52, demanding a Law to authorize the Cabinet of the Ministry of Home Affairs, to define in details the Jewish question (by King Boris 111)	Sofia Jul. 4, 1942
13. A Law authorizing the Cabinet to settle42 the Jewish question	Sofia Jul. 9, 19
14. Decree No. 68 (King Boris 111), with approval of the Order for changing amendments in the Law for Special Tax	Sofia Jul. 28, 1942
15. Decree 69 (King Boris 111), with approval of Order to an amendment to the Law Against Speculations in the Jewish Real Estate	Sofia Jul. 28, 1942
16. Order No. 2 (A. Belev, Secretary of Department of Jewish Affairs) on Item 22, authorizing the cabinet for settlement of the Jewish Question	Sofia Sep. 4, 1942
17. Definition of the Jewish privileged strata on, Order 3, item 33 in Law for Protection of the	

Nation (A. Belev)   Sofia Sep. 4,1942
18. Order No. 5 (A. Belev) for economic sanctions,
on item 45, of the Order for settlement of the
Jewish question   Sofia Sep. 8, 1942
19. Order (by A. Belev) for the levels of rents
for Jewish people   Sofia Sep. 11, 1942
20. Order No. 8 (A. Belev), precise rents
on rents for Jewish people   Sofia Sep. 12, 1942
21. Order (part) for curfew and limitations of
movement of Jews (Chief of Police in Veles)   Veles Sep. 14, 1942
22. Order No. 32 (A. Belev) obliging all
Jews to wear the Star of David   Sofia Sep. 23, 1942
23. Directives (A. Belev) to consistories,
of Jewish Councils on their management   Sofia Oct. 21, 1942
24. Instructions (A. Belev) to consistories,
of Jewish Councils, regarding the Law,
for wearing badges   Sofia Oct. 21, 1942
25. Orders (A. Belev) to consistories of
Jewish councils to submit precise lists of
Jewish businesses   Sofia Oct. 31, 1942
26. Regulations (A. Belev) for management
councils of Jewish   Sofia Oct. 31, 1942
27. Order No. 255 (A. Belev) for limitation
of income and expenditures of Jewish councils   Sofia Nov. 2, 1942
28. Order 362 (A. Belev), on item 4 of the
Regulations for expenditures of the Jewish
Council Fund   Sofia Nov. 10, 1942
29. Regulations (Department of Jewish
Affairs) for distribution and expenditure of
finances of the Jewish Council Fund   Sofia Nov. 18, 1942
30. Order No. 462 (A. Belev) regulating
expenditures of finances of Jews, deposited
in the Bulgarian National Bank   Sofia Nov. 23, 1942
31. Names of Jews (I. Zahariev) whose accounts   Skopje Nov. 27, 1942
have been frozen
32. Instructions (Department for Jewish Affairs)
to Jewish councils on determination the wages
and salaries   Sofia Nov. 27, 1942
33. Instructions (Department of the Jewish
Affairs) on the budget for 1943   Sofia Dec. 11, 1942
34. Order (A. Belev) putting in charge the

Jewish Council in Skopje for Gjevgelija   Sofia Dec.31, 1942
35. Additional instructions (A. Belev) on permanent
residence of Jewish people   Sofia 1942
36. Order (Department of Jewish Affairs
) to prohibit Jews visiting public places,
restaurants etc. in Skopje   Sofia Jan. 4, 1943
37. Order (Department of Jewish Affairs)
prohibiting Jews to stay in hotels   Sofia Jan. 5, 1943
38. Order (A. Belev) regulating control of
Jewish properties   Sofia Jan. 12, 1943
39. Instructions (A. Belev) on rents   Sofia Jan. 14, 1943
40. Order (Department of Jewish
Affairs) regulating Jewish movement   Sofia Jan. 15, 1943
41. Note (Department of Jewish Affairs)
forbidding Jews to visit public places   Sofia Jan. 21, 1943
42. Adolf Bekerle (German ambassador)
on the persecutions of Jews   Sofia Jan. 22, 1943
43. Report (A. Belev) on the deportation
of the Jews from Macedonia   Sofia Feb. 2, 1943
44. Demands (A. Belev) all Jewish rents to be
deposited in the National Bank of Bulgaria   Sofia Feb. 5, 1943
45. Demand (Department of Jewish Affairs)
of list of all Jews   Sofia Feb. 9, 1943
46. Decision report from T. Daneker (National
Security of Third Reich) of the Bulgarian
cabinet for the deportations of Jews in
Macedonia and Aegean belt   Sofia Feb. 16, 1943
47. Order (A. Belev) for strict araha payment
of all Jews   Sofia Feb.20, 1943
48. Agreement for deportation of 20.000 Jews   Sofia Feb.22, 1943
from Macedonia and Trace (A. Belev and T. Daneker)
49. Decisions (Department of Bulgaria) on
deportation of the Jews from Macedonia, and
the Aegean belt, with confiscations   Sofia Mar. 2, 1943
50. Decision (Cabinet of Bulgaria) to confiscate
all Jewish properties   Sofia Mar. 2, 1943
51. A plan (Department of Jewish Affairs) for
collection of the Jews from Aegean coastal belt   Sofia Mar. 4, 1943
52. Minister of Home Affairs (P. Gabrovski
) report on the agreement (A. Belev and T. Daneker)
for deportation of 20,000 Jews, from

Macedonia and Thrace, and establishment of temporary concentration camp in Skopje	Sofia Mar. 1943
53. Order (Department of Jewish Affairs) of a temporary concentration camp	Sofia Mar. 1943
54. Orders No. 1 and 2 (P. Draganov, Commander of the temporary camp in Skopje	Skopje Mar. 8, 1943
55. Order No. 865 (A-Belev) for liquidation of the properties of the deported Jews	Sofia Mar. 13, 1943
56. Instructions (G-Djambazov, delegate of Dept. of Bitola Jewish Affairs) for the properties sale of the deported Jews	Mar. 24, 1943
57-Order No.339 (D. Baev, Director of Skopje District Office), on estimating the "damage" caused by the Jews in the concentration camp "Monopol"	Skopje Mar. 30, 1943\
57. Ribbentrop-King Boris III talks on the Jewish question	Berlin Apr. 4, 1943\,
58.Report of the German police in Niska Banja, , about the transport of Jews from Skopje to Treblinka	Niska Banja Apr.3 Apr. 7, Apr. 12, 1943
59. Order 1283 (A. Belev) on procedures for the sale of Jewish valuables	Sofia Apr. 19, 1943
60. Order (A. Belev) for collection of araha	Sofia Apr. 19, 1943
61. Order (Dept. Jewish Affairs) for the sale of Jewish properties to be obeyed	Sofia Apr. 19, 1943\
62. Order (A. Belev) - all properties of deported Jews (Bitola, Skopje, Aegean District) to be sold to Bulgarian Agriculture and Cooperative Bank, and the confiscated properties to be sold in favor of the state.	Sofia Apr. 21, 1943\

REFERENCES

1. Z. Kolonomos and V. Veskovich Vangeli: The Jews in Macedonia During the Second World War (1941-1945). Macedonian Academy of Sciences and Arts, Skopje 1986. 2 Volumes.
2. A. Matkovski: A History of the Jews in Macedonia. Macedonian Reviews Editions. Skopje 1982.
3. E. Benbassa and A. Rodriguez: Juifs des Balkans. Editions la decouverte. Paris 1993.

4. S.A. Rosanes: The History of the Jews in Turkey and the Middle East. Rav Kook Institute, Husijatin, Tel Aviv-Sofia-Jerusalem 1907-1945, 6 volumes.
5. Aaron Assa: Macedonia and Jewish People. Macedonian Reviews Editions. Skopje, 1994.
Harry Nissimov: By the skin of our teeth. IK "Kolumb'92", Sofia, 1995.

Skopje, 11.27.98

POLAND

Delegation Statement

The Polish delegation that took part in Washington Conference on Holocaust Assets in December 1998 has submitted to all delegations the detailed materials concerning all the problems discussed at the conference. The document is a shortened copy of texts on most important issues from the above-mentioned volume. Due to the shortage of space not all issues have been raised so please refer to the original materials for a comprehensive view of Polish side on these matters.

The Polish delegation has made a promise to prepare and be a host to the similar conference on restitution of communal property in post-communist countries of the Eastern Europe. The Polish Government shares the opinion of U.S. Under Secretary of State, Mr. Stuart E. Eizenstat, that the issue of restitution of communal property must be seen in respect to all religious communities like the Protestant, Catholic and Jewish communities that lost their property because of WW II and later the communist rule. The conference will be prepared jointly by the Chancellery of the President of Poland and the Chancellery of the Prime Minister of Poland. In order to ensure the proper preparation the government of Poland suggests November 1999 as the best suitable date to hold the conference.

It is also very important to recall that Polish delegation wants to play an active part in the new body called the Task Force for International Cooperation on Holocaust Education, Remembrance and Research. Polish Government is extremely interested in this idea and gives it unquestionable support.

INSURANCE MARKET IN THE REPUBLIC OF POLAND BEFORE AND AFTER WORLD WAR II

Before the Second World War there was a well developed insurance market in Poland. In the territory of the Republic of Poland there were 79 insurance companies operating in 1939.

After the end of the Second World War the assets of the insurance companies existing before the Second World War in Poland were not nationalized, but the process of liquidation was carried out. With respect to insurance companies the Act of Parliament dated January 3, 1946 on the taking over by the State of the basic sectors of the national economy was not in force. On January 3, 1947 a Decree on the regulation of property and personal insurance was published. From the day of the entry in force of this decree, that is from January 3, 1947 the domestic and foreign private insurance companies irrespective of their legal form have lost the right to further conduct insurance business.

The permit for the continuation of the conduct of business within the scope defined in this decree was granted only to two insurance companies existing before the Second World War, namely: The Reinsurance Company „Warta" S.A. in Warsaw and Powszechny Zakład Ubezpieczeń Wzajemnych (General Mutual Insurance Company - PZUW). These two companies became State owned.

With respect to the remaining companies the liquidator of Polish private insurance companies had to be the Powszechny Zakład Ubezpieczeń Wzajemnych (the General Mutual Insurance Company - PZUW) which was later on transformed into the State Insurance Company of Poland - PZU, and the liquidator of the foreign insurance companies operating in the territory of Poland had to be the main representative of the foreign insurance company or the liquidator appointed ex officio by the court.

On the other hand, with respect to insurance companies underwriting exclusively personal insurance, the liquidation of their operations had to be carried out by insurance companies for personal insurance which had to be set up especially for this purpose. However, these insurance companies were never created. With respect to insurance companies whose liquidation was not finished, for any reasons, Państwowy Zakład Ubezpieczeń (the State Insurance Company of Poland – PZU) became their liquidator. PZUW had taken over the management and the assets of insurance companies being in liquidation from their companies' bodies. In the liquidation process the legal provisions generally in force were applied in order to ensure the correctness of the carrying out of the procedure/ proceedings.

Altogether PZUW carried out the liquidation of 26 insurance companies. With respect to the two larger mutual insurance companies operating in Poland before the Second World War, that is: „Dniestr" Mutual Insurance Company in Lwów and, „Karpatia" Mutual Life Insurance Company in Lwów, the liquidation proceedings were not carried out as their assets remained in the territories which after the Second World War have not belonged to the territory of the Polish State.

Before the Second World War there were six foreign insurance companies operating in Poland through their own representations. On the basis of the Act of Parliament dated January 3, 1946 on the taking over by the State of the basic sectors of the national economy, the nationalization of two German insurance companies had to take place. Also with respect to these companies liquidation proceedings were carried out. At the moment of the liquidation it was stated that neither of the two did own immovable property. The only movable property of Aachen-München fire insurance company located in Katowice was intended to cover the dismissal money for the employees. All the securities of the two companies were lost during the period of the German occupation or were transported to Germany.

The owners of the policies of the British insurance companies: „Alliance" and „Prudential", living abroad were told to request for the payment of indemnities resulting from these policies at the Head Office of the company in London. This was done on the basis of the Polish-British Financial Agreement dated November 11, 1954 which declared that they did not benefit from the satisfaction of their claims with the funds located in Poland. Similarly the owners of the policies of Italian insurance companies, „Assicurazioni Generali" and „Riunione Adriatica di Sicurta", living abroad were told to go to the Head Office in Triest, but although negotiations took place several times in 1959, 1972 and 1977, Poland did not sign a bilateral financial agreement with Italy in this respect. For the owners of the policies of the above mentioned British and Italian insurance companies in Poland, the payments on the basis of these policies were covered/ paid by the Polish State with the amounts obtained from the assets of these companies located in Poland. No claims concerning the two German companies were registered.

In the majority of the cases the only real element of the assets of the insurance companies being liquidated were the real estate which survived the war. These were mostly urban real Estate whose value was defined according to approximate technical standards taking into account the technical condition of these pieces of real estate including the war destruction.

The value of the securities which consisted mainly of bonds issued by the State before the war, by the association of communes and by other institutions dealing with long-term credit, such as Bank Gospodarstwa Krajowego (The Bank for Domestic Economy), Towarzystwo Kredytowe Ziemskie (Land Credit Company), etc. was assumed as being equal to zero, because these loans were not reimbursed, and the bonds had no real value. The valuation of other securities was made taking into account the provisions of the agreements on indemnification concluded by Poland with other countries and taking into account the principle of reciprocity.

The valuation both of assets and of liabilities was homogeneous for domestic companies domestic companies with foreign shareholding as well as for foreign insurance companies operating in Poland. Also claims resulting from policies were treated identically both in case of Polish citizens living in Poland and abroad and in case of citizens of other countries (with exception of claims of persons living abroad which were addressed to foreign insurance companies, British and Italian insurance companies - the explanation has been given above).

According to the data that survived the Second World War there were approximately 275 insurance contracts in 1939 concluded for a total amount of 640 million zloties. The indemnities resulting from the policies of the insurance companies existing before the war and being liquidated were paid after the submission of the original policy or of the evidence/vouchers of the payment of premium until August 1939, and each case was examined separately (separate liquidation report). The liabilities resulting from insurance contracts with respect to the persons entitled were paid according to the principles defined in the general conditions of insurance. However, if the total amount of these liabilities was not covered by the balance-sheet value of the assets of the estate, the payments were made proportionally to the existing funds.

Of course in case of life insurance, the death-taking place in the conditions of Holocaust was considered as a death connected with acts of war. However, it results from the files of the liquidation that although the particular general conditions of insurance excluded the payment of indemnity in case of death occurring in connection with acts of war, the indemnities were paid to all persons submitting claims resulting from concluded insurance contracts - the amount of payments depending on persons-survivors or the recipient heirs of the policies.

Poland, as a country occupied by Germany during the Second World War and whose citizens suffered deeply under the Hitler's occupation has not obtained the full payment of indemnities for the victims of nazi crimes from Germany. On the other hand, there was no indemnification program for the victims of the Holocaust.

One has however to stress that on October 16, 1991 as a result of an agreement between the Government of the Republic of Poland and the Government of the Republic of Germany a foundation called „Polish-

German Reconciliation" was set up. This foundation operates according to the legal principles being in force in the Republic of Poland. The Foundation Reconciliation grants financial assistance having the nature of a single benefit. The assistance granted by the foundation, however, is not an indemnity and may not be considered as damages for all the injuries suffered. Polish citizens are entitled to request for financial assistance out of the funds of the foundation. **These citizens include Polish citizens of Jewish origin, who were alive on January 8, 1992, who have submitted an application personally, who have their permanent residence in the territory of the Republic of Poland and who are the victims of special nazi persecutions.**

It is important to stress once again that in Poland there was a liquidation of the assets of the insurance companies existing before the Second World War that was carried out in accordance with law, and there was no nationalization.

THE PROBLEM OF RESTITUTION OF MONETARY GOLD TO POLAND

The Tripartite Commission for the Restitution of the Monetary Gold which adjourned on July 25, 1998 in its final task sent, to the countries that in 1947 submitted their claims to the Nazi gold restitution, statements informing them about the remaining gold pool for particular countries and the necessity of their final distribution. According to the Commission's calculations, Poland was to receive 1.206,228 ounces of pure gold and 4.782,90 sterling pounds – the sum remaining after the undistributed parts of monetary gold. The calculations were accompanied with the proposal from the three governments of the United States, Great Britain and France which made up the Commission to contribute the remaining gold, including Poland's share, to the Nazi Victims Relief Fund – founded in order to bring relief to those victims who presently live in difficult conditions. This Fund, to be managed by non-governmental organizations, was established in New York on the basis of the agreement between the government of Great Britain and the Management Board of the Federal Reserve Bank in N.Y.

The Ambassador of the Republic of Poland in Brussels, which was the city where the Commission held its headquarters, signed the according voucher for received gold and the given amount of money, while Minister of the State Treasury during the London Conference on the Nazi gold of December 2 – 4, 1997 made an offering of a contribution to this Fund. The transfer of the money took place on July 2, 1998.

THE DORMANT SWISS ACCOUNTS IN THE CASE OF POLAND

The Governments of Poland and Switzerland in the Polish-Swiss Compensation Agreement of 1949, which among others included two treaties: 1) *On the Exchange of Goods and Forms of Payment;* and 2) *On the Matter of Recompensatory Damages for Swiss Transactions in Poland* decided upon the restitution of bank accounts and the deposits from insurance policies in Swiss banks by Polish citizens who had died or disappeared during the Second World War. On the basis of the said agreement the Poland was given money in the total amount of 480.391,65 Swiss francs with nearly 96,6% having been transferred only in 1970, fifteen years after the first payment of 16.347,10 Swiss francs in 1960. Along with the money the Swiss government delivered the documentation which included the **available** data concerning the owners of bank accounts or insurance policies whose accounts or claims were liquidated by the transfer of agreed-upon sums to Poland in 1960 and 1975. However, the information supplied by Swiss side was incomplete often only with the surname and the place of residence of the account holder as any meaningful information.

Despite that Polish government on January 7, 1997 made the decision to return money to the rightful holders or their heirs. Several complementing actions to correct the gaps in the documentation were taken including the setting up of the Interdepartmental Disbursement from the Dormant Accounts Task Team which included representatives from the Ministry of State Treasury, Ministry of Foreign Affairs and Ministry of Justice. The Ministry of Finance published on December 8 and 9, 1997 the advertisements in Poland's two largest nationwide newspapers as well as in Its Internet site (www.prezydent.pl) calling upon all persons interested in making a claim to contact the Ministry of Finance, Office of Property Claims with the aim of establishing a procedure to satisfy the outstanding claims. (It should be noted that in order to facilitate the identification of „interested persons" - who are often heirs of the original owners - the Ministry of Finance prepared a special publication of all the documentation received from the Swiss government which is available upon request in all Polish embassies, and will be sent to all interested persons upon request). Thanks to all the actions new information was recovered however, in some cases not all adequate data was retrieved.

In December 97 a Report by Ministry of Finance was introduced on the subject of procedure of claims inquiries from the National Treasury regarding the liquidation of dormant Swiss accounts. Those requesting the disbursements have to present their claim through administrative procedure to the Minister of Finance with an attached petition documenting the justification of their claim. In case of heirs of the holders of accounts and insurance policies it is necessary to attach to the petition a legal copy of the Polish court's judgement on the status of the inheritance. It is verified as to its validity and then decision for the disbursement payment is made. Such decision is the basis for the conclusion of the contract with the claimants. In those cases where the claimants' claims are satisfactorily determined to be valid, the Ministry of Finance will authorize the Director of the Office of Property Claims, together with the Office's Chief Accountant, to enter into a settlement agreement with said claimants setting forth the amount of the claim to be liquidated according the documentation delivered by the Swiss government and the exchange rate of Swiss francs into Polish zloties on the date of the agreement. In the event of a dispute concerning either the basis of the claim, the amount, or especially the method of indexing the original sum, the claimants are authorized to commence an appropriate judicial action in the General Court against the Treasury Department of the Ministry of Finance. As of December 1, 1998, out of 16 petitions for disbursements, 13 settlement agreements have been signed with heirs of the holders of lost accounts that were identified on the basis of the documentation delivered by the Swiss government in November 1997. Additional claims are currently being processed.

Persons who have financial claims stemming from Swiss accounts held by themselves or their ancestors, the names of whom do not appear in the documentation delivered by the Swiss government to Poland, are encouraged to contact the firm Ernst and Young, having its headquarters in Budapest, which is involved in the search for satisfying such claims.

REPRIVATIZATION IN POLAND

One of the ongoing problems of Poland as democratic country is how to repair the damage done to people deprived of their imposition of Communist rule in Poland. It seemed at first to be easy to solve, but very soon it proved that due scope of the problem it will be very difficult to grasp the essence of reprivatization and complete it successfully. The initial ideas were influenced by the notion that the continuity of Polish statehood must be preserved and further by the constitutional provision of Article 2 of the new Polish Constitution of April 2, 1997 stating that "the Republic of Poland is a democratic state ruled by law and implementing the principle of social justice. Consequently all statutes of 1944-1989 period remained in force with principle of constitutional state of "rule by law being understood that any compensation for the wrong done to citizens should be restricted to the cases in which property had been appropriated by the state with infringements of the Communist laws.

Since 1989 there have been several projects of reprivatization bills starting with earliest initiatives of the higher house of Parliament – Senate of so-called "small reprivatization" to the latest ones of Freedom Union and the other by President Lech Wałęsa, both rejected by Sejm – the lower chamber of Parliament, so none has successfully gone through the legislative path yet. This is at least partly due to the different ideas towards the reprivatization. The most important questions concerning here were included in the papers delivered by Polish Delegation to all national delegations at the Conference. **All the new projects under preparation have a provision, which ensures that restitution will include among others all former citizens of Poland who no longer live in Poland.**

The Polish Government that took office after the general elections of fall 1997 instructed the Ministry of the Treasury to resume work on the draft of the reprivatization statute. The latest proposals of the issues included in the draft were also included in the above mentioned papers.

COMMUNAL PROPERTY RESTITUTION IN POLAND

After World War II the established system of government in Poland was based on and followed the Soviet model. A new type of property was introduced: this was called the socialist property, which meant common property of state and of the cooperative. This new type was given preferential treatment especially in regards to the protection of property laws. The role of private property was degraded. Ownership of many private properties due to so-called nationalization bills and expropriations was shifted to various persons.

In response to the transitions that took place in Poland in 1989, the entire system of governance including the legal system went under principal changes. The return of protection of property rights in its rightful place created a place for the new legal system. This took place under new Constitution of the Republic of Poland, passed on April 2, 1997 (Articles 21 & 64). These articles regard property rights and their protection as the founding stone for the new political and economic system. Therefore the new legal system of the Republic of Poland marks the return of property rights into the status they held before World War II.

The process of property restitution to the rightful owners already began in 1989. There are many reasons why the process of restitution is much more complicated in Poland than in other Central European State. Most important of them being: size of the achieved property nationalization and expropriations, shift of the Polish borders to the West and the migrations of million of people that accompanied such a change. The problem gets much more attention in papers delivered by Polish Delegation at the Washington Conference. The size of the performed property changes means today that the total recovery to the WW II status seems to be unrealistic. This remark does not pertain only to Jewish property but equally to any other, disregarding the owner's ethnicity. Scanning through laws passed in the after war period suggests that there were no special circumstances attached to Jewish property rights status. Therefore, based on legal means, there is no special distinction made as to Jewish property status.

In 1989 the new Polish State began the process of restoring friendly relations with Jewish State. This need of normalization of relations with the Jewish State but also with the Jewish Diaspora based on democratic principles gave the problem of Jewish property restitution a political dimension.

The first law that regulates the restitution of property to Jewish Owners was passed on January 20, 1997. It set the relation of the State towards religious Jewish communities in the Republic of Poland. This Law was a part of a package of bills describing the relation of the State towards different religious organizations. The thorough description can be found in the above mentioned papers. The compensation of Jewish property, based on this bill, is considered in Poland as an important step for normalizing Polish-Jewish relations. It can even be considered as a turning point in the relations of the State towards the entire problem of Jewish restitution. The 1997 law created legal limitations of property restitution for Jewish communities. These limitations permit, following the logic of restitution, the restitution of property to the past owners, i.e. Jewish Communities. A new proposal allowing other subjects than Jewish communities to receive property, which belonged to these Jewish communities, would mean creating the rights to the property restitution principles that are used in the relation of the state in these matters to other religious communities.

The sketched issues of property restitution for Jewish communities and other Jewish religious organizations are only a small part of even a bigger. If the problem of property restitution for Jewish communities is very complex; then the problem of property restitution to persons and legal persons creates even a larger challenge for the Polish legislators.

A more thorough view of the problem is included in the papers prepared by Polish Delegation, mentioned in the above text several times.

ACCESS TO POLISH ARCHIVES

Once upon a time Poland could be proud of its archives but the history of our country in the last two centuries – the partition of our territory for 123 years and two World Wars had an irreversible and of course negative impact on the integrity of the assets of the Polish archives. However it is important to mention here that countless wars that had through centuries rolled over Polish lands had not caused such horrid losses like the ones that occurred during WW II only. These losses affected all existing kinds of archives – state, local-government, church, private as well as archival collections in the National Library and in the private libraries of the great aristocratic Polish families. Several key factors contributed to that destruction. Direct military operations affected archive assets in September 1939; during the Warsaw uprising of 1944; and during the liberating operations of the Soviet Army and the Polish Armed Forces in 1944 and 1945. Beside that the total number of losses must be increased to include materials that were removed and plundered by the occupiers. Despite the 50 years that passed since the end of WW II many of these records are still stored in foreign countries and the majority of them were not even accessible for Polish Scholars until 1991. Thus the number of assets is limited.

Documents and other archive materials are primarily stored in state archives. The network of state archives is composed of archives directly subordinated to the Chief Director of State Archives, as a central organ of state administration, and of others.

The „Law on the national archive assets and archives" of July 14, 1983 regulates the general principles of access to archive materials stored in state archives. It determines that archive materials are made accessible to institutions and individuals for scientific, cultural, technical and economic purposes after 30 years from their creation, on condition that this does not infringe legally protected interests of the State and citizens. Permission to use archive materials is granted by the director of the relevant state archive and in the case of foreigners - the Chief Director of State Archives. Further information can be found in the papers of Polish Delegation prepared for the Washington Conference. The restrictions that may arise – applying to both Polish citizens and foreigners – stem from the legal principle of protection of the State and citizens. When granting permission for the use òf materials, directors of state archives and, in some cases, the Chief Director of State Archives must also take into account other legal regulations, in particular protection of so-called personal goods, law on protection of state and professional secrets of 1982 and the 1997 law on protection of personal data.

Research institutions make their archive materials free of charge. Charges are levied – according to a price list determined by the Chief Director of State Archives – for copying of records and for the time lost in finding materials inaccurately described by interested persons.

EDUCATIONAL ACTIVITIES OF THE AUSCHWITZ-BIRKENAU MUSEUM

From the very beginning of the Museum there have been educational activities addressed to the future, to guiding youth so that the tragic past of Auschwitz would not be repeated. The overriding task of those who created the Museum fifty years ago was, however to commemorate the boundless sufferings and the deaths of all who died, in the gas chambers immediately after being brought to the camp or later as a result of the atrocious conditions that prevailed.

Auschwitz symbolizes all the evil bred by hatred and contempt in interpersonal relations, and in social life by violence and coercion, racism and lack of respect for the other peoples. For this reason the place should be an international center for the education, where new educational methods will be developed through the joint efforts of the best specialists, where Polish and foreign teachers can obtain help and practical guidelines, together with a broad assortment of suggested methodological materials.

Interest in the subject of Auschwitz is growing around the world, and special centers for teacher and student training are being established in many countries. Because this process is coupled with the history of the Auschwitz camp and other Nazi camps where Jews were killed en masse during WW II in German-occupied Poland, Poland is compelled to be the center for this research. Since Auschwitz functions in the world as a symbol, it is essential for the Auschwitz-Birkenau Memorial and Museum to become, as quickly as possible, an important center for education about the history of Auschwitz, the Holocaust, and also the history of the Jews in Poland. In this regard the Museum is working with other institutions involved with this subject matter, but a lack of resources has prevented many initiatives and plans from being implemented so far.

For deeper study of these all the programs prepared and conducted by the Auschwitz-Birkenau Museum in Oświęcim please refer to the papers mentioned in previous sections of this paper.

RUSSIA

The General Goals of the Conference and the Looted Art Problem

Statement by
Ambassador Valentin Kopteltsev
HEAD OF DELEGATION

Plenary Session on Nazi Confiscated Art Issues

Chairman, Ladies and Gentlemen,

1. Russia favors the humane idea of seeking possibilities to provide aid to victims of the Nazis, regardless of their nationality, who have not previously received such aid in sufficient volumes and require it due to their health conditions and low income.

2. The establishment and operation of the New York International Fund for Needy Victims of Nazi Persecution is valued positively. Due to its current economic conditions Russia is now unable to become a donor of this Fund, however it anticipates that the Fund's resources will be used to provide aid to the citizens of Russia and other Republics of the former USSR. Russian authorities and non-government organizations are prepared to cooperate with the Fund in the distribution of such aid. It is important in this respect to take into account the disproportionate allocation of aid that has so far been provided to the Nazi victims in the West, Russia and other Republics of the former USSR.

3. In accordance with the Russian law Russia will continue the search for cultural values confiscated by the Nazis from their victims, and continue publishing their list. The law provides that claims for these values could be submitted only within the 18- month period beginning from April 21, 1998. Since the work in the archives as well as attribution of the retrieved works of art is difficult and time-consuming the Russian Government will be ready to discuss these issues even after the expiration of the above period.

4. Compilation by the interested parties of the catalogue of values missing from the private collections of the victims of the Nazis and transferring it to the Russian side to organize offset search activities would accelerate the work of the Russian experts to identify the unknown values.

5. We are ready to accept a large-scale research program focusing on preconditions, practices and consequences of the Nazi <<Holocaust>> policy and to conduct on this basis a research in the Russian archives and cultural institutions on the Nazi gold issue and displaced cultural values. We hope that other countries of the former Soviet Union, whose national property was plundered by the Nazis, could adhere to this program.

6. In case of failure to locate the former owners of the cultural values among the victims of the Nazis or their direct inheritors, Russia proposes to consider these values property of the states where they are currently located, and use them for providing aid to the victims of Nazism and war in this countries. In this context we would be able to support the Eleven General Principles with Regard to Nazi-confiscated Art circulated here if the word <<direct>> would be set before the word <<heirs>> in articles VII., VIII. and X. of these Principles.

7. Due to the immense damage caused by the Nazism to the cultural property of the former Soviet Union, Russia urges the participants of the Washington conference and the entire world community to do everything possible to locate these cultural values and return them to countries from which they were stolen. For this purpose, Mr. Chairman, I convey to you the first volume of a series of catalogues of cultural values looted from the territory of Russia during World War II.

Thank you.

SLOVAK REPUBLIC

Delegation Statement

One of the critical duties resulting from political changes in 1989 for the Czech and Slovak Federal Republic and since 1993 for Slovak Republic as one of successors of Czecho-Slovakia was the mitigation of injustices of the past. It was necessary to compensate the victims of Nazi persecution during the World War II and at the same time to compensate injustices of the communist regime 1948-89. Quite naturally, these laws could not eliminate all cases of treatment. However, this was a successful practical start to mitigate the cases of violations of fundamental rights and freedoms which, as far as its extent and impact on public funds concern, can hardly be matched to any other country of the former communist block. The rehabilitation and restitution proceedings, so vitally important for the emerging democracy, have been nearly completed. The federal and the national authorities which initiated these proceedings in the early 1990's should be credited with a considerable recognition for their commitment. Democratic forces coming forward after the period of violations of political and property rights should always lead those proceedings.

Looking at the problem from the aspect of time, it was necessary to compensate victims of communist persecution from 1948-89, including compensation of victims of deportations to soviet concentration and work camps (GULAGs) in post war period. That is why appropriate acts were adopted in former Czech and Slovak Federal Republic. The basic framework consisted of: Act n.119/90 on Judicial Rehabilitation, Act n.403/90 on Mitigation of Consequences of Results of Some Property Injustices (restitution act), Act n.87/1990 on Extra Judicial Rehabilitation, Act n.229/91 on Conversion of Some Ownership Relations to Land and other Agricultural Property, Slovak National Council Act n.319/1991 on Mitigation of some Propriety and other Injustices and on Competence of Authorities of the Slovak Republic in the field of extra judicial rehabilitation.

All these acts were subsumed into the legal order of the Slovak Republic after 1993. The adoption of National Council of the Slovak

Republic's Act n.125/1996 on Immorality and Illegality of Communist System represented a moral satisfaction to all victims of communist persecution.

The adoption of the National Council of the Slovak Republic's Act n.282/1993 of 27 October 1993 on Mitigation of Some Property Injustices Inflicted to Churches and Religious Communities was the base for compensation of victims of Nazi persecution. The range of entitled persons is determined in §1 of the aforesaid act. In this paragraph the peremptory period concerning deprivation of movable and immovable property of religious communities in breach to the principles of democratic society and relevant covenants on civil, political, economic, social, and cultural rights is determined. The law maker took into account that the religious communities became victims of persecution mostly after The World War II and that is why the peremptory period was determined for these communities from 8 May 1945 to 1 January 1990. At the same time it was necessary to take into account that an extensive Jewish community had existed before the World War II on the Slovak territory. This community was systematically destroyed between 1939 - 45. That was the reason for explicit determination of peremptory period by lawmakers for Jewish religious communities in §1 of aforesaid act. The peremptory period for Jewish religious community has been determined since 2 November 1939 to 1 January 1990. Movable and immovable propriety is the object of return of propriety to the entitled persons who are the churches and religious communities or their parts, with legal personality registered by state, resident on the territory of the Slovak Republic. The entitled church organization or religious community had one year for claiming their property from the entity which possessed or disposed with the property in question. If such entity failed to make an agreement with a church organization of a religious community to return the property within ninety days of the submission of the claim, the entitled person could turn to court within fifteen months. In civil or administrative proceedings church or religious organizations were exempted from payment of administrative and judicial costs. Any expenses arising from restitution, e.g. in surveying the estate, were reimbursed by the State as fixed by law. According to the reports of the Ministry of Culture under the auspices of which the restitution of property of religious communities occurred, no major problems were encountered. In the restitution of the property of Jewish congregation, the Ministry of Culture provided consultation services which resulted mostly in fruitful restitutions.

The act presumes that the state takes the primary responsibility for the compensation of injustices: *" The responsible persons are state, municipality, legal persons established by the state or municipality and legal persons established by the law who are managing the state or municipal propriety or are administering and possessing such propriety to the day of effect of this law..."* (§3 part 1).

The responsible persons are also natural persons who have acquired the propriety in accordance with §4 of the aforesaid act, and also if these persons have acquired the property contrary to regulations which were in effect at that time.

At the same time it has been determined in this paragraph which categories of propriety do not fall within the scope of the law: *" ...except a) legal persons with foreign interest and commercial corporations where the associates are exclusively natural persons. This exception is obsolete if the propriety is acquired from legal persons after 1 January 1990; b) foreign states."*

Preparing this act, the lawmaker paid the diligence to the fact that there is some property which should be returned in accordance with the act, but in reality it is not possible to return such property and that's why it is necessary to exclude such property from the act (§7), or in reasonable event to limit the free dispensability with the property by entitled person (§11).

The mitigation of injustices caused by the Nazi persecution cannot be limited only to property injustices, it has to be above all a direct compensation of victims of persecution and reprisals. In these days the act on compensation of some injustices caused by Nazi persecution during the World War II is under preparation. The draft law anticipates financial compensation and bonuses to the retirement benefits to persons deported to and detained in concentration camps, and also to their family survivors.

The draft act determines the entitled persons in its §2 part 3 and 4, and §3 part 2 and 3. These are persons directly sanctioned by deportations into concentration camps, or sanctioned by other Nazi repressive actions in period 1939-45. If there are no such persons, their bereaved spouses and children are entitled and if there are neither those persons, their parents are entitled. The preliminary assessment of expenditures needed for compensations is 500.000.000 SK (it is approximately 16.000.000 USD).

Quite obviously, the debates on the act focused mainly on financial resources necessary for payment to the entitled persons. Extensive considerations have been given to the assistance in anticipation from the German Government, that launched the plan of compensation of victims of Nazi persecution in several European Countries including the Czech Republic. The new Government, according to a statement by Vice-Prime Minister in charge of the Legislative Board, will reconsider the draft law prepared during the preceding parliamentary period. Such proposal may become a key topic for the ongoing discussion, and in particular for its immediate presentation for a parliamentary debate.

In the preparation of and the debate on the new bill regulating the compensation of victims of Nazi persecution, the appropriate governmental authorities in Slovakia will have to consider the following:

1. the time factor – the passage of the law cannot be delayed in view of the age of entitled persons, and also in view of the fact that this will be the last law on the compensation adopted after 1989, even though the period of violation of human rights and freedoms preceded the period of 1948-89, in which alleviation of the injuries and injustice have been granted;

2. The cooperation with the interested non-governmental institutions, i.e. communication with the Slovak Union of Fascist Resistance, the Central Union of Jewish Religious Communities should become a basis for drafting the bill corresponding to the nature of injuries and suffering;

3. financial factor – the financial resources, as one of the fundamental conditions for this compensation of victims must be a priority in the process of the completion of rehabilitation and restitution processes in Slovakia.

In addition to these measures the Government of the Slovak Republic at its session on 26 May 1998 took into consideration that the Tripartite Commission for Restitution of Monetary Gold had returned 5.312,108 ounces of fine gold in value of approximately 1,6 mil. USD to the Slovak Republic. The Government of the Slovak Republic agreed that this amount of gold will be used for compensation of Slovak victims of Nazi persecution and at the same time the Slovak Republic will take part in Nazi Persecutee Relief Fund. From the amount of fine gold the 3/4 part (1,2 mil. USD) will be used for direct compensation for victims of Nazi persecution in accordance with the prepared compensation act and 1/4 (approximately 400.000 USD) will be used as contribution of the Slovak Republic to the Nazi Persecutee Relief Fund established at the London Conference on Nazi Gold in December 1997.

The Slovak National Archives concluded an agreement on cooperation with the Holocaust Memorial Museum enabling to provide a large number of copies of documents concerning various aspects of the Holocaust period, as well as facts related to that period.

These facts evidence the effort of the Government of the Slovak Republic to ensure by internal measures the compensation of victims of Nazi persecution to the greatest possible degree. At the same time it is necessary to mention that Slovak victims of Nazi persecution, as compared with other victims, have not yet received any compensation for their sufferings from German authorities, although the Federal Republic of Germany made a symbolic gesture in the form of so called „Hirsch initiative" for some countries of Central and Eastern Europe, granting simple humanitarian aid for some categories of victims of Nazi persecution.

Slovak victims of Nazi persecution are still hoping that the Federal Republic of Germany will act in the same manner as it did with respect to all other victims of Nazi persecution duly compensated by German authorities.

REPUBLIC OF SLOVENIA

Delegation Statement

The Delegation of the Republic of Slovenia to the Washington Conference on Holocaust-Era Assets has the honor to announce that the Government of the Republic of Slovenia adopted the decision that it renounces its share of the gold pool of the Tripartite Commission for the Restitution of the Monetary Gold to the benefit of the Nazi Persecutee Relief Fund.

The text of the decision is as follows:

The Government of the Republic of Slovenia herewith adopts the following decision:

The Republic of Slovenia, as one of equal successor states to the former SFR of Yugoslavia, renounces its share of the gold pool of the Tripartite Commission for the Restitution of Monetary Gold – which was due to the former SFR of Yugoslavia – to the benefit of the International Fund for Needy Victims of Nazi Persecution (Nazi Persecutee Relief Fund), established at the London Conference on Nazi Gold held from 2 to 4 December 19.97, and, within the said Fund, to the benefit of non-governmental organizations in the Republic of Slovenia to aid individual victims of Nazi Persecution.

The share renounced by the Republic of Slovenia (for which it has already been established or will be established that it belongs to the Republic of Slovenia as an equal successor to the former SFR of Yugoslavia) is equivalent to 16.39% of the share of the gold pool – which was due to the former SFR of Yugoslavia – being formerly held by Tripartite Commission for the restitution of Monetary Gold, and now held jointly in the names of the Governments of France, the United Kingdom and the United States of America in the Bank of England.

The two non-governmental organizations in the Republic of Slovenia to the benefit of which the Republic of Slovenia renounces its share of the gold pool are the Slovenian Red Cross and the Slovenian Karitas which are obliged to allocate the funds acquired from the International Fund for Needy Victims Of Nazi Persecution (Nazi

Persecutee Relief Fund) either for the programs of aid to individual victims of Nazi persecution or for relevant educational programs.

SPAIN

Activities of the Spanish Commission on Holocaust-Era Assets

The Spanish commission was established by Royal Decree of July 11, 1997, with the aim of investigating the role of Spain in its economic relations with the Third Reich during the Second World War.

The Commission carried out research focused on the transactions of gold during the war and by December 97 it had already drafted a provisional report. The report was introduced, along with its conclusions, in the London Conference.

The final report was presented to the Government of Spain in April 1998, along with a series of recommendations. It concluded that Spain had bought gold during the Second World War, mainly from the Swiss National Bank, the Bank of Portugal and the Bank of England. It also concluded that only a small part of the gold acquired in those years came directly from Germany.

The report also studied the negotiations that took place between the Spanish Authorities and the Allies after the war, that led to an Agreement in execution of which Spain returned the amount of gold that, according to the investigations conducted at the time, had been looted by the Nazis.

At a later stage, the Spanish Commission presented two additional reports: the first one on the German insurance companies in Spain during the Second World War, and the second on the works of art bought or sold in Spain during the war.

The research on the German insurance companies was carried out in the archives of the Spanish Foreign Ministry and the Bank of Spain. The conclusions are as follows: during the war, German insurance firms in Spain increased both their capital and their customer base. Most of these customers as well as the signatories of the insurance policies were citizens of Spain or Spanish companies. Nothing came out in the research that points to any problem of non-payment of the policies during or after the war. There is no documentary trace of any claim whatsoever that affected either Spanish citizens, Jewish or non Jewish, or foreign nationals.

After the war, and following the recommendations and resolutions of the Allies, German goods and property in Spain, including the assets and liabilities of all German firms, were embargoed by the Spanish Authorities. Of the eighteen companies so embargoed, four were completely expropriated and liquidated.

Both the Report on Insurance and the Report on Works of Art, as did the Report on Gold Transactions from Central Europe, coincided in their conclusions: the role of Spain was very limited.

Indeed, in what pertains to works of art – and apart from smuggled items, difficult to trace – the cases registered are few in number and of minor importance. It was estimated that only one per cent of all the art dealers operating in Europe did business in Spain at the time. Therefore, this issue was barely examined in the course of the negotiations between the Spanish Government and the Allies at the end of the war.

The only case worth noticing is that of Alois Miedl, Göring's art dealer, who brought to Spain a total of twenty-two painting, that were deposited in the Tax Exempt Warehouse in Bilbao (Northern Spain). What happened to these paintings after 1949 is not known. Eight of the twenty-two paintings belonged to the Goudstikker Collection. The origin of the other fourteen is not known to this day.

Having reached the aforementioned conclusions, the Spanish Commission, well aware and sharing in the global feeling on the horrors of the Jewish Holocaust, shared also by many Sefardim, and keeping in mind the links and common culture and origin of the latter with Spain and the Spanish people, proposed to the Government of Spain – and the latter approved the proposal – to provide two hundred and fifty million Pesetas to the Nazi Persecutee Relief Fund, with the specific proviso that the money would be applied to the needs of the Sefardim.

Washington, D.C. December 1st, 1998

SWEDEN

Statement by
Mr. Salomo Berlinger
SPECIAL ADVISER TO THE COMMISSION ON JEWISH ASSETS IN SWEDEN
AT THE TIME OF THE SECOND WORLD WAR
MEMBER OF THE SWEDISH DELEGATION

Sweden does definitely not belong to the countries that were on the headlines with Nazi-confiscated art. Nevertheless, we considered it our duty to make a thorough investigation also of this subject in our Commission.

The Swedish Commission therefore appointed a special project group to work with art and insurance. Because of the limited time at disposal, let me just mention that among the actions taken we have interviewed a number of trade organizations dealing with art, Art associations, auction houses, transport- and storage companies, active during that period. We have advertised in daily newspapers in order to obtain information from the public and we have sent a questionnaire to every member of the Jewish Communities in Sweden.

The Project Group has through a number of experts conducted research in various public archives in Sweden and abroad and made a thorough study of the leading art museums in Sweden including the National Museum of Fine Arts in Stockholm. Purchases during and shortly after the war of international art were checked. Relatively few pieces of international art were purchased. There were however some purchases and donations of art works which the Nazis regarded as "Entartete Kunst".

The fact that there was no obligation to supply information about previous owners and that our researchers for that reason noted several examples of missing links in the documentation did not make our work easier. Even more complicated was the research done in private archives and galleries. However the lack of evidence or proof so far of dealings with looted art does not stop us from continuing our investigations.

Let me also state that we have a close look - as much as one can look into private collections - into possible looted art works, emanating from Göring and brought to Sweden by or to his relatives and friends, a very tough task for our Commission.

We have naturally also closely followed the international activities, particularly in the United States, to trace and find looted Jewish art. As a conclusion at this stage can be said that the investigations so far have not yielded any concrete and convincing examples of acquisitions of looted or confiscated works of art belonging to Jews in Sweden. However some traces have been found and we hope that with the co-operation we can get from abroad and from this conference – including the establishment of the Art Loss Register – we can finish our work with a good conscience. The final report of our commission and its conclusion will be submitted at the end of February 1999.

SWITZERLAND

Introductory Declaration

By Ambassador Thomas G. Borer
HEAD OF DELEGATION

Mr. Chairman, Mrs. Secretary of State, Mr. Foreign Secretary, Mr. Under Secretary of State, Honorable Delegates:

I would like to begin by expressing my great appreciation that this Conference is being held and that my country has been invited as an active participant. It is an honor for me and my delegation to be here, and I would like to thank the U.S. Government and the Holocaust Museum for making this important event possible. My country sees this Conference as a unique opportunity for all those concerned to pool their knowledge and to work together to achieve a deeper understanding of the historical questions related to the Holocaust era still awaiting answers. As the previous conference on Nazi gold held in London last year has shown, the task of establishing historical facts on these extremely delicate and complex issues is colossal and requires close international cooperation. We sincerely hope that the Conference will make a major contribution to clarifying the historical context of looted art, insurance policies, communal property, libraries, and archives.

We also especially welcome the fact that the Conference will pay special attention to Holocaust education, remembrance, and research. This dimension of the Conference is of particular importance: The memory of the victims and the sufferings of the survivors place a duty on all of us to keep remembering, for our conscious awareness of the mechanisms of history and of the roots of human evil is all we have to protect us against a resurgence of such monstrous insanity. Tragically, the passage of time is irreversible, and, as time goes by, this duty to remember takes on a new dimension: As the Holocaust survivors are approaching the end of their lives, the day will come when we won't have direct testimony at our disposal anymore. It is therefore important to develop ways and means of remembrance and sensitization. Even though Switzerland was largely spared the unspeakable horrors of World War II, it shares with other nations the commitment to remember and remain alert. To this end, it has undertaken a large number of initiatives at the cultural, educational, and political level. Switzerland – which has a long-standing tradition of peaceful coexistence of different languages, cultures, and faiths – is ready and willing to share with others its experiences in this field in order for us all to ensure that future generations will never be able to say "We didn't know..."

Therefore, I would like to express the sincere hope that this Conference will offer us the opportunity to pursue a constructive dialogue on how to advance towards a greater understanding of our common past in order to build a better future.

Mr. Chairman, Honorable Delegates,

Since 1996, Switzerland has been implementing an unprecedented series of measures to come to terms with the painful and recurring questions which have remained unanswered since 1945. Our objective is to shed light on the role Switzerland played in the context of World War II and on open questions related to any dormant accounts, looted art works and insurance policies that may still be held in Switzerland. My country has also demonstrated its profound sense of compassion towards the survivors of this unspeakable tragedy in the history of mankind by setting up a humanitarian fund endowed with Sfr. 275 million. These efforts have gained international recognition, and Under-Secretary of State Eizenstat will allow me to quote him when he stated some weeks ago: *"Switzerland continues to take the lead among the wartime neutral nations in the commitment it has made to provide justice in concrete ways."*

Although the role played by Switzerland with regard to unclaimed insurance policies or looted art is quite modest in comparison, our genuine will to cooperate has also been demonstrated by the leading role played by Swiss insurance companies in setting up an International Experts Commission. Its mandate is to address the difficult problem of World War II insurance policies. By the same token, Switzerland is undertaking detailed investigations with regard to looted art, a topic which is currently being investigated by the Bergier Commission. Furthermore, the delicate issue of combating any manifestation of anti-Semitism and of promoting tolerance among civilian society is being addressed by the Swiss government in the same resolute manner, as the recently released report by the Federal Commission against Racism illustrates. This serious and objective report has been unanimously praised for its candor and quality. Abraham Foxman, Anti-Defamation

League National Director, referred to the report in the following terms: *"The Swiss report should serve as a model for countries confronting their problems with anti-Semitism. We hope other nations and institutions will follow the Swiss example as they examine their wartime role and anti-Semitism in their society".*

By focusing all its efforts on carrying out these and other measures efficiently and rapidly, Switzerland has demonstrated an unambiguous and profound commitment to dealing with this issue. My Government would like to take the opportunity of expressing its hope that our discussions over the next three days will be held in a spirit of openness and objectivity, and that we will always bear in mind the common goal of our endeavor: Justice for the victims and awareness for the future, for the tragedy of the Holocaust shall never repeat itself.

Mr. Chairman, honorable delegates, thank you for your attention.

Delegation Statement

The following paper sums up the position of the Swiss government with regard to topics on the agenda of the Washington Conference on Holocaust-Era Assets.

I. REVIEW OF GOLD ISSUES

More than 53 years ago, in September 1945, the Swiss National Bank (SNB) provided the U.S. Legation in Berne with a statistical overview of gold transactions it had carried out during World War II with the central banks of 16 countries. These data have been confirmed since by each subsequent historical investigation. The gold purchased from the German Reichsbank amounted to $280 million, clearly less than the gold purchased from the Allies ($523 million). By the end of the war, the SNB had resold two thirds of the gold it had acquired from the Reichsbank.

While negotiating in spring 1946 with Switzerland in Washington, the Allies were informed extensively of the gold transactions. The result of these negotiations was a political agreement in the interest of both sides, representing governments only. On the gold issue, Switzerland agreed to pay $58 million to the Allies, whereas the latter waived all claims against Switzerland which could result from taking delivery of gold from the Reichsbank during the war.

It cannot be disputed that Switzerland completely fulfilled its obligations under the agreement. It paid the sums agreed to with the Allies both for gold acquired from Germany during World War II and for liquidation of German assets.

Moreover, neither the two Eizenstat reports (two studies on the conduct of wartime neutrals headed by U.S. Undersecretary of State Stuart Eizenstat and published in May 1997 and June 1998) nor the interim report on gold transactions published in May 1998 by the Bergier Commission (an independent body of Swiss and foreign experts established to examine Switzerland's history before, during, and after the war) raised historical arguments justifying the reopening of the Washington Agreement. On the contrary, they confirmed that the Allies were fully informed of all wartime gold transactions between the SNB and the German Reichsbank. The Bergier interim report even confirmed that the amount of looted gold acquired by the SNB was in fact *lower* than estimates the Allies made at that time.

One should not forget that, while legally binding, the Washington Agreement includes a political dimension. As in the case of the negotiations the Allied conducted with other neutral countries, this agreement resulted from concessions accepted by both sides. It involved four related issues: restitution of gold, liquidation of German private assets in Switzerland, abolition of blacklists affecting Swiss firms in the USA, and unfreezing of Swiss assets in the USA. It is thus clear that any renegotiation would imply a renewed discussion of all these issues and not simply of the gold question. For example, this would be the case with Swiss assets frozen by the US government during the war. Their unfreezing was also part of the Washington Agreement. At the time, the US claimed that about $100 million of those assets could not be certified and consequently confiscated those assets.

In any case, the 18 signatory countries of the Washington Agreement declared that "they waive (...) all claims against the Government of Switzerland and the SNB in connection with gold acquired during the war from Germany by Switzerland. All questions relative to such gold will thus be regulated." This unmistakably clear language made the accord a final global settlement.

In May 1997, the first Eizenstat report was released. It includes some assertions that go beyond a serious historical analysis and hence give rise to inaccurate interpretations. To begin with, neutrality is referred to as having fundamentally collided with morality. Such criticism is based on a premise that neutrality between those states defending what is good and those incarnating evil is immoral. It applies a latter day moral judgment to positions taken in the midst of war that is alien to and inconsistent with the tenets of international law that applied at the time. Significantly, all criticism of Swiss neutrality during the ensuing Cold War is avoided in the report. It must be emphasized that Swiss neutrality during World War II was aimed at protecting the country from conflict in order to safeguard the independence and survival of the population. These goals are the responsibility and priority of any sovereign nation. This policy also allowed Switzerland to become a haven for tens of thousands of refugees. It is true that the report indicates that Swiss neutrality benefited the Allies on many occasions, for instance, with regard to protection of tens of thousands of British and US prisoners of war.

When considered as a whole, neutrality implied a delicate balance between the pressure to adjust to the new order of the time and to resist its abhorrent ideology. If Switzerland had not remained neutral and, as a result, suffered the fate of France or Belgium, would anyone – including the Allies and Holocaust victims – have been better off? Clearly, the answer is "no".

A second historically unfounded reproach formulated against Switzerland touches on the alleged Swiss contribution to prolonging the war, which is said to have caused the death of tens of thousands of civilians and soldiers. Yet the report contains no corroborating evidence of this allegation. One might also ask what made the war possible in the first place. Even without coming back to such decisive stages as the Munich Conference of 1938 and the Hitler-Stalin Pact on the eve of the war, some simple facts put into true proportions the role of Switzerland, a country of only 4 million inhabitants during the war years.

It is today estimated that the total cost of the German war effort approached $850 billion. The Swiss share – including all financial and commercial transactions – amounted to 0.5% of this amount. Although bled white after Stalingrad, Germany was still able to launch murderous offensives such as the occupation of Italy in September of 1943, of Hungary in March 1944, and the Battle of the Bulge in December 1994. What made these last-ditch efforts possible has nothing to do with Swiss supplies, but everything to do with the last throes of a fanatical and brutal regime. In contrast, in a daring effort of mediation, Swiss intermediaries negotiated the surrender of all German troops in Italy, numbering one million men, a week before the end of the war in Europe. A modest shortening perhaps, but how many lives were spared?

At the London Gold Conference, which took place in December 1997, participants agreed that the results of the research on gold transactions with Nazi Germany must be shared at the international level and that this research process should continue.

At this international meeting, the *Bergier Commission* presented a substantial contribution, the *Statistical Review with Commentary*. In May 1998, it released an interim Report on *Switzerland and Gold Transactions in the Second World War*. According to U.S. Undersecretary Eizenstat, both reports «*demonstrate the integrity and the probity of the work of the Commission.*»

The interim report fully confirms the amounts of SNB gold transactions, as they have been known since the end of World War II as well as historical facts already published in the literature. But it also reveals new and tragic facts: a few gold ingots delivered by the

Reichsbank to its deposit in Berne, which were not distinguishable from the others, contained some 120 kgs of fine gold seized by the Nazis from extermination-camp victims. Although the Commission did not find any evidence that the responsible SNB parties had or could have had knowledge of this, the Swiss government declared itself shocked at this finding, since this victim gold stands for the immeasurable suffering the Nazis inflicted on victims of their persecution.

The question of victim gold requires further historical investigations on an international scale. The Swiss Independent Commission of Experts ("Bergier Commission") has always worked in that perspective. The Swiss Government welcomes all efforts from other countries and interested organizations. Therefore, it decided recently to publish a summary of the Commission's interim report. It is convinced that the Swiss people are entitled to know the truth about Switzerland's past, be it positive or negative.

Finally, mention should be made of the "Swiss Fund for Needy Victims of the Holocaust". The Fund was endowed with roughly $200 million through the contributions of Swiss banks, other private-sector companies, and the SNB. The Fund was set up in 1997 to support needy survivors of the Holocaust and their families. Switzerland welcomes the fact that other countries have decided to follow this path by creating an "International Nazi Persecutee Relief Fund".

II. OVERVIEW OF HOLOCAUST-ERA INSURANCE CLAIMS

The question of Holocaust-era insurance claims was revived not long ago and has not yet become the subject of extensive research. Thus Switzerland welcomes the opportunity to debate this important matter.

In order to gauge the relative relevance of this topic for Switzerland, the following facts need to be recalled:

Four Swiss insurance companies *(Basler, Swiss Life, Vita, and Winterthur)* had a branch in Germany long before Hitler came to power. About 80 German companies dominated the German market, whereas the four Swiss companies had a market share which did not exceed 2 to 3 percent. No Swiss life-insurance company was established in Central or Eastern Europe at the time.

Notwithstanding these facts, both the Swiss Government and the Swiss insurance companies concerned are fully committed to clarifying all open questions and providing active support for this process.

Since 1996, Swiss insurance companies have been searching intensively for policies which may have been held by Holocaust victims. Committed to find the owners of any World War II policy that may exist, they launched intensive searches in their archives and set up information mechanisms, such as cost-free "help lines" interested individuals can call to give or receive information on such policies.

The Swiss insurance companies have also been at the forefront of international efforts to establish an international commission of investigation which will examine all policies drawn up between 1920 and 1945 which have remained unclaimed since World War II. It should be mentioned that the Swiss companies were the first to sign the related Memorandum of Understanding, thus giving a clear sign of their genuine commitment to and support for this international effort.

The Swiss authorities welcome these initiatives, which clearly reflect a strong will to find a satisfactory solution to all remaining questions concerning World War II. The Swiss government further called on the Conference to actively support the work of the newly constituted International Commission of Investigation (IC), for it is only through international cooperation that satisfying answers can be found to this complex issue. On the other hand, this cooperative approach is incompatible with confrontational methods such as the pending class-action law suits and threats of sanctions. The Swiss government rejects such methods and urges that they be discarded in the process.

III. SWITZERLAND'S ROLE IN THE TRADE OF ART WORKS STOLEN BY THE NAZIS

1. Situation at the outset

Given its location in the heart of Europe, its highly developed infrastructure, and good international connections, Switzerland has been an important art market since the end of World War I. The Swiss art market participated in the boom of the 1920s with annual import values between SFr. 4 and 7 million. Like the economy as a whole, the Swiss art market was then heavily affected by the Depression of the 1930s. During World War II, borders remained closed, and imports as well as exports of art works declined sharply, with import values of between SFr. 1.9 million in 1939 and SFr. 219,000 in 1945 and export values between SFr. 1,142,000 and SFr. 16,000. Even in the 1950s, import values of art objects did not attain the level of the 1920s.

2. "Degenerate" art in Germany sold abroad

With Hitler's accession to power, many art works and artists were considered "degenerate"[1] by the Nazi regime. Following a decree issued by Goebbels on 30 June 1937, the "degenerate" art works could be removed from German public museums, and the most valuable of them could be sold abroad on the international market in exchange for foreign currencies.[2]

Such a sale took place in Switzerland on 30 June 1939 in Lucerne where the internationally known Galerie Fischer put up for auction 126 paintings and sculptures by great modern masters removed from the German public museums: Braque, van Gogh, Picasso, Klee, Matisse, Kokoschka, and 31 other artists. Out of the 350 persons attending the auction, 40 bought two thirds of the art works. The works were mainly sold to buyers from Switzerland, Belgium, and the United States.

3. Switzerland, a safe haven for endangered art works and artists

Before and during World War II, Switzerland became a secure deposit location, either temporarily or permanently, for endangered art works and artists. Stephanie Barron (Los Angeles County Museum of Art) wrote with reference to Helmut F. Pfanner[3]: *"After Hitler's rise to power, neutral Switzerland became a haven, albeit temporarily, for German artists (and collectors who emigrated to keep their collections intact), writers, musicians, actors, theatrical directors, and other refugees. Many settled in Swiss cities, hoping to pursue their careers with relatively little disruption. Some stayed only long enough to make arrangements to emigrate elsewhere in Europe or to Palestine or the United States. Some remained permanently; others returned to Germany after the war"*.

Robert von Hirsch transferred his first-class collection from Frankfurt/Main to Basel in 1933; he obtained the right to export it with a

---

[1] Impressionists, expressionists, fauvists, cubists, and surrealists.
[2] The rest was kept for "terror exhibitions" or destroyed.
[3] "The Role of Switzerland for Refugees" in *The Muses Flee Hitler,* edited by Jarrel C. Jackman and Carla M. Borden, Washington, DC, 1983, p. 243

present to Hermann Goering[4]. In 1941, he donated Gauguin's major work *Te matete* (1892) to the city of Basel in gratitude for accepting him as a refugee. The Austrian painter, writer, and humanist Oskar Kokoschka transited through Switzerland for his emigration from Czechoslovakia to England in 1938. Another example is the Dutch art dealer Nathan Katz who was able to flee to Switzerland, thanks to Swiss mediation in 1941.[5]

4. LOOTED ART WORKS IN SWITZERLAND

In neutral and democratic Switzerland, the rule of law prevailed during the whole period of World War II. As a result of closed borders, trading or dealing with art works in Switzerland was difficult. As indicated above, imports and exports of art works declined sharply during the war. Nevertheless, objects were shipped to and through Switzerland, for instance, by smuggling or through diplomatic pouches of the German legation and consulates.

Indeed, some art dealers, among them Theodor Fischer, took advantage of the situation and dealt with art of dubious origin. Fischer sold looted objects to collector Emil G. Bührle, an industrialist living in Zurich. Another well-known collector, Oskar Reinhart, in Winterthur wanted to avoid entanglements through dubious dealings and devoted great attention to the origin of the art works he was interested in acquiring. In 1958, he bequeathed his collection to the Swiss Confederation. In a study published in May 1998, the *Federal Office of Culture* concluded that no object found in Reinhart's collection had been acquired through illegal dealings.

5. Restitution efforts after World War II

The British Wing Commander and art historian Douglas Cooper, who belonged to the Monuments, Fine Arts, and Archives (MFAA) branch of the Allied armed forces, was sent to Switzerland in February 1945 to investigate the matter of stolen art works. He traveled freely

---

[4] Cranach's *Judgment of Paris*. Cf. J.W.Wille in "*Masterpieces*" from the Robert von Hirsch sale at Sotheby's". London, 1978, p. 5.

[5] Cf. A. Venema, *Kunsthandel in Nederland, 1940-1945*, ("Art Dealing in the Netherlands, 1940-1945"), pp. 254 ff.

through the country and spoke with all who had rank and names in art dealing. His investigation led him to compile a list of 77 art works stolen by the Nazis. Cooper's list formed the basis for the looted-art suits before the Swiss Supreme Court.

The Swiss federal government, aware of looted art works in Europe, instituted special measures in order to return looted art works to their rightful owners or their heirs: on 10 December 1945 and 22 February 1946, two Federal Council decrees initiated and facilitated the process of restitution. The first decree remained in effect until 31 December 1947. A special looted-objects chamber of the Federal Supreme Court was designated as the sole and exclusive authority responsible for looted goods. The 77 stolen art works on Cooper's list were recovered and subsequently returned to their owners. More than half of the works belonged to the well-known Parisian art dealer Paul Rosenberg and the rest to art dealers and collectors like the Parisian Bernheim-Jeune and Levy de Benzion and a British citizen established in Paris, Alphonse Kann. These paintings were bought by Theodor Fischer, of which he resold 12 to Emil G. Bührle.

It must be assumed that the art works mentioned represent less than the total number of stolen art objects sold in or having passed through Switzerland during World War II. Since a number of such works were sent to Switzerland by German diplomatic pouch, it remains very difficult to estimate the number of unreported cases of looted art works having ended up in or transited through Switzerland. However, in relation to restitution problems other countries face today, it is safe to assume that despite Switzerland's relatively important role as an art market during the war, the number of stolen art works that might still be located in Switzerland should be limited. Indeed, Marc Masurovsky, an expert on the American safe-haven policy, asserts that after the war thousands of paintings found their way from Europe to South and North America.[6] This seems confirmed by the number of art works of dubious

---

[6] *"American and British intelligence reports have detailed the presence of substantial collections transiting through Cuba, Venezuela, and Argentina, en route to the United States. According to American officials based in France in 1945 and 1946, export controls were so lax between Western Europe and the Western Hemisphere that they held special meetings to figure out ways of tightening them in order to prevent looted art from finding a safe haven in the U.S. or Latin America. The closing down in late 1946 of Allied commissions searching for looted art, the shift in priorities in the European theater from reparations to reconstruction, the lack of highly skilled individuals to screen art works bound for the Western Hemisphere in search of looted items, all these*

origin that emerged in the USA and may be hanging in American museums or possessed by private collectors. Research on this topic has just begun and should continue.

6. CURRENT RESEARCH EFFORTS

In the context of the present international debate on assets and other questions dating from the World War II period, Switzerland has taken concrete steps to clarify any open questions concerning looted art. In August 1998, the *Federal Office of Culture* published a study concluding that no object in collections belonging to the Swiss Confederation was found which had been acquired through illegal dealings. Another study on development of the Swiss art market between 1930 and 1955 will be published on 11 December 1998. In addition, the Independent Commission of Experts "Switzerland – Second World War" is mandated by the government to investigate this subject systematically and comprehensively and will put it in a historical and international context.

Furthermore, the Swiss authorities have taken concrete measures to address the issue of stolen art. At the federal level and based on the report drafted by the independent historian Thomas Buomberger, the Federal Office of Culture (FOC) will accept, from mid-January 1999, inquiries in connection with looted art dating from the period of World War II. This "Contact Bureau for Looted Art" will serve mainly as a contact office to register and pass on inquiries.

The FOC will examine possible inquiries that might affect the federal collections. If cases of unlawful acquisition were identified in the process, the possibility of restitution or compensation would have to be clarified immediately.

Moreover, the FOC has invited the cantons and Swiss museums to address the issue of looted art works and to check the provenance of their collections as the federal authorities have already done.

Finally, the FOC is prepared to call upon other institutions or organizations in Switzerland to comply with possible internationally

---

factors allow us to postulate that from August 1944 to July 1946, an untold number of paintings and drawings – perhaps numbering in the thousand – found their way out of Europe and into North and South American collections." Testimony of Marc Masurovsky, before the Committee on Banking and Financial Services. U.S. House of Representatives, 25 June 1997 agreed recommendations similar to guidelines of the American Association of Art Museum Directors and to support those responsible for implementing such recommendations, in particular with regard to publishing lists.

All international research, inventory, and publication efforts deserve our basic support. The same applies to opening all relevant archives. In this respect, one has to note that access to files from the federal inventory is granted liberally in Switzerland. These files are in principle accessible up to 1963. As to access to other archives, we strongly support all networking efforts at the national and international level.

Switzerland welcomes the current efforts towards closer cooperation in the context of looted art. It is in this spirit that the Swiss delegation has played an active role in order to facilitate a consensus on the 11 principles on restitution of Nazi looted art proposed at the Washington Conference.

IV. HOLOCAUST EDUCATION, REMEMBRANCE, AND RESEARCH

This century has produced more victims, more fallen soldiers, more murdered citizens and slain civilians, more dislodged minorities, more tortured people, more flayed and starved human beings, more political prisoners, and more refugees than we even could have imagined. Within this sad enumeration of atrocities, the Nazi crimes against humanity are unparalleled. They remain the symbol of the most complete denial of what we call humanity. As such, they stand before us as a constant warning never to let history repeat itself.

As time goes by, this duty to remember takes on a new dimension: As the Holocaust survivors are approaching the end of their lives, the day will come when we will have no direct testimony at our disposal anymore. It is therefore important to develop ways and means of remembrance and sensitivity. The place where we are gathered today is a perfect example of what is possible to pursue for this important purpose.

Remembering the Holocaust should not be seen as a way of constantly looking back at the past but as an important basis for discussion on issues relating to humanity, democracy, and equality, the Holocaust being a reference or starting point. An intelligent and sensitive way to do Holocaust teaching has much to tell us about tolerance, about freedom, about peace, about ourselves.

Switzerland is committed to this effort towards the future. This is also the reason why the Swiss delegation has proposed an important initiative to the States gathered at the Conference: The Swiss Delegation has <u>invited the participants</u> in the Washington Conference on Holocaust-Era Assets <u>to welcome</u>, during the concluding plenary session, <u>the Swiss government's proposal to host a governmental conference on the fight against use of the Internet for racist, anti-Semitic, or hate purposes</u>.

In recent years, the Internet has considerably developed. The web acts as a media, discussion forum, educational tool, and market place. However, the Internet is also used – or rather abused – as a most favored means of propaganda, in particular by racist and anti-Semitic activists, many of whom disseminate the "Auschwitz lie" theory. This is all the more worrying as the web appeals to and is used by younger generations.

As a concrete example, we can mention the plagiarism of the Swedish "Living History" project web site. Those who deny the Holocaust have recently set up an almost identical home page in order to spread their revisionist message by creating confusion.

More generally, the Swiss Federal Police recorded 700 racist, anti-Semitic, or revisionist websites in 1997. None was based in Switzerland, as dissemination of racist and anti-Semitic propaganda is strictly forbidden in our country. However, as the Internet has no borders, prohibition in specific countries is not a viable solution, for hate propaganda can be disseminated via foreign providers and anonymous parties. The need for international cooperation in this field is thus obvious.

While we are discussing Holocaust remembrance and education, the Swiss delegation wishes to stress the importance of preventing distribution of racist and anti-Semitic propaganda through the Internet: more and more youngsters use the Internet every day as a primary source of information and as an educational tool. As such, it is a critical task for every nation to contain the spread of hate propaganda on the web.

This Conference carries a huge moral burden. While work in the fields of remembrance and education is essential, the Conference should go further. In our opinion: this Conference shall send an important signal: A signal showing that the participants will not allow use of new technologies to deny a past that should never be repeated.

Switzerland and World War II:
A General Presentation

1. A wide-spread image depicted Switzerland during World War II as an **island** in continental Europe preserved from Nazi terror and war devastation by **divine providence**. It is hardly necessary to say that such an image does not correspond to reality.

Lying at the crossroads of big powers of continental Europe, Switzerland had a centuries-long experience of avoiding implication in wars. As a matter of fact, military, political and economic factors - and not divine providence - preserved the territorial integrity of the country, its democratic institutions, its democratic values, its cultural variety and the life of the about 300,000 refugees admitted, including 28,000 of Jewish confession. Up to 450,000 men served simultaneously in the Swiss Army, which corresponded to more then 10 percent of the population. They were ready to resist to any foreign military attack. The German General Staff had prepared detailed operations plans for attacking Switzerland, as those known under the code name of *Tannenbaum*.

If Switzerland was not preserved by divine providence but by a series of man-made factors, we should add it was, indeed, not an island. There was no ocean between this little democratic country of 4 million inhabitants and Europe dominated by the Axis powers, their Allies and the countries they occupied (**see map** of Europe in early 1943). Or, using Undersecretary Eizenstat's words: *"Alone among the neutrals, Switzerland was totally encircled by the Axis powers and the countries they occupied."*

2. Switzerland's **economy** was very useful for Germany. First of all, we should not forget that Germany was Switzerland's main trade partner since long before World War II. These economic relations subsisting during the war were not in contradiction with the longstanding neutrality status of Switzerland recognized by international law. Switzerland had no choice but to deal economically with its potential aggressor in order to maintain its independence. This policy was simply a non-heroic way to survive.

The commercial links with Germany did not make Switzerland richer: real national income diminished considerably between 1939 and

1945. But they raise an important question: did they contribute to prolong World War II? Apart from the impossibility to answer this question on a scientific-historical basis, we have to consider the quantitative data and keep the sense of proportion. Gold sold by the German Reichsbank to the Swiss banks amounted to 0.1 percent of the Reich's total war costs. Swiss war material sold to Germany amounted to a percent still less important. Gold and war material operations were conducted with both belligerent camps.

3. The rise of German power in Europe had a dampening effect on export trade relations for Switzerland, a land short of raw materials and energy. It meant an increasing economic dependence on its trade partner, thereby increasing Switzerland's exposure to German blackmail according to the prevailing military and political situation. Despite these extremely difficult conditions, the scope of trade transacted with the Allies amounted to one third of that carried out with the Axis. By the way, Berlin repeatedly demanded that Bern completely sever these economic ties. Without success.

In consequence, Switzerland was in a **highly difficult position** until the end of 1944, when France was completely freed. But even in April 1945, a powerful German army was still occupying Northern Italy, at the Southern border of Switzerland. The Swiss were sensitive to the catastrophe under way out of their borders. They demonstrated from 1944 concrete and material solidarity with European countries hit by the war: the *Swiss donation to war victims* consecrated about 200 million Swiss francs to relief projects and to the hospitalization in Switzerland of more than 10,000 victims of the war. This important effort was acknowledged by the US Government, which, in a document from 1950[1], stated: *"Switzerland's economic contribution to European recovery, begun before the Marshall Plan was inaugurated, has been substantial. Since the end of the war the Swiss Government has extended over $187,000,000 in credits to other ERP countries. Additional private credits from Swiss banks come to approximately an equal amount. Coupled with purely charitable gifts for international relief and welfare, Switzerland's aggregate contribution to European relief and rehabilitation amounts to half a billion dollars, a significant sum for a small country whose total yearly national income is less than $4 billion."*

---

[1] *Foreign Relations of the United States*, 1950, Volume III, p. 1586.

4. In the last two years, distorted views of Switzerland and its people were disseminated by some media. According to one critic accusation, the Swiss were said to have had great sympathy towards the Nazis. If this had been true, the country would have been easily annexed to the Third Reich. In the Foreword of his Second historical report, Undersecretary Stuart Eizenstat underlines the historical truth: *"The Swiss people were overwhelmingly sympathetic to the Allies, even against the backdrop of Switzerland's strict neutrality"*.

* * *

5. After the end of the war, Switzerland assumed its **responsibilities** on several issues. The gold claims were definitely settled with the Allies here in Washington. German assets were liquidated in conformity with agreements concluded with the Allies in 1946 and 1952. Legal dispositions concerning the return of looted assets to their rightful owners and concerning heirless assets were taken. However, as elsewhere, the United States of America included, these measures were taken in the spirit of the postwar period, and their implementation was not perfect.

6. During the past two years, Switzerland took a series of measures in the spirit of **truth, justice and solidarity**.

- First, as an expression of solidarity and thanks to contributions from Swiss banks, private-sector companies, and the Swiss National Bank, the Swiss Fund for Needy Victims of the Holocaust was set up to support needy survivors of the Holocaust and their families. The Fund was endowed with approximately $200 million. Thus far, over $26.7 million has been paid to more than 30,000 Holocaust victims. Of the remaining funds, about $37.1 million are already granted for payment, mainly to survivors in the USA. Additional applications totaling SFr. 7 million ($5.10 million) are pending. A further installment of about $60 million will be paid to the WJRO in Jerusalem for needy Holocaust survivors in Israel as soon as a distribution channel is made available.

- Second, an International Independent Commission of Experts is examining historical and legal aspects of Switzerland's role as a financial center before, during, and after the war years. The Commission has released an intermediate report on the Swiss National Bank's gold transactions. A second intermediate report on refugee policy is to be published in 1999.

- Third, the Swiss Bankers' Association published in July and October 1997 several lists of names of foreign and Swiss holders of unclaimed accounts. More than 16,500 people have registered and lodged claims to date on lists of foreign holders of dormant accounts. Moreover, the Swiss banks set up an **independent Claims Resolution Foundation** to provide an international and objective forum to adjudicate claims on dormant accounts of foreigners from the period prior to 1945. Up to 15 Swiss and foreign arbitrators with experience in international adjudication preside over a fast-track procedure to hear claims cost-free to the claimants under relaxed standards of proof that recognize the difficulty of presenting evidence under the tragic circumstances of the Holocaust and World War II. As a concrete result, the first 58 payments of dormant accounts were made by the end of September 1998. Settlement of all claims could occur within a year.

- Fourth, a **Committee of Eminent Persons headed by Paul Volcker** was set up in May 1996. Its mandate is to investigate all unclaimed assets in Swiss banks by Nazi victims which have not yet been identified. The Committee's objective is to complete the major elements of its investigation by the end of this year. The final report is to be released in 1999.

- Fifth, another project bears witness to Switzerland's commitment to strengthen our humanitarian tradition and solidarity: the Swiss Foundation for Solidarity, with a planned annual budget of several hundred million Swiss francs. The main purpose of the Swiss Foundation for Solidarity is to contribute to a future in human dignity, including for those suffering from or threatened by poverty or violence, in Switzerland and abroad.

Finally, in connection with the discussion on Switzerland's role during and immediately after World War II, Swiss citizens have expressed their solidarity and, in keeping with the humanitarian tradition of our country, offered proof of it through various campaigns.

The **Solidarity Association/Foundation for Holocaust Victims**: an initiative of a high school in Berne. Since the beginning of 1997, more than SFr. 140,000 have been donated and presented to relief agencies that care for Holocaust victims. An example: a gift of SFr. 50,000 to the **AMCHA** (National Israeli Center for Psychosocial Support of Survivors of the Holocaust and the Second Generation)

Foundation for Humanity and Justice: Collected SFr. 2 million for needy victims of the Nazi regime and their descendents. Individuals and projects were previously supported by SFr. 800,000.

Fund in Favor of Holocaust Survivors and Jewish People in Distress: Mobilized resources for Holocaust survivors and their descendents (SFr. 270,000).

With these measures, Switzerland has shown that it is not suppressing its past but rather learning from it, as we work toward a future of peace and solidarity. We are fully committed to righting the wrongs that may have been done with these appropriate moral and financial answers.

* * *

7. In May 1998, **Under Secretary Stuart Eizenstat acclaimed the Swiss efforts**: "*No country is undertaking more comprehensive research than Switzerland through its historical commission headed by Professor Jean-François Bergier. (...) Switzerland continues to take the lead among the wartime neutral nations in the commitment it has made to provide justice in concrete ways. It is important to recognize, amidst all the criticism and controversy, the breadth and depth of the Swiss effort*".

Three months later, a settlement was agreed upon in New York between plaintiffs and the two Swiss banks concerned by Class actions. It is our sincere hope that following this settlement, a just distribution plan can be established shortly and that the Holocaust victims will soon benefit from those payments. We appreciate that this settlement has in general led to a fairer and less polemic debate about Switzerland's past.

We hope that such a fairness, which we have always asked for, will be respected in the future.

The Bank's settlement does in no way affect **the strong determination of the Swiss Government and the Swiss people to pursue the implementation of the measures of truth, justice and solidarity.**

Switzerland's Role in the Trade of Art Works Stolen by the Nazis

1. SITUATION AT THE OUTSET

Given its location in the heart of Europe, its highly developed infrastructure and good international connections, Switzerland has been an important art market since the end of World War I. It experienced a peak in 1920 when art works valued at about SFr. 11 million were imported. Although imports of art works declined in the following years, the Swiss art market participated in the boom of the 1920s with annual import values between SFr. 4 and 7 million. Like the entire economy, art dealing was greatly affected by the Depression of the 1930s. During World War II, borders were closed, and imports as well as exports of art works declined sharply, with import values of between SFr. 1.9 million in 1939 and SFr. 219,000 in 1945 and export values between SFr. 1,142,000 and SFr. 16,000. Even in the 1950s, import values of art objects did not attain the level of the 1920s.

2. "DEGENERATE" ART IN GERMANY SOLD ABROAD

With Hitler's accession to power, many art works and artists were considered "degenerate"[1] by the Nazi regime. Following a decree issued by Goebbels on 30 June 1937, the "degenerate" art works could be removed from German public museums, and the most valuable of them could be sold abroad on the international market in exchange for foreign currencies.[2]

Such a sale took place in Switzerland on 30 June 1939 at the Grand Hôtel National in Lucerne when the internationally known Galerie Fischer put up for auction 126 paintings and sculptures by great modern masters removed from the German public museums: Braque, van Gogh, Picasso, Klee, Matisse, Kokoschka, and 31 other artists. Out of the 350 people who were invited, 40 bought two thirds of the art works. The

---

[1] Impressionists, expressionists, fauvists, cubists, and surrealists.
[2] The rest was kept for "terror exhibitions" or destroyed.

works were mainly sold to buyers from Switzerland, Belgium, and the United States.

3. SWITZERLAND, A SAFE-HAVEN FOR ENDANGERED ART WORKS AND ARTISTS

Before and during World War II, Switzerland became a secure deposit location, either temporarily or permanently, for endangered art works and artists. Stephanie Barron (Los Angeles County Museum of Art) wrote with reference to Helmut F. Pfanner[3]:

> *"After Hitler's rise to power, neutral Switzerland became a haven, albeit temporarily, for German artists (and collectors who emigrated to keep their collections intact), writers, musicians, actors, theatrical directors, and other refugees. Many settled in Swiss cities, hoping to pursue their careers with relatively little disruption. Some stayed only long enough to make arrangements to emigrate elsewhere in Europe or to Palestine or the United States. Some remained permanently; others returned to Germany after the war".*

Robert von Hirsch transferred his first-class collection from Frankfurt/Main to Basel in 1933; he obtained the right to export it with a present to Hermann Goering[4]. In 1941, he donated Gauguin's major work *Te matete* (1892) to the city of Basel in gratitude for accepting him as a refugee. The Austrian painter, writer, and humanist Oskar Kokoschka transited through Switzerland for his emigration from Czechoslovakia to England in 1938. Another example is the Dutch art dealer Nathan Katz who was able to flee to Switzerland, thanks to Swiss mediation in 1941.[5]

---

[3] "The Role of Switzerland for Refugees" in *The Muses Flee Hitler* edited by Jarrel C. Jackman and Carla M. Borden, Washington, DC, 1983, p. 243

[4] Cranach's *Judgment of Paris*. Cf. J.W.Wille in "*Masterpieces*" from the Robert von Hirsch sale at Sotheby's". London, 1978, p. 5.

[5] Cf. A. Venema, *Kunsthandel in Nederland, 1940-1945*, ("Art Dealing in the Netherlands, 1940-1945"), pp. 254 ff.

4. LOOTED ART WORKS IN SWITZERLAND

In neutral and democratic Switzerland, the rule of law prevailed during the whole period of World War II. As a result of closed borders, trading or dealing with art works in Switzerland was difficult. As indicated before, imports and exports of art works declined sharply during the war. Nevertheless, objects were shipped to and through Switzerland, for instance, by smuggling or through diplomatic pouches of the German legation and consulates.

Indeed, some art dealers, among them Theodor Fischer, took advantage of the situation and dealt with art of dubious origin. Fischer sold some looted objects to collector Emil G. Bührle, a rich industrialist living in Zurich. Another well-known collector, Oskar Reinhart, in Winterthur wanted to avoid entanglements through dubious dealings and devoted great attention to the origin of the art works he was interested in acquiring. In 1958 he bequeathed his collection to the Swiss Confederation. In its study published in May 1998, the *Federal Office of Culture* concluded that no object found in the Reinhart's collection had been acquired through illegal dealings.

5. RESTITUTION EFFORTS AFTER WORLD WAR II

At the end of the war, the British Wing Commander and art historian Douglas Cooper, who belonged to the Monuments, Fine Arts, and Archives (MFAA) branch of the Allied armed forces, was sent to Switzerland in February 1945 in order to investigate the matter of stolen art works. He traveled freely through the country and spoke with all who had rank and names in art dealing. His investigation led him to compile a list of 77 art works stolen by the Nazis. Cooper's list formed the basis for the looted-art suits before the Swiss Supreme Court.

The Swiss federal government, aware of plundering of art works in Europe, instituted the following measures in order to restitute looted art works to their rightful owners or their heirs: on 10 December 1945 and 22 February 1946, two Federal Council decrees initiated a process to restitute stolen art works. The first one remained in effect until 31 December 1947. The looted-objects chamber of the Federal Supreme Court was designated as the sole and exclusive authority responsible for looted objects. The 77 stolen art works on Cooper's list were recovered and subsequently restored to their owners. More than half of the works belonged to the well-known Parisian art dealer Paul Rosenberg and the others to art dealers and collectors like the Parisian Bernheim-Jeune and Levy de Benzion and a British citizen established in Paris, Alphonse Kann. These paintings were bought by Theodor Fischer from whom Emil G. Bührle acquired 12 of them.

These art works do not represent the whole amount of stolen art objects sold in Switzerland during World War II. Since a number of them were sent to Switzerland by German diplomatic pouch, it remains very difficult to estimate how many other looted art works ended up in or transited through Switzerland. However, in relation to problems related to restitution that other countries face today, it is safe to assume that despite Switzerland's relatively important role in the art market during the war, the number of stolen art works that might still be located in Switzerland should be limited. Indeed, Marc Masurovsky, one of the best-known experts on the American safe-haven policy, asserts that after the war thousands of paintings found their way from Europe to South and North America.[6] This seems confirmed by the number of art works of dubious origin that emerged in the USA and may be hanging in American museums or possessed by private collectors. Research on this topic has just begun and should be investigated further.

---

[6] *"American and British intelligence reports have detailed the presence of substantial collections transiting through Cuba, Venezuela, and Argentina, en route to the United States. According to American officials based in France in 1945 and 1946, export controls were so lax between Western Europe and the Western Hemisphere, that they held special meetings to figure out ways of tightening them in order to prevent looted art from finding a safehaven in the U.S. or Latin America. The closing down in late 1946 of Allied commissions searching for looted art, the shift in priorities in the European theater from reparations to reconstruction, the lack of highly skilled individuals to screen art works bound for the Western Hemisphere in search of looted items, all these factors allow us to postulate that from August 1944 to July 1946, an untold number of paintings and drawings – perhaps numbering in the thousand – found their way out of Europe and into North and South American collections."* Testimony of Marc Masurovsky, before the Committee on Banking and Financial Services. U.S. House of Representatives, 25 June 1997

6. CURRENT RESEARCH EFFORTS

In the context of the present international debate on assets and other questions dating from the World War II period, Switzerland has taken concrete steps to clarify any open questions on looted art: the *Federal Office of Culture* already published in August 1998 a study concluding that no object in collections belonging to the Swiss Confederation was found which had been acquired through illegal dealings. Another study on the development of the Swiss art market between 1930 and 1955 will be published on 11 December 1998. In addition, the Independent Commission of Experts "Switzerland – Second World War" is mandated by the government to investigate this subject systematically and comprehensively and will put it in a historical and international context.

Concrete steps have also been taken: At the Federal level and based on the Buomberger report, the Federal Office of Culture (BAK) will accept, from mid-January 1999, inquiries in connection with looted art dating from the period of World War II. This "Contact Bureau for Looted Art" will serve mainly as a contact office to register and pass on inquiries.

Possible inquiries that might affect the Federal collections will be examined by the Office. If cases of unlawful acquisition were identified in the process, the possibility of restitution or compensation would have to be clarified immediately.

Moreover, the Federal Office of Culture has invited the Cantons and the Swiss Museums to address the issue of looted art works and to check the provenance of their collections as the Federal authorities have already done.

Furthermore, the Federal Office of Culture is prepared to call upon other institutions or organizations in Switzerland to comply with possible internationally agreed recommendations similar to the guidelines of the American Association of Art Museum Directors and to support those responsible for implementing such recommendations, in particular with regard to publishing lists.

All international research, inventory and publication efforts deserve our basic support. The same applies to opening all relevant archives. Here I wish to note that access to files from the Federal inventory is granted liberally in Switzerland. These files are in principle accessible up to 1963. As to the access to other archives, we strongly support all networking efforts at the national and international level.

Teaching Tolerance

Initiatives to Promote Educational, Cultural and Political Tolerance in Switzerland
November 1998

INTRODUCTION

The heat and acrimony that permeated the controversy about Switzerland's role before, during and after World War II have largely died down. We hope that the nation can now get down to examining this period of its history in the necessary calm and with the commitment that this task requires. The most important issue is to find out the truth, while bearing in mind that truth within the framework of history is always more complex than simple scientific truth. Both the Swiss government and parliament have expressed the firm wish that questions should be asked openly, investigated thoroughly and with the maximum transparency, and answered without reservations. This task is essential; it is in the interests of our country, especially of future generations.

The results of the Commission of Independent Experts (Bergier Commission) will make an important contribution to this process. It is essential that its findings are discussed as widely as possible among the Swiss public, and especially among the younger generation. It is important that the discussions cover both the negative as well as the numerous positive aspects of the Swiss response.

However, this wide-ranging dialogue should not deal only with the past. Even though Switzerland was largely spared the unspeakable horrors of the Second World War, it shares with other nations an obligation to remember and to remain alert, so that such a tragedy can never happen again. To this end, a large number of initiatives in the areas of culture and education have already been taken in Switzerland - a country which has long been the home of communities with different languages and faiths. This document lists and briefly describes these initiatives, some of which are of long-standing. They have been selected on the basis of their particular relevance to current efforts to reappraise our history and to generate more awareness of the importance of promoting tolerance and the fight against racism and anti-Semitism.

POLITICAL AND CULTURAL EVENTS

- In 1997, a number of federal parliamentarians including the President and the Vice-President of the Swiss Confederation set up a group against anti-Semitism.

  This multi-party group is committed to and supports activities against anti-Semitism both in politics and society.

- On 14 May 1998, the President of the Swiss Confederation, Flavio Cotti, gave a major policy speech entitled **Tolerance in a Democracy** at the National Congress of Teachers and Educationalists in Zurich.

  This speech, which condemned all forms of racism, anti-Semitism and intolerance as counter to Swiss secular values, had a strong impact in the media and on the public.

- During 1998, as part of the 150th anniversary celebrations of the Swiss constitution, a traveling exhibition entitled **Tolerance 98, a game with limits** is touring all the different linguistic regions of Switzerland.

  This multi-lingual exhibition invites viewers to analyze the topic of tolerance for themselves. Stands, stories, pictures, listening stations, interactive experiments, workshops, framework events and an illustrated multi-lingual magazine as well as live and Internet discussions supplement and accompany the exhibition.   *More information is available on: http://www.tolerance.ch

- On 18 November 1998, the Vice-President of the Swiss Confederation, Ruth Dreifuss, inaugurated the exhibition **Visas for Life** in Bern.

  This exhibition shows for the first time in Switzerland how the Swiss consul Carl Lutz, the police captain, Paul Grüninger, and a dozen other courageous diplomats from Germany, China, Holland, Italy, Japan, Portugal, Sweden, Hungary and the USA saved persecuted people from the Nazi gas chambers. Together these courageous people saved between 150,000 and 200,000 people, many of them Jews. *The exhibition will last until 2 December 1998.

- In June 1998, an exhibition **Les chemins de passage (Escape routes)** was opened in Geneva.

  This meticulously presented exhibition, illustrates the clandestine routes through which "guides" led refugees towards Switzerland – the last remaining haven of liberty on the continent. The exhibition has also been mounted in other cities throughout Switzerland.

- The **Lutz-Born-Wallenberg monument** is due to be unveiled soon in front of the House of Human Rights in Geneva.

  It will honor three exceptional people who distinguished themselves helping refugees during the Second World War. A monument commemorating the gratitude of refugees who were admitted into Switzerland during the Second World War may also be erected in Geneva at the initiative of a group of these refugees.

- A number of cinemas, including the Kellerkino in Bern, have shown **a series of films on the theme *Jewish Stories*.**

  *We mention, in particular, the showing of the film by Walo Deuber **Spuren verschwinden, Nachträge ins Europäische Gedächtnis**, which, as its title indicates, traces the important history of Jewish culture in Eastern Europe.*

- A traveling exhibition, entitled ***Swiss Jews,*** is currently shown across the country.

This exhibition presents the origin and diversity of the history of the Jews in Switzerland.

- Last but not least, a project for a ***Center for Tolerance,*** initiated by a Jewish-Gentile committee is well under way.

The idea is to present the issues of tolerance, combating racism and anti-Semitism, and to promote coexistence with a focus on the Holocaust. The Center would house a permanent exhibition and would also organize temporary exhibitions, seminars and conferences. It would target on schools, teachers, youth associations, as well as be open to the general public. The project is planned to be completed in two to three years. The Center will probably be located in Bern.

INITIATIVES AND PROJECTS IN EDUCATION

Sociological, historical and educational background material

- **"Le rôle de la Suisse durant la Seconde Guerre mondiale, Bibliographie choisie", ("Switzerland's role during the Second World War, selected bibliography"),** published by the Federal Office of Culture, 1997.

This exhaustive 227-page bibliography on Switzerland during WWII presents various works on topics such as refugee policy, dormant accounts, Switzerland's relations with Germany and with the Allies, Switzerland's defense army, and domestic policy. This volume stresses the educational aspects of the works it lists as well as on their particular relevance. It contains brief summaries of their contents and critical reviews. It is useful to anyone interested in these subjects and especially to teachers and researchers.

- **Medienpaket Rassismus (Media package on racism)**

This new set of teaching materials on racism, anti-Semitism and tolerance was launched in April 1998 by the Foundation for Education and Tolerance, the foundation against racism and anti-Semitism, and the Pestalozzianum Center in Zurich. It consists of modern educational material, and includes a basic manual and a file of teaching materials and aids, as well as a video on the topic of racism and tolerance entitled Colors of Schweiz. It is intended for secondary school teachers, who have been familiarized with it at special seminars, and is being progressively distributed throughout schools in German-speaking Switzerland. It has been so successful that projects are now under way to adapt it to Switzerland's other national languages, French and Italian.

- **"Geschichte des Judaismus in der Schweiz" ("History of Judaism in Switzerland")**

This work will be published by the specialist publisher of educational and school publications, Lehrmittelverlag.

- **"Anti-Semitism in Switzerland"**

This is a report on past and current manifestations of anti-Semitism, with recommendations for counter-measures.

It was published in November 1998, in French, German, Italian and English by the Swiss Federal Commission against Racism. The Anti-Defamation League in New York called the report "Honest, Hard-hitting and realistic". ADL national Director Abraham H. Foxman, further said: "The Swiss report should serve as a model for countries confronting their problems with anti-Semitism. We hope other nations and institutions will follow the Swiss example as they examine their wartime role and anti-Semitism in their society"

- **"Le Livre Noir et Blanc" ("The Black and White Book")**

*This book, aimed at primary school pupils, is accompanied by a teaching manual **"Tous différends, tous égaux" ("All different, all equal").***

It was produced and published in 1993 by three associations: la Déclaration de Berne (The Bern Declaration), le Comité suisse pour l'UNICEF (The Swiss Committee for UNICEF), and le Service école-tiers monde (The Service for Schools and the Third- World).

- **"Odyssea: Accueils et approches interculturelles" ("Odyssea: Intercultural Welcomes and Approches")**

  This reference manual on intercultural teaching methods, including preventing racism was written by the educationalist, Christiane Perregaux, and published in 1994 in French, German and Italian by la Commission romande des moyens d'enseignement et d'apprentissage (the French-speaking Swiss Commission on methods of teaching and learning). It is used in Schools throughout Switzerland.

- **"Rassistische Vorfälle in der Schweiz, eine Chronologie und eine Einschätzung" ("Incidents of racism in Switzerland, a chronology and evaluation"), published** annually by the Gesellschaft Minderheiten in der Schweiz (The Society of Minorities in Switzerland) and the Foundation against Racism.

  This work contains detailed accounts of incidents and other information concerning racism, xenophobia and anti-Semitism that have occurred during the past year. It gives statistics on legal proceedings, based on Art. 261 bis of the Swiss Penal Code (the anti-racist law), brought against such acts, and on the resulting judgments. It also contains research-based findings on how to prevent such incidents.

- **Summarized version of the Interim Report by the Independent Commission of Experts Switzerland - Second World War on Gold transactions in Switzerland during WWII**

  The Swiss Government has decided to publish the main points of the Bergier Interim Report on gold transactions in the form of a free booklet. This booklet will be published in German, French, Italian and English. It will provide an account of this important investigation, and will be easily accessible to a wide public.

- **"Die Schweiz im Zweitem Weltkrieg" ("Switzerland during the Second World War")**

  The editors of the Journal of Swiss Teachers are planning to devote an edition of their Journal to the subject of Switzerland and the Second World War.

This special edition, intended for teachers, will contain research-based contributions on various subjects related to Switzerland and the Second World War, and will include a chapter on teaching about the Holocaust. Each chapter will be accompanied by notes giving advice and teaching ideas.

- **"Aussenpolitik, Die Schweiz in der Welt von heute und morgen, 1997" ("Foreign policy, Switzerland in today's and tomorrow's world, 1997")**

This school text book on Swiss foreign policy, edited by the Swiss Foreign Policy Society in conjunction with the Conférence des Directeurs cantonaux de l'instruction publique (CDIP) (Swiss Conference of Cantonal Ministers of Education), is aimed at students at secondary schools. It contains a chapter devoted to the discussions of Switzerland's role before, during and after the Second World War.

At the end of 1998, the Swiss Conference of Cantonal Ministers of Education studied the question of teaching the issues of the Holocaust and tolerance at its annual general meeting. In particular, it recalled its 1991 Déclaration sur l'enseignement à la tolérance (Declaration on the Teaching of Tolerance), as well as the report "Racisme et école" (Racism and Schools) of its educational commission."

- **List of refugees admitted into Switzerland during World War II (to be published)**

The Swiss government is planning to publish an exhaustive list of the 51,000 or more civilian refugees who were admitted into Switzerland between 1939 and 1945.

Awards and Prizes

- **Fischhof Prize**

This prize (named after a WWII refugee in Switzerland) rewards institutions or individuals who have distinguished themselves in fighting racism, xenophobia or anti-Semitism. It is awarded by the

"Gesellschaft Minderheiten in der Schweiz" (Society of Minorities in Switzerland) and the Foundation against Racism and Anti-Semitism.

- **Max und Erika Gideon School Prize**

    This prize rewards school pupils and teachers who have distinguished themselves in fighting racism, xenophobia or anti-Semitism. It is awarded by the "Gesellschaft Minderheiten in der Schweiz" and the Foundation against Racism and Anti-Semitism.

Other recent initiatives and studies

- Working Group on the fight against racism and anti-Semitism on the Web

    The Swiss federal authorities together with Internet providers in Switzerland have just set up a working group to study the problem of racism on the Internet. This aims to contribute to the fight against the dissemination (mostly from abroad) of racist or pornographic pages on the Web. The Working Group will present a list of joint proposals at the beginning of 1999.

- **Exchange programs and seminars**

    Numerous exchange programs for teachers and pupils have taken place. The last one involved 27 intermediate-school teachers from the French-speaking part of Switzerland, who attended a continuing-education seminar at the Yad Vashem Holocaust Center in Jerusalem.

    Besides field trips and visits to memorials, the program included seminars and presentations on the history of Judaism, anti-Semitism and the Holocaust, as well as on current forms of anti-Semitism. Teachers learned to teach the subject of the Holocaust to children, and to adapt their methodolgy to various age groups. Contacts with Holocaust survivors who talked about their experiences, made a deep impression on the Swiss teachers. This program showed that teaching history is not simply a matter of presenting facts but must also touch on the issue of human suffering. The participants received specific teaching material on this subject.

- **Various events** at schools and universities have been set up **to generate awareness about the problems of racism, xenophobia and anti-Semitism.**

  *These include lectures given by Holocaust survivors and visits to extermination camps in Germany and Poland. In September 1997, the Central Office of Continuing Education for Teachers in Bern organized a seminar called: "Switzerland and the Second World War", at which more than 100 teachers participated. On 2 March 1998, a meeting of Swiss and Israeli students entitled **On the threshold of a new century** enabled the participants to discuss the subject of the Holocaust, its significance and its dimensions.*

- **A seminar on anti-Semitism** *organized for history and philosophy teachers by the Coopération Intercommunautaire contre l'antisémitisme et la Diffamation (CICAD) (Committee against Anti-Semitism and Defamation) was held in the summer of 1998.*

- **An international colloquium on the subject of racism and anti-Semitism** was held at the Institute of Comparative Law in Lausanne in October 1998.

  More than 100 people attended, several of whom were specialists from Eastern European countries which are confronted with acute problems of intolerance and even inter-ethnic violence.   In her opening address, the Vice-President of the Swiss Federal Council, Ruth Dreifuss declared the fight against racism a permanent task of the state, and emphasized that society must maintain a constant guard against it.

- **Evaluation studies on teaching methods for the prevention of racism and anti-Semitism**

  Two studies on preventing xenophobia, racism and violence were conducted in 1995 and 1997 among selected groups of 17 to 19 year-old students from Swiss vocational schools in Switzerland.

  The projects focused on tolerance and understanding of asylum seekers and their situation, on the role of foreign workers in Switzerland, and on increasing awareness of both the Jewish religion and the Holocaust. One of the main conclusions of these projects was that direct contact with people who have first-hand experience of suffering is the most effective way of changing attitudes because it appeals more to pupils' hearts than to their minds.

- In 1996, the Federal Commission against Racism launched a media campaign **called Der Schöne Schein (Fine Appearances)**, to fight racism and anti-Semitism.

This campaign, which aimed to teach tolerance and prevent racism, received the Gold Medal of the United Nations Department of Public Information, as well as the Swiss Art Directors Club prize for the best campaign of the year.

- Between July and August 1997, a six-part documentary series entitled **Die Schweiz im Schatten des Dritten Reichs (Switzerland in the shadow of the Third Reich),** produced by the German television channel DRS was broadcasted on Swiss national television.

BODIES, FOUNDATIONS AND OTHERS NGOS ACTIVE IN THIS FIELD (NON-EXHAUSTIVE):

- *Federal Commission against Racism*
- *Stiftung gegen Rassismus und Antisemitismus*
- *Gesellschaft Minderheiten in der Schweiz*
- *Stiftung Erziehung zur Toleranz*
- *Coopération Intercommunautaire contre l'antisémitisme et la Diffamation (CICAD).*
- *Ligue internationale contre le racisme et l'antisémitisme (LICRA)*
- *Stiftung Bildung und Entwcklung*
- *Akademie der Menschenrechte*
- *Christlich-Jüdische Arbeitsgemeinschaft*
- *Centre contact Suisse-Immigrés*
- *Forum contre le racisme*
- *Institut für Unterrichtsfragen und Lehrerinnenfortbildung*
- *Komitee "Stop dem Rassismus"*

- *Service d'information antiraciste*
- *Zentrum für Antisemitismus-Forschung*
- *SOS Racisme*
- *Association romande contre le racisme (ACOR)*
- *Asylkoordination Schweiz*
- *Bewegung für eine offene demokratische Schweiz*
- *Konfliktophon*
- *Schweizerischer Evangelischer Kirchenbund – Kontaktstelle Menschenrechte*
- *TiKK – SOS – Team für interkulturelle Konflikte unf Gewalt*
- *Déclaration de Berne*
- *Comité suisse pour l'UNICEF*
- *Service école Suisse Tiers-monde*

Proposal on the Fight Against the Use of the Internet for Racist, Anti-Semitic or Hate Purposes

The Swiss Delegation would like to invite the participants in the Washington Conference on Holocaust-Era Assets to welcome, during the concluding plenary session, the Swiss government's proposal to host a governmental conference on the fight against the use of the Internet for racist, anti-Semitic or hate purposes.

- The Washington Conference represents an important milestone in the discussion about Holocaust remembrance and education. However, this duty to remember the Holocaust should not only be seen as a way of looking back to the past, but as an important basis for promoting tolerance for the future.

- The Internet has become an invaluable tool for students, educators, the media and the market-place. However, it has also provided a platform for racist, anti-Semitic, and revisionist activists, many of which disseminate the "Auschwitz lie" theory. This is all the more worrying as the web appeals to and is used by younger generations.

- More generally, the Swiss Federal police recorded 700 racist, anti-Semitic or revisionist websites in 1997. None was based in Switzerland, as the dissemination of racist and anti-Semitic propaganda is strictly forbidden in our country. However, as the Internet has no borders, prohibition in specific countries is not a viable solution, for hate propaganda can be disseminated via foreign providers and anonymizers. The need for international cooperation in this field is thus obvious.

- While we are discussing here Holocaust remembrance and education, the Swiss delegation wishes to stress the importance of preventing the distribution of racist and anti-Semitic propaganda through the Internet: more and more youngsters use the Internet every day as a primary source of information and as an educational tool. As such, it is a critical task for every nation to contain the spread of hate propaganda on the web.

- This Conference carries a huge moral weight. While work in the fields of remembrance and education is essential, the Conference should go further. In our opinion, this Conference could send an important signal: A signal showing that the participants will not allow the use of new technologies in order to deny a past that should never repeat.

SWISS PROPOSAL FOR THE CHAIRMAN'S CONCLUDING REMARKS

"THE PARTICIPANTS WELCOMED THE SWISS GOVERNMENT'S PROPOSAL TO HOST A GOVERNMENTAL CONFERENCE ON THE FIGHT AGAINST THE USE OF THE INTERNET FOR RACIST, ANTI-SEMITIC OR HATE PURPOSES".

Independent Commission of Experts "Switzerland – Second World War"

The Swiss Insurance Industry during the Second World War:
Research Issues – Initial Results – Perspectives

1. GENERAL QUESTIONS

Contrary to the tendency of the general public to regard insurance as an extension of banking, questions relevant for the banking sector cannot simply be transferred to the insurance industry. A good example is dormant life insurance policies which are frequently compared with dormant bank accounts, although in contrast to bank accounts, every insurance contract is limited in duration and has a clear expiration date. After ten years the statute of limitations has expired and claims are therefore considered lapsed.

It is clear that detailed legal settlements still have to be resolved. Although insurance companies have violated existing laws in only a few cases, they were readily able to conform to changing legal norms during the Nazi era, and at war's end, they were often able to obstruct Jewish claimants and other policy holders using questionable arguments.

Furthermore, public interest has focused on the settlement of claims after the Crystal Night pogrom. Even this issue is usually viewed narrowly. Although the companies' behavior towards policy holders was formally correct, the arguments used by insurance companies to reject claims by the insured as well as those made by the Nazi German state were problematic. (The Nazi state had tried to submit and collect claims on behalf of the insured with limited success.)

The questions of corporate insurance policy and commercial practice before, during, and especially after the Second World War are broader. They include issues of accommodation and resistance, of taking advantage of maneuvering room, of behavior towards victims and perpetrators – even within their own ranks – as well as to Allied demands.

The question of the development of the insurance business is closely linked to these issues: How did specific Nazi measures affect the course of insurance industry business? What were the pressures and what were the additional business opportunities that the war created for insurers? One specific aspect of insurance companies' business that must be examined is financial transactions between Germany and foreign countries. These transfers not only reflect the general course of business, but also often give information about the routine behavior of corporations toward the Third Reich and its leaders.

The problem of so-called "Aryanization" constitute another major focus of research. What role did insurance companies play in restructuring ownership as well as in dealing with its own staff, management, or officers in the context of German "racial policies"? These issues are often closely linked to the acquisition of Jewish real estate under forced liquidation procedures.

The last problem involves reinsurance. Our knowledge about this subject is especially meager. Two complex issues predominate: (1) the guarantee bonds issued by reinsurers on life insurance policies of later victims of the Nazis, and, (2) the risks which were knowingly or unknowingly reinsured by companies within the Nazi Reich.

2. ARCHIVAL SOURCES: THE CASE OF SWITZERLAND

The scope of the ICE's mandate enables it to conduct research in Swiss corporate insurance archives. Despite substantial gaps, more records are available than originally anticipated. However, this has not eliminated the difficulties of access, since the companies have sometimes misunderstood the quantity and nature of the records available. Moreover, not all corporate historical records have indices or inventories. In instances where no archives are available, it is possible to go to public archival holdings in Switzerland as well as abroad. However, gaps are also encountered here.

Access to files in the archives of Swiss insurance companies is also frequently difficult. The Commission is not able to obtain an overview of the existing collections without basic archival order or finding aids.

3. INTERIM FINDINGS IN SWITZERLAND

The economic significance of the Swiss insurance industry and especially its foreign business has not been adequately understood until now. Although Swiss insurance companies usually only held small market shares abroad, combined they contributed essentially to the premium income -- depending on the line of insurance business between 25 and 90 percent -- and also to the profit of individual companies. Moreover, a somewhat differentiated examination shows that Swiss businesses possessed comparatively high market shares of specific products and segments. Finally, it must be emphasized that after the war began, Swiss insurers were practically the only foreign suppliers (and in the life insurance business the only one) to the German economy.

Although we do not yet have the complete range of proven data, we know that the Swiss insurance market increased in significance for the German economy during the war. On the one hand, this is because of its strong, internationally-oriented reinsurance, where for all intents practically only Swiss companies were able to underwrite these policies. On the other hand, during the war Swiss insurance companies administered German insurance contracts in a fiduciary capacity and thus made it possible for those companies to continue their insurance relations despite embargo. Furthermore, early precautions taken by German authorities for the postwar period emphasize the importance given to the Swiss insurance industry for the reconstruction of Germany.

There were also close, personal relations between the leading representatives of German and Swiss companies that existed parallel to their business relationships. Moreover, Swiss insurance companies interested in business with Nazi Germany had, at their disposal, good contacts with important individuals in the Third Reich. They were always able to negotiate favorable solutions. The question here is whether or not room for maneuverability was completely exhausted or whether the valid interests of their clients were sacrificed to corporate self-interest. In any case, insurance business with Germany developed favorably under existing conditions. At least part of the profits could be transferred to Switzerland.

Because the insurance companies that were active in Germany were implicated in Nazi looting policies (forced surrender or repurchase), it is safe to assume that within the insurance industry there was a high level of knowledge about developments inside Germany. It is not known how broad this knowledge was within the insurance industry, and why barely any concrete evidence of this can be found in surviving business records.

It is also known that as a rule, claims made by the insured were handled strictly according to formal criteria, irrespective of their personal fate. Within various corporations, there was the tendency to insinuate that claimants who were harmed by Nazi measures were being intentionally dishonest when they made claims to their insurance company.

4. OPEN QUESTIONS

The history of insurance and its corporate history have not been adequately researched. This gap means that new methodological studies are required. How can we achieve concrete answers about the insured, whom we do not know and whose existence is not even certain? How do we compare economic data developed under changing criteria? What are the relevant parameters for assessing this or any other development?

Moreover, there are open questions particularly about the economic, political, and legal framework For example, the preferential treatment of the insurance traffic within clearing cannot be sufficiently substantiated. Many technical insurance questions also await answers and it is often difficult to locate specialists familiar with the procedures used at that time. The most important questions are about confiscated and possibly dormant insurance assets. These are not only questions of an historical or legal nature. All of these questions lead finally to the same basic question: Can apparent injustice be the norm and can it be made the norm just because it carries the cloak of legality?

5. INTERNATIONAL COOPERATION

Intensive cooperation is particularly important for this subject, since it is not widely studied. Contact with similar corporate history research projects initiated by German firms, in the framework of the recent discussions about the Second World War era, has been more productive for the ICE than cooperation with purely academic researchers. These projects are more advanced than academic research, and they have also benefited from very favorable financial sponsorship and access to records. However, the Swiss insurance industry is not the focal point of these foreign projects. It is therefore hoped that these already existing contacts can be intensified and extended to most insurance companies which operated in Nazi Germany and occupied Europe. It would be desirable if universities would include these projects, integrating them as new areas of research in their curriculum. Nevertheless, this will only be possible when the insurance companies' private archives are opened for research in general.

INDEPENDENT COMMISSION OF EXPERTS "SWITZERLAND – SECOND WORLD WAR"

Gold Transactions of Nazi Germany
Research Issues – Initial Results – Perspectives

1. GENERAL ISSUES

For a long time, the public and historical research have been only peripherally concerned with German looted gold during the Second World War. This situation has changed decisively during the past few years. Gold has become the symbol of Nazi crimes because of extensive and increasing public interest in the Holocaust.

Public debate focused initially on Switzerland. Since then other countries, commercial banks, and corporations have been in the critics' line of fire. The investigation of German "gold policies" has become an international affair.

2. THE ICE INTERIM GOLD REPORT

The Independent Commission of Experts: Switzerland—Second World War (hereafter ICE), created in late 1996, decided its goal was to document as precisely as possible gold transactions between Germany and Switzerland during the Second World War. For this purpose, the Commission compiled the most significant statistics for its first interim report.

The report is entitled "Switzerland and Gold Transactions in the Second World War." It was published in May 1998 in four languages and reached the following conclusions:

1. Our approach was not to examine gold looted by the Nazi regime by looking at its results, but to start with the robbery and thus follow the process of exploitation. This approach seemed more appropriate for the ethical as well as the historical requirements of the subject.
2. The interim report is based on extensive material from diverse archival sources. Until now, Switzerland's role in the German gold

trade has usually been traced from the Swiss point of view. The ICE has analyzed this role from both domestic and outside perspectives. It is for this reason that the Commission employs research teams in foreign countries. Private corporate archives in Switzerland as well as public archives in the United States, Germany, Great Britain, Poland, and Russia were consulted.

3. We concluded that Swiss commercial banks clearly received more gold from Germany than was previously assumed. Moreover, the behavior of Swiss banks and insurance companies showed that as financial creditors they had substantial interest in preserving the solvency of the German state. This probably increased pressure on the directorate of the Swiss National Bank (SNB) to accept gold from Germany, even if its origins were dubious, despite Allied warnings against its acceptance. We know today, beyond a doubt, that the SNB clearly knew from the beginning of 1941 that the Reichsbank had amassed disturbing quantities of looted gold.

4. Switzerland functioned as the most important "gold hub" for the Nazi regime. About four-fifths of German gold deliveries abroad were processed through Switzerland. As a result, gold from the murdered and surviving victims of Nazi genocide reached Switzerland. Based on current knowledge, the SNB received only a fraction of this gold. Furthermore, it could not be proven that the leadership of the SNB was informed about the origin of this gold. Nevertheless, in retrospect, it must be stated explicitly that the directorate of the SNB regarded its relations with the Reichsbank for the most part as "business as usual," and that until the end of the war, the SNB failed to distance itself from the German Central Bank.

3. THE CURRENT DEBATE

The ICE interim report has stimulated a lively response in Switzerland and abroad.

The Commission held an academic conference about the financial history of Nazi Germany at the University of Bielefeld. Based on the results of our interim report, questions were formulated that will enable specific research to proceed, thus increasing our level of knowledge. Important new information is also found in the published second Eizenstat report, as well as in studies published by Sweden, Argentina, and Luxembourg.

4. OPEN RESEARCH QUESTIONS

The principal questions, still remaining open, that require research are:

1. Various aspects of gold transactions between the SS Central Office for Economy and Administration and the Reichsbank still require clarification. It is not clear why some gold ingots, deposited in the Reichsbank by SS Captain Bruno Melmer, had high levels of purity. The rationale for smelting gold in some concentration camps is also not known. It is also unclear what routes were used to transport gold from the East across customs' borders into Germany. It is unlikely that the remaining existing documentation will enable us fully to trace the routes of victim gold.

2. A scientific history of the Reichsbank has yet to be written. The close linkages between the Reichsbank and Nazi financial and economic policy also necessitates that gold not be separated from the wider context of the currency situation and political framework of that time.

5. INTERNATIONAL COOPERATION

Interpretations based on specific national positions fail to understand the complexity of gold transactions during the Second World War. This is connected with the fact that gold is fungible and, that therefore, it is possible to obscure its origins. The leaders of Nazi Germany systematically took advantage of this fact when they robbed their victims and systematically exploited such stolen goods.

The international dimensions of gold transactions during the Second World War does not mean the relativization of individual countries' profits and responsibilities. Only within the framework of empirically sound comparisons can national idiosyncrasies be revealed and hasty moralizing be replaced by differentiated interpretations.

INDEPENDENT COMMISSION OF EXPERTS "SWITZERLAND – SECOND WORLD WAR"

Report on Switzerland's Refugee Policy
Research Issues – Initial Results – Perspectives

BACKGROUND

The Independent Commission of Experts: Switzerland - World War II (hereafter ICE) will issue an interim report in 1999 about Switzerland's refugee policy. Although Switzerland was only one of many possible havens for those fleeing Nazi German persecution before 1939, it became the major potential sanctuary for Jews fleeing Nazi German despoliation and deportation operations after 1940. Because of its geographical proximity to Germany and Austria and to occupied territories in France, and later Italy, Swiss restrictionism has been a central concern in historiography about refugee policy. As early as 1957, the official Swiss report by Carl Ludwig provided details about the "J" stamp in 1938 and the closure of Swiss borders in mid-August 1942.[1] Swiss anxieties about *Überfremdung* --"being overrun with foreigners" -- frequently prevailed over moral or humanitarian concerns. The massive number of political, economic, and racial refugees in flight from German, Italian, and Spanish fascisms during the 1930s resulted in growing emigration restrictions in most western countries, including Switzerland. Moreover, the interaction of Nazi policies with the responses of other governments reveals global patterns fluctuating between hostility, benign neglect, and occasional sympathy. These policy variants, in turn, depended on local prejudices, economic apprehensions, political constraints, and bureaucratic procedures.

---

[1] See Carl Ludwig, Die Flüchtlingspolitik der Schweiz seit 1933 bis zur Gegenwart: Bericht an den Bundesrat zuhanden der eidgenössischen Räte (Bern, 1957).

STRUCTURE OF THE ICE FUTURE REFUGEE REPORT

The major segments of the 1999 ICE refugee report will include discussion of:
1. Historiography, sources, and refugee categories;
2. the political and institutional framework of Swiss refugee policy;
3. economic and legal aspects;
4. 1938 as a turning point closing the door to refugees, including the Evian conference, the "J" stamp, and the closure of borders in August 1942;
5. Swiss governmental knowledge of Nazi German policies, 1941-1944;
6. refoulement, expulsion, or acceptance of refugees, 1939-1945;
7. refugee life in Switzerland;
8. international and national charitable organizations in Switzerland, including American licensing procedures for refugee relief work by these agencies during the war;
9. financial aspects of refugee policy in Switzerland, including mandatory deposits of a "bond" [*Kaution*] for temporary residence and the issuance of "tolerance permits" [*Toleranzbewilligungen*];
10. the problems of quantification and refugee statistics; and
11. postwar refugee policy in Switzerland.

THE "J" STAMP

Until 1938, Switzerland nominally maintained its traditional policy of asylum for refugees admitting 10,000-12,000 refugees between 1933 and 1938. Refugee policies were initially decentralized and vested with the cantons rather than with federal authorities, although refugee policy was increasingly centralized after 1938. Refugees were usually not allowed to work and were generally under police surveillance. Moreover, they had no access to their finances during their stay in Switzerland, although mandatory security deposits were required before certificates of residence could be issued.

Escalating German measures against Jews, political dissidents, Jehovah's Witnesses, and Roma and Sinti limited employment possibilities and accelerated their impoverishment inside Nazi Germany.

Cumulative Nazi exclusionary legislation, employment discrimination, and economic restrictions also resulted in denaturalization and impoverishment. This made many refugees unwelcome as residents or transients in potential European countries of exile, including Switzerland.

German territorial changes in 1938, with the incorporation of Austria and the Sudetenland, resulted in the eviction and attempted flight of thousands of native and refugee Jews from these regions. Switzerland had a common border with both Nazi Germany and incorporated Austria, and fearing a deluge of Austrian Jewish and stateless refugees, the Swiss Federal Council ordered visa requirements reinstated initially for Austrian passport holders and later for all refugees. Lengthy negotiations from April to October 1938 between the Swiss Police, the Swiss Legation in Berlin, and the German Foreign Office, resulted on October 5, 1938, in a German decree ordering every German and Austrian Jew to hand in their passport inside the German Reich and at German consulates or missions abroad to receive a special 3 cm. high red "J" stamp on the left-hand side of the first passport page. ("J" stood for *Jude* - "Jew"). On October 4, 1938, the Swiss police announced that Germans bearing passports indicating they were not Aryans would require special authorization to enter Switzerland.

The spontaneous emigration of Jews from Germany after 1933 accelerated by 1938 under concerted official pressure. Although historians have usually held only Switzerland responsible for the invention of the "J" stamp, it is clear that Germany had already introduced a black "J" stamp on domestic identity cards during the late summer of 1938. Regulations for resident registration inside Germany were amended on July 23, 1938, requiring all German and Austrian Jews to carry special identification papers inside the Reich.[2] This identity card was subsequently stamped with a black "J." Moreover, the German Security Service had already considered in January 1937 "marking Jewish passports, for use only inside Germany," but delayed implementation "so that foreign consulates would not deny visas to

---

[2]   See David Martin Luebke and Sybil Milton, "Locating the Victim: An Overview of Census-taking, Tabulation Technology, and Persecution in Nazi Germany," IEEE Annals of the History of Computing 16, no.3 (Fall 1994): 30-31. See also "Bekanntmachung über den Kennkartenzwang vom 23. Juli 1938," Reichsgesetzblatt 1938, I:922.

holders of such passports."[3] Such blatant measures would have nullified official German policy to expedite Jewish emigration.

By August 1938, Germany had also introduced new "name" legislation, requiring the addition of the middle names "Israel" or "Sara" on all official Jewish documents, including identity cards and passports. Nevertheless, Swiss diplomatic pressure resulted in the acceleration of German measures explicitly identifying Jews on their passports, thereby inhibiting possibilities of flight and asylum. Similarly, the Swedish-German passport agreement of October 15, 1938, restricted the entry of specified "persons" without passport validation into Sweden.[4] Concurrent Italian racial legislation also led Italian border police to ask all German and Austrian passport holders crossing an Italian border in late 1938 if they had Jewish names.

The question of Swiss responsibility for the "J" stamp must also include precedents before 1933. After 1910, a pencil "J" had been affixed on some naturalization requests by East European Jews in Switzerland. By the end of World War I, a red-ink stamp of the Star of David in a circle as well as the letter 'J' was sometimes placed on such files. Although it is impossible to prove direct continuities of Swiss knowledge and police personnel between the end of World War I and 1938, the earlier use of the "J" may have been a precedent for 1938.[5]

After the war started, the Swiss Federal Council ordered on October 17, 1939, that foreigners who entered Switzerland illegally would be immediately expelled to the countries from which they came, with the exception of deserters and recognized political refugees. During the war years, Jewish refugees also faced political expediency, indifference, and open hostility in other allied and neutral nations. Restrictive American immigration policies, British hostility to Jewish resettlement in Palestine, and international apathy doomed most Jews and many Roma and Sinti („Gypsies") to death in the ghettos and concentration camps of occupied Europe. In October 1943, the Swiss

---

[3] See Michael Wildt, ed., Die Judenpolitik des SD, 1935 bis 1938: Eine Dokumentation (Munich, 1995), p. 100. See also Bundesarchiv Berlin, R58/956.
[4] See Paul A. Levine, From Indifference to Activism: Swedish Diplomacy and the Holocaust, 1938-1944 (Uppsala, 1996), chap. 5. See also Schweizerisches Bundesarchiv Bern, E 2001 (D) 2/114.
[5] See Marc Perrenoud, "Problèmes d'intégration et de naturalisation des Juifs dans le canton de Neuchatel, 1871-1955," in Pierre Centlivres, Devenir Suisse: Adhésion et diversité culturelle des étrangers en Suisse (Geneva, 1990), pp. 82-83.

opened the Italian border to increasing numbers of civilian and military refugees, including Jews. In the final stages of the war by early 1945, the inevitability of German military defeat resulted in German offers for releasing Jews to safety in Switzerland for ransom in money, goods, or postwar alibis against war crimes prosecution. In 1944, 1,686 Hungarian Jews arrived in Switzerland from Bergen-Belsen and in early February 1945, 1,200 Jews from Theresienstadt entered Switzerland. The costs of their support were absorbed by the Swiss Jewish community, the American Jewish Joint Distribution Committee, and the Swiss Society to Assist Jewish Refugees. It must also be remembered that the Swiss consul in Budapest, Carl Lutz, worked together with Raoul Wallenberg to save the lives of many thousands of Jews. The legacy of Swiss refugee policy is mixed with relatively tolerant behavior in 1933 and after 1944, but with severe restrictionism during the critical period from 1939 to 1943.

OPEN QUESTIONS

The 1999 ICE refugee report will try to clarify the financial aspects of refugee life in Switzerland, including whether mandatory security deposits reverted to the depositors or their heirs. The magnitude and handling of refugee "surety" accounts and related assets are being researched by the Independent Experts Commission as part of the refugee report in 1999.

Other issues include the quantification of refugees in Switzerland between 1939 and 1946. Partial statistics of refugees rejected at the border reveal that at least 24,000 refugees were denied entry to Switzerland. Additionally, 14,500 visa applications at Swiss embassies and consulates were denied.[6] There is a high probability that these statistics include duplications, since those who did not receive visas may

---

[6]   See Guido Koller, "Die schweizerische Flüchtlingspolitik im Zweiten Weltkrieg," in Schweizerisches Bundesarchiv, ed., Fluchtgelder, Raubgut und nachrichtenlose Vermögen: Wissenstand und Forschungsperspektiven (Bern, 1997), pp. 44-49.

also have been turned away from borders. The clarification of these questions and the personal fates behind these statistics are part of the ICE's current research agenda.

TURKEY

Delegation Statement on Holocaust-Era Assets

Turkey is one of the few countries in the world where the Jews have never been persecuted. Indeed, it was the Ottoman Empire which sent its powerful Mediterranean fleet to save thousands of Jews from Spanish Inquisition in 1492. These Jews were then settled in various parts of the Ottoman Empire, almost all in urban areas in Istanbul, Salonica, the coastline as well as the Balkan provinces at that time. Following the collapse of the Ottoman Empire, many of these Jewish communities left behind were not always as lucky, since many of them were to be exterminated either during the Second World War or even before. It is not, therefore, surprising that so many Jewish communities retreated together with their Turkish and Moslem neighbors from the territories the Ottoman Empire evacuated especially in the Balkans. And this joyful co-existence between the Jews in Turkey and the rest of the Turkish population continued during the Second World War.

Moreover, during the difficult years of the war, Turkey acted as a guardian of the Jewish communities who were chucked out of Europe by the Nazis. All evidence confirms that Turkey played a significant role in a variety of ways in rescuing Jews from the Nazis during the Holocaust. Turkish diplomats throughout Nazi occupied territories in Western Europe did all they could, sometimes even acting beyond what their diplomatic status allowed them, to protect and save Turkish citizen Jews, as well as their properties. The Jewish Agency which established itself in Istanbul due to Turkey's proximity to the Nazi occupied South Eastern and Eastern Europe worked freely during the war, and saved and directed thousands of Jews through to Palestine through a number of ways. As Professor Stanford Shaw pointed out in his book *Turkey and the Holocaust,* **"Turkey...came to constitute a true bridge to Palestine, a transit center that enabled Jews being persecuted in their own countries to go on to the Holy Land."**

Further evidence in Turkish and the International Committee of the Red Cross (ICRC) archives in Geneva points to the fact that Turkish authorities allowed the passage of Jewish refugees even without an official permission by British authorities to enter Palestine. The Jewish Agency conducted these rescue operations, some of which were certainly carried out in a clandestine manner, with the tacit approval of the Turkish authorities. According to many scholars who have written on the subject, the number of Jews saved by Turkey during the Second World War goes up to a hundred thousand, if not more.

One other important point to be borne in mind about Turkey's policy during the war regarding the plight of the Jews is that hundreds of Jewish intellectuals, in particular the Jewish academics of German origin, found refuge in Turkey for a long time. In fact, many German Jewish professors made their way down to Turkey well before the outbreak of the war in order to escape persecution in Germany at the hands of the Nazis, and stayed over for several more years after the end of the war. Some of them even decided to remain in Turkey altogether. And several of them later published their memoirs, which talk of a friendly country to Jews not only during the war but in general.

Therefore, Turkey would never have expected to have been included in the list of the countries which were in one way or the other involved in the transaction of Nazi gold and related issues. In a sense, Turkey was quite surprised at the allegations in the reports published by the US Department of State. Nevertheless, Turkey took the matter seriously and a Cabinet Minister was assigned by the Prime Minister to deal with the matter, who in turn immediately set up a Commission of Experts, composed of high ranking officials from the Ministry of Foreign Affairs (hereafter MFA), the Central Bank of the Republic of Turkey (hereafter CBRT), academics, historians and members of the Turkish Jewish Community. The Commission has conducted extensive research in the Turkish and foreign archives, and is still carrying on with their research on some detailed aspects of the issues. The Commission's findings have been brought to the attention of the officials who prepared the previous reports, and historian members of the Turkish Commission and Dr. William Slany, the State Department Historian, have agreed to write reports, articles and even books on these matters.

Nonetheless, until those publications come out, the Turkish Commission would like to clarify all the allegations regarding Turkey in the previous reports, which blamed Turkey on three counts: Nazi gold, Turkey's sale of chromium to Germany between 1942 and 1943 for about twelve months during the Second World War and German assets held by Turkey after Ankara declared war on Nazi Germany and returned gratis to the Federal Republic of Germany in the second part of the 1950s.

A) THE NAZI GOLD ISSUE

It is clearly inferred from the latest publications that the gold assets looted by Germany during the Second World War were used to finance the German war machine, and several countries became involved in this process by facilitating Germany's transactions through the looted gold. However, Turkey is unjustifiably mentioned among the countries alleged to have been implicated in this whole affair. It seems that this accusation against Turkey mostly stemmed from the fact that Turkey's gold assets increased considerably from the end of 1938 to the end of the Second World War. Indeed, the gold assets of the CBRT increased from a level of 27.4 metric tons in 1939 to 216.2 metric tons by the end of 1945. In other words, the total increase was about 188.8 metric tons. This increase seems to have led to speculations that perhaps a large part of it was to do with the Nazi gold.

However, this assumption does not seem to be borne out by archive documents. If anything, figures of the State Statistical Institute clearly demonstrate that during the period in question Turkey's foreign trade surplus went up to 341.5 million US Dollars during the Second World War, and that much of this surplus was invested in gold by the Turkish government to meet the constant demand for foreign currency and to protect its foreign holdings against possible depreciation under war conditions. And, should this amount be fully translated into gold, the total would have made 300 metric tons of gold.

At first sight, this might look a bit odd, given that Turkey had experienced almost a constant trade deficit in the years previous to the outbreak of the war. Nonetheless, the point to be borne in mind is that, although Turkey managed to remain outside the war, it was one of the very few countries which could not escape from the devastating effects of the war, particularly in economic terms. For instance, Turkey's trade with the outside world shrank considerably during the war years. However, perhaps paradoxically, Turkey's current account in relation to its foreign trade underwent an impressive surplus during these years, not least because the country, feeling the war clouds on its borders, was careful not to spare much money for imports, and also because all those countries who used to export to Turkey found themselves in the war, and in a sense Turkey lost a number of its trading partners. In addition, in 1940, impressive increase in the cotton harvest and coal production together with the discovery of oil fields also contributed, to a large extent, to tilting the balance in the foreign trade in favor of Turkey. The trade agreement Turkey signed with Britain in December 1940 also appears to have contributed to Turkey's foreign trade surplus. All the money Turkey earned from its exports were kept in corresponding banks mostly in North America and partly in Europe. According to an agreement between the CBRT and the Swiss National Bank (hereafter SNB) signed in 1942, the latter would automatically invest foreign exchange deposits of the CBRT with the SNB into gold, when the amount exceeded certain limits, or would make the payment from the gold when the amount dropped under a certain agreed limit.

The CBRT records account for the movement of every piece of gold purchased by Turkey during the Second World War. The following is a brief account of all these gold movements: For instance, records in the CBRT indicate clearly that 55.7 metric tons of this increase in the gold reserves of Turkey, 29.6 per cent of the total increase, came from the gold bars that the Turkish Treasury was able to buy from Banque de France thanks to a credit facility of the British government of 15 million pounds through the Bank of England. Initial research into the British archive documents in the Public Record Office (hereafter PRO) in London under catalogues FO371 for the year 1939 explains extensively how the credit facility was arranged between Ankara and London as part of a financial package to Turkey. The records of the CBRT and of PRO also explain how the purchase of this gold was made and how it was brought over to Turkey. According to the documents, this gold, having been purchased from Banque de France with British credit and brought over to Turkey, was deposited with the CBRT to form collateral for the future cash demands of the Treasury during the war.

From the records of the Board of Directors of the CBRT, it is obvious that with the advent of the Second World War, the CBRT adopted a policy of transferring all its gold assets entrusted with its correspondent banks in Europe to North America, in particular, to the USA. These records make it clear that a large bulk of Turkey's gold purchases was made through the CBRT's correspondent banks abroad. Indeed, the total amount, 127.2 metric tons which the CBRT's correspondents bought during this period account for 67.6 per cent of the total increase in gold assets.

The CBRT records also track down the rest of the gold increase, 5.0 metric tons, which was bought abroad in two separate instances and brought over to Turkey in two parties. The first party, 2.0 metric tons, was purchased in the form of bars, from Reichsbank in 1942 prior to the Allied Declaration of January the 5th, 1943, and the payment for the purchase was made through the accounts of the CBRT with SNB and Sveriges Riksbank. The second party was the acquisition of 249 bars, approximately 3.0 metric tons in 1943. The records of the Board of Directors of the CBRT dated May 5th and May 21st of 1943, with reference numbers of 2662 and 2681 respectively, the minutes of the meetings of the CBRT's Board of Directors, the strongroom records of the CBRT, as well as related SNB documents explain the purchase and the transfer of the gold in full detail. According to this documentation, the CBRT was planning to buy gold for SFR 10.000.000 at the beginning of May 1943. However, due to the high transportation cost which was likely to incur under war conditions, the Board later decided to increase the amount to SFR 15.000.000 in order to reduce the transportation cost per kilogram. At that point Reichsbank offered to sell gold for SFR 5.000 per kilogram which was found to be more expensive than the offer of the SNB, 4.920.63 per kilogram. Moreover, in compliance with the Allied Declaration of 1943 which forbade all countries from buying gold from Germany, the Board of the CBRT looked at possibilities of entrusting it with the Bank for International Settlements (BIS) to be safeguarded or of purchasing the desired gold from the USA against Swiss Franks, and finally came to the conclusion that the gold should be purchased from SNB. Accordingly, the SNB purchased 3.048,40672 kilograms of gold on behalf of CBRT for SFR 15.000.081 on May 8th, 1943.

Though the gold was bought, its transportation presented certain difficulties. While Turkey was in search of ways to bring it home, an option emerged whereby the Reichsbank would supply 249 bars of gold weighing 3.047.32 kilograms in total to Turkey against the gold purchased by SNB on behalf of CBRT. This offer was accepted by the CBRT and in order to finalize the transaction, the CBRT instructed the SNB on May 25th, 1943, to transfer the gold it had bought earlier on behalf of the CBRT to Reichsbank. From these records, it is clear that for all intents and purposes, the CBRT acted in this whole matter in good faith. According to the records of the CBRT, the gold supplied by Reichsbank in return for the transfer of the gold SNB bought on behalf of the CBRT was used in minting commemorative coins by the Turkish State Mint during 1944-1946.

The 243 kilograms of gold bars and 32.000 gold coins handed over by the German Embassy in Ankara to the Swiss Embassy and finally to the Turkish authorities when Turkey declared war on Nazi Germany in 1945 were kept on consignment basis by the CBRT. These gold bars and coins were fully returned to the German side (Deutsche Bank, Dresdner Bank and the German government) by the Ministry of Finance in June and November 1960 under the provisions of an economic protocol signed between Turkey and the Federal Republic of Germany within the context of NATO solidarity.

From the documents of the Bank of England, it became clear that the CBRT approached the Bank of England about the possibility of re-smelting 8 tons of bars of varied and relatively low fineness and 3 tons of miscellaneous coinage in 1947. However, the Bank of England declined this request at the time, on the grounds that it was concerned that perhaps these were either fully or partly the looted gold. Finally, in 1952 the CBRT made an arrangement with the Bank of England about the re-smelting of 8.706 kilograms of gold bars of varied and relatively low fineness. The strongroom records of the CBRT clearly indicate that these gold bars re-smelted in London were either the bars purchased between 1931 and 1939 by the CBRT or the ones received from the Ministry of Finance in 1934 to back up the bank notes in circulation under the provisions of Article 6 of Act No. 1715 of the CBRT. In other words, all that gold re-smelted in London had nothing to do with Nazi gold.

Meanwhile, it is interesting to note that according to a number of Turkish and Polish documents Turkey became a place of safekeeping for most of the Balkan countries during the war. For instance, 70.0 metric tons of Polish gold was saved by Turkey and transferred to free Syria with the assistance of Turkish authorities. In addition, US$ 3.000.000 of the Kingdom of Yugoslavia were kept on consignment basis in Turkey during the war. Needless to say, these assets would have been looted by the Nazi authorities to finance their military campaigns, otherwise.

B) CHROMIUM ISSUE

On a related matter, that of the German purchase of chromium from Turkey during the Second World War, mentioned in the report of the US State Department published on June 3rd, 1997, the records of the Turkish Foreign Ministry, as well as British archive material and books based on British documents challenge the allegation that Turkey sold Germany large quantities of chromium in order to keep the German war machine going. Indeed, even a cursory look at the report published by the State Department reveals that the subject was examined only in light of American documents starting from 1941, after the US declaration of war on Germany.

But it was a matter extensively discussed between Britain and France on the one hand, and Turkey, on the other, from the beginning of the war onwards. It is possible to track down all the negotiations between

Ankara and London regarding the chromium issue both through the Turkish Foreign Ministry records and all the archive material in PRO. In order to understand what happened, the Turkish Commission Experts carried out extensive research in various Turkish Archives.

The truth of the matter is that Turkey allied itself to Britain and France through formal alliance treaties at the outbreak of the Second World War. And although Turkey remained non-belligerent during much of the war until 1945, which is when it declared war on Germany, Turkey continued its close cooperation with Britain and France throughout the war. For instance, if Turkey had been selling chromium to Germany without the knowledge and consent of Britain, the latter would probably have refused to come up with a financial assistance package to Turkey after the beginning of the war, and without the credit facility rendered to Turkey, the CBRT would not have been able to purchase gold from Banque de France.

The following is a brief summary of what took place. Having realized that the Soviet Union could no longer be trusted after the Soviet Foreign Minister, Molotov, had struck a Non-Aggression Pact with his German counterpart, Ribbentrop, on 23rd August, 1939, Turkey allied itself to Britain and France through a Tripartite Alliance Agreement of Mutual Defense despite German preponderance both in economic and military terms in the Balkans and Central-Eastern Europe, areas very close to Turkey. In addition to this Tripartite Agreement, a Special Accord was also signed on the same day which offered economic aid by Britain and France to Turkey. Almost simultaneously, Turkey informed Germany that it could not renew its trade agreement with the latter until and unless Germany sorted out its differences with France and Britain and signed a trade agreement with them. Turkey also informed Germany that it was not to prolong the trade agreement with Germany the two countries had signed on 26th of July 1938. Not surprisingly, all the trade between Turkey and Germany came to an abrupt end on the 1st of September 1939, the day the war broke out.

Since Turkey broke off its economic relations with Germany, it negotiated with Britain and France as to how to sell its products, primarily chromium which was a major export item, to these allies. In fact, breaking-off with Germany had been part of the deal. In the course of the negotiations within the framework of the Tripartite Agreement and the Special Accord among Turkey, Britain and France, Secretary General of the Turkish Foreign Ministry, Numan Menemencioglu, visited both Paris and London soon after the outbreak of the war, and he made an offer to the Allies in December 1939 while he was still in London:

Britain and France should purchase all Turkey's chromium for a period of fifteen years, corresponding to the duration of the Tripartite Agreement. But, as Britain was purchasing its chromium from several countries, mostly its colonies, it turned down this offer, on the grounds that the duration of the agreement would be too long. Instead, Britain proposed that London and Paris governments should buy all Turkish chromium for a period of two years, after which time the matter would be taken up again between the three countries. And Turkey accepted this offer, however grudgingly it may have been, and the Chrome Trade Agreement was signed in Paris on January 8th, 1940, between these three allies. According to this deal, France was to buy 4/15 and England 11/15 of Turkey's total chromium production of 250.000 tons. This agreement also stipulated (Article 6) that Turkey could sell its surplus chromium production to third countries, particularly to the USA, on condition that Britain and France approve the sale beforehand. The Agreement, which was concluded only for two years, could be renewed, but only for one more year, between the signatories.

It seems clear from the documentation both at the MFA as well as PRO that the Turkish side wished to prolong the trade for a much longer period than only one more year when the two years term expired. However, Britain appeared quite unwilling for a longer extension of the agreement, while France had already been overrun by Nazi Germany. Professor W.N. Medlicott, the famous late British historian who conducted extensive research into British archives laments this decision on the part of the British government. According to him, Numan Menemencioglu made a bold attempt on 21st of December, 1941 in arguing that Turkey's agreement with Britain and France to sell chromium to these allies should continue for a period of twenty years. Sadly, however, this was turned down by the British government. As Professor Medlicott put it: **"later events showed that the British would have been well-advised to tie up Turkish chrome for a longer period."**

Meanwhile, Germany had approached Turkey with an offer to buy Turkey's chromium. Having secured Britain's agreement within the context of the Chromium Trade Agreement between Turkey, on the one hand, and Britain and France, on the other, and in particular in accordance with Article 6 of that Agreement, Turkey agreed to the sale of chromium to Germany by signing a chrome agreement with that country on 9th October, 1941. It is perhaps important to note that, by that stage, the USA was still a neutral country. Even then, Turkey was very cautious with Germany. It inserted a clause in the Agreement which stipulated that Turkish chromium deliveries to Germany could start only after January 1943, the termination of the Tripartite Chrome Agreement and one year extension. And when the actual deliveries began, all the transaction was done on the basis of barter, particularly war material to Turkey, avoiding any Nazi gold.

The documentation in the MFA makes it clear that the whole deal with Germany was carried out in close consultation with the British government. When, in fact, the British government asked for clarification in September 1943, the Turkish Foreign Ministry instructed the Turkish Embassy in London to remind the British authorities that the German Chrome Agreement had been signed with the approval of the British government, and that the British had expressed the view at that time that the requirements put forward for the sale of the chromium to Germany were drafted by Turkey in such a way as to make it quite difficult for the Germans to carry forward the plan in full-swing.

When the allies requested of Turkey that chromium deliveries to Germany be stopped, Turkey immediately complied with that request on 24th April, 1944 and discontinued the chromium trade with Germany though the chrome agreement with that country had not yet expired. Few months later in August 1944, Turkey severed all its diplomatic relations with Germany. It is interesting to note that almost a year later, April 1945, the Swedish Embassy protecting Germany's interests in Ankara handed in a Note to the Turkish Foreign Ministry, saying that the Krupp Company in Germany had decided to annul the chrome agreement with Turkey in the absence of any chromium deliveries to Germany.

There is further evidence which clearly indicates that Turkey acted in this whole matter of the chromium in good faith and in accordance with the letter and spirit of the Alliance Treaty which it had signed earlier with Britain and France. For instance, according to the agreement between Turkey on the one side, and Britain and France on the other, Turkey was to have sold all its chromium to these two countries for as long as the agreement was in effect, an obligation which Turkey duly respected and undertook. When France came under German occupation and the Vichy government was set up, which collaborated with Nazi Germany, Turkey, instead of going on to supply the so-called government of France with chromium, discontinued shipments to France, and directed instead the chromium deliveries to England who assumed the French share. All this refutes the allegations that Turkey contributed to the ongoing German war machine by selling large quantities of chromium to Germany during the war.

It is important to note that all this is documented by large bulks of documents in various Turkish archives, that initial research into the archive material in PRO does confirm this assessment, and that Turkish Commission Experts' research into the material in PRO will resume in early 1999 with a view to writing a detailed report on all aspects of the chromium issue.

C) THE ISSUE OF THE GERMAN ASSETS

The issue of the German assets seized at the end of the Second World War by Turkey as a victor country has also been turned into a matter of unfounded allegation against Turkey. The truth of the matter is the following: Turkey broke off its diplomatic relations with Germany in August 1944, and, later, in 1945 declared war on Nazi Germany. As a result, all the German assets, including the embassy and consular buildings and the German school in Istanbul were seized by Turkey as enemy property. These German assets also included 243 kilograms of gold bars and 32.000 gold coins handed over by the German Embassy in Ankara to the Swiss Embassy when the German Ambassador was leaving, and finally to the Turkish authorities when Turkey declared war on Nazi Germany in 1945. It is important to note that these gold bars and coins were kept under the CBRT's care by Turkey on a consignment basis.

Turkey at the time thought that when the general procedures as to how to deal with these assets became established, it would handle the matter accordingly, since Ankara was to make war claims against Germany. Oddly enough, however, Turkey was not invited to the Paris Conference for Reparations in 1946 although it had duly declared war on Nazi Germany. Therefore, Turkey acted on its own to handle both matters of Turkish claims against Germany and the German assets seized in Turkey, following Turkey's declaration of war on Germany and Japan. The Agreement which came out of the Paris Conference for Reparations in January 1946, established the modalities of the liquidation of German assets. Upon the conclusion of this Agreement, the Allies approached Turkey which, in turn, informed the former rightfully that it was not bound by international agreements which it had not signed, and which it had taken no part in framing. Turkey duly expressed the view and registered its position accordingly that it **"maintains sole jurisdiction over its program of German external assets and enemy property,**

and that the proceeds of the liquidation be used first to satisfy Turkish war claims against Germany."

In fact, the Allies left it to Turkey to deal with this matter directly by excluding Turkey from the Paris Reparation Conference in which 18 countries had participated. In the previous reports on the issue published by the State Department, there was a reference to a remark (pages 136-137) by a US delegate, Seymour Rubin, in the Conference on Economic Security held in Paris between 27th of April and 7th May 1948. Mr. Rubin, according to the documents used to prepare that report, mentioned Turkey in relation to the termination of efforts on the liquidation of German assets in some countries, including Turkey.

But closer scrutiny of American documents suggests that a very important State Department document was omitted in preparation of that report. In a telegram sent by the State Department to the US Embassy in Ankara dated 8th April, 1948, twenty days before the Paris Conference on Economic Security was held, the State Department was recommending to the US Embassy in Ankara that Turkey be treated as a special case with regard to the seized German assets. The Turkish Commission Experts have already brought this document to the attention of the officials who prepared the report.

According to the documentation, Turkey maintained its position that it should deal directly with this issue because it had not been invited to the Paris Reparation Conference. In the end, Turkey gave up its war claims against Germany who had by then become Turkey's ally in NATO, and all the German assets estimated by the Allies at about 50 to 70 million Dollars were returned gratis to the Federal Republic of Germany by the Turkish government within the context of NATO solidarity in the second half of the 1950s. The gold bars and coins handed over to Turkey by the Swiss Embassy in Ankara were also returned in full amount to the German side (Deutsche Bank, Dresdner Bank and the German government) by the Ministry of Finance in June and November 1960 under the provisions of an economic protocol signed between Turkey and the Federal Republic of Germany, again, within the context of NATO solidarity.

UKRAINE

Delegation Statement

The broad and fruitful discussion begun a year ago at the London International Conference continues today in Washington. It is endeavoring to set new parameters, that would allow us to declare new claims, backed by evidence and calculations carried out by our experts.

A year ago, an experts group on the "Nazi Gold" problem was established in Ukraine. Its primary goal was to examine all available sources of information in Ukraine and abroad. With the active assistance of local archivists, members of the group have studied documents in the state archives of Ukraine, in the archives of the Autonomous Republic of Crimea, in 19 regional archives, in the state archives of the Russian Federation (Moscow), in the Central Repository of Historical-Documentary Collections (Moscow), in the Federal Archives in Berlin — altogether some 500 archival collections have been accessed and more than 500,000 pages of documents checked.

What were the venues of the Ukrainian share in the Third Reich's capital formation?

FINANCIAL POLICIES OF THE OCCUPIERS, COMPULSORY PAYMENTS, FUNCTIONING OF THE BANKING SYSTEM:

The Nazis worked vigorously and broadly. The collection of precious metals and currencies was carried out by forcing the inhabitants of Ukraine to sell these at a very low fixed rate. (An order to this effect was issued in August, 1942).

Earlier, in June, 1942, a new monetary unit — the karbovanets — was introduced in Ukraine. By April, 1943, more than 2,000 million Soviet rubles were exchanged for the karbovantsi. This was equal to 200 million Reichsmarks. All payments for forcibly bought precious metals and currencies were made in karbovantsi.

The exchange operations for the Soviet rubles were done at extortionate rates – much lower than the rate in use by the German Reichsbank at the time.

Sale of government bonds was widespread and residents were forced to buy these bonds. In Bukovyna, for example (then under Romanian occupation) state obligations were sold beginning in 1941. The archives contain lists of inhabitants compelled to buy these bonds.

One should also note such measures of capital formation as taxes, penalties, contributions and other compulsory payments. Preliminary data we have gathered shows that the population of Ukraine made payments in excess of 2,500 thousand rubles; Ukrainian government data show that these payments amounted to 2,600 thousand rubles, about 46 million Reichsmarks, 195 million karbovantsi, 14.4 million zlotys.

THE FUNCTIONING OF THE BANK SYSTEM:

Analysis of the operations of banks and other financial structures and organizations within the Reichscommisariat of Ukraine shows an increase in the volume of financial activity. We have data on account balances in the Central Economic Bank during the final stages of occupation. The liabilities of this bank were not paid to the creditors. As the result, there was a windfall of 7,290 million karbovantsi. More than 5,500 million karbovantsi or 550 million Reichsmarks were not paid to the creditors of the Economic Bank network.

UKRAINIAN SLAVE LABORERS IN GERMANY:

One should not overlook the use of the bank system for the so-called "savings" of the slave laborers from Ukraine, who were compelled to transfer home some of their earnings made in the Reich. What were the practical results of this? The Central Economic Bank of Ukraine, which operated in the Reichscommissariat of Ukraine, received 191.1 million karbovantsi or 19.11 million Reichsmarks in deposits, or money withheld from the Ukrainian slave laborers. This amount should be added to the money removed from inhabitants of the territories that constitute present-day Ukraine.

While the amounts transferred from the meager earnings of individual people in penal servitude were insignificant (they were receiving inadequate payment for their hard labor), the total sum is impressive. We have no right to disregard it.

Also worthy of note should be the accumulation of Nazi assets through obligatory insurance of workers. The Reich minister of labor issued an order in April, 1942, that business owners should make monthly contributions of 4 Reichsmarks to local hospitals or treasuries for every employee's health care. We estimate that the total paid for every Ukrainian slave laborer amounted to 200 million Reichsmarks. Since these amounts were taken out of the earnings of the slave laborers working under intolerable conditions, they should be included in the compensatory requirements for Nazi victims.

ROBBERIES DURING ARRESTS, EXECUTIONS AND VARIOUS RETALIATORY ACTIONS:

Capital formation in the form of gold and precious metals was done not only through "spontaneous" robbery, but also in the process of "scheduled" robbery during arrests, executions, removal to concentration camps and other retaliatory actions. The valuables thus confiscated were registered at the trophies reception posts of the Reich Treasury. They came from German army units and from detention camps on the territory of occupied countries, including the Soviet Union.

To date we have studied trophies records from the USSR and from camps in Poland, Germany and other occupied territories where our citizens were interned. The money and gold were transferred to the German Reichsbank whose records also were examined. These records provide a concrete data on the Ukrainian share of the "Nazi gold." Currencies were recorded in Reichsmarks, but the value of jewelry was not estimated. It was recorded as so many pieces or so many kilograms of jewelry, and not specified whether the pieces were made of gold or silver or some other precious metal.

The total amount of currencies and gold coins taken from the Soviet Union was more than 1,800 million Reichsmarks. In addition, the records show more than 1,210 kilograms of jewelry, made up of 1,123,525 individual items. The significant part of these came from Ukraine. Almost 70,000 gold rubles and coins of other currencies were registered with indications of their Ukrainian origin. Similarly, some 7,000 valuable items, separately recorded 588 gold items and about 110 kilograms of jewelry suggest that they came from Ukraine. But we are convinced that the share of valuables confiscated in Ukraine is much higher, as numerous records don't show where the items originated.

Clearly, not all the stolen valuables reached the Reich Treasury. But the analysis of the trophies reception post records is very important for the establishment of appropriate parameters. Research in the archives of the trophies reception post of the Reich Treasury (Bundesarchives in Berlin) will continue.

RESEARCH IN UKRAINE

We continue to examine affidavits gathered by local assistance groups of the State Emergency Commission, which would provide data on property confiscation and on the suffering of Ukrainian population during the German occupation.

Plans call for a compilation of a list of citizens who have had their jewelry confiscated by the Nazis. Also, testimony and interrogation records of persons who returned from slave labor camps and prisoner of war camps about living conditions in Germany -- some 1,300,000 pages -- is available in the State archives. This material came from the Security Service, Ministry of Internal Affairs and Ministry of Defense of Ukraine.

OUR CONCLUSIONS AND PROPOSALS

1. Ukraine, where more than 600,000 Nazi victims still live, supports the world community with regard to a fair distribution of Nazi assets gained during the Holocaust era among the survivors of that era. We would like to see the creation of a fund as suggested by the United States and Great Britain for the support the victims of Nazi persecution until the end of their days, and wish to note that the people characterized at the London conference as "double victims" tend to die sooner. It is our view that this problem is complex and requires a complex solution, rather than a one-time humanitarian assistance.

2. The most urgent task for the benefit of Nazi victims – citizens of Ukraine and other new independent states on the territory of the former USSR – is the establishment of fair compensatory payments to them by the Federal Republic of Germany, the successor state of the Third Reich. This we emphatically reiterate. The payments should be made on a non-discriminatory basis not just to one category of persons (industrial slave laborers, for example), but to all categories of victims of

the National-Socialist persecution, including inmates of concentration camps, Gestapo prisoners, inhabitants of ghettos, persons compelled to work in hard-labor factories. To accomplish this, negotiations have to be undertaken with Germany and appropriate agreements concluded. In this respect we look to the attention and understanding of the new German government.

3. From Ukraine's point of view, "Nazi Gold" should not be defined only as stolen gold and other precious metals, but as a concept that in a broad sense characterizes the process of the Reich's capital formation during the Second World War. We thus take into consideration not only direct confiscation of valuables, but also the systematic fiscal policy in occupied territories, use of compulsory labor and removal of Ukraine's material resources. This approach corresponds with the orientation of the present conference. When we speak of "Nazi Gold" we mean Nazi assets gained during the Holocaust.

4. Our approach to this problem may differ from those of other European nations, but there is a reason: Ukraine had existed within the totalitarian system of the Soviet Union. Under conditions of this system, inhabitants of the greater part of Ukraine, on the eve of Nazi occupation, had no property rights, no bank accounts, no assets in bank safe deposit boxes. The only thing they were allowed to have were personal belongings and modest savings. We should remember, however, that during the Second World War millions of small streams of fine jewelry, ornaments, rings, watches, crosses, tooth caps merged into a mighty river of gold that became the Nazi assets of the Third Reich. The western lands of Ukraine, on the other hand, which became a part of the Soviet Union in 1939-40, did have the attributes of countries under whose rule these lands existed until that time. It is our position, therefore, that inhabitants of Eastern Halychyna, Bukovyna and Transnistria who survived the war and Holocaust should be compensated the same way as those of other European countries for their losses of bank savings, insurance, property and the like.

5. We confirm our readiness to cooperate with the world community in a full information exchange. Based on the principles of open society, we will make available all the materials in our archives that had been inaccessible before Ukraine's independence not only to foreign, but even domestic experts.

6. We support the idea of establishing an international archival directory on problems of Nazi assets and we stand ready to participate in planning such database. This directory, accessible through a world computer network, would be a worthy representation of the world

community's unity on the threshold of the third millennium. Moreover, it would have not only a practical significance, but also serve as a memorial to the victims of the Nazis and to remind the future generations of the Nazi horrors.

7. Ukraine supports the creation of a permanent advisory body made up of various experts, who would work on the problems of Nazi assets.

The delegation of Ukraine has come to the Washington conference with a fervent desire to promote practical achievements in its work, first and foremost – a fair division of Nazi assets, fair compensatory payments to the victims of Nazi persecution.

FIVE BASIC GROUPS OF THE ARCHIVAL DOCUMENTS

- Archives of the state government bodies;
- Archives of regional government bodies;
- Archives of the invaders' authority;
- Archives of the underground in Ukraine;
- Collections of documents.

The first group contains the instructive materials, correspondence of the chief Party and Soviet authorities of the Ukrainian Soviet Republic concerned with organizing the inventory of losses and damage caused in the time of the German occupation of the territory of republic, mass decimation of the civilians and prisoners of war, compulsory export of products, works or goods to Germany. The documents establishing or detaining carried out in areas of Ukraine including enterprises, establishments, organizations, citizens; the robbery of church property, museums, scientific and educational institutions: the export of objects of material and cultural values to Germany, Romania, are stored at the treasury of Council of the Peoples Commissars (CPC), the State or dared commission attached to the Ukrainian CPC, the Central statistical Department on the return of the equipment, property and valuables attached to the Ukrainian CPC (1943-1947). At the treasury of some People's Commissars there are certifications on the damages in various branches of the economy, health care, culture, overall data, registers, and acts proving the damage.

The second group is submitted by the documents of regional government bodies. Among them there are information, certifications, acts of regional certifications commissions of assistance to the Emergency State commission of the USSR on the establishment and investigation of invaders' crimes; citizens' petitions on the damage caused lists of the destroyed occupied settlements, citizens put to death or exported to Germany for slave labor; information on concentration camps, ghetto on the territory of Ukraine, etc.

The third group of the documents - has the greatest potential research value for studying occupation policy. It includes the documentary materials of the ruling government bodies such as the Reich safety services, Reich commissariat of Ukraine, Halychyna district; local general - commissariat, local and regional authorities, material on banks, police, different firms and organizations: the Reich Head Monetary Department - the Trophies Service, the German Reichsbank, the Economic banks in Ukraine, the agricultural banks, the Reich Society on auditing the occupied enterprises of the eastern areas of the Soviet Union, and material on concentration camps.

The fourth group includes the documents of the Ukrainian Headquarters for underground movements (UHGM), associations, and other groupings in which there is information on atrocities, crimes and robberies carried out by the Nazis.

The document collections according to their origin which characterize the Nazi regime in the occupied territory of Ukraine, the results of investigations of crimes and damage caused by the invaders, surveys of republican Emergency state commission concerned with the fifth group.

In general the archival base presented contains a sufficient volume of information to allow for scientific research of the problem.

UNITED STATES OF AMERICA

Overview of the Washington Conference Principles on Nazi-Confiscated Art

Stuart E. Eizenstat
UNDER SECRETARY OF STATE FOR ECONOMIC, BUSINESS AND
AGRICULTURAL AFFAIRS

Intervention during the Plenary Session: Overview of Nazi-Confiscated Art Issues

I want to thank all of our speakers for their extremely impressive and well-documented presentations. The work of Jonathan Petropoulos and Lynn Nicholas represent the outpouring of new scholarship about the cultural consequences of the Holocaust by scholars and archivists in many countries. We now have a better, more factual understanding about the massive displacement of art that took place in Europe during the Holocaust period. We know how the Nazis, in their expropriation of artworks and other assets, took a first step toward the destruction of an entire people. We understand the way in which well-meaning restitution efforts after the War were ended prematurely by international political considerations related to a focus on the Cold War.

From Mr. Kulishov's presentation, we have a renewed appreciation of the suffering the Russian people endured during the War. We welcome the Russian Federation's participation in the efforts of the international community to come to terms with issues relating to Nazi-confiscated art. And we look forward to hearing how the Duma exempted from its nationalization law art that the Nazis had confiscated from religious organizations, charitable institutions, and individuals due to their race, religion or national affiliation.

Ambassador Lauder has spoken from his perspective as a former diplomat, as a knowledgeable collector, and as a distinguished leader in the art world and the international Jewish community on the need for principles and guidelines for returning Nazi-confiscated art to its rightful owners.

Herr Bacher has explained the pioneering legislation last month by Austria, which can serve as a model for the return of Nazi-confiscated art. And Rusty Powell, Director of the National Gallery of Art here in Washington, has explained the genesis of the guidelines issued by the task force of the Association of Art Museum Directors.

When you think how much art was moved around during the War, in the midst of the bombings and movements of whole armies, it is amazing so much survived. It survived because there were German officers who disobeyed the Fuehrer's orders to burn Paris; because there were the dedicated "Monuments Men" among the Allied forces, who managed to find millions of hidden works that were disintegrating; and because there were civilians on both sides of the conflict who took risks to save art from destruction because they saw it as a glory of our civilization.

For decades, the search for Nazi-confiscated art was the lonely effort of survivors of the Holocaust and their families, aided by organizations devoted to their welfare. In the last few years, it has become a serious international issue. In country after country, public displays of this art have set off intensive controversy, touching on sensitive memories and inflaming ancient prejudices, casting a cloud over the international art market, threatening beneficial cultural exchange and reopening the wounds of World War II at a time when our nations are trying to construct new partnerships to serve us in the next century.

We must use this Conference to give new vigor to the work of restitution, so that people who have been deprived of their property for most of their lives can find justice. It will not be easy. Those were times of great confusion. The provenance of much of this art is not fully clear. Memories are fading, lives are drawing to a close. There are also innocent purchasers involved, who also must be heard if justice is to be served.

The purpose of our discussions at this Conference is not to blame any nation or group of nations. Our purpose is more constructive. We want to understand what happened to these works of art; to share the positive steps' nations have begun to take; and to learn about the new methods of archival research, the exciting new technologies for matching art with claims and the useful new methods of resolving disputes without lengthy and costly lawsuits.

Specifically, we shall discuss the general principles relating to Nazi-confiscated art that we included in a discussion paper we provided you during our consultations in the months preceding the Conference. Some of these principles were inspired by the guidelines, noted by Mr. Powell, prepared for American museums to use in dealing with Holocaust-era art.   Others reflect constructive initiatives of European governments and museums.

I am convinced that with the background we have been provided here, we can accept the opportunity and the responsibility to forge a consensus around these principles and make a commitment to finish this work.

Explanation of the Washington Conference Principles on Nazi-Confiscated Art

Stuart E. Eizenstat
UNDER SECRETARY OF STATE FOR ECONOMIC, BUSINESS AND
AGRICULTURAL AFFAIRS

Intervention during the Break-out Session: Principles to Address Nazi-Confiscated Art

I have been impressed - indeed I have been almost overwhelmed - by the way this Conference has evolved so far. We have moved from sadness and moral outrage, through a clearheaded definition of the issues and the problems, to a strong determination to resolve the issues, with more and more countries making commitments to do far more than what has been done up to now.

This is especially true as regards art. I was immensely pleased yesterday afternoon, when the chairman of the Russian delegation in effect opened a new chapter in restitution for his country. I was also immensely gratified as one delegation after another has committed itself to the principles of open archives, full accounting, and international cooperation in helping victims and their families find lost art.

The U.S. Government is very hopeful that out of our discussions here will come a consensus on broad principles that can guide us down this road. There are some difficult steps to take, but I hope we can take them in a spirit of mutual respect and cooperation among all nations and all concerned institutions.

After we announced at the London Conference on Nazi Gold that the United States would host a follow-up conference on other Nazi-confiscated assets and that art would have a prominent place on the agenda, the U.S. Government surveyed what was being done by various countries and other interested parties both in Europe and in this Hemisphere. We noted the actions being taken by a number of countries, such as France and the Netherlands, to identify Nazi-confiscated art and, in the case of Austria, to provide a comprehensive solution by which art can be returned to pre-War owners, notwithstanding former legal barriers such as the statute of limitations.

Several weeks ago, we prepared a discussion paper laying out eleven general principles, which was used as the basis of extensive consultations and which all of you have today. These principles are not, in themselves, a solution. They are a means by which nations can fashion their own solutions consistent with their own legal systems. The principles try to capture the spirit of this Conference for nations to use in this task.

If these principles are properly applied, the discovery of Nazi-confiscated art will no longer be a matter of chance. Instead, there will be an organized international effort - voluntary in nature but backed by strong moral commitment - to search provenance and uncover stolen art. This is a shared effort on the part of governments, NGOs, museums, auctioneers and dealers.

Claimants who have long been ignored will be encouraged and actively assisted in making claims. Those who research claims will no longer find that files are closed. There will be open archives everywhere in the world, easily usable by researchers. Issues of ownership will no longer be decided solely by endless, expensive, winner-take-all litigation. Instead, there will be enhanced opportunities for mediations, arbitrations and negotiated settlements, so that the art world and cultural exchange will be steadily freed from the taint of Nazi confiscation.

Let me add that, in light of the announcement yesterday by the Russian Federation that it will participate in developing a database, open archives to researchers, extend the period in which Holocaust survivors can apply for return of their art and support the principles suggested to this conference, I am confident that some of the greatest collections in the world will be returned to their rightful owners and a vast storehouse of information about other works will open up as well.

The first three principles envision a massive cooperative effort to trace this art. We call upon museums to search the provenance of their holdings, on governments to open up their World War 11 and related archives to private researchers, for commercial galleries and auction houses to seek information, document, and make available what information they have. It is important to locate what was confiscated. It is equally important to know what was not confiscated, or what was restituted to the pre-War owners. The taint of "stolen art" should not be applied to works that do not deserve it.

Researchers in Switzerland, Austria, the Netherlands and France are at work today tracing the provenance of artworks in their national collections.   The international auction houses have redoubled their provenance investigations.   Non-governmental organizations have launched projects to find lost art and help survivors and their families in the painful task of remembering what they owned and when and how it was seized.   The guidelines issued by the American Association of Art Museum Directors and the Museum Directors Conference of the United Kingdom call for institutions to research their collections and make them available as well to outside researchers.   These are practices that are consistent with these principles. More and more nations are adopting them.

The fourth principle deals with gaps and ambiguities in the provenance of works.   The vast displacement of art, the destruction of many records and the furtive nature of the international market during the War mean there must be some leeway in establishing provenance. Where there is no bill of sale, a diary entry or an insurance listing might be acceptable evidence of pre-War ownership. If a work is not on a Nazi confiscation list, it may be in the archives of the "monuments men" or the secret inventories of the French Resistance or in other archival collections.

Conversely, there may be circumstantial evidence that works were not stolen but sold at market, or restituted to families and subsequently sold.   Provenance work is not easy.   But I can say from experience that neither was it easy to trace the movement of Nazi gold. Some said it would be impossible.   Yet in two years of hard work we were able to do it, as was the Swiss Bergier Commission.

The next three principles -- numbers 5, 6, and 7 -- deal with publicizing the information and encouraging resolution of the issues. They include circulating photos of the art and information about it everywhere in the world, through the traditional media and on the new electronic media.   Maximum publicity will tell survivors and their families if their art still exists.   It will also tell the international art community if questions still exist about a given work.   I applaud the government of France for its initiative in displaying on the Internet a portion of the unclaimed art restituted to France by the Allied military authorities, the so-called MNR collection.   An impressive number of other nations and non-governmental organizations are also preparing databases and their own web sites.

The Internet is a powerful tool, but as anyone who uses it knows, it can be overwhelming.   With that in mind, we suggest the eventual establishment, as a cooperative project, of a central registry -- in effect, a digital collecting point -- of information about Nazi-confiscated art.   This will greatly help museums and collectors avoid acquiring stolen objects and assist the victims of the theft in locating their losses. A number of countries and institutions are making details of their archival holdings and access information available on their dedicated web sites.

The U.S. National Archives and Records Administration has placed its finding aid to Holocaust-era art on the Internet. We encourage all governments, museums, art dealers and other institutions to join in this effort. On-line repositories could include lists of losses that have not been restituted; lists of unclaimed items, and information that will help individuals research and make claims. They should be linked for easier access. In posting information on the Internet, institutions should bear in mind the benefits of adhering to common standards. For example, Object I.D., which is already gaining worldwide acceptance and is available in many languages, sets forth minimum descriptive data for uniquely identifying a work of art.

After existing art works have been matched with documented losses, comes the delicate process of reconciling competing equities of ownership to produce a just and fair solution -- the subject of the 8th and 9th principles. We can begin by recognizing that as a moral matter, we should not apply rules designed for commercial transactions of societies that operate under the rule of law to people whose property and very lives were taken by one of the most profoundly illegal regimes the world has ever known.

In this regard, the U.S. Government applauds the courageous decision of the government of Austria to return art held in its federal museums and collections to surviving pre-War owners and their rightful heirs notwithstanding legal defenses. We hope other European governments will follow Austria's example in their own way, so they can complete the restitution process their predecessors left in abeyance after the war.

The leadership of the art world is moving in the same direction. The Art Dealers Association of America has flatly stated its members will not knowingly purchase or sell Nazi-confiscated art. The guidelines of the Museum Directors Associations, in both the United States and the United Kingdom, call on museums not to acquire such art until ownership questions are resolved.

Practices such as these recognize the fact that the public enjoys works of art because they represent the highest achievements of our civilization. They are proud of their museums and public collections. They do not want this pride to be clouded by unresolved claims of the Holocaust.

As the desire to do justice grows stronger, we hope that collectors of art will use the Internet to look at their holdings and then look into their own hearts and decide what to do. They may follow the example of two families in Brazil. One owned a Picasso, the other a Monet. Knowing these works had passed through a wartime dealer notorious for his dealings with the Nazis, they voluntarily put them at the disposal of the Jewish community of Sao Paulo pending discovery of the rightful owners.

To illustrate the 8th principle, that solutions should be flexible and just, I commend to you the recent settlement of the disputed ownership of a painting by Degas, "Landscape With Smokestack." The claimant family produced a fairly clear record of ownership. The owner had paid full value with no knowledge of the wartime provenance. Both were in a position to wage a legal battle that could have gone on for years. Instead, they settled on partial payment for the family and donation of the work to the Art Institute of Chicago, where the public could enjoy it and a label accompanying the work acknowledged both parties. Art claims do not have to be winner-take-all propositions, which produce prolonged struggles in the courts, and drain the resources of both parties. In an atmosphere of good will, a wide range of solutions is there to be found.

There are additional opportunities when the original owner is found to have died without heirs, the subject of the ninth principle. The art could be sold with the proceeds going to victims of the Holocaust and Jewish communities around the world. Or it could be displayed in museums and identified in ways that educate the public about the cultural losses of the Holocaust.

The 10th principle states that to ensure objectivity and to enhance public confidence in their work, commissions in this field should have members from outside the government, such as art experts, historians and representatives of communities which were victims of the Holocaust and, where appropriate, distinguished persons from other countries.

The final principle - which I suggest today for the first time - speaks to the need to give the other principles vitality. Nations should take specific measures to apply these principles so they can more quickly accomplish our mutual goals. For example, they should strive to develop internal processes, making use of alternative dispute resolution mechanisms, to restitute looted property.

While the proceedings of the Conference will be published shortly, they will remain open until the end of the millennium so that nations may submit reports on the progress they have made to put these principles into effect.

In conclusion, the most important test for any country today is not only what it did or failed to do in the past, but what it is doing and will do to face the past honestly and make amends for what was done. The U.S. Government supports these principles as an action plan to resolve a difficult, longstanding, embarrassing problem. I urge the delegates to this Conference to form a consensus around them so that the enthusiasm we have generated can result in real action.

The American philosopher Ralph Waldo Emerson once said, "Every genuine work of art has as much reason for being as the earth and the sea." It is to cap the glory of art with the crown of justice that we try to finish our work today.

Art Databases and Archives

Stuart E. Eizenstat
UNDER SECRETARY OF STATE FOR ECONOMIC, BUSINESS AND
AGRICULTURAL AFFAIRS

Intervention during Break-out Session: Identification of Art,
Archives and Databases

Mr. Chairman and delegates to the Conference:

On behalf of the host delegation, I want to thank our presenters:

Connie Lowenthal of the Commission for Art Recovery, who is using her skills to help so many individuals press their claims for return of their property;

Ron Tauber of the Art Loss Register, who has assembled the largest registry of stolen art in the world and has offered to make the resources and experience of his company available to survivors and their families without cost;

Gil Edelson, who speaks for American art dealers, who will be so important to implementing whatever recommendations come out of this Conference;

Konstantin Akinsha, whose patient work in Russian archives opened a new chapter in this story and whose new Project of Documentation of Wartime Losses is another important part of the solution; and

Ori Soltes, whose work in the past with the Klutznick National Jewish Museum helped to move this issue forward.

It is obvious from these presentations that technology and history are coming together to create an opportunity we cannot afford to miss.

After World War II, most of the survivors of the Holocaust were too concerned with putting their lives back together to undertake the difficult task of locating their stolen artworks. Much of the art displaced during the War was presumed lost. The vast majority of the claims that were made were not for restitution, but for monetary compensation.

Decades later, when the Cold War finally ended and archives previously closed were opened up, we learned that some of what was presumed to be destroyed had actually survived. The discovery of missing art in Eastern Europe, along with the aging of the survivors themselves, gives both new hope and new urgency to the search.

The search itself did not grow easier. It still involved going through tens of thousands of feet of records, in many different archives, in several different languages, in countries stretched over half the earth. Very few survivors could afford this. Even those who could, found that many doors were still closed and many paths led nowhere.

All that is beginning to change. What has been achieved on gold, and the equally important progress on insurance, show that nations want to heal the remaining wounds of World War II with speed and with justice. You should know that the five governments comprising the International Task Force on Holocaust Education, Remembrance and Research will present their own recommendation to the Conference that all nations commit themselves to opening up, by the end of next year, all public and private archives on the Holocaust in general, and Holocaust assets in particular. I hope the Conference will make a similar commitment to the principle of open archives and fully accessible records on art.

I hope you will explore ways to speed up archival research on art. An excellent example is the finding aid that has been developed by the National Archives here in the United States. The Archives' holdings of Nazi records, war crimes trials transcripts, and Allied Occupation documents is vast. In it are records of the Nazi organizations engaged in art looting; also the records of postwar restitution, including efforts to locate looted assets. The finding aid, available on the Internet, helps researchers who are searching for missing art and provenance information determine what records exist, what they contain, and where they are located. It leads them down to the right stack area, the row and even the shelf. Archival personnel are available to offer additional assistance.

It is possible, through the power of the new technology, to give all survivors and their families the research capability that up to now has been available to just a few. France has already used the Internet to publicize the collection of unclaimed art recovered after the War that it holds in custody. Many of you have expressed an interest in linkups, so that someone with a documentation claim can put their information on a website and match it against the inventories of works which were confiscated but are still unclaimed. Or will allow those who deal in art to check the wartime provenance of works they are interested in to see if a documented claim exists.

The web site of the U.S. Holocaust Memorial Museum provides listings of information on Nazi-confiscated art (www.ushmm.gov) including the National Archives finding aid. A number of countries and institutions are making details of their archival holdings and access information available on their dedicated web sites, linked to this central web site managed by the Holocaust Museum. We encourage all governments, museums, art dealers and other institutions to join in this effort to link information on Nazi-confiscated art and to help the long overdue resolution of outstanding ownership issues.

All of this will require cooperation, a willingness to share data, and careful monitoring. None of us wants this information to be used in ways that impede the free flow of commerce or restrict cultural exchange between nations. Nor need it. Private organizations and police authorities look for stolen art all the time. Their efforts actually help to stabilize the market. A speedy resolution of claims arising from Nazi-confiscation will free the world of art from the uncertainty and threats of litigation that have troubled its workings and eliminated impediments to international cultural exchange, which benefits all out citizens.

We have the means and we have the will to bring justice after so many years. I know your discussions, conducted in that spirit, will make a significant contribution to that goal.

U.S. Support for the International Commission on Holocaust Era Insurance Claims

Stuart E. Eizenstat
UNDER SECRETARY OF STATE FOR ECONOMIC, BUSINESS AND AGRICULTURAL AFFAIRS

Intervention during the Break-out Session: Solutions – Addressing Claims and Providing Humanitarian Relief

The International Commission (or the IC) has the strong support of the U.S. Government because: the IC brings together many of the interested parties in a cooperative, non-confrontational process; the IC includes the important survivor organizations; the IC will foster a fact-based effort to resolve Holocaust insurance claims promptly and fairly, and without resorting to lengthy litigation; and the IC seeks practical solutions to resolve the issue of heirless insurance assets.

The IC is already functioning. It has had two meetings during which much has been accomplished. The IC selected former Secretary of State Lawrence Eagleburger as its chairman. At the November 11 meeting chaired by Mr. Eagleburger, the IC established five Working Groups to resolve specific issues.

The insurance companies on the IC pledged $90 million as an act of good faith. Disbursement of the $90 million will be decided either on the basis of the claims adjudication procedures or for humanitarian relief projects approved by the Commission.

The IC is committed to resolving all claims on the basis of expedited claims requirements over the next two years, or less. This timetable is far superior to lengthy litigation. The IC also has the support of the major companies and key governments. I believe we can achieve far more through cooperation rather than confrontation.

The International Commission has the strong support of the U.S. Government. I hope other companies and other insurance regulators will also join this effort. I hope this Conference can agree to express strong support for the International Commission and urge other companies and governments to join this process.

The Need for Others to Join the International Commission on Holocaust Era Insurance Claims

Stuart E. Eizenstat

UNDER SECRETARY OF STATE FOR ECONOMIC, BUSINESS AND AGRICULTURAL AFFAIRS

Intervention during the Break-out Session: Solutions – Addressing Claims and Providing Humanitarian Relief

We commend the six insurers that have voluntarily agreed to join the International Commission: Allianz, Generali, AXA, Zurich, Winterthur, and Basler.

These companies are fully committed to the IC process and are also supporting our goals here at the Washington Conference. These companies recognize the importance of our work here today, particularly with respect to assuring prompt justice for Holocaust survivors. The companies are also committed to open archives.

However, these six companies together are not the only companies that sold policies during the Holocaust era. Indeed, these companies estimate their market share from that era to be about 30 percent of the total.

The Washington Conference should encourage other insurers to join the IC process. In this regard, we welcome the informal expressions of interest by some Central and East European governments in IC. The interest of these governments is further evidence of their commitment to modernize and adapt their laws and markets to Western norms.

In addition, we hope that Austrian insurance companies, which are not represented on the International Commission at this time, will also join this process.

In this regard, Lawrence Eagleburger, the Chairman of the International Commission, has indicated that he will be traveling to Vienna and to Central and East European capitals to encourage others to join this process.

The U.S. Government strongly supports this effort by Chairman Eagleburger.   I hope delegations here today will assure that former Secretary Eagleburger is received at the highest level in your capitals.

Archival Openness

Stuart E. Eizenstat
UNDER SECRETARY OF STATE FOR ECONOMIC, BUSINESS AND
AGRICULTURAL AFFAIRS

Intervention during the Break-out Session: Archives and Books

I want to thank all of my colleagues here on the panel with me today: Thank you to Ambassador Amigues for his remarks here and I wish to commend him for the leadership role of France in winding down the Tripartite Gold Commission and establishing in Paris at the Foreign Ministry the complete archives of the Commission for all to see and examine. And, as I have gladly acknowledged in other places, I want to thank Gill Bennett for taking the first steps more than two years ago in beginning the reporting on Nazi gold. I also want to thank Dr. Büttner for showing such outstanding leadership not only in seeing that the German archives were opened but in encouraging and assisting researchers in their use. We have also heard from Dr. Bergier, author of the remarkably penetrating and courageous study of the role of Switzerland and Swiss banks in the financing of the Nazi war effort; I thank him for appearing here with us today.

I must also thank Michael Kurtz of the U.S. National Archives and Records Administration, whose team spearheaded the massive declassification effort that has proved so invaluable not only to the U.S. interagency project but to all the researchers from the historical commissions represented here. NARA archivists continue to provide extraordinary assistance and information to the many governmental and private researchers who have traveled to the Archives to consult documents available nowhere else in the world.

The world has seen an amazing outpouring of scholarship on Holocaust-era assets over the past several years. The examination of long sequestered or neglected historical records on the tragic events of a half century ago, taken together with greater national will in many countries to face the often disturbing contents of these records, are making such important research possible.

National commissions in more than 16 nations have given structure and impetus to this research and, above all, an urgency to complete the review soon enough to give assistance to remaining survivors of the Nazi depredations. Working within the framework of these commissions and their diverse mandates or more directly under the aegis of governments and organizations, historians and other experts have sifted through 50-year old records in central government archives, local government records, and the private papers of individuals and commercial organizations. The research has reached beyond national boundaries, and it has allowed the comparison of the recollections of the occupied and the oppressed with those of their Nazi conquerors and oppressors. And the published results of this research has had its national and even international audiences, and has fostered the expectation and need for a full, unflinching account of the decisions and events of the past as they affected both governments and individuals.

I think we all must acknowledge, with astonishment and pride, just how much important research has been done and how many new archival sources have been opened by the governments of the nations committed to our common task as a result of the work of the various national commissions. I cannot fail to mention the truly remarkable measures taken by my own government: making available and fully accessible to researchers by May of 1997 at the National Archives more than 15 million pages of documents-nearly a million pages of which were declassified almost on the spot to facilitate their public availability. And the work has gone forward without pause at the National Archives with new and important files being found, described, and made available for research.

Despite the rising tide of research in archives and collections around the world on monetary gold and financial assets of various sorts, some subjects remain to be examined with the same authority and thoroughness. Some of these subjects-like looted art and other cultural objects and insurance policies-are uniquely difficult to subject to clear and unambiguous accounting. We are trying at this Conference to advance our international understanding of the dimensions of these matters. The full disclosure of the historical record on these complex issues and others, such as communal property, requires a further, continuous effort to open and make broadly accessible to researchers the wide range of historical sources from which judgments can be made and justice can arise.

Much has been done to at last open the record of the past, but much remains to be done by governments and institutions that retain some portion of the shared recollection of the events of 50 years ago. There are files and collections still to be found and identified; there are files and archives to which access must be made more responsive to the reasonable needs of researchers, and there are files and collections that must be declassified and exposed to the light of scholarly scrutiny.

The International Task Force on Holocaust Education, Remembrance and Research is presenting a declaration that calls on all nations participating in the conference to join in taking steps to ensure the fullest possible openness and accessibility of archives bearing on the fate of Nazi looted assets. The opening of these archives by the end of next year should be the target of all of us participating here. As we enter the new millennium, we must reaffirm and reinforce the commitment of humanity to learn from its history.

WORLD JEWISH RESTITUTION ORGANIZATION

Report of the W.J.R.O.
Jerusalem, November 1, 1998

Submitted by
Ambassador Naphtali Lavie
VICE CHAIRMAN OF THE EXECUTIVE

The World Jewish Restitution Organization which was established at the end of 1992 by nine major world Jewish organizations, in coordination with the Government of Israel, engaged eight governments of Central, Northern and Eastern Europe in negotiations for the restitution of Jewish communal and public properties which were confiscated and/or nationalized by the Nazi occupation regime and by the Communist authorities. Unfortunately, most of the respective governments demonstrated a negative attitude toward the claims WJRO presented.

POLAND:

In May 1993, WJRO started its operations in Warsaw, at meetings with representatives of the Government of Poland, in coordination with the Union of Jewish Religious Communities in this country. Since then WJRO negotiated with five consecutive governments in Poland. WJRO requested the Polish government to enact a law in favor of restitution of the communal and public properties which belonged to over 1500 Jewish communities in Poland prior to September 1, 1939, similar to the laws enacted in favor of the various Christian denominations.

In February 1997, the Polish Parliament enacted a law regulating the relations of the State and the Jewish Communities, which includes a chapter dealing with the restitution of Jewish properties. However this chapter is far from satisfying the basic claims of the Jewish Communities. Moreover, the attempts to settle the restitution issue within the abovementioned law negates all the possibilities to claim and receive the vast number of properties, which for many years served the 3.5 million Jews of Poland, about 10% of the total population of Poland. In March 1946, the Polish Government appropriated these properties according to a Government decree, which transferred to the Government the ownership of all properties defined as enemy property, which is Jewish property the Government inherited from the Nazi occupants of Poland, who confiscated it from the legitimate Jewish owners.

Two memorandums protesting the negative attitude of this law were submitted to the Government of Poland in 1997, and in 1998, by WJRO and the World Federation of Polish Jews. Until this date no response has been received.

WJRO compiled a list of approximately 6000 communal properties such as synagogues, schools, hospitals, senior citizens' homes, orphanages and other institutions of religious, cultural and social services which belonged to the Jewish Community but the Polish Government ignores this claim. Instead, the government recognizes the rights of the existing nine remnant communities and the Union of these communities to file claims to regulatory committees which have been established for the purpose of restitution. Until the end of October 1998, less than one hundred claims have been dealt with and only a few of them have been finalized and returned to Jewish ownership.

THE CZECH REPUBLIC:

In the Czech Republic (Bohemia and Moravia) there existed before W.W.II a vibrant Jewish Community of approximately 100,000 people. Today there are less than 3000 Jews in the whole Czech Republic.

Taking a slightly different approach of the one demonstrated by Poland, the Government of the Czech Republic was more flexible in accepting a small number of claims submitted by the local Jewish Community. The Community claimed approximately 200 properties hoping that by minimizing its claim the Government will be willing to restitute this number of properties in spite of the fact that WJRO has prepared a list of over 1000 communal and public properties which belonged to the Jewish Communities in the Czech Republic in 1939. So far only a small number of communal properties have been restituted.

SLOVAKIA:

The Jewish population in Slovakia numbered about 120,000 before W.W.II. Today there are 14 Jewish Communities in Slovakia with a population of approximately 2000 Jews.

The Slovak Government was more forthcoming than its previous partner in the Czechoslovak Federation, the Czech Republic. The Government of Slovakia enacted in November 1993, a law for the restitution of Jewish communal properties which is almost identical to the law enacted in favor of the various Christian denominations in Slovakia.

WJRO in coordination with the local Jewish Communities prepared a list of nearly 1000 communal and public properties belonging to the Jewish Community in Slovakia. The Federation of Jewish Communities in Bratislava submitted claims of over 800 properties including cemeteries, but only 360 have been restituted, most of them cemeteries. Some 250 cases are pending ruling of the local courts.

HUNGARY:

WJRO together with the Federation of the Jewish Communities submitted a list which constituted about 3000 communal properties in the country which served the Jewish Communities of a population of nearly 700,000 Jews before the Holocaust. Today the estimates of the existing Jewish Community in Hungary are between 70,000 and 110,000 Jews.

After many attempts by WJRO, made in coordination with the Federation of Jewish Communities in Hungary, with previous governments in Hungary, the last government in Budapest agreed to regulate the issue of restitution of communal and public Jewish properties within a law enacted in parliament which called for the establishment of a joint Foundation for restitution. The Foundation, with the participation of representatives of the Hungarian Government, the local Jewish Communities and Organizations and WJRO, began its operations some months ago but at this stage less than ten properties have been restituted to this Foundation.

Recently, on October 1, 1998, the Hungarian Government signed an agreement with the Jewish Community to settle the claim of the community for communal real estate. According to the settlement the Jewish Community will waive its claim of 152 properties, value of HUF13,511 billion   ($60,000,000) and in return will receive a government annual allocation of about $3 million, for religious, educational and charitable activities of the community.

The agreement does not refer to the list of 3000 communal properties WJRO together with the Jewish Community submitted to the Government already in 1995.

ROMANIA:

An agreement had been reached between WJRO and the Government of Romania in September 1997 to establish a joint Foundation by WJRO and the Federation of Jewish Communities in Romania. This Foundation is entitled to claim and to receive the properties that belonged to the Jewish Communities. According to the list WJRO prepared, there are approximately 3000 communal properties in Romania which belonged to the Communities and served their needs at the time where there were over 800,000 Jews in Romania. Some 400,000 Jews of Romania survived the Holocaust and most of them immigrated to Israel. Only about 12,000 Jews live today in Romania. The Foundation which was established by WJRO and the Federation of Jewish Communities in Romania has been registered in the Court in Bucharest according to the Romanian law, and at present, October 1998, over 20 properties are in the process of being transferred to the ownership to the Foundation.

THE UKRAINE:

Several attempts were made in the last five years to convince the Government of the Ukraine to restitute the Jewish communal properties which were left in the Ukraine. The President of WJRO, Mr. Edgar M. Bronfman, and the Chairman of the Executive, Dr. Israel Singer, met with the former President and the current President of the Ukraine and discussed at length the moral and legal claim to the communal properties in the Ukraine, but no positive results have been reached.

In January 1995, Vice Chairman of WJRO Naphtali Lavie, and Chairman of the Jewish Community in Ukraine, Joseph Zissel, submitted a memorandum to Deputy Prime Minister, Prof. Ivan Kuras, claiming the restitution of Jewish communal property, but no response has been received.

Since there are today in the Ukraine approximately 300,000 compared to about 2 million Jews who lived in that area (including Eastern Poland and parts of Romania that were annexed by the Ukraine), the government gave back a small number of synagogues to the existing Jewish Communities, but there is no positive attitude of this government to restitute the Jewish properties that served the local communities.

CROATIA:

Several attempts made by WJRO to the government of Croatia have not produced any results. The Government of Croatia holds on to Jewish communal properties and is not willing to negotiate any possible solution to this problem.

ESTONIA, LATVIA AND LITHUANIA:

The Government of Estonia is forthcoming on its own initiative towards the claims of the Jewish Community, which numbers approximately 2,500 Jews, for its few properties.

The Latvian Government, as well, is positive in its attitude toward individual claims for restitution. According to the existing law, which passed legislation in the Latvian Government in 1989, every person who possessed private property in Latvia can claim and receive the property without any limitations, unlike the procedures practiced in Poland and the Czech Republic where individuals can claim their property only if they prove their citizenship and residency in the country.

As for communal and public properties the Latvian Government expressed its willingness to restitute such properties by a joint Foundation to be established by WJRO and the local Jewish Communities, which number about 15,000 Jews out of about 100,000 who lived there before W.W.II.

The situation in Lithuania is rather negative compared to the one in Latvia. Of a population of about 250,000 Jews who lived in Lithuania before the war, there are today between 5,000 to 7,000 Jews living in

Lithuania. The Lithuanian Government did not respond positively to attempts being made by representatives of WJRO who negotiated with the Government, in Vilnius and in Jerusalem.

NORWAY:

Unlike other countries in Europe, which were and still are reluctant to deal positively with restitution claims, the Government of Norway demonstrated a constructive attitude toward the claims presented by the Jewish Community and WJRO.

Last month the Norwegian government submitted to the Parliament a bill concerning a restitution package which will allocate $60 million to Holocaust survivors, for the Jewish Community, for projects of Jewish heritage and for the establishment of a center for tolerance, to fight racism and anti-Semitism. This government decision was made following appeals by the local Jewish community and WJRO and ongoing negotiations during the last two years.

Nazi-Confiscated Art Issues

Dr. Jonathan Petropoulos

PROFESSOR, DEPARTMENT OF HISTORY, LOYOLA COLLEGE, MD
UNITED STATES

Art Looting during the Third Reich: An Overview with Recommendations for Further Research

Plenary Session on Nazi-Confiscated Art Issues

It is an honor to be here to speak to you today. In many respects it is the highpoint of the over fifteen years I have spent working on this issue of artworks looted by the Nazis. This is a vast topic, too much for any one book, or even any one person to cover. Put simply, the Nazis plundered so many objects over such a large geographical area that it requires a collaborative effort to reconstruct this history. The project of determining what was plundered and what subsequently happened to these objects must be a team effort. And in fact, this is the way the work has proceeded. Many scholars have added pieces to the puzzle, and we are just now starting to assemble a complete picture. In my work I have focused on the Nazi plundering agencies[1]; Lynn Nicholas and Michael Kurtz have worked on the restitution process[2]; Hector Feliciano concentrated on specific collections in Western Europe which were

---

[1] Jonathan Petropoulos, Art as Politics in the Third Reich (Chapel Hill: The University of North Carolina Press). Also, The Faustian Bargain: The Art World in Nazi Germany (New York/Oxford: Oxford University Press, forthcoming, 1999).

[2] Lynn Nicholas, The Rape of Europa: The Fate of Europe's Treasures in the Third Reich and the Second World War (New York: Alfred Knopf, 1994); and Michael Kurtz, Nazi Contraband: American Policy on the Return of European Cultural Treasures (New York: Garland, 1985).

plundered[3]; Thomas Buomberger has been examining the Swiss connection to this history[4]; Wolfgang Eichwede and his team in Bremen have explored looting on the Eastern Front[5]; Konstantin Akinsha, Gregori Kozlov, and Sylvia Hochfield unearthed the history of the Soviet Red Army trophy brigades[6]; Willi Korte and Bill Honan showed that the American G.I.s also stole works during and after the war[7]; and one could go on and on (my apologies to those left off this brief list).[8] Certain events, notably the symposium "The Spoils of War" which was held in New York in 1995 have facilitated this cooperation, and I am pleased to say that there has generally been conscientious teamwork within the

---

[3] Hector Feliciano, The Lost Museum: The Nazi Conspiracy to Steal the World's Greatest Works of Art (New York: Basic Books, 1997).

[4] Thomas Buomberger, Raubkunst -- Kunstraub: Die Schweiz und der Handel mit gestohlene Kulturgüter zur Zeit des Zweiten Weltkrieges (Zürich: Orell Füssli, 1998).

[5] See Wolfgang Eichwede and Ulrike Hartung, eds., "Betr.: Sicherstellung": NS-Kunstraub in der Sowjetunion (Hamburg: Edition Temmen, 1998); and Ulrike Hartung, Raubzüge in der Sowjetunion. Das Sonderkommando Künsberg 1941-1943 (Bremen: Edition Temmen, 1997).

[6] Konstantin Akinsha and Gregori Kozlov with Sylvia Hochfield, Beautiful Loot: The Soviet Plunder of Europe's Art Treasures (New York: Random House, 1995).

[7] William Honan, Treasure Hunt: A New York Reporter Tracks the Quedlinburg Hoard (New York: Delta, 1997). Also on this theme, see Kenneth Alford, The Spoils of World War II: The American Military's Role in the Stealing of Europe's Treasures (New York: Birch Lane, 1994).

[8] Other especially important studies include: Willem de Vries, Einsatzstab Reichsleiter Rosenberg, Sonderstab Musik: The Confiscation of Music in the Occupied Countries of Western Europe during World War II (Ann Arbor: The University of Michigan Press, 1997); Wolfgang Eichwede and Ulrike Hartung, eds., "Betr. Sicherstellung": NS-Kunstraub in der Sowjetunion (Bremen: Edition Temmen, 1998); Mathias Frehner, ed., Das Geschäft mit der Raubkunst. Fakten, Thesen, Hintergründe (Zurich: Neue Zurcher Zeitung, 1998); Günther Haase, Kunstraub und Kunstschutz: Eine Dokumentation (Hildesheim: Georg Olms, 1991); Ulrike Hartung, Raubzüe in der Sowjetunion. Das Sonderkommando Küsberg, 1941-1943 (Bremen: Edition Temmen, 1997); Ernst Kubin, Sonderauftrag Linz: Die Kunstsammlung Adolf Hitler. Eine Thriller der Kulturgeschichte (Vienna: Orac, 1989); Jakob Kurz, Kunstraub in Europa, 1938-1945 (Hamburg: Facta Oblita, 1989); Peter Manasse, Verschleppte Archive und Bibliotheken. Die Täigkeiten des Einsatzstab Rosenberg wärend des Zweiten Weltkrieges (St. Ingbert: Röhrig Universitätsverlag, 1997); Matila Simon, The Battle of the Louvre: The Struggle to Save French Art in World War II (New York: Hawthorn, 1971).

scholarly community.[9] I make a plea today to broaden this circle of cooperation so as to also include museum administrators and curators, gallery owners, and government officials. If we are to continue to make progress in writing this history and effecting a just restitution of the displaced artworks, it must be a collaborative venture among individuals in all of these spheres.

I have been asked to speak on the National Socialists' actions with respect to artworks – an immense topic that is impossible to cover in ten minutes. But I would start with the following observation: the Nazis used art instrumentally as a part of their larger political and ideological project. Their policies with respect to art are inextricably linked to efforts to seize power within Germany, to conquer the European continent, and to execute their genocidal program. From the beginning, Hitler and the other Nazi Party leaders realized that artistic issues could be used to attract supporters. The Party Program of 1920 contained provisions about art (namely, that modern art should be viewed as "degenerate" and alien to the German people). By 1930, the Nazi leaders had learned to utilize artistic issues as a means of attacking political enemies. In Thuringia, where a Nazi had been appointed Minister of Education (Kultusminister), the target was the left, whom they associated with modernism – and indeed, they effectively forced the relocation of the Bauhaus from Dessau to Berlin. By the mid-1930s, the Nazi leaders were using art policies in their war against the Jews: the traveling Degenerate Art Exhibition, which opened in 1937, contained caustic anti-Semitic messages, and the expropriation of Jewish collections, which became more common around the same time, represented an important escalation of this war. Both developments were, as many have noted, part of the process of dehumanizing the Jews undertaken by the Nazis. Finally, the Nazis' project of seizing artworks from foreign lands that they viewed as Germanic was an expression of their geopolitical goals: the "Poland is really Germany" school of thought, which sought to seize objects deemed German and eradicate indigenous Polish culture, is but one example. In short, the Nazis' cultural policies – and specifically their efforts to loot artworks – were inextricably bound with the war and Holocaust, and this gives the project

---

[9] Elizabeth Simpson, ed., The Spoils of War: World War II and Its Aftermath: The Loss, Reappearance, and Recovery of Cultural Property (New York: Harry Abrams, 1997).

of restitution special urgency. One Polish scholar has made this linkage as he recently called for "material restitution and moral indemnity."[10]

I think it helpful to outline the different categories of Nazi plunder here at the outset; in part to gain a sense of the cultural objects that were displaced, but also to communicate with more specificity how the looting fit into the Nazis' ideological agenda. The first seizures involved modern art – works labeled "degenerate" – from state collections. This began by order of both Propaganda Minister Joseph Goebbels and Adolf Hitler in 1937 and resulted in the removal of over 17,000 works from German museums (though certain objects actually belonged to private individuals and were seized with no legal basis).[11] While we do not know the fate of all these works – many were sent abroad and some were burned in Berlin – it is important to note that there have thus far been no claims on these works. The Nazis passed a law, dated May 31st 1938, which legalized the sale of artworks purged from state collections. German officials in the postwar period have recognized this law – or at least not filed claims or sought restitution. I have heard that some German museum directors and curators do not agree with this policy and would like to see their institutions pursue certain artworks that had been purged by the Nazis. But to repeat, there have been no claims made on these works and the task until now has been simply to ascertain the fate of these works (the first comprehensive list of the 17,000 purged pieces surfaced only last year in London).

The second category concerns artworks taken from German and Austrian Jews. Very often artworks were seized as part of Nazi Aryanization measures: the taking over of Jewish-owned businesses, including art galleries. This happened first in Germany on a limited scale, and then was "perfected" in Vienna by Adolf Eichmann and his cohorts who oversaw a "one stop" emigration office. This is part of what scholars have termed the "Viennese model." These works, if found, should be restituted to former owners or their heirs.

The third category is the property belonging to Jews outside the Reich. This includes, in order of seizure, the property of Jews in Poland, France, the Benelux countries, Greece, and subsequently the rest of Eastern Europe. The Nazis established a network of agencies to carry

---

[10] Jan Pruszynski, "Poland: The War Losses, Cultural Heritage, and Cultural Legitimacy," in Simpson, ed., The Spoils of War, 52.

[11] See the case of private property in the custody of the Berlin National Gallery discussed by Anja Heuss, "Das Schicksal der jüdischen Kunstsammlung von Ismar Littmann," in Neue Zürcher Zeitung 188 (17 August 1998), 23.

out these operations: from Heinrich Himmler and Reinhard Heydrich's SS and security agencies (as well as their ancestral research organization, the Ahnenerbe) to Alfred Rosenberg's Special Staff (the Einsatzstab Reichsleiter Rosenberg or ERR) to Kajetan Mühlmann's commandos in Poland and his office in the Netherlands. Works from this category, of course, should be restituted.

Category four concerns artworks that belonged to non-Jews living outside Germany. The majority of these cases occurred in Eastern Europe: in Poland, the Protectorate of Bohemia and Moravia, Hungary, and the former Soviet Union. Very often the victims were aristocrats, such as the Czartoryskis and the Lanckoronskis. This was part of the Germanification program in Eastern Europe, although greed was also a significant factor.[12]

Category five is the property belonging to religious organizations. This would include synagogues (much of the Judaica was sent to Prague in preparation for the museum to document a deceased Jewish culture).[13] Catholic churches in Eastern Europe and Free Masons' temples in all the occupied lands also fell victim to the Nazis' plundering commandos.

Category six is the property of the state. The Nazis refrained from the wholesale expropriation of state collections in Western Europe, and most of the state property that was seized came from the East. The Soviets did not undertake evacuations as quickly as they might have – such behavior was at times viewed as defeatist thinking – and they lost many artworks as a result.

These are the six main categories, but they do not necessarily cover all the losses incurred. For example, families that were implicated in the July 20th, 1944 plot to assassinate Hitler also had artworks confiscated (although the amount of property is much smaller than with the categories noted above). Beyond the issue of categories, the question remains, how many works did the Nazis plunder? Obviously, this depends on how one counts cultural objects. Does one calculate every coin in a collection? What does one do with books, rugs, ·church bells,

---

[12] See Jonathan Petropoulos, "'People Turned to Ashes, Their Property Did Not': Plundering and the Pursuit of Profit during the Holocaust," in Geoffrey Giles and Eberhard Jäckel, eds., The Genesis of Nazi Policy (Cambridge/New York: Cambridge University Press, forthcoming 1999).

[13] A good treatment of plundered Judaica can be found in David Altshuler, ed., The Precious Legacy: Judaic Treasures from the Czechoslovak State Collections (Washington, DC: National Gallery of Art, 1983).

furniture, and other types of cultural property? Added to this problem, there has been a tendency for individuals – in particular government officials – to estimate numbers without adequate documentation. Because of the lack of consensus on how to count cultural objects, the estimates vary greatly. Even with respect to the restitution of objects by the U.S.A. through their Central Collecting Points, the number of returned objects ranges from 250,000 to several million.[14] In terms of paintings, sculptures, and objets d'art – that is, the fine art which serves as one of the focal points of this conference – my own estimate is that the Nazis looted approximately one hundred and fifty thousand art objects in Western Europe and about a half million works in Eastern Europe. But I would underscore the imprecise and even speculative nature of these estimates.

There is a similar lack of precision with respect to the number of artworks still considered missing. Again, all sorts of numbers are thrown about: one scholar claims that in France alone, "many tens of thousands of works stolen are missing today."[15] But when one puts together lists of specific objects, the numbers shrink considerably.[16] There is still much research to be done.

I would like to talk very briefly about how one does research into the Nazis' looting – and how one tries to ascertain what is still missing. This is a topic that will be taken up in greater detail in Friday's symposium at the National Archives, but the methods may be outlined here. The most important source of information is the national archives of the combatant nations – including the U.S.A. Here can be found copies of the Art Looting Investigation Unit reports, the foundation for all research into displaced cultural property during World War II. Important as they are, however, these reports contain mistakes (errors that tend to be passed along by scholars). Furthermore, these reports, which were written right after the war, do not specify the current location of the artworks involved. Provincial archives often contain useful

---

[14] For the figure of 250,000, see Haase, Kunstraub und Kunstschutz, 243. For the figure of millions, see Lynn Nicholas, "World War II and the Displacement of Art and Cultural Property," in Simpson, ed., The Spoils of War, 43.

[15] Feliciano, The Lost Museum, 4.

[16] The Belgian authorities claim 3,273 documented cultural objects to still be missing, and this includes furniture. But furniture comprises only 5 percent of this list; clearly this number should be much higher and this is a reflection of the lack of precise information about such objects, Jacques Lust, The Spoils of War Removed From Belgium During World War II, in Elizabeth Simpson, ed., The Spoils of War, 62.

information – especially about the Aryanization of collections. However, they are often closed to researchers (the French records have been notoriously difficult to access), and again, they rarely reveal the present disposition of the works. Museum archives constitute another resource – one, I would add, that is largely untapped. To date, relatively little of the information contained in museum archives has been incorporated into the literature on looted art. And this information, in contrast to that in historical archives, often has direct bearing on the current disposition of the artworks. Museum archivists are not always fully aware of what is in these records.[17] I also understand that many museums do not give access to the files in their individual curatorial departments: it is these "deep files" which contain information about dealers, prices, tax deductions, lawsuits, and so forth. In addition, there are the records of commercial galleries. Again, these files have been largely neglected. Yes, there are certain firms that have cooperated with researchers. The Rosenbergs in New York, for example, have allowed Lynn Nicholas, Hector Feliciano, and me to work with their papers. But the Rosenbergs are fairly exceptional (and they are also victims trying to regain lost works).[18] Finally, there are the records of private individuals. In this category I would place collectors, but also witnesses and perpetrators. The latter – for example, individuals who catalogued plunder for the ERR in the Jeu de Paume – have actually assisted a number of scholars. But the participants in the looting program are dying off and the window of opportunity is closing quickly.

In terms of research, I urge a more systematic effort to utilize the records in these latter categories, and in particular, those in museums and galleries. These are where we will find the documents that will permit us to determine the current location of artworks. It is therefore essential that researchers and the individuals who oversee these records develop a

---

[17] See Jonathan Petropoulos, "Exposing Deep Files," in ARTnews (January 1999), 143-44.
[18] Note that a few other galleries have also been willing to cooperate with researchers: the Galerie Fischer in Lucerne has generally made its files available to researchers, as has the Kornfeld Gallery in New York. See Buomberger, Raubkunst, 18.

cooperative relationship. As most scholars who have worked in archives know, a helpful archivist can be a godsend. And I have found that many, indeed most, archivists really do want to help. This must be a team effort, and the connection of this history to the Holocaust renders it a moral imperative: we must all try to do the right thing.

As a practical suggestion, it would be extremely useful to establish some mechanism by which researchers can become more aware of the archival resources. What is needed is a central office or agency that could collect a list of museums, galleries, and individuals who are prepared to open their records. If they could also create finding aids and send them to this office, that would help. There are various possibilities for a central office: it could be at the U.S. Holocaust Memorial Museum's Center for Advanced Holocaust Studies (something of a complement to the database of survivor testimony that has been created). Or, it could be in a new office which has just been formed called the Council of Art Restitution and Research Organizations (CARRO for short). This is a board comprised of representatives of the various organizations working on the subject of cultural property displaced as a result of World War II: the Holocaust Art Restitution Project (or HARP), the Commission for Art Recovery of the World Jewish Congress, a new organization called The Project for the Documentation of Wartime Cultural Losses (of which I am a member), and so forth. CARRO might be the right place for a central register of institutions and individuals prepared to help. The point is that we must do what we can to facilitate teamwork and share information. We are now at a special juncture in history – after the Cold War but with survivors still among us – and we must make a concerted effort to learn as much as we can about this history and effect a just restitution of this displaced cultural property.

I would note in closing that this project of ascertaining precisely what was plundered by the Nazis is just one of the three major tasks that are necessary to bring closure to this history. Additionally, we need more comprehensive international agreements to facilitate the repatriation of artworks, and we need a more precise and consistent legal framework in order to settle the claims. Only through a combination of research, diplomacy, and legal reform can the issue of displaced cultural property be resolved.

Ms. Lynn H. Nicholas
INDEPENDENT SCHOLAR
UNITED STATES

Plenary Session on Nazi-Confiscated Art Issues

The events of World War II led to the greatest displacement of works of art in history. By early 1943 art specialists in the Allied nations were quite aware of the Nazi confiscations and purchases of art objects and their governments had declared all such activity illegal. They realized also that these objects, as well as the national collections of all the belligerents, most of which had been removed from their normal locations, would be in great danger in the planned invasions of Europe. It was only with considerable difficulty that military commanders were persuaded to attach a small group of art officers to their staffs. The primary duty of these officers was to prevent damage to historic monuments and to salvage and secure movable works of art. While the protection of buildings and monuments in the battle zones was often impossible, the salvage of movable works, which they accomplished in the chaos of war-torn Western Europe, was nothing short of miraculous.

In the Western countries responsibility for movable works of art was returned to the local authorities as soon as those areas were liberated from German control. But the situation within the borders of the Third Reich was quite different. For here the arts officers were required to deal not only with the German national collections, but with the vast quantities of cultural objects confiscated within Germany and brought from other countries. The objects were found in thousands of hiding places and refuges. Under the most arduous conditions they were secured and gradually taken to Collecting Points set up by each Allied Command within its own Zone of occupation. Despite endless international meetings, no coordinated Allied policy was ever developed to deal with these objects. The restitution policies of the Western Allies and of the USSR were, therefore, very different.

The Western Occupation authorities did not wish to handle individual claims, and it became Western policy to return an object to the country from which it had been removed. Books, paintings, furniture and every other kind of object, by the thousands, were sorted and returned to both East and West. There were a few notable exceptions to this rule (such as the Lubomirski drawings from Lvov) which affected items taken from Eastern European nations. In the Western nations the works were turned over to recuperation commissions which then dealt with individual claims. Soviet Trophy Commission officers, on the other hand, were instructed to take valuable works of art, regardless of ownership, back to the USSR. In the fifties the Soviet Union returned large quantities of art to state collections in Eastern Europe, but, as a form of reparation for the immense damage done to their cultural heritage by the Nazis, the nations of the former USSR still retain a considerable number of objects from both public and private collections in the West, including some confiscated by Nazi agencies from Jewish owners.

In the years immediately following World War II the recuperation commissions of the Western nations, staffed by a group of extremely dedicated officials, and the agencies which superceded them, returned tens of thousands of works to individual claimants. Heirless works, mainly from Jewish communal holdings, were given over to Jewish successor organizations for worldwide distribution. And in the mid-sixties the West German government compensated many claimants for a percentage of their unrecovered art losses.

But, after a time, the art restitution process, like so many other World War II issues, though never officially terminated in countries such as France, lost ground to the pressures of the Cold War and the desire to return to life as usual. After the great bulk of objects had been returned, and as the number of claims declined, both interest and funding diminished, leaving a quantity of works in the hands of European government agencies and museums where many still remain. These works come from many sources, not always Holocaust related: some are objects that were not returned to the previous owner because they had been sold willingly to the Nazis. Other items were abandoned by collaborationist dealers and may or may not have been confiscated. A great many, of course, are works confiscated from Jewish collections both known and unknown. Why certain works from known collections, sometimes very prominent ones, were not claimed or returned is difficult to understand. Indeed, from today's perspective, a number of the adjudications made by the recuperation commissions after the war seem overly legalistic and unfair, and efforts are underway in several countries to review them and to revive the entire restitution process. I am sure that you will hear more about this activity from the individual delegations.

But not all displaced art was recovered by the allied agencies. Items which were fed into the art trade, stolen by Nazi operatives from their own agencies, or looted by soldiers and civilians of every nation, went underground and have been dispersed all over the world. This unrecovered art is the most difficult category to deal with, for we do not know where or exactly what it is until it suddenly appears in a museum or on the market and is recognized.

There is, at the present time, still no easy way for the layman to check the status of a work about which he has suspicions. The inventories and files relating to claims and confiscations compiled at the end of the war had for the most part been relegated to storage and were in disorder. A tremendous amount of work has been done in the last five years to reconstitute and re-examine these files and a number of catalogs of missing works have already been published. But much more consolidation of records is necessary, and the remaining sealed archives must be opened. The usefulness of internationally linked databases using all these records is obvious, ' These databases should not only include what is known to be missing a listing of works that have been returned could eliminate weeks of expensive research and prevent false accusations. The present agreements of museums and dealer's associations to vet their holdings would be greatly expedited by more precise tools of inquiry.

The recovery of art assets is really a dual problem: some claims concern only governments and others concern individuals. Governments can negotiate via diplomatic channels, but the greatest problem facing the individual claimant is the method to be used for recovery. By now works can be anywhere in the world and the laws of different jurisdictions are not uniform. The gathering of documentation in different countries, often by very expensive lawyers with no particular knowledge of the milieu in which the confiscation or sale occurred, can take years. Detailed documentation *is* necessary, however, because although works of art are individual, identifiable objects, there are many of them and they are easily confused. It is, therefore, usually necessary to determine if the claimant was the real owner, if the parties are talking about the same object, or, for example, 'whether or not the work was restituted long ago and then resold.

There is no question that any work that can be shown beyond a reasonable doubt to have been confiscated, stolen, or sold unwillingly should be returned to its former owners or their heirs. Ideally the determination of the validity of a claim should be made by an international panel of experts. But this, I feel, is not enough, for, realistically, some 50 years after the fact, some thought should be given to the present holder of the work, who may not have anything to do with the original confiscator or receiver of stolen goods. By now, proving absolutely that something was or was not a good faith acquisition is extremely difficult. Here I believe that government intervention is necessary in order to limit the bitter and expensive litigation, which seems to accompany even the most valid claim. A government might, for instance, give some sort of tax relief to someone who willingly returns an object belonging to a valid claimant.

Above all, I believe we must not forget the human and historical context in which Second World War losses occurred. Nor should we ignore the great efforts of restitution which were made at the end of the war. That work was not finished, and now it is up to us to complete the task and correct any injustices, and to do so in an equitable and civilized manner.

Dr. Ernst Bacher

CHAIRMAN, AUSTRIAN ART COMMISSION
AUSTRIA

Restitution of Works of Art in Austria: State of the Provenance Research November 1998

Plenary Session on Nazi-Confiscated Art Issues

After 1945, the Republic of Austria passed in the years 1946-1949 a total of seven restitution laws, two laws for the settlement of claims regarding art and cultural heritage (1969 and 1986) and the amendment passed in 1995 for the so-called "Mauerbach Sale", an auction of Nazi-confiscated works of art, to benefit Holocaust victims, 1996.

By January 1, 1949 over 13.000 art objects had been returned to their rightful owners or their legitimate heirs of the over 18.500 items which had been seized during the Nazi era or which had been voluntarily given up to air-raid shelters. Restitution of the remaining objects was spread out over the subsequent years to 1996.

The archives of the Federal Office for Monuments Preservation (*Bundesdenkmalamt*) alone contain around 120.000 documents designated as "Restitution Materials" (decrees, various departmental and institutional files, lists, correspondence, etc.). This figure does not include further documentation in museums and collections as well as in various ministries.

At the beginning of 1998 Federal Minister Elisabeth Gehrer established a "Commission for Provenance Research" which was charged with working through the historical material on the theme of looted art at the Bundesdenkmalamt and in State Museums and Collections. The goal of this very extensive historic survey was to shed some light on the events of the looting during the period 1938-1945 and to establish which dubious acquisitions may have been made by public collections during that time. Furthermore, the restitution procedures of the immediate post-war period are to be examined; from today's point of view, there are known accessions by museums and collections as a result of the Export Ban which, by today's standards are no longer supportable.

In the early 1990's the Bundesdenkmalamt had already begun systematic cataloguing and archiving- organizing the restitution material in its keeping. Since 1998, these holdings are being researched individually from a chronological and a subject view. There are three main categories:

Salvage materials, part of the extensive system of air-raid shelters; from 1943, valuable art and cultural heritage – both seized and voluntarily given up for protection – stored in some 200 Viennese and Lower Austrian castles, monasteries, churches and parish-houses until after 1945.

General material concerning the security, seizure, and distribution of largely Jewish and monastery collections by the Nazis as well as their restitution after 1945.

Documentary material (ca. 1.000 documents) with information and data pertaining to persons connected with works of art and art collections.

All these materials are presently being archivally organized, foliated, re-housed and indexed so that a user is able to obtain primary resource material in a concise and focussed manner (synopses, indexes, information on size/extent of holdings, index of names, index by medium, etc.).

Parallel to the research and organization of looted art and restitution documentation at the Bundesdenkmalamt (Austrian Federal Office for the Care of Monuments), the archives of the following State Museums and Collections are also being searched: Kunsthistorisches Museum (Museum of Fine Arts), Graphische Sammlung Albertina (Albertina Collection of Graphic Arts), Österreichische Galerie, Österreichisches Museum für Angewandte Kunst (Austrian Museum of Applied Arts), Österreichische Nationalbibliothek (Austrian National Library), Naturhistorisches Museum (Museum of Natural History), Museum für Völkerkunde (Museum of Ethnography), Österreichisches Theatermuseum (Austrian Theatre Museum), Technisches Museum für Industrie und Gewerbe (Technical Museum), Museum des 20. Jahrhunderts (Museum of 20t-Century Art), Heeresgeschichtliches Museum (Military Museum), Bundesmobiliendepot (State Furniture

Collection); Pathologisch-Anatomisches Bundesmuseum (Anatomical Museum).

The results of the provenance research in the Bundesdenkmalamt as well as in the museums and collections will enable a better view of the events during 1938 and 1945 and subsequent post-war period, and are primarily geared at gleaning information about questionable acquisitions. These facts will provide the basis and historic evidence for the legislation governing the "Restitution of Works of Art from Austrian State Museums and Collections" and its implementation.

Passed by Parliament on November 5, 1998, this federal law creates the legal basis for the restitution of artistic and cultural artifacts to the original owners or their legitimate heirs mortis causa according to the following criteria: artistic and cultural artifacts which were kept as a result of applications for export permits and were accessioned by state museums and collections as "gifts" or "endowment". All those art objects falling into this category were already subjects of restitution claims, were indeed returned to their owners and are consequently well documented. In return for the issue of an export permit under the laws prohibiting artwork exports, potential exporters agreed to "donate" several of the items to Austrian museums and collections. From today's point of view and because of the fact, that in both the laws (1986 and 1995) governing the clarification of artistic and cultural artifacts the application of the directives of the law prohibiting exports were specifically excluded, the practices of the past are indefensible.

Artistic and cultural artifacts which, although they became state property legitimately had nonetheless been the subject of legal proceedings in the terms of the so-called Nullification Law (*Nichtigkeitsgesetz*) of 1946 (nullification of legal proceedings and other actions that occurred during the German occupation of Austria) which itself is thus void. This includes questionable purchases during the 1938-1945 period, as well as acquisitions after the war: e.g. in the post-war period museum directors purchased works of art in good faith in the art market from authorized dealers, whereby only later were doubts raised about the integrity of the provenance. Cases such as this have come to light in the course of the provenance research.

Artistic and cultural artifacts which, despite all efforts involved in their restitution couldn't be returned to their original owners or their legitimate heirs and were thus transferred to state ownership as unclaimed property. Also such indications came to light in the course of our provenance research.

In all these cases the new law will rescind the export ban.

To execute this law an advisory panel has been established at the Federal Ministry for Education and Cultural Affairs which will advise the Minister authorized to transfer the items upon identifying those persons legally qualified to receive the works of art.

In the cases where no original owners or their legitimate heirs *mortis causa* can be ascertained for art objects, then these objects will be transferred to the "National Fund of the Republic of Austria for the Victims of Nazi Terror" for beneficial disposal.

As well as the professional staff of the *Bundesdenkmalamt* and the mentioned Museums and Collections who have already been entrusted with this work, free-lance researchers have also been taken as the Federal Ministry for Education and Cultural Affairs has made special positions available in order to accelerate progress.

By November, 1998 about one third (ca. 40.000 documents) of the restitution material in the *Bundesdenkmalamt's* archives) have been reviewed. Progress in the above-mentioned museums and collections varies; in those collections e.g. the Kunsthistorisches Museum, where provenance has been researched for a number of years, the documentation (containing 500 pages) has already been completed in 1998. Other institutions will take longer to complete the project.

The brief to research provenance in the form described above applies only to the state museums and collections. Nonetheless, the Provincial museums (Historisches Museum der Stadt Wien, Landesmuseum Joanneum in Graz, Tiroler Landesmuseum Ferdinaneum in Innsbruck, Residenzgalerie Salzburg, Oberösterreichisches Landesmuseum in Linz etc.) have joined the research project and have similarly begun to organize and search their archives from this perspective.

The first results of the Commission's work deal with artistic and cultural property which had been previously held back from restitution claim cases by the export prohibition law, and which thus came into the possession of Austrian state museums and collections.

This is the actual situation of provenance research in Austria. The next steps to execute the mentioned legislation governing the "Restitution of Works of Art from Austrian State Museums and Collections" will start within the next month.

For questions please contact:
Univ. Prof. Dr. Ernst BACHER
Leiter der Kommission für Provenienzforschung
Bundesdenkmalamt
Hofburg, Säulenstiege
A-1010 Wien
Tel.: 0043 1 53 415-200 or 201
FAX: 0043 153 415-252
e-mail: denkmal@bmuvie.gv.at

Mr. Valeriy D. Kulishov

CHIEF OF THE OFFICE OF RESTITUTION, DEPARTMENT FOR THE
PRESERVATION OF CULTURAL ASSETS, MINISTRY OF CULTURE
RUSSIA

*Statement translated from the original Russian by the
U.S. Department of State Office of Language Services, Translating Division*

Plenary Session on Nazi-Confiscated Art Issues

First of all, allow me, on behalf of the Russian Delegation, to express our profound support for the goals and objectives of the Washington Conference. We must not forget that among the more than 20 million Soviet citizens who perished during the last war there were more than two million Jewish victims of the Holocaust.

As we understand it, one of the main objectives of this conference is to develop international cooperation among all interested states in searching for and identifying cultural assets that the Nazis confiscated from their victims during the years of the Holocaust. As we see it, this objective involves Russia, as the successor to the Soviet Union, in the following way: by decision of the allies in the anti-Hitlerite coalition, the Soviet High Command was the supreme authority in the Soviet Zone of occupation and was thus responsible for restitution of allied property, including property belonging to victims of the Holocaust, from all of occupied East Germany.

The difficult foreign policy situation of the post-war period, which culminated in the "cold war", as well as the atmosphere of secrecy that surrounded and still surrounds the repositories of Russian museums where so-called "trophy art" is kept, gave rise to the following assumption: German cultural assets removed to the territory of the Soviet Union after World War II as compensation for the enormous cultural losses suffered as a result of the German occupation might also include cultural assets confiscated by the Nazis from victims of the Holocaust.

Before turning to an analysis of this assumption, I feel I should remind you of the mechanism employed by the Nazis for depriving Holocaust victims of their property. As you are well aware, this mechanism varied depending on the country of occupation. In France, for example, cultural assets confiscated from Jews became the property of the French State. The Nazis insisted on "open" public auctions and formally acknowledged that the French authorities had precedence in selecting artworks for French museums; this was the case with part of the confiscated Schloss collection, which was selected for the Louvre. In Austria artworks confiscated from Jews were simply distributed among the future Führermuseum in Linz and various Austrian museums. Ostmark, as Austria was then called, was considered to be 100 percent Aryan, and there were no complaints.

The cultural assets of Holocaust victims in Poland or the Soviet Union became the property of the German state. For us such concepts as "forced sale" and "ostensibly voluntary transaction" are purely abstract ideas. There were no sales – forced or otherwise. There was only flagrant robbery accompanied by the physical annihilation of the victims.

After the confiscation of Jewish property in France, Belgium and the Netherlands, generally carried out by special units of the ERR – the "Einsatskommando [rectē: Einsatzstab] Reichsleiter Rosenberg" – the very best artworks were selected by special agents for the future Hitler museum in Linz. The special agents whose job was to satisfy the art demands of other Nazi leaders, primarily Hermann Goering, were equally active. These Nazi agents, especially the former director of the Dresden Gallery, Hans Posse, did their jobs very professionally. Artworks selected for the Führermuseum in Linz were shipped to specially equipped collection points, located mainly in the Austrian Alps. These collection points were discovered by special units of the U.S. Army. Everything that either disappeared or was not found in the American Zone should be sought in the West. It is unlikely that these works could have found their way to the East.

Everything that was not looted by Hitler's special agents in the occupied countries of Western Europe was sold at auction. This applied mainly to good, but not museum-quality, works, worthy of private collections. At the auctions Germans readily purchased these items, taking advantage of the artificially high exchange rate of the German mark in relation to the other currencies of occupied Western Europe. Given the wartime situation, some of the assets in this category could, theoretically, have found their way to the eastern part of Germany.

As I have already noted, in the occupied areas of the Soviet Union the Nazis simply looted their victims before sending them to the gas chambers. In this connection, one should bear in mind that in western Ukraine, for example, some wealthy Jews owned quite valuable art collections that contained works of good, though not museum, quality. Of course, these were not on a par with the collections of Rothschild, Schloss, Mannheimer, Bondy, and others, and were thus of no particular interest to Hitler and Goering's special agents. These were plundered by the lowest level Nazis and all these works vanished in the direction of the West. Representatives of the Extraordinary State Commission were never able to determine exactly what was in the private collections looted by the Nazis and, accordingly, to identify even a part of them in the Soviet Zone of occupied Germany.

It is necessary to bear in mind one other circumstance. By the end of the war the cultural assets confiscated by the Nazis from their victims in the East were literally burning a hole in the pockets of those who had possession of them. They could have become material evidence of their current owners' complicity in Nazi crimes in the East. It is not surprising that these individuals tried to get rid of them at any cost. There is no doubt that these artworks ultimately found their way to the West. The facts uncovered to date confirm this.

As an example of how the Soviet Union fulfilled its obligations to its allies in returning allied property, in general, that was found in the Soviet zone, and the property of Holocaust victims in particular, allow me to cite some data from the summary report on the activities of the Restitution Office of the Reparations, Deliveries, and Restitution Directorate of the Soviet Military Administration in Germany (SMAG) for 1946. Specifically, the report states the following:

- SMAG activities in searching for and identifying property in the Soviet Zone, including cultural assets looted by the Germans, in the territory of the Soviet Union and allied countries, were carried out in conformity with the laws and directives of the Allied Control Council, and with SMAG orders and directives;
- the Office's activities in this area were closely coordinated with the Committee on Restitution Procedures of the Allied Control Council;
- for the reporting period the Restitution Office received 869 restitution requests to search for and determine the ownership of property subject to restitution from the Soviet Zone of occupied Germany from the following allied states: France, Poland, Czechoslovakia, Yugoslavia, the Netherlands, Norway, Belgium, and Denmark;

- 87,131 items of equipment and property subject to restitution were identified in the Soviet Zone in 1946; these included 33,552 cultural artifacts (this figure includes books);
- of the above amount of allied property that was identified, 40,584 items belonged to the Soviet Union;
- it was established that the rest of the property (46,597 items) belonged to the following allied countries: Poland (38,892), Czechoslovakia (5,123), the Netherlands (955), France (761), Belgium (101), Norway (23), Yugoslavia (14), Denmark (1);
- it proved impossible to determine whether the remaining 677 items of equipment and other property belonged to the state or to some other party;
- in accordance with the Quadripartite Procedures for Restitution, adopted by the Allied Control Council, all the equipment and property that had been identified was turned over to the appropriate allied countries.

The report lists the most important items of equipment and other property that were returned to the allied countries. This list is far from complete, but I would like to point out that the list of restored property greatly exceeds the list of restitution claims received by the Soviet Military Administration from the Allies.

This list also refers to cultural assets that were returned to victims of the Holocaust. A large organ from a Prague synagogue was returned to Czechoslovakia. In addition to the well-known Armistice monument from Compiègne, the collections of paintings that had belonged to French citizens Léonard Lévy, Paul Denique, and Pierre Maurice [names transliterated from Russian] were returned.

In searching for and identifying cultural assets that belonged to the allies and their citizens, the Soviet Military Administration in Germany could proceed only on the basis of restitution claims submitted by the interested countries and backed up by documentation. In the case of state property this was relatively simple. It was much more difficult in the case of property belonging to Holocaust victims. Nevertheless, I can solemnly state that Russian archives do not contain any information or documents which would indicate that the Soviet Military Administration knowingly or intentionally kept property that belonged to Holocaust victims, including cultural assets, when it was aware of the origin of these items.

Because of the complex and confused circumstances surrounding the post-war fate of cultural assets confiscated by the Nazis from victims of the Holocaust, which subsequently ended up in the hands of other physical and juridical persons, including the museums of some Western and Eastern countries, it is extremely urgent that we establish, through joint efforts, an international database that would be accessible to all interested private citizens and organizations: above all, Holocaust victims and their direct heirs and legal successors.   Russia is fully prepared to take part in establishing this database and, for that purpose, to provide relevant documents from Russian archives.

Recently a great deal has been said about the new Russian law on cultural assets that were removed and are currently located in the repositories of Russian museums. The law does in fact establish Russia's right of ownership in cultural assets that were taken to Russia as compensation for its enormous cultural losses. But I can assure you that in Russia there is no law which would stand in the way of just and legitimate restitution of cultural assets confiscated by the Nazis if convincing evidence that they belong to Holocaust victims is provided.

Ambassador Ronald S. Lauder

CHAIRMAN OF THE BOARD, MUSEUM OF MODERN ART
UNITED STATES

Plenary Session on Nazi-Confiscated Art Issues

When I was asked to be Chairman of the Commission for Art Recovery for the World Jewish Congress, I knew it would be a difficult task, but nothing prepared me for what lay ahead.

As you have just heard, although a great deal of art was found in salt mines, warehouses, trucks and trains, and many pieces were returned to the countries from which they were stolen – approximately 50% - 110,000 pieces of art worth between ten and thirty billion dollars today are still missing.

It is my belief, because of these large numbers, that <u>every</u> institution, art museum and private collection has some of these missing works.

I question how many great institutions have held works of art for 50 years, knowing that what they have held didn't belong to them, but to Jewish families. It is only now that they are being forced to take some action, action that they should have taken many, many years ago. How many homes have works of art hanging on their walls from Jewish families?

In France, after the war, many works were returned to prominent Jewish families. However, 15,000 works of art remained unclaimed, from which the French government allowed the museums in France to select the 2,000 best works, and the remaining 13,000 were auctioned off. Where is the record of these sales? Who benefited? These 2,000 works that remained in French museums have a special number.

France stopped trying to find owners after 1959. It was only in 1997, after being reminded by Hector Feliciano, that an exhibition was held, and a list was published of these 2,000 works. It is time for the provisional and temporary custody of the French museums to end. These works should be returned to the families who owned them, and where no families can be found, an auction should be held and the Jewish Communities of France should benefit.

The Austrian government took a giant step forward when it decided to hold an auction in 1996 of the works stored since the war at

Mauerbach. Today there is a complete search being done by the government of Austria itself of the holdings of all its federal museums. Research is being done to find the owners of the paintings that were taken between 1938 and 1945.

The Netherlands also has works for which no owners were found: they were placed in the care of the Netherlands Art Foundation. Although they knew that there were objects in the museums that were stolen from Jewish families, it was only after other countries started to do their research that the Netherlands decided to look for pre-war owners. They now have identified 3,900 works of art, and the government estimates it will take three years to complete the research project. It can be done in 6 months. An auction should be held.

Germany also received art that it knew came from Jewish families. Did they try to find the owners or their heirs? No. They simply set up a trust: the Gemälde Treuhand Verwaltung and distributed it among museums.

In the Czech Republic, the museum in Brno acknowledges that it has art once in the collection of the late Arthur Feldmann, whose grandson, Uri Peled, now lives in Israel. Mr. Peled maintains, correctly, that his family's collection of old master prints and drawings was looted by the Nazis. These works were subsequently nationalized by Czechoslovakia and the Slovakian Museum. They have refused to return the Feldmann works in their possession.

In Hungary, a portion of the collection of the Hatvany family is now in the Museum of Fine Arts in Budapest. The Hatvany heirs are getting nowhere in their efforts. Sixty years later!

A great portion of the art that was not deemed appropriate for German museums or for the new museum that was being created in Linz, was sold through dealers to Switzerland. Douglas Cooper, the British investigator, reported in 1945 that Switzerland had been the prime destination. He identified quite a number of private collectors and sixteen dealers in Switzerland who trafficked in Nazi-looted art. Chief among these was Theodore Fischer, auctioneer and dealer, and Emil Bührle, industrialist and collector. Paul Rosenberg, the eminent French Jewish art dealer whose collection had been looted from a bank vault in Libourne, traced thirteen of his pictures to Bührle. (He had to bring a court case to strike a deal, in which Bührle bought from Paul Rosenberg the stolen Rosenberg pictures Bührle had already bought.)

Since Switzerland was neutral, the Allies could not monitor trade there. No one knows how many looted works were sent to Switzerland. Switzerland's recent investigation into the past of the art owned by the

Swiss Confederation is a step in the right direction. But it doesn't even touch on the holdings of the majority of Swiss museums, private foundations or private collections.

No one knows how many "hot" works are in Swiss bank vaults or free ports – even today.

No one knows how many works went <u>through</u> neutral Switzerland to Spain, Portugal, Argentina, Brazil, Venezuela, and from there to the United States and other collecting countries.

In the United States, there are many works of art that have come here right after the war and into the 1950's and 1960's through a second or third party.

The United States is perhaps the most active country in finding works of art through its Association of Art Museum Directors, ("AAMD"). They met this past June and worked out guidelines for a complete and thorough investigation of the provenance of all art for all their museums, to determine if any of their works of art could have been looted works from the Nazi era.

Perhaps the most important job my Commission is doing is working on a database, so that we can cross-reference all works of art looted during the Nazi era. And we will have as close as possible a complete list.

This summer we did an experiment. We began to see what we could uncover by going through catalogues: catalogues of permanent collections and special exhibitions. My staff went to over 225 books of museum collections and catalogues and found more than 1,700 works that could be war loot. It is clearly much more widespread than museum directors had thought.

We have a list of Nazi collaborators. Any work with those names in the ownership history could be unrecovered Nazi loot. We are comparing this art with claims from families, and we'll let them know if there is a match.

We invite you to send us the information, and we would welcome your cooperation. But if you do not want to work with us in this way, we will review all your publications anyway and find the works with dubious provenance.

In the fifty years since the end of the war, the art world forgot, maybe it chose to forget, the Nazi depredations – but we will not. Some of the most notorious names appear in scholarly catalogues. Goering's name is there! The Linz Museum is there! In some German museum catalogues, the provenance states that the art was "taken from the possession of Jews between 1933 and 1945!" I hope that this is an honest way of serving notice to possible claimants, and I have been told that the museum will soon contact the Commission. Perhaps we can work together to find the heirs to these paintings.

Some of the names of the most famous looted collections appear in published provenances. Were all these works of art restituted and legitimately re-sold? Of course not. There is either a collective amnesia or a brazen openness in including these names in the published provenances. But there they are. And they will go into the Commission's database to be matched against art claimed by looted families.

It is time for museums to set the same standard for ownership that they expect of themselves for authenticity. Is the art genuine? Is the art genuinely theirs?

Together, in the next few years, we must find out. We must set the record straight, and put art back in the hands of the families from whom it was stolen, simply because they were Jewish. For many members of this generation, art is the only connection they have to members of their family who perished in the Holocaust.

These works of art that were looted are the last "prisoners of war." We do not want to wait. We will find these works of art – now.

Mr. Earl A. Powell, III

DIRECTOR, NATIONAL GALLERY OF ART
UNITED STATES

Plenary Session on Nazi-Confiscated Art Issues

I would like to thank you for this opportunity to speak today to discuss the important subject of restitution of works of art seized during the Third Reich. We join our museum colleagues in expressing our profound concern for the victims whose artistic treasures were pillaged during the holocaust. The National Gallery has been involved since the end of World War II with the international effort to recover the looted works. On June 23, 1943, President Roosevelt established the Roberts Commission to promote the preservation of cultural properties and to protect Europe's treasures in war-ravaged areas. An independent presidential commission, it was headquartered at the National Gallery and several Gallery officials as well as those from the Metropolitan Museum of Art and other institutions served on this Commission. The Commission promoted the establishment of the Monuments, Fine Arts and Archives (MFAA) section of the U.S. Army in post-war Germany which, among other things, established "collecting points" where art objects retrieved from the Nazis could be inventoried and protected before their restitution.

Certain records of these and other restitution activities are available for research at the National Gallery Archives. Copies of the glass slides and gelatin negatives of the roughly 60,000 works of art in one of the Army collecting points, called the "Munich Collecting Point," are available for research in our Photo Archives. As a matter of interest, the historian and author, Lynn Nicholas, spent much time in our archives while researching her book, The Rape of Europa: The Fate of Europe's Treasures in the Third Reich and the Second World War. The last several years have brought forth an extraordinary amount of new scholarship regarding the fate of many cultural treasures during and after this terrible period. But more is needed and we are hopeful that new revelations will shed further—and much needed—scholarly light on this subject.

The National Gallery follows the practice of American art museums of publishing annually a list of all acquisitions. In addition, the Gallery has undertaken an extensive project, which began over a decade ago and which will take years to complete, of the publication of a projected thirty-volume detailed systematic catalogue of its entire collection. Each volume, written by Gallery curators or other scholars, is devoted to a particular school of painting, sculpture or decorative arts area with comprehensive, scholarly essays on each work articulating the history, style, content, and context with technical notes and artist biographies, summarizing and expanding upon the literature in the field. Ten of these volumes have been published, three more will come out in 1998, and the other volumes are in progress. Additionally, research on works of art in the Gallery's collection is often available in special exhibition catalogues. As all of this new scholarly research is published, the details regarding the history of ownership, or provenance, are added to our curatorial records which are open to researchers. In an effort to make as much information as possible available to the public around the world, the National Gallery launched its World Wide Web Site a year ago. A cornerstone of the site is the collection section, which contains detailed provenance information on thousands of works of art in the National Gallery collection.

It is a time consuming, expensive kind of research. We are currently looking into a claim involving a work that was restituted by the allied military government after the war. In this case the claim involves legitimacy of ownership. The work in question is one of more than 20 drawings by Durer from the Lubomirski Collection which were returned in the 1940s to a lineal descendant of the family which originally owned them. This gentleman subsequently sold the drawings to several purchasers in good faith. These works are now held in many public and private collections in this country and abroad. The complexity of the case, which involves rightful ownership, dates back to 1823 and involves conflicting claims from more than one institution, and shifting national boundaries. This is the only claim received to date by the National Gallery. We are pressing on in our efforts to complete as thoroughly as possible the necessary provenance research. It is a complicated and time consuming task, which we trust will result in due course in a just resolution of the claim. Should any other claim arise we will treat it with the same commitment to establish the facts and achieve a resolution. The National Gallery, along with other museum directors, participated in the Association of Art Museum Directors' Task Force dedicated to finding solutions to these complex problems. We welcome the opportunity to join with our colleagues in the museum community to explore ways of continuing restitution as new information becomes available.

Dr. Wojciech Kowalski

PROFESSOR, FACULTY OF LAW, UNIVERSITY OF SILESIA
POLAND

Restitution Policy of the Polish Government Post-war to Present

Break-out Session on Nazi-Confiscated Art Issues: Government
Restitution Policies, Postwar to Present

Polish cultural heritage suffered severe losses in the course of the 19th and early 20th centuries; thus, when the restitution policy was framed after World War Two, Poland, unlike many other states, could fall back on its previous 'wide' experience in this field. The only difference between World War Two and the former global war, or, other historical perturbations was the range of damage to cultural property and degree to which the plunder was organized,[1] surpassing all previously suffered

---

[1] Cultural looting was carried out on the formal basis of special Nazi decrees issued for occupied Poland and later for other countries in occupied Europe. See, for example, full text of such "laws" issued for occupied Poland, W. Kowalski: Art Treasures and War. A Study on the Restitution of Looted Cultural Property Pursuant Public International Law. Leicester 1998, annex 1 and 2, p. 91-92. For other countries see: R. Lemkin: Axis Rule in Occupied Europe. Washington 1944. As an illustration of the character of these "laws" referring to private property only two paragraphs of one of them only can be given. Regulation concerning confiscation of the works of art in the German-occupied Poland dated 16 December 1939:
"Para 1: Public possession of the works of art in the German-occupied Poland is hereby confiscated for the sake of public benefit and use (...).
Para 2: The term of public possession of the works of art, (...) refers to: 1. Private collections of the works of art, which are subject to registration and security procedures undertaken by the appointed commissioner to protect their cultural and historical value, 2. The works of art in the exclusive possession of

losses.[2] The fate of Jewish assets could be given as the best example here.

For these reasons, the first attempts to formulate the concept of liquidating the effects that the War had on Polish culture were initiated right from the start - two months after the War broke out. It is at that time that the first conspiracy group was organized to register the damage inflicted upon culture and the losses resulting from the Nazi invasion of Poland in September 1939. Soon the group, called the Department of the Liquidation of the Effects of War, became an official agency of the Polish Government in Exile in London, which operated in conspiracy in the Nazi-occupied Poland. Also, in the structure of the Government in Exile itself, Bureau of Revendication of Cultural Losses was established, which, irrespective of considerable obstacles, remained in touch with the above mentioned Department which operated in Poland. The data on the losses and on the occupant's policy[3] that was thus obtained made it possible for the Bureau of Revendication of Cultural Losses to initiate the actions to be undertaken by the Allied agencies, for example, by the Conference of the Allied Ministers of Education which worked in London since 1942 until 1945.

In view of the above, it should be noticed that the Polish restitution policy began to emerge very early and was mainly focused on

---

the Church, except for the property needed for everyday liturgy." W. Kowalski, op. cit, p. 91.

Introduction of such "laws" constituted, without any question, severe breach of International Law of War. See, for example: I. Brownlie: International Law and the Use of Force by States. Oxford 1963, A. McNair, A. Watts: Legal Effects of War. Cambridge 1966. I. Brownlie: Principles of Public International Law. Oxford 1979.

[2] On the scale of damage and losses see, for example: G. Mihan: Looted Treasure: Germany's Raid on Art. London 1944, Tentative List of Jewish Cultural Treasures in Axis-Occupied Countries. Jewish Social Studies 1946, Vol. 8, no 1. Supplement, W. Tomkiewicz: Catalogue of Paintings Removed from Poland by the German Occupation Authorities During the Years 1939-1945. Vol. 1. Foreign Paintings. Warsaw 1950, Vol. 2. Polish Paintings. Warsaw 1953. B. Bieńkowska: Losses of Polish Libraries During World War II. Warsaw 1994. L. H. Nicholas: The Rape of Europe. The Fate of Europe's Treasures in the Third Reich and the Second World War. New York 1994.

[3] On the basis of the information on losses received this way, Charles Estreicher, head of the Bureau, was able to produce and publish their first account before the end of war. See: Ch. Estreicher (ed.): Cultural Losses of Poland, Index of Polish Losses During the German Occupation 1939-1943. London 1944.

two agencies: the one operating in the Nazi-occupied Poland- that is to say, directly at the scene of the crime, and the other one in London, which, at that time, was an important co-operation center for the Allies. I emphasize these facts, as they had a fundamental impact on the approach of the two agencies towards the principles upon which they framed their respective restitution policies.[4]

The circles operating in secret in Poland favored the postulate of reparations. Being everyday witness to the range of the inflicted damage[5] and the methods that the occupational administration and several Nazi agencies specialized in looting[6] employed, home-based organizations could not possibly imagine any other alternative way of indemnity. As cultural property was damaged and removed from Poland with no trace of documentation, and such activities were organized on massive scale, effective restitution seemed irrelevant or practically impossible. Moreover, in the process of organized removal of cultural property from Poland, the Nazis were interested to keep only the most valuable works of art, allocating the majority of plundered cultural objects to sale through special agencies, such as Haupttreuhandstelle Ost, HTO (Central Trustees Office, East).[7] In view of this, the circles involved in the issue

---

[4] The process of formulating these policies and arguments raised during relevant discussions, see: W. Kowalski: Liquidation of the Effects of World War II in the Area of Culture. Warsaw 1994, see in particular chapter I entitled: Concept of the Redress of Losses in the Field of Culture put forth by Polish Centres before the end of War, p. 15 et seq.

[5] The first full report of the Nazi's cultural policy in occupied Poland based on their evidence was published in London in 1945. See: The Nazi-Kultur in Poland by Several Authors of Necessity Temporarily Anonymous (Written in Warsaw Under the German Occupation) London , HMSO, 1945.

[6] Today we would rather say - specialized in cultural cleansing. These agencies included, among other organizations, SS art branch called Ahnenerbe (Ancestral Heritage) and Einsatzstab Reichsleiter Rosenberg (ERR). Rosenberg was formally instructed by Hitler to "transport to Germany cultural goods which appear valuable to him and to safeguard them there". NA, RG 260/411, Keitel to CIC France, September 17, 1940. L. H. Nicholas: The Rape..., p. 125. For more information on the activity of SS Ahnenerbe, see: H. Lehmann-Haupt: "Cultural Looting of the Ahnenerbe". Office of Military Government for Germany (US), Berlin, March 1, 1948, no. 183. On the role of both these agencies see several remarks and facts given by L. H. Nicholas: The Rape.....

[7] To illustrate the scope and scale of the HTO activity, it is enough to quote a fragment of one of its executive orders:

of reparation considered different options of the same, practically impossible solution. Was there and is there any way to compensate the loss of as unique objects as only the works of art can be?

For example, while considering what kind of indemnity could be claimed for the destruction of the Royal Castle in Warsaw, deliberations were made how many paintings could have been bought by a Polish king in the 18th century with the money that had been used for extension works on this castle. Several sources could even name which paintings could have been bought, basing their estimations on the actual works, which had been purchased at that time by a Prussian king. Furthermore, because the paintings in question were still kept in Berlin, it was argued that they should be claimed as compensation for the damaged Royal Castle.[8] Under such circumstances, the only realistic solution of repairing the inflicted damage seemed to be the reparations 'payable' in cultural property.

Unlike the organizations operating in Poland, the Polish Government in Exile in London had a different view on liquidating the effects of the War. On the one hand, it was difficult for them to fully understand the extent of damage and plunder, as they had not witnessed it in their own eyes. Living in the times of the omnipresence of mass

---

"I. In order to fortify Germanism and the defense of the Reich, confiscation is ordered (...) of all objects mentioned in point II of this order on confiscation, found in the territories which have (...) become a component part of the Reich, as well as those found in the Governmentship General (occupied central part of Poland, add. W. K.) providing that these objects do not belong to the Reichsdeutsch or the Volksdeutsch (two kinds of German citizenship, add. W. K.), or that the Reichsdeutsch and Volksdeutsch do not own more than 75% of the rights to the property. Most particularly, subject to confiscation are all objects mentioned in point II found in archives, museums, public collections, and in Polish or Jewish possession, but whose security and appropriate treatment lies in German interest.
II. 1. Objects of historical and prehistoric provenience, records, books, documents important for research on the history of civilization and public life, and those particularly relevant to the question of German contribution to the historic, cultural and economic development of the country as well as documents of importance to current history. 2. Objects of artistic, cultural and historic value, such as paintings, sculptures, furniture, rugs, crystal pieces, books, etc. 3. Objects of interior decorations and objects of precious metals". Document of December 15, 1939. Further quotations: W. Kowalski: Liquidation..p. 20.
[8] For more detailed description of these discussions see: W. Kowalski: Liquidation... p. 28-29.

media, one must remember that people acting in conspiracy under the Nazi occupation could not possibly take photographs or make films. However, on the other hand, any reparation proposals put forward before the Allied bodies had to be realistic. Neither the political practice of the states concerned, nor the international law recognized, at that time, reparations in the form of cultural property. The only precedent in this matter was made in Art. 247 of the Versailles Treaty, under which such reparations were stipulated in favor of Belgium only and in purely symbolic form.[9] Although some far-reaching reparation proposals were every now and then presented in England or the USA, including, for example, a postulate to seize the German collections and divide them among the injured states, these were only public opinion[10] or private bodies' postulates.[11] The respective governments were much more moderate in their views. Due to political reasons, obvious reparation claims tended to be limited and intermediate solutions were looked for instead.

---

[9] Art. 247 of the Versailles Treaty, as well as the whole issue of cultural reparations after the World War I is discussed in detail in W. Kowalski: Art Treasures ....p. 33 et seq. See also detailed report on the negotiations which led to the formulation of art. 247 in: P. Burnett: Reparation at the Paris Peace Conference from the Standpoint of the American Delegation. New York 1940.

[10] Rather radical stand of the British opinion was, for example, expressed in "The Daily Telegraph" of March 16, 1943. A. E. Russel wrote that: ".increasing attention is rightly being paid to the unparalleled looting committed by the Germans in the occupied countries of Europe; looting not only of war materials, live stock and food, but of major works of art and uncountable humbler of treasures...Whereby the galleries of German cities contain large and well catalogued collections of works of art and craftsmanship of all kinds and of all countries, and of immense value. I suggest that at the end of the war an International Restitution Committee should take possession of all such collections with the view of distributing their contents between the various ravaged nations. The confiscation should be sweeping, so that empty museums and galleries would be a permanent reminder to the Germans that war does not pay and a comptemptous rejection of their impudent claim to be the guardians of Europe's culture."

[11] In the USA one of such opinions was formulated by the Study Group of the Council of Foreign Relations. They found proper, that "In default of restoration of property which is of exceptional historical, artistic, or cultural value, the Axis nations must substitute equivalent property of their own". A Memorandum on the Restitution or Indemnification of Property Seized, Damaged, or Destroyed During World War II. In: Council of Foreign Relations. The Postwar Settlement of Property Rights. New York 1945.

As Poland and Germany had been in close neighborhood for ages and the cultures of the two nations intermingled in the course of the centuries, one solution was self-evident. If the reparations could be paid to Poland neither in German cultural property, which anyway was not welcome in our country at that time, nor in world famous masterpieces, which was politically unrealistic, the advanced claims would have to concern the Polish cultural heritage which had been kept, in quite a few cases, in German museums for several centuries. Following such reasoning, actual attempts were made to prepare the claims for such form of reparations, registered in the files of the Department of the Liquidation of the effects of War operating in conspiracy. For example, it was expected that numerous military accessories of Polish origin would be handed over to Poland, as well as portraits of Polish historical persons and some collections which had been purchased in Poland.

Another way of making good considered as feasible was in kind restitution. On the basis of the exemplary in-kind restitution stipulated in the Versailles Treaty, the proposal involved the compensation of irretrievably lost cultural property by the works of art of equivalent importance.

As a result of such reasoning, final drafts of some clauses of the peace treaty were formulated by the Ministry in the Polish Government in Exile, which was responsible for the preparation of the Polish proposals for a peace conference. The drafts are the best representation of the restitution concept adopted as an official standpoint the Polish Party before 1945.

This gave priority to absolute restitution. Considering the circumstances of the plunder, which was often made for the private benefit of German soldiers or civil occupational authorities, the draft of the peace treaty obligated the German Party to hand over all the Nazi documentation concerning cultural property, including the registers and inventories kept in German museums, etc.[12] In-kind restitution was

---

[12] Art. 3 of this Draft stated that since there were: "very many instances of robbery of property by the German military and German officials who took advantage of their position as the occupant for their own private use and due to the resultant difficulty in finding these objects in Germany for they were not included in any collections or government warehouses, German was under obligation to order a compulsory registration in order to return the works of art, historic objects of the art and crafts industry, historic mementos, cult objects, books, documents, etc, seized in Poland by the said persons." W. Kowalski: Liquidation...p. 40.

considered as the next priority. This solution involved handing over the works of art of equivalent value or importance, to compensate for irretrievably lost cultural property, or, to rebuild historically important works of architecture.[13] The most comprehensive provision of the draft was devoted to reparations of cultural heritage. The adopted principle stipulated the supremacy of cultural reparations over any other reparations, which was highlighted by a separation of the cultural reparation postulates form the chapter devoted to reparations in general.[14] The postulate was supported with a list of claimed works of art, at the top of which the cultural property of Polish origin was placed, and next, different objects kept mainly in Berlin or Dresden museums successively.[15] I would also like to recall yet another interesting postulate that, although proposed by one of the experts, had never been included in the draft. It was a plan to create an international museum of the plundered works of art, consisting of those object that had been found but could not be returned to their rightful owners, as it was impossible to determine who the owners were. According to the plan, this, so-called, "Common Exchange Museum" was not supposed to have a permanent base; instead, the idea was to transfer the museum collection from town to town among the injured countries every few years. The crucial reasoning behind this concept was a kind of "indirect" return of the cultural heritage looted from a nation which had, quite probably, been deprived of the objects

---

[13] The relevant provision of the Draft was formulated as follows: "Germany has bound itself to restore historic secular and church buildings as well as monuments that had been destroyed by military operations and due to the special orders issued upon their cessation (torn down, remodeled, etc.). Art. 4. W. Kowalski: Liquidation...p. 41

[14] This idea is reflected by the art. 1 of the Draft which reads: „Reparations and requital for losses in the field of culture (...) for a clearly distinct area of obligation and have priority over and above all other categories of imposed obligations". W. Kowalski: Liquidation...p. 41.

[15] Art. 5 of the Draft provided in this respect: "For the deliberate destruction and damage, and for the loss of cultural property in the area of museum art collections and artistic furnishings of the destroyed buildings, Germany is obliged by the provisions regarding reparations and requital to deliver works of art and objects of the arts and crafts industry in the number and type specified in the enclosed Annex, in that the ill will of the Germans as well as the enormous value of this property for the Polish nation is taken into consideration". W. Kowalski: Liquidation... p. 41. See also detailed description of the Annex, p. 42-43.

After the war operations stopped in 1945, the Soviet-dependent government took power in Poland but, in general, this had no influence on the restitution concept formulated before the War was over. Obviously, for political reasons, it was addressed to Germany only, although even then it was difficult to conceal the massive removal of cultural property by the Red Army from the formerly German lands which were already granted to Poland, not to mention the tragic fate experienced by the cultural heritage left in the former Polish eastern territories taken over USSR. The above mentioned restitution principles were adopted by the Ministry of Culture and Arts and had to be presented to the Allies by the Ministry of Foreign Affairs as Poland's official proposal.

The basic postulate was still absolute restitution of the objects that could be identified. This postulate was the only one that was ever executed in practice but only to limited extent. Its fulfillment was largely possible thanks to the American military administration of the relevant Occupation Zone in Germany, where most of the Polish cultural property of great value was found, having been removed by the Nazis from Cracow, Warsaw, etc. Due to good co-operation in this field, 34 362 cultural objects were returned to Poland in 1945 and 1946. As far as the second postulate of in-kind restitution was concerned, initially, there was also a chance to achieve it thanks to the attitude of the American government, which at least up to the year 1947, was the only one that supported such form of restitution. Thus, the principle of in-kind restitution was introduced to the Definition of Restitution adopted by the Control Council for Germany in 1947 as its official legal standpoint to give grounds for the in-kind restitution proceedings in all the four occupation zones. According to point 3 of this document, "As to goods of unique character, restitution of which is impossible, a special instruction will fix the categories of goods which will be subject to replacement, the nature of these replacements and the conditions under which such goods could be replaced by equivalent objects." On the basis of this indication, the Polish government approached the American military authorities with a list of 64 paintings to be granted to Poland as compensation for the paintings removed from our country by the Nazis. However, 1947 was the year of the beginning of the Cold War, which put an end to the chance of executing the provisions made previously by the Allies. The reparation proposals turned to be entirely unacceptable in practice for purely political reasons.

At that time, the Polish Ministry of Culture and Arts had already some preliminary data on the war losses,[16] and prepared comprehensive general postulates of reparations and restitution claims from Germany. Apart from the facilities to the damaged theatres, operas, libraries and other cultural institutions, the claims comprised lists of works of art grouped in different categories, including, for example: paintings of various schools, old furniture, ceramics, tapestry, etc.[17] The lists were made in view of the objects to be found in the Dresden Gallery, which, at that time was kept in the Soviet territory. The Polish Ministry of Culture and Arts assumed that if Poland was to receive 15 % of the reparations due to the USSR under the Berlin Treaty provisions, the same portion of the Dresden Gallery collection could be claimed as well. Finally, this postulate, just as the whole concept of reparations, were never officially presented. Apart from some obvious political obstacles, the Polish authorities at that time paid much more attention to economic reparations, with particular focus on the industrial ones.

Following the ensuing unfavorable political climate, restitution proposals were gradually limited, until, in principle, they became a historical issue. As a result of these developments, in the early 1950s the Bureau of Revindication and Reparations in the Ministry of Culture and Arts was closed. Thus, the inventory of the War losses was discontinued, stopping at the figure of 516 000 cultural objects including those that had been completely damaged. The last attempt at restitution measures undertaken at that time was the 1953 proposal made by the Polish Party to exchange 117 German works of art for the 18th century architectural designs of Warsaw buildings which were required to rebuild the city so much damaged in World War Two. Irrespective of definite agreements

---

[16] For more details on the methods used in collecting information about the losses and their assessment, see: W. Kowalski: Liquidation..p. 67 et seq. According to official report presented by Ambassador Wierbłowski at the meeting of the Deputy Ministers of Foreign Affaires in London in 1947, Poland lost 43 % of the cultural property owned in 1939. For example, the National Museum in Warsaw lost 100% of ancient art, 78% of Polish paintings, 58% of foreign paintings, and 75% of the applied art.

[17] For example, the lists include the following entries: from the Kaiser Friedrich-Museum in Berlin: 45 paintings of the 14th and 15th century Italian school, 62 paintings of the 16th to 18th century Italian school, 10 paintings of the 17th century Spanish school, from the Neues Museum in Berlin: 3 Egyptian granite sarcophagi, 10 Egyptian stone sarcophagi, 15 alabaster Egyptian vases, 10 Roman busts, 100 Greek vases, etc, etc. For further entries see: W. Kowalski: Liquidation...p. 82-83.

made between Poland and East Germany on the diplomatic level, the exchange had a unilateral character only - the German Party accepted the paintings with proper solemnity but never gave the promised designs.

Due to the political changes initiated in Poland in the late 1980s the problem of the liquidation of the effects of the Second World War has revived as an issue of diplomatic negotiations. In the case of Poland that means reopening of 'old' matters still to be settled with Germany and we may say, 'new' matters related to Russia and other states in the East of Europe, with which this dialogue could be entered into only nowadays. In 1991 probably the last attempt was made to list the losses suffered by Polish culture in World War Two. Up to the day on which I am making this speech, the inventory has recorded 52 038 items altogether. This figure includes single works of art and whole collections. In terms of categories it covers, for example: 4600 paintings by Polish masters, 3 730 paintings by foreign masters, 2363 pieces of sculpture, 3 250 gold-work objects, etc.

Irrespective of the future figure by which the present statistics will be increased, it has always been evident that this task is impossible to achieve as a whole. The documentation concerning cultural property damaged or removed by the Nazis from Poland is incomplete as a result of the methods by means of which the plunder and damage were made. Therefore, if it is impossible to calculate the losses, how can they be directly repaired?

Under such circumstances, what restitution policy should my government adopt?

Because of the main focus of our conference, my remarks will cover only the relations with Germany. For obvious reasons, I cannot answer this question in full detail, but generally it would be my suggestion to adopt the following principles.

On the one hand, the losses are still remembered in Poland and they are still easily and clearly visible in many places and many cultural institutions, so their character is not purely historical.

On the other hand, the restitution policy should also be determined by the present and future political relations between Poland and Germany, totally different from the political climate of the times when the above discussed rigid restitution and reparations concepts were formulated. Our present relations have been designated by 'the treaty on good neighborhood policy and friendly co-operation'[18] signed several years ago between the two countries and I am convinced that the suggestive wording of this title is not only formal. In my opinion, the issue of the lost cultural heritage seems to be the last unresolved problem concerning the effects of the War. However, the way in which this issue is to be settled should by no means disturb our good relations; conversely, it should show that our two countries are capable of settling even the most difficult disputes so the good relations between us are permanent and long-lasting.

What will probably remain out of the old restitution concepts is the expectation to receive back all the cultural property that was subject of unlawful removal and can be restituted now. As far as other aspects of the policy of liquidating the war effects is concerned, it should be based on the general principles laid down in the above-mentioned treaty. First and foremost, Art. 28[19] stipulates that Poland and Germany will co-

---

[18] Treaty between the Republic of Poland and the Federal Republic of Germany on good neighborhood policy and friendly cooperation signed in Bonn on June 17, 1991.

[19] Art. 28 reads as follows:

"1. The contracting Parties will co-operate in the field of the preservation and protection of European cultural heritage. They will protect monuments.

2. The contracting Parties will assure particular care for located on their respective territories places and cultural properties, which are the evidence of historical events and of cultural and scientific traditions and achievements of other Party, and will assure full access to them or will take steps to assure such

operate in the field of the protection of European cultural heritage. It also includes the obligation of both parties to protect the objects of Polish heritage that have been preserved Germany, as well as German heritage located in Poland. As section 2 of the said Article emphasizes, these efforts should be undertaken 'in the spirit of concord and reconciliation', which, if really accepted by the two Parties, shall definitely facilitate the settlement of even the most difficult issues connected with cultural property and archival material.

---

access in case it is not in the State's competence. Above mentioned places and cultural properties are under legal protection of both Parties. Contracting Parties will undertake initiatives in this respect in the spirit of concord and reconciliation.

3. The contracting Parties will strive to resolve in the same spirit the problems related to the cultural goods and archives starting with individual cases".

Dr. Oliver Rathkolb

KREISKY ARCHIVES AND INSTITUTE FOR CONTEMPORARY HISTORY,
UNIVERSITY OF VIENNA
AUSTRIA

From 'Legacy of Shame' to New Debates over Nazi Looted Art

Break-out Session on Nazi-Confiscated Art Issues: Government
Restitution Policies, Postwar to Present

1) INTERNATIONAL DEBATES 1984/1985

A few years before the Waldheim-Debate – in 1984 – Andrew
Decker criticized the "Austrian Style" of restitution of art work stolen by
the National Socialists after 1938, and he primarily focused on items
stored in a monastery outside Vienna (Mauerbach), which had been
turned over by the US authorities in Germany after they passed on the
supervision over the Central Art Collecting Point in Munich to the
Germans in 1951.[1] These remaining 8,500 pictures, drawings and books
have still not been restituted partly due to the rather unprofessional and
reluctant handling by low level Austrian authorities to trace down the
owners (e.g., limiting the publishing of the list in the Austrian
government newspaper "Wiener Zeitung" in 1969, which is barely read
outside Austrian government circles) and the unwillingness of politicians
to solve the issue by passing a law in the parliament until July 1995 (in

---

[1] Andrew Decker, "A Legacy of Shame," *ARTnews 83* (December 1984): 55-75;
see also Andrew Decker, "How Things Work in Austria: Stolen Works of Art,"
ARTnews 92 (Summer 1993): 198-200. and Herbert Haupt, *Das
Kunsthistorische Museum. Die Geschichte des Hauses am Ring. Hundert Jahre
im Spiegel der Ereignisse* (Wien: 1991). More precisely Josephine Leistra, "The
Mauerbach Case," *Spoils of War*, .3 (December 1996): 22-27.

1969 the Austrian parliament only agreed to enlarge the acceptance of claims until the end of 1972).[2]

On Christmas Eve 1997, however, the international media began to respond to a new debate. This time it focused on specific individual Nazi era art claims by two families concerning two paintings from the Austrian expressionist Schiele. The paintings were on display in the Museum of Modern Art in New York on loan from the private (state subsidized) Leopold Foundation.[3] On January 7, 1998, the Manhattan District Attorney confiscated the two paintings ("Portrait of Wally" and "Dead City") starting a criminal investigation into the ownership of the paintings and providing evidence for a possible trial before a grand jury.[4]

It should be noted that this incident was not only a side show of the "Swiss Nazi Gold Bank" discussion but became part of a much broader debate in the US dealing with the sometimes dubious ownership of alleged Nazi loot on display in several museums in the US and Canada - paintings claimed by heirs of Holocaust victims.[5] Before the "Austrian incident" the "Holocaust Art Restitution Project" was established in Washington, D.C. and the World Jewish Congress established a "Commission for Art Recovery." This commission is chaired by former US Ambassador to Austria, Ronald Lauder, who also happens to be the chairman of the MOMA.

In order to place the various events into a broader perspective I shall try to analyze some of the historical reasons for the most recent discussions. These discussions culminated in an international media debate and a new – much more concerned – political debate in Austria with an unexpected outcome. I cannot go into more details, why it took nearly 10 years to solve the issue, although on the level of the key decision makers like then Chancellor Fred Sinowatz and Minister of Finance Franz Vranitzky, who in 1986 became Chancellor, the option of an auction in favor of the Jewish community in Vienna and Jewish organizations has been already agreed upon. The original idea along these lines have been proposed in early 1980 by then Chancellor Bruno

---

[2] Paul Grosz, "Introduction," in Christie's, The Mauerbach Benefit Sale, Vienna, October 29-30, 1996, Auction 5638.
[3] New York Times, 24 December 1997.
[4] New York Times, 8 January 1998.
[5] Boston Globe, 24 July 1997.

Kreisky and Minister of Science and Research Hertha Firnberg.[6] In the following article I shall try to analyze briefly some of the 1945 ff. roots of these public debates of the 1980s and early 1990s.

2) NATIONAL RESTITUTION FIRST - US ART RESTITUTION POLICIES AFTER 1945

One of the central problems of postwar art restitution certainly is the policy question of how to administer the return of stolen art in Austria. On May 8, 1945, US troops took over authority over the greatest collection of Nazi loot in Austria in the Alt Aussee salt mine (and other repositories nearby like the Lauffen mine in Bad Ischl) which contained works of art (7,000 paintings and drawings, and approximately 3,000 other items)[7] – stolen and sometimes bought from all Nazi occupied Europe to become part of the "Führermuseum" in Linz – a project close to the heart of Hitler himself.[8] Austrian resistance fighters and Austrian museum experts had already taken care of the art treasures and prevented the destruction by National Socialist and SS hard-liners.[9]

A considerable portion of the Alt Aussee loot was of "Austrian" origin – some 700 paintings belonging to the Rothschild family and 500 paintings belonging to other Jewish families. Although the Rothschilds and the other collectors and/or their heirs had been brutally forced out of Austria by 1938 by the Nazi regime thereby taking their art treasures,

---

[6] Bruno Aigner, Information für Heinz Fischer, 20 June 1985 and Sinowatz to Vranitzky, 4 July 1985, Bruno Kreisky Archives Foundation, Vienna, Franz Vranitzky Archives, Mag. Krammer, Box Mauerbach.

[7] United States Allied Commission Austria, *The Rehabilitation of Austria, 1945-1947*, Vol. III, Vienna (no publisher and no date, app. 1950) 67. (more details concerning the legal and political aspects of preserving art 1918-1945 in: Eva Frodl-Kraft, Gefährdetes Erbe. Österreichs Denkmalschutz und Denkmalpflege 1918-1945 im Prisma der Zeitgeschichte, Wien, 1997).

[8] Charles de Jaeger, *The Linz File. Hitler's Plunder of Europe's Art (Exeter: Webb and Bower, 1981)*, 19 and with more sophisticated analysis and academic research by Jonathan Petropoulos, *Art as Politics in the Third Reich* (Chapel Hill: The University of North Carolina Press, 1996). See also Lynn H. Nicholas, *The Rape of Europe. The Fate of Europe's Treasures in the Third Reich and the Second World War* (New York: Knopf, 1994), 346-350.

[9] Katharina Hammer, *Glanz im Dunkel. Die Bergung von Kunstschätzen im Salzkammergut am Ende des 2. Weltkrieges* (Wien: Bundesverlag, 1986), 119-166.

these properties still were considered Austrian property and therefore turned over to the Austrian government and subordinate administrative institutions to carry out the restitution (e.g., Finanzlandesdirektionen, in charge of the legal matters, and the Bundesdenkmalamt acting as the overall art custodian). Due to criminal activities of individual art experts (many of them active in the white-washing and expropriation machinery of the Nazi regime) the Provisional government under State Chancellor Karl Renner decided as early as 22 August 1945 to establish a "Vermögenssicherungsamt" under the control of the Ministry of the Interior.[10] According to experts art objects worth 200,000.000 "Reichsmark" have "changed" owners during April and August 1945.

3) THE "RANSOM" CASES OF THE ROTHSCHILDS' AND LEDERER'S RESTITUTION CLAIM:

After the so-called "Anschluß" of Austria in 1938 "Reichsdeutsche" officials especially - both from the Gestapo and the cultural administration (including Austrian museum experts) confiscated a large number of art collections from Jewish owners (among them well known collections like the collections of Alfons Rothschild, Louis Rothschild, Rudolf Gutmann, Oskar Pick, T. Goldmann, Felix Haas, etc.), which were stored in the "Zentraldepot" in the Vienna Hofburg and were reserved for the "Führermuseum" in Linz. In 1941 this depot was transferred to Kremsmünster and parts of the local deposit in Hohenfurth were moved to Alt Aussee in February 1944.

When the Austrian Bundesdenkmalamt was authorized by US authorities and the Allied Commission to take over the individual restitution responsibilities the prewar legal framework again began to influence the transfers. Since 1918 a special Export Control Law ("Ausfuhrverbotsgesetz"), amended in 1923, enabled the Bundesdenkmalamt to decide which art treasures were allowed to leave the country, ignoring the nationality of the owners. This meant, however, that after 1945 – despite the fact that Jewish owners with Austrian

---

[10] Staatsratsprotokoll, 22 August 1945, Archiv der Republik, Wien, Sammlung Staats- und Ministerratsprotokolle post 1945; the author owes this reference to Dr. Theodor Venus, Vienna. More details concerning the legal and political aspects of preserving art 1918-1945 in: Eva Frodl-Kraft, Gefährdetes Erbe. Österreichs Denkmalschutz und Denkmalpflege 1918-1945 im Prisma der Zeitgeschichte, Wien 1997.

nationality who had been persecuted and many of them killed in the Shoah (nearly one third of the Jewish Segment of Austrian society) have lost their citizenship automatically (!) – suddenly the traditional Austrian legal order began to overrule the National Socialist atrocities and individual pains and material losses as if nothing has happened. These treasures again were considered "Austrian" and an integrate part of the Austrian cultural heritage. In the pragmatic restitution procedure this meant that the original owners had first to prove their ownership – which under the circumstances of exile, imprisonment and the Second World War was very difficult to fulfill.

In the case of large collections like the collections of the Rothschilds this was a relatively easy task, since the "curators" have even produced a printed catalogue in 1939 (classified top secret and printed in a very limited number). It became difficult when the "legal owners" wanted to export their property because only a very few wanted to return at this stage (as most of the Austrian authorities and many Austrians were eager to keep the surviving Austrian Jews out of the country). In a "Restitution Compromise" (Rückstellungsvergleich) the lawyer of Clarice de Rothschild for example agreed that from 16 art objects, held by the Ferdinandeum in Innsbruck 14 will be restituted (including an export license), 2 will be turned over by Ms. Rothschild (1 to the Albertina and 1 to the Ferdinandeum).[11] The same procedure was used when dealing with old music instruments of the Rothschild collections although here most of the instruments stayed with the Kunsthistorisches Museum as a permanent loan.[12]

4) 'OTHER' RESTITUTIONS OF ART OBJECTS AND EXPORT CONTROL

Another case illustrating the rather shabby habit of restitution after 1945 in the field of arts is the equestrian painting of Bellini from the Sarah Lederer Collection. Ernst Lederer, a well known art historian, has been "dazu bewogen" (induced) to "donate" this valuable painting to the Republic of Austria in return for an export license for a fragment of the large Lederer collection which was destroyed at the end of the war by SS

---

[11] GZ 29.036/47, Archiv der Republik, Wien, Bundesministerium für Unterricht, Box 99.

[12] GZ 29.102/47, Archiv der Republik, Wien, Bundesministerium für Unterricht, Box 165.

troops at Schloß Immendorf (including famous paintings by Klimt and Schiele) or like the textiles and drawings disappeared during 1938-1940.[13] In such a case Austrian courts would refuse to accept any claims for compensation. The famous Klimt Fries in the Lederer collection was, however, not included in the export license, and it took until the 1970s when Chancellor Bruno Kreisky himself started negotiations for the Republic of Austria to buy the Klimt Fries from Lederer.[14] When Erich Lederer had tried to get back the Bellini painting in the 1950s the Austrian Ministry for Education refused, although a confidential internal evaluation of the Ministry opposed to the use of the Export Control Law for such deals ("Vorgang immerhin im Ausfuhrverbotsgesetz nicht gedeckt"). The Minister, Heinrich Drimmel, himself decided not to restitute, but at least admitted that the Export Control law should be changed.

This rather strange – and from my point of view both immoral and illegal procedure – has been developed before 1938 and accepted by the collectors (e.g., in the case of the Rothschilds), but after the Holocaust, exile and emigration and the Second World War restitution issues should not be effected by such "deals" since the State of Austria has lost the right to decide about the fate of properties of the Jewish minority so brutally persecuted both by fellow citizens and German Nazis and even after 1945 were deprived of their citizenship (they had to apply again for Austrian citizenship and needed a permanent residence in Austria, a procedure which however has been changed in the recent years as one of the positive consequences of the Waldheim debate).

It would be a falsification to state that the Republic of Austria after 1945 did not restitute property to former citizens in exile, but by doing so used a rather complicated legal procedure, executed sometimes by a highly passive or even resenting bureaucracy.[15] The main reason, however, why restitution issues and "Jewish claims" (concerning heirless property, advocated by Jewish organizations) became such sensitive issues both within the Austrian political debate and in the concrete

---

[13] Erich Lederer, Archiv der Republik, Wien, Bundesministerium für Unterricht, Sammelmappen, K 131.

[14] Bruno Kreisky, *Der Mensch im Mittelpunkt. Der Memoiren dritter Teil*, ed. Oliver Rathkolb, Johannes Kunz und Margit Schmidt (Wien: Kremayr & Scheriau, 1996), 44f.

[15] Compare for more details on this issue Brigitte Bailer, *Wiedergutmachung - kein Thema. Österreich und die Opfer des Nationalsozialismus* (Wien: Löcker), 1993.

handling of individual cases can be traced down in the political perceptions of some of the "fathers" of the Second Republic like the Chancellor Karl Renner, who in his first political memorandum in April 1945 pleaded for restitution of the Jewish property ("Rückgabe des geraubten Judengutes"[16]) not in favor of the individuals, but in favor of a restitution fund, which would distribute shares to the individuals in order to hinder a massive return of the exiles ("um ein massenhaftes, plötzliche Zurückfluten der Vertriebenen zu verhindern"). The legal Department of the Austrian Foreign Office refused to accept a legal obligation with regard to Jewish claims since the Austrian state was not considered being the legal successor of the Nazi regime; only due to "political reasons" restitution should be granted under the presumption that National Socialist Germany alone was considered responsible for the Holocaust and World War II and seen as "the" perpetrator.

"Aryanized" property was secured as early as May 1945, but it took until 1946 and the following 6 restitution laws to provide the legal framework for this ambivalent approach of "restitution" due to political reasons. The state of Austria until very recently considered herself a victim of National Socialism and Germany, a myth which began to erode during the Waldheim debate in 1986 and was buried at least officially by Chancellor Franz Vranitzky in 1993.

To come back to the return of stolen art, it is correct to say that the large and famous collections have been restituted to their owners if they were found in 1945 in one of the repositories. The right to export could be "organized" as shown above, although in some cases in the first months after the end of the war and before Austrian bureaucracy took over restitution responsibilities, direct restitution was executed. A good example is the Gutmann collection: Rudolf Gutmann, a Canadian citizen, identified his property in 1946 in Alt Aussee and his Austrian lawyer needed only an export permission from the Ministry of Finance, which was granted.

---

[16] Österreichisches Institut für Zeitgeschichte, Archiv - Nachlaß Karl Renner, NL 1-3, Do 721, Mappe 9.

5) THE PROBLEM OF LOST ART

5a) The "Eastern" Problem

But even in the case of Gutmann he ran into trouble when he tried to seek restitution of 41 Rembrandt engravings which were transferred to Germany by one of Hitler's art experts, Posse, and in 1945 were confiscated by the Red Army. Official applications were not successful, so then he tried to bribe Eastern German officials with $20,000 since the engravings have shown up in the Soviet Zone of Occupation in Germany. It could not yet be clarified whether he was successful – in 1957 they were still missing – but his problem is a typical one in the postwar era. Thousands of art objects were at first confiscated in Austria and then transferred to "Reichsdeutschland," both for party functionaries and private individuals.

There does exist a list of losses concerning private (mostly Jewish) collections dated 1957 and Austrian museums and monasteries[17]

---

[17] List of public property
Kunsthistorisches Museum, Wien
Graphische Sammlung Albertina, Wien
Historisches Museum der Stadt Wien
Stadt Salzburg
Mozarteum Salzburg
Österreichische Bergbaumuseen
Österreichisches Apothekermuseum, Wien
Zisterzienser Stift Heiligenkreuz, NÖ

List of private (mostly, but not exclusively) Jewish property
Nachlaß Rudolf von Alt
Dr. Biermann
Carl Blaas
Dr. Josef und Gusti Blauhorn
Ferdinand Bloch-Bauer
Oscar Bondy
Margarete Buchstab
Karoline Czeczowiczka
Ernst Duschinsky
Hortense Eissler
Valerie Eissler
David Goldmann
Dr. Philipp von Gomperz
Rudolf Gutmann

since bureaucracy kept track of those cultural treasures which were borrowed for decoration in National Socialist offices or in private residences of party leaders like "Karinhall" of Hermann Göring (only few could traced down like two of these tapestries from Karinhall in

---

Dr. Otto Habsburg-Lothringen
Dr. Felix Haas
Henriette Hainisch
Bruno Jellinek
Karpeles-Schenker
Stephan Kerlin
Dr. Norbert u. S. Klinger
Nettie Königstein
Dr. Felix Kornfeld
Moriz von Kuffner
Henriette Lainzer
Graf Anton Lanckoronski
Prinz Eduard Liechtenstein
Margit Löffler
Leidinger (Hanna Rhode)
Fritz Mandl
Franz Matsch
Egger Möllwald
Berta Morelli
Benno Moser
Kunsthandlung Nehammer-Prinz
(Kunsthändler Oskar Hamel)
Kunsthandlung Plobner
Albert Pollak
Ernst Pollak
Frau Reichel
Alphons Rothschild
Louis Rothschild
Schiff-Suvero
Arthur Spitzer
Dr. Alfons Thorsch
Hedwig und Viktor Wimpfen
Georg A. Wolf
Kunsthandlung Wolfrum
Paul und Andy Zsolnay
Ing. Herbert Zucker-Hale

Poland, which were restituted to the Kunsthistorisches Museum in 1976)[18].

5b) The whitewashing problem

Not only the Cold War hindered the search for stolen art post 1945, but so did the fact that some Nazi party functionaries have been able to hide their – mostly – stolen art treasures (most of them did not show up in the postwar era). An illustrative case is Baldur von Schirach, the former Hitler Youth leader and later Reichsleiter and Gauleiter in Vienna. In 1942 he had bought from the Vugesta (Verwaltungsstelle für Umzugsgüter jüdischer Emigranten), an agency of the Gestapo, confiscated Jewish property to the value of Reichsmark 42,092 [19](obviously partly through the Dorotheum, the state owned Austrian auction house, which was heavily used for "whitewashing" and selling machinery for looted art objects which were not under "Führervorbehalt," being reserved for Adolf Hitler). Among other objects he "bought" was a Lucas Cranach, Madonna with Child, from the confiscated Gomperz collection – which is still missing. Was it taken by Schirach, who in 1948 declared that he did not know about the original owner, or was it stolen in 1945 from the Schirach Villa in Vienna – either by Austrians or by Russian soldiers or confiscated by the Red Army, or did he sell it through his family to a collector/art dealer overseas?

This "selling" constitutes one of the major problems for the location of stolen art post 1945 on an individual basis, since the Monuments, Fine Arts and Archives Section of the US occupation forces both in Germany and Austria concentrated on the large collections which were deposited in several salt mines and castles throughout Austria to be protected against air-raids. By May 1948 nearly 2.5 million objects,

---

[18] Gerhard Sailer, "Austria," *Spoils of War*, International Newsletter, .3 (December 1996), 35; again published in Elisabeth Simpson, ed. "The Spoils of War. World War II and Its Aftermath: The Loss, Reappearance and Recovery of Cultural Property" (New York: Harry N. Abrams, 1997), 88-91. In a rather strange analysis Gerhard Sailer omits the theft of Jewish-owned artworks so that the editors had to refer to this immoral and shameful chapter of recent cultural history in a separate editorial remark.

[19] Bernard B. Traper, Transcript of interrogation, National Archives, Record Group 260, ACA Austria, Box 365 Folder: R&R 51.

including 468,000 paintings, drawings and sculptures had been restituted by US authorities in Germany.[20] The Alt Aussee art works have been secured and partly transferred to Munich and as far as Austrian property was concerned mostly brought to Vienna under the custody of the Bundesdenkmalamt. As referred to above US authorities did not deal with individual restitution cases. According to the Bundesdenkmalamt 10,000 works from different repositories have been restituted under the title of "Jewish property."[21]

6) HEIRLESS PROPERTY

As documented on the basis of individual cases in the 1984 article by Andrew Decker the real long range political problem in the Austrian restitution story was the' fact that in 1969 8,422 objects in Austrian care were still not restituted, and the deadline for the claims was extended to December 31, 1970 after public intervention by Simon Wiesenthal - but still was limited and due to rather poor public relation only 71 objects could be returned.

No active policy has been worked out to trace down at least the names of the owners of this "heirless property," although Sophie Lillie, one of the young experts consulted for the Christie's auction in 1996 clearly recognized the possibility to read "the inscriptions on the back of the canvases and frames. 'Aryanization' numbers, inventory numbers from secret Nazi depots and/or gallery labels chronicle a kind of unconscious history of Mauerbach, revealing or concealing in codified form the stations of theft ...".[22] I, however, do not agree with Hector Feliciano, that all, or most, owners and/or their heirs could have been traced down even in 1996 by active research.[23] The chances to identify the original owners would have been relatively high – especially by using the original lists gathered by US officials and experts after 1945 and material stored in German and Austrian archives. At the same time it is obvious that a large segment of these art objects did belong to people who did not survive the Holocaust.

---

[20] John Dornberg, "The Mounting Embarrassment of Germany's Nazi Treasures," *ARTnews* 87 (September 1988), 138.

[21] Hammer, Glanz, 258.

[22] Unpublished research proposal by Sophie Lillie, September 1996.

[23] Hector Feliciano, *Spoils of War* 3 (December 1996), 25f

The auction in 1996 was a financial success – due to well prepared sponsoring activities by the US Jewish Community on the first day – and a wise political decision, turning over the ownership of the Mauerbach collection to the Jewish Community of Vienna. The sale brought a total of ATS 155,166,810 and the net profit will go to people who suffered under National Socialism and/or their descendants in need of material assistance.

The handling of the Mauerbach case by Austrian bureaucrats and some politicians since the 1960s, however, reveals a strange mixture of ignorance and stubbornness to admit the Nazi policies and brutal Austrian collaboration on all levels and the postwar problems of restitution. Symbolic for this policy was the tendency to close Mauerbach like a fortress to the public, which in return increased the fantasy of American journalists and led to conflicts with the French Embassy by refusing French curators (e.g., Pierre Rosenberg, now director of the Louvre) in 1973 to see the Mauerbach collection when trying to locate lost French art objects. In 1987 at least 17 paintings were shown to members of a French claim commission, the rest kept closed by the Ministry of Finance.[24]

On the one hand Austrian politicians especially – already decades before the Waldheim debate – have feared a public debate about Austrians taking part in the Nazi machinery of the Holocaust, which means primarily that they feared negative press reports in the United States (overestimating the political interest in Jewish issues in the US in the 1960s, but obviously influenced by perceptions which came close to the "Jüdische Weltverschwörung" ("Jewish Conspiracy against the World") and the influence of Jewish journalists on the "Eastcoast," propagated by the Nazis. At the same time they feared an Austrian debate about Jewish property which would again reveal an even stronger Austrian contribution to the execution of the National Socialist persecutions and, on the side of the former members of the NSDAP, would lead to opposition to one of the two leading parties. Frankly put, politicians of the Great Coalition after 1945 (up to the early sixties) always tried to postpone the settlement of the Jewish claims and if they were not hard pressed by the Allies, especially the US, would even have postponed the restitution procedures. Highly sensitive issues like the return of rented (not owned) apartments, pensions, bank accounts, etc., were always excluded due to opposition from the voters. It should be noted here, that the Department of State, too, did not press the Austrians

---

[24] Hector Feliciano, *Spoils of War* 3 (December 1996), 25f.

hard on the "Jewish Claims issue" (compared with claims of US oil firms), although the settlement of these claims was part of the Austrian State Treaty. The State Department even took over the negotiation initiative from the Jewish organizations in 1958/59 and settled the claims on a rather low financial level.[25]

This explains why since the 1960s this issue of "heirless property," too, did not move – no one wanted really to stir up the issue, because no one wanted a political debate which then would result in the unmasking of the myth of the Austrian victimization under National Socialism (although on an individual basis many non-Jewish Austrians, too have suffered under the Hitler regime or have been killed). In the field of the "stolen art" this certainly reveals the collaboration of art dealers, auction houses, museum experts and curators in the mostly organized plunder of art collections of their Jewish fellow citizens, as well as the fact that many fellow citizens – many of them not members of the NSDAP – stole art objects from Austrian Jews, and tried to hide the truth after 1945. Still today there is a tendency in self descriptions of museums and the Bundesdenkmalamt to hide the truth or to smoothen this brutal chapter of Austrian cultural history and again present the Germans as the overall Nazi perpetrators. Fortunately, the political debate has moved forward.

As an appendix, however, it must be noted that the "human factor" should be more important when analyzing the spoils of the war and talking about restitution. Still the value of forced labor and the human factor should be of much higher importance both in analytical and legal debates. Still the "thieves" are more guilty than the "middle men" who sold or bought stolen art. On the other hand the historical debate moved on also dealing with the post-1945 history of the Nazi war loots. Art objects are an important component of national memories and images. Therefore historical reflections concerning the cultural heritage of museum and private owners ought to be part of an open-minded democratic memory.

This new trend in 1998, certainly a positive result of the Waldheim-Debate and the increasing knowledge about the atrocities of the Nazi regime and the Austrian collaborators, is best exemplified by the debate following the seizure of the two Schiele paintings in the MOMA in January 1998. At first the public and political debate in Austria concentrated on the ownership of the two paintings – at least in

---

[25] Oliver Rathkolb, *Washington ruft Wien. US Großmachtpolitik und Österreich, 1953-1963* (Wien: Böhlau, 1997), 212-232.

the case of the "Wally-Portrait." This issue was cleared in favor of correct transactions leading up to Leopold.[26]

On January 14, 1998, the Austrian Minister of Education, Elisabeth Gehrer, asked for a comprehensive examination of all transactions in Austrians museums during 1938-1945, but it took until the end of February that the internal commission was set up. Since then the debate has shifted from the 2 Schiele cases to the broader debate about immoral treatment received by major collectors like the Rothschilds and their heirs post-1945 (unearthed by the author of this article and made public in an article in "Der Standard," January 14, 1998). But it took another month (until a series in the same newspaper appeared on looted art from the Nazi period) that this fact really became an issue. Reluctantly even the director of the Kunsthistorisches Museum, Winfried Seipel, now pleaded for the return of plundered art work.[27] In the 1960s, however, an inter-ministerial committee turned down requests of the widow of Louis Rothschild, Hildegard Countess Auersperg, who tried to regain the 4 valuable oil paintings from her late husband's collection.[28] And still in 1974 Austrian bureaucracy turned down efforts to solve this problem of immoral trade-offs.

There are still many smoking guns in Austria's Nazi past, but obviously a new generation of journalists, academics and politicians are prepared to face this past and unearth the truth – even if this hurts not only the national memory, but also means concrete efforts for restitution of material losses. The new political trend in Austria – certainly a positive result of the Waldheim-Debate and the growing broader knowledge about the atrocities of the Nazi regime and the Austrian collaborators - is best exemplified by the debate following the seizure of the two Schiele paintings in the MOMA in January 1998. In the first weeks the public and political debate in Austria concentrated on the ownership of the two paintings.

In a broader context the Austrian Minister of Education, Elisabeth Gehrer, asked for an overall examination of all deals in Austrians museums during 1938-1945 on January 14, 1998. In the meantime the debate has shifted from the 2 Schiele cases to the broader debate about immoral deals with the major collectors like the Rothschilds and their heirs post 1945, a fact by the way unearthed by the author of this article and made public in an article in "Der Standard", 14 January

[26] News 4/98, 140.
[27] Boston Globe, 5 March 1998.
[28] Archiv des Bundesdenkmalamtes, Wien, Karton 52.

1998: Large collections were restituted to the owners but under the then existing "Export Prohibition Law" they were forced to trade in selected art objects (chosen by the state museum officials and worth in some cases 10% of the whole collection) in order to obtain an export license.

But it took another month in 1998 (until a series in the same newspaper appeared on looted art from the Nazi period) that this fact really became an issue and even the director of the Kunsthistorisches museum, Winfried Seipel now, pleaded for the return of these immoral trade offs.[29] In the 1960s, however, an inter-ministerial committee turned down requests of the widow of Louis Rothschild, Hildegard Countess Auersperg, who tried to regain the 4 valuable oil paintings from her late husband's collection. And still in 1974 Austrian bureaucracy blocked efforts to solve this problem of immoral trade-off.

Still enough smoking guns are buried in Austria's Nazi past, but obviously a new generation of journalists, academics and politicians are prepared to face this past and unearth the truth - even if this hurts not only the national memory, but also means concrete efforts for restitution of material losses. On November 5, 1998 the National Council of the Austrian Parliament unanimously passed a law to restitute looted art from the Nazi period (including the immoral trade off since the export prohibition law has been amended not to include these objects previously). Since this law is limited to State owned collections provincial and municipal authorities have established research commissions to screen their collections after Nazi looted art (e.g. the Historical Museum of Vienna or the museums of the City and of the Province of Upper Austria in Linz, etc.).

---

[29] For the "Kunsthistorische Museum" see the unpublished report by Herbert Haupt in cooperation with Lydia Göbl, Die Veränderungen im Inventarbestand des Kunsthistorischen Museums während der Nazizeit und in den Jahren bis zum Staatsvertrag 1955 ("Widmungen"), Wien June 1998. This report is the first one of a series from the "National Museums" and seems to be intended to be published. Dr. Haupt takes a very different position on postwar restitution issues than outlined in his previous book "Das Kunsthistorische Museum." Die Geschichte des Hauses am Ring. Hundert Jahre im Spiegel Historischer Ereignisse, Wien 1991. Other forthcoming publications are a series of articles on the Nazi art loot in Austria from a research conference before the Mauerbach sale, edited by Theodor Brückler (Böhlau Verlag, Vienna, Spring 1999) and an enlarged version of the articles by Hubertus Czernin (in cooperation with Gabriele Anderl and Thomas Trenkler) for "The Standard," which will appear in the Molden Verlag in Vienna (January 1999).

THE PROBLEM OF "LOST LOOTED ART" RECONSIDERED:

Therefore it seems now important to focus on those art objects which never have been located by the Allied authorities immediately after the end of the war and which have only been partly destroyed. In order to document this future research focus which needs stronger international networking and cooperation of European (Eastern Central European and Western European) and American, Canadian museums, art dealers and collectors as well as a functioning internet data base, I shall present two concrete cases: One bases on the research of Oliver Kühschelm who traced down three art objects which had belonged to the collection of Philipp Gomperz in the Moravian Gallery in Brno, Czech Republic, which had been confiscated in 1942 (only 30 of the 85 art objects looted by the German Reich have been restituted after 1945). Another painting from the Gomperz collection, a Luca Cranach with Child, was „bought" by the Vienna Reichsleiter Baldur von Schirach and sold by a New Yorker art dealer after 1952, who refused to identify the buyer of the stolen object. My own research on the Lederer Collection unearthed concrete evidence that 44 etchings by Rembrandt have been looted in 1938 and only 3 could be returned after 1945. 41 have been taken by Hitler's special commissioner for the "Führer Museum" in Linz to the Dresdner Gallery in 1941, and seemed to have still existed in the first postwar years. An extensive research by the director of the gallery, Dr. Wolfgang Holler in November 1998 did not unearth more information on the whereabouts of these Rembrandt etchings, but they could have been transported to the Soviet Union and were not part of the returned art works after 1957.

The Cold War hindered a European wide research effort concerning looted art by the Nazi regime, a fact which can be documented in numerous cases. Therefore it seems to be of utmost importance to include Eastern Central European and if possible Russian national and provincial/municipal collections into a database approach of "lost looted art." In order to start with this approach concerning "art objects" looted on the territory of Austria during 1938 and 1945 (including partly the immediate postwar loot) I placed a 60 page list of more than one thousand missing art objects (both from public, but primarily private ownership) into the world wide web (http://members.vienna.at/kreisky/naziartloot/). This list has been collected by the Bundesdenkmalamt and the Ministry of Education in 1957 – which means that maybe a few of these objects have been restituted in the meantime, but the overall percentage is still missing.

This presentation is based on a paper presented at the German Studies Association Conference (September 26, 1997), Washington, D.C., with the panel "Kunstraub and Memory" and rewritten for this Holocaust era conference.

Mr. Richard Bevins

HISTORIAN, LIBRARY AND RECORDS DEPARTMENT, FOREIGN AND
COMMONWEALTH OFFICE
UNITED KINGDOM

Britain and the Restitution of Art Looted from Occupied Countries during the Second World War

Break-out Session on Nazi-Confiscated Art Issues: Government
Restitution Policies

Although the course of the war meant Britain's art treasures
escaped the plundering inflicted on the collections of occupied Europe,
the UK played a significant role in shaping the wartime Allied response
to the art losses suffered by her European Allies and in attempts to make
good those losses after the defeat of Germany in May 1945. Almost from
the moment in 1942 when officials and others in London began to
consider how to respond to news about the fate of works of art in
territories occupied by Germany, the governing assumption was that a
relatively simple process of returning identifiable property subject to an
act of dispossession by the enemy would follow the liberation of the
occupied countries and the defeat of Germany. Implementing such a
restitution policy, however, was not a simple matter.

Those developing restitution policy generally regarded works of
art in theory as a distinct category, thanks to their unique and easily
identifiable character and the intangible values attached to them, but their
restitution could not in practice proceed in isolation. Tempting though it
was to deal with works of art in advance of resolving a myriad of
contentious claims from newly-liberated countries for essential and
scarce items like railway locomotives and factory equipment, progress,
or lack of it, on the wider problems of restitution and reparations in the
end determined the success of efforts to restore looted art to its original

owners or their heirs. It took the 4 Occupying Powers in Germany until 1946 to reach agreement on a definition of restitution, and then to agree on how to interpret this definition. Only then was it settled precisely what kind of property was eligible for restitution, how restitution would relate to reparation, what procedure to follow to process claims and what to do if a particular item was not available for restitution. Restitution of some of the most easily identifiable examples of the looted art found in the British Zone of Germany had gone ahead on a provisional basis in advance of these agreements being reached in the Allied Control Council (ACC) but a proper legal and administrative process existed only after they had been concluded.

The Allies' basic intention to do something in response to Germany's exploitation of Occupied Europe had first been expressed formally in the *Inter-Allied Declaration against Acts of Dispossession Committed in Territories under Enemy Occupation or Control* issued by Britain and 16 other governments of the United Nations on 5 January 1943. Britain had been prompted to instigate discussions during 1942 on such a Declaration with her Allies by a growing awareness of the scale on which Germany was conducting a systematic looting of the Continent's material and cultural assets and the accompanying realization that the easy disposal of many of these assets in neutral countries was aiding her war effort. In their Declaration the signatories stated their determination to "combat and defeat the plundering by the enemy Powers of the territories which have been overrun or brought under enemy control" and reserved their rights "to declare invalid any transfers of, or dealings with, property, rights and interests of any description whatsoever which are, or have been, situated in the territories which have come under the occupation or control, direct or indirect, of the Governments with which they are at war". The Declaration was silent on *how* the Allies might "combat and defeat" the plundering of Occupied Europe and at that stage of the war there was in fact very little that could be done to enforce it. Foreign Office officials recognized that effective action could only follow victory over Germany, but those taking and disposing of looted art had been placed on notice that the Allies intended to counter their efforts.

For the remainder of 1943 little could be done in London except continue to collect information about art losses and begin preparations for when the Allies were in a position to take physical control of Germany's plunder. On the military side this saw the creation by the Civil Affairs Directorate of the War Office of Monuments, Fine Arts and Archives (MFA & A) branches to be attached to the Headquarters of each the Allied Armies. These were intended primarily to accompany advancing troops and direct efforts towards avoiding damage to cultural objects in the battlezone and take looted art left behind by retreating enemy forces into protective custody. British policy planning began in earnest following the establishment of the Macmillan Committee in the spring of 1944 in the run up to the invasion of Normandy. This was an independent non-governmental body of art experts appointed at the direction of the Prime Minister which met under the chairmanship of Lord Macmillan, a distinguished QC and a Trustee of the British Museum. The Committee, whose formal title was the British Committee on the Preservation and Restitution of Works of Art, Archives and other Material in Enemy Hands, met 11 times between May 1944 and April 1946 (all but 3 of its meetings were held before the end of 1944). It was directed: "to be at the service of His Majesty's Government in connection with the post-war restitution of monuments, works of art, and archives misappropriated by enemy governments or individuals in the course of the war"; to co-operate with the Roberts Commission (which had been set up with a similar brief in the USA) and other sources of relevant information and expertise and "to investigate and consider the technical problems (other than legal) of restitution." Despite this focus on restitution in its terms of reference, at its outset the Committee was preoccupied with preparations to preserve and protect artworks, monuments, churches etc likely to be at risk during the imminent fighting in Northern France.

Not until the summer of 1944 did it turn its attention to the development of the outlines of a restitution policy for looted art. The Committee submitted a number of informal papers to the Prime Minister and Foreign Secretary on, for example, the need for an international body to oversee the claims process, undertake searches for lost works and act as a central clearing-house of information. The Committee's thinking did not always chime with that of Whitehall- Anthony Eden told the Committee that it would impossible for any international body that was set up to act independently of the military or civilian authorities in occupied Germany. A rather plaintive request from Lord Macmillan to Eden in September 1944 for "some guidance from you as to the direction which [the Committee's] further work should take so as best to fulfil the purpose of their appointment" hints at the rather marginal impact of the Committee's work and its decline into semi-obscurity in 1945.

By the spring of that year, when the Rhine was about to be crossed by the Allied Armies advancing from the West and the Russians were within reach of Berlin in the East, a significant amount was known in London about *how* the Germans had stripped many of Western Europe's art collections. This knowledge principally concerned the organizations and some of the individuals responsible for the looting and was derived from the information gathered by the network operated by Britain's Ministry of Economic Warfare to support the economic blockade of Germany, supplemented by information acquired in the liberated territories. Contrasting examples of what was available are the individual reports based on intelligence sources about the activities of the notorious Alios Miedel, art agent for Goering, who arrived in Spain in the autumn of 1944 with 2 large American cars and a large number of paintings from Holland, including works by Rubens and Van Dyck and a short paper summarizing German efforts to loot art prepared for the information of the British Legation in Berne in February 1945 in advance of the first visit by a member of the MFA & A branch to Switzerland to trace looted art.

Although this knowledge of *how* the Germans had looted art often included information about what had been taken from particular, usually high-profile, collections, the MFA & A branches fanning out across a defeated Germany naturally did not know *what* looted art they would find in the devastated country or whether it would have survived the fighting and the bombing, whether it had been hidden in Germany, dispersed amongst German cultural institutions, passed into private hands or sold in neutral countries. It was only when they were in possession of the country and able to divert attention from the immediate task of preserving vulnerable sites from further damage to discovering caches of looted art and relevant archives that the first decisions were made on how to deal with the looted art in Allied hands.

The War Office issued an interim directive to the Deputy Commander-in-Chief of the British Zone of Germany, General Robertson, on 14 August. This set out interim measures for the restitution of identifiable works of art which had been subject to an act of dispossession by the enemy and had been located in the territory from which they were subsequently removed at the date of the German invasion of that territory. The directive was confined to works of art whose "identification is prima facie obvious and whose ownership is a matter of common knowledge" and to those works known by the staff of the British Element of the Control Commission to be in the British Zone. Inquiries about other works were only to be pursued where circumstances permitted and information about art covered by the directive was to be passed direct to the national government concerned. The directive had been inspired by Lt-Colonel Sir Leonard Wooley (head of the MFA & A branch) in June in response to the public announcement by SHAEF shortly after the conclusion of hostilities that the bulk, perhaps 90%, of the art looted by Germany in Western Europe had been recovered, in the 586 art deposits found by Allied forces. The FO endorsed Wooley's initiative, noting "It is fantastic that we should not be able to hand looted works of art back to their owners, when their origin is known to all the world" and accepted the risk that going ahead with this kind of interim arrangement for art would expose the Control Commission to unwelcome pressure to agree to similar arrangements for all looted property.

Despite this kind of support, and the effort that went into framing the procedure set out in the directive in as simple a fashion a possible, almost no works of art had been restituted from the British Zone by the end of the year. Part of the explanation for this can be found in the two problems that were raised by the Control Commission shortly after receipt of the separate War Office telegrams containing the directives on interim measures for the restitution of looted art and other property. The first problem was that the War Office directive placed responsibility for handling claims on a Restitution, Deliveries and Reparation Division of the Control Commission which did not yet exist. The second, and more fundamental, problem was raised by the Control Commission's request for a definition of "an act of dispossession . . . i.e. to what extent is payment made by Germans in money or in kind for removed goods to be taken into consideration in deciding whether property is loot."

The War Office answered this on 18 September by saying goods should be included in the interim restitution directive irrespective of whether they were paid for by the Germans. The Control Commission appears, however, to have hesitated at the implications of following such a sweeping directive. In a letter to HS Gregory of the Trading with the Enemy Department of 27 November on the subject of works of art purchased by Germany during the war, Wooley agreed that "to regard all sales to Germans by citizens of the occupied countries as having been made under duress would widen the issues unduly and establish a very dangerous precedent." He considered that "there are only about a dozen objects in the whole British Zone which are really loot coming under the definition given in SUGRA 18, but there are a very great numbers of objects [elsewhere he referred to many "thousands of second-grade" Dutch paintings in the British Zone] which do come under that definition but were purchased and not directly looted." A great deal of pressure was being placed on the UK by the newly-liberated countries of Western Europe on the subject of restitution in general and "purchased and not directly looted" art was a prominent grievance cited by the Netherlands and France when making their case in London. On 4 December Coulson described restitution in a letter to Sir William Strang (Political Adviser to the Commander-in-Chief of the British Zone) as a "burning political question" and said he was "very much afraid that things are boiling up for a good row."

It was this political background that prompted officials in the British Zone to ignore the continuing lack of a 4 Power agreement on a definition of restitution, ease the practical and administrative difficulties that had been hindering any implementation of SUGRA 18 and proceed with the return to the Netherlands in early 1946 of a substantial quantity of looted but purchased art and looted church bells. January 1946 also saw the Allied Control Council reach agreement on a definition of restitution.

The Control Council had been split primarily by differences between the French and Soviet Delegations, who had sharply differing views on the share of German resources that should be devoted to restitution as opposed to reparation. The French were much less interested than the Russians in reparation and sought to broaden the spread of restitution by arguing for the return of all property removed to Germany. Conversely, the Russians argued that only goods removed *by force* should be eligible for restitution, for the less that was restituted the more that was available for reparation. The chief British and American concern was to see that whatever was recovered from Germany did not so weaken her that she would become a burden to them; in practice this meant they leant more to the Russian than the French point of view. This came out particularly clearly in their desire to restrict the extent to which goods could be replaced by German equivalents if restitution of the original was impossible. The definition agreed by the Allied Control Council on 21 January conceded little to the French position. After reaffirming that the question of restitution to Allied countries "must be examined, in all cases, in light of the declaration of 5 January 1943" the text stated that restitution "will be limited in the first instance to identifiable goods . . . taken by the enemy by force. . . . Also falling under [this] measure of restitution are identifiable goods produced during the period of occupation and which have been obtained by force." However, all other property removed by the enemy was eligible for restitution only to the extent consistent with reparations. The definition went on provide for replacement of "goods of a unique character" subject to certain unspecified special instructions and conditions and concluded by noting that contact on all restitution questions would be with the government of the country where the objects were looted.

This agreement enabled the restitution of property taken from occupied countries and found in Germany to proceed on a legal basis. After its conclusion the Control Commission authorities in the British Zone were able to move rapidly to return, especially to the governments of the Netherlands, Belgium and France, the vast mass of the works of art which the Control Commission had taken custody of. It was the responsibility of the government of the country from which the art had been taken to allocate returned art to individuals and determine to what extent an individual claiming restitution had in fact collaborated in selling a work to the occupying power.

More problematic than the art which had come into the custody of the Commission authorities was art in private German hands. Steps were taken to compel individuals to reveal details of property they had acquired from occupied countries during the war and to enforce the ban on the sale, transfer and export of such property. Searches were carried out for particular items alleged to have been looted. Special provision was made to enable claimant countries to send teams of investigating officers into the Zone, something which the Dutch had pressed for in view of the enormous amount of art removed by purchase from the Netherlands and their well-founded suspicion that a substantial proportion of it was in private hands in the British Zone. Tracing such art and returning it to its original owners was a task of a different magnitude to the process of returning the collections which had come under British control in the immediate aftermath of Germany's collapse. In comparison returning the works of art gathered in the main British Collecting Point at Celle was relatively straightforward once the legal framework had been agreed given the easily identifiable nature of much of this art and the discovery of many of the records which the Germans had kept of their looting.

A second category of art whose restitution remained difficult even after the ACC had settled on a definition in January 1946 was of course art which had been transferred to the neutral countries during the war. Though the Allies had, in a declaration of 5 June 1945 assumed supreme authority in Germany and claimed the right to exercise control over German assets abroad in the Communiqué of the Potsdam Conference issued on 2 August 1945, such authority was extremely difficult to apply in practice. The Allies had limited leverage over the neutrals and attempts to apply the claimed right to dispose of looted assets deposited in their countries were fiercely resisted.

Substantial information was available in London as the war drew to an end to suggest that Switzerland had been prominent amongst those neutrals receiving art looted by the Germans. Accordingly, Squadron Leader Cooper, of the MFA and A Branch, was dispatched there in February 1945 to investigate this trade. His reports of this visit, and a second, longer, one he made in the autumn of that year, give a vivid account of the involvement of a number of Swiss dealers in efforts by several individual Germans, most notably Goering, to build up collections of looted art.

In his first report, Cooper detailed his efforts to identify some of the looted art which had reached Switzerland and through what channels and set in train further investigations to be carried out by the Legation. He noted that it appeared that very few people were involved in the traffic in looted art in Switzerland and that he had not discovered anything linking Swiss museums or the more important collectors to looted art. Although he had spoken to most of those involved in the trafficking, and amassed considerable evidence about which works had passed through their hands, he was unsure what had happened to looted art once it reached Switzerland and considered there was no limit to the quantity of works of art which may been deposited by, or was being held for, those who involved themselves in handling the loot. By the time he completed his second report he was able to give a more authoritative account of art looted from Allied nationals and discovered in Switzerland. In his description of the negotiations Allied officials had held with the Swiss (in which he had taken part) to secure the right for the owners of looted assets to try to recover their property from Switzerland, Cooper revealed the practical and legal obstacles to be surmounted in any attempt at restitution of art from Switzerland.

The story of British policy towards restitution of looted art mirrors that of restitution in general. At the war's end restitution was one of the most pressing problems confronting both the governments of the newly-liberated countries which had suffered so terribly and the Occupying Powers in Germany. But these governments had other equally pressing problems- securing reparations for some of their material losses, demobilization, the needs of millions of displaced persons, how to feed, house and pacify a devastated Germany for example. Many of these problems demanded solutions which conflicted in some way with an ideal restitution policy. In the circumstances of 1945 and 1946, restitution of looted art from the British Zone of Germany was an immense, intractable, task. The task was not completed down to the last painting, some individuals were certainly left with cause for grievance, but intensive effort had resulted in much effective restitution of art to governments of the countries from which it had been taken. The Western Allies' recognition that they had not been able to complete the task of restitution meant that the Bonn Conventions (signed in 1952 and effective from 1955) which terminated the Occupation regime in western Germany included provision for the Federal Republic to establish an Agency to handle outstanding matters relating to the restitution of cultural property.

Mr. Nikolai Gubenko

DEPUTY CHAIRMAN, COMMITTEE ON CULTURE, STATE DUMA
RUSSIA

Break-out Session on Nazi-Confiscated Art Issues: Government
Restitution Policies: Postwar to Present

Ladies and gentlemen,

Each one of us, who participates in this conference, bears a great responsibility because it touches interests of two sides: of victims and their executioners, the good and evil. We cannot permit any ambiguity, any streamlining.

The organizers of the conference asked me to clarify certain details of the Law "On cultural Treasures Transferred to the Union of Soviet Socialist Republics as a result of the World War II and Located on the Territory of the Russian Federation" adopted by the Russian parliament. During the procedure of drafting the law (and it took three years), the Law was attacked by mass-media, government officials and public figures of Germany. I cannot, but admire the unanimity with which certain European countries supported Germany in its negative reaction to the Law.

This reminds me the unanimity of certain countries on the eve of the World War II. It is known, that one of the main objectives of this war, criminal from the point of view of the international law, was the genocide against the Slavic, as well as Jewish races. "One of the main assignments, said Hitler, is to halt the growth of the Slavic race. I have the right to dispose of millions from the sub-race, who are multiplying like worms." Fieldmarshal Reihenau, in an order to the Nazi army wrote: "The principal objective of the campaign against the Jewish-Bolshevik system is the outright destruction of its power and influence of European culture. No historic or art treasures of the East have any significance." "An outrage and tyranny will be on extremely fitting form of government for the people of the USSR," - seconded him relchsleiter Rosenberg, the one who headed the Department, which robbed our museums, libraries and churches. The "Ost" plan emphasized: "The matter not only deals with the destruction of government. More important, is the destruction of Russians as nation."

27 million killed, of them - 2 million Jewish compatriots; 1710 (Seventeen hundred and ten) fully or partly destroyed cities, 70000 (seventy thousand) villages, 1670 (sixteen hundred and seventy) ruined churches and mosques, 532 synagogues, 237 chapels, 427 destroyed or looted museums, nearly 200 (two hundred) million destroyed and stolen books, more than 600,000 (six hundred thousand) lost cultural works. This is the amount of the USSR's losses in the World War II. At the Nuremberg Process the Soviet Union offered 39 volumes of documentary evidence of the destruction and looting of its cultural property. What other country could provide such evidence?!

And in the context of the problem we envisage here, a discriminative approach towards peoples of the USSR-victims of the Nazis is not permissible, because the Soviet Union suffered the most.

Russia has a normal right to compensation. But because the mass media is attacking our international rights with regards to our Law I would like to present to you the arguments of Parliament of the Russian Federation.

Fascist Germany and its partners in crime can console themselves in the hope that the international rights lag behind the moral principles of humanity; that the criminal actions which took place 53 years ago will no longer be considered criminal from the legal point of view. I reject this assumption.

The law is based on the international legal principles and other acts, specified in article 2 of the Law. Among the conference materials is the English translation made by US experts.

All these international legal acts are maintained for all aspects on transferred cultural treasures, retain their validity for property relations developed in response to these documents. The property rights of Russia including the right to transferred cultural values acquired as compensation for caused damaged emerge just from these documents.

The grounds for this statement are in the peace treaties with former enemy states signed in 1947. For instance, the Paragraph one (1) of Clause 79 (seventy nine) of the peace treaty with Italy that is identical in relevant aspects to similar treaties with Bulgaria, Hungary and Romania states: "Every Allied power shall possess the right to take, retain, abolish or initiate any other action in respect of property, rights and interests in a whole that for a day of entry into force of the present treaty shall be located at its territory and belong to Italy or Italian citizens, and also use this property or its gain for the purposes this power considers as desirable."

It follows that the instruction of the Allied powers concerning property of former enemy states and their citizens found at their territory was the term of the peace treaty. This standard does not contain any exception concerning cultural values.

The fact of refusal of former enemy states of any claims towards Allied powers confirms this conclusion.

For example, item 1 of article 76 of the Peace Agreement with Italy, identical to the corresponding articles of the Peace Agreements with Bulgaria, Hungary and Finland, states (I quote): "On behalf of the Italian Government and the Italian citizens, Italy gives up all claims of all natures to the Allied and United Powers, which were associated directly with the war afforded by measures taken in the result of the War in Europe after the first September 1939."

1 can remind you of one more document adopted by the Control Council in April 1947. The document "Quadrilateral Procedure of Restitution," stipulated: "If the restitution of the object itself is impossible, the right of the exacting side to restitution is satisfied by compensation from German property with articles equivalent value." It is clearly obvious, that in these cases the substituted object became the property of the exacting side. The same condition was applied to the Peace Agreement signed in 1947 with the axis countries.

Item 9 of article 75 of the Peace Agreement with Italy (as well as the Peace Agreements with Bulgaria and other satellite countries) envisages: "If in individual cases, it is impossible for Italy to restitute cultural objects - taken by the Italian army from the territory of a United Nation - which have artistic, historical and archaeological value, then Italy must compensate that United Nation with similar objects with approximately equivalent values."

Therefore, according to the abovementioned acts, the Soviet Union had the right to confiscate and own the cultural treasures of former hostile states.

At the same time the former hostile countries confirmed their denial of claims of all nature, including those dealing with assets, to the Allied Powers and the United Nations.

One of the opponents of the Law Mr. Kurt Zir from the Zurich University ironically noted, that "Russia discovered new sources of international public law." It is not astonishing, that Russia "discovered" the documents of the Control Council in Germany and the Peace Agreement of 1947, signed by the governments of many countries, but it is really astonishing, that these acts are still ignored by many opponents of the Russian Law, who in their critical remarks first of all cite the declarations, conventions of UNESCO and other acts of international law of the 50's - 70's being fully aware that no legal document is retroactive.

Furthermore, you know that not every Allied Power and states of the anti-Hitler coalition had rights for restitution. In the resolutions of the Control Council from the 17th of April 1946 it was clearly indicated: "The right for restitution is granted only to the states, which were completely or partially occupied." For example, the United States of America has no right to claim any restitution, because its territory was not occupied. Much less Germany has no right to claim restitution, because it carries the biggest responsibility for waging the cruelest war in the history of mankind.

The discussion about the legitimate nature of the acts of the Control Council possessing absolute legal and executive power at the territory of Germany can be considered groundless. Their competence and efficiency were confirmed in the Joint Declaration by the governments of the German Democratic Republic and Federal Republic of Germany, addressed on the 12th of September 1990 to the ministers of international affairs of the USSR, Great Britain, USA and France. This Declaration states: "The measures on withdrawal of assets, adopted on the basis of the rights and supremacy of the occupational authorities (in 1945-1949) are irreversible. The German government, considering the historic development, takes this into evidence and will not publish the regulatory acts, which may contradict the above cited part of the Joint Declaration."

For lack of time, I will briefly touch upon some principles of the Law, in order to fulfill the recommendations of our conference. Although, when put into practice, these recommendations do not possess any measures of enforcement. The process of restitution of the cultural treasures is, to a greater extent, a problem of bilateral relations, where the main source of jurisdiction and the only act to become law is the treaty, the agreement between the countries.

Article 8 of the Law clearly defined the transferred cultural values, which is not included in the definition of the property of the Russian State and can be conveyed to the other countries and individuals.

Firstly, these are cultural values, with regard to which the interested state will provide evidence that it demanded its restitution before expiration of the terms, determined by the Peace Agreements with Bulgaria, Hungary, Italy, Romania, Finland. The council of ministers of the USSR determined the term in the Soviet zone of occupation in Germany - the 1st of February 1950.

Second, cultural values, which belonged to religious organizations and private charity organizations, which did not serve the interests of Nazism.

Third, cultural treasures, which belonged to the individuals, deprived of these assets because of their active fight with Nazism. In this includes those who were involved in national defense from occupation and those who were taken for their race, religion and national origin.

In accordance with recommendations of the Council of Europe, cultural treasures, representing family relies, may be given to the representatives of the families, that owned them.

Taking into account the legal character of the retrieval of cultural treasures in 1945-1949, which took place only at the government level of the interested countries, the law maintains the established rules. The law states: "Claims on transferred cultural treasures... can be made by the government of the state, who makes a claim of these treasures, strictly to the government of the Russian Federation; claims of individuals and legal entities, municipal organs, social and other organizations and corporations will not be accepted."

And finally, the German side consistently proclaims that they have none of our treasures on their territory. Nevertheless, in 1990 the weekly magazine "Zeit" wrote: "The Russians were robbed twice, first by fascist Germany and then by their allies. 80% fell to Americans. The English, French and Russians were satisfied with 20%." The relations between USA and Russia are too delicate now that I would not like to elaborate on this subject for the lack of time. I admit that "Zeit" has dispersed this information with the purpose that search of Russian values shall be directed on the wrong track.

It is hard to imagine that Germans did not know the location of the transferred Russian cultural treasures or even the direction they traveled with respect to its territory.

I won't be amazed, if cultural treasures of the victims of the Holocaust are hidden in the same "coves," as the cultural treasures removed from the Soviet Union.

In June of 1945 the prominent representatives of scientific and cultural communities of our country - actor Mihoels, writers Bergemson, Sutskover, the academicians Obnorskii, Lebedev, Shishmarev, professors Greenberg and Feter - turned to Stalin with the following letter: "Dear Joseph Vissarionovich! The Germans have destroyed all the Jewish book depositories on all territories, which they temporarily occupied. They carried away manuscripts that were centuries old, antiquity works, and rare books of great value. The basis for further study of Jewish culture in the USSR is seriously damaged. We believe that in conjunction with the decisions of the Crimean Conference that ordered the Germans to compensate by nature all the distraction they inflicted. Germany firstly should be obliged to return to the USSR all that was stolen and taken to Germany; Secondly, to remove the monuments of Hebrew culture stored in book archives of Berlin, Munich, Frankfurt, and Leipzig and transferred them to the corresponding libraries and museums of the USSR."

Hundreds of thousands of similar letters came from the Ukrainians, Russians, Tartars and representatives of hundreds of other nationalities which where victims of Hitler's genocide.

One year ago, when our Law was not yet adopted, Russian mass media conducted a research of public opinion. The result was unanimous. 86% supported the Law. And it is natural, because the language of this Law is the language of justice.

Those who perished are gone. In the same Jews there are Russians, French, a lot of other nationalities all together. They are my father, Ukrainian, who went to the front when I was yet in mother's belly. They are my mother, Russian, who has been hanged by Germans in Odessa because she hid Jews, when I was eleven months old. They are dead victims. We must think about today's people. It will be a shame to divide into "ours" and "aliens" those victims who survived. We must unite all efforts aimed at just compensation for every victim of the tragedy regardless of nationality.

Mrs. Charlotte E. van Rappard-Boon

HEAD INSPECTOR, MINISTRY OF EDUCATION, CULTURE AND SCIENCE
THE NETHERLANDS

The Fate of Works of Art in the Netherlands During and After World War II

Break-out Session on Nazi-Confiscated Art Issues: Government
Restitution Policies, Postwar to Present

Just before World War II the once thriving art trade in the Netherlands came to a virtual standstill due to the economic circumstances and the threat of the war. At the start of 1940 most art dealers were in the possession of large stocks of works which had remained unsold for some years. On the other hand, in the Netherlands the possession of works of art in private hands was not restricted to the rich and very rich bourgeoisie but, as was the case in the seventeenth century, many moderately prosperous middle class families possessed one or more good quality paintings, Chinese blue and white ceramics and other precious antiques. Amongst these families was a large number of families of Jewish descent who, thanks to the open Dutch society which had welcomed them in the times when they were persecuted elsewhere, had flourished in the trade and the liberal professions.

These two factors form part of the explanation why the disappearance of works of art from the Netherlands to Nazi Germany - whether by looting, confiscation or sale - took place on such an unprecedented scale.

As happened in France, already during the German occupation Dutch art historians started compiling lists of works of art which they knew to have left the country. Also, already during the war the exiled Dutch Government in London prepared an extensive and complex set of measures with regard to legal restitution. One of these Dutch measures forbade to sell Dutch assets, including objects of art, to the enemy without prior permission.

As soon as the war ended, efforts to track down works of art in Germany and to return them to their original owners were gathered together in a single service, called the Netherlands Art Property Foundation (SNK). This service cooperated closely with the allied forces in Germany, especially with the Monuments and Fine Arts & Archives Service (MFA&A). On the basis of detailed lists made up from forms in which missing works of art were reported, the Allies tried to find as many works of art as possible. These forms were based in requests by private persons and on information compiled by the Foundation itself from the administration of objects confiscated by the Germans, on transport lists of works looted by the Germans or by firms which collaborated with them and on records of sales by auction houses and art dealers. These efforts were often severely hampered - as ours are still today - due to the fact that only well-known works of art were known in detailed descriptions detailed enough to recognize them easily or were even photographed.

Identification of a work of art listed for example: as "Farmers making merry at a tavern by the workshop of van Ostade" without any measurements of further description, is an extremely fortuitous business. Hundreds of paintings must exist answering to this kind of caption. Thus mistakes in identification of objects were made and not always corrected afterwards. Also, works of art that were nearly impossible to identify, mostly decorative art, were shipped back to the country that seemed the most likely to be their country of origin. In this way most Delft blue-and-white tiles were sent to Holland though they might as well have come for example form a French collection.

All the same, seeing how people in the office of the Art Foundation worked in those years, when Holland was recovering from its great war losses and money and means to run an adequate administration were scarce, one is filled with admiration. Without a computer, but using an endless amount of paper files and lists ordered according the artist names, original owners, art dealers or auction houses they reconstructed the provenance of many works of art.

The Foundation recovered many thousands of objects of art and returned them to their rightful owners, and also organized "viewing days" for people to identify their property. Many objects which were recovered, were works that had been sold during the occupation by the art trade violating Dutch law. These objects became in principle the property of the Dutch State. Objects for which the owner could not be found or for which claims could not be recognized because of lack of proof came under the custodianship of the State. What remained, after restitutions to the owners and after sale of part of the objects, was registered in the 1950's and forms the so called NK-collection of the Dutch State. Details about the work of the Netherlands Art Property Foundation can be found in the introduction of the report Origins Unknown.

This report, which is available here today, was published by the Dutch Government in April 1998. It also describes the methods of investigation which we use today. Recently questions concerning these remaining works of art have been asked. Might not modern methods of research, use of database and vast modern documentation systems such as that of Netherlands Institute for Art History enable us to find more information about original owners than was previously possible? The pilot study was done for a hundred works of art, both paintings and decorative art. Because sufficient new details concerning the provenance of these objects were found, the Dutch government decided to extend the study to comprise all objects of the NK-collection which were recuperated after the war. Of course, after all these years much of the documentation which might have helped is lost or destroyed, but by gathering circumstantial evidence from catalogues of pre-war exhibitions, of private collections, of art dealers administrations, of insurance lists, etc. links might be found which were lost before.

Because a work of art can mean an extremely personal tie with the past and can have great emotional value for a family, the Dutch government plans to proceed on a case by case basis regarding the restitution of works of art of the NK-collection. It is still possible for a private person to file a claim on an object in the NK-collection, provided it regards a work of art which has not been previously claimed and of which sufficient proof of the original ownership can be found. Also earlier claims which were not accepted before can be filed again if substantial new facts have come to light. This year two paintings have already proved to belong the Jewish families that did not file claims after the War. These paintings are being returned to their rightful owners.

The works of art of which no new facts concerning their provenance are found during the investigation, will stay available in the future if new facts come to light.

Works of art in the possession of private owners who are in good faith, are in principle protected by Dutch Civil Law. However, in these cases possible claimants and present owners can apply to the Netherlands Institute for Art History and our office, for more information concerning provenance and possible postwar claims. Possible solutions for these cases could include arbitration and a decision by common consent along the lines similar to the American Museums Association.

In the same way as the State Government is researching its collections, the Dutch museums under the aegis of the Dutch Museum Association are researching the acquisitions made during the war and in the after-war years, to investigate whether they acquired objects which were looted or confiscated by the enemy from Jewish owners. The museums are conducting their own research aided by the Inspectorate for Cultural Heritage which checks the museum data and adds facts which it has found during its own research.

If there is any evidence that objects were Nazi confiscated Jewish property, it is expected that the governing bodies of the Museums, will make every effort to ensure that they are returned to their original owners of their heirs.

With regard to the timetable of the state and museums investigation, the museum investigation will be finished and published next year. The State investigation will be finished in three years time and its interim-results will be published during those years in regular reports.

Further details about the investigations and about restitution of art objects can be found in several leaflets which we brought with us.

We hope these investigations solve most outstanding questions about the provenance of art objects, though truth commands us to say that some of these will probably never be answered.

Colonel Seymour J. Pomrenze

FIRST DIRECTOR, OFFENBACH ARCHIVAL DEPOT
UNITED STATES

Personal Reminiscences of the Offenbach Archival Depot, 1946-49: Fulfilling International and Moral Obligations

Break-out Session on Nazi-Confiscated Art Issues: Identification of Art, Archives and Databases

INTRODUCTION

In late February 1946, my colleague First Lieutenant Leslie 1. Poste, a Library and Archives specialist, drove me through a blinding snowstorm to Offenbach. En route, Lt. Poste briefed me on the Offenbach Collection Point's origins, his role in selecting a building within the I.G. Farben complex on the Main River, and his concern that restitution operations be expedited in accordance with military regulations. Since its establishm:nt in July 1945, the operation had yet to restitute any materials.

Lt. Poste also reviewed the operations of Hitler's Einsatzstab Reichsleiter Rosenberg (ERR) and its educational branch the Institut zur Erforschung der Judenfrage (Institute to Research the Jewish Question). The ERR, backed by German military forces, had traced Jewish, Masonic, Socialist, and other anti-Nazi cultural objects throughout Germany and Nazi-occupied Europe and had deposited them in many places, especially in Frankfurt am Main in the Rothschild Library, Hungen and Hirzenhain in Hesse, and all over Bavaria. The ERR targets ranged from occupied Ukraine to the French-Spanish border and from Greece to the British Isle of Man. The ERR even raided Italy, an axis power. After Kristallnacht, the ERR collected items to save and use them for Nazism.

Lt. Poste also described the U.S. combat and occupation operations to protect and restitute the looted collections. He and other Museums Fine Arts and Archives personnel felt the collections at the Rothschild Library and other places should be moved to a single large, secure facility. The I.G. Farben building at Offenbach was their site of choice.

FIRST IMPRESSIONS OF OFFENBACH

My first impressions of the Offenbach Collecting Point were overwhelming and amazing at once. As I stood before a seemingly endless sea of crates and books, I thought what a horrible mess! What could I do with all these materials? How could I carry out my assignment successfully? Beyond the mess, however, was an even larger mission. Indeed, the only action possible was to return the items to their owners as quickly as possible.

The Offenbach Collecting Point was housed in well-guarded five-story concrete building suitable for use as a warehouse following repairs. Inside, however, there were only six or seven Germans, headed by an U.S. civilian with displaced person status, who did very little. Many crates, packages, stacks, and loose piles covered several floors. Clearly, the operation was not being run effectively. My mission was to revive this organization in order to accomplish my mission successfully. Hence I launched the following actions.

THE OFFENBACH ARCHIVAL DEPOT

The Offenbach Archival Depot was officially established under military directive, in conjunction with Monuments, Fine Arts and Archives Wiesbaden, on March 2, 1946. As Director of the Offenbach Archival Depot (OAD), I received extensive authority and broad mission responsibilities within Greater Hesse. The operation's new designation indicated my function as archivist. Archival principles, such as restoration of the original order, were crucial at this stage. As part of the directive, an organization chart served as a blueprint for action by three branch chiefs responsible for administrative, operations, and liaisons, respectively.

The OAD needed many hardworking personnel, and requested about 50 people a week throughout March 1946 from the local German employment office. By March 28, the OAD had nearly 180 employees. Good working conditions were essential. Heat, light, clean floors, repaired windows, and heavy-duty shelves were provided. U.S. sources requisitioned and supplied enough coal and gasoline. And the large OAD maintenance staff - about 30 - did an excellent job of ensuring a pleasant working environment in the depot.

The I.G. Farben complex had security staff on site, as did the OAD. Together, security watched employees for theft items, particularly small books that were easy to hide. Some thefts did occur - some were detected, others were not. Spot checks of OAD employees were also conducted. Some staff members were even strip-searched. Moreover, internal telephones on each floor were activated through an OAD switchboard.

SORTING, IDENTIFYING, PRESERVING

The OAD received tons of materials from Frankfurt, Hirzenhain, Hungen, and many other German locations. By March 25, 1946, the OAD had processed - received and/or shipped - over 1.8 million items contained in 2,351 crates, stacks, packages, and piles.

Crates, stacks, packages, and piles bearing some indication of the country of origin were spot checked and set inside pending restitution claims. Following some classification by country and by language, the semi-identifiable piles awaited further processing. The unidentifiable books and other materials were left alone until an opportunity arose for careful study by competent persons - professionals like Professor Pinson, Chaplain Isaiah Rackovsky, Rabbi Maurice Liber, Dr. Gershom Scholem, Lucy Dawidowitcz, and knowledgeable displaced person volunteers. Much thought was given to improving and expediting the identification process. My successor, Captain Isaac Bencowitz, who began to intern at Offenbach in April 1946, designed a somewhat unique system, which I called the "Bencowitz sorting system," identifying books from ex libris bookplates or stamps found inside book jackets.

Many books and documents required care and preservation as a result of mishandling, damage during transit, water, mold, and neglect. The OAD did not possess any equipment or materials for care and preservation. Luckily, I learned that one of the employees - a former monk - had worked with documents at a religious order. I assigned him to devise homemade care and preservation techniques. One method he used for drying wet books and documents involved hanging them from clothespins and applying extra heat. The technique worked very well.

RESTITUTION

What did the OAD accomplish? As of August 1947 some 2,000,000 books and other identifiable materials had been restituted and distributed. I am proud - at this late state - to relate to you that the United States restituted well over 93 percent of the Nazi-looted materials. Five countries -Germany (Berlin), the Netherlands, France, the USSR, and Italy received the following quantities of materials: Germany (Berlin), 700,000; The Netherlands, 329,000; France, 328,000; the USSR, 232,000; and Italy, 225,000.

In addition to items restituted to governments, the YIVO Institute for Jewish Research with worldwide headquarters in New York received 92,000 items. Under direction of the U.S. State Department, I supervised the return of these materials to the United States in June 1947. The American Jewish Joint Distribution Committee distributed, on loan, of 24,000 books to the Displaced Persons; and the Library of Congress Mission received some 20,000 books. German institutions other than the Preussisches Staatsbibliothek received 50,000 items; Poland 25,000; and Belgium, Czechoslovakia, United Kingdom, Greece, Hungary, and Yugoslavia each received less than 10,000 items.

OAD HISTORY

Both Isaac Bencowitz and I understood Offenbach's importance and the need for an historical record of its activities. We wrote detailed, factual monthly reports. We prepared pictorial albums - I did the first one, and Bencowitz did three others. We saved correspondence relating to OAD operations, including liaison relationships. These items are on deposit in over 20 archival boxes in the U.S. National Archives in Washington, D.C. as well as deposited with Yad Vashem in Israel.

Bencowitz also recorded his experiences in his diary, from which I share an eloquent entry describing the signification of Offenbach's history:

I would walk into the loose document room to take a look at the things there and find it impossible to tear myself away from the fascinating piles of letters, folders, and little personal bundles. Not that what you held in your hand was so engrossing, but rather what the next intriguing item might be. Or, in the sorting room, I would come upon a box of books which the sorters had brought together, like scattered sheep into one fold - books from a library which once had been in some distant town in Poland, or an extinct Yeshiva. There was something sad and mournful about these volumes ... as if they were whispering a tale of yearning and hope since obliterated... I would find myself straightening out these books and arranging them in the boxes with a personal sense of tenderness as if they had belonged to someone dear to me, someone recently deceased

AFTER OFFENBACH

I returned to Offenbach in 1947 on assignment for the Library of Congress Mission to arrange the transfer to New York of the vast YIVO archives. Later, I briefly participated in restituting the Collegio Rabbinico de Firenze's historic library, including the incunabula, to Italy. I have remained involved in restitution efforts throughout most of my military service, primarily as the U.S. Department of Defense Representative to the U.S. Interagency Committee on Captured ("Seized") Records and other restitution-related assignments. I worked with German representatives of Konrad Adenauer to return German military records. I also participated briefly in the transfer of the U.S. Army Berlin Documents Center to the State Department, which have been turned over to the German government.

In retrospect, Offenbach proved to be a most unusual and challenging assignment - a high point in my 35 years of military and civilian service. Offenbach was a very unusual part of what I call the "cultural Holocaust." Participating at Offenbach on the greatest book restitution in history now seems truly providential. I share Lt. Poste's sentiments that,

Facts and figures on the Offenbach Archival Depot fail to reveal the intensely moving story of this phase of

restitution activity. Through the depot passed the remnants of age-old cultures, and particularly of a culture which survived despite the vicissitudes of interminable persecutions and periodic massacres. These books and objects were what was left of the hundreds of Jewish institutions of learning, of Jewish communities, wiped out by the Holocaust. Few can fathom the depth of the Jewish tragedy of which remnants stood as a sad memorial.

CONCLUSION AND OUTLOOK

In closing, I am inspired by actions of the international community to convene at the Washington Conference on Holocaust-Era Assets to resolve lingering issues of restitution and archival access. To this end, I support and encourage efforts to identify items improperly restituted, and to negotiate with rightful owners for redistribution of such materials. in addition, I recommend governments and institutions -examine and report the fate of restituted materials as well as prepare inventories and provide access to archival materials restituted vis-à-vis Offenbach.

It is at this exciting moment in history, that silent archives where facts have gathered dust and awaited the avenging moment of their revelation may at long last find voice.

Dr. Constance Lowenthal
DIRECTOR, COMMISSION FOR ART RECOVERY,
WORLD JEWISH CONGRESS
WORLD JEWISH RESTITUTION ORGANIZATION
UNITED STATES

Break-out Session on Nazi-Confiscated Art Issues: Identification of Art, Archives and Databases

The Commission for Art Recovery was formed to reunite pre-war owners (or their heirs) with art that was looted from them by the Nazis and their collaborators. It will also locate and recover heirless art for the benefit of Jewish communities.

The formation of the Commission was announced at a meeting of the World Jewish Restitution Organization in September 1997. It operates through the World Jewish Congress - American Section. Ronald S. Lauder is the Chairman.

I began as director in mid-January 1998. The Commission has a staff of five. Menachem Rosensaft serves as Special Counsel.

The problem we seek to address is familiar to everyone attending this conference. Much has been written about, and our speakers in the plenary session have already described, Nazi art confiscations from private collections and from Jewish art dealers' inventories.

Nazi art thefts were a violation of international law at the time they took place, even though the Third Reich enacted laws to give the appearance of legality to some transactions. Knowledge of this led to the Allies' Declaration of London, which suggested that nullifying forced sales would be important. Taking spoils violated Article 56 of the 1907 Hague Convention, to which Germany was party. Nazi confiscations of cultural property were crimes at the Nuremberg Trials.

In addition, these thefts were inextricably linked to genocide. Often the looting immediately preceded the escape of the victims, or for the less fortunate, their deportation and extermination.

Some plunder was official, and some was the result of aggressive collecting by high level Nazi officials like von Ribbenntrop and Hermann Goering. During the German occupation of France, Goering regularly visited the Jeu de Paume, the little museum on the Place de la Concorde. New shipments of art seized from Jews arrived every day.

During his frequent visits, Goering made his choices, and his initials were stamped in the margin of the inventories of seized Jewish collections next to those items that he wanted.

The western Allies were well aware of the looting and investigated it after the war. It is well known that the Allies found vast stores of art in caves and mines. Some belonged to Germany's museums, but much of it was confiscated art destined for Hitler's planned museum in Linz. They also found traincars near Berchtesgaden filled with art amassed by Goering.

Some art that the Nazis looted from Jews was found, at the end of the war, in the Soviet sector. This was not returned; Soviet policy determined that Red Army Trophy Brigades would remove it to the former Soviet Union. Collections of Hungarian Jews, for example those of the Hatvany and Herzog families, are today in Russia, looted first by the Nazis and later taken by the Soviets.

The western Allies returned, and could only return, what was found on German territory after the war. Art confiscated from German, French, and Belgian Jews that had already been absorbed by the art market, through Jew auctions and wartime trades, was untouched by these efforts.

The first step in re-uniting Jewish confiscation victims with their art is to identify it. This is called for in the Principles circulated by Under Secretary Eizenstat's office. The Commission for Art Recovery has designed a computer database to assist in ways that were not possible until now. The New York State Banking Department Holocaust Claims Processing Office is using the same software, and the two organizations are sharing all information.

The simple concept of the database is a matching of "Lost and Found" art that is executed in a very sophisticated way. The Commission's database will match claimed works of art with published works whose whereabouts are usually known and whose provenances give reason to believe that they might have been looted. The software developed for the Commission by Gallery Systems, Inc. is unique in this ability.

We are soliciting information from claimants on the art they lost. Often their descriptive information is insufficient to identify it. Of course, people who fled the Nazis were unlikely to have carried detailed inventories of their collections with them. One claimant's Austrian mother made her inventory from memory in the London Underground during the Blitz.

The Commission developed its claim form with the help of colleagues at the Art Loss Register and the New York State Banking Department Holocaust Claims Processing Office. Claimants may contact the Commission's office or download claim forms from our website (www.wjc-artrecovery.org).

We also ask for accurate information about the various names, residences, and dates of birth of the victims.

To help improve the quality of information for claimants, we will cross-index claimant family names with those in Nazi looting records and with names of homeowners insurance policyholders whose policies had art schedules. If the names match, we will then obtain copies of the Nazi inventories or the insurance art schedules and fill in the descriptive information. Even if a grandchild-claimant is unaware that his family had insurance, we may be able to get a list of art and antiques from an old insurance policy. These are fairly detailed inventories that can supplement claimants' recollections and strengthen a case.

Our criteria for describing art are compatible with museum standards and the Getty Information Institute's "Object ID", which is used by many types of organizations that need to identify art, including: law enforcement agencies, insurers, etc. Our database will also use two authority vocabularies developed by the Getty Information Institute for geographic names (Thesaurus of Geographic Names - TGN) and for artists' names (Union List of Artists' Names - ULAN). These computer aids make it possible to find the works of an artist even though his name may have many variants, i.e. Michelangelo Merisi is known in Italian and in English as Caravaggio, in French as le Caravage. Jan Brueghel (or Bruegel) the Younger was also known as "Velvet" Brueghel. Likewise, place names vary in languages and time, but our computer will recognize that Lemberg is Lvov is Lviv.

We are now officially accepting claims, but even before a public announcement, the Commission received correspondence and telephone calls from 55 families whose losses occurred in eight countries: Austria, Czechoslovakia, France, Germany, Italy, The Netherlands, Poland, and Yugoslavia. We have met with relatives of Alphonse Kann, Jacques Goudstikker, Jacques Helft, and Georges Wildenstein.

To develop our catalog list of Found art, we drew up a list of the names of looted families and art agents and middlemen mentioned in the reports of the Office of Strategic Services investigators and in "The Rape of Europa" by Lynn Nicholas and "The Lost Museum" by Hector Felicianc

Since many looted works of art were sold and entered the art market before the war was over, we guessed that some portion of the highest quality works would be published. Our staff went to the library and looked for provenances that included the names on our list or were simply blank for the critical years. These are works that could be matched with art sought by our claimants. We began with catalogues of permanent collections and exhibitions assembled from museums and private collections. Our research team will go on to catalogues raisonnes (the scholarly publications that include all the works of a particular artist), and other exhibition catalogues.

In just four months, after consulting about 220 books, we found over 1,700 possible matches. The scholars who prepared these catalogues have included such names as Goering, the Fuhrer Museum in Linz, Hans Wendland, apparently without self-consciousness. The Commission's findings reveal that these works are more numerous than previously assumed. When museums said they thought the problem was small, they were sincere. I believe that most current possessors have no idea of the art's tainted past. I believe that many of the scholars who included names of once notorious dealers in published provenances simply didn't recognize the names as having a connection with Nazi art looting.

The Commission's customized software will compare works of art with works of art and report possible matches to us, based on the number of category characteristics they share, categories like artist's name, subject, medium, approximate size. Even if the art matches on all criteria, this only means that further research is necessary. It may be a looted work of art that was never returned or it might be a recovered object which was sold legitimately by the pre-War owners.

The working database will neither be on the Internet nor "published." We are happy to share claimed art information with other restitution organizations and with the art market. We would welcome the opportunity to add other lists of claimed art to ours. We also welcome lists from museums of works whose provenance has gaps during the critical years, or has names of persons involved in the trade of Nazi-looted art.

The Commission has an agreement with the Art Loss Register to share information about the art claimed so that those works of art will be checked against the upcoming auction sales at the major houses (the Art Loss Register checks about 400,000 auction lots annually). This was arranged early on, so we designed our database for ease of electronic information transfer. We are open to discussions about sharing information with other organizations. As I mentioned, the New York State Banking Department Holocaust Claims Processing Office has chosen to use the Commission's database.

I have held talks with people in the art world (museums, dealers, auction houses), with law enforcement agencies, government officials, and art restitution groups. I believe this is essential. The solution to this problem requires cooperation across the board internationally, in the public and private sector, in the art trade and insurance industry.

An Advisory Committee for the database is in formation. Its members include Jane Kallir, President of Galerie St. Etienne and an expert on Egon Schiele; Robert Bergman, Director of the Cleveland Museum of Art; Charles Moffett, Sotheby's Vice President for Impressionist & Modern Paintings and a former curator and museum director.

In the coming months I expect to work with scholars of international law and others to study and develop Principles of Return to guide the Commission's work. The Principles put forward for adoption by this conference do not apply readily to looted art held by private individuals. Yet, I believe that most works of art that we will find will be in the hands of good faith purchasers who, under European legal systems, acquire good title. Many of the looted works have changed hands several or many times since 1945, and many of the buyers would be considered good faith purchasers under law. I am well aware of the difference between European law and that in the United States, Canada, and the United Kingdom. Here a thief cannot pass good title, but time limits may curtail a victim's rights. In Europe, a good faith purchase confers good title.

Some heirless works may be found in museums. We need to develop policy on heirless art (a) when there is one work of art in a private or public collection, and (b) when countries have not returned art to pre-war owners and a large number of works is under a single, national administration.

In spite of the complexities that surround this problem which we have inherited, I am hopeful that new research, new identification techniques, and a new will shall resolve it – a will demonstrated by this Conference. Our joint efforts can help to correct the inequities we have tolerated for too long.

Mr. Ronald S. Tauber

CHAIRMAN, THE ART LOSS REGISTER, INC.
UNITED STATES

Restitution of Looted Art: A Practical Approach

Break-out Session 01. Nazi-Confiscated Art Issues: Identification of
Art, Archives and Databases

This Conference on Holocaust era assets has the opportunity not only to formulate general principles, but also to encourage practical steps to help restitute looted art to rightful owners. I am the Chairman of the Art Loss Register Inc. which represents the world's largest private database of stolen art. The company was formed principally by the art and insurance industries in order to help identify and recover stolen art, to deter the trade in stolen art and to provide a central checkpoint to prospective purchasers and lenders. The database now comprises more than 100,000 items reported to have been stolen worldwide, and each year the Art Loss Register examines 400,000 auction lots to uncover stolen or looted items. Auction houses participating in this screening program include Sotheby's, Christie's, Phillips, Bonhams, Dorotheum (Vienna), Lempertz (Cologne), Bukowskis (Stockholm), Villa Grisebach (Berlin), and Finarte (Milan).

The majority of items on our database consists of contemporary thefts. Earlier this year, however, with the financial support of certain of our shareholders, principally Sotheby's and Aon Corporation, we began the expansion of our activity relating to Holocaust era assets. Based on our extensive experience in helping to recover stolen and missing art, we are convinced that a practical approach will result in identification and recovery of looted art. In general, the practical approach relies on two steps. First, to the fullest extent possible, all items of looted art should be entered on a database open to all organizations working in this area. Second, items on the database should be continuously checked against art entering the commercial market at the point of sale.

There is at present no single international listing of looted art and many of the existing publications, produced mainly just after the war, are now inevitably out of date. Our aim, working with others, is to create as complete a database as possible of works of art looted by the Nazis, Soviets, or others from public or private collections, preferably, though not exclusively, with claims attached. The Art Loss Register has carefully built bridges to the World Jewish Congress Commission for Art Recovery, the New York State Holocaust Claims Processing Office and the Holocaust Art Restitution Project. Our efforts represent an unusual level of cooperation between the private sector, government and philanthropic agencies. We are exchanging data and have succeeded in creating a unified Wartime Losses Claims Form.

Claims are accepted where there is a reasonable chance of identifying the item and the claim is judged to be authentic. Additional validation of claims would be required at the point of identification. During the past year, 560 Holocaust looted artworks have been reported to the Art Loss Register to add to the approximately 4,000 missing artworks from museum collections from Belgium, France, Germany, Hungary, Italy and Poland. All registrations of looted art from private individuals are free of charge, and the ALR will not charge its customary recovery fee when it is able to identify an individual's looted artwork in an auction house catalog or elsewhere.

The diversity of the art reported to us during the past year is striking. We registered on our database a portrait by Paul Gauguin of his son, Emile. This painting was seized by the Nazis from the collection of Jakob Goldschmidt in the early 1930's. The painting was sold at the Hans Lange auction house in September 1941 with other works confiscated from Jewish collections to raise money for the Hitler Jugend. We have also registered Impressionist pictures from the Paul Rosenberg collection; a Marieschi painting looted by the Gestapo in Vienna in 1940; a series of five hunting tapestries seized from the Berlin Oppenheimer collection on the orders of Hermann Goering; a collection of Dutch Old Masters apparently seized by Allied troops in Austria in 1945; and other paintings seized as war loot by the Red Army.

The first pillar of the practical approach, then, is the creation of a comprehensive database. The second pillar is the continuous examination of the commercial art market. Our staff of twenty examines auction house catalogs from around the world, responds to dealer, customs and police inquiries and is identifying the location of a stolen item nearly every day. Since our formation in 1991, we have recovered in excess of $75 million in value. To illustrate the effectiveness of our process, during just the past eighteen months we identified a Manet, a Monet, two Picassos, a Giacometti, and a de Kooning among many other items of lesser value; some of these pictures were reported stolen more than twenty years ago. In our view, as the database of looted art grows, we will be able to make significant matches in the commercial marketplace. Please understand that the auction houses are totally supportive of our efforts. They are not concerned that we will cause the withdrawal of some lots from sale. Quite the contrary, their business requirement is that a comprehensive data base be built as quickly as possible so that they can be assured that they do not offer looted art for sale in their salerooms.

As I have said, The Art Loss Register is committed to providing a pragmatic response to the task of identifying and, where possible, returning looted art to its rightful owners. We recommend that this Conference urge the adoption of the following practical guidelines with respect to the purchase, sale and ownership of works of art:

First, commercial sellers – galleries and auctioneers – should undertake due diligence, prior to sale, to determine the rightful provenance of a work of art through consultation with relevant databases and appropriate experts on art looting. The screening by the ALR each year of approximately 400,000 auction lots against the database of claims is a key part of this process. Increasingly, galleries are also using our service. The ALR is underpinning the screening program by providing the auction houses with a research effort that highlights pieces in catalogs whose provenance suggests that the item may have been looted and might therefore be problematic.

Second unless it is clear that the seller has already done so, a potential purchaser of art should consult the databases and appropriate experts to determine the rightful provenance of the item in question.

The third recommendation concerns works of art held by public and quasi-public institutions. The ALR is helping the museum community conduct due diligence with respect to the acquisition and display of works of art. In the United States, approximately twenty museums – including the Chicago Art Institute, the Metropolitan Museum of Art, the Museum of Modern Art, the Boston Museum of Fine Arts, the National Gallery of Art in Washington, the Indianapolis Art Museum and the Cleveland Museum of Art – are checking acquisitions, donations or existing exhibits against the ALR database. Many museums are already searching their holdings to determine whether any of the works may constitute looted art. We recommend that every museum and public institution be urged to conduct a rigorous self-examination of its

538   WASHINGTON CONFERENCE ON HOLOCAUST-ERA ASSETS

holdings in line with the statement adopted by the American Association of Museum Directors in Worcester this past June. These institutions should then create an inventory of "problem" pictures where the provenance is unclear or has problematic gaps. The creation of such an inventory of "problem" pictures, stored alongside the register of losses, would allow researchers and others to focus on potentially looted works.

This Conference serves an important purpose. Nothing that we do today can compensate for the catastrophes imposed by the Nazis on the Jewish people and so many others during the Holocaust era. We must do what we can, however. And we can and must see to it that all practical steps are taken to return stolen property to its rightful owners.

Ronald S. Tauber is the Chairman of The Art Loss Register, Inc. He is a former partner of the investment banking firm of Goldman, Sachs & Co. and a former partner of Stroock & Stroock & Lavan, a New York law firm.

Gilbert S. Edelson

ADMINISTRATIVE VICE PRESIDENT AND COUNSEL,
ART DEALERS ASSOCIATION OF AMERICA
UNITED STATES

Break-out Session on Nazi-Confiscated Art Issues: Identification of
Art, Archives and Databases

I speak today as a representative of the Art Dealers Association
of America which is known as ADAA.   ADAA is a non-profit
association of America's leading dealers in works of fine art, that is
painting, sculpture and works on paper from the early Renaissance to the
present.

ADAA's members are sensitive to the issues involved in Nazi-
looted art.   Many art dealers and their families, including past and
present ADAA members, were victims of Nazi persecution.   Their
inventory and their private collections were looted. Some perished, some
were imprisoned in concentration camps, some came to the United States
where they have made important contributions to the cultural life of this
nation.

We don't know precisely how many works were looted by the
Nazis. We don't know precisely how many looted works were returned
to their rightful owners. We don't know how many looted works were
not returned, or where they are now. We will never have complete
answers to these questions, but we must do everything in our power to
assemble the information. We can speculate and debate, but it is more
important that we act, that we get on with the work to be done in this
country. What is that work? I suggest the following:

First, we must stop all traffic in unrestituted Nazi-looted art.

Second, we must seek to identify works which are subject to
claims, and their owners.

Third, we must seek to resolve claims fairly and expeditiously.

First, as I have said, all traffic in unrestituted art must be ended.
To that effect ADAA has pledged that its members will not knowingly
sell such works.

ADAA members will continue to research the history of the
works of art which they offer. That research will be professionally
conducted by individuals uniquely qualified to do so by virtue of their

specialized knowledge and experience. ADAA members know that research into a provenance is not a title search and that there are frequently gaps in a work's provenance for perfectly legitimate reasons. They are also aware of the fact that because certain dealers' or collectors' names appear in a provenance does not necessarily mean that the work was looted and not restituted. I should note at this point, as a slight digression, that ADAA members will continue to assist museums which make inquiries about the provenance of works in their collections.

Our second task is the identification of unrestituted works and their owners. Many months ago, in testimony at the hearings so ably conducted by Congressman Leach, we said that the single most effective tool which dealers, collectors and museums could utilize in determining whether a given work of art has been stolen is a reliable, central source of information about its identity and the identity of any claimants to the work. We urged the creation of a central database containing that information.

We understand that such a database is now being created and will be maintained by the World Jewish Congress' Commission on Art Recovery under the effective leadership of Connie Lowenthal. ADAA will, of course, fully cooperate with this enterprise. One of our members, Jane Kallir, has been invited to join the advisory committee. She and other ADAA members will make their expertise in works of art and their experience in the field of stolen art available to the World Jewish Congress. We urge all other interested parties to do likewise in the hope that the database will be as complete as possible and fully operational at an early date. ADAA members will, of course, avail themselves of this important facility. They will also be consulting the Art Loss Register which is taking a very active and commendable role in the maintenance of a database of stolen works of art, now including Nazi-looted art.

I note that the FBI has placed information about stolen works of art on the Internet, where it is widely and freely available. I hope that the database on Nazi-looted art will also be on the Internet.

We believe that the first priority of a database ought to be the assembly and dissemination of claims by victims or their families of specific, identified works. We also believe it important that any claimed work be identified as precisely as possible.

Our next task is the resolution of claims. In the United States, our experience in the resolution of claims of ownership has thus far been limited. In the past 40 years, there have been only four or five court cases of which I am aware which involve Nazi-looted art.

Even on the basis of our limited experience, however, we know that a case involving Nazi-looted art can involve difficult and complex issues of law and fact. In such a case, a purchaser in good faith may be sued by the original owner, from whom the work was stolen. One of two innocent parties will be hurt.

American law favors the original owner. Under our jurisprudence good title to a stolen work does not pass. The European legal system, however, favors the good faith purchaser. Even in the United States the law varies from state to state on such issues as the applicable statute of limitations.

Likewise, any case involving Nazi-looted art may present difficult factual problems. After all, the claimed work was looted more than 50 years ago. Identification of the work may involve special problems. Witnesses may be gone; memories may be bad.

Any lawsuit is therefore likely to be lengthy and expensive. The costs could exceed the value of the work. And there is something else which serves to make such a case longer and more expensive — passion. I know of no lawsuit which engenders more passion, this side of the bedroom, than an action involving a work of art, especially one involving possession of the work.

We therefore urge the parties to any claim involving Nazi-looted art to consider mechanisms which exist for resolving claims without the necessity of litigation, such as mediation, arbitration and alternative dispute resolution. There have been suggestions that such cases be resolved by a commission or committee of experts. I would not agree. It must be kept in mind that each case is fact specific, and that it will therefore be decided on the basis of its unique facts. Each case will therefore require different expertise, which may be beyond the competence of a single committee. There are no "art experts"; there are only experts in specific and limited fields. Moreover, to the extent possible, the parties should be able to choose their own mediator, arbitrator or such other aide in the non-judicial resolution of a claim.

ADAA and its members are prepared to make their expertise available at no cost to parties who attempt to settle claims without litigation. Resolving such disputes promptly, fairly and inexpensively is in the base interest not only of the parties involved but of the entire art community.

Dr. Konstantin Akinsha

RESEARCH DIRECTOR,
PROJECT OF DOCUMENTATION OF WARTIME CULTURAL LOSSES
UNITED STATES

Break-out Session on Nazi-Confiscated Art Issues: Identification of
Art, Archives and Databases

The establishment of different databases, collecting information
about art works looted during WWII, is now a popular topic within the
circle of scholars and representatives of organizations and groups
involved in the search for the 'disappeared' cultural property of the
victims of the holocaust. There are many plans and ideas to create a
"total" database, which will include all possible claims and information
about nearly every artwork looted during the war. Unfortunately such an
undertaking doesn't appear very realistic. When we are addressing the
problem of the cultural property lost during the war, we are talking about
hundreds of thousands of paintings and objets d'art. It is difficult to
believe that tomorrow some organization will be ready to collect such a
quantity of information from archives throughout Europe and put it into
computer format.

Much more productive are the efforts of some European
countries (for example Austria) to post Internet lists of claims collected
by the governments in the first post-war years. However, not all
European governments are ready to make such information public. They
have a good reason. In many countries (for example the Netherlands,
Belgium, France, Austria) a portion of the art works returned by the
Allies after the end of the war was sold through government organized
auctions. The ground for such sales was that the "owners" of the pieces
were never found. However in many cases provenance of the works of
art proposed for sale was not carefully checked.

Today the traditional argument against putting information about
post-war claims in the public domain is that such a step could violate the
privacy of claimants. It seems, however that the real reason behind the
secrecy is different: to avoid scandals that could start if some art works,
sold by the governments after the war, will be recognized and claimed by
their real owners. The majority of recently established databases are of a
practical, workaday nature. Their task is to collect information about

claims and to provide detailed descriptions of the disappeared art works. However, not only "practical" databases could be of help in the research and understanding of the Nazi looting of Europe. No less important is historic research, which could have both a practical and academic value. Unfortunately, the Nazi looting of European culture is a part of the history of the 20th century, as it is a part of art history and the history of taste. Without detailed research of this dark chapter of our past, we will never understand it in its complexity.

I represent the Project of Documentation of Wartime Cultural Losses, an academic organization, the task of which is to research and to put in the public domain information about the confiscation and removal of cultural property during the war. We recently opened our web site, which you can find at the address: *doc.proj@loyola.edu*. The first project put by us on the web is dedicated to the looting of the Jewish collections of France. It includes reproductions of some documents of the notorious Arbeitsgruppe Louvre of the Einzatzstab Reichsleiter Rosenberg, responsible for confiscation of the Jewish art treasures in occupied France. In addition to lists of confiscated paintings selected for the Hitler museum in Linz and the private collection of Field marshal Herman Goering, we put on our web site photographs of exhibitions of looted art organized by the Nazis in Jeu de Paume, then the collecting point of the stolen masterpieces. These photos, proudly produced for the ERR files, were never published before. Using albums of photographs of thousands of paintings and objets d'art confiscated in France, which were presented by Alfred Rosenberg to Adolf Hitler, we succeeded to recognize art works put on display in the Jeu de Paume. You can see a virtual reconstruction of the notorious Nazi exhibitions of stolen art on our web site. By clicking on artworks displayed in the halls of Jeu de Paume, you will receive enlarged photos of them and information from which collection they were confiscated. At the moment we are researching the routes of the Nazi traffic of art works to Spain and South America at the end of WWII. Soon the results of this research will become available on our web site.

The Documentation Project is beginning research of the history and collections of the Hitler Museum in Linz. We hope to compose a complete catalogue of the most important Nazi collection of looted art in wartime Europe. We believe that if such information were available to the public it could be not only benefit historians and art historians but could prevent unpleasant scandals connected with the appearance of art works with Fuhrer museum inventory numbers on the international art market. For complete research of the looting of cultural property during WWII Russian archives are extremely valuable.

I was surprised today by the statement of Mr. Kulishov, a representative of the Russian delegation, that Russian archives are open to researchers. It is not true. They are even more closed than in the beginning of the 90s. Mr. Kulishov quoted in his speech some documents from the Archive of the Soviet Military Administration of Germany – until this day independent researchers had no chance to cross its threshold. The notorious "Osobi" (Special) Archive – the collection of documents confiscated by the Red Army in the occupied European countries – remains closed to historians. Access to such museum archives as the archive of the Hermitage or the archive of the Pushkin Museum is strictly limited. Mr. Kulishov said that he has no information about Jewish cultural property kept in Russian special depositories. I want to give just a few examples - unique paintings from the collections of Hatvany and Herzog, Jewish families from Budapest, confiscated by the infamous Eichmann are today in the Pushkin Museum. The paintings, which include masterpieces of Goya, El Greco, Manet and Degas, were found by the Red Army in a little town Regensburg near Berlin and transported to Russia. Until this day a collection of the Torah scrolls confiscated by the Nazis in Hungary is collecting dust in the library of Nizhni Novgorod. In Moscow archives such as the archive of the Rotschild family, confiscated by the Gestapo in Vienna, and the archive of David Herzog, a professor of the Würzburg University and a member of the Rabbinate of Würzburg, whose house was burned out by the Nazis, are kept in the "Osobi" archive. It is possible to multiply such examples.

Today Russian representatives told us that according to the law on "cultural property removed to the territory of the Russian Federation in a result of WWII" adopted by the Duma, but not signed by president Yeltsin, Jews whose property was confiscated by the Nazis and than removed to the USSR can claim it back. But it is difficult to claim something if you don't know where it is. In the mid 50s, when the Soviet government was preparing to return the collections of the Dresden Gallery and other East German museums, the content of the Soviet secret depositories of art works confiscated in the occupied countries of Europe was checked. It was discovered that more than 1000 paintings stored in the vaults of the Hermitage and the Pushkin Museum had no provenance. Soviet experts had no idea about provenance of thousands of works on paper, sculptures, tapestries, and objects of furniture. It is possible to guess that some of them belonged to obscure and not well documented

German private collections. But a possibility that these "ownerless" art pieces, found on the territories of the Third Reich after the end of the war, once belonged to the European Jews is very high.

If Russian officials really want to return property to Holocaust victims and their survivors, they have to give an international art experts the opportunity to see and research these artworks of "unknown origin" that are now stored in different museum depositories. In his speech Mr. Kulishov mentioned that the Russian Federation will be happy to participate international efforts on the establishment of databases, which could help to trace art pieces disappeared during the war. Russia has a good chance to help the research of the Nazi confiscation of art. In the end of the war many important Nazi archives, which could now shed new light on the looting of the European culture, were confiscated by the Soviet forces and transported to Moscow. Among such collections are documentation of Sonderauftrag Linz (the organization responsible for collecting art works for the Hitler museum) which includes personal diaries of Hans Posse, the first curator of the Fuhrer collection. Important documents of ERR, the archive of SS and other valuable sources are still hidden in Russian archives. The open access to this documentation could be of great help for the researchers working to create databases of looted art.

Mr. Ori Z. Soltes

FORMER DIRECTOR, KLUTZNICK NATIONAL JEWISH MUSEUM
UNITED STATES

Spoliated and Restitutable Art and Their Databases

Break-out Session on Nazi-Confiscated Art Issues: Identification of Art, Archives and Databases

The following talking points note what I and my colleagues believe are the key issues that require consideration if an equitable resolution of this complex problem, both with respect to individual claimants and with respect to human history, is to take place. These points attempts to take into consideration the rights of claimants, which rights seem elsewhere to be missing in a conference which has as its most notable lack the presence (which is to say the *absence*) of claimant representatives — and has offered certain pre-digested conclusions from its outset, from the alleged number of objects stolen from Jews to conclusions about "what claimants should want and get" in lieu of their works of art.

1. No single database can ever be infallibly complete on this subject, due to the vastness and far-flung nature of the material, the lapse of time between the Nazi era and our own and the vagaries of human memory and human record-keeping. Certainly a registry such as that which currently exists, the Art Loss Register, has proven itself flawed with respect to stolen works both within and outside the Holocaust context — this I note not as a criticism, for the percentage rate of success for ALR is very high, but as a statement of historical fact and as a reminder that no one entity can accomplish it all.

2. Nonetheless, a database as a *beginning* point, not as an *end*point, is extremely desirable: the longer we wait to begin *doing* something, the more mired the issues become in impossibilities. The first

priority, to quote my colleague in the *Holocaust Art Restitution Project*, Marc Masurovsky, is "to create a list of Holocaust art losses on all unsettled Holocaust art claims arising from the Second World War which were filed with the American occupation military government of Germany and Austria between 1945 and 1951." Most such data are contained, in fact, in one record group at the National Archives, here in College Park, MD, and HARP has already done some of the leg work.

3. ' The next crucial series of phases would include the consolidation of this list with the claims currently being processed though various agencies, such as the Commission on Art Recovery, (whose chairman, Ron Lauder, reiterated CAR's commitment to championing the cause of claimants, yesterday), the Art Loss Registry (which has, as its Holocaust claims Director, Sarah Jackson, mentioned yesterday, begun to process such claims *gratis*), and the Holocaust Claims Processing Office (which has received scores of inquiries over the past several months). It would also include – and this is obviously of equal significance – the cooperation of all such countries, including the United States, who would order the complete declassification of all archival documents, civil and military, which have to do with Holocaust art thefts and their recovery after war's end. This the French have begun to do at last, and this the Russians – specifically, Valeriy Kulishov, of the Ministry of Culture – vowed, in yesterday's afternoon plenary session, to do. Presumably that sincere gesture can and will be echoed by similar acts of willingness to be accessible, on the part of other countries with archives that would help further to clarify the relationship between claimants and that which they would claim.

4. Each country would, then, ultimately, produce a registry of restitutable items located in their public holdings. For example, if, as is by now common knowledge, the French possess some 2,000 such works, these would be publicized in order to encourage claimants to come forth. In any case, the consolidation of all of these national and institutional registries would – and could, for the technology to do so is there – be consolidated, matching up unresolved claims with items still held in public institutions.

5. The residual would constitute the core of heirless cultural property. But the effort, if it is to be pro-active and not essentially passive, would go and could go further. All heirless property – property with no recognized claimant assigned to it – would be set aside and an effort made to locate claimants. This would require a substantial outreach campaign – but the precedent of the use of print, electronic and on-line media to facilitate such a massive search, is there, having already had a

"dry run" in the search for claimants with regard to Swiss bank accounts. Such a project could be managed jointly by organizations that are already in place to accomplish the various aspects of such an enterprise. Financing for this could be half public and half private. Some funds, for example, could come from the Holocaust Victims Redress Act of 1998, sponsored by Congressman Leach. Half could come from funds raised by the Jewish community, most of whose major organizations have claimed serious interest in this matter. The total of $10 million is not beyond reach, and would support a process that will take 5 to 7 years to complete.

   6. But for this to succeed, the kind of cooperation and sincere dedication that was evident 53 years ago in the efforts of the Art Restitution Commissions will have to resurface. Congressional legislation on a bi-partisan basis would have to support it. Museums, auctions houses, dealers and collectors must actively support the creation and distribution of the above-described international registry, look into their collections and their souls and continue to champion multi-sourced due diligence as we move between past and future. Practically, this means discontinuing the campaign on the part of some members of the art world to alter New York State legislation and undercut the rights of Holocaust claimants; to gut current law and oversimplify the issue of restitution by referring its questions to a simple and single database. It means cooperation on the part of such groups, rather than seeking to reduce the rights of claimants either to a time-specific window in which to lodge a claim or to a process of adjudication that denies them the right ever to reclaim their works of art. (Indeed that same attempt at problem-reduction also proposes to respond to any and all claims by means of a penny for dollar cash settlement. This banalizes the issue and equates works of art *qua* family heirlooms with old shoes and used tires). It means not hiding the demand for due diligence behind the false claim that the art market will revert to economic chaos if the pursuit of claims is ongoing and if multi-sourced due diligence in purchasing, auctioning, gifting or lending of works of art is demanded. This assertion is false for the obvious reason that, if art were *not* big business, and if art movement did *not* continue *even* while people were being destroyed by the *millions* half a century ago, the problem which we are addressing would not exist, and thus there is no reason to suppose that multi-sourced due diligence will significantly disturb, much less destroy the flow of art.

   7. Where the matter of difficulties to resolve issues of restitution are concerned we applaud the notion of a group to arbitrate claims and keep the struggle out of the law courts. The question is who should serve

on such an important team, so that it be balanced and fair. I would suggest that it might include not only two art historians, two lawyers and two museum professionals, two claimant representatives, two Holocaust researchers, as well as one or perhaps two individual(s) from congress, but also a journalist – someone like a Morley Safer – who is committed to yielding just conclusions in such matters but with clearly no partisan ax to grind. Moreover, the goal of such a team should be to consider the claimant's desire as to *how*, if a claim is validated, it should be resolved, and not simply the penny for dollar restitution that has been proposed and ignores the *human*, as opposed to art market reality of claimants' claims. This means *not* assuming, as a point of departure, that claimants will be happy to settle for cash rather than art, which is insulting to them and unsubstantiated. This can surely be an *option*, but neither the *only* option nor the desired *goal*. Moreover, the notion that has been put forth, that such cashification (my own word; forgive the neologism) of claims could be funded by redirecting the Holocaust Victims Redress Act Funds in *that* direction is inherently fallacious since, if the moneys intended for research – precisely to help *answer* complicated provenance questions – are eliminated, then the ability of the team to makes its determinations will be severely undercut, and with that ability, its very *raison d'être* demolished.

8. Such a team would have as a goal the assertion of claimant rights even as it would not assume that a claim was automatically valid, but would seek, bolstered by the expertise of its members, to determine that validity. Moreover, two different further categories of difficulties would confront it. One sort is where the holder of a work of art is a private collector; the other is where the holder is a public institution – be it a museum or a government. In both cases, some compensation to a good-faith purchaser might be necessary. In the first instance, compensation might come in the form of government intervention: offering a tax-break, for example, to the purchaser required to give up his/her work of art, could be a solution. In the latter instance, the team could further help broker an agreement between claimant and museum that would permit the museum to cede title to the claimant, but allow the work of art in question to remain, on long-term loan, in the hands and on the walls of the institution in question – thus no museum would be threatened by the sudden loss of massive parts of its collections – where it would hang side-by-side with heirless works. Similarly, all such works would have text panels explaining the painful history of ownership with has left a hole in their provenance, and educating the public about a subject which is an integral part of human history – and about which

there is at present virtually no education inside or outside of museums (a serious contradiction of the educational mission of museums, it seems to me). Such works would hang side-by-side with the wonderful array of works of art lucky enough to have had no part in this grim chapter of art history.

9. At issue, then, is both the resolving of claimant matters that have emerged out of the past, together with the restrengthening of our resolve to connect yet unidentified claimants with their objects; and maintaining our resolve with regard to multi-sourced due diligence matters in the future. We have a historic opportunity to restore, even after so many decades, some of what was forcibly taken half a century ago as part of an extraordinary outburst of genocidal fervor, and more fundamentally, to begin writing the last chapter of Holocaust history and give it a reasonably happy ending. And we have the opportunity to assure that the *failure* of due diligence over the past half century, which has yielded problematic claims questions today, will be replaced by an unequivocal willingness – mirroring that exhibited by our nation in 1946, and eventually and unaccountably abandoned over the years which followed – to do the morally responsible thing. I hope that we have the courage and conviction to write that last chapter with justice and humility, as we face simultaneously back on the past and toward the future.

Thank you for your attention.

Mr. Philippe De Montebello
DIRECTOR, METROPOLITAN MUSEUM OF ART,
U.S. ASSOCIATION OF ART MUSEUM DIRECTORS TASK FORCE
UNITED STATES

Break-out Session on Nazi-Confiscated Art Issues: Principles to
Address Nazi-Confiscated Art

Thank-you, Congressman Leach:

It is a pleasure to appear before you again, as I did last February before the House Banking Committee that you chair, to have yet another opportunity to discuss the guidelines that American art museums have adopted in *principle* – and also set in motion *in practice* –that is, to deal fairly, forthrightly, and comprehensively with the issue of spoliated art from the Nazi/World War II era in Europe.

These guiding principles have now been in effect in the United States for six months. My colleagues here from Europe have had a chance to review the document and they have expressed general agreement with its content. Some have indicated that they, too, will be adopting similar guiding policies, adapted to their own country's situation.

When I testified on Capitol Hill 10 months ago, you may recall, I did so not only as Director of the Metropolitan Museum, but as Chairman of a Task Force of the Association of Art Museum Directors, assigned specifically to devise a comprehensive policy on this issue. I indicated then that our Task Force, composed of nine other art museum directors, would report back within four months with a policy to guide to art museums in North America. And this we did.

On June 4, at the AAMD annual meeting in Worcester, Massachusetts the Task Force report was discussed extensively, fully endorsed, and adopted unanimously. We coalesced around a broad set of principles, guidelines, and recommendations to deal proactively with the issue of works of art confiscated during the Nazi regime and not restituted to their legitimate owners or their heirs.

I will not read the entire report at this time. For whomever wishes it, I have copies of it as well as of the public announcement that accompanied its release last June 4th.

In the 10 minutes allotted me I'll offer a brief summary of the substance of the Task Force guidelines, and provide an update on how one museum at least, the Metropolitan, has moved to put the report's words into action.

Principally, the Task Force Report called on American art museums to begin to conduct a comprehensive review of their collections to ascertain if any works may have been unlawfully confiscated during the Nazi/World War II era, and never subsequently returned.

We agreed that to do so, we would make maximum use of traditional research from scholars, donors, auction houses, dealers, and of course, all of the standard literature, all of whom –or which-- might shed information on provenance hitherto unavailable or unrecorded. And we agreed that we must also take advantage of high-technology databases and computer linkages that are scheduled to be established by various third parties – computerized records that promise wider access to, and more reliable cross-referencing of, previously dispersed data: I cite, for example, plans for such an undertaking by the Commission for Art Recovery, established by the World Jewish Congress.

Such databases promise the possibility of a future in which claimants and art museums alike can use the Internet to gather and compare all available information about the provenance of a work of art --now all widely dispersed--as well as the existence of any known past or present challenges to ownership. It is in these databases, ultimately, that lies the best hope of dovetailing information and access to hitherto unknown information – not only claims, I hasten to add, but possible postwar restitution or entirely proper subsequent sales.

Our report also, called on art museums to respond promptly to any and all claims by owners or heirs of allegedly confiscated art, and proposed resolving such matters "in an equitable, appropriate, and mutually agreeable manner," ideally utilizing the avenue of mediation to help resolve claims, most of which, it was acknowledged would be *sui generis*.

Finally the Task Force guidelines recommended seeking as much provenance information as possible in the future before accepting gifts, bequests, and making purchases; and it discouraged borrowing works of art for loan exhibitions that were known to have been illegally confiscated during the Nazi/World War II era and never restituted.

By taking these concrete actions, art museums placed themselves firmly on record as committed to acting swiftly and proactively to conduct the necessary research that will help us learn more about works for which full ownership records have remained stubbornly unavailable –

hidden, for example, in this nation's own previously classified World War II documents, or in the Soviet Union and Eastern Europe.

Therein, incidentally, lies the key to a critical difference that exists between Swiss or Italian bank or insurance companies and the American Art Museum, a difference that is too often blurred. Indeed "omnibus" conferences such as this one --and I do not contest its enormous merits, encourages such blurring: namely, the implied equating of works of art somehow "secreted" in museums with "hidden" financial assets. I think everyone knows that this equation is patently absurd --nor, incidentally, were U.S. museums acquiring art in Europe during the Nazi era-- but rhetoric does get out of hand in this highly emotional arena. Of course, a mountain of books, journals, catalogues, press releases, and similar materials testifies to the contrary, and to museums' propensity for *celebrating* their collections, not *hiding* them.

The fact is, museums proudly announce acquisitions – the Met has joyously recorded in recent weeks the purchase of works by Jasper Johns and Van Gogh – and frankly, if my press office had not generated considerable press attention, internationally, someone would now be looking for other work! And of course, museums display new acquisitions prominently in their galleries, indeed all new acquisitions at the Met have a special and highly visible blue sticker on the label. Museums publish their art in widely-read illustrated catalogues, as well as in scholarly journals, and lend them to special exhibitions all over the world. They can be seen on ubiquitous postcards and posters that decorate dormitory rooms at colleges all over the country. We are, to mix a metaphor, an open book...when it comes to new acquisitions *or* the ongoing scholarship and research to which we also subject works of art that have long resided in our collections.

All that said, and I assure you that I offer this reminder of *past* practices strictly as a useful prologue to *future* practices, let me report on our progress in fulfilling the mandate of the Task Force I chaired.

The work is exhaustive. Frankly, it is also exhausting – of resources, time, and human energy alike. But it proceeds. It will not, however, be done overnight; indeed no amount or money or industry at this point could guarantee the swift completion of the task: too much vital information is still unavailable. In most large museums at least, the systematic examination of indices, acquisition records, and entry cards, some of them written generations ago in now-fading ink, is an inherently slow and painstaking process. But it has begun: The Metropolitan Museum's own curatorial departments –there are 18, entrusted with over 2 million works of art, are reviewing the records of all works of art acquired since the war and they report regularly to me and to the office of the Secretary and Council's. The Met is in the process of creating an illustrated, computerized collections management system, a project that will permit even greater access to the Museum's works of art. But this effort, too, is far from complete.

We continue to do our research, index card by index card, collection by collection – and I am assured that other museums are doing so as well. Our ability to fill in all the blanks in the provenance is likely to depend, in part, on unpredictable outside factors, such as the publication of further declassified, or previously unknown records, and their eventual, and indispensable ordering by archivists. As a case in point I would note that just a few weeks ago, a secretly compiled report of the OSS listing more than 2,000 people who allegedly handled art looted by the Nazis, was again made public, and again made news. There may be other such reports yet unopened.

I would caution, too, that it will unavoidably take time to construct the kind of databanks necessary to make a much-needed high-tech, cross-referencing archive function usefully. As is well known, no web site is more valuable than the data it contains. And I must point out, hopefully to good effect in this international forum, that the cooperation of European art museums, and of course, of their governments, in this data-building effort will be crucial to the success of any future data base.

I have probably exceeded my allotted time, Mr. Chairman. But to summarize: the AAMD has adopted a policy; American museums are committed to a comprehensive review of their provenance records, and many have undertaken them; we await eagerly the day when computerized data bases will provide easily accessed information on claims and restitution; we believe that many of our colleagues in Europe support this approach and are prepared to follow it themselves, a vital step toward crucial cooperative research; and we hope that whatever classified material remains shrouded in secrecy, here and abroad, can finally see the light of day to further illuminate our efforts.

Ladies and gentlemen, we believe in no principles more than those of fair title and public access to works of art. They have guided our policies of collecting and exhibiting art for generations. We are committed to re-examining our own records to ensure that neither goal is overlooked in the promotion of the other. And we welcome the notion that such an effort should be, as it now appears to be, a truly global one.

On the issue of the spoliation of art in the World War II/Nazi era, the genie is, at last, out of the bottle, and no resistance, apathy, or silence can ever fit it back inside again. We trust that all those who would right so hideous a wrong will work to insure that information is sought, disseminated, and shared, legitimate claims addressed, and that great art, untainted by lingering doubts on its ownership, will remain available to the widest possible audiences.

Thank you.

Mrs. Françoise Cachin
Director, the Museums of France
FRANCE

Issues of Unclear Provenance and Principles to Address Nazi-Confiscated Art

Break-out Session on Nazi-Confiscated Art Issues: Principles to
Address Nazi-Confiscated Art

Ladies and Gentlemen:

Because this session is dedicated to the provenance of artwork,
the difficulties we are faced with, and the experience already acquired in
this area, Mr. Amigues, the Director of Archives and Records at the
Foreign Ministry, and myself have decided to present the work of each of
our agencies conjointly, since the Foreign Affairs and the Museums have
continually collaborated in this area, the Quai d'Orsay being in charge of
investigating restitution request cases, and the State-owned museums
being the custodians of the MNR artwork as well as the experts in history
and art.

In introduction, I simply want to recall the role played by the
Management of the Museums of France as early as during the war in
protecting the French private heritage. This approach has facilitated later
searches and restitution: the handling of private collections, particularly
Jewish-owned, as part of State-owned collections when evacuated early
in the conflict, the fictitious recording of threatened private collections in
the inventory of public collections as a measure of protection, Rose
Valland's courageous deeds in the Galerie du Jeu de Paume which had
become a sorting center for the collections looted by the ERR, the
involvement Jacques Jaujard, who was director of the State-owned
Museums, in this resistance and subsequently in the creation of the
Commission for Art Retrieval, as well the involvement of the curators of
the Louvre in the searches made for restitution and in setting-up a

directory of Despoiled Assets, are some of the widely recognized historical facts.

What may not be as widely known, but is important to recall so as to understand the present situation, is the fact that the artwork referred to as "MNR" was put under the custody of the Museums of France, in accordance with the Decree of September 30, 1949. These paintings, totaling 2,058 pieces, have not been claimed. They could not be returned since their origin was unknown. The 1949 Decree called for these paintings to be exhibited: this was accomplished between 1950 and 1954 at the Chateau of Compiègne to allow potential owners to come forward and claim the artwork.

That same Decree also called for these paintings to be registered on temporary inventories, separate from state-owned collections: this was done in each department of the public museums involved (paintings, sculptures, drawings, objets d'art, etc.).

However, one of the provisions of the 1949 Decree was not fulfilled: the setting, through legislation, of a deadline for claiming this artwork. Since this deadline was never established, the Museums of France have always kept the MNRs available for possible claimants, a deed recently recognized in a dual appraisal of both our Chancery and our State Council. Thanks to the research made by former members of the Artistic Retrieval Commission, particularly by Rose Valland, about thirty additional paintings were recovered in the 1950's in addition to the 45,400 paintings retrieved after the war. After the Compiègne exhibition, and because all the paintings could not be permanently exhibited, the MNRs were distributed among State-owned museums and stored in provincial museums and government property. Even though part of this artwork is stored in custodial museums, the MNRs remain listed in state-owned collections catalogs, particularly those of the Louvre and the museum of Orsay, and also in the catalogs of temporary exhibitions of MNR artwork.

However, in the past several years, we have entered a new phase in the way we perceive the tragic events of World War II. I believe that this is because the generation of victims and witnesses of atrocities from that period has led way to new generations for whom duty of justice and memory prevail. This is also related to specific events, such as the fall of the Berlin Wall which brought back the despoiling issue back to the table, again revealing to us, among other things, that a considerable amount of artwork had nearly been ignored right until then.

Historians, such as Mrs. Lynn Nicholas, whose very enlightening speech you heard yesterday and whose book was translated into French in 1995, journalists, such as Eric Conan and Yves Stavridès, who were the first ones in France to expose the subject of looted art in the weekly "L'Express," or even Hector Feliciano, in his book Le Musée Disparu ("The Missing Museum") helped draw the attention of the public power's opinion on these issues.

The Management of the Museums of France itself very soon became eager to inform the public and answer questions. It is in this intent that, in November 1996, it held an international colloquium titled "Looting and restitution. The fate of the artwork that was removed from France during World War II." About fifteen experts as well as French and foreign witnesses came to speak about the events that took place during the Occupation and in the post-war period, and the current dealing with the issue of despoiled artwork in France and other countries. At the same time, we set up a database on the Internet, on the server of the French Ministry of Culture, listing the complete catalog of MNR artwork along with pictures.

With the help of the research we have been conducting to find a "pedigree" for each of these pieces of art, a research that I will soon share with you, this catalog has been continually updated since then.

Finally, in the spring of 1997, we held an exhibition of MNR artwork at the Louvre, the Center Georges Pompidou, the Orsay museum, the Sèvres museum, the castle of Versailles, and in about one hundred other provincial museums. Many MNRs are already on permanent display at these museums, but we also wanted to boost viewing. Over the next few months, millions of inquiries were made into our database, and during the exhibition, we received a large number of calls from Jewish and non-Jewish families who had lost artworks during the war. Unfortunately, less than ten of these claims pertained to MNR artwork. Since then however, five MNR pieces were returned to their legitimate owners: paintings from Foujita, Gleizes, Picabia and Utrillo, and a drawing from Granet. However, I think it is important to underline that four of these art pieces were not claimed by the families after the war.

As I indicated earlier, we have begun a large scale investigation on the history of each of these MNR art pieces. Since 1997, this investigation has benefited from the support of a Commission created on the initiative of the Prime Minister in order to investigate the despoiling of Jewish assets in France. This Commission is chaired by Mr. Jean Mattéoli. About ten researchers thus undertook the task of systematically analyzing publications, particularly descriptive catalogs and mostly archives. In fact, we are also researching additional resources provided by:

- the Art Retrieval Commission archives in Paris;
- the Office of Private Assets archives in Paris;
- the collecting points archives kept here in Washington at the National Archives,
- the German intelligence archives, particularly the Einsatzstab Reichsleiter Rosenberg (EER) that are available for consultation in Koblenz.

Also, we will soon begin researching archives kept in Berlin, as well as, I hope, a number of private records collections.

However, this work is facing obvious difficulties, from which I will list at least three:

- First of all, 2000 pieces are being researched. Their origin could not immediately be established after the war by the Art Retrieval Commission experts, such as Rose Valland and Carl Dreyfus, although they had direct knowledge of their contemporaries' collections and the tribulations undergone by them.
- Many of the often substandard quality paintings could not be traced back. Even the iconography, such as landscapes or unidentifiable portraits, was of little help.
- Research conducted on the 1,000 pieces other than paintings, such as sculptures, antic objects, furniture, tapestries, ceramics, is even more complex because these objects are particularly difficult to identify due to descriptions such as: "cup made of Sèvres porcelain," "Chest," "wing chair," etc.

The detailed results of these searches, which have nonetheless progressed significantly, will be included in a report currently being prepared by the Commission chaired by Mr. Jean Mattéoli. I can however give you today an initial overview of the conclusions that we reached.

Apart from a certain number of very clear-cut cases, which do not cast any doubt about their itinerary during the war, numerous questions remain about the history of many MNRs. For example, the origin of most of the 38 MNR exposed at the National Art Museum/Center Georges Pompidou remains unknown in spite of lengthy research conducted by this museum's curatorship. As for 980 older paintings that were studied by a team from the Louvre, the research indicates that most were bought from art dealers, at public sales at the

Drouot Hotel, or directly from French individuals by German museums such as those of Essen, Wuppertal, Dusseldorf, Vienna, and the museum that Hitler had planned to put in Linz, etc., dealers, brokers, dignitaries and Reich officials, without it being possible to determine the conditions that this artwork was sold under. It is likely, even certain, that others were despoiled or looted, but for now, the owners' identity remains unknown.

CONCLUSION

It is our intention that, regardless of what happened, the results of this research, which will be led to a completion in spite of difficulties, be made available to the public to the largest extent possible. Hence, I can announce to you that, in addition to the database made available on the Internet over the past two years, and which is regularly updated, we plan to release of a series of publications over the upcoming years: as early as next year, a catalog of MNR paintings will be released, including over 1000 pieces, and, another one containing other objets categories will appear in 2000. The purpose of these researches and publications is to ease recovery and restitution. In this regard, all the MNR artwork, proven to have been despoiled and the provenance of which will have been established, will evidently be returned to their legitimate owners. For those whose origin is uncertain or questionable, it is the duty of the Mattéoli Commission to make proposals about their fate to the French government. The government will then make the appropriate decisions.

It is my opinion that, as the many requests directed to us during the exhibitions of Spring 1997 demonstrated, we should expect more new developments on the artwork that disappeared before and right after the war than that found and kept in French museums under the name of MNR. In fact, a number of masterpieces from the famous SCHLOSS collection, from instance, reappeared on the market over the last few years. We tend to believe that, if we continue to be watchful, these types of discoveries will increase over the upcoming years. Finally, should I remind that large sets of artwork, even masterpieces, still remain "frozen" in some countries.

I will now let Mr. Louis Amigues speak and describe in much detail the restitution requests currently underway.

Ambassador Louis Amigues

DIRECTOR, ARCHIVES AND RECORDS, MINISTRY OF FOREIGN AFFAIRS
FRANCE

Break-out Session on Nazi-Confiscated Art Issues: Principles to
Address Nazi-Confiscated Art

Ladies and Gentlemen,

As Mrs. Cachin just reminded you, the Ministry of Foreign
Affairs is in charge of recovering the cultural assets that were despoiled
by the Nazis.

Restitution requests should thus be made to the Foreign Ministry.
Petitioners should provide supporting evidence of their filiation with the
persons that were despoiled, or the bases for their entitlement. Once
proof is established, they will receive a complimentary copy of all the
documents that apply to them, from the archives of the Ministry of
Foreign Affairs.

If necessary, the Ministry of Foreign Affairs can submit a
petition to a French-German working group that was established in 1992,
for the restoration of cultural assets. Two requirements must be met.
First, the petition must be a reopening of a restitution petition already
filed before 1956, because the German delegation will only consider
petitions filed prior to this date. However, we have not renounced to
submit cases that did not meet this requirement. Second, a minimum
amount of pertinent information must support the petition.

There are currently around 80 families despoiled during World
War II that have sent requests for information or petitions to the Quai
d'Orsay.

To handle these matters, the Ministry of Foreign Affairs
possesses in its own right two archival collections: one contains about
750 files, most of which came from the Art Retrieval Commission's
archives given by the Management of the Museums of France at the end
of 1991. The other belongs to the Office of Private Assets and Interests,
an organization that was put under the authority of the Foreign Ministry,
and which took over the Art Retrieval Commission in 1950.

In accordance with French law, these archives are confidential
for a period of 60 years, meaning that they cannot be disclosed, because
they contain private information that may affect people's lives. I will add

that, if necessary, it is always possible to have access to other archives collections.

It goes without saying, however it should be reminded, that all this activity occurs in consultation with other ministries and in narrow cooperation with the Museums of France. Among these institutions, and I insist on this point, there is no divergence on the essential. By that, I mean that the despoiled artwork that has been kept since the war or that was recently recovered has the vocation of being returned to those legitimately entitled to a restitution. However, differences of opinion may arise about the assessment that should be made on certain elements of the case.

This is usual, and there are established procedures to reach a decision. However, let me point out that ever since I began working on these cases, I have never encountered this type of situation.

This restitution work is facing several difficulties today. These difficulties essentially pertain to:

- The time elapsed since the occurrence of events makes the research very chancy, even impossible;-The lack of information or the vagueness of the information provided on the assets under petition, for instance, description of the artwork, circumstances of the looting (place, date), the lack of a claim after the war, etc.
- The journey of the artwork: did it travel commercially, and under what conditions? Right after the war, a series of official texts addressed the issue of returning despoiled assets. The issue of trading with the enemy was also addressed, allowing for the artwork bought by the Nazis to be returned. A Commission was put in charge of ruling, on a case by case basis, on the conditions under which the sales had occurred and whether they should be annulled or not.
- The absence of information on the owners of the retrieved artwork;
- The uncertainty of knowing whether a piece of art that belonged to someone before the war was still under this person's possession at the time of despoiling;
- In determining who are the heirs or eligible recipients;
- On the considerations associated with other State legislation on this issue, and the position of other States on this problem. It is not because laws and international agreements exist that a solution to the cases presented will be found.

What conclusions can we draw from our experience?

I have four main conclusions:

The necessity of rigor. It must be applied to both the research work and the decision that will be made, and that largely relies on the results of the research. A restitution can only occur if it is based on elements of proof, not on mere assumptions. A litigation opposing two families is underway, one family is disputing the ownership of artwork that was returned to the other family after the war. This example can only strengthen our resolve.

Observance of the law. Our work is done within the framework of domestic and international laws, from which we cannot depart.

The necessity of cooperation between all parties involved. Up until now, emphasis was put on the responsibility of the public powers. It is evident that this responsibility is real. However, I must underline that private institutions, dealers, auctioneers, and even individuals must equally demonstrate responsibility, even if, up until now, this is something that was not as widely discussed. It is very important to be able to have access to those records. Although this is not something required by the law in France, we are calling for voluntary cooperation.

The acknowledgment that each case is unique. No case is like another. Naturally, there can be some general rules, and I just recalled some of them. However, experience proves that there is no formula that will generally rule favorably on these restitution requests.

If you wish, I am ready to illustrate my words with a few examples.

I thank you for your attention.

Ms. Sharon Page

TATE GALLERY
CHAIR OF WORKING GROUP ON NAZI SPOLIATION OF ART,
NATIONAL MUSEUMS AND GALLERIES' DIRECTORS CONFERENCE
UNITED KINGDOM

UK National Museums and Galleries Statement

Break-out Session on Nazi-Confiscated Art Issues: Principles to
Address Nazi-Confiscated Art

I am speaking today as a representative of the United Kingdom's
National Museum Directors' Conference. I am particularly privileged to
be representing some of the UK's major cultural institutions and to be
here among so many influential figures in the international cultural
world.

I ought to start by telling you something about the Conference,
which is a voluntary association of 26 national institutions who receive
funding from central government. Its members include 20 museums and
3 national libraries and it is these institutions which I represent today.

In June this year, the Conference set up a working party to
develop a statement of principles and consider what we in the UK should
do about works of art that may have been confiscated from their owners
during the Holocaust and the Second World War. I must stress that no
UK national institutions have received any claims from owners
dispossessed of works of art during this period. However, following
discussions with Chris Smith, the Secretary of State for Culture, Media
and Sport, Lord Janner, Chairman of the Holocaust Educational Trust
and colleagues in the USA, France and the Netherlands, it was agreed
that confiscated art was a subject which deserved serious attention.

As a lawyer in a major art gallery with a keen interest in cultural
history, I was delighted to be asked by my director, Nicholas Serota, to
chair the working party, which included representatives from the Victoria
and Albert Museum, the British Museum, the National Gallery and the

Imperial War Museum. The statement which I am introducing today results from the working party's efforts and has been endorsed by all the directors represented by the Conference.

Before I give you an outline of the key points in our statement, I would like to give those of you who are not familiar with UK national institutions some idea of the diverse size and content of the collections they hold. It might also help if I painted a brief picture of the environment in which these institutions operate, as I believe it is pertinent to the way the principles and actions contained in our statement will be implemented.

To give you two examples – I work at the Tate Gallery in London which holds the national collection of British art and 20th century international art. Our collection currently totals about 60,000 works as well as related archive material. The Victoria and Albert Museum, on the other hand, has collections which illustrate and document the history of art, craft and design. With numbers in the millions rather than thousands, their collections include not just paintings, prints and sculpture, but also ceramics, furniture and costume.

However, although our collections vary enormously in size and scope, we have a number of important characteristics in common. We are all governed by act of parliament or Royal Charter which set out our various aims, objectives and powers, including – and this is particularly important to the topic under review today – our powers to dispose of works in our collections.

Most of our institutions are governed by Boards of Trustees who must act in line with their founding statute or charter as well as their fiduciary duties as trustees. The nature of our aims, objectives and powers reflects the fact that our collections were created and have been largely maintained as a result of significant public funding and are held in trust for the British people. Of particular relevance I believe to our debate today, is the fact that a central objective of the majority of our institutions is to provide access to our collections, to increase public enjoyment and understanding and promote education and scholarship.

Finally, as with many publicly funded cultural institutions, resources are tight. This is particularly significant as many of us are in the midst of major millennium related building projects. The Tate, for example, is in the midst of two capital building projects costing in the region of £160 million, half of which we have to raise through private donations.

This is a complex environment in which the principles and actions I am introducing today will be implemented. But I must emphasize that the Conference is committed to carrying them through and I hope that by taking part in this conference, I will learn much that will help us in realizing this commitment.

So to the statement itself. Essentially it outlines the broad principles and proposed actions agreed by the Conference. However, more importantly, it also calls for the production of more detailed practical guidance on specific issues such as surveying and researching collections and handling claims.

The next big challenge for my working party is to roll up its sleeves and address these practical issues. Our aim is to produce guidelines which we hope can be used, not just by the major national institutions, but also by the many other museums and galleries throughout the UK.

The statement makes clear from the outset that the Conference deplores the confiscation of works of art which constituted one of the many horrors of the Holocaust and the Second World War. It also emphasizes our commitment to existing UK guidance issued by the Museums Association, which stresses the need for rigorous procedures to ensure that works of art which may have been stolen or illegally exported are not acquired or exhibited.

This statement also makes clear the Conference's commitment to working with other institutions and organizations, both nationally and internationally, in order to increase awareness and understanding of the facts surrounding the fate of works of art during this period.

The Conference, together with the UK government through the Department of Culture, Media and Sport and other cultural agencies, is committed to promoting access to its public collections. In addition to physical access, this includes promoting research and scholarship and providing wide access to collections information.

The statement, therefore, urges a practical approach to reviewing and making accessible information about its collections – including information about provenance. It accepts that the level and scope of that research and publication must take into account the size and nature of the collections concerned and the resources available. However, the statement encourages institutions to develop and publicize their own plans outlining what they hope to achieve.

Information sharing is, of course, key, and one of the major impediments to research into art confiscated during this period is lack of access to information. One practical initiative already underway in a number of institutions is to make collections information available using information technology. The Tate, for example, has set up a web site with the primary aim of making accessible information about all works in our collection to the widest possible audience. To date, 35,000 works from our collection are on the web site, 8,000 of them illustrated. Use of information technology could easily be broadened to include the results of research in this area and to keep records of claims and inquiries.

A very practical step recommended by the statement is that all institutions should nominate a person as the main point of contact for inquiries on confiscated art and potential claims. This person could also keep a central record of research being undertaken. Most of our institutions have already nominated their own contacts and a list is kept centrally by the Conference's administration. In this way, it is hoped that potential claims can be handled quickly and sensitively.

This statement sets outline steps for checking provenance for new acquisitions and appropriate procedures for loans. We are confident that our institutions already have rigorous procedures in these areas, but I hope that my working party will be able to call on new research and checking procedures so that practical guidance can be developed that focuses in particular on the problem of confiscated art.

Finally, this statement anticipates the development of detailed guidance on how our institutions should handle claims. The challenge for the Conference will be to guide institutions in understanding the complexity of the issues involved on a case by case basis and how to reconcile the interests of individuals with their responsibilities as national public institutions.

Fundamental to the success of these initiatives is the involvement of all those in the art world. I hope that participation in the Conference this week will take us some steps further in our understanding of this most complex of issues.

Prof. Dr. Carla Schulz-Hoffmann

DEPUTY GENERAL DIRECTOR,
BAVARIAN STATE PAINTINGS COLLECTION
GERMANY

Break-out Session on Nazi-Confiscated Art Issues: Principles to
Address Nazi-Confiscated Art

Ladies and Gentlemen:

May I express my gratitude to the American Government and the organizers of the Washington Conference to be able to take part in this important and valuable conference. Let me begin with a statement that, even though it should be clear without saying, needs underlining and stressing again and again: Remembrance of what has been done in the name of my country is the first and everlasting basis, has to be the self-evident moral issue with utmost priority, This surely can not remain a theoretical topos favored in privacy. Instead everything possible should be done to at least parallel this with practical work - meaning in my special field as an art historian and deputy general director of the Bavarian States Collections in Munich - meaning in my field with practical work regarding sorrow research on the issues involved, openness to questioning and awareness of the responsibility to put into open light whatever seems to be held doubtful, And to keep in mind that there is no justified "statute of limitation" for an eternal injustice that didn't have any limits.

Working in Munich for one of the major European museum institutions surely has a special meaning in this historical context. In Munich as the capital of the Nazi movement Hitler opened, as you all know, on July 18th 1937 the "House of German Art" and on the following day in the direct neighborhood of this monumental building the so called "degenerate art" exhibition, a show that was not only disastrous for all modem Art in Germany bur more so was used as a diabolical alibi and a murderous tool for all the Nazi terror that reaches far beyond words.

And it goes without saying that our institution had the responsibility to work on a first comprehensive reconstruction of this fatal exhibition. In 1987 Peter-Klaus Schuster, now general director of the Bavarian States collections, put together, mainly in a sorrowly researched catalogue, the history and implications of the "degenerate art show" - a project which raised controversy as well as it initiated a lot of scholarly research on the issue. But this only implies one of the several aspects of "Nazi confiscated art" - an aspect even though that should not be underestimated - as it meant nothing less than the confiscation of free expression of creativeness and thus in the end - of humanity.

After World War II Munich again was the center of another issue linked with Nationalsozialism - the question of confiscated works of art and their repatriation- The officers of the Monuments, Fine Arts and Archives Services, shortly the "MFA and A," were charged with locating the German repositories of art and archives, protecting them from loss and deterioration as well as returning looted objects. A number of Allied collecting points were established of which the largest was the Central Art Collecting Point in Munich. Craig Hugh Smyth, than a young naval lieutenant (and later director of the Harvard University Center for Italian Renaissance Studies), was given the task of administering this vast and sensitive operation. Round about 700,000 works of art found in Germany and Austria were collected and usually returned to their owners or their heirs. In September 1951, the Collecting Points were closed down and the remaining objects were handed over to the "Trcuhandverwaltung für Kulturgut" (i.e. "Trustee Administration for Cultural Property") that continued the restitution work until its closure in December 1962. But still some 3,000 works remained unidentified and are kept in different museums and museum related institution till a legitimate owner can be traced.

Regardless of this since some years now a data collecting office is established at the German Government as well as at the Coordination Office of the Federal States for the Return of Cultural Property, now situated in Magdeburg (Saxony-Anhalt) and financed by all 16 states together.

This recently intensified effort to clarify the still doubtful art properties became even more important especially after reunification with regard to the new States, the former "German Democratic Republic." There still is an ongoing research with questionnaires and catalogues of lost art send to German museums. Even though till now the results for identifying confiscated property mainly had negative results, the efforts will be continued.

One example showing the complicated situation can be seen in an important body of works of art having been on deposit since 1972 in the "Alte Nationalgalerie" of East Berlin and after reunification given to France in 1991 till the real owner is found. The 28 paintings and works on paper by artists as Delacroix, Courbet, Monet, Gauguin, Renoir etc. since today could not be returned to their legal owners even though an exhibition with venues in Berlin and Paris was made to trace them. The story, as far as it could be clarified, was, that a priest (Solbach) had a soldier in confession who told him that he had been given a suitcase with valuable art works by a German officer in France who wanted to get it back after the war. The soldier, evidently stricken by bad conscience, handed the suitcase over to the priest who gave it to DDR officials in Halle in 1972, wherefrom it went to the East Berlin collections and could be restituted to the French authorities after reunification. Hopefully this unsolved riddle still can be clarified - showing once and again the importance of world-wide data information.

Yesterday Mr. Rusty Powell quoted the necessity for research work including provenance checks in each museum. I would dare saying that this largely has been done in German governmental museums for art works in question till the end of the 19th century including roughly impressionism. 20th century art is surely not as sorrowly covered. In Munich we just finished the catalogue raisonné of the Brücke collection and in a few months, the Klee collection - till now without any now results concerning questionable property, But of course every work of art coming to the collection - regardless if it is an acquisition or a donation - has been and will be checked for any hint to a doubtful provenance.

Thus I widely share the view emphasized in the Statement of Principles and Guidelines developed by the American Association of Art Museum Directors outlined by Philippe de Montebello and discussed as well in the international "Réunion des Musées Nationaux," the international meeting of museum directors. Everything helpful and useful to trace and return art property confiscated by the Nazis should be done keeping in mind that here a "statute of limitations" never can be a justified question. And with regard to this conference one result for me personally is to strengthen our efforts to clarify museum provenances especially for works which came to the collection after 1937 till today and thus to contribute as far as possible to a restitution of works of art confiscated during the Holocaust-Era to their legal owners and heirs.

Holocaust-Era Insurance Claims

Prof. Gerald D. Feldman

PROFESSOR OF HISTORY, UNIVERSITY OF CALIFORNIA, BERKELEY AND
FELLOW, AMERICAN ACADEMY IN BERLIN
UNITED STATES

Nazi Confiscation of Insurance Policy Assets

Plenary Session on Holocaust-Era Insurance Claims

This description of the confiscation of the insurance policies of Jews and other designated enemies of the National Socialist State is based on my research for a book that will appear in English and German on the Allianz AG, the German Insurance Industry, and the National Socialist regime. I wish to make it clear that I have been asked to undertake this study, as an independent scholar with no obligation to Allianz beyond producing a professional work of history. The confiscation of Jewish insurance policies and related measures constitute only a part of my study of the relations between the company and the regime, and I am in no way personally or professionally engaged in the search for unclaimed and unpaid policies. I study insurance policies, whether compensated or uncompensated, primarily for information about the relations between the company and its Jewish customers. This said, the processes by which the Nazis despoiled Jews of their insurance assets are of great importance to my work, and I shall do my best to clarify them. I shall concentrate on life insurance policies with a face value of between 10,000 and 100,000 Reichsmark, that is, the larger type of policy that constituted a substantial investment and asset. I should note that policies above 30,000 RM were extremely rare. Finally, I will say a word about postwar compensation programs. Let me emphasize that these are necessarily very summary remarks, and I will expand on some of the points made here and deal with some of the other issues in the breakout sessions.

I think it important to point out at the very beginning that life insurance was a popular form of saving and investment for middle class and upper middle class German Jews who made their careers as merchants, lawyers, and doctors. Most of the persons whose policies I have examined fell within these professional categories. Typical life insurance policies examined by me ran for about twenty years and had a face value between ten thousand and thirty thousand Reichsmark at maturity. They constituted a form of capital investment, having a growing repurchase value that usually included dividends paid by the companies. Because of the experience of hyperinflation in 1922-1923, many of policies I have seen which were taken out in the mid-1920s were denominated in gold, fine gold, or supposedly secure foreign currencies, above all, the dollar and Swiss franc. Most of these policies were voluntarily converted to Reichsmark in the early 1930s, while conversion became mandatory in August 1938.

In thinking about Nazi confiscation of insurance, I find it useful to distinguish between indirect and direct confiscation. Prior to the outbreak of war in 1939, the primary means by which Jews were deprived of their insurance, that is, the expectations they entertained when they took out insurance and the proceeds available to them from their insurance, were indirect. On the one hand, the increasing economic pressure on the Jews caused by loss of means of livelihood through various impositions and restrictions on their economic activity made it impossible for many of them to pay their premiums and also compelled them to monetize their insurance assets. Also, insofar as they decided to emigrate, they needed all the money they could get to pay the costs of emigration and to pay the Reich Flight Tax (Reichsfluchtsteuer), a measure introduced in 1931, that is, before the Nazis came to power, to prevent flight of capital. The tax had been deliberately revised in 1934 to enable the regime to exploit emigrating Jews by taxing away a quarter of all their assets. The situation became qualitatively more severe after the Pogrom of November 9/10, 1938 because of the billion RM "Atonement Tax" (Sühneleistung) on assets imposed on the Jews and the systematic measures then taken to drive Jews from German economic life. As a result of the increased radicalization of National Socialist expropriation measures, panic took hold among Jewish policyholders, and there was a flood of repurchases. The evidence I have seen shows that the Allianz paid promptly and correctly to their Jewish policyholders, and this would seem to be true of the other major companies. Such payment was in any case required of all companies, no matter how large the number of Jewish policyholders they had, by the Reich Supervisory Office for Insurance (Reichsaufsichtsamt für Versicherung).

The fact that the insurance companies paid out the repurchase price, however, does not mean that the Jews had full and free access to their money. Jews who planned to emigrate normally had to state their intention to the authorities and, in certain instances, transform their bank accounts into blocked emigrant accounts (<u>Auswanderersperrkonten</u>) from which they could only withdraw funds with the permission of the tax authorities upon certification that they had paid the Flight Tax and the Asset Tax and any other taxes that may have been due. In some cases the revenue offices simply ordered the blocking of the accounts of Jews who had not fully paid their taxes or who were liable to further taxation. Insurance proceeds were paid into such accounts at the instructions of the insured, who in effect had no other choice but to issue such instructions. In other cases, the insured simply instructed the insurance company to pay insurance proceeds directly to the financial authorities. Finally, even if Jews could gain access to their funds, the exchange controls made it impossible for them to take more than a very limited sum of money outside Germany so that many emigrating Jews retained money in the blocked emigrant account, sometimes for the use of relatives remaining in Germany. In any case, by 1939, the processes of indirect confiscation as I have described them had thus become barely distinguishable from those of direct confiscation.

Nevertheless, the direct confiscation of Jewish insurance assets had different foundations from the indirect confiscation in connection with tax and other currency and financial obligations discussed until now. The basis for such confiscation already existed in the Law for the Seizure of Assets of Enemies of the People and the State (<u>Gesetz über die Einziehung volks- und staatsfeindlichen Vermögens</u>) of July 14, 1933 which, along with an accompanying law on termination of the citizenship of such persons (<u>Gesetz über Wiederruf von Einbürgerungen und Aberkennung der deutschen Staatsangehörigkeit</u>), allowed the government to confiscate the assets of Communists and other designated enemies of the regime. Some use of this legislation was made to confiscate Jewish assets throughout the 1930s, particularly of Jews who had emigrated and those who had aroused the ire of the regime through their activities abroad. The names of those deprived of citizenship were normally published in the official government journal (<u>Reichsanzeiger</u>), and the Gestapo then proceeded to inform the relevant bank and insurance organizations that the assets of these persons were confiscated and were to be turned over to the financial authorities. In the case of insurance, this meant that the repurchase value was to be calculated and the sum transferred to the designated Revenue Office.

The reporting and confiscation of Jewish assets was turned into a requirement by the 11th Decree of the Reich Citizenship Law of November 25, 1941 (11. Verordnung zum Reichsbürgergesetz), which mandated the confiscation of all Jewish assets for Jews regularly residing abroad. By this time, of course, most of those who had not emigrated had been deported to concentration camps in the East, which constituted "residing abroad," and were now systematically deprived of their citizenship and property. Indeed, the decree was directly connected with the effort to deport all Jews remaining in the Reich who had not already been deported that had begun earlier in the month. Under Paragraph 7 of the decree, organizations and persons who had control of such assets – insurance companies, for example – were required to report them within a very short period of time.   It cannot be said that the insurance companies showed any enthusiasm for this decree, not because of discernible moral or ethical considerations, but because they had neither the personnel nor the resources to identify the Jewish policies in their possession, many of which were free of premiums and thus of constant bookkeeping requirements and were not easily identifiable as Jewish. The records I have seen suggest that the initiative usually came from the Gestapo and other authorities, which turned up with the names of the Jews, announced the deprivation of their citizenship, and then used the information collected on their assets to contact the insurance companies and order payment of the repurchase value to the Regional Revenue Office in which the Jews had resided. I think it important to recognize that insurance at this point was among the lesser assets subject to seizure since the moneys in question had already been surrendered in one form or another by the general despoliation of the Jews and their forced emigration in 1933-1939.

In the case of German Jews, therefore, postwar restitution for insurance was primarily concerned with compensation for prematurely terminated policies and the proceeds of policies subsequently seized from insurers and blocked bank accounts. The payments were made by the government under the postwar restitution and compensation agreements. Under the compensation laws, the insurance companies, including foreign companies operating in Germany, were responsible for checking their files for the policies of former Jewish customers and calculating the amounts to be paid by the government.

Swiss and insurance companies of other countries allowed to do business in Germany were subject to the confiscatory regulations and decrees I have described, as, after 1938-1939, were the Italian companies operating in Austria and then in the Sudetenland and in so-called

Protectorate of Bohemia and Moravia. Swiss companies argued during and after the war that the German government, not they, was liable for the Jewish insurance monies they had paid out to the National Socialist regime. In the case of law suits against the Swiss both during and after the war, U.S. courts ruled against the Jewish claimants in favor of the Swiss insurance companies, although back in Switzerland, Swiss courts ruled in favor of Jewish claimants in cases where their policies specifically stated that payment could be made either in Germany or in Switzerland. Italian companies have denied payment obligation on the claims of customers in Poland and the former Czechoslovakia by of the socialization of their assets in those countries after the war. The Austrians issued an Insurance Reconstruction Law in September 1955 requiring that claims for all insurance contracts issued prior to January 1, 1946 would be paid on the basis of a reduction of the claim by 60%. The Dutch apparently were able to transfer stolen insurance assets from their collection point in the bank of Lippmann, Rosenthal & Co., which had been aryanized by the Nazis and used for such purposes, to the relevant insurance companies and mandated settlements with their Jewish customers. Manifestly, we are thus confronted with very diverse practices and solutions with respect to compensation of Jewish insurance assets, which run the gamut from the absence of any compensation in the former Communist countries to varieties of compensation in Germany, Austria, and the Netherlands.

Mr. Glenn Pomeroy

NORTH DAKOTA COMMISSIONER OF INSURANCE
PRESIDENT, NATIONAL ASSOCIATION OF INSURANCE COMMISSIONERS
UNITED STATES

Plenary Session on Holocaust-Era Insurance Claims

Thank you, Ambassador Olson.

It is a great honor to be here, to work with you, and be a part of this historic undertaking.

My colleague, New York Superintendent of Insurance, Neil Levin and I hope to briefly outline steps U.S. Insurance Regulators have taken throughout this past year with respect to insurance issues. In particular, we have had a very productive summer and fall as we have worked hard in search of a solution to the issue of unpaid Holocaust era insurance claims.

First of all, I need to briefly describe U.S. Regulatory environment for insurance.

In the U.S., this industry is not regulated at the national level, here in Washington, D.C., but is regulated by the states. Each state has a primary regulator for the insurance sold there. That person is responsible for licensing the companies and agents that sell in that state and oversee the products that are sold there. Each state is assisted in their individual effort by the collective effort of the National Association of Insurance Commissioners, the NAIC. The NAIC is a membership organization that brings all states together for various voluntary efforts such as developing model laws or facilitating joint enforcement activity.

Last year, with the publicity surrounding the restitution of Holocaust-era assets from Swiss banks, the issue of unpaid insurance policies began to draw national attention as well. A growing body of public evidence suggested that several major insurance companies had sold policies to people of Jewish faith in the 1920s and 30s, but they had never paid a claim on those policies to the rightful parties...the insured.

In September of 1997, the NAIC created a Working Group to investigate these issues and identify the appropriate role for the NAIC and the states in the search for justice – helping Holocaust survivors and their heirs resolve claims stemming from policies sold during the Holocaust era.

The Working Group began by holding a series of hearings around the country. I attended our first hearing held here in Washington, D.C., last fall. My colleagues and I listened first hand to the personal accounts of several Holocaust survivors whose parents had been sold either a life policy, property policy, or dowry policy. The purchasers of these policies, generally the parents of the persons who testified, perished in the concentration camps at the hands of the Nazis. They left behind children who, though they managed to somehow survive the Holocaust, had never managed all these years later to be adequately compensated under the insurance policy purchased by their parents.

The hearing was a powerful experience for all of us. We sat with Holocaust survivors and looked into their eyes as they fought through their emotions to tell us their stories. A woman, for example, who recalled the day long ago when a door to door salesman came by to sell her father and insurance policy. How thrilled he was that notwithstanding the discriminatory practices then targeted at the Jewish community, here was one company that wanted his business. She recalled for us the circumstances surrounding the murder of her parents, her own survival, and her unsuccessful efforts over the last several years to receive just compensation under the policy.

And so, after conducting several hearings through the country, this past Spring, the NAIC decide to establish a committee of nine states and work toward the establishment of an International Commission to resolve unpaid claims to Holocaust survivors and their heirs.

Given the importance of this issue to all the states, as President of the NAIC, I was asked to head up this effort and I asked Superintendent Levin to serve as Vice Chair. As he and I and other colleagues from around the country, many of whom are also here today, began our work this spring, for me personally, there were two particularly inspiring moments that gave direction to the passion that all of us felt for this cause.

The first came in early May when this new committee of State Insurance Commissioners met in New York and met with Rabbi Israel Singer. Rabbi Singer, in his own powerful and articulate way, encouraged us to be guided by achieving an outcome that was both swift and fair. Swift because for Holocaust survivors still living we don't have time to debate or litigate this matter for the next ten years. Fair because as we heard last night and this morning this is not about money this is about justice. This is about doing what we can to obtain justice – now!!

Work with the companies, Rabbi Singer implored, and the honorable men and women who now run them. Let cooperation and collaboration be our cornerstone and not confrontation because if confrontation is the chosen path, no one will win and everyone will lose. Rabbi Singer's words meant a great deal to our committee and we have tried to honor them with our actions.

For me, the second defining moment came in June, when I had the opportunity at the planning session for this conference, to visit personally with Ben Mead who heads the American Gathering of Holocaust Survivors and who, with his granddaughter, led the Remembrance Service last evening. Ben told me that it was this wish that when people today work on these issues, that they always remember that we are not talking about academic issues, or not just talking about abstract numbers, but real people, who lived and worked and dreamed – and who purchased insurance policies as part of their dreams for the future – a future that would never come.

Ben told me his own story. As Rabbi Singer mentioned, Ben's family didn't have much money, sometimes they even had to forgo a trip to the grocery store. But, they would always make their weekly insurance payments. Ben told me how he, as a little boy, was the only child in the neighborhood who didn't have a bicycle, his family couldn't afford it, and yet his father made sure the insurance payment was made – every week.

Now, here in the U.S., I'm from North Dakota. As I began this involvement, I was aware that perhaps only one survivor resided in my state and, sadly, she passed away this summer. Obviously, this issue is not one that impacts directly the people in my state – but that doesn't matter – not anymore. Not when I think about my friend Ben Mead, and think about when he was a young boy with parents who loved him but were taken from him – forever.

I think about my own young son, and I realize that I am personally connected to this issue now in a way that is powerful and profound – even a little difficult to explain.

And so, we worked throughout the summer to create an International Commission. Through a "Memorandum of Understanding," which has now been signed by six insurance companies and over 40 states, an agreement was reached in August and the Commission was formed.

This Commission is made up of representatives from the insurance regulators, both U.S. and Europe, the companies, the survivor organizations, and the State of Israel. The goal is to work with collaboration rather than confrontation.

Superintendent Levin will explain in more detail about the Commission, its process, and how it will approach its task to achieve the moral accounting that must take place now, before it is too late.

Yes, this is difficult. And, yes this is complicated. We are talking about horrible activity that occurred over 50 years ago. In so many cases, policyholders were murdered and all their records destroyed. Many companies have since either been taken over by the Nazis or nationalized by Eastern European governments in the years following World War II.

But, these difficulties are tiny and insignificant compared to the tremendous responsibility we now bear – the tremendous opportunity we now have – to achieve, under our watch, a measure of justice by working with others who share our responsibility and our opportunity.

Through the work of the International Commission, we have created the process to get the job done. And now, the Commission must to its work.

Thank you.

Mr. Neil D. Levin

SUPERINTENDENT, NEW YORK STATE INSURANCE DEPARTMENT AND
VICE CHAIR, NAIC INTERNATIONAL HOLOCAUST COMMISSION
TASK FORCE
UNITED STATES

Plenary Session on Holocaust-Era Insurance Claims

Thank you, Commissioner Pomeroy.

It is a great honor to be here and to be part of this historic conference.

As you all recall this conference began with comments by Ambassador Eizenstat and Mr. Wiesel who spoke so eloquently about the moral and ethical imperatives for addressing issues which have been lingering for over 50 years. This was followed by Secretary of State Albright's personal and moving plea to give people back their history. I would like to take a few moments to speak about how the International Commission will strive to do this.

The theme of this conference is voluntary action based on a moral foundation. This also is the theme of the International Commission. The Commission is composed of thirteen members, all of whom have joined voluntarily: Three representatives from the United States commissioners, three representatives from the international Jewish and survivor organizations and six representatives from the European insurance companies and regulators. There are also three observer spots for the survivor and Jewish groups, an observer spot for the State Department and an observer spot for the European Economic Commission.

The International Commission has already begun meeting and has initiated its work. As part of its mandate, the International Commission will oversee an audit process and is currently developing an audit program. However, we are going to learn from the successes and problems of the Volcker Committee. The Commission is committed to a "top-down" review and will not expend millions of dollars combing through every shred of paper in Europe. Further, the Commission is committed to using the work of auditors the companies have already hired if that work meets an appropriate standard in order to avoid unnecessary costs. At all times we will be attempting to maximize recovery for Holocaust victims and minimize expenditures for auditors and lawyers.

Further, the Commission is committed to a claims driven process and is currently setting up a claims resolution process with a 1-800 number to receive and process claims. Our goal is for the complete process to be user friendly. The claims process will operate with relaxed standards of proof that will acknowledge the passage of time and the practical difficulties of the survivors, their beneficiaries and heirs in locating relevant documents.

The Commission will work to resolve all of the claims within two years and payments to survivors and their heirs will be made throughout the Commission's two-year investigation.

The Commission has also created a humanitarian fund and a fund to deal with nationalized claims and claims against companies that are no longer in existence. We are proud to be able to say that we already have an upfront contribution of $90 million from the insurance companies towards those funds. The Commission plans to move quickly to determine how these amounts will be allocated to Holocaust victims. Further, the insurance companies have committed to pay the expenses of the Commission so that no money is taken away from survivors.

In addition, Mr. Eagleburger and the U.S. State Department will lead an effort to encourage other insurance companies and foreign governments to participate in the Commission.   Today we are making an appeal to the 44 countries represented here to participate in this Commission. I would like to personally commend the six companies that are participating in the International Commission yet unfortunately they only represent 25% of the market during that time period. Not one company has come forward that is not doing business in the United States. I must ask the question why? There is a moral and ethical obligation to aid in this effort to restore and rewrite history for the survivors.

We should end the 20th Century differently than it began -- with a global community with a strong conscience -- a community that is unafraid to remember and is committed to moral and ethical renewal. We must commit to open our archives to take steps to make them accessible and to commit to preserve these archives. Just recently I was able to learn about my own personal history through access to archives in Belarus and the Ukraine. This is the least we can do for all of the survivors.

As we were reminded by Elie Weisel, Secretary of State Albright and Under Secretary of State Eizenstat, our efforts here today are about a lot more than money.   They are about a gesture of restitution and contrition, rewriting history and letting the victims witness before they die, the support of the governments around the world who sat by silently for far too long.

Thank you, and I look forward to working with all of you in this effort.

Mr. Herbert Hansmeyer

MEMBER OF THE BOARD OF MANAGEMENT
ALLIANZ AG

Plenary Session on Holocaust-Era Insurance Claims

Mr. Bindenagel, Secretary Eagleburger, Judge Mikva, distinguished Ladies and Gentlemen,

I would like to extend my sincere thanks to you for the opportunity to participate in the Washington Conference on Holocaust-Era Assets on behalf of Allianz AG. The topic of insurance policies held by the victims of the Holocaust is very challenging and not at all comparable to the dormant accounts in Swiss banks - not only because many countries - each with its own history and political and legal aspects - are involved, but also because insurance itself is a rather complex area of business.

I would be pleased if I could contribute some information to Conference participants for their discussion of Holocaust-era insurance claims.

Allow me to begin by emphasizing that Allianz AG is committed to achieving clarity on this issue. Furthermore, it is, and has always been, our policy to pay all legitimate claims of our policyholders. This is naturally also the case for unsettled claims of our company from Holocaust survivors and their families.

In this respect, we are determined that justice is done. It is for this reason that Allianz AG is a participant in the International Commission under the chairmanship of Secretary Eagleburger. At this juncture, I would like to express my personal and my company's thanks to him for taking on this difficult task. Under his guidance this commission will certainly bring us all a step closer to our common pursuit of a just resolution. In this respect, I would also like to express my personal appreciation to the U.S. State Department and the U.S. Holocaust Memorial Museum for organizing this important international forum. This, too, will certainly help us all achieve clarity on the factual circumstances before, during and in the aftermath of the Second World War.

That many insurance claims might have remained unpaid after the Second World War came, quite frankly, as a surprise to Allianz AG. Even more surprising to us was the accusation - made in no uncertain terms in the New York lawsuit that for more than 50 years we had not paid claims to victims of Nazi persecution. This, ladies and gentlemen, is quite simply untrue. It is vitally important that those of us seeking to address these issues in a constructive manner realize this.

The reason that the lawsuit came as a surprise to us - and let me emphasize this clearly - was that we did know that, as far as Germany is concerned, most insurance claims had been previously paid fairly and correctly, the majority of them before the war. In addition, the majority of cases were included in post-war compensation programs and treaties among the nations involved in the war. It was our understanding that these programs - initiated after World War II by the Allied governments and continued to this day by the Federal Republic of Germany had, in fact, settled all claims. The restitution laws were exceedingly comprehensive and did include claims on insurance policies. In short, we had to assume that the combined efforts of the Allied governments and the Federal Republic - with the assistance of the German insurance sector - had made it highly unlikely that claims remained unsettled.

However, when the lawsuit was filed, it became clear that there were unanswered questions around already settled policies but even more about nationalized policies, particularly in Eastern Europe. As many of the participants here today know, Allianz sought from the very beginning to be open for a constructive dialogue. Above all, we stated quite clearly our commitment to treat this with the highest level of integrity. We see this as our responsibility to all policyholders past and present.

Many of you are aware of our efforts in this area. In April 1997, we established 24-hour helpline call centers in North America, Europe and Israel to enable potential claimants to contact us directly with inquiries in the most unbureaucratic manner possible. We asked Arthur Andersen to conduct an independent audit of relevant file inventories in Germany in order to see whether policies had, contrary to our knowledge, remained unsettled. And we invited Professor Feldman, renowned expert of history at the University of California at Berkeley, to research our company's history independently and publish his findings.

We further sought to come to a dialogue with the US insurance commissioners and the organizations that have represented Holocaust survivors for decades, seeking to find together a constructive means of addressing the concerns of all involved. The result of these talks was the establishment in August of the International Commission, chaired by Secretary Eagleburger.

We are committed to creating a very sound international process for settling potentially open insurance claims. Ladies and gentlemen, I am personally convinced that we are together- on the right path toward a swift and just resolution of these issues.

Nonetheless, we have observed that discussions remain partially hindered by lingering problems of perception on the issues involved. This is, in some respect, understandable. As I said, the technical side of insurance is difficult to understand, and has been made even more complex by the passage of more than 50 years since the events under consideration took place. Additionally, these issues involve many countries across Europe West and East all with their diverse legal and historical aspects.

Especially for Eastern Europe, it is not easy to get to the hard facts of the fate of policies because the insurance companies and their branches were nationalized after the war. Still, we must make this effort.

Because of Allianz AG's position as the largest insurer in Germany both today and in the early decades of this century our focus has naturally been primarily on Germany. The independent audits I have already mentioned were conducted initially on the file inventories of Allianz Lebensversicherungs-AG, our German life insurance subsidiary. They were then extended to inventories held by Vereinte Leben, a German life insurance company acquired by Allianz AG in 1996.

The auditors faced a daunting task; under consideration were more than one point four million individual paper files on policies issued between 1920 and 1945. No separate file inventories for people persecuted by Germany's Nazi regime existed, and the files have not in any way been computerized.

Identification of victims of the Holocaust was particularly difficult. Methods for identification using direct and circumstantial evidence contained in the files had first to be developed. Finally, Arthur Andersen provided us with a clear evaluation of the status of files, giving us an assessment on what happened to those insurance policies and how our companies have dealt with them.

The audit results showed that, of the files examined, the vast majority of policies were, in fact, previously paid out at the request and into the accounts of individual policyholders. Some 70 percent of the files audited involved cases in which the policy had been canceled prematurely and been cashed in. Again, almost all were cancelled by the policyholder, while cancellations on Nazi Government order were rather rare.

Ladies and gentlemen, in considering these facts from the view of an insurance company which of course we must do if we truly want clarity on insurance issues, we should not lose sight of other important aspects as well.

In the years leading up to World War II, Jewish people in Germany came under increasing pressure from the Nazi regime. That regime first sought to exclude Jews from the economic, social and political life of Germany, then sought to plunder their property, and ultimately perpetrated one of the most heinous crimes against humanity ever recorded - the Holocaust.

Thus, when people sought to cash in their life insurance policies, they may have done so in a desperate effort to alleviate increasing financial burdens from unjust levies and taxes, or to facilitate emigration. They did so in order to escape no uncertain peril to their lives. This is a fact that cannot and should not be left out.

It is for this reason that the postwar German government provided compensation not only for the value of policies confiscated by the Nazi regime in the late 1930s and through 1945, but also for instances in which people suffered a financial loss on policies cashed in early. Our research has shown that around 70 percent of the Jewish files of our companies were later made part of the German government's restitution and compensation programs.

And let us be quite clear on this, neither the insurance customers themselves nor the insurers benefited in any way when people cashed in and thus canceled their insurance policies. But it was and still is the responsibility of an insurer to pay the cash value on a policy at cancellation if requested. It may be interesting to note that recently conducted audits of the German Insurance Department have shown that, in such cases, our company not only paid, but paid quickly, in some instances hand-delivering insurance payments to peoples homes. Thus the Nazi government's efforts to directly seize Jewish assets under expropriation laws were quite frequently unsuccessful because the policies were previously paid out or, if they were still in force, carried loans and prepayments, leaving sometimes only very little, if anything at all, for the Nazi regime to confiscate.

The question remains, though: Despite earlier payments and comprehensive compensation programs, is it still possible that some policies remained unsettled? The answer is yes, but only in the small number of cases where the beneficiary or heir could not be found by the companies in the turmoil after the war or did not claim under a policy in the compensation proceedings.

Did the companies keep the money, as was the case with the dormant accounts? The answer is no they did not. After the war all German life insurance companies were technically bankrupt and kept alive through government subsidies the so-called equalization funds - which exactly matched their liabilities. The German Insurance Department conducted audits for a period of 18 years on these subsidies. If the liability did not materialize, then the subsidy had to be paid back to the government. Therefore the companies could not enrich themselves with funds due under unsettled policies. In other words, there are no dormant assets from unclaimed policies.

Despite this fact, it is our firm belief that policies that remained truly unsettled should be paid regardless of statutes of limitations and bureaucratic red tape. This has always been our policy, and it remains our policy as part of our voluntary participation in the International Commission.

We still have a great deal of work to do in achieving clarity on all these issues. This is particularly true in terms of efforts to address claim payments that were hindered by the chaos in which Europe found itself during and after the War waves of emigration, the rebuilding of entire countries and, especially, the nationalization of the private insurance industry in a number of countries in Eastern Europe. Determining how to address these issues will take some time. However, as a further sign of our commitment to assisting Holocaust survivors, the International Commission has created funds that will be available to support needy survivors whose claims may be complicated by such factors.

Ladies and gentlemen, I remain personally convinced that we can best achieve our common goal of justice and clarity through continued dialogue between companies, regulators, claimants and, of course, governments. Again I would like to express my appreciation for this conferences efforts and offer Allianz AG's assurances that we share your goals and will continue to support all constructive efforts to address these issues.

Thank you.

Prof. Gerald D. Feldman

PROFESSOR OF HISTORY, UNIVERSITY OF CALIFORNIA, BERKELEY AND
FELLOW, AMERICAN ACADEMY IN BERLIN
UNITED STATES

Confiscation of Insurance Assets: Special Issues

Break-out Session on Holocaust-Era Insurance: Historical Overview,
Nazi Confiscation of Insurance Policy Assets

In my presentation to the Plenary Session, I sought to outline the basic manner in which German-Jewish assets were confiscated. I distinguished between indirect and direct confiscation. The former was the consequence of the economic deprivation experienced by Jews through loss of livelihood, the financial needs arising from decisions to emigrate, and financial impositions upon Jews. Thus, many of the proceeds received from the repurchase of insurance policies ended up in blocked accounts or at various Finance Ministry revenue offices either, in the first case, as a guarantee that they would pay their taxes or, in the second, in actual payment of those taxes. Direct confiscation took place under decrees allowing the State to deprive Jews who had emigrated or who had been deported in the East of their citizenship and confiscate their assets. It was systematized under the 11th Decree of the Reich Citizenship Law which mandated that insurance companies, banks and other institutions holding Jewish assets actually report them to the financial authorities so that they could be confiscated and threatened penalties for non-compliance.

What I want to do now is to flesh out some of these points, addressing in particular some of the more technical issues involved and the behavior of the insurance companies in these processes. To begin with, I would like to make the point that Jews were valued customers until the regime turned them into poor customers and bad risks. In 1935, for example, Allianz sent around a circular to its branches and daughter companies asking that it be alerted to the names of persons who were emigrating, to Switzerland, Palestine, or elsewhere, so that the companies connected with Allianz in those countries could try to keep these customers. Such a circular would have been inconceivable two years later, but it is revealing of the effort to sustain a measure of normal business practice in an increasingly abnormal situation. Similarly, the correspondence in the policies I have seen demonstrate a desire to maintain as much of the worth of the policies as possible under the circumstances. Many Jewish customers moved very slowly in giving up their insurance. Finding themselves unable to pay premiums, they often turned their policies into paid-up policies, which maintained at least the present worth of the policies. Thus, in the case of a twenty-year policy converted in its seventh year, the value would be about thirty percent of what it would have been had it come to term. Conversion, however, also kept the way open for a return to the old policy and full value if premium payments were resumed. Some Jewish policyholders were very uncertain as to what to do and, as far as I can tell from the correspondence I have seen, they received objective and straightforward advice with respect to borrowing on their policies and the details of buying them back if that seemed necessary to the customer.

Clearly it is very much to the interest of any insurer to have its customers hold on to their policies until they come to term since the profit made on prematurely terminated policies was either negligible or non-existent. In some cases there was even a loss. German companies, unlike their American counterparts, did not impose surrender charges. The cash surrender value of a twenty-year policy after seven years was slightly below twenty percent. Obviously it was much more to the interest of the customer not to take the disproportionate loss on present and expected value entailed in buying a policy back. Insurance companies that tried to hold on to their Jewish customers, therefore, were doing so at the very least because it was in their interest. By 1937-1939, however, this was becoming increasingly pointless. The introduction of the Four-Year rearmament program at the end of 1936 made Field Marshall Hermann Göring, who was its head, particularly anxious to mobilize Jewish assets, while radical elements in the National Socialist Party put increasing pressure on Jews as well. Jews could no longer afford to pay premiums and were increasingly inclined to emigrate. There was a veritable flood of cash-ins beginning in mid-1937, and a particularly dramatic development following the November Pogrom. The statistical findings of Allianz tend to confirm the impressionistic findings of my reading of the policies. Cancellations shortened the average life of policies by about half, that is, from 20 to 10 years, thereby diminishing the average cash value of Jewish policies to about 38% of anticipated full value. In the end, cancellations far outweighed conversion to paid-up policies. Of the Jewish policies sampled, 69% were cancelled, while only 17% were converted. There is good evidence that the shift from indirect to direct expropriation took place in the latter part of 1939 and early 1940 before it was legally imposed in late 1941. Most Jews holding insurance, therefore, cashed in their policies by force of circumstances prior to 1940.

The flood of repurchases in 1937-1939 obviously was a cash drain on the insurers, and given the way Jews were treated in Germany, one naturally raises the question as to whether insurers tried to deny Jewish customers immediate access to their money. I have found no such evidence with respect to Allianz. There was at least one case, the Isar Insurance Company, which tried to gain government permission to convert Jewish policies into premium free policies rather than pay out the repurchase value. Isar was peculiar in that it had a particularly large number of Jewish policyholders acquired when it took over the German block of the business of the Austrian Phoenix company, which had gone bankrupt in 1936. Isar, however, was denied permission to withhold payments for repurchase by the Reich Supervisory Office for insurance and paid out two million marks to Jewish policyholders in 1938-1939. Leaving aside legal niceties, this was of course quite logical quite once one reflects on National Socialist intentions. Robbing the Jews of their insurance assets required their monetization, whether by the Jews themselves or, as in the case of direct confiscation, by the government. The regime had nothing to gain by leaving such assets in the hands of the insurance companies.

Let me now expand somewhat on one of the most confusing of all the issues connected with the insurance question both with regard to the policies and with regard to compensation question, namely, currencies and their worth. This problem is especially difficult for Americans, who have experienced neither a hyperinflation nor the introduction of a new currency in this century. The Germans have undergone this experience twice, first in 1922-1923, and then in 1945-1948. In the first case, the new Reichsmark was denominated at a ratio of 4.2 trillion paper marks to one dollar or a trillion paper marks to one Reichsmark. In the second case, the now old Reichsmark was denominated at ten RM to one DM in the currency reform of 1948. I want to concentrate here on the interwar currency issues and their implications for insurance and will talk about the postwar currency reform with respect to the compensation issue in the breakout session devoted to that problem.

Given the fate of the German mark, it is understandable that after 1923 many Germans did not want to take out insurance companies denominated in Reichsmark but rather wanted policies denominated in real values, gold mark values. These took various forms. Some policies were denominated in fine gold, this being measured as 1/2790 kilograms fine gold equaling one gold mark or, at a minimum, one Reichsmark, thereby insuring the customer receipt of at least the Reichsmark equivalent in fine gold. Policies denominated in gold marks were presumed to be on a dollar basis, that is 4.2 gold marks to the dollar, thereby allegedly insuring customer whatever the real value might be in Reichsmark. Other policies were denominated in dollars or Swiss franc. Some of them even took out their policies with Swiss or other foreign companies operating in Germany for good measure. What they did not anticipate, however, was the currency instability of the Great Depression, especially after September 1931, when England went off the gold standard. The Germans did not go off the gold standard in theory but they effectively did so in practice by introducing exchange controls during the banking crisis of July 1931. With the end of currency convertibility, it was very much to the German advantage to have insurance assets denominated in RM, and a good case could be made that this was also to the advantage of insurance policyholders after the United States devalued the dollar by 41% in January 1934 and the Swiss devalued their currency by 35% in 1936. Companies like Allianz offered their customers the opportunity to convert their dollar and gold denominated policies at the old rate of 4.2 RM to the dollar rather than at 2.5 marks to the RM, which became the new exchange rate. Not surprisingly, most customers took advantage of this offer before conversion to a Reichsmark basis became compulsory in August 26, 1938. It is important to bear in mind that this was not a policy aimed specifically against Jews. All German insurance policy holders were subject to these conversions. The real purpose was for the government to get more hard currency for the Four Year Plan, and insurers were compelled to convert the hard currency they had used to cover their gold mark obligations into Reichsmark and then to invest these Reichsmark in Reich bonds.

The damage done to Jews in connection with these currency issues was a product of the exchange control restrictions first introduced in July 1931, that is before the Nazis came to power, and then progressively made more severe after 1933 so that emigrating Jews could not take more than a very limited amount of their money out of the country. The Reichsmarks Jews had left after paying their various taxes and for the costs of their emigration had to be converted at a very unfavorable rate at the Gold Discount Bank, so that Jews could usually take no more than a pittance of their cash assets out of the country. The alternative was to leave a blocked account in Germany. This meant that insurance proceeds often had to be retained in Germany in an emigrant blocked account. The emigrant could arrange to have money paid to his relatives in Germany from such an account but could not use such money for himself or have it transferred since he had become a "non-resident" (Devisenausländer) with respect to currency matters.

The 11th Decree of the Reich Citizenship Law of November 1941 not only mandated the confiscation of all such accounts and the face value of all insurance policies of Jews remaining in Germany but also made banks and insurance companies liable for reporting these assets within six months. It received further elaboration in the 13th Decree of the Reich Citizenship Law issued on July 1, 1943 which ordered that the assets of all deceased Jews were the property of the Reich. The 89 insurance companies operating in the Reich in 1941 had over five million policies and were undergoing manpower rationalization because of the war effort. There was no effective way of going through these policies systematically to find Jews, and there are of course many names, Rosenberg, for example, that could be Jewish. For this reason, the Reich Group for the Insurance Industry regularly sought extensions and exemption from penalties for delays in compliance. These were granted only on a rather short-term basis and with the proviso that the company would have to pay interest on the delivery of insurance assets after the deadline. Whatever the efforts at compliance, my sense is that actual confiscation depended on the Gestapo reporting names and policy numbers, these often being at its disposal because of the requirement after April 1938 that Jews report all their assets. Once such confiscation instructions came in, the insurance companies were no less "correct" in calculating and delivering the repurchase value of the policies to the Revenue Offices than they had been in doing so for the rightful owners of the policies in earlier years.

Finally, as I noted in the plenary session, the confiscation of Jewish insurance assets spread as the Third Reich expanded. The areas incorporated in the Reich, beginning with Austria, and going on to the Czech lands, the Polish areas outside the General Government, and Alsace-Lorraine. The confiscation of Jewish assets in Austria seems to have been pursued with particular vigor, and this shows up in Austrian files dealing with insurance issues. I have not yet done much work on the seizure of Jewish insurance assets in the occupied areas during the war. Various decrees issued by the military authorities and or civilian authorities in the occupied areas of France, in Belgium and Luxembourg in 1941 and 1942 also mandated the seizure of assets of Jews who had fled and emigrated. In this way, the expropriation of Jewish insurance assets by the National Socialist regime became a European-wide phenomenon.

Mr. Tomas Jelinek
OFFICE OF THE PRESIDENT
CZECH REPUBLIC

Insurance in the Nazi Occupied Czech Lands: Preliminary Findings[1]

Break-out Session on Holocaust-Era Insurance: Historical Overview, Nazi Confiscation of Insurance Policy Assets

An overview of the insurance industry during the Second World War in the territories of what is now the Czech Republic is presented, with the emphasis on the fate of the life insurance policies of the Holocaust victims. The first chapter characterizes the Czechoslovak insurance industry before the Second World War. The second chapter deals with the period between 1938 and 1945, including the occupation of the "Sudetenland" and the consequent establishment of the "Protectorate of Bohemia and Moravia."

THE INSURANCE INDUSTRY BEFORE WWII

Inter-war Czechoslovakia[2] was one of the most industrialized countries in Central and Southeastern Europe.[3] Its economy was highly dependent on the exportation of goods, following from the fact that 70% of the industrial production of the former Habsburg Empire was concentrated in the Czechoslovak territory, though only 26% of the

---

[1] Prepared for the Washington Conference on Holocaust-Era Assets in 1998. Based on the findings of the Czech Working Group on Holocaust Insurance.
[2] Czechoslovakia was established on October 28, 1918. It consisted of 21% of the former Austro-Hungarian Empire: Bohemia, Moravia, Slovakia, Silesia, Ruthenia (Transcarpathia).
[3] The former Hapsburg Empire

Empire's population lived there. After the disintegration of the Habsburg Empire common market, the newly-born Czechoslovak state was faced with the challenge of finding foreign markets for Czechoslovak goods. In order for the economy to survive, at least 30% of industrial production needed to be exported.[4] Upon reaching this level of exportation, Czechoslovakia became one among ten member states of the League of Nations with the highest industrial product per capita and was also one of the seven biggest weapon suppliers in the world.

Before the Second World War, Czechoslovakia was, in many respects, a modern and dynamic state which was able to maintain its democratic system throughout the rise of authoritarian regimes in the region. However, one cannot claim that inter-war Czechoslovakia was a free market economy. From the turn of the century, banks already had controlling influence over numerous industries and had become a primary force in furthering oligopolistic business organizations. The links between banks and industrial and commercial enterprises limited competition by internalizing functions of the market.[5] The most famous example of such an arrangement was Zivnostenska banka, which spread its influence not only in Czechoslovakia, but also throughout Southeastern Europe. After the world economic crises of the early thirties, a strict exchange control and other protectionist measures were introduced in Czechoslovakia, as they were in many countries in the region.[6] Most of the industry was organized through cartel agreements.

Inter-war Czechoslovakia was an important intermediator between western economies, namely Britain and France, and Southeastern Europe. In the same period Western entrepreneurs were competing with German companies for their share of the Czechoslovak market. Consequently, German capital tried to extend its influence in order to undermine Czechoslovak economic connections with Western countries and allies in the region. While the principal direct investors in inter-war Czechoslovakia were Great Britain and France, German entrepreneurs obtained their influence through cartel agreements.[7]

The Insurance sector in inter-war Czechoslovakia was comparable to the insurance industry in any developed country. There was a tradition of availability of all types of insurance, and

---

[4] Teichová 1994a, p.25.
[5] Teichová 1994b, p.84.
[6] Teichová 1994b, p.90.
[7] For details see Teichová 1994a and compare this argument, particularly in the insurance industry, with Axis Penetration of European Insurance (1943) p.15-16.

Czechoslovakia had very strong international ties. Foreign companies controlled much of the industry within the country (for data on life insurance see Table 1), while the business share of Czechoslovak companies abroad was negligible.

The insurance industry went through a number of troublesome transitions following the First World War. The first was the period of transformation which occurred during the division of the territories of the Austro-Hungarian Empire. At this time, Czechoslovakia was faced with the task of creating an independent Czechoslovak insurance sector. The second difficult period for the insurance industry resulted from the economic crises of the nineteen-thirties, during which the growth of new businesses slowed, the total sum of premiums decreased, and administrative costs increased. The third tumultuous period for the Czechoslovak insurance sector was the result of the collapse of the Fenix Insurance Company in 1936, which greatly undermined the public's trust in the insurance industry. The incident required that the state, together with the insurance sector, consolidate Fenix. The total loss was Kc 1,450 million,[8] and the regulatory organization of the insurance industry had to be entirely revised.

Table 1 - The Life Insurance Sector during 1933-1936 (in millions of Kc)

Year	Domestic insurance companies					Foreign insurance companies				
	Total sum of direct and indirect business									
	Insured capital	Premium		Pay out		Insured capital	Premium		Pay out	
		Gross	Net	Gross	Net		Gross	Net	Gross	Net
1934	9 626	471	361	146	115	6 398	304	233	120	92
1935	9583	431	327	170	130	4 142	189	142	72	53
1936	9606	441	341	168	131	4 261	195	146	76	56

Source: Kral 1937, p.130.

For the purpose of our current attempt to resolve the issue of the insurance policies of Holocaust victims, it is important to be familiar

---

[8] Kral 1937, p.39.

with the following main legal regulations of insurance activities before World War Two.

In 1924, the Ministry of the Interior, which was responsible for the supervision of the insurance sector, issued a regulation forbidding insurance companies to denominate their policies in other than Czechoslovak currency. In 1933, the same was done for policies denominated in gold. Also in 1933, insurance clients complained about the unjust calculation of reduced insurance policies. Their compensation by different companies was resolved by a regulation which stated that those conditions had to be written on every life policy.

The most important legal change in the inter-war period was the *Law on securing the claims of insurance companies' clients and concerning state supervision (No.147/1934)*. This law mandated a necessary level of reserve funds for insurance payments. The reserve funds had to be held separately from the rest of the property of the insurance companies. However, in the case of foreign companies, the law permitted locally licensed branches of foreign companies to manage the funds.

At the end of 1937, there were 48 domestic insurance companies in Czechoslovakia. 24 had foreign direct investors. The total sum of foreign holdings was Kc 32.8 million, 40% of the basic capital of all companies with foreign participation. The most active companies were Italian companies with a direct investment of Kc 20.8 million, followed by German and Swiss companies with the direct investment of Kc 8 million and Kc 4 million, respectively.[9]

In 1938, there were 28 domestic and 6 foreign life insurance companies in Czechoslovakia (for details see Appendix 2). The average life insurance policy face value was Kc 13,142 in domestic companies, and 28,869 K in foreign companies. There were about 1.255 million people insured with Czechoslovak companies, while foreign insurance companies insured about 161,000 clients.

THE INSURANCE INDUSTRY IN THE YEARS 1938-1945[10]

The question of property claims against Czechoslovakia was raised immediately after Nazi German annexation of the so called

---

[9] Teichova 1994 a, p.34-41.

[10] For basic information about the history of the Protectorate see Appendix 1.

udetenland. Though the main concern was the division of the gold and
ard currency reserves of the Czechoslovak Central Bank, the insurance
ndustry was also subject to division. All insurance business in the
udetenland was transferred from Czechoslovak companies to German,
austrian, Italian or Swiss insurance companies (see Table 2). Although
n international agreement about the division of insurance business
etween Nazi Germany and Czechoslovakia was under preparation
efore March 15, 1939, the final separation was carried over by June 30,
939, three month after the occupation of the rest of the Czech territory.
ccording to the rules proclaimed by the Nazi administration all
nsurance policies signed prior to October 10, 1938 at the territory of the
ormer Czechoslovakia (i.e. deadline for final separation of the
Sudetenland") belonged to the insurance companies in the Protectorate
' the insurance company had established headquarters in the
Protectorate" before December 31, 1938 and if the insured object was in
ne same territory by this date. At the same time the insurance business in
lovakia and in the areas annexed by Poland and Hungary had to be
eparated.

The vast majority of the Jewish population of "Sudetenland"
scaped and moved to the territory remaining under Czechoslovak
ontrol. One can assume that the fate of the insurance policies and other
roperty of those who remained was identical to that of Jews from
iermany and Austria, where policies and other property were
onfiscated by the Reich.   In 1943, the total premium income of
nsurance companies in Sudetenland was estimated to be approximately
3 million RM in life insurance and about 30 million RM in general
nsurance.[11]

Table 2 Transfer of Czechoslovak Insurance Activities in Sudetenland

Name of original company	Taken over by	
	Life Insurance	General Insurance
Albrechticka		Sudetendeutsche Union Versicherungs - A.G.
Cechoslovia	Donau-Concordia, Lebensvers. - A.G.	Moravsko-slezska Brno
Ceska vzajemna	Victoria zu Berlin	

---

[11] Axis penetration of European Insurance (1943), p.30.

Ceskomoravska	Riunione	Schles. Feuer-Vers.-Gesellschaft
Elbe - Schaden		Albingia, Vers. - A.G.
Hasicska	Manheimer Lebensvers. - Gesell., A.G.	Gothaer Feuerversicherungs-bank
Koruna	Rothenburger Lebensvers., A.G.	Sudetendeutsche Union Versicherungs - A.G.
Kvas	Donau-Concordia, Lebensvers. - A.G.	Donau-Concordia Allgemeine Versicherung-A.G. Erste Allg. Unfall-u. Schadens Vers. Gesellschaft
Lipa	Donau-Concordia, Lebensvers. - A.G.	Sudetendeutsche Union Versicherungs - A.G.
Loyd	Terra, Spar-u.Lebensvers.A.G.	Moravsko-slezska Brno
Merkur	Donau-Concordia, Lebensvers. - A.G.	Deutsche Algemeine Versicherungs - A.G. Allgemeine Unfall- u. Haftpflicht-Vers.- A.G.
Moldavia-Generali-Sekuritas		Erste Allg. Unfall-u. Schadens Vers. Gesellschaft
Narodni	Manheimer Lebensvers. - Gesell., A.G.	Sudetendeutsche Union Versicherungs - A.G.
Patria	Donau-Concordia, Lebensvers. - A.G.	Sudetendeutsche Union Versicherungs - A.G.
Plananska		Allgemeine Elementar Versicherungs-A.G.
Praha	Rothenburger Lebensvers., A.G.	Aachener u. Munchener Feuer-Vers.-Ges.
Prazska mestska	Rothenburger Lebensvers., A.G.	Moravsko-slezska Brno
Prvni ceska		Victoria, Feuer-Vers.-A.G. Leipziger Hagel-Vers.-A.G. Wiener Alianz, Vers.-A.G.
Rolnicka	Manheimer Lebensvers. - Gesell., A.G.	Manheimer Vers.-Ges. Wiener Alianz, Vers.-A.G.
Slavia	Alianz Lebensversicherungs, A.G.	Alianz, Vers.-A.G. Wiener Alianz, Vers.-A.G. Bayerische Vers.-Bank, A.G. Kraft-Vers.-A.G.
Slovanska	Donau-Concordia,	Moravsko-slezska Brno

	Lebensvers. - A.G.	
Vorsorge	Volksfursorge, Lebensvers. A.G.	
Vseobecna	Deutsche Herold, Volks-u. Lebensvers. - A.G.	Sudetendeutsche Union Versicherungs - A.G.
Zemska zivotni	Offentl. Vers. - Anstalt der Sachs. Sparkassen	Offentliche-rechtliche Sachversicherungsanstalt

Source: Marvan (1993), p.314

In order to understand more about the background the following review shows control of individual companies by several foreign insurance concerns and groups operating in Czechoslovakia and "Sudetenland" at the end of 1938.[12]

1. Italian Group
Assicurazioni Generali Concern
Assicurazioni Generali for Czechoslovakia
Moldavia Generali
Securitas
Prvni ceska zajistovaci banka (First Czech Reinsurance Bank)
Riunione Adriatica di Sicurta Concern
Riunione Adriatica di Sicurta for Czechoslovakia
Ceskoslovenska pojistovna (Continental)

2. French Group
La Nationale - Vie
La Nationale - Incedie

3. Swiss Group
Basilejska dopravni pojistovna
Basilejska pozarni pojistovna
Svycarska narodni pojistovna
Helvetia
Concern of Zurich, Unfall-und Schaden-Vers. A.G.
Merkur
Concern of Schweizerische Ruckversicherunge-Ges.
Kotva
Dunaj
Concordia

---

[12] Document from Ceska pojistovna Archive dated Oct. 8, 1938.

4. British Group
Anglo-Elementar

5. German Group
Concern of Victoria in Berlin
Victoria-Leben
Concern of Leipziger Feuer-Vers.Ges.
Union
Muncher Ruckversicherung-Ges. (group of interests)
Cechoslavia
Slovanska pojistovna
Evropska pojistovaci spolecnost

After the Nazi occupation of the rest of Czechoslovakia at the beginning of the Second World War, the insurance companies from nations at war with Nazi Germany halted all their activity in the "Protectorate Bohemia and Moravia". Their business was taken over by German companies (for example, the Anglo-Elementar Insurance Company was taken over by Colonia from Cologne).

A few weeks after the occupation, the first insurance regulation was introduced aiming directly at Jews. On April 29, 1939, a meeting took place between representatives of the Ministry of the Interior, the (formerly Czechoslovak) National Bank, and representatives of the Deutsche Reichsbank. Consequently, the Ministry of Interior issued a circular "Regulation of insurance conditions of non-Aryan policyholders" (No.18623/39-16) declaring both that Jews could only receive their insurance payments to accounts in a selected group of banks, and that these bank accounts would be regulated by the state. Jews were not allowed to change conditions of their insurance policies (e.g. cession, changing of the beneficiary, etc.). [13] Exceptions could be granted by the Ministry of Interior with the consent of the National Bank. However, this regulation did not specify who should be considered Jewish. Later on, in the letter of Association of Czechoslovak Insurance Companies to all its members (dated April 17, 1939) in order to overcome this problem, it was specified that every client had to sign a statement about his/her *Aryan origin*. In the circular of the Ministry of Interior (No. 23728/39-16) from April 27, 1939 it was stated that Jewish clients can be honored the cash benefits up to K 5,000 by their insurance companies without the preliminary permission of the Ministry of Interior and the National Bank.

---

[13] State Central Archive MV-SR k.6352

Any benefit exceeding K 5,000 could be honored without such a permission only on condition that the money was used as a remittance of public services, taxes, fees etc. and transferred directly to the public revenue office. We have found several documents of Star Insurance Company showing that such payments were realized. We may even argue that this company tried to help Jewish clients in order to give them some cash and its clerks calculated their benefits in such a way that they would not exceed K 5,000.[14]

In June 21, 1939 the "Reichsprotektor for Bohemia and Moravia" issued a decree about the Jewish property. For the purpose of our discussion it is important that since that time the Jewish origin was defined according to the Nurnberg laws at the territory of "Protectorate". Almost all property had to be registered by July 31, 1939[15] and it fell under the control of "Protectorate". Another important regulation (No. 25761/39) which significantly influenced the treatment of Jewish clients by insurance companies was issued by the Revisory Department of Finance Ministry in January 23, 1940. It was generally stated that all payments to Jews have to go to their bank accounts, which were under state control.[16] With this stricter regime the limited possibility for Jews to cash directly their insurance policies, which had been in place so far, was abolished. All individual requests of non-Aryan insurants concerning their policies had to be submitted to the Revisory Department of Finance Ministry for individual consideration. The Ministry of Interior made the final decision on the individual applications based on the reference from Finance Ministry.[17]

Application of all these regulations was so complicated that the Association of Insurance Companies published a special guide for insurance industry with respect to Jewish laws. This guide was very detailed and it also dealt with "mixed marriage households" (i.e. Aryan with non-Aryan). By law, Jews could only withdraw up to K 3,000 from their bank accounts per month. However, they were obliged to pay from this amount premiums of their private insurance policies up to the limit of K 750 per month. If the total of the premium payments exceeded K

---

[14] State Central Archive, Ministry of Interior (No.1197/40-16).

[15] The definition of Jewish property was very flexible (e.g. what was Jewish company or a company under the Jewish influence) and it was estimated about 20 billions K.

[16] This regulation was reflected in the circular of Interior Ministry (No.6055/40-16).

[17] State Central Archive, Ministry of Interior (No.23293/40).

750, a person could apply to the Revisory Department for the permission of a higher limit for monthly withdrawal. The guide was written in 1941 by Regierungsassesor Herbert Schmerling, an official from the Revisory Department (Department No.16) of the Finance Ministry. This Department was deeply involved in the agenda of Jewish property. An important role in the expropriation of Jewish property in "Protectorate" was played by Reichsbankrat Walther Untermohle who cooperated closely with Department No.16 . As a member of the Economic Department in the Office of the Reichsprotektor Untermohle was later responsible for the Property Office (details see below).

Supervision of the Insurance Industry

The Insurance industry in the "Protectorate" was supervised by the Ministry of Interior until January 15, 1942. At that time, the responsibility was passed to the Ministry of Economy and Labor which was under the direct control of Nazi Germany. Beginning with May 15, 1941, the insurance industry in the "Protectorate" was centralized in a manner identical to the situation in Nazi Germany. The entire industry was controlled through a central institution, the Central Association of Private Insurance in Bohemia and Moravia (Zentralverband der Vertragsversicherung in Bohmen und Maren), which was designed to serve as an intermediate between the insurance industry and the government. Two economic divisions were established under this association: one for life insurance and the other for general insurance. The chairman and vice-chairman of the association were appointed by the Minister of the Interior (later by the Minister of Economy and Labor). German citizen Robert Rozenkranz, previously a special envoy of the Reichsprotektor in the organization of the Protectorate insurance industry, was the first chairman to be appointed. Circulars of the Association are a very good source of information on the development of the insurance industry during the "Protectorate," particularly concerning the issue of confiscations during the Protectorate (see Appendix 3).

Jewish emigration

At the beginning of the "Protectorate" the Jewish emigration was still viewed by the German authorities as a main "solution of the Jewish question." Expropriation of the property of Jewish emigrants was organized in order to strengthen expansion of German banks and industrial groups in the "Protectorate." Already in March 29, 1939 it was agreed by the representatives of German banks, German Ministry of Economy, Gestapo, and Sicherheitsdienst that Jews would be allowed to emigrate only if they left their property by a German bank. Otherwise Gestapo would not allow them to emigrate.[18] Jews seeking the emigration permit also had to deposit their private insurance policies at an authorized bank.[19] However private insurance policies could be used to cover the emigration tax if the emigrant and did not have other means.

The official Jewish emigration was organized by the Center for Jewish Emigration (Zentralstelle fur judische Auswanderung)[20] which was founded by the Hitler-appointed, German Reichsprotektor Konstantin von Neurath in July 15, 1939. This institution was supervised by the chief of Sicherheitsdienst Walter Stahlecker, and it was closely cooperating with Adolf Eichmann in the Berlin Gestapo Headquarters. In order to manage the Center's property the Emigration Fund for Bohemia and Moravia (Auswanderungsfond) was established in March 5, 1940. The occupation authorities intended to use this Fund to support the German settlement of the "Protectorate"[21]. The Center issued 16,782 passports till the first quarter of 1941. According to the report of the Prague Jewish Community from 1942, 25,977 Jews left the Protectorate between March 15, 1939 and November 30, 1942.

The insurance policies of people who emigrated illegal or "broke the law" in any other way were confiscated by Gestapo. This applied to all the former Czechoslovak citizens who decided to leave the "Protectorate" and even to those who left before the Nazi German occupation.

With the beginning of deportations of Jews to concentration camps and ghettos, the Center for Jewish Emigration was responsible for confiscation of their assets. People asked to register for transport had to declare again all their property including their private belongings (e.g. suits, furniture, food rations vouchers, etc.). They were forced to give the power of attorney to the Center for Jewish Emigration to administer this property.

---

[18] Karny (1991), p.34.
[19] Zajisteni zidovskeho majetku (1941), Vol. VIII., p.6.
[20] It was renamed as Center for Solving of the Jewish Question (Zentralamt fur die Regelung der Judenfrage) in August 12, 1942.
[21] Karny (1991), p.64.

Property Office

Since the beginning of the occupation the Gestapo, which ordered the confiscation of assets of the people and organizations which were declared the "enemies of the Reich", had to look after this property as well. However, with the growing volume of assets, this was more and more difficult to manage (in March 1941 the total of the confiscated property was estimated to be K 10 billion). To free Gestapo for its original mission on September 2, 1941, the reichsprotector established the Property Office (Vermogensamt) to administer the confiscated property. As far as the insurance policies are concerned there is a report of the Prague Gestapo Headquarters from July 1, 1942 which states that K 54.4 million of repurchase value were confiscated from insurance companies in the Protectorate. The report gives the following breakdown:

Assicurazioni Generali in Trieste	K 20,172,418
Victoria Berlin	K 13,470,549
Riunione Adriatica	K 5,959,330
Star-Versicherungsanstalt	K 4,676,389
Prager Stadt. Versicherunsanstalt	K 2,700,589
Anker (Kotva)	K 2,548,180
Slavia	K 2,136,240

There were other 22 insurance companies on the list, but the amount of money confiscated from them ranged only between K 500 to K 500,000. We do not know whether the Gestapo headquarters in Brno filed separate reports or whether the Prague office reported for the whole "Protectorate". It is likely that most of the policies were life insurance policies, for the following reasons. The first, Generali, Victoria, Anker (Kotva), and Star were licensed only for life insurance business. The second, life insurance was the most common form of capitalized insurance policies.

CONCLUSION

The research done so far reveals the set of rules used by the Nazis to control insurance in the "Protectorate". The rights over the confiscated policies were transferred to Gestapo (later the Property Office) or the Center for Jewish Emigration. There is an evidence that hese institutions were not required to have the original insurance agreement to receive the payments.[22] The history of the cash flows from confiscated policies is not yet fully documented. The archive of the former Czech Escomt Bank and of the Dresdner Bank could reveal the evidence of these transactions. The recent search in the archive of the Czech Union Bank (Deutsche Bank Group) so far uncovered documentary evidence of the transfers of the Holocaust victims' insurance policies to the Property Office and to the Emigration Fund.

The Czech Working Group on Holocaust Era Insurance comprises of the representatives of President Havel's Office, of the Federation of Jewish Communities in the Czech Republic, the Czech Insurance Company, the Finance Ministry, and the Ministry of foreign Affairs. In the past year the Czech authorities have been cooperating with the US insurance regulators namely with the Holocaust Claims Project of the Washington State Insurance Commissioner's Office. We hope that the creation of the international commission of Holocaust insurance will further enhance the international cooperation in this field.

References

Board of Economic Warfare, 1943, Axis Penetration of European Insurance, US National Archives.

Chmela, Leopold, 1946, Hospodáøská okupace Èeskoslovenska její metody a dùsledky (Znalecký posudek v procesu s K.H.Frankem), Orbis - Praha.

Karny, Miroslav, 1991, Konecne reseni - genocida ceskych zidu, Academia

Král, Eduard (ed.), 1937, Èeskoslovenské soukromé pojiš ovnictví v letech 1934 - 36, Nákladem Svazu èsl. assekuraèníkù.

Král, Václav, 1958, Otázky hospodáøského a sociálního vývoje v èeských zemích v letech 1938 - 1945 Vol.I, II, III, Nakladatelství Èeskolovenské akademie vìd.

Marvan, Miroslav, Chaloupecký Josef, 1993, Dìjiny pojiš ovnictví v Èeskoslovensku
1918 - 1945, Èeská pojiš ovna.

Marvan, Miroslav, Chaloupecký Josef, 1997, Dìjiny pojiš ovnictví v Èeskoslovensku

---

[22] See in Appendix 3 the Document No.4.

1945 - 1992, Èeská pojiš ovna.
Shirer, William L., 1960, The Rise and Fall of the Third Reich: A History of Nazi Germany, Ballantine - New York.
Teichová, Alice, 1998, Nìmecká hospodáøská politika v èeských zemích v letech 1939-1945, VŠE studie z hospodáøských dìjin (English version in,..., Cambridge Press 1998).
Teichová, Alice, 1994a, Mezinárodní kapitál a Èeskoslovensko v letech 1918 - 1938, UK Karolinum.
Teichová, Alice, 1994b, Interwar Capital Markets in Central and Southeastern Europe, p.81-91, in: Der Markt im MittelEuropa der Zwischenkriegszeit, UK Karolinum, 1997.
Vencovský, František. 1998, Mnichov 1938 - poèátek mìnové a finanèní devastace èeské ekonomiky, in: Finance a úvìr 9/98, Economia - Praha.

APPENDIX 1

Historical Background of the Protectorate
(based on Mastny, Vojtech, 1971, The Czechs Under Nazi Rule: The Failure of National Resistance, 1939-42, Columbia U.P. - New York, pp.55-76)

Following the signing of the Munich Treaty, the Second Czechoslovak Republic came into existence on September 30, 1938. The Republic existed for less than six months, for on March 15, 1939, when Hitler invaded and occupied the Czech lands. During the Second Republic, the border areas of Bohemia and Moravia, known also as the Sudetenland, were forced to surrender to Nazi Germany.

Based on the extent to which the Protectorate's economic and military infrastructure was incorporated into the Reich, one can divide the Protectorate era into two periods. The first period, which extends from the Protectorate's creation in March, 1939, until the end of 1942, has been characterized as a "strict system of [economic and military] controls" which allowed for a certain amount of personal, economic, and political autonomy among Protectorate citizens. The Reich market was intended to "supplement rather than substitute for the traditional Western markets." However, anti-Semitic and anti-Communist legislation was put into effect, and there was a substantial expansion of German business interests into the territory. From the end of 1942 until the end of the war, the Protectorate economy and military were used primarily for Reich purposes, and the Protectorate became an integral part of the Reich's economic infrastructure.

Preparation for the "seizure of arms and for the control of defense industries" began at least three months before the invasion on March fifteenth. Therefore, though the political infrastructure of the protectorate was largely "improvised," the economic organization of the Protectorate, along with the military organization, was handled with extreme precision. The Czech lands were viewed as a valuable military and economic center for the Reich, as well as a source of liquid assets which could be converted into "sorely needed" foreign currency.

The Nazis had direct economic control through two networks; The Economics Department in the Office of the Protector, which was a "prolonged arm" of the Berlin Ministry of Economics, and through military contracting.   The Central Office for Public Contracts coordinated the military production with other programs.   The entire store of Czech weapons and ammunition was secured and sent to Germany.   All defense plants were inspected, and managers were required to provide data about input and output capacity in meticulous questionnaires.   Over two-hundred thousand patents and technical designs were usurped by the Germans, and power stations and gas works stations were taken over. Czech companies were forced to sell part of their stock at prices dictated by Germans, or to create a German majority among stockholders by increasing their capital. The Hermann Goring works acquired capital control over the Czech leading suppliers of arms in the Protectorate, Škoda and Brunner Waffen, and over Poldi and Vitkovice, the largest steel producers.

Before the war, the Nazis had preceded ruthlessly to satisfy their immediate needs in the Protectorate by seizing arms and trying to put gold and foreign exchange at their command. As a long-term economic policy, however, they avoided measures which would drive the Czechs to desperation. German firms kept their activities within strict limits, under the watchful eye of Hans Kehrl, a high official of the Reich Ministry of Economics, who tried to prevent excesses which would cause disruptions. The system left the Czechs enough room for their own economic activity.

All the same, it cannot be forgotten that the Protectorate was a militarily occupied territory. Although the Nazis did not insist upon total economic mobilization during the first two years of the occupation, they nevertheless transformed the newly created Czech institutions into instruments subject to their own control. They only needed to impose their own appointees in the Central Associations to make use of the sweeping powers provided by the system. There were frequent incidents of arbitrary interference on an administrative level. In several cases, the Nazi supervisors ordered local Czech authorities to submit all business correspondence for their approval or even insisted on the use of German for the conduct of business in local Czech agencies.

APPENDIX 2

List of life insurance companies in 1936:

Domestic companies:
1. Concordia
2. Cechoslovakia
3. Ceska vzajemna zivotni
4. Domov a Slovakia
5. Fenix (Star)
6. Hasicska
7. Karpatia
8. Koruna
9. Legie
10. Loyd
11. Merkur
12. Narodni
13. Patria
14. Pece
15. Pojistovna prumyslu kvasneho
16. Praha
17. Prazska mestska a Prazska mestska zivotni a duchodova
18. Prudentia
19. Republikanska
20. Labe zivotni
21. Rolnicka
22. Slavia
23. Slovanska
24. Slovenska
25. Union
26. Vseobecna
27. Zemska

Foreign companies:
1. Assicurazioni Generali - Italy
2. Donau (Dunaj)- Austria
3. Anker (Kotva) - Austria
4. La Nationale - France
5. Riunione Adriatica - Italy
6. Victoria - Germany

APPENDIX 3

Circulars of Central Association of Private Insurance in Bohemia and Moravia

1. Ia-44/42 Topic: Confiscation of Insurance Policies
2. Ia-51/42 Topic: Confiscation of Insurance Policies
3. Ia-17/43 Topic: Confiscation of Insurance Policies
4. Ia-23/43 Topic: Form of the Property Office which enables confiscation without insurance policy agreement
5. Ia-2/43 Topic: List from Gestapo- confiscated property

Mr. Rudolph Gerlach

DEPARTMENT CHIEF, GERMAN FEDERAL REGULATORY
AGENCY FOR INSURANCE PRACTICES
GERMANY

Break-out Session on Holocaust-Era Insurance: Postwar
Government Compensation Programs and Nationalization

1.   I take the pleasure to be one of the presenters on postwar government compensation programs and nationalizations. I am no historian but an officer of the German insurance supervisory authority. I have been working on insurance issues of Holocaust victims for nearly a year, as Chair of the BAV Working Group on Holocaust Issues and lately as a member of the International Commission. My work is dealing with insurance in Germany. Therefore I shall concentrate my remarks on compensation and nationalization of insurance companies there.

There is little to say about nationalization of insurance business in Germany, because it occurred only in East Germany, while insurance business, like other businesses, remained in the private sector in West Germany. In East Germany private insurance companies were expropriated and liquidated while new state owned companies under public law were set up. So the in West Germany still existing private companies lost all their assets in the East.

2.   This panel concerns life insurance contracts of victims of the Holocaust. Potentially there might be claims against insurance companies or there might be claims for compensation against the German state.

2.1 Insurance claims:

In most cases prior to 1941 after cancellation of the insurance contract by the Jewish policyholder the surrender value had been paid to the policyholder. Legal consequence was: The contractual relationship has expired by performance, the insurance company has been released from its obligation to perform. In the lapse of time and increasing of persecution the bank accounts of victims were frozen, so payments on these accounts could not reach their holders anymore. Later on the insurance companies were forced by Nazi law to turn over all surrender values and all other payments to the German state. Therefore the life insurance companies generally have not been enriched by Jewish life insurance contracts. Unpaid claims are conceivable only in cases in which the contract had not been recognized as such with a Jewish policyholder.

The German Federal Supreme Court decided in 1953 that the expropriations were at no time lawful and were unlawful even at the time when they were formally effective. In paying to the Reich the surrender value, which the Reich had expropriated, insurers were released from their obligation. Claims of the persons concerned deriving from the unlawful nature of the acts of the Reich in expropriating property could be asserted under the restitution and compensation laws.

2.2 Compensation Programs:

2.2.1 Different programs were set up, first under Military government, later under government of the German "Länder" to return property that had been taken by Nazi government from victims (restitution) or to compensate for loss of freedom, health, income, and property or other financial losses (compensation).

After establishing the Federal Republic of Germany the German government assumed responsibility for the injustices of the Nazis and proposed legislation to continue these programs. It entered into discussions with the State of Israel that lead to the Israel-German Treaty of 1952. Finally a restitution law and a compensation law were enacted by the German parliament.

The most important of these laws is the latter, the Federal Compensation Law of 1956. It provides compensation not only to victims of the Holocaust but to victims of all kinds of Nazi persecution. This law contains special provisions dealing with life insurance policies: Provisions on entitlement, the procedure, and the calculation.

The restitution and compensation program was run very efficiently with the help and support from foreign official authorities as well as private organizations. The compensation authorities had to inquire abroad if they needed information. There were lawyers who specialized in this area. Information on the compensation program was made public in the media both in Germany and in foreign countries. Jewish organizations were involved as well. They were entitled to receive proceeds if no heir could be found. They also supported the fact-finding and provided assistance to claimants.

Both, life insurance companies and the German federal insurance supervisory authority, took part in the compensation procedure. The companies on request of the compensation agencies were obliged to answer all questions they were asked by the agencies. The compensation agencies also had to perform hearings with the insurance supervisory authority. The supervisory authority performed audits of the insurance companies for many years in order to confirm that the calculations were right. The vast majority of policies belonging to victims of the Holocaust were included in these programs (over 70 %).

Calculations and assumptions favored victims. The basic premise of the compensation procedure was that a victim of the Holocaust should be treated as if no persecution had ever taken place. The amount of compensation was determined following the policy terms, considering currency conversion and providing additional grants. Only unpaid premiums and payments that the policyholder himself had received were de- ducted. Payments to government authorities were not considered.

According to the compensation program, claimants were put on the same, or a better, footing than West German citizens who had not been persecuted. The file examinations have shown that most policies were cancelled by the policyholders themselves, in many other cases the premium payment stopped. In an insurance case with no persecution involved, the policyholder would receive much less due to this fact. Not so the compensation law. The compensation for the policy was based on the face value of the policy, that is the full amount of the insurance. Only then, unpaid premiums and payments to the policyholder were deducted. Payments to the policyholder were deducted only insofar as they actually benefited the claimant.

In a given example, which has been approved by an actuary in my working group and which is attached to my paper, the victim of Nazi persecution is preferred to a non-victim considerably. He receives 2,510 DM, the latter only 815 DM, that is less than a third. Since the victim of Nazism has received full compensation, according to the applying rules there is no legal basis for further claims concerning the same insurance policy.

2.2.2 Applications for compensation payments for financial loss with regard to life insurance policies pursuant to the specific laws could be made for a total of 13 years. The laws provided a cutoff date for applications at the end of 1969. A reinstatement may be possible, if the victim or the heirs can show that they did not know of the relevant facts without any fault of their own.

According to the Law to compensate victims of National Socialist persecution of 1994, which was enacted following German reunification, applications for compensation can now be made also by inhabitants of former East Germany, who had not been entitled for compensation before the reunification.

2.2.3   According to calculations of the German Ministry of Finance as of 1 January 1998 (s. "Frankfurter Allgemeine Zeitung", 8 Sept. 1998) German public administration has paid out through compensation and restitution programs 102,1 Billion DM. Future payments, especially pension payments, will amount to approximately additional 24 Billion DM. Further payments come out of an agreement between the Federal Government and the Jewish Claims Conference concerning the establishment of a Fund of 200 Million DM for the aid of Jewish victims of the Holocaust in Eastern Europe, who are needy and have not received any compensation yet.

ATTACHMENT
GERMAN COMPENSATION LAW
Sample comparison calculations
Base data:

Sum insured:	Reichsmark 10,000
Birth date	June 1, 1895
Begin of insurance	June 1, 1925
Maturity date	June 1, 1960
Compensation proceeding (if any)	June 1, 1960

Example I: No victim of Nazi-persecution

Termination of premium payment:	June 1938
At maturity date (1960) policyholder is alive	
Payout:	815.70 DM

Example II: Victim of Nazi persecution

Cancellation of contract and confiscation of surrender value by Nazis
June 1938
At maturity date (1960) policyholder is alive
Payout: 2,516.50 DM

ATTACHMENT
DETAILED CALCULATION EXAMPLE I AND II:

Example I: No victim of Nazi persecution
sum insured   10,000 RM
conversion to non-contributory policy (1938): 4,240 RM

	i. e.	DM	424
profit participation and dividends:		DM	138.20
old savings compensation		DM	253.50
		DM	815.70
deductions:			
premiums		DM	0.

Total benefit paid out in 1960	**DM**	**815.70**
to policyholder by insurance company		

Example II: Victim of Nazi persecution
sum insured: 10,000 RM
cancellation of policy (1938), confiscation of   proceeds by Nazis
        surrender value: 2,110 RM

but: face value considered conversion of face value - RM - into face value DM

assuming (fictive) premium payments	DM	4,250
profit participation and dividends:	DM	892.50
old savings compensation	DM	429.00
		5,571.50

deductions:
no deduction of confiscated amount

premiums payable in RM converted 1:10	DM 231.40
premiums payable in DM after 1948	DM 2,823.60
Total benefit paid out 1960	**DM 2,516.50**
to policyholder by compensation office	

Dr. Tamás Földi

DIRECTOR OF THE PUBLIC POLICY INSTITUTE
HUNGARY

Insurance Claims in a Historical Context with a Special Regard to the Holocaust in Hungary

Break-out Session on Holocaust-Era Insurance: Postwar
Government Compensation Programs and Nationalization

SUMMARY

Recent emergence of claims by Holocaust survivors on property lost during or after the Holocaust era is a consequence of the end of the fall of communism in Eastern Europe. This made possible the reparation for human and material losses in East-European countries and gave a rise to claims by Holocaust survivors for lost assets, as well as, for those assets which were owned by the victims of the Holocaust.

In the early seventies Germany paid reparation to individual survivors who lived in Hungary but they received relatively low amounts.

Hungarian governments prior to 1990 made only vague declarations on reparation but were effectively reluctant to pay, although Hungary had also an own share in the Holocaust misdeeds. The reluctance was due mainly to political reasons but the relatively low income level of the general public, the potential claims of non-Jewish civilians were also a hindrances in this respect, aggravated by the fact that Hungary had in the afterwar period a relatively large Jewish origin population which is still today about 80, 000 - 100,000.

First the largest postwar inflation and later the liquidation of private insurance companies made impossible payments to owners of life insurance policies based on contracts concluded prior to 1945. Heirs of Holocaust victims shared in this respect the fate of other citizens of the country. Capital collected by mostly directly or indirectly foreign-owned insurance companies could have been served as a basis for paying insurance claims, since the loss of their Hungarian affiliates and partners was insignificant in relation to their total capital. On the other hand similar claims could have been raised by other Hungarian citizens who owned insurance policies.

Recently beyond the general rules of reparation of the victims of totalitarian regimes the Hungarian government acknowledged a special responsibility towards the remaining Jewish population and pays an additional [pension] to Holocaust survivors. The extension of the respective Public Foundation by those assets which belonged to victims without legal successors would be a justified and feasible way of satisfying claims. According to the Hungarian legal principles individuals have no more domestic legal title to claim for assets lost since such claims by individuals were settled paramountly through the Hungarian reparation legislation after 1990. This legislation covering several acts and amendments tried to balance the payment capacity of the country and the justified claims, but did not involve the reparation of losses of insurance policy holders.

> Motto: "A peace loving man ... does not allow perverting his or others' truth, clear rights, doing out of his and others' *deserved claims*[1] by no kind of brute force, intimidation, dissuasion, and dirty tricks. (From the "Ten Commandments of Policy Conduct of a Peace Loving Man" by István Bibó).[2]

INTRODUCTION

Claims by Holocaust survivors and by victims of other crimes against humanity committed by totalitarian regimes pose a number of difficult questions. Several approaches to such problems can be applied parallely, which do not overlap each other. The most general approach is

---

[1] italics by the author of this paper

[2] *István Bibó* (1911-1979) one of the most eminent political thinkers, cabinet minister during the 1956 revolution.

the ethical one which condemns all crimes and justifies all claims regardless to law or historical circumstances. Nevertheless, even this approach cannot be totally refused as non-valid. The legal approach often yields another judgment than the ethical one by taking into account specific points of views that may be disregarded by a general ethical approach. There exist a difference between the retrospective judgment of the question and that taking into consideration specific historical circumstances. This paper applies the last mentioned approach and tries to reveal historical facts and describe circumstances contemporary to the misdeeds, thus putting the question into a historical context.

Just from this point of view it is almost unavoidable to raise the question why claims by Holocaust survivors came to the foreground of interest after more than 50 years. Possible explanations of this are manyfold. It can be hardly denied that the collapse of the Soviet Empire contributed to the revival of such claims since Jews living in the satellite countries alongside with the victims of communism have the right to be compensated. This is the more topical since in these countries Holocaust survivors did not get a reparation adequate to their human and personal losses neither from their home country nor from Germany. Namely Germany satisfied such claims to a restricted degree because the justified suspicion that the reparation provided, will help more the communist governments suffering of an acute shortage of Western currency than Holocaust survivors. Other countries that hold assets of Holocaust survivors shared this assumption. Another argument for the restricted reparation paid to Jews in the East European countries was that in many cases the governments of the countries concerned were themselves accomplices in crimes committed against Jewry by the German Nazis.

Reparation was put on the agenda almost immediately after the fall of communism. Although the solutions were different in methods and extent in the various countries of Eastern Europe, the start of the process activated also those survivors of Holocaust who emigrated to the West after the war and also those who avoided persecution by emigrating before the extermination started but left behind large assets in the countries concerned. Many victims of the Holocaust and the persecution prior to it placed their assets in the banks of third countries. Another source of claims can be attributed to the fact that after the end of WW2 the victorious occupying powers confiscated in Germany or in other countries such precious goods that belonged originally to people of Jewish origin (gold, artifacts) but were previously confiscated by the authorities of the countries concerned. Historical investigations which were hindered prior to 1989 because of the bipolarity of international relations and also the reglementations of archives, not to open their records prior to 50 years after they were deposited, then proved the existence of such goods. These investigations proved also that some countries accepted the offer by communist countries in secret talks to withhold originally Jewish property as a kind of reparation for losses they suffered by nationalization of their property by communist governments. Thus the fall of communism in Europe put the whole question under a new light. Perhaps a psychological momentum can also be [found] behind the new wave of claims. Immediately after the war many survivors were happy because of having avoided the worst consequences of persecution and did not take so much care about their losses. By now even the youngest survivors of the Holocaust are becoming elderly people. They would not like to miss the last chance to get a reparation for their material or pecuniary losses. Many of them are in need of a supplementary source of income in retirement especially in East-Central- Europe.

THE HISTORICAL BACKGROUND

1. Hungary was occupied by German troops at March 19, 1944. In April 1944 a number of legal acts were issued that deprived the Jewish origin population, which enjoyed until then a relative good position in Hungary in comparison to other German occupied or satellite countries, of their human and civil rights. Their wealth was conscribed and practically confiscated[3]. Except Budapest Jews, over 440,000 persons were deported during the summer of 1944 to Auschwitz, Germany and Austria. Out of them over 150,000 including 10,000 from Budapest came from the present territory of Hungary. Further 90,000 – 100,000 were deported after the mass deportation. As a consequence 200-210,000 people of the present territory and a quarter of million from the rest of the territories under transitory Hungarian rule lost their lives.

Human losses were caused also by the Soviets. The estimated number of those who died in Russian POW camps reached 20,000.

---

[3] The latter measure was taken by the Government Decree 1944. 1600/ME on the registration and freezing of the property of Jews. In *Magyar Közlöny*. Official Gazetteer. vol. 1944. (in Hungarian.)

The number of survivors at the present territory of Hungary was about a quarter of million and at the other territories only about 75,000.[4] This ratio does not express real proportions of losses at the present territory of Hungary since many Jews fled from last mentioned territories to the present territory of the country.

Almost every deportee and most of those who were not deported lost their movable properties or at least a considerable part of it.

Statistical evidence is neither available of the number of those who lost their lives and had life insurance policies nor of the number of those survivors who were the potential heirs of those insured. Nevertheless, since the death toll was higher at the less developed territories of the country than the average, one may assume that more insured persons' legal successors survived, than of those who were not insured and perished by the Holocaust.

Although most of the human losses occurred after the German occupation of Hungary, losses of the Jewish origin population started already before that period and affected not only those living within the present borders of Hungary but also those who became subject to Hungarian authorities as a result of the expansion of Hungarian territories between 1938 and 1941 on account of Czechoslovakia, Romania and Yugoslavia. Over 40,000 lives were lost as a result of two major measures taken by the Hungarian government:

- From July 1941 those who could not prove their Hungarian citizenship were deported to the German occupied former Polish territories which led finally to their execution by the SS. Many lives were lost due to the lack of food and shelter and the cruelty of Ukrainian Nazis, who tortured them during the deportation march. Later this measure was annulled.

- From 1939 on Jews were excluded of the normal military service and forming for them labor service units has started which arrived to a climax in 1944. People of Jewish origin called up to these units wear their own civil clothing and the adaptation to changing weather was made possible only with a help of their families, if at all. When Hungary entered the anti-Russian war labor service units were transported to places which became the theater of war (Ukraine) and were simple by their circumstances much more exposed to losses of their lives than ordinary soldiers, not to speak of the wide-spread brutality of Hungarian soldiers who were their guards. It is difficult to distinguish between the

---

[4] For data above see Stark Tamás: *Jewry during the Catastrophy Period and after the Liberation 1939-1955*. MTA Történettudományi Intézete. Budapest 1995. 109 p. (in Hungarian)

losses which occurred by their deprived situation and the losses caused by military actions and the hard winter. Nevertheless the fact that in 1942 actions were taken by the Hungarian Ministry of Defense to refrain brutality proves that many human losses were caused by other reasons than winter and warfare.[5]

2. From October 1944 up to April 1945 the present territory of Hungary became a theater of war. War damages, confiscation of material and pecuniary goods by both fighting foreign armies caused a loss of 40 per cent of the estimated national wealth of the country in 1944. 0,7 per cent of these losses were suffered by social insurance and private insurance companies that made out in absolute terms USD 30 million of 1938 value. National income which was in the prewar years much below the European average fell down in 1945/46 to the half of that of the previous year, and in the next year it arrived only to 60 per cent of base period. Due to human losses suffered per capita national income decreased somewhat less.

3. The foreign balance of the country was characterized by a total prewar debt of USD 578 million in October 1945, and Hungary had to pay as reparation according to the peace treaty of Paris after deducing the later decreases USD 131 million at 1945 prices. According to the Potsdam Agreement in 1945, Hungary lost its 280 million USD liabilities with Germany accumulated by wartime exports, while the claims by Germany making out a value of USD 30 million were ceded to Soviet-Russia.[6]

4. Foreign and domestic debts, as well, as money emission by the Soviet army and the emission of the pengö currency by the National Bank of Hungary to cover current government expenditure and overall shortages caused a hyperinflation of unprecedented height, which totally ruined the actual currency system of the country. The process was halted only in 1946 by introducing a new currency, the forint.[7]

---

[5] The concise history of the Holocaust in Hungary is described by Braham, Randolph: *The Politics of Genocide. The Holocaust in Hungary.* Vol.1-2. New York 1981. Columbia University Press. 1269 p.

[6] Petö Iván - Szakács Sándor: *The history of the Hungarian economy of four decades 1945-1985.* Vol. 1. The reconstruction and the period of directive planning. Budapest 1985. Közgazdasági és Jogi Könyvkiadó. pp. 17-25. (in Hungarian)

[7] Ausch Sándor: *Inflation and stabilization in the years 1945-1946.* Budapest 1958. Kossuth Könyvkiadó. 190 p. (in Hungarian) and Petö-Szakács op. cit. 43-76.

The total collapse of the pengö currency freed the government of the obligation to convert pengö notes to the new currency issued.[8]

5. Changes in property rights started immediately after the liberation by the Russian Army of a substantial part of the Hungarian territory of the Nazi rule. First, land was deprived of owners of large landed estates by the land reform that distributed land among landless rural population or nationalized it. Nationalization of non-agricultural private property started also in 1945 with the mines, then at the end of 1946 the five biggest metallurgy and engineering companies, as well as the major electric power stations were put under government's economic control.[9]

But already prior to this, owners of companies in the manufacturing industry were deprived of their right of disposition by the Soviet Army, the mostly communist lead worker's councils, government commissioners and the legal actions by the government.[10]

In 1947 the eight largest banks and 344 other banks and companies were nationalized. Further major steps of nationalization included after March 1948 the manufacturing industry and wholesale trade later on retail trade. Also the largest part of small and medium sized companies was either nationalized or forced into government controlled co-operatives.

As a result of large-scale nationalization in 1948 joint stock companies were transformed to national enterprises their stocks and other securities issued by them became invalid. So the Stock Exchange having been reopened in 1946 was closed in 1948 too.[11]

In 1952 urban and larger non-urban residential estate was also nationalized.[12] Private sector was reduced also by the forced collectivization and as a result, its share fell under 5 per cent of the produced GDP.

The confiscation of most of the movable and all immovable property of emigrants was an additional violation against property rights

---

[8] See: Pető-Szakács op. cit. 62.

[9] See: Pető-Szakács op. cit. 37-75.

[10] Földi Tamás: First steps of restriction of capitalists' property rights in the Hungarian manufacturing industry (up to the Fall 1945) in *Közgazdasági Szemle*. Vol.10. no. 4. April 1963 pp. 385-398 (in Hungarian)

Documents on the history of Hungarian manufacturing industry 1945-1946. In *Levéltári Közlemények*. Vol. 31. 1961. pp. 205-262 (in Hungarian)

[11] See: Pető-Szakács op. cit. pp. 76-103

[12] Decree issued by the Presidential Council 4/1952 *Magyar Közlöny.* Official Gazetteer. February 17, 1952 (in Hungarian)

that lasted throughout the whole Communist era. Emigration was rather widespread among middle class people regardless to their ethnic origin.

About 40,000 Jews left Hungary before the Communist regime closed the borders in 1949. In 1956, when a massive emigration took place having embraced all strata of the society, further 20-25 thousand Jews left the country.[13]

Some thousands left Hungary between 1956 and 1989 mostly illegally, since the regime tolerated emigration to a very small extent. Many of them were of Jewish origin. Emigration did not stop even after 1989 but remained without legal consequences.

SITUATION OF THE INSURANCE SECTOR UNTIL 1948

1. The number of insurance companies enlisted in the Insurance Yearbook for 1943/1944 was 36.[14]

Prewar insurance companies were of a larger number since the affiliates of British insurance companies having had their registered head office outside Hungary stopped their activities after Hungary declared war against Britain in 1941. Their assets and liabilities were transferred to the remaining insurance companies. The total number of insurance companies in Hungary with head office registered abroad, prior to 1941 was 22.[15]

Wartime inflation affected the insurance sector as well.[16] Severe losses were caused to insurance companies due to war damages of office buildings and residential real estate owned by them, different kinds of confiscation by the occupying foreign powers, the freezing of their bank accounts, hyperinflation that hit their securities. The latter loss was the more significant since during the war insurance companies were obliged to purchase government bonds which totally lost their value. Also the devaluation of their real estate fortune added to the dramatic situation. Their assets ceased to bring yields even after the stabilization since rental prices were fixed at a low level and no revaluation act was issued to convert security values to the new currency. Insurance companies after

---

[13] See: Stark op. cit. p. 107

[14] *Hungarian Insurance Yearbook*. Vol. 35. 1943-1944. Budapest 1943. 346 p (in Hungarian)

[15] Verbal information by Dr. Gál Nyáry, legal adviser to the Center of Credit Institutes Corp.

[16] *Hungarian Insurance Yearbook*, 1943-1944 pp 124-127.

the massive nationalization did not dispose anymore with reserves to pay. In spite of the optimistic statements of an author, who as the editor remarks was an eminent expert hiding under a pseudonym, insurance companies were near to bankruptcy. To be honest to that unknown person one has to admit that those tasks which he attached to his forecast could not be fulfilled in the coming years.[17]

3. According to the last mentioned source 17 domestic and 10 foreign insurance companies were active at the insurance market. After 1945 the number of insurance companies decreased as consequence of the take-over of nine German and Austrian owned insurance companies by the Russian owned but in Hungary registered East-European Insurance Corp., which followed from the decisions of the Potsdam Agreement. Four of them were of Austrian and four of German property, the remaining one was registered in Budapest, but since belonging to the confiscated Anker shared the latter's fate. Among these Allianz, Anker and Victoria merits a special mentioning. Generali, Adria being of Italian ownership were among those foreign insurance companies that maintained their businesses after 1945 too. Those Austrian insurance companies in which British, Italian or Hungarian participation could be indicated were exempt of the confiscation. Both Italian companies participated in Hungarian insurance companies as well.[18]

According to another source, published almost simultaneously, the number of private insurance companies was only 22 out of which seven were foreign-owned already in prewar time and two others had new Russian owners. The difference can be attributed to different starting points: whether these sources quoted items that were figuring at the Registry Court or they refer only to those which actually made businesses.[19]

Russian owned companies were transferred to the Hungarian State late 1954. Insurance companies merged with the Hungarian State Insurance Company.

---

[17] *Hungarian Insurance Compass, 1947.* Vol. 11. Budapest 1947. Apor Sándor. pp. 18-22. (in Hungarian)

[18] *Hungarian Insurance Compass 1947.* pp. 123-161. and the information provided by *Dr.* Nyáry

[19] *Business Financial and Stock Exchange Compass for the years 1947/1948.* Ed. by János Kallós. Budapest 1948. Kallós Albert pp. 249-257.

COLD NATIONALIZATION OF INSURANCE COMPANIES

1. Against the common belief insurance companies were never nationalized, they existed formally until 1950. What happened was a process that may be called "cold nationalization". This included the liquidation by legal force of insurance companies. The executor of the liquidation was the Hungarian government and the State took over also the real estate assets of insurance companies in 1950, i.e. two years before the general nationalization of urban residential estate.[20]

2. The "cold nationalization" started with merging insurance companies into 10 which were to be liquidated. Their accounts are still managed by the Pénzintézeti Központ Rt. (Center of Money Institutions Inc.) an existing financial institution under government control.

3. During the liquidation insurance companies were forced to hand over their assets and liabilities - except those related to life insurance - to the newly established State Insurance national enterprise. Nevertheless the latter did not become neither a proprietor - being merely an administrator of the balances mentioned - nor a *de iure* successor of the liquidated companies.

4. The recently established foreign insurance companies in Hungary did not claim for being a legal successor of their pre-1950 companies since the latters were *de facto* liquidated by the Hungarian government.

5. However it is an open question how much of the assets of the foreign owned insurance companies could be saved by hidden financial transactions of the consequences of cold nationalization or of the take-over of their assets by the Soviets.

6. Finally holders of pre 1945 insurance policies did not receive any return on their capital accumulated.

SPECIAL ISSUES RELATING TO LIFE INSURANCE

1. Foreign companies' role in life insurance business has decreased in the interwar period. In 1928 their share was still almost 52.5 per cent while up to 1938 this share has reduced to 27.6 per cent,

---

[20] 4247/1949 Government decree amended by the 113/1950 MT Government decree on the liquidation of some enterprises and 2444/1950 MT Government decree on the property rights, management recording and trade of state owned immovable property. See the respective volumes of *Magyar Közlöny*.

although the total revenue of insurance premia did not reach the 1930 level up to 1940. The decrease of foreign share was mainly due to the bankruptcy of the Austrian Phoenix Insurance Corp., a major actor in the life insurance business whose assets were taken over by a company registered among Hungarian insurance companies. Another factor of the decrease was the enlargement of the territory of Hungary after 1939 where mostly Hungary based companies could raise their share in insurance business although to a lesser extent in life insurance than in the total insurance business.[21]

2. Until 1941 *vis major* clauses were valid for life and property insurance. In 1941 a decree expanded the validity of life insurance to loss of human life caused by war events against a minimum extra payment out of which a fund was established to cover the expenses of insurance companies. (This extension did not relate to property insurance.)

No distinction was made in this respect between Jews and non-Jews. This situation lasted until the German occupation of Hungary. In comparison to other compatriots Jews were *de iure* handicapped in insurance matters in the period between March 19, 1944 and April, 1945.[22]

Nevertheless, actual conditions restricted the possibility to raise such claims to a minimum, since the time lag between the start of such losses and the deprivation of rights was too short for raising by documents well established claims.

3. Prior to the stabilization in 1946 a decree generally prohibited both active and passive insurance payments. Insurance policy holders' rights were severely restricted in order to bring their claims in line with remained payment capacity of the insurance companies. The revaluation was fixed in pengö and adópengö (a money substitute). The decree contained also the potential prolongation of the payment of dues to maintain insurance contract of those who could fulfill their obligations. This decree seemed to save but actually paralyzed the life insurance sector.[23]

This legal action was not only aimed at the restriction of surplus money outflow not controlled by the National Bank, but also caused by the fact that insurance companies lost most of their assets.

---

[21] *Hungarian Insurance Yearbook 1943-1944.* pp. 124-130.

[22] Verbal information by Dr. Gál *Nyáry*

[23] Government decree 6400/1946 ME on the revaluation of life insurance claims. *Magyar Közlöny.* Official gazeteer. 1946. no. 127. June 6. (in Hungarian)

According to a cautious criticism of the decree by the anonymous contemporary author already cited the revaluation life insurance policies was still unripe for a final judgment, since those who issued the decree did not take into consideration the disastrous situation of insurance companies which are not able to collect capital only to cover the risks involved in life insurance.[24]

This fact was reflected by the amendment of the 6400/1946 which prolonged the procedure of revaluation up to mid-1947. Simultaneously it was allowed to pay rents in monthly installments at a fixed rate corresponding to 1/5 of the nominal pengö value valid at the end of 1944.[25] Nevertheless an actual revaluation did not take place and as a consequence no payments were possible.

During the liquidation of insurance companies life insurance was exempt of the annihilation, but even this did not change the situation of insurance policy holders.

According to some estimations the present value of the life insurance claims by victims of Holocaust is about USD 2.5 billion.[26] According to our own calculations some 80,000 Jewish origin people had life insurance policies.

Only quite recently and only foreign insurance companies admitted their responsibility for claims of former policy holders and an agreement was reached with the Italian insurance company Generali that shows a willingness to pay a lump sum of USD 100 million as compensation. The discussion is still going on with Generali and also the German Allianz is involved in such discussions.[27]

---

[24] See *Hungarian Insurance Yearbook* p. 21.
[25] Government decree 12.640/1946 ME on the revaluation of claims arising from life insurance contracts aminding the decree 6.400/1946 ME.
[26] The Endless Story. Recent development of reparation matters. In *Szombat* 1998 no. 8. p. 18.
[27] The Endless Story cited above

THE TREATMENT OF THE COMPENSATION OF PEOPLE OF JEWISH ORIGIN UNTIL 1990[28]

1. The first postwar Hungarian government acknowledged the responsibility of the Hungarian State in face of the Jewish origin people who lost their lives and/or property. This statement was never really followed by government actions prior to the fall of the communist regime. The Provisional National Government elected by the Provisional National Assembly late 1944 established already in 1945 the Government Commissariat for Relinquished Goods. Among the goals to be followed figured the task to use relinquished goods without a legal heir for the partial reparation of those who suffered damages due to deportation, but this task was never accomplished. Goods left behind by Hungarian Nazis or of those who took a refuge to Germany when Russian Army neared and the inheritance of deportees were equally treated.[29]

2. In 1946 a law was adopted by the Parliament on the establishment of a "Jewish Restitution Fund" which was designed to take over the property of those who lost their lives during the persecutions and had no legal successors. It should have been the goal of this Fund first to collect Jewish property, then to sell it and to support the survivors of persecution from the acquired capital. The property to be collected should have covered all movable and immovable property. Implementing this law started only after the Paris Peace Treaty was signed.[30]

3. The Paris Peace Treaty signed by the actually communist led Hungarian government in early1947 obliged Hungary to hand over the property of the non-survivors without a legal successor to organizations

---

[28] A summary review of the reparation process up to 1998 is presented by the paper of Feldmájer Péter: Bitter Restitution. *Szombat.* English edition 1998. pp. 2-5., in Hungarian a more detailed account is given by the recent manuscript of Lea Feldmájer, entitled *"The History of the Reparation of the Jewish Community from the Jewish Restitution Fund to the Hungarian Jewish Heritage Public Foundation".* 14 p. + supplements 10 p.

[29] Ács Gábor: The non-restituted fund. In *Szombat.* 1995. no. 7. p. 3. (in Hungarian)

[30] Act 1946. XXV on denouncing and mildering the consequences of the persecution suffered by teh Hungarian Jews. *Corpus Iuris Hungarici, 1946.* Ed. by Vincenti G. - Gál L. Budapest no date. Franklin Társulat pp. 104-106. reprinted in Gonda, László: *Jewry in Hungary 1526-1945.* Budapest 1992. Századvég Kiadó. pp. 299-304. Government decree 3200/1947 ME published in the respective volume of *Magyar Közlöny.*

of survivors in order to support them. This was in line with the formerly mentioned Hungarian law but even this has not been really implemented although the Jewish Restitution Fund started its operation in October 1947. In 1948 an inventory on proprietorless goods was compiled which is still to be found in the archives of the Center for Credit Institutes Corp. The sales of relinquished goods started after a long delay in 1949. Until mid-1953 the Fund sold properties in a value of almost 3 million forint legally equal to less than USD 300.000. The legal title of collection and sales of immovable goods were largely hit by the nationalization of residential estate that comprised also those immovables, which belonged to the potential assets of the Fund. The sad story of the Fund ended in 1954, when its assets were transferred to the State Office of Ecclesiastic Affairs, which sold later on step by step the relinquished properties. This process lasted until 1981. Incomes were used to cover the expenses arising of the legal obligation of the government which confiscated the wealth of the Jewish Community, to fund current activities of the Jewish religious communities. A part of this wealth was nationalized.[31]

Communist governments argued such a way that all citizens enjoy social care there is no reason to create differences among citizens according to past injuries. Facts behind this hypocritical stand show that while reforming the pension system, pensions were determined regardless to employment prior to 1945, a term which was prolonged in 1959 up to 1929. This meant that if somebody achieved pensioner age (60 years) as born in 1899 and worked between 1913 and 1929 these 17 years were not regarded as active period. A hidden additional deficiency of this new act was that between 1929 and 1933 a massive unemployment had existed in Hungary which in fact for many shortened the respective period by further years. In contrast to members of small business co-operatives who were included to pension schemes already in 1951, private small shopkeepers were embraced by the pension system not before 1962 and private retail traders even later, in 1970. These facts clearly show that instead of the social care principle the promotion of nationalization and government control was the leading principle of the pension system. It can be added that many people of Jewish origin belonged to the handicapped categories.[32]

---

[31] Ács Gábor op. cit. pp. 4-5.
[32] For the data see General Directorate of Nation-wide Social Security: *Four Decades of Social Security 1945-1985.* Budapest 1985. Népszava Könyv és Lapkiadó. pp. 11-14.

4. The Hungarian government did not return confiscated Jewish owned precious metals which were taken over at the end of the war by the French and US army without a claim for the property and returned to the National Bank of Hungary after the Paris Peace Treaty became valid i.e. in 1947 and in 1948. Later these were sold by government-controlled agencies. (For further developments see the next chapter.)

5. In 1971 between German authorities and the Budapest-based Organization for Promoting the Interests of People Persecuted by Nazism in Hungary an agreement was concluded about the reparation to be paid for Jewish origin people who were Hungarian residents at the beginning of the year. Accordingly the Organization which stood under communist control collected claims and received German reparation. A sum of 97 million German Mark was transferred in three installments and converted at an unrealistically low but legally valid exchange rate to the Hungarian currency and paid out with deduction of expenses to 60,000 claimants. Those who were subject to inhumane medical experiments received a special reparation.[33] Some German companies paid compensation to former slave laborers who served in their factories (e.g. I.G. Farbenindustrie).

6. The failure of the Jewish Restitution Fund was of epochal importance. The number of people to be compensated decreased not only by emigration but also by natural mortality. This contributed to the decrease of Holocaust claimants during the last more than 50 years. When comparing data of survivors i.e. potential claimants was 325,000 just after the war, in 1957 under ceteris paribus circumstances still over 200 thousand claimants should have been satisfied. In 1971 German reparation involved merely 60,000 people and the present number of Holocaust claimants is below 20,000 Lea Feldmájer rightly puts an emphasize on the loss which Hungarian Jewry suffered due to the lack of implementation of the respective laws of 1946/1947.[34] The reluctance of the post-war reparation of Holocaust survivors had another consequence as well. During the period between 1947 and at least the beginning of the eighties so many other injuries were committed by the communist governments that they diminished the relative weight of the anti-Semitism driven sins of the former governments, not to speak of those

---

[33] Government decree 21/1971 on the satisfaction of some reparation claims by the National Organization for Promoting the Interest of People Persecuted by Nazism in Hungary. in *Magyar Közlöny* 1971. pp. 489-490. Documents from the Archives of the Alliance of Jewish Communities in Hungary.

[34] Feldmájer, Lea op. cit.

who suffered under both totalitarian regimes (forged trials, intra-country deportation, confiscation, nationalization).

THE GENERAL PRINCIPLES OF REPARATION OF MATERIAL LOSSES CAUSED BY TOTALITARIAN REGIMES IN HUNGARY

1. The laws issued after the political change in 1990 admitted the responsibility of the Hungarian government for losses caused by the legal actions of governments contradicting their responsibility to observe human rights and general principles of law.

2. Simultaneously Hungarian legislation rejected the principle of direct reprivatization i.e. to reestablish the property right of former owners - except the constructed immovable formerly owned by churches - in order to avoid endless and overcomplicated claims by more than one owner for the same property and because of the changes in those immovable properties during the time passed. (Some were demolished, other were hugely expanded etc.) Law making avoided also to follow the principle of general and unified compensation based on citizen's rights. The law expressed a strive for determining claimants right case by case. This determination ended in most cases in providing persons having suffered persecution and/or material losses and their legal successors with "reparation bills" that were intended for use to buy consumer goods, to purchase immovable, or rights generating income, to sell them at secondary market. These bills are traded at the Stock Exchange and underwent considerable changes in actual value between 20 and 90 per cent of the nominal value.

3. A further restriction in Hungarian law making is that legal persons are excluded from the reparation process. Thus only natural persons acquired the right to be compensated.

4. Also those foreign residents or citizens fall under reparation laws who lived in Hungary during the periods of persecution and suffered human and material losses.

5. In order to balance the payment capacity of the country and the justified claims the amount of reparation is fixed at a low proportion of the lost value.

THE REPARATION FOR PEOPLE OF JEWISH ORIGIN AFTER 1990[35]

1. In general the rules of reparation of the losses suffered by people of Jewish origin do not differ from those relating to people who suffered losses because other causes than racial discrimination. But this is the final result of a prolonged discussion on Jewish claims, which started at a zero point. Decisions by the Court of Constitution remedied deficiencies of the original reparation acts. E.g. claims due to military work service accomplished within the borders of Hungary were initially not regarded as legal title for reparation. This was amended by a later act.

2. In 1993 the Court of Constitution after having investigated the story of the Hungarian Jewish gold took a decision which excluded the individual reparation of the former owners of the confiscated gold. The part of this, which belonged to persons without a legal successor and was sold by the State, is to be involved into the reparation in favor of the propriety of a fund for Jewish reparation, an organization the creation of which delayed until 1996.[36]

3. In 1996 the Hungarian Jewish Heritage Public Foundation was established to which an annually fixed amount should be allocated by the Budget and from this the survivors can obtain an age dependent monthly support paid out through the Pension Fund.[37]

According to a message from New York dated June 7, 1997, the Hungarian government transferred an amount of USD 28 million to the World Jewish Congress, out of which the estimate 20.000 Hungarian Holocaust survivors will receive a regular monthly aid.[38]

4. So far as the reparation of foreign residents is concerned the following data are available.

---

[35] See Feldmájer Péter op. cit.

[36] Court of constitution decision 16/1993 AB (III. 12.)

[37] See *Szombat* 1996. no. 10. pp. 6-8.

[38] http://www.internet.hu/zsido/zsh 24 htm Untitled

Table 1. Reparation of foreign residents by cases and in the percentage of the total reparation payments

Reparation by titles	No. of cases	Paid amounts
Reparation of personal losses	596,019	56,249,116 thousand forints
out of which foreign residents	33.13 %	35.95 %
USA	16,855	2.71 %
Israel	11,980	0.80 %
Germany	7,709	2.862 %
Reparation of lost assets	1,429,494	80,920,422 thousand forints
out of which foreign residents	72,859	12.62%
USA	11,388	2.13%
Israel	3,808	0.04%
Germany	29,548	5.14%

Source: Kárpótlás és kárrendezés Magyarországon 1989-1998 (Reparation and Setting of Claims on Losses 1989-1998), Budapest, 1998, Napvilág Publisher, pp. 685-693.

The interpretation of these data needs further investigation. It can be supposed that a reasonable number of US claims fulfilled were raised by non-Jews, while the data relating to Germany overwhelmingly reflect claims raised by those German residents who were deported as a consequence of the Postdam agreement.

5. Swiss banks and the government transferred a lump sum of USD 8 million to the Hungarian Jewish Heritage Fund.

6. Recently also the German government shows a willingness to pay for Holocaust survivors living in Hungary, although the requirements set for the entitlement are far from being satisfactory, not to speak of the procedural side.

CONCLUDING REMARKS

The problems of the reparation for people of Jewish origin is far of the final solution. The following reasons make this solution difficult:
- the economic and of living level of Hungary and especially the lability of the equilibrium of the central budget,
- the moral and real argument by people of Jewish origin that their losses were disproportionate higher than those of non-Jews, also

backed by the fact that many of them suffered under both totalitarian regimes,
- the in part open, in part hidden anti-Semitism existing in the country with the second largest Jewish community in Europe (about 80-100 thousand). Politicians in Hungary are afraid of the expansion of anti-Semitism in the light of a special treatment of Jewish losses in a country where almost each citizen suffered material losses especially after 1944, when Hungary became a theater of war and as a consequence of the four decades of communism. This circumstance is considered also by the Hungarian Jewish community which is relatively moderate in claiming for additional reparation under new legal titles. (e.g. the author of this paper has no information about claims against Hungarian companies or their legal successors, which enjoyed the benefit of military labor service in their war-time production activities. A reason for this is that many of those who accomplished such a service were that time happy to avoid harder circumstances than those which prevailed in most of these factories, not to speak about those cases, where the original owners of the workplaces were themselves, Jews. This is not a speculative example but relates to a concrete situation well known by the author of this paper).
- the rivalry among Jewish organizations and especially the differences between those in Hungary and abroad,
- the fact that most of the people of Jewish origin who suffered persecution have no real contact with any of the Jewish organizations participating in the discussion to solve the problems,
- the reluctance of those who should pay compensation for the wealth they acquired as a consequence of the Holocaust without hard pressures. Recent readiness to fulfill such claims is due to avoiding further humiliation of those institutions which were involved in withholding Jewish property or compensation for the gains that can be attributed to forced services by Jews during the period of persecution.

A way out of the present situation could be that those foreign insurance companies still existing and having been participated to a large extent in Hungarian life insurance business should take the responsibility for compensating the proven heirs of life insurance policy holders or the Hungarian Jewish Heritage Foundation. Their payments would compensate the capital collected prior to 1944 by companies which they owned directly or indirectly. Such payments could contribute to the compensation of survivors, whose number is diminishing day by day and also to the preservation of Jewish cultural heritage and the constructed objects belonging to it.

Finally, it has to be admitted that research on Holocaust insurance claims necessitates further investigation of historical records. This research should be accomplished in the near future. Such a research requires substantial efforts that cannot be based exclusively on voluntary work. Therefore, I suggest that a reasonable and proportionate amount of the compensation paid or to be paid in the future by insurance companies should be allocated for promoting the respective research. This proposal is taking into account the difficulties of identifying insured Jews and expresses also the intention to preserve the names of victims also this way.

Acknowledgments
are due by the author of this paper to Lea Feldmájer, law student, Dr. Péter Feldmájer, president of the Alliance of Jewish Communities in Hungary, Mrs. Zsuzsa Földi, collaborator to the Library of the Central Statistical Office of Hungary, Dr. Gál Nyáry, legal adviser to the Center for Credit Institutions Corp. Budapest, Dr. Béla Révész, lecturer at the University of Szeged, and staff member of the Public Policy Institute, for their assistance collecting documentary material for this paper. For the errors or omissions the author bears the only responsibility. I am also grateful to Professor Márton Tardos MP, who called my attention to this topic.

About the author
Born in Budapest in 1929. He is of Jewish origin and survived in the ghetto in Budapest. After having graduated at the Hungarian University of Economic Sciences in 1952, received six years later his Doctor title in economic history. Between 1956 and 1963 he published a series of papers on the economic history of the postwar period. He was employed over thirty years by the Hungarian Academy of Sciences and even today is the editor in chief of its English language economic journal. At present besides being the director of a private foundation based public policy institute, he is also the head of a research group assisted by the National Scientific Research Foundation (OTKA) investigating the reparation process in Hungary. His main publication is a two volume trilingual encyclopedic dictionary on comparative economic systems published in 1992 in Munich, London, New York.

Address: Public Policy Institute, Budapest 1132 Visegrádi u.4. fsz.4. Hungary.
Tel./fax: (361) 239 1951, 239 1199 E-mail: ptia@mail.matav.hu

Prof. Vojtech Mastny

SENIOR RESEARCH SCHOLAR
WOODROW WILSON INTERNATIONAL CENTER

The Impact of Post-World War II Nationalizations and Expropriations in East Central Europe on Holocaust-Related Assets

Break-out Session on Holocaust-Era Insurance: Postwar
Government Compensation Programs and Nationalization

The purpose of this presentation is to examine and evaluate the developments in the countries of East Central Europe where communist regimes were established after World War II with regard to the causes and consequences of the policies of nationalization and expropriation relevant to the holocaust-related Jewish assets.

The imposition of communism on East Central Europe after the defeat of Nazi Germany created a situation there radically different from that in Western Europe, where the end of the war meant political liberation, restoration of the rule of law, and continuity of the market economy. The East Central European developments, which brought widespread political, economic, and social damage, were complicated by the fact that the introduction of Soviet-style communist systems as it eventually took place after a brief period of genuine or sham coalition governments had not originally been planned to be implemented in the ways and at the time it was. There was less design than most contemporaries believed during the Cold War, thus making the proper understanding of the transitional period both crucial and difficult. The consequences were disastrous all the same—not only for the peoples concerned and the European order, but ultimately also for the local communist regimes and the Soviet Union as well.

Since the conditions in all countries were not the same, also the patterns of their development during the critical postwar years were often quite different. Until the conclusion of the 1947 peace treaties with the defeated countries in Europe except Germany, the distinction between enemy and allied nations accounted for much of the difference. Germany, Italy, Hungary, Romania, and Bulgaria were in the former, Poland, Czechoslovakia, and Yugoslavia in the latter category, Austria straddling uneasily both because of its having been an integral part of Nazi Germany yet classified by the Allies for reasons of political expediency as its victim, entitled to be reconstituted as a separate state. In practice, the distinction was less respected albeit more readily invoked by the Soviet Union than by the West—primarily for the sake of economic exploitation.

Taking into account the political and economic changes that took place, there were three distinct stages of development:

1. The immediate post-hostilities period, lasting approximately until the end of 1945, characterized by widespread lawlessness and chaos, during which nationalization and expropriation measures were often taken haphazardly and inconsistently.

2. The transitional period of from 1946 to 1948, when nationalizations and expropriations were put into effect as a result of deliberate, though not necessarily systematic policies, introduced in ostensibly legal fashion by governments in which communists exercised important, sometimes decisive, influence but did not hold exclusive power.

3. Sovietization since 1948, when the Stalinist system was purposefully imposed by the local communists on behalf of the Soviet Union in all the areas where Moscow was firmly in control, namely, Poland, Czechoslovakia, Hungary, Romania, and Bulgaria, as well as—with limitations given by concern about the Western powers participating in the control of Germany—in the Soviet zone of Germany and the Soviet-occupied part of Austria, though not in Yugoslavia where such a system had already been introduced by the local communists on their own initiative.

The outstanding features of the first period were indiscriminate looting and violence by the advancing Red Army, the full dimensions of which have only recently been revealed from evidence in former Soviet and other communist archives.[1] In this respect, the difference between occupied and supposedly liberated countries was more in degree than in kind. Property deemed to belong to Germans and their allies, to persons labeled as Fascists or collaborators, and to other arbitrarily described

---

[1]Norman N. Naimark, *The Russians in Germany: A History of the Soviet Zone of Occupation, 1945-1949* (Cambridge: Harvard University Press, 1995).

enemies was stolen, carried away, or simply destroyed. The Red Army systematically dismantled and transported to the Soviet Union industrial plants in not only the Soviet zone of Germany but also other territories it had overrun. From Hungary, for example, the entire equipment and inventory of the partly US-owned Tungsram electric company, known as the flagship of the country's industry, was shipped away by Soviet troops in 600 railroad cars.[2]

There was a measure of spontaneity in what was happening: the Vienna populace, for example, started looting the city's leading department store, formerly Jewish-owned, even before Soviet soldiers came to finish the job.[3] Everywhere individuals used the opportunity to settle personal scores, or simply acted out of greed. The victims were by no means merely Germans, let alone Nazis. They included Hungarians living in Czechoslovakia, and sometimes anyone who spoke German, occasionally even returning Jewish inmates of Nazi concentration camps whose native tongue happened to be German, and German anti-Fascists.

Much of the lawlessness, however, was not only tolerated but also encouraged by the Soviet authorities and local communist parties. This was particularly the case in the defeated countries that were at the mercy of the new occupation power, but was also common in the ostensibly liberated Poland and Czechoslovakia, where provisional coalition governments – unelected but not yet fully controlled by communists – were allowed to perform administrative functions. The resulting policies were not necessarily consistent. Different Soviet agencies in occupied Germany often operated at cross purposes and in other countries the activities of local communists were at first not sufficiently coordinated with Moscow. Politically, the Soviet Union was trying to win the victims of Nazism on its side, yet economically it was antagonizing them by its rapacity. It turned over formerly German territories to Poland, yet not before clearing away most of the movable assets.

In Hungary, Poland, Czechoslovakia, as well as the Soviet zone of Germany, the first radical economic measure was land reform, implemented under direct Soviet pressure. Arguably, the breaking up of large estates and redistribution of land were long overdue; however, the

[2]László Borhi, *The Merchants of the Kremlin: Soviet Economic Penetration in Hungary*, Cold War International History Project Working Paper, forthcoming (Washington: Woodrow Wilson International Center for Scholars, 1999), pp. 7-8.
[3]Guenter Bischof, *The Leverage of the Weak: Austria in the First Cold War, 1945-1955* (Basingstoke: Macmillan, 1999), pp. 16, 36.

manner in which the land reform was conducted and its consequences were destructive rather than constructive. The goal was to break the power of the old landowning classes without giving the security of tenure to farmers; in Czechoslovakia, much of the confiscated land became state rather than private property. Eventually, temporary beneficiaries of the land reforms fell victim to the Stalinist collectivization of agriculture.

Czechoslovakia was also the country where the nationalization of industry and business, including private insurance, started first—as early as the fall of 1945. Aimed primarily but not exclusively at supposed national enemies and traitors, it was introduced by a series of presidential decrees, and implemented before being ratified by the later elected parliament. Reminiscing on the manner in which nationalization started, the chief of the communist-controlled Czechoslovak labor unions Antonín Zápotocký later observed that "had the party not begun pursuing nationalization regardless of established laws, it would not have compelled the noncommunist government to issue the nationalization decrees . . . . We had to teach people that it was not possible to maintain the old legality . . . but that it was important to violate it."[4]

As an emergency measure—which later proved permanent—the post-World War II governments moved quickly to freeze bank accounts and insurance policies, denominated in deeply depreciated currencies. Access was allowed only in exceptional cases, to be determined by the authorities, and was seldom granted. All claims had to be reported, sometimes within an unreasonably short time limit, after which the state assumed the right to dispose with them.[5] In Hungary, they were effectively extinguished in August 1946 as a result of revaluation following the currency reform that had ended the worst hyperinflation history had seen.

The notion of "enemy assets" was used to justify arbitrary seizure of property. All that belonged to the defeated Germans was war booty in the Soviet view. Hence the Soviets opposed the nationalization pursued by Austria's non-communist government, with parliamentary support by the communists, which was intended to save the country's enterprises from being claimed by the Soviets as German-owned. Everywhere the alleged German assets included property stolen by the

---

[4] *Rudé právo* [Prague], 31 January 1953.

[5] "Dekret presidenta republiky o znárodn_ní soukromých pojiš_oven" [Decree by the President of the Republic on the Nationalization of Private Insurance Firms], 24 October 1945, *Sbírka zákon_ a na_ízení* [Collection of Laws and Ordinances], 1945, no. 103, pp. 224-31.

Nazis from Jews who had perished in the holocaust or emigrated. The newly installed governments—whether or not controlled by the communists—made little, if any, effort to identify, much less indemnify, the original owners, few of whom were inclined to file claims in such an unpropitious time.

The policy, or rather the lack of policy, of the postwar governments was consistent with their official line against anti-Semitism, which precluded singling out Jews as a special category, and was facilitated by the willingness of those surviving Jews who chose not to emigrate to assimilate and adapt to the new order. This willingness, encouraged by the Soviet Union's image as liberator from Nazism, also helps to explain the prominence of Jews in the new government administrations and communist party apparatus, especially pronounced in countries where relatively higher numbers of Jews survived, notably Hungary, but also in Poland and in Czechoslovakia.[6]

In traditionally anti-Semitic countries, such as Poland, anti-communism and anti-Semitism often merged. The notorious Kielce pogrom of June 1946, carried out with the complicity of the police, has long been regarded a provocation by the communist-controlled Warsaw regime calculated to discredit its political opponents in the forthcoming elections; from new evidence it appears more like a spontaneous outburst that the regime had not anticipated and was unprepared to handle.[7] All considered, whether victims or accomplices of the emerging communist regimes, Jews in East Central Europe remained in a precarious position.

Once the immediate postwar chaos subsided, the support for the idea of nationalization, which extended wide across the political spectrum in East Central Europe, did not substantially differ from its popularity much of Western Europe. This was the time when the bankruptcy of old-fashioned capitalism in the Great Depression was still a fresh memory, when the notion that capitalists had precipitated the war in order to profit from it enjoyed its superficial attraction, and when the public ownership of the key sectors of the economy was therefore widely regarded as not only politically correct but also socially just and economically beneficial. In such countries as Great Britain and France,

---

[6]Charles Gati, "A Note on Communists and the Jewish Question in Hungary," in his *Hungary and the Soviet Bloc* (Durham: Duke University Press, 1986), pp. 100-107; Michael Checinski, *Poland: Communism, Nationalism, Anti-Semitism* (New York: Karz-Cohl, 1982), pp. 76-82.

[7]Andrzej Paczkowski, *Pó_ wieku dziejów Polski, 1939-1989* [Half a Century of Polish History] (Warsaw: Wydawnictwo Naukowe PWN, 1998), pp. 190-93.

nationalizations of key economic branches believed to be in the public interest were carried out by non-communist governments.

In East Central Europe, too, nationalization was by no means supported only by the Soviets and the communists, nor were these always the ones promoting it most eagerly. In Czechoslovakia, it was the social democratic minister of industry, Bohumír Laušman, who urged immediate complete nationalization at a time when the communist prime minister Klement Gottwald described such a policy as "madness." In Gottwald's opinion, the need was for the establishment of clear boundaries between the nationalized and the private sectors in order to ensure "juridical security."[8] Under the guidance they had been receiving from Moscow, the East Central European communists did not envisage the abolition of private enterprise within any particular time frame; in fact, they saw in its preservation a key feature distinguishing their "new democracies" from the Soviet system.[9]

The distinction conformed with the concept of "national roads to socialism," supported actively promoted by the Soviet Union. This did imply eventual abolition of private enterprise though without a time frame; at issue, for the time being, were the different ways in which this ideological goal could be accomplished. On that subject, there were genuine discussions among communists in each country, particularly lively in Poland, as well as genuine differences between countries, which set especially apart East Germany—where Moscow regarded the preservation of private enterprise an indispensable prerequisite for Germany's reunification under Soviet auspices.[10] Thus, even though there was no design, the policies steered by Moscow converged toward the ideologically defined communist economic model whose attainment was to be determined by politics rather than by economics.

In the event, the pace proved faster than originally anticipated. It was forced by the mounting Cold War confrontation between East and West, which Stalin had neither wanted not expected yet precipitated all the same, and by the diminishing utility for him of the East Central

[8]Josef Korbel, *The Communist Subversion of Czechoslovakia, 1938-1948: The Failure of Coexistence* (Princeton: Princeton University Press, 1959), pp. 163-64.

[9]Benon Dymek, *PZPR, 1948-1954* [The Polish United Workers' Party, 1948-1954] (Warsaw: Pa_stwowe Wydawnictwo Naukowe, 1989), pp. 19-45.

[10]Wilfried Loth, *Stalins ungeliebtes Kind: Warum Moskau die DDR nicht wollte* (Berlin: Rowohlt, 1994), pp. 142-48.

European coalition governments, whose viability he had overestimated.[11] But the economic transformation still preserved some specific features in each country even after the political turnabout had taken place. These included in Poland the creation of particularly large state enterprises, in Czechoslovakia the nationalization of smaller units than elsewhere, in Hungary the establishment of the most elaborate system of state control. The prevailing pattern was that of controlling and restricting but not yet abolishing private enterprise. This was, as Zápotocký's proclaimed it, "a national revolution, not a social revolution . . . . it does not socialize, it nationalizes. It does not set out to abolish private capitalist enterprises, it puts them under control."[12]

In this political and legal limbo, the private insurance industry, together with banking, found itself in a more difficult predicament than other economic branches. It became victim of the notion that it was the state's obligation to provide for the protection of individuals as well as the society against accidental damages and losses. The communists considered the state, with its greater available resources and the supposedly superior wisdom of its planners, more suitable to discharge that obligation than could any private enterprise, guided by the principle of profit. They caricatured capitalist insurance firms as inherently dishonest.

Once private enterprise was proclaimed both economically and morally inferior to public enterprise, it could only be made beneficial to the people if protected against its worse instincts. In practice, this meant cutting credit and imposing a system of regulations which, along with the depreciation of currency, made doing sound business increasingly difficult. As a result, most private firms became "trapped in an impasse of shortage of money and credits, fixed prices, increasing taxation, and accumulating deficit," yet were forbidden to stop production.[13]

It was a tribute to the vitality of the remaining private enterprise, the largely uninterrupted continuity of economic expertise, and the still unimpaired willingness of the population to work hard that the ideological experimentation, made worse by the drying up of foreign economic assistance other than UNRRA because of the incipient Cold

[11]Vojtech Mastny, *The Cold War and Soviet Insecurity: The Stalin Years* (New York: Oxford University Press, 1996), pp. 23-29.

[12]Antonín Zápotocký, *Po staru se _it nedá* [We Cannot Live the Old Way] (Prague: Práce, 1949), p. 66.

[13]Iván T. Berend and György Ránki, *The Hungarian Economy in the Twentieth Century* (New York: St. Martin's Press, 1985), p. 193.

War, did not prevent a remarkably fast postwar recovery. This was particularly impressive in Hungary after its 1946 currency reform. By 1948-49, Hungary, Poland, and Czechoslovakia achieved the production levels, though not the standard of living, that had existed before the war.

The catastrophe that followed was the result of the imposition from the outside of the Soviet model, with its rigid planning, distorted priorities, disincentives for individual initiative, and reliance on compulsion. The economic change that took place in 1948-49 was the direct consequence not of the communist seizure of political power—which had occurred gradually or abruptly in the different countries already before—but rather of the abandonment by the communists themselves of the concept of "national roads to socialism." This happened during the second half of 1948 at direct Soviet pressure in response to the Stalin-Tito break, which led Yugoslavia on its own, anti-Soviet road, as well as to the incipient recovery of Western Europe under the Marshall Plan, which prompted Moscow to organize its European dependencies into an economic grouping of its own, the Comecon.

The introduction of the Stalinist economic model, aimed at wiping out the last vestiges of private enterprise, was done in a fashion calculated to make a reversal, much less restitution, all but impossible; the advent of socialism Soviet-style was understood by its architects as marking the irresistible march of history. Whether the preferred way of eliminating foreign business interests was liquidation (as in Poland and Hungary) or takeover (as in Czechoslovakia), there was an intended break in continuity, conducive to regarding past claims and records as obsolete, and discarding them accordingly. In any case, the assets were confiscated by the state.

The state monopolized all insurance, formally assuming all liabilities of both local and foreign-based companies. In Poland, the introduction in the fall of 1948 of the Soviet banking model, with its management by the ministry of finance through the monopoly of the central bank supplemented by specialized banks for particular kinds of domestic and foreign operations, coincided with the transfer of all insurance surpluses into the state budget. As the Cold War progressed in the early 1950s, the Stalinist regimes also obliterated all Western economic presence in a campaign which assumed particularly vicious forms in Hungary—the country where such presence used to be more extensive than elsewhere. Not only were Western enterprises and other assets confiscated without compensation, but also local and even foreign employees of Western firms were framed as "saboteurs" and paraded at show trials, before being condemned to long prison sentences and eventually released for ransom.[14]

The trials prominently featured some of the communist officials who had previously been instrumental in enforcing the now superseded partial nationalization policies or had been involved in the similarly obsolete Soviet assistance to Israel in 1948, which had failed to meet Stalin's expectations. In that operation, which had been erroneously calculated to manipulate the Jewish state against the West while also being conducted for profit, Czechoslovakia had played the key role as a Soviet subsidiary.[15] Accordingly, as was Stalin's habit, its communist officials of Jewish origin who had been involved in the operation had to pay for his miscalculation. But his victims also included fanatical anti-Zionists, such as the deputy Czechoslovak minister of finance notorious among applicants for emigration to Israel for extorting from them their remaining property for the benefit of the state.[16]

By 1953 Stalin, having exhausted the utility of his Jewish disciples among Eastern European communists, followed in Hitler's footsteps by conducting a violent anti-Semitic campaign which was possibly intended to culminate in genocide.[17] Yet since the campaign was cut short by his death, the Jews remaining in East Central Europe were not singled out for a persecution anywhere comparable to Hitler's. Instead they suffered much like all subjects of the communist regimes from the policies of pauperization that were the end product of the Sovietization of the economy and its militarization since 1950. Periodic confiscations of private savings by means of "currency reforms" were part and parcel of the system. The reforms in Poland in 1950 and in Czechoslovakia in 1953 included, among other measures, the final cancellation of all insurance policies, which had until then been formally blocked.

During the subsequent periods of détente, the post-Stalinist regimes tried reluctantly to satisfy Western demands for compensation for nationalized foreign property, and agreements to that effect were

---

[14]Borhi, *The Merchants of the Kremlin*, pp. 49-52.

[15]Ji_í Dufek, Karel Kaplan, and Vladimír Šlosar, *_eskoslovensko a Israel v letech 1947-1953* [Czechoslovakia and Israel in 1947-1953] (Prague: Institute for Contemporary History, 1993).

[16]Meir Cotic, *The Prague Trial: The First Anti-Zionist Show Trial in the Communist Bloc* (New York: Herzl Press, 1987), pp. 225-26.

[17]Louis Rapoport, *Stalin's War against the Jews: The Doctors' Plot and the Soviet Solution* (New York: Free Press, 1990).

concluded with the United States as well as with other Western countries. Not all of the communist countries concluded such agreements with all the Western governments involved, and the common feature of the settlements achieved was the gross inadequacy of the lump sums paid as final compensation for all losses. Disbursement of these sums was left up to the recipient governments, which followed different practices in different countries. Indemnifying claimants who had come forward, the Western governments did not make any particular efforts to identify and compensate original Jewish or other owners of the properties nationalized by the communists if claims had not been advanced.

The democratic and pro-Western governments that emerged in East Central Europe from the wreckage of the communist regimes in 1989 have not considered compensation of insurance or other claims from the pre-communist era a high priority. Not only did they find themselves financially strapped by inheriting economies mismanaged by their predecessors, but they have also been faced with a flood of more recent claims by victims of communism, which understandably commanded immediate attention. Thus Poland has partly paid off its own residents for their prewar insurance policies, despite the extensive destruction of the pertinent records, but excluded from compensation anyone living abroad. To illustrate the complexity of the tangle on the example of Czechoslovakia, claims have been pursued against it by the expelled Sudeten Germans, some of whom had been beneficiaries of Nazi-stolen Jewish property, before themselves losing this and other property to the Czechoslovak state, for which losses they were later partly indemnified, though not by the Czechoslovak but by the West German government, which in turn seeks compensation from the Czech and Slovak Republics as the legal successors of the extinct Czechoslovak state—compensation to be balanced against restitution claims for the damage caused by Germans in these countries during World War II.

The main conclusions to be drawn from the historical analysis of the exceedingly complex situation that has evolved since World War II are the following:

First: Unlike in Western Europe, in the countries that became communist the post-1945 developments have not created clearly identifiable winners and losers, but only different categories of losers, Jewish and others, including the respective populations along with their governments, besides the foreign firms unlucky enough to have done business in the area.

Second: The distinctiveness of the injustices suffered by Jews in East Central Europe after 1945 is blurred in comparison with the unique catastrophe of the holocaust that had taken place before.

Third: The destruction or disappearance of assets as a result of the communist-engineered political, economic, and social upheaval and the irrationality of the ideologically motivated policies that had caused it have made a fair restitution of the damage difficult if not impossible.

Fourth: Such a situation makes not only legal claims very difficult to substantiate, much less enforce, but makes also moral claims less clear cut and persuasive than those arising from the Nazi-inflicted injustices during World War II. Accordingly, except in the case of clearly identifiable owners, compensation is a matter of philanthropy, which by differentiating between Jewish and non-Jewish victims of communism would risk reawakening in East Central Europe's fragile democracies the very scourge of anti-Semitism that has fortunately been receding.

Ms. Elzbieta Turkowska-Tyrluk

VICE PRESIDENT, POWSECHNY ZAKLAD UBEZPIECZEN (PZU)
POLAND

Break-out Session on Holocaust-Era Insurance: Postwar
Government Compensation Programs and Nationalizations

1. Before World War II, a widely developed insurance market existed in Poland. In 1839, 79 insurance agencies were active, on the territory of the Polish People's Republic, that is;

- 15 joint stock companies, in this two companies in liquidation and two, in relation to which under the judgement of the court of second instance bankrupt was announced;
- 10 counter – insurance agencies, conducting business on a broader level, of which two placed in liquidation;
- 42 small counter – insurance agencies, of which only one was a life counter – insurance agency. From among the small counter – insurance agencies five just before the second world war were placed in liquidation;
- 5 public insurance agencies;
- Postal Savings Bank as a public corporation performing the insurance business;
- 6 foreign insurance agencies: two English, two Italian, two German.

2. After the end of World War II, pre-war insurance agency estates were not nationalized, but their liquidation was executed. In relation to the insurance agencies, the act from the 3rd of January 1946, concerning the main branches of national economies, becoming the property of the State, was not in force. (Law Gazette Nr. 3, item 17, with later changes.)

On the 3rd of January 1947 a decree the ordering of personal and property insurance (L. G. Nr.5 it. 230). From the day the decree comes into force, that is the 3rd of January 1947, the local and foreign, private insurance agencies, regardless of their legal condition, have lost their right for a further conduct of the insurance business.

Only two pre-war insurance agencies received a license for conducting business, in the scope, settled in the decree, that is:

1) Warta Reassurance Company J.S.C. in Warsaw and
2) Polish General Counter-Insurance, of which both were nationalized.

In connection with the rest of the agencies the liquidation was to be conducted by the Polish General Counter-Insurance, later transformed into the Polish National Insurance, and for the foreign agencies, active on Polish territory, the main representative of the foreign insurance agency or the liquidation will be assigned by the court in virtue of its office.

However, in connection with insurance agencies, which are engaged only in personal insurance, the liquidation of their operations was to be performed by special, personal insurance agencies, which were brought into being, but were never created.

However, for agencies, of which the liquidation, for whatever reasons, was not completed on the strength of the decree's regulations, from 1947, according to [sec.] 2 act 1 orders of the Minister of Finance from the 29th of June 1959 on the principles and the course of insurance agencies liquidation, which lost the right of conducting the insurance business (L.G. Nr. 40, it. 211), the liquidator assigned was the Polish National Insurance.

In accordance with this, the Polish General Counter-Insurance took over the management and property of the liquidated insurance companies from their hitherto authorities. The liquidation was conducted on the basis of liquidation plans confirmed by the Minister of Finance, and during the liquidation, to ensure a proper realization of the proceedings, generally valid legal regulations were employed.

Notwithstanding the property connections in the joint stock capital between some liquidated agencies, principles of the separate character of property in relation to each of the agencies were strictly abided. In connection with this, separate balance-sheets, plans of satisfying creditors, reports of liquidation, etc. were prepared.

Jointly the Polish General Counter-Insurance conducted the liquidation of 25 insurance agencies that is:

- three public insurance agencies,
- six larger counter-insurance agencies,
- one small counter-insurance agency
- ten joint stock companies, in this one with the lone stock of Polish Capital,

- six foreign insurance agencies (two German, two English, and two Italian).

In relation to two of the "larger" counter-insurance agencies, operating in Poland before the war, that is:
- "Dniestr" Counter-Insurance Agency in Lwów
- "Karpatia" Counter, Life Insurance Agency in Lwów

Liquidation procedures were not conducted, as all the property was left on the territory, which did not enter into the composition of the territory of the Polish State.

From among the small counter-insurance companies only one was liquidated, as investigations conducted by the Polish General Counter-Insurance showed, that no property was left by these companies for which the investigation ought to be conducted, or the existing property was not sufficient to cover the costs of liquidation.

At this moment I would like to remark, that as far as the local companies, also with foreign contribution of capital were brought to trial in all virtues only up to the amount of property possessed in the balance, the foreign companies operating in Poland were brought to trial on the strength of art. 74 of the Polish Republic's President order from the 26th of January 1928 concerning supervision of insurance (L.G. Nr. 9 it. 64) their whole property, the one found in Poland as well as the property outside its borders. In practice this meant securing the rights of creditors and the insured, as well as the right to demand the existing commitments from the Head Office of the insurance company.

As I have mentioned earlier, six foreign insurance companies, through the meditation of main agencies, operated in Poland before the War.

In spite of provisions art. 2 para. 1 of the act from 3rd of January 1946 about the state taking over the main branches of national economies (L. G. Nr. 3 it. 17) on the strength which the nationalization of German insurance companies was to take place, also in relation to them liquidation procedures were conducted.

During the procedure of their liquidation it was ascertained, that:
1) The Bavarian Insurance Company - German Joined Stock Company - Headquarters in Katowice did not possess any movables or real estates in Poland. No claims in connection with liquidated company were registered, both in virtue of the insurance contracts entered before the war, as well as in virtue of workers' and other debts.
2) Aachen-Munich Insurance Company against the headquarters in Katowice also did not possess any real estates and the company's

movables found in Katowice were assigned for covering the workers' compensation.

Both companies' securities were not lost during the occupation period of were removed from Germany.

Owner of English insurance companies policies: "Alliance" and "Prudential" settled abroad, they were directed to collect the payments from these policies at the company's headquarters in London, as on the Polish-English financial contract from the 11th of November 1954 they did not provide from the funds found in Poland.

Similarly the owners of insurance policies of Italian companies "Assicurazioni Generali" and "Riuniona Adriatica di Sicurta" who settled abroad were directed to the Headquarters in Triest, Poland, however, in spite of numerous negotiations: in 1959, in 1972 and in 1977, in this scope, did not sign a mutual, financial agreement with Italy.

In Poland, for the owners of the above-mentioned English and Italian insurance companies, the payments from the policies were covered by the Polish State from the sums gained from the properties of those companies in Poland.

3. In a great majority of causes the one real element of assets of the liquidated insurance companies were the real estates, usually urban, saved after the war, of which the value was calculated according to the technical estimated norms, taking into the account the technical state of those real estates and also the destruction caused by the war.

The value of the securities, into which composition entered mostly pre-war bonds issued by the state, communal union and other long term credit institutions, such as the Bank of Local Economy, Land Credit Associations etc. was accepted as zero, because these loans were not repaid, and the bonds did not possess no real value.

The valuation of other bonds was done taking under consideration: decisions of indemnification contracts entered by Poland with other countries together on mutual terms.

To the passive debts of the liquidated companies were assigned mostly: the costs of liquidation, commitments from the insurance policies, taxes, stamp duties, other possible commitments and claims in virtue of shares or stocks.

Pricing both the assets and passive debts was unified both for the local companies, local companies with foreign stock capital and the foreign insurance companies operating in Poland. Also the claims in virtue of the owned policies were treated equally both in the case of Polish citizens in the country and abroad, and citizens of other countries (apart from claims from persons living abroad directed to English and Italian companies – justification as above).

The repayments from policies present by persons living abroad were transferred abroad, in accordance with the contemporary law, only after achieving a foreign permit. Depending on whether Poland signed a mutual contract with a given country in the scope of foreign circulation, money could be transferred either to the policy owner's country or transferred only to the blocked accounts of foreigners in Poland, to use in Poland.

4. Orders of the Minister of Finance from the 29th of June 1958, in the case of the principles and the course of liquidation of the insurance companies, which lost the right of conducting the insurance business originally anticipated, (section 3, act 1) that creditors of the liquidated insurance companies should, if they have not done this in the course of the hitherto liquidation operations, notify his liquidator in writing of his claims, within the period of six months, counting from the day of this orders coming into force, that is the 21st of January 1960.

In accordance with section 10 of the objective orders the responsibility for announcing in a widely read, daily newspaper the place and appointed time of the beginning and end of payments and imparting information on this subject by the Polish National Insurance, was imposed on the liquidator.

This condition was fulfilled by the PNI, which printed numerous notices about conducting liquidation procedures of pre-war insurance companies, both in the Polish Monitor and few other daily newspapers of an all-Polish and local range, such as "Trybuna Ludu," Zycle Warszawy," Rzeczpospolita."

The time of submitting claims was prolonged three times, in turn from the 31st July 1961, 30th June 1964 and finally till the 30th October 1979, in relation to the claims directed to the two last, Italian insurance companies:

1) ITALIAN JOINT STOCK COMPANY National assurance in Triest – Assicurazioni Generali Triesta, Management for the Republic of Poland in Warsaw;

2) ITALIAN JOINT STOCK COMPANY Riuniona Adriatica di Sicurta, Adriatic Insurance Company in Triest, Management for the Republic of Poland in Warsaw;

Only these two insurance companies were not yet liquidated in the course of the hitherto conducted procedures (notice from April 1979).

5. Compensation from the policies of the pre-war liquidated insurance companies were repaid after presenting the original policy and evidence of the share payments from August 1939, and each case was dealt with separately (separate liquidation check-ups).

Commitments from the insurance contracts in relation to the authorized persons, were regulated according to principles defined in the general conditions of insurance, but if the total sum of those commitments did not have coverage in the balance sum of the property of the given liquidation mass, the payments were placed in proportion with the existing funds.

The assignation of insurance sums in relation to the policies stated in zlotych in gold, and made out before the 8th of November 1927, was done by re-counting, first on the strength of the law itself in ratio 1 zloty in gold equals 1.72 zloty in circulation, and then the new sum was accepted as the nominal sum of the policy on the 31st of August 1939, composing the basis for later calculations, according to generally valid principles and it was re-counted into zloty in relation 1:1, not taking into account the height of the parity in the given pre-war period.

In the above way the recountings of the given group of policies did not refer to the policies with the amount in zloty in gold, but made up by different insurance companies following the date of the President orders from the 5th November 1927, in connection with change of the monetary system, coming into force, as these policies were calculated according to the relation 1 zloty in gold equals 1 zloty in circulation.

Policies stated in foreign currencies, if it had not yet been done on the strength of the law itself till the 1st of August 1934, were re-counted into zloty according to suitable in-force regulations.

In every case the final sum of the policy was calculated according to regulations of the orders of the Cabinet from the 27th of June 1958 regarding the definition of the ratio of re- counting claims from insurance contracts of liquidated insurance companies (L.G. Nr. 38, it. 243).

6. Naturally, in the case of life Insurance, death suffered as the result of the Holocaust was treated as death resisted to war procedures. From the liquidation papers it appears, that in spite of excluding the repayment of compensation in the case of death suffered as the result of war procedures by particular insurance conditions, the compensations were repaid to everyone who submitted the claim in virtue of the entered insurance contracts.

While repaying the policies qualified for repayment it was admitted, that in reality the insured stopped to pay shares from the 1st September 1939. As the cessation occurred without any fault on the part of the insured, but was the result of that created by the occupant, in Poland conditions, making it impossible for the citizens to pay the shares, it was accepted that the responsibility of insurance companies is not suspended and will last till the end of the war, that is till the 9th of May 1945.

And so the insured, who lived past the day of the 9th of May 1945, were repaid the insurance sum decreased in proportion to the period for which the premiums were paid before the 1st of September 1939 and the full period of the insurance, with deductions of policy loans.

At the repayment also the heirs of the dead during the War, were repaid the full sum of insurance, after the deduction of the possible loans and overdue premiums (generally for half of the war period).

7. Poland as a country occupied by Germany during World War II and which citizens suffered a great deal from the hands of the Nazi occupant, up till this day did not get the full settlement of compensation for the victims of the Nazi crimes on the part of Germany. No compensation program existed for the victims of Holocaust.

It should, however, be noticed that on the 16th of October 1991 as the cause of an agreement between the Republic of Poland's Government and the German Federal Republic, a foundation, "The Polish-German Reconciliation" was founded, which operated according to the legal regulations in force in the Republic of Poland.

On the strength of the above-mentioned agreement, the GFR Government, actuated by humanitarian reasons, donated 500 million DM for granting help to the victims who especially suffered by Nazi persecutions.

The "Reconciliation" Foundation grants financial help, one time performance character. The help granted by the Foundation is not a compensation and cannot be treated as satisfaction for all the suffered wrongs.

Polish citizens, as well as those of Jewish origin, alive on the 8th of January 1992, who in personally deposed the application, living permanently on the Republic of Poland's territory, and being victims of special Nazi persecution, have the right of soliciting for the financial help from the Foundation's means, these are:

- stay in the Nazi concentration camps, ghettos and prisons;

- stay in the so-called Polenlagr, which are severe work camps for Poles in Slaak;
- deportations from the place of settlement and forcing over the period of over 6 months to work for the benefits of the Third Reich;
- repressions during the stay in Stalaga;
- persecutions toward children (which during them turned 16):
  a) born in the concentration camps, ghettos, prisons and the children of the Holocaust.
  b) taken away from parents for purposes of Germanization, deported to work camps, forced to work at the place of stay; children, whose both parents were taken to concentration camps, imprisoned or to compulsory work, and which, were through this devoid of parental care, as well as those born in the Third Reich as the children of compulsory workers.

To finish I would once more like to emphasize, that in Poland, occurred a liquidation of property of pre-war insurance companies, in accordance with the law, and not their nationalization. This fact for a great number of the authorized, on the basis of insurance contracts entered before the Second World War, made possible the execution of their rights.

Prof. Gerald D. Feldman

PROFESSOR OF HISTORY, UNIVERSITY OF CALIFORNIA, BERKELEY AND
FELLOW, AMERICAN ACADEMY IN BERLIN
UNITED STATES

Compensation and Restitution: Special Issues

Break-out Session on Holocaust-Era Insurance: Unpaid Claims

My purpose in these remarks is to try to expand somewhat on the ways in which restitution and compensation for insurance were carried out following the German defeat in 1945. As was the case with respect to confiscation, so with respect to compensation and restitution, it is very important to understand the role played by currency and exchange regulations as well as by inflation and currency reform. Even before Germany had been fully occupied, the Supreme Commander of the Allied Forces had issued Law No. 53, which contained exchange regulations that, among other things, banned the payment of life insurance policies for persons living outside of Germany. While this measure was obviously aimed at preventing National Socialists and Germans abroad from getting access to their assets, it also prevented Jewish and anti-Nazi emigrants from collecting on their life insurance as well. Indeed, it was only in June 1950, that is, two years after the currency reform, that the Allies were prepared to entertain individual requests for payments of insurance to persons living abroad. Ironically, however, these had to be paid on a blocked DM account. Procedures were relaxed in 1951, and these peculiar restrictions were terminated with the London Agreement of 1953. Nevertheless, DM blocked accounts remained non-convertible until July 1958, that is, just five months before the DM became fully convertible.

The currency reform of June 21, 1948 determined both the currency in which insurance policies were to be denominated in the future and the currency in which insurance compensation was finally to be denominated. The optical impression of some Jewish émigré getting

79.87 DM in 1957 on a 5,000 RM policy taken out in 1925 is one that is likely to produce irritation and even rage, especially when one is used to today's price levels and when one considers the great success and wealth of German insurance companies at the present time. My job as an historian, however, is to try to reconstruct past times and make what happened then intelligible. Insurance is a liquid asset, and inflation inevitably favors those holding material assets over those holding liquid assets. By the time of the currency reform, the RM was virtually worthless, and cigarettes were actually being used as a currency. In fact, as at the end of the hyperinflation in 1923, people were turning to barter, trading eggs, for example, for a dental examination. All currency reforms involve an arbitrary decision about the relationship between the old currency and the new. In 1923-1924, the German government set the ratio of paper marks to the dollar at 4.2 trillion to 1, lopped off twelve zeros and pegged the RM at 4.2 to 1, which was the old parity. In 1948, when convertibility was not of significance, the value was simply set at 10 RM to 1 DM. The important thing was to create confidence by creating a new currency, limiting the amount of currency in circulation, and thereby inducing people to make goods available and get back to work. All insurance policies, indeed all liquid assets, non-Jewish as well as Jewish, were thus reduced to a tenth of their previous nominal value, but the purpose was to create a real value. One of the most important guarantees of such real value was the continued Allied occupation, and it was indeed the occupation authorities in the West which helped to insure the control of the currency and mandated its rapid acceptance. The currency reform must be viewed as an event that made compensation of liquid assets possible with real as opposed to worthless money. It goes without saying, of course, that the National Socialist regime was responsible for the necessity of currency reform, but in this instance they had despoiled everyone by bankrupting the nation in order to help pay for the war.

This also helps to explain why it was the German Federal Republic, not the insurance companies, which took over the responsibility for compensation and restitution that developed following the treaties with Israel and the Claims Conference of 1952 and the London Agreement of 1953. The insurance companies had been compelled to invest heavily in German State bonds (Reichsanleihe), and these were worthless. Prior to the currency reform the insurance companies were limited in the amounts they could pay out to policyholders by the occupation authorities, and their resumption of operations depended on state guarantees. In effect, they were rendered dependent on the government for past obligations and reliant upon new business for any future success they might have. The one significant obligation remaining to them was to search their files for Jewish policyholders when called upon to do so and to calculate compensation claims according to the formula devised by the Federal Compensation Office. As far as I can tell, they performed this task quite diligently, charging the government about 9.50 DM for their labors.

As Dr. Gerlach has pointed out in his paper, compensation to victims of National Socialism for insurance losses was based on the presupposition that they would have maintained their insurance policies, that is, paid their premiums and collected the full value of insurance when the policy came to term were it not for their persecution. Values and premiums for the period prior to the currency reform were calculated in RM and then recalculated in DM. For the period after June 1948, both values and premiums were calculated in DM. Since he has already described and illustrated the method used, I shall not repeat what he said here. Instead, let me turn very briefly to what happened in the Soviet Occupation Zone of Germany and the former GDR and say a few words about Austria. The Soviets liquidated all the old insurance companies in 1945, took over their assets, and created state companies. Policyholders were given the option of contracting a new policy with these companies that would automatically reinstate their old policies. The right to make claims against the old insurers was denied. This remained the state of affairs until the collapse of the GDR. The Unification Treaty of August 1990 has made provision for a new regulation of claims arising from the war, but such legislation has not yet been issued. This does not, however, preclude individual agreements between insured and previous insurers.

Finally, let me turn to the Austrian case. Between 1959 and 1964, the Federal Government of Germany entered into a series of bilateral agreements with a variety of countries for the purposes of compensation of victims of Nazism. In the case of Austria, 102 million DM was given, 96 million DM of which was used to compensate loss of income of victims of Nazi persecution and to compensate victims in other countries, while the remaining 6 million were to compensate for lost property. Austria had nothing comparable to the German compensation legislation. Insofar as insurance was concerned, the Austrians confronted a situation similar to that of the Germans in that their insurance companies were insolvent at war's end. An Insurance Transition Law of 1946 limited the amount companies could pay out, while the Österreichisches Versicherungs AG, which was a successor to the Phoenix--a special case because of its bankruptcy in 1936--and was in particularly dire straits, was barred from making any payments on policies paid up prior to May 1, 1946 and was limited in what it could pay out on policies that were still active. These restraints were eased as the condition of the Austrian economy stabilized. The Insurance Reconstruction Law of September 8, 1955 mandated that claims regarding life insurance policies created after January 1, 1946 would be paid in full, while those created before that date would be reduced by 60%. The payment of the latter policies was to be made possible by government bonds and cash advances. All policies were to be converted into Austrian currency. A special fund was set up in 1955 for Phoenix annuitants providing three million shillings annually. It is interesting to note, in conclusion, that there were complaints about these arrangements by victims of the National Socialist regime at the time and that the Austrian government was charged with violating the Austrian State Treaty. The U.S. Embassy in Vienna, however, took the position that "It is the opinion of the Embassy that the foregoing laws are ameliorative and not confiscatory in nature. Insofar as the insolvent 'Phoenix' Insurance Company is concerned, the laws were designed to rehabilitate it and to save its assets for the benefit of all its policy holders and may be characterized as bankruptcy or reorganization legislation."[1] Whether this is a valid judgement or not is difficult for me to say without further study, but I think it is interesting as a reflection of attitudes at the time and provides some perspective from which to judge the far more extensive and elaborate arrangements made by the German Government with respect to compensation and restitution of victims of National Socialism in the realm of insurance.

---

[1] James K. Penfield, Minister-Counselor of Embassy to the Department of State, November 10, 1955, National Archives of the United States, RG 59, 863.08/11-1955, Box 4792. I am grateful to Dr. Oliver Rathkolb for bringing this document to my attention.

Ms. Catherine A. Lillie

DIRECTOR, HOLOCAUST CLAIMS PROCESSING OFFICE,
NEW YORK STATE BANKING DEPARTMENT
UNITED STATES

Government Compensation Programs and Unpaid Claims

Break-out Session on Holocaust-Era Insurance: Unpaid Claims

Thank you for this opportunity to present the work of the Holocaust Claims Processing Office. The HCPO was established by Governor Pataki in September 1997 as a division of the New York State Banking Department. It grew out of the NYSBD's investigation into the wartime activities of SBC's, UBS's and Credit Suisse's New York Agencies and was initially intended to assist claimants with unresolved claims against Swiss financial institutions. However, it soon became apparent that our claimants also needed help with other types of claims, most notably insurance claims. Therefore, the HCPO added claims for unpaid insurance policies written in Europe in the pre-war and Holocaust-Era to its mission. The mandate did not end there. Today, the HCPO assists claimants with a vast array of claims: the majority still reference Swiss banks and European insurance companies, but there is an ever increasing number of claimants filing claims for lost, looted or stolen art, as well as for assets deposited with European financial institutions, be they Austrian, British, Dutch, French, German, or Italian.

Overall, the HCPO has handled in excess of 5,000 inquiries in the past year. Of these, 2,600 have been insurance-related inquiries from 22 countries and 43 states. These inquiries have generated 1,300 claims from 18 countries and 36 states. The majority of insurance claims have come in from the US, Canada, the United Kingdom and Australia; the majority of domestic claims are not surprisingly from NY, IL, CA, FL, NJ, and TX. But, essentially, it is true that wherever people fled to in the 1930s and 1940s, we now have claimants, be that as close as Canada or as far afield as Australia or Israel. What started off as an additional service that we wanted to offer survivors and their heirs with banking claims has now turned out to be half the work the office does on any given day, and on some days well more.

I hasten to point out, however, that while there are 1,300 claimants, this actually means that we have claims for more than 1,900 insured persons. The reason is simple. in many instances, individuals had multiple policies. In other instances, the claimant may well be the sole survivor of a sizable family, the members of which were well-insured, or just insured. Either way, many of our cases refer to more than one policy.

Claims currently filed with the HCPO reference a little more than 100 companies as identified by claimants. The HCPO is currently trying to determine how many successor companies are in fact involved. It may be as few as two dozen. The most frequently cited companies remain Generali, Phönix, RAS, Victoria, Allianz, Anker, Basler and Donau. But claimants have also identified Barmenia, Fonciere, Gerling, Hermes, Isar, Lloyds, Merkur, Nordstern, ÖVAG, Swiss Life, Star and Vita, to name but a few. We have actual policy documents in every imaginable Central European language for some of these, and policy numbers for many many more.

I have given much thought to how to best give you a sense of where these policies were written, not just by whom. But the frequent border changes in Central Europe that you are all aware of make this challenging. When going back to reconstruct how many Polish, Czech, Romanian, Hungarian or even Austrian claims the HCPO currently has on its books the first question one must ask is at what point in time, according to which borders? Roughly speaking in terms of pre-1938 borders the majority of our claims are Austrian, Polish, Czech and Hungarian. There is also a handful of Romanian, Yugoslav and Bessarabian claims, some of which are rather well documented. In terms of post-1945 borders, however, the countries involved are more numerous.

But numbers don't tell the whole story. Our experience has been far more complex than this. We have an exceptional team of multi-lingual professionals with a wide array of talents who process written and verbal inquiries and claims in eight different languages, drawing on their knowledge of European history, as well as their banking, insurance and legal backgrounds. Our staff provides assistance in a variety of ways: preparing the claims either by appointment or over the telephone. They assist in securing documentation where claimants do not have appropriate documents; they research successor companies where these

ıre not known. They then continue on and submit claims to the
ıppropriate companies, and European regulatory authorities. The
ıltimate goal is to alleviate the burden and cost that claimants have
ɔncountered when proceeding on their own.

Claims range from the purely anecdotal, through the detailed that
ıre merely lacking the original paperwork, to the partially or even fully
ɹocumented cases. For the most part we are dealing with life, dowry, and
ɔducation policies, as well as the occasional annuity, property, fire,
ɹealth and pension policies. Unlike the Swiss Bank cases that we have
worked on (where only 10-15% of account holders can be linked to a
specific bank), almost 50% of the policyholders can be linked to an
insurance company.

Those who cannot provide documentation do know significant
details. What sorts of details are these? Claimants know there was
insurance; they even recall purchasing it, and they remember perhaps the
name of the agent and location. They can remember the piggy bank
sporting a company logo, which they received when purchasing a policy.
Some have memories of a fearful and frenzied attempt to bury their
documents while in the ghetto -- the only available form of safekeeping.
Unfortunately in many cases this desperate ruse failed. They remember
accompanying parents to medical exams, or to photographers for dowry
policy photographs. We have claimants who accompanied their father, an
insurance salesman, on sales trips. And we have a claimant with very
vivid memories of Generali Christmas parties in Warsaw -- both her
father and grandfather were senior managers of the Polish subsidiary of
this Italian insurance company.

We have devoted a lot of time and energy to listening very
carefully to our claimants. Often, the details that may lead us to connect
the insured to the company that wrote the policy are not apparent in the
information supplied on the claim form the HCPO uses. But extensive
follow up conversations frequently reveal a degree of detail that emerges
in the retelling of highly traumatic events. Details such as the piggy
bank, which I know was red and domed, and German. The claimant can
even place the logo on it. Unfortunately the one detail that is missing is
an accurate description of that logo. But I am hopeful that one day soon a
claimant will walk in, lamenting the loss of the paper policy but
proffering a red, domed piggy bank as proof.

Documentation, and by this I mean actual paper documentation,
where it exists is no less vivid. There are of course the handwritten lists
kept by families that itemized their assets. Moreover, claimants have pre-
war and wartime confirmation letters from insurance companies

referencing policy numbers and policies. In some cases we have seen postwar confirmation of the existence of policies, and clarification of who received the proceeds during the war. One claimant's father owned two life insurance policies written by Basler. They were seized by the Nazi government in 1942 in accordance with the 11th ordinance of the Reich's citizenship law (25 Nov 1941) because he was "abroad". To the best of our knowledge, the policyholder never received restitution from the German government. This is not an isolated case.

In 46% of cases the claimants can provide some sort of link to the company that originally wrote the policy. These are predominantly life and dowry policies; in some instances there are also some property, fire, health and pension insurance policies. I stress "originally" wrote the policy because needless to say, in many instances that is only a starting point. We have had many claims for Phönix policies, written all over central and Eastern Europe. As you are all well aware, Phönix went bankrupt in 1936 and companies scrambled to carve up Phönix's holdings and incorporate the portfolios into their own. Thus, the Austrian Phönix portfolio was incorporated into OVAG, the German portfolio into Isar, the Czech portfolio into Star, the Polish portfolio into the PZU, and so on. For policies written in contested geographical areas such as Trans-Carpathia, this was often just the first move and far from the last, making successor companies difficult to research. The pre-war Nazi consolidation of the insurance industry and the post-war reconstruction of this industry add to the difficulties encountered in successor company research, and nationalization issues that pertain to policies purchased in Eastern Europe are no less complex.

The chopping and changing of company holdings is not the only hurdle to successful research. The vast array of companies in pre-war Europe, the tendency to buy locally, from subsidiaries of larger, more prominent companies, complicates matters further. Moreover, Europe is a vast place. In order to do business effectively, it had to be conducted in a dozen languages, through local subsidiaries or branch offices. Thus, although the companies most frequently cited by claimants are Generali, Phönix, RAS, Victoria, Allianz, Der Anker, Basler, and Donau, they are mentioned in a variety of different languages, frequently referring to a local company that was backed by a home office in Vienna or Prague, Trieste or Berlin.

But linguistic confusion is not just prevalent when trying to determine company names. It is also apparent when trying to verify claimants' personal details. On the whole, people stayed put as borders were moved around them, dominant languages and currencies changed, etc. Contested territories switched backwards and forwards between Czechoslovakia, Hungary and Romania. Our claimants have documents that show their names, addresses, dates of birth and value of their policies in three different languages and currencies. Until recently one of my favorite examples was the claimant who provided documentation from Cluj, Kolosvar and Klausenburg – all the exact same place in present-day Romania. But I have recently been told by an archivist at Yad Vashem that Nagy Szolosz offers a far greater challenge – it has 26 variations!

In other examples claimants have come in convinced that the policies they are seeking were written by one company and the HCPO's research has been able to determine that it was in fact quite another. How do we do this? Let me give an example. A claimant, originally from Vienna, came into the HCPO relatively certain that his father's life insurance policy was written by Der Anker or Phönix. A reasonable assumption, given the size of these companies and the fact that the policy was purchased in Vienna. Neither Der Anker nor Austria Lebensversicherung (the Phönix successor) had any record. So the HCPO researched this claimant's father's tax records. The Vermögensverzeichnis on file at the Austrian Federal Archives revealed a Victoria life insurance policy, and even cited its repurchase value as of July 1938. Again, this is not an isolated case.

Another example is a claimant who contacted the HCPO over a year ago. She has her Anker dowry policy purchased by her mother in Czechoslovakia in the late 1930s to ensure an adequate dowry of 50,000 Czech Crowns. By the time the claimant found the HCPO she had already been married and widowed twice, all without ever receiving the dowry her mother had intended for her. To add insult to injury, this claimant has not only the actual policy, but also every premium receipt for every payment made, all the way into the ghetto and from there to the camps. The claimant here is the sole survivor of a sizeable family and this policy is the only link that remains to that pre-war world. Anker's home office in Vienna has consistently refused to offer payment on this policy because it claims not to be the legal successor to the policy. Instead, it prefers to present itself as a fellow victim, claiming to have lost all its assets to nationalization in the former Czechoslovakia and Hungary. Over the years, the Czech authorities have repeatedly asserted that these policies were seized by the Nazis. Moreover, in this case, where the policy was written in a contested territory, it was apparently transferred to Hungarian portfolios. In any case, the German or the Hungarian governments are cited as the more appropriate places to address these claims. In this way, claimants have been sent from pillar to post for over 50 years.

It is true that some of these claims were settled in the 1940s, 1950s and 1960s and restitution was indeed received by some. But in the chaos of postwar Europe some policyholders and their heirs were missed, even in Western Europe. While German insurance companies have provided assistance with Western European claims that were missed in the post-war period, policies written by Eastern European subsidiaries or branches of Austrian, Italian or German and French companies are generally refused. Companies cite nationalization decrees in Czechoslovakia, Hungary and Poland, as a result of which they lost their assets. Moreover, parent companies claim to have lost their archives along with their other assets in nationalization. This explanation has been offered even in cases where claimants have supplied the original policy and premium payment receipts. Without their original archives, some companies have been extremely unwilling to consider assessing the value of policies presented to them.

The reasons are fairly self-explanatory of course, and have been outlined by Prof. Feldman in the past. Jews were dispossessed of their assets in a variety of ways, some more direct than others were. There was outright seizure of the policy by the Gestapo after "flight" to the East, but there was also surrender to the tax authorities to cover a variety of punitive taxes. Or there was repurchase by the policyholder/insured in an attempt to fund emigration. Or there was the failure to meet premium payments, because of loss of livelihood for example. We have certainly received very detailed information from a variety of insurance companies listing loans that were taken out against policies, or illustrating how failure to maintain premium payments resulted in a loss of value of the insurance policy. Or citing repurchase dates and amounts. Unfortunately, some of these repurchases occurred after the policyholder had already been incarcerated or had perished in a concentration camp. Alternatively, there are considerable payment details that have come out of Austrian insurance companies listing exact payment dates and amounts in the 1950s. While this information is very welcome, it is also hugely problematic: the companies cannot tell us who received those payments in the 1950s, yet the heirs can confirm that the insured were murdered 15 years earlier.

So where do matters stand now, from the claimants' perspective? Before the creation of the International Commission on Holocaust-Era Insurance Claims chaired by Lawrence Eagleburger, the HCPO had been offered ten settlements, covering a total of 19 policies. To date none of our claimants have accepted the offers, and a brief overview may explain why. The offers range from a low of $50 to a high of $3,000, but all combined add up to just under $10,000. Vastly different approaches to valuation are of course the reason for these enormous disparities. One of our claimants who purchased a policy in 1923 in Berlin for a one-time payment of 5,000,000 marks and a final payout of 10,000,000 in 1948 has discovered that the policy is not worth the paper it is written on. Not only was there a period of currency stabilization just after he purchased his policy (Germany was struggling with hyperinflation, after all), but then there was the creation of the Reichsmark. And the creation of the Deutschmark in 1948 three months before his policy was due wiped out any remaining value.

Similarly, Austrian companies have been very adept at calculating the value of the policies they wrote in the 1930s. First the Schilling replaced the Krone. Then the Reichsmark was introduced, only to be replaced with the new Schilling after the war. All these changes must be accounted for. However, companies have then proceeded to offer no interest for the fifty-plus years that followed these conversions. Thus, claimants feel that insult has been added to injury when their four policies are assessed at a total of $50 despite being written in gold Schillings or gold dollars.

In many instances, companies have insisted, even where policy documents remain, that they cannot assess the value of the asset on the basis of these documents alone. Or they have assumed that, where repurchase values were listed on asset declaration forms such as the Vermögensverzeichnis, that payment was made. Who received it remains for someone else to determine The company's liability has been removed. Usually these letters end with the suggestion that there may well be more documentation elsewhere.

I will readily admit that the historian in me loves this continued quest for more and more documentary evidence and detail. I am often dumbfounded by the documents that claimants can provide, by the stories of how paper was safeguarded or rescued. I am frequently amazed at the detail that can be found on tax forms and the like if one is prepared to look. And I could happily go on at great length about individual cases that the HCPO has handled in the past year. But to be perfectly candid, the historian in me is also confronted daily with a terrible conflict inherent to this subject matter: the inevitable mortality of the generation of survivors still with us. Our claimants are getting older every day. Their health is not improving. That other part of me, the part that carries the responsibility for the HCPO and its claimants, is far more enamoured with the concept of speedily arrived at "rough" justice. Many have been trying to arrive at resolution for more than half a century. If they are to witness any closure for themselves, we must all work to achieve it sooner rather than later.

Mr. Bobby Brown

ADVISER TO THE PRIME MINISTER FOR DIASPORA AFFAIRS,
PRIME MINISTER'S OFFICE
ISRAEL

Break-out Session on Holocaust-Era Insurance: Unpaid Claims

Ladies and Gentlemen:

I come to you as the Representative of an ancient people whose history has been stolen.

Since World War II, the entire Jewish people have moved from their countries of origin. Ask a Frenchman in Paris or an Italian in Milano or a German in Berlin where their ancestors lie and they will take you to the local cemetery and show you the graves of their forefathers. They can show you the town records, the church registry and the family bible, which lists their family tree. Almost no Jew today lives in the same town as his grandparents. We have lost our history. We no longer remember the maiden names of our grandmothers or the number of uncles and cousins that we lost.

But much of that "history" was written in a most unusual historical record - in the ledgers and policy information of European insurance companies. There lie the maiden names, the occupations, the addresses of the former homes and the names of the children designated to inherit those policies.

We never assigned insurance companies the task of holding our history; we never thought that they would record our families' stories but they did - and with the ferocious appetite of some Rip Van Winkle, reawakened and with a thirst for knowledge that had been denied too long - we now come forward and say: Give us the history that you hold; give us the life stories of our forefathers. Tell us who we are; tell us what happened; return to us our heritage; publish the names.

I come to you today with a message of hope; hope that we had given up for lost; hope from the places which we thought were lost forever.

A Jewish family having survived the ravages of the First World War begins to build a new life for itself in the unstable political and economic climate of Eastern or Central Europe. They buy a life insurance policy from a trusted neighbor and friend. It is bought as a way of saving for the uncertain days ahead. It is bought as a pension plan; It is bought to pay for the wedding of that most precious of treasures – a daughter. Slowly, the sky fills with the clouds of hatred, racism, political instability and economic upheaval. Discrimination begins. Job loss.   Education denied. Degradation and violence. Our family seeks an escape but the "civilized world" has turned its back and refused them entrance. The confiscations, the destruction, the "round-up," the trains, the ghettos, the dogs, the helmets, and the cursing. The selection, the camps, the beatings, the starvation, the disease and death.

And yet, the hope that maybe, if the children live, a policy issued in better times, will be there for a new life for the children – that after the darkness, a new day of security and a new beginning for the precious remnant that survives.

As the voltage on the electrified fences is turned off and the gates opened, as a new life must be started from the ashes and tears, a recollection of that policy, issued during better times, comes to mind.   It is the key to the door of opportunity; it is the first step on a tall staircase; it is the past reaching out to help the future – AND IT IS DENIED.

This was the story of many. It was the story of Herman Klein, the proprietor of the Budapest factory of the Parker Pen Company who lost his home, his furniture, his business, and his family. In 1947, Herman Klein spent many nights completing the forms at the Register of Enemy Debts in his new home in Palestine. He listed every possession in the hope that his property would be restored. He included the linen shutters on the kitchen windows of his Budapest home, the washbasin with pipe fittings, the gold bracelet, tie clip, ladies ring and medallion, totaling 69 grams of gold and the 88 fountain pens that were stolen from Herman Klein, the former Head of the Parker Pen Company. He carefully listed his insurance policies

Providencia Insurance Company, Budapest	Herman Klein	Policy No 52418	Issued 22 February 1937
Providencia Insurance Company Budapest	Herman Klein	Policy no. 52412	Issued19 February 1937
Generali Insurance Company, Budapest	Herman Klein	Policy no. 64620	Issued 24 October 1929

Generali Insurance Company, Budapest	Herman Klein	Policy No. 74490	Issued 24 February 1934

Phonix Insurance Company	Herman Klein	Policy no. 530258	Issued 22 December 1932

Herman Klein carefully notes on the yellowed form that his policy states that all currencies are convertible to gold. Herman Klein never again saw his linen shutters, never again saw his 88 pens and never received any payment for his insurance policies.

Erwin Steiner, was born in Budapest on the 6 June 1888. Erwin sat with his insurance agent on September 9, 1927 and took out this policy (holds up copy of Generali policy).

It is clearly stated on this policy that in 20 years Mr. Steiner would receive 1,000 "New York" dollars; his monthly premium would be $14.92. But Mr. Steiner was to die in the crematoria at Auschwitz in 1944 and when Mr. Steiner's surviving son applied to receive his father's bequest, he was denied because his father had stopped paying his premiums. In the depth of the camps struggling each day for a crust of bread and wome watery soup, Erwin no longer had any possibility to pay $14.92 each month.

An insurance policy is a contract of faith where one side promises to pay premiums and the other side promises protection, a future and hope. For many Jews, it was that future, that hope and that protection that kept them going another day, and another day, in the very Gates of Hell.

I am a child of survivors. I am a proud representative of the reborn State of Israel - reborn from the ashes of European Jewry and I am full of hope. Because I have the honor to be Israel's representative on the International Commission on Holocaust Era Claims, I am full of hope that the heirs of Herman Klein, the Parker Pen manufacturer from Budapest, and the heirs of Erwin Steiner, whose ashes were lost through the chimneys of Auschwitz, will regain the dignity that has been denied them. The world will quickly forget the words we say here, but will never forget the justice we seek to achieve here.

I – with this Conference – am full of hope.

Communal Property

Stuart E. Eizenstat

UNDER SECRETARY OF STATE FOR ECONOMIC, BUSINESS,
AND AGRICULTURAL AFFAIRS
UNITED STATES

Plenary Session on Nazi-Confiscated Communal Property

Mr. Chairman, I want to thank you for agreeing to preside over our sessions on communal property today. As Chairman of the House International Relations Committee, you have proudly been one of the leaders on this issue in the United States Congress. Through the hearings that you have chaired you have brought public attention to the opportunity we have had since the end of the Cold War to right this injustice. You have focused on the progress achieved by the new democracies in Central and Eastern Europe as well as on the obstacles which make early resolution of these claims difficult. Your efforts have provided a real service to the international community.

Earlier in this conference we reviewed the looted gold issue and commenced our dialogue on insurance and art. We now turn to communal property, that is the land, buildings and religious artifacts owned by religious organizations and other community-based groups in Central and Eastern Europe prior to World War II. This property has a significant value; returning it to its rightful owners, or compensating owners, will correct yet another of the injustices of the Holocaust era.

Before going into the communal property issue in more detail, I want to mention briefly the twin issue of private property. In planning this Conference, we concluded that the private property issue was too complex to be dealt with adequately in the time available. I do not want to leave the impression, however, that by omitting private property we are somehow downgrading or ignoring that issue. The contrary is the case. Omitting private claims from the agenda of this Conference acknowledges the complexities which those claims pose and the need to consider that issue in a different context. But it is essential that governments make a start to return private – or pay compensation.

Communal property was one of the early targets of the Nazi regime. By expropriating churches, synagogues and other community-controlled property – such as community centers and schools – the Nazis denied religious communities the temporal facilities which held those communities together. After the war, the authoritarian regimes that succeeded to power nationalized the property, compounding the persecution of the Nazis. In the former Soviet Union, the communist government expropriated property as part of Stalin's effort to eliminate religion from Soviet life. Religious objects, such as Torah scrolls and artifacts of a religious nature, also fell victim to authoritarian regimes both during and after World War II.

While the circumstances of each parcel of real estate and artifact are different, the component parts of the communal property issue share a common characteristic: governments improperly took this property from the rightful owners without compensation. Now it is our common responsibility to ensure that, finally, justice is done.

Addressing these issues in a forthright and sympathetic manner is part of the broader process of moving to closure on the questions left open after World War II and which merely became more complicated during the Cold War. For those states which gained independence as a result of the collapse of the Soviet Union, dealing with these issues is part of the broader challenge of building democratic institutions and establishing the rule of law.

As many of you know, the issue of communal property restitution has a special importance for me. Since 1995, I have had the privilege of leading a U.S. government initiative to promote the just resolution of this issue. My role as special envoy has brought me both satisfaction and frustration. Satisfaction during visits to communities of Holocaust survivors in Central and Eastern Europe which have endured 50 years of oppression under Nazi and Communist governments. Satisfaction to see that many are rebuilding their communities. Frustration that these double victims – who lost nearly everything to the Nazis and who endured another 40 years of repression under communist governments – continue to see justice delayed.

The U.S. Government encourages the return of communal property, and supports the revitalization of religious and other communities. We want to see schools and community centers included in the process. We encourage governments to establish equitable, transparent and non-discriminatory procedures to evaluate specific claims, and to work closely with local religious communities to resolve those claims. We feel that cemeteries should never be desecrated or used for any other purpose – to maintain in dignity those buried there.

Let me cite one example of a restitution success story which I believe is symbolic of the kind of property transfer which can benefit us all. Part-of the commemoration of the 60th anniversary of Kristallnacht last month was the re-dedication of a small synagogue in Oswiecim, Poland. The name may not be familiar to many of you but the German name of that town, Auschwitz, is all too well-known. Here, a short distance from the infamous Nazi death camp, the Polish Jewish community has used Poland's new restitution law to reclaim one of the city's former synagogues, used for a commercial purpose in more recent years. Together with a small nearby house, the synagogue will serve as a museum to show the daily life of Oswiecim's once substantial Jewish population during the pre-Nazi period. The restoration of this synagogue in an area which is the symbol of the Holocaust shows how a well-conceived, carefully administered restitution law can work.

Progress has been made on this subject in many countries. Recent legislation in Poland and Hungary has laid a solid foundation for sound restitution programs. Hungary established a public foundation to claim and receive communal property, and also established a fund which will pay Holocaust survivors small monthly pensions. Other countries are actively dealing with this issue.

But while a start has been made, we should be under no illusion about the difficulties of this task. As the Department's Special Envoy for Property Restitution in Central and Eastern Europe, I have visited eleven countries, many more than once, to address this issue.

More recently, my colleague, Ambassador Henry Clarke, visited several countries to gain a more detailed appreciation of the complexities of restituting communal property. We have both been impressed with the progress which has been made in many instances. At the same time, we have observed obstacles which make the resolution of this issue a daunting task.

For example, despite the commitment of national governments to restitution, local governments often block implementation. In some countries laws on restitution apply only to narrowly defined religious properties, leaving out the far more numerous communal properties such as schools and community centers that were and are so important to these communities. The legitimate interests of the current tenants can be used to block progress. Access to records that can help clarify claims is often difficult. Complex and costly legal procedures can discourage claimants. The issue of who should receive and manage restituted property can generate controversy and slow the process.

We have made clear that we support a process of communal property restitution that reflects a commitment to religious freedom and tolerance, a sense of justice, and the concept that property can be expropriated only through due process and for prompt and effective compensation. I think the governments represented here today share those basic tenets. But while we seek consistent standards for restitution, we also recognize the widely divergent circumstances that exist where this property is located and the need to take these circumstances fully into account. It appears obvious that no single grand solution will work effectively in all countries.

However, my hope is that to guide our efforts we can agree on a system of principles along the following lines:

First, we want to encourage national governments to take the necessary steps to ensure that restitution policies established by the national government are implemented at regional and municipal levels of government. Differences between various levels of government should not thwart the effort to return property to legitimate owners. Having a federal government ourselves, we recognize the constitutional and legal problems which can arise on issues having implications at both national and local levels. Nevertheless, I would hope that we in this Conference could agree that the resolution of this issue requires each country to have some uniformity of policy and administrative practice in this area.

Secondly, as a general principle, communal property should be eligible for restitution irrespective of whether the property had a religious or a secular use. There may be cases of secular property such as extensive agricultural land or factories for which restitution is not possible. Fair treatment may require new legislation which more properly defines and describes property eligible for restitution.

Thirdly, legal procedures for filing claims should be clear and simple. Complex legal procedures delay or deny the justice we all seek in resolving communal property issues. Those preparing claims should have easy access to archives.

Fourthly, we should encourage the establishment of foundations jointly managed by local communities and international groups to aid in the preparation of claims and to administer restituted property, where these are needed to assist the local communities. Such foundations enable international groups to share the burdens, and potentially some of the benefits, of the restituted property.

Finally, elected governments must make provisions for the present occupants of restituted property. In most cases, those now using property wrongfully seized in the past had no hand in its original expropriation. We therefore urge governments to establish procedures that will allow for the restitution of as many properties as possible, and that take into account legitimate needs of the current tenants.

We hope that a consensus on principles can give new impetus to the encouraging initiatives already underway in many countries, and that this intergovernmental forum can be a catalyst for many other belated efforts to address this unfinished business of the twentieth century. With a bit of good will and some imagination, we will be able to implement these or similar principles to resolve communal property claims.

The traumatic events of the 1930's and 1940'sr followed by the long period of totalitarian communist rule, destroyed trust within religious communities, among religious communities and between religious communities and governments. A successful communal property restitution process will help to re-establish trust, understanding and acceptance at all these levels.

The issue will not simply vanish; the fact that we are discussing it more than fifty years after the war is ample evidence that this question has considerable staying power. What could occur, of course, is that delay and obfuscation could simply run the clock out on Holocaust survivors, most of whom are already elderly. I think I speak for the countries represented here when I say that to delay justice further would dishonor us all. We have a clear obligation, which we must meet now. The right and honorable solution is to deal with this issue in an expeditious manner, and to do so through a process that is transparent, fair and nondiscriminatory. This will take courage, vision and persistence. Given the passage of over fifty years, absolute justice may not be obtainable for either the original owners or the current occupants of disputed real property. But producing a measure of justice for thousands who suffered most will help all of us to come to terms with history as we end the 20th Century and begin a new millennium.

I believe that we should proceed from the premise that this is a problem which can be solved. With that as our starting point, I am confidant that we can reach mutually agreeable formulas for bringing this issue to closure. I look forward to a profitable exchange of views in this morning's plenary, and in the breakout session this afternoon.

Mr. Ignatz Bubis
PRESIDENT
EUROPEAN JEWISH CONGRESS

*Statement translated from the original German by the
U.S. Department of State Office of Language Services, Translating Division*

Plenary Session on Nazi-Confiscated Communal Property

Mr. Mikva, Mr. Gilman, Mr. Eizenstat, Ladies and Gentlemen:

Let me first of all ask your understanding for giving my speech in German, because I find it easier to express myself clearly in that language. I shall limit my remarks to matters relating to restitution of real estate property in the Federal Republic [of Germany] and the countries of the former East Bloc.

It is bad enough that it has taken us more than 50 years after the end of the nazi dictatorship to talk about this.

In Western Europe in general, and especially in the Federal Republic, there have been laws on compensation for the injustices suffered and the restitution of assets. As far as real estate is concerned, this has been implemented in an exemplary fashion in the Federal Republic and has long since been concluded. After the unification of the two German states, the Federal Republic undertook treaty obligations to return real properties to their former Jewish owners in the same manner, or to provide compensation, with restitution being given priority vis-à-vis compensation. A large part of these restitutions has already been carried out, and where this was not possible, compensation has been provided. It is true that there are a few cases left to decide, but they, too, are nearing completion. Among the cases yet to be decided are, among other things, emergency sales forced on the Jewish communities by the former rulers of the former GDR.

Formerly, the Jewish communities in Germany were very rich. Today, the new Jewish communities are very poor and consist mostly of refugees or their descendents. Without support form the federal government and the federal states, the existence of the Jewish communities today would be in jeopardy. This, too, is a consequence of the nazi dictatorship that is still being felt to this day. Without the help of the federal government and the federal states, even the rebuilding of synagogues would be impossible.

As concerns the countries of the former East Bloc, restitution is coming along very unevenly. Some countries, as for instance Ukraine, categorically refuse to return former Jewish real estate, be it private or communal. One must take into account in this connection that the expropriations took place as early as in the 1920s, after the formation of the Soviet Union. Other countries, such as the Czech Republic, Slovakia, and Poland, are at least partially willing to return communal real estate, though not private properties. The fairest agreements could be concluded and implemented with Hungary. It is true that there are positive agreements with Romania, but none of them have been implemented so far. I am mentioning all of this in order to make clear how differently compensation and restitution matters are handled in different places.

It may be true that one or the other country can claim that the statute of limitations has run out, however, this should not have anything to do with the moral aspect. Today, hundreds of thousands of refugees are living in foreign countries and are still dependent on assistance by charitable organizations. These people must receive assistance through compensation for heir-less assets.

Another subject is the archives, which very often could shed light on possessions and property. In this regard, I would like to appeal to all countries to open their archives to research in order to facilitate justice.

In conclusion, I would like to thank the initiators of this Conference, especially the Congress and the Senate, as well as the U.S. Administration. Special appreciation is also owed to the Department of State, and especially to Stuart Eizenstat, who began working on this matter years ago, when he was still ambassador to the EU in Brussels.

Thank you for your attention.

Ms. Erzsébet Pék
SECOND SECRETARY, MINISTRY OF FOREIGN AFFAIRS
HUNGARY

Plenary Session on Nazi-Confiscated Communal Property

As the representative of the Republic of Hungary I would like to express my government's gratitude to the United States Holocaust Memorial Museum and the United States Department of State for hosting the Conference. My delegation is well aware of the complexity and difficulty of the issues to be solved. At the same time, we are of the view that this Conference presents an excellent opportunity to evaluate the historical facts and will contribute to finding a just resolution for the Holocaust injustices.

In Hungary, during the five decades under totalitarian political regimes, the property rights of a great number of citizens have been gravely violated. After the historical changes of 1989-1990 it has been the obligation of the Hungarian State to recognize and protect private property and to compensate the citizens for wrongful acts caused by the State. Within this context the Hungarian Parliament has enacted two fundamental laws, Act XXV of 1991 on partial compensation for damages unlawfully caused by the State to properties owned by the citizens aggrieved by the application of regulations enacted after June 8, 1949, and Act XXIV of 1992 for the damages caused by regulations, enacted between May 1, 1939 and June 8, 1949. These acts provided compensation to all persons whose property had been injured either by the racial discriminating regulations enacted after May 1, 1939, or by the measures of nationalization. According to the above mentioned two acts, partial compensation was due not only to Hungarian citizens, but also to persons who had been Hungarian citizens when the injury occurred, to persons who had been aggrieved in connection with deprivation of their Hungarian citizenship, and to those non-Hungarian citizens who had their ordinary residence in Hungary on December 31, 1990. If the claimant had deceased, his descendant, or in absence of such, the surviving spouse was entitled to lay claim for compensation. With the enactment of Act XXIV of 1992, Hungary also fulfilled its obligations under Art. 27. par. I of the Paris Peace Treaty, according to which

Hungary was required to pay fair compensation to persons who aggrieved damages due to their race or religion.

At the same time, the Hungarian Constitutional Court in a decision in 1993 stated that the implementation of Art. 27. par. 2 of the Paris Peace Treaty was still missing. That paragraph of the Peace Treaty obliged Hungary to transfer the claims of the former owners without legal successors to the interest organizations of the victims. The Constitutional Court gave notice to the Parliament to lift this unconstitutional state. In order to execute the above decision of the Constitutional Court, the Hungarian Parliament enacted Act X of 1997 by which the National Jewish Indemnification Fund was established by the Government. For the purposes of the Fund the Government gave indemnification vouchers of 4 billion forints transferable into life annuity, the distribution of which is to be decided by the Board of Trustees. In 1997 life annuity of 900,000 million forints were distributed, in 1998 1.8 billion, and in 1999 2.3 billion is planned in the budget. At the same time the government transferred the ownership of 7 real estates and 10 objects of art and has ensured a yearly budgetary contribution to the operational expenses of the Fund. Through the enactment of Act X of 1997 and the establishment of the Fund the Republic of Hungary fulfilled its obligation taken under Art 27 par. 2 of the Paris Peace Treaty.

A further obligation of the State was to compensate the churches for the damages unlawfully caused by the State. The basic principle of the legislation was to enable the churches to again fulfill their social role freely, without restrictions. In order to create the material and financial conditions, necessary to the fulfillment of their activities, the Hungarian Parliament has enacted Act XXII of 1991 on the settlement of the ownership relations of the properties owned by the churches. In connection with this Act it must be stressed that the measures of nationalization applied after January 1, 1948 affected all churches, and as the Hungarian Government repealed the discriminating decrees after the war, the application of nationalization in 1948 did not relate to Holocaust.

The Act, based on functional principles, made it possible for the churches to submit claims for compensation for damages caused by application of regulations enacted after January 1, 1948, on condition that the claimed real estates were used for religious, educational, social-health care or cultural purposes before the nationalization and the churches intended to use them for the same purposes. In the interest of settling the ownership relations of the real estates, a Commission was set up, comprised of the representatives of the Government and the concerned churches. On the basis of the claims of the churches the Commission drew up the list of the real estates to be returned. The commission submitted the list to the Government for approval. Having approved, the Parliament determined the sum to be expended on the settlement. The Act made it also possible that the churches, instead of the claimed immovable, could obtain, on agreement, an adequate real estate or financial compensation.

In September 1996 negotiations started between the Government of the Republic of Hungary and the representatives of the Holy See on the financing of the civil and religious activity of the Catholic Church and among others on the settlement of the ownership of the former Catholic property. The Agreement was signed on 20th June, 1997 by the Prime Minister of the Republic of Hungary and the competent state secretary of the Holy See. According to the agreement, the Catholic Church renounced its compensation claim of 42 billion forints, on condition that the Hungarian Government pay annuity which is to be used for financing its religious activity.

The Agreement served as a basis for a comprehensive legislative process, involving the settlement of the ownership of the churches, according to which the Parliament modified the above Act, making it possible for the churches that their claims which were to be compensated not in kind, but not yet returned, or compensated can be transferred into annuity on the basis of an agreement between the Government and the concerned church. According to the claims submitted by the churches till 30th June, 1998, the basis of the annuity of the Catholic Church is the above mentioned 42 billion forints, 6.66 billion of the Hungarian Reformed Church, 4.2 billion of the Hungarian Evangelical Church and 13, 511 billion of the Association of the Hungarian Jewish Communities. The first agreement on the transfer of the claims into annuity was signed with the Association of the Hungarian Jewish Communities in October of this year.

The total number of the claims submitted by the churches is 7221. About 1000 cases were settled by direct agreement. The number of claims settled by government decision exceeds 1065. On the basis of the above decisions, 20 billion forints were paid between 1992-97 and the Government undertook to pay further 14 billion forints as compensation due till 2001. 3380 of the submitted claims remain to be settled. 1200 of these claims were renounced by the Catholic Church for the above-mentioned annuity. The Agreement between the Government of the Republic of Hungary and the Association of the Hungarian Jewish

Communities settled 157 claims. Preparation of similar agreements with the other churches is in progress.

Mr. Saul Kagan

EXECUTIVE VICE PRESIDENT
CONFERENCE ON JEWISH MATERIAL
CLAIMS AGAINST GERMANY

Plenary Session on Nazi-Confiscated Communal Property

Last month the world marked the 60th anniversary of the burning of the synagogues in Germany and Austria by Nazi mobs. This was the most extreme demonstration- of the Nazi plans to destroy the Jewish communities of Germany and Austria. As we know now, the Nazis intended not only to murder the Jews but to destroy their communities – the schools, synagogues, the old age homes, and all of the institutions of the millennium of vibrant Jewish life, culture, and traditions in Europe.

As the Third Reich conquered most of Europe, the design to destroy Jewish lives and life was brutal and merciless. The three million strong Jewish community of Poland was practically obliterated. This was the largest Jewish community in Europe and the heart of the Jewish world at that time.

As the war ended and the world awoke to the immensity of the Holocaust and began to confront the human and social carnage, we were faced with two enormous tasks: first. to bind the wounds and resettle the survivors, and, second, to establish the principle that one should not profit from murder and pillage. To paraphrase the biblical admonition: "You shall not murder-and inherit."

Immediately after the war the major Jewish organizations turned to the victorious Allies, primarily to the United States to secure restitution for Jewish property in Germany. As a result of these efforts the United States military government introduced in November, 1947, 51 years ago, the first property restitution legislation on German soil. One of the historic achievements of this law was the recognition of the principle that heirless and unclaimed property of Nazi victims should not become the property of the successor state of the Third Reich. This was a revolutionary development in international law acknowledging that ordinary legal principles could not be applied when dealing with the consequences of this enormous tragedy.

The United States military government law provided for the designation of a successor organization to recover heirless and unclaimed property in the American occupation Zone and to use the proceeds for the benefit of survivors. Following the enactment of this law, we established the first Jewish successor organization, which recovered private and communal property in the American occupation zone. Later, similar laws were enacted by British and French military government for their respective occupation zones, as well as West Berlin. No such legislation was enacted in the Soviet zone of occupation. One of the first things we did was to use proceeds to buy prefabricated housing for the concentration camp survivors living in tents in Israel in the first year of its independence.

After the German Federal Republic came formally into existence in 1949, and thereafter, the principles of the Allied restitution legislation were subsequently incorporated into its national law.

A major task for the successor organizations was the recovery of the property of the Jewish communities and organizations such as synagogues, old age homes, hospitals, schools, cemeteries, and other institutional property.

We turned over to. the newly constituted Jewish communities the buildings that they needed for the use of their community, such as synagogues and community centers. We also established the principle of sharing the proceeds with the local communities and the needs of the survivors who were rebuilding their lives and communities elsewhere.

Four decades later, upon the unification of Germany, the Claims Conference succeeded in obtaining restitution legislation along similar principles for property subject to forced sale or confiscation during the Nazi period in the former East Germany. Following the precedent of West Germany, the Claims Conference worked out with the Central Council of Jewish communities in Germany a sharing agreement for the proceeds from the sale of the assets of the former Jewish communities and organizations of East Germany.

Although the task of recovery of Jewish communal property in the former East Germany is far from complete, the principles and experience that guided us in Germany can serve as a model for similar measures in the many other countries that have not as yet fully faced the historic and moral responsibility to return Jewish communal property.

This is the challenge which the governments concerned must meet promptly. The legal principles and the methods for restitution of such property have already been tested. The needs of the local Jewish communities and Holocaust survivors around the world are great.

It is tragic that many governments have not as yet responded to this challenge. We expect this conference to bring about the universal acceptance of the principle that Jewish communal property must be restituted and where in some specific instances restitution may not be feasible, properly compensated.

We expect the implementation of this principle to be encouraged and monitored by whatever mechanism will be evolved as a follow-up to this conference. This will be the ultimate test of the determination of the world community to help restore Jewish life which the Nazis set out to destroy.

Rabbi Andrew Baker

DIRECTOR, EUROPEAN AFFAIRS
AMERICAN JEWISH COMMITTEE

Jewish Communal Property

Plenary Session on Nazi-Confiscated Communal Property

"Why now?" seems to be the question that is most frequently asked. After fifty years have passed, why now is so much attention being given to the question of Holocaust assets. Why now is this conference taking place? Each of us is, perhaps, both asking and being asked this question. There are many answers to "Why now," but no single answer serves to explain it. The passing of eye-witnessed events into history; the last opportunity to address the injustices of the survivor generation; the popularizing through movies and television of stories once ignored; the need to get things straight before the close of the century? We may not be able to answer the question, Why now?, with any satisfaction, but we should be able to say what *now* we can do about it.

Fifty years ago, after the Nazis were defeated it was fair to conclude that much of Central and Eastern Europe would remain irredeemably inhospitable to Jewish life. In Germany and Austria, for example, Allied occupation forces took stock of the small number of Jewish survivors, the adverse conditions, the high level of anti-Semitism still present in society, and determined that no effort should be made to encourage former Jewish residents to return. In fact, those present would be offered assistance to emigrate. Pogroms in Poland and elsewhere which left thousands of returning Jews dead at the hands of their former gentile neighbors sent a similar message. The future for those who survived the Holocaust would be found in other places—primarily in Israel and America.

It is hard not to imagine what we might have been able to do *if* this conference took place fifty years ago. All of those assets which we are discussing this week—insurance policies, bank accounts, looted gold—could have been directed to the benefit of these survivors when they would have done the most good, as they were starting new lives in new places and when the trauma was most severe. All of the difficulties in the passing years of identifying assets, of sifting through lost and discarded and incomplete records, of trying to match accounts with claimants and their heirs, would have been so much less. The work would have been much simpler; the benefit for Holocaust survivors so much greater. But, fifty years ago, no one was ready to do what we are prepared to do today.

We know there are survivors in need, and they deserve to be helped now. Everyone agrees with this statement, but it appears to be the beginning and not the end of problems and controversy, as help is delayed and as organizations and lawyers and governments vie with each other to be the conduit for this aid. Meanwhile, the cynicism increases and the embarrassing private battles become public news. This, too, will be part of the discussion at this conference, even if it goes on only in the corridors rather than the official sessions.

We know that even now, at this late date, we should make every effort to find the heirs of newly-identified assets. Works of art, insurance policies and bank accounts may still have legal claimants. Fifty years of neglect and resistance make this a difficult and time-consuming task, and the cost may far exceed the actual assets identified. But, if this enterprise really is about justice and not just about money—a sentiment that seems increasingly challenged by the day-to-day statements of some—we need to follow this path.

Still, there is something wrong if all we succeed in doing is reckoning the accounts fifty years late. There ought to be some things we can do *now* that go further. After all, the very changes that have occurred in many of the countries represented at this conference are much greater than just open archives and a willingness to look at history. The problems we are examining and trying to redress can also be a bridge to the future. This possibility may be most evident in the difficult and still largely-unresolved area of Jewish communal property restitution.

It was only in this last decade that one could even imagine the possibility that what was once Jewish property in the Communist nations of Central and Eastern Europe might again pass into Jewish hands. But, the euphoria which greeted the fall of the Berlin Wall and the successful and largely peaceful revolutions which brought democracy to these countries was not easily shared in the Jewish world. More frequently, our assessment resembled those reached in 1945. After the destruction of the Holocaust and decades of Communist tyranny and state-sponsored anti-Semitism, what future could there be for Jewish life in these countries? These were still inhospitable places, to be sure. And if Jewish communal property could now be restituted, the heirs—or at least the proper heirs—would be found in America and Israel. Not only were these the places where the majority of Jewish survivors had settled, but they were still the places where the Jewish future was thought to be located.

In these last half-dozen years we have acted in various and contradictory ways. We have provided support for the communal, religious and educational revival of Jewish life in Central and Eastern Europe, and we have encouraged the brightest of them to make *aliyah* to Israel. We have put political and moral pressure on their governments to restitute Jewish property, and we have fought with local Jewish communities over this property. In the meantime, very little has happened in the area of restitution, but a great deal has happened nonetheless.

In almost all of these countries Jewish life has "revived." We can still debate the long-term prognosis, but they're off life-support systems and out of intensive care. They are small; they are poor; they are disadvantaged. Let us acknowledge after all that these communities, too, are *survivors*. But, they believe they have a future in their respective countries, and they are acting on that belief. They face enormous challenges, and they still confront anti-Semitism in the societies around them. But, they also, for the most part, have governments that want to see them succeed. And they have at least some fellow citizens who believe it is in their own best interests to build a pluralist society in which Jews and other minorities can feel at home.

However, their survival will depend on their resources. And these resources will need to come from the restitution of communal property. So far, the efforts have been difficult and the results have been disappointing. In some countries we have seen only a handful of formerly religious properties returned to the Jewish community. Even in the best of situations the gains have been modest.

Last year, legislation was enacted which provides for the return to the Jewish community in Poland of former religious property. Property is reclaimed through a cumbersome and costly process, and much communal property is excluded under the law. Instead, it involves primarily synagogues and cemeteries, and the latter, which are in need of repair and restoration, are a financial burden, not a benefit to the small community.

Legislation was never adopted in the Czech Republic. Its Jewish community identified only two hundred communal properties--a fraction of the pre-war total--for which it sought restitution. While the Federal government offered verbal support, decisions were left to individual municipalities, and after several years about half of these properties have been returned. Only in these last few days, has the government created a commission to examine ways in which the Jewish community might receive back or receive compensation for the remaining properties.

In Hungary, which has the largest Jewish community of Central Europe, an agreement was reached only this October, which provides for financial compensation in the form of an annual payment, determined to be a percentage of the communal property value. This will provide the Jewish community with several million dollars a year to help it address the needs of over 100,000 Hungarian Jews.

In these communities and in others, restitution efforts were initially aided by the work of the World Jewish Restitution Organization, which drew public attention to this need and assisted in the cataloguing of former Jewish properties. The WJRO also enunciated the position that world Jewry is the correct heir to the full pre-war assets of Jewish communities that had numbered in the millions. But, such assets are not now being and perhaps never will be restituted to the local Jewish communities or to international Jewish organizations. Nevertheless, this has not precluded tensions to grow and adversarial relationships to develop. What should have been a collaborative and cooperative relationship has all too often turned into a fight over who is the rightful owner of property not yet being returned.

It is correct to insist that the governments in these new democracies have a moral obligation to return all former Jewish communal and private property, and no one should dispute that heirless assets ought to be the inheritance of the Jewish community worldwide. But, at the very least and in the "short term" which is unfortunately not very short, resources should first be directed to aid the reviving Jewish communities and to maintain the cemeteries and other historical sits of pre-war Jewry in Europe.

Perhaps, this is the area in which the surrounding non-Jewish world can also play a role. Reclaiming these sites, reclaiming history, is also a means of reclaiming memory and educating ourselves and others. This is critical for a new generation of Jews who choose to make their homes in Central and Eastern Europe, but valuable, too, for their non-Jewish neighbors. In the end, tangible assets must pass to the rightful inheritor. But, these other "assets"--the assets of history, the assets of memory, the detailed knowledge that a culturally rich and vibrant Jewish community once flourished where now only small remnants, but at least and remarkably so small remnants, live on--these assets can be shared. If we work together, we can also make them a bridge between Jews and non-Jews, a bridge between present and future generations.

Mr. Jerzy Kichler

PRESIDENT, UNION OF JEWISH RELIGIOUS CONGREGATIONS IN POLAND
POLAND

Restitution of Jewish Communal Property in Poland (Status as of November 23, 1998)

Break-out Session on Communal Property: Progress and Challenges

1. INTRODUCTION

The continuity of the Polish Jewish communities was interrupted by World War II and by the changes that came into being soon after the end of the War. In 1945, the Polish Communist government permitted the re-establishment of Jewish communities as cultural societies only. Regulation #3 of February 6, 1945 denied them legal personality. Thus, unlike the situation in other Soviet satellite countries, where Jews were permitted to own some communal property, all Jewish communal property was legally considered abandoned property and on that basis confiscated by the State.

2. CURRENT STATUS OF THE JEWISH RELIGIOUS CONGREGATIONS

Nine Autonomous JRCs (in Warsaw, Krakow, Lódz, Wroclaw, Katowice, Bielsko-Biala, Gdansk, Szezecin, and Legnica), and seven affiliates connected with different JRCs (in Walbrzych, Dzierzoniów, Zary, Bytom, Czestochowa, Lublin, Poznan) exist today. Their number, after a steady downwards trend over the last 30 years, has again started to grow, when last year the Warsaw JRC and the Pozna affiliate were set up. The Union of Jewish Religious Communities in Poland is a coordinating body for all the JRCs.

The Communities and their affiliates operate synagogues, prayer houses, and kosher kitchens, run welfare and educational programs. Since up to now they had no independent revenue, all this activity was made possible through grant and organizational support from the Joint Distribution Committee and the Ronald S. Lauder Foundation. The former supplies the main budget of the JRCs, while the latter supplements it and runs youth clubs, summer and winter camps and a school and a kindergarten in Warsaw. A second school will open this fall in Wroclaw. The JRCs also take care of Jewish cemeteries and historical monuments they have title to.

There Union has prepared a program of reviving of Jewish life in Poland, which postulates the setting up of Jewish Community centers and schools in all the main towns where Jewish communities exist, as well as expanding services for the sick and elderly, with new day-care centers, retirement homes and medical facilities. The program covers also the preservation of unused Jewish cemeteries and historical monuments.

3. LEGAL SITUATION

The Law on the relationship between the State and the Jewish Religious communities was submitted by the Government to Parliament on February 20, 1997, passed and signed by the President soon thereafter, and effective as of May 11 of the same year. It was published in the Official Gazette (Dziennik Ustaw) on April 24, 1997 as Item #41.

This law grants the Jewish communities legal status similar to that they enjoyed in Poland before World War II, and identical tot hat which applies to all the eleven recognized cults today. All relevant laws to that effect had been passed in the post-Communist period, the first being that on the relationship between the State and the Catholic church, passed in 1989. This law is based on previous legal solutions dealing with kehilloth existing on Polish territory, especially a regulation issued by the President of Poland in 1927.

This law deals mainly with the issues of taxation of the Jewish community, the status of Rabbis and Hazzanim, Jewish holidays as paid vacation days, etc. It has historical significance, inasmuch as it will allow the return to the Polish Jewish community of a part of its material heritage, thereby enabling it greater self-sufficiency. The goal of this law is to make Jewish continuity in Poland possible, and to regulate issues of preservation of the spiritual and material heritage of Polish Jews.

3. RESTITUTION OF JEWISH COMMUNAL PROPERTY

In accordance with Article 29 of the law, property that was in the use of the Jewish community on the day of May 11, 1997, becomes its property, no matter to whom it belonged at that moment, and what was previously located there. On the basis of this regulation, three properties have been returned already, including the Nozyk Synagogue in Warsaw, the premier temple of Polish Judaism.

Article 30 deals with Jewish communal property and the property of other formally registered Jewish religious organizations, held by its owners before the war on what is now Polish territory. These properties can now be reclaimed by member communities of the Union of Jewish Religious Communities in Poland.

Paragraph 1of that Article concerns that part of current Polish territory which was contained within Polish borders as of September 1, 1939. Here, Jewish Religious Communities may claim ownership of cemeteries and synagogues. In respect to synagogues, a property may be claimed even if it is now an empty plot or if there is another building built over it (p.1). If the actual building or plot of land cannot be returned, financial compensation can be offered. In the case of other relevant buildings used for religious, cultural, educational or charitable purposes, the property can be returned only if the original building is still standing. In the case of cemeteries, only the actual plot can be returned and no financial compensation will be offered. If a property was sold to a third party before the restitution claim had been filed, it cannot be returned.

Paragraph 2 deals with the issue of the Western Territories (former Germany) that were incorporated by Poland after World War II on the basis of treaties made by the Allies. The difference with Paragraph 1 in claiming properties there is as follows: (a) the property has to have belonged to the Jewish community, or another religious Jewish organization on January 30, 1933, i.e., before the Nazis came to power; and (b) the local Jewish community now existing there and claiming it has to prove that the property will be used for religious, cultural, educational or charitable activities (except cemeteries, synagogues and kehillot offices buildings where it must not to be proved). If the property cannot be returned, there is no way to receive compensation.

With the help of the Jewish Historical Institute in Warsaw a list has been made of Jewish cemeteries (about 1,000), still existing synagogues (about 300), buildings of different institutions: hospitals, mikvaot, schools, etc. (about 100).

In order to file their claims, Jewish Religious Communities have to gather the appropriate documentation: proofs of legal status of the property before the war (maps, registers, land registry books, proofs of ownership); certificates of present legal status (documents as above together with the maps presenting changes that came into being – property division, etc.). In the case of properties that used to belong to a Jewish organization other than the Jewish Community, documents that prove its religious purpose have to be gathered (statutes, experts opinion, testimonies).

The gathering of such documents is obviously very difficult due to the effects of the Shoah and other man-made and natural disasters. Therefore, any documentation and testimonies that will lead to the location of Jewish communal property will be very helpful and appreciated.

4. RESTITUTION PROCESS

The return of Jewish property is based on the work of a specially assembled Regulation Commission which functions as an arbitration court. The commission was set up by a Decree of the Minister of Internal Affairs and Administration on October 10, 1997. Its body is composed of six people (three from the said Ministry and three from the Union of Jewish religious Communities).

The period of sending complete applications to the Regulatory Commission is 5 years; the deadline is May 2002.

To date, 217 applications have been submitted to the Regulation commission. Of those, 182 applications have been acted upon, other have been returned to applicant because of incomplete documentation, and decisions have been made in the case of 23 (positively 16, negatively 6, given to voivoda decision 1) – including 5 cemeteries, 8 synagogues. Moreover, the boards of the communities in Warsaw and in Wroclaw were given by the respective Governors (Voivods) legal title to the buildings they use.

The proper implementation of the law is a historical challenge for the community – our future depends on it. The restitution of communal properties should finally bring to an end the suffering and humiliation experienced by Polish Jews and Jewish organizations during and after World War II.

5. JEWISH COMMUNITIES OF POLAND AND THE WJRO

The law states that, as far as restitution and other relations are concerned, the Jewish Religious Communities in Poland are the sole partner of the Polish State. Only the Communities can file restitution claims. Any changes to that law would require not only amending the act itself, but also probably making amendments to laws pertaining to the relationship of the State to other recognized cults, since all should be constitutionally equal.

Cooperation with the WJRO is a basic requirement for the Jewish Religious Communities of Poland. The Board of the Union of Jewish Religious Communities in Poland (UJRCP) sees in the setting up of a conjoint foundation with the WJRO an expression of our shared responsibility for the heritage of Polish Jews. However, the principles of such foundation cannot violate the continuity of the rights of the communities in Poland, both in respect to their property and to their autonomy, nor can they contradict Polish law.

In April 1998 a Memorandum of Understanding was signed by Israel Singer representing the WJRO and Jerzy Kichler representing the UJRCP. This Memorandum is the base for the establishing of a conjoint foundation. A negotiating tem finished at present a work to elaborate the billow of the joint foundation. With help of the foundation, the process of restitution of Jewish properties in Poland should not only lead to the proper revival of the Jewish community of Poland and to covering the needs of the Communities, but should also enable the participation of all Polish Jewish living outside of Poland in that process.

Mr. Michael Lewan

CHAIRMAN, UNITED STATES COMMISSION FOR THE PRESERVATION
OF AMERICA'S HERITAGE ABROAD
UNITED STATES

Break-out Session on Communal Property: Progress and Challenges

"May we live in interesting times." The sentiment expressed by the old Polish proverb certainly applies to all of us concerned with the return of communal property. Today, more than a half-century since the defeat of fascism and a decade after the fall of communism, the nations of Eastern and Central Europe and grappling with their past. They need help. This is truly a time for strong and supportive American leadership and friendship.

My name is Michael Lewan and I have been appointed twice by President Bill Clinton to Chair the United States Commission for the Preservation of America's Heritage Abroad. The Commission was founded in recognition that the United States, as a nation of immigrants, has its values rooted in lands distant in miles and time. As a people, we believe that the fabric of our society is strengthened by visible reminders of our ancestral past. The history, culture, politics, sociology, economy, and religion of our forefathers have stamped upon our souls an indelible mark of character. As the years go by, Americans need to see the sites, hear the echoes, touch the tombstones, feel the pain, and relive the joy of our ancestral past. How else can we understand the present or prepare for the future?

The Commission's charge is to encourage the preservation and protection of communal properties. Specifically, the buildings, monuments, collections and cemeteries connected with the heritage of Americans from the 22 countries that comprise Eastern and Central Europe and the former Soviet Republic. Americans who trace their family roots to these cultures are, for the first time, able to visit the churches, synagogues, cemeteries, and monuments to which they have binding ties.

What they see often shocks and saddens them. The Nazi extermination of six million Jews and so many other innocents extended to physical places as well. Schools, libraries, museums, and social halls were all expropriated.   Synagogues, churches, and cemeteries were especially sought out for vandalism or destruction.

The Communists continued this wanton behavior. Buildings and graveyards were bulldozed to make room for development. Those sites that escaped were left to suffer the ravages of time and natures. Many, if not most, important sites passed into oblivion.

Some did survive. Today there exist hundreds of synagogues, churches, cemeteries, and other places in desperate need of attention. They stand now not as a reminder of death and decay, but as a testament to the strength and substance of those vital, vibrant souls that once prayed, sang, studied, danced, and lived within their walls. Some sites are artistic treasures and deserve restoration on that basis, some are sacred and demand the highest degree of devotion.

Our Commission has spent much time and energy preserving and protecting Jewish cemeteries. To take care of the dead is the highest calling. A mitzvah. An obligation. The Book of Ruth teaches, "Blessed is he by God, for his kindness to the living as well as the dead." (Ruth 2:20).

Central to our work as participants in the Holocaust Assets Conference must be the legal and spiritual status of these Jewish cemeteries.   The United States Commission for the Preservation of America's Heritage Abroad stands undivided in this regard.   Jewish cemeteries are sacred; they cannot be sold; their soil must not be disturbed; their sanctity must be respected by all.

It is my hope that in its deliberations on the status of communal properties that special consideration is given to cemeteries. Clearly there are challenges. As economies of the region prosper, these sacred plots of land will become increasingly valuable. Pressures to sell and develop these sites will grow. Legitimate social service needs will be held as a reason to destroy these old graveyards. These are monetary temptations that must be resisted.

The Commission acknowledges that few if any Jewish citizens remain to care for these sites, and that the Diaspora cannot provide the needed resources to tend the graves. With this in mind, the Commission respectfully recommends that "national communal property restitution" laws be passed that returns all cemeteries to the remnant Jewish communities.   This will protect them from sale or unbridled development.

We also suggest that a certain percentage of funds realized from the sale or lease of other communal property be set aside for the perpetual care of these cemeteries. This we believe is the framework for a right and proper solution. It respects not only the land on which so many are buried, but indeed is a symbol that on this land once lived a people that contributed mightily to the fabric of their society, their religion and their country.

The United States Commission for the Preservation of America's Heritage Abroad will continue to use all its influence on governments, NGOs and all parties involved to ensure that we find the ways and means to preserve and protect these sacred places for all eternity.

The historic and moral importance of the Commission's work is clear. We must help the emerging democracies of Europe settle old debts and begin anew by building on the foundations of yesterday to create a better tomorrow.

Tomorrow...Listen to the haunting words of Elie Wiesel, "Teachers and their pupils; mothers and their infants; rabbis and their followers rich and poor; learned and illiterate; prince and beggar all pushed inexorably toward death. "Father," a young boy asks, "is it painful to die?" Father replies, "Think of something else my son, think of tomorrow."

My friends Jew and Gentile alike, we are that tomorrow.

So, as we continue our work to repair, restore, recompense, and return, let us commit together to use whatever resources come available to build a future that honors the past. For the age-old values, traditions, and observances so critical to survival must never be lost as new generations make their way.

This is our legacy. This is our burden. This is our tomorrow.

Archives, Books and the Role of Historical Commissions

Mrs. Gill Bennett

CHIEF HISTORIAN, FOREIGN & COMMONWEALTH OFFICE
UNITED KINGDOM

British and Allied Restitution Policy during and after the Second World War

Plenary Session on Archives, Books and Historical Commissions

During the Second World War, the major Allies - the United Kingdom, United States of America and the Soviet Union - were naturally more concerned with winning the war and bringing hostilities to an end than they were with forward planning to attempt to repair the damage done by that devastating conflict. Nonetheless, the documentary evidence shows that postwar planning began to take shape as early as 1941-42, long before the end of the war could be foreseen; and that restitution, by which was meant restoring the stolen property belonging to European governments, was seen as an issue with early priority when hostilities ended. The British and American governments, at least, took the view that it should be far easier to reach agreement on restitution than on reparations, and that restitution could be settled at an early stage. It became a bone of contention between all three major Allies, and between them and the European powers who had been occupied by Germany and her allies.[1]

In Britain, serious consideration of postwar restitution was prompted at an early stage by the representatives of the occupied countries who based themselves in London. Exiled from their countries, their principal concern in anticipating the end of hostilities was the

---

[1] Cf. *Documents on British Policy Overseas* (hereafter *DBPO*), Series I, Volume V (HMSO, 1990), Preface, p.xiv: 'In practice the problem...caused at least as much damage to British relations with the liberated countries as an other matter in clearing up after the war.'

recovery and restoration of their property and assets. In May 1941 the Czechoslovak Minister for Foreign Affairs, Jan Masaryk, wrote to Frank Roberts at the Foreign Office regarding the seizure by the German occupying forces of Czechoslovak shares and securities, and asking the British government to draw the attention of neutral governments to the fact that the sale or Purchase of such securities would not be recognized by the Czechoslovak government.[2] At about the same time, the Ministry of Economic Welfare suggested that joint action be taken by the Allied governments to discourage the purchase by neutrals of securities seized by Germany in occupied territories. Although it was decided at an interdepartmental meeting in July 1941 that the question of Allied declaration should be deferred "until the machinery of Allied cooperation, which was still in its initial stages, had had been developed rather further,"[3] These two initiatives led to further consultation within the British government and with the US government, and formed the basis of the Inter-Allied Declaration against Acts of Dispossession Committed in Territories under Enemy Occupation or Control issued on 5 January 1943 by British and 16 other governments of the United Nations.[4] Allied postwar restitution policies were based upon that Declaration, which was intended as a "general statement of the attitude of the governments concerned towards the acts of dispossession...practiced by the enemy powers in the territories which they have occupied or brought under their control by their successive aggressions against the free peoples of the world."[5]

The records show that the Allied governments were well aware of the concerns of the occupied territories and appreciated the importance of helping them to recover their looted property, both to enable their economic reconstruction and in order to lessen possible resentment against the three Great Powers who might be seen to be deciding policies without consultation with them. The major Allies were, however, also concerned with protecting their own postwar interests as powers who had borne the brunt of prosecuting the war and paying for it: this was

---

[2] Letter of 21 May 1941, C 5610/550/12.

[3] Record of interdepartmental meeting held at the Foreign Office on 8 July 1941, C 7081/550/12.

[4] The Declaration was published as Cmd. 6418 of 1943. See also FCO history Note No. 11, *Nazi Gold: Information from the British Archives* (hereafter *Nazi Gold*) Revised end. January 1997, pp.4-5.

[5] Draft guidance note on the proposed Allied Declaration, 21 November 1942, W 15270/108/64.

particularly true in the case of the Soviet Union, which had experienced invasion and human and material loss on a vast scale, and was now determined to extract maximum compensation. Even for the UK and US, who had not been occupied, the costs had been great, the UK in particular having been brought to a 'financial Dunkirk' by her war effort.[6] The sweeping measures of restitution sought by the smaller allies, which included compensation for spoliation and the impressment of goods and services from Germany, would have a damaging effect on the reparation claims of the Big Three: as a memorandum prepared in the British government's Trading with the Enemy Department in April 1944 noted, it was "clear that the small disarmed Allies are seeking to obtain for themselves certain drastic powers in priority to the general reparation claims of all the Allies."[7]

These concerns confirmed the major Allies consensus that restitution and reparation should, be treated as separate, if coordinated issues. They were not in agreement, however, as to the relationship between the two issues and even how they should be defined. Although there was a shared understanding that restitution meant the return or replacement of property lost or looted as a result of Nazi aggression, they held strong and differing views on whether restitution policies should encompass only property seized by force, or should include property found by the Germans on occupation or paid for by them in forced or voluntary sale. The definition was crucial to the linked issue of reparation, that, is of using German assets to pay back those who had footed the bill for the war, for the more that was included in restitution, the less would be available for reparation shares for the Allies. Nevertheless, restitution and reparation were not discussed at the same meetings. The Allies agreed that talks on restitution should be relegated to the Allied Reparation Commission, ostensibly because the subject was too technical and complicated to be dealt with at major international meetings such as the Potsdam Conference of July 1945, where France was not represented; but also because reparation was the issue on which agreement was most eagerly sought after (particularly by the Soviet

---

[6] A phrase used by Lord Keynes, the distinguished economist and advisor to HM Treasury, in a paper of 13 August 1945 entitled 'Our Overseas Financial Prospects': see *DBPO*, Series I, Volume III, *Britain and America: Negotiation of the United States Loan, 3 August-7 December 1945* (UMSO, 1986), enclosure in No. 6.
[7] TWED memo., Bank of England records.

Union), and which was thought to be the most politically sensitive and potentially difficult to resolve.

Another complication was presented by the lack of agreement between the Allies on what sort of Germany would emerge from the war, an issue of vital importance to restitution policy. Would Germany be a single economic unit, or divided?[8] An industrialized state, or reduced to pastoral status as envisioned by US Treasury Secretary Morgenthau in 1944?[9] These questions had a direct bearing on what might be available from Germany in terms of restitution. The Soviet Union was clear in the view that Germany must be stripped and de-industrialized, but Britain, and to a lesser degree the United States, was uneasily aware of the potential financial burden that would fall on her in supporting a crippled Germany with no economic life of its own. France was equally clear that Germany must not retain any form of central administration, and with the other occupied countries, wished to get back her looted possessions from Germany as soon as possible, in addition to obtaining essential supplies from her.

The UK, US, France and other occupied countries generally agreed on the desirability of tackling restitution before reparation, partly in order to speed up the movement of essential supplies from Germany, and partly to remove restitutable items before the remainder were calculated for the division of reparation shares: as Mr. Coulson of the Foreign wrote to Mr. Playfair of the Treasury in February 1944, "if we leave restitution until too late, there may be a danger that property belonging to other countries will be handed over as deliveries in kind."[10] French Foreign Minister Georges Bidault, urging the Council of Foreign Ministers in September 1945 towards the speedy adoption of restitution policies, put it even more succinctly, "reparations from Germany should be levied on German property and not on Allied property stolen by the Germans."[11]

---

[8] On the question of 'one Germany or Two', see *DBPO*, Series I, Volume I, *The Conference at Postdam, July-August 1945* (HMSO, 1984), Nos 153 and 164.

[9] For British views on the plan for the pastorialization of Gemany (printed in *Foreign Relations of the United States (FRUS), the Conference at Quebec 1944*, pp. 101 – 5) advanced by Mr. Mongenthau in 1944, sec Sir. L. Underwood, *British Foreign Policy in the Second World* (London, 1970), vol.V., pp. 222-9.

[10] Letter of 23 February 1944, U 1322/104/70.

[11] See *DBPO*, Series I, Volume II, *Conferences and Conversations 1945: London, Washington and Moscow* (HMSO, 1985), No. 128.

President Truman, meanwhile, had expressed the view that "the required coordination between reparations and restitution shall not act to retard unnecessarily (1) the withdrawal from Germany in the form of restitution or any other form of supplies badly needed by Allied Nations for their economic reconstruction or (2) the return of works of art to those nations from which they were taken."[12] None of these approaches, however, was satisfactory to the Soviet Union, whose chief aim was to obtain as much as possible in reparations before restitution claims were dealt with, to ensure maximum profit from the operation. Consequently, the Soviet negotiators dealing with the definition of restitution and draft directives to implement restitution played their hand long and obstructively, so that by the end of June 1945 the US government, exasperated with the delay, unilaterally launched a limited program of restitution from their zone of Germany (restricted mainly to the return of identifiable works of art – the one area where there was general agreement to restitution) to the governments of Allied nations and the removal from Germany of supplies needed by Allied governments for their economic reconstruction.[13]

Although protesting the US action ("This subject is one on which it is most desirable to work out a policy common to all four zones, particular in view of the wider aim to secure the treatment of Germany as an economic unit"), the British authorities moved towards a similar policy in their own zone, acting on a directive issued by the War Office on 14 August.[14] Stressing that these were interim measures to be taken while a formal policy was being worked out, the British Control Commission was ordered to deliver to Allied governments identifiable plant, equipment, livestock and valuables "in respect of which there is satisfactory evidence that the property was located in the territory of the Ally concerned and was the subject of an act of dispossessions by the enemy." Despite this directive, implementation proved problematic and long-drawn out, and the British government was subject to considerable criticism from the formerly occupied countries, who blamed the British military authorities for the delay in restoring looted property.[15] Meanwhile, the Soviet government stripped their own zone of Germany and extracted as much in reparation from the other zones as they could.

---

[12] Message from US ARC representative Pauley to Eisenhower, 27 June 1945, FRUS, The Conference at Berlin, vol. I, pp. 514-15.
[13] Ibid.
[14] DBPO, Series I, Volume V, No. 6.
[15] See, for example, DBPO, Series I, Volume I, No., 584.

British and American efforts to carry out restitution policies from their zones of Germany continued into the winter of 1945. The formerly occupied countries were allowed to send inspecting teams in to look for their property while policies were worked out at an intergovernmental level for the restitution of gold, money and securities.[16]   The quadripartite control machinery addressed, if slowly and with difficulty, the question of restitution, and by 1948 elaborate quadripartite machinery was in place.   Meanwhile, thc Occupation authorities in Germany worked tirelessly to develop and implement policies that would enable people in the Zones to keep alive and recover, where possible, the necessities of survival: agricultural implements; livestock; and raw material for essential industries.   The documentation on their efforts reveals frustration, prevarication, administrative obstruction and political stalemate.   On another level, however, it shows men and women working in a new and very difficult situation to help in practical ways where they could.

As the above summary account shows, the concern of the Allied governments during and after the war was directed towards restituting property to governments, not to individuals.   They all accepted the principle set out by the US delegation at Potsdam in a resolution of 22 July: "All questions of restitution shall be dealt with on behalf of the injured property owners by the State of which they are citizens, unless such State shall make other arrangements with the State from whose territories the property was removed."[17]   Discussion of restitution in the 1990s is naturally focused on individual losses suffered by those who survived the conflict, or their heirs, a who may now need help.   At the time, however, the Allied governments were concerned with inter-governmental policies, not individual property, on the premise that there was no prospect of restoring individual property until a nation's economic life were restarted and the urgent priorities of food, fuel, and shelter addressed.   The archival evidence reveals intergovernmental talks and negotiations, not records of individual cases.   That came later, when the governments had signed the reparations agreement at Potsdam and begun to settle between themselves questions of mutual debt and

---

[16] See *Nazi Gold I*, and also Fco history Note No. 12, *Nazi Gold: Information from the British Archives Part II: Monetray Gold, Non-Monetary Gold and the Tripartite Gold Commission* (May 1997).

[17] *FRUS, ibid.*, pp.542-.

repayment.[18] This focus did not mean that governments were unaware or uncaring of the terrible price that the Second World War had exacted on a personal level from millions of their citizens. But it did mean that their first priority was to restore some kind of political and economic normality in Europe, so that people could stay alive through the winter, and re-establish a base from which to rebuild their lives.

---

[18] For an account of the postwar payments agreements and debt settlements negotiated between Britain and her Allies and former enemies, see the Anneses to FCO History Note No. 13, *British Policy Towards Enemy Property during the Second World War* (April 1998).

Dr. Michael J. Kurtz

ASSISTANT ARCHIVIST
NATIONAL ARCHIVES AND RECORDS ADMINISTRATION
UNITED STATES

Searching for Truth: The Relationship Between National Archives and Independent Commissions

Plenary Session on Archives, Books and Historical Commissions

This morning I would like to discuss the relationship between national archives and independent commissions in the search for an accurate historical record of what transpired during the Holocaust-era to Jewish and other looted assets. I will use the experience of the U.S. National Archives and Records Administration (NARA) as a case study in discussing issues that affect access to the historical record. Hopefully, our experience will offer some insights into the complementary roles of national archives and the various independent commissions investigating events of the Holocaust and World War II eras. For success in establishing an accurate historical record and rectifying past injustices lies to a very great extent in the relationship between national archives and independent commissions.

I would like to begin by quoting from a letter to the editor of Time magazine (March 17, 1997) by John W. Carlin, Archivist of the United States.

"Everyone should understand the role of records in establishing rights and legitimate identities and liberties. The dramatic case of the search for Nazi gold is an excellent example of the value of records not only in documenting historical facts but also in preserving essential evidence. For us at the National Archives and Records Administration, the role of preserving and providing access to this essential evidence of history is at the core of our mission."

Indeed, NARA's holdings of records relating to all looted assets - gold, art, insurance, dormant accounts - and the ability to make those records available in a timely manner has demonstrated the value not only for the United States but to peoples, governments, and organizations in other countries. Though methods of operations may vary from country to country, all national archives share a common vision of preserving the historical record and making it available for historical and objective scrutiny. In pursuing this vision the various national archives and nations represented here share in NARA's experience of assisting the search for truth even in other countries.

Let me share NARA's experience in providing access to records relating to Holocaust-era looted assets; and something of what can be expected by those national archives in the early stages of research and reference activities.

The search for what became known as "Nazi Gold" records began in March 1996, when researchers from Senator Alfonse D'Amato's office began coming to Archives II at College Park looking for records relating to World War II-era dormant bank accounts of Jews in Swiss banks. Within weeks the research expanded into issues surrounding looted Nazi gold and other assets. By midsummer 1996, the research room at College Park was the host to at least 15 researchers daily - sometimes as many as 25 - conducting research in "Nazi Gold" records. These records, contained within 30 record groups and comprising some 15 million pages of documentation, were like a magnet, drawing increasing numbers of researchers as the summer progressed.

In the early fall of 1996, President Clinton asked then Under Secretary of Commerce Stuart E. Eizenstat, who also served as Special Envoy of the Department of State on Property Restitution in Central and Eastern Europe, to prepare a report that would "describe, to the fullest extent possible, U.S. and Allied efforts to recover and restore this gold [gold the Nazis looted from the central banks of occupied Europe, as well as gold taken from individual victims of Nazi persecution] and other assets stolen by Nazi Germany." Eizenstat, in October, formed an 11-agency Interagency Group on Nazi Assets, including NARA, to do the research and produce the report, under the direction of William Z. Slany, Historian, Department of State. Slany formed his research team, consisting of researchers from the Departments of Defense, Treasury, Justice, and State, the U.S. Holocaust Memorial Museum, the Central Intelligence Agency, and the Federal Reserve Board. They soon made Archives II their home.

This cross-government research effort, mandated by the President, focused attention and effort in a manner that lower-level efforts could never have achieved. The search for accountability and justice requires leadership and support from the highest political levels. The efforts of national archives and independent commissions will not be successful without this type of support and on-going commitment.

During the next five months the demands on NARA's staff were enormous. Not only were both government and non-government researchers making relentless demands for records, often the same records at the same time, but also relevant records from the World War II-era were accessioned from the Department of the Treasury in November 1996, and the Federal Reserve Board in March 1997, and declassified under great pressure to make them immediately available.

While research was being conducted during the fall of 1996 and the following winter, the media discovered that an important aspect of the "Nazi Gold" story was NARA: its records, its staff, and its researchers. Thus, journalists and documentary film makers began appearing on a regular basis during the winter of 1996-1997, and the first stories highlighting NARA's role appeared in November 1996 in *USA Today* and in early February, 1997, in *Le Monde*. *Time* also ran a cover story in late February regarding the quest for records relating to "Nazi Gold."

NARA management and staff realized that their work would receive unprecedented scrutiny, a factor promising the possibility of reward or peril. The work of all national archives and independent commissions can expect similar scrutiny and accountability for its professional performance.

THE NARA-SWISS CONNECTION

Starting in the winter of 1996-1997 and continuing since, Archives II has become a gathering place for prominent individuals representing various groups involved in the "Nazi Gold" and looted assets phenomenon. This has been particularly true of the Swiss, because their country was the initial and primary focus of the "Nazi Gold" story. The NARA connection to the Swiss has become a very close one, in part, because of an agreement between the United States and Swiss governments. This agreement, signed in early 1997, by Under Secretary Eizenstat and Ambassador Thomas Borer, head of the Swiss

Federal Task Force, provided that their respective countries, including national archives, would closely cooperate.

Among the Swiss visiting Archives II have been a member of the Swiss Federal Task Force; a member of the Swiss Parliament; the first secretary of the Swiss Bankers Association; the chairman of the Independent Commission of Experts (looking into all facets of World War II Switzerland), and four commission members; and, members of the Swiss Embassy staff. Researchers representing the Swiss Bankers Association began their research at Archives II in spring of 1996, and were joined in July 1997, by a four-member research team from the Bergier Commission. Other researchers, including accountants from the Volcker Committee (created by the Swiss Bankers Association and the World Jewish Congress to investigate deposits made in Swiss banks by victims of Nazi persecution), have also found NARA a useful source of information.

During the past two years NARA and the Swiss Federal Archives have developed close ties. There have been frequent communications between Dr. Christoph Graf, the Director of the Swiss Federal Archives, and NARA. In November 1997, Dr. Greg Bradsher, NARA coordinator of Holocaust-era research, visited Dr. Graf and the Swiss Federal Archives in Bern. He also met with Madeleine Kunin, America's Ambassador to Switzerland, and Jacques Picard, a member of the Swiss Independent Commission of Experts, to discuss ongoing research and NARA's critical role in what President Clinton stated was one of the aims of his Administration - to "bring whatever measure of justice might be possible to Holocaust survivors, their families, and the heirs of those who perished."

THE MEDIA INTEREST

By the spring of 1997, NARA had become a magnet for the media as well as researchers. The media, unable to obtain stories from those government historians researching and drafting the first Eizenstat Report, found that much of the document base upon which the report would be derived was in NARA. Not only were the documents reviewed and filmed, but researchers and NARA staff members were interviewed. Feature stories appeared in *The New York Times*, *The Washington Times*, *The Jewish Times*, and *The Cleveland Plain Dealer*, among other newspapers.

Also, major periodicals such as *Newsweek* and *US News & World Report* contacted NARA for information. The History Channel, the Arts and Entertainment Network, the Public Broadcasting System, and the Cable News Network ran specials based on interviews with NARA staff and researchers. Press interest has continued since May 1997. ABC News, Dateline NBC and a wide variety of print and visual media have regularly contacted NARA, as have Swiss TV, Swedish Public Radio, and numerous film makers, newspapers and magazines.

THE FIRST EIZENSTAT REPORT

On May 7, 1997, the Interagency Group on Nazi Assets, headed by Ambassador Eizenstat, issued its report entitled *U.S. and Allied Efforts To Recover and Restore Gold and Other Assets Stolen or Hidden by Germany During World War II: Preliminary Study.* The report, based primarily on NARA's holdings, was quite critical of the Swiss and the other World War II neutrals. The author of the report acknowledged NARA's contributions to the completion of the report. In his preface he wrote "All of the research depended directly upon the unfailing support, assistance, and encouragement of the Archivist of the United States and the staff of the National Archives and Records Administration. Our work simply could not have been carried out without this assistance... It is to the credit of the National Archives staff that the needs of all researchers-government and private, domestic and foreign-were met with unfailing courtesy and without disruption to research schedules."

My point in quoting this complimentary statement is to highlight the key points on which NARA's performance was judged; opening all pertinent records and providing equal access, in a timely manner, to all researchers. These are the key points on which any national archives will be judged.

SPECIAL FINDING AIDS

The issue of equal access depends on the researchers' ability to navigate through often voluminous records, many untouched for decades. Finding aids are indispensable tools in this effort. If such finding aids do not exist, in all likelihood they will need to be created. This was certainly NARA's experience.

With the help of NARA staff and others, Dr. Bradsher prepared a 300-page finding aid to the records at Archives II. This finding aid served as the appendix to the Interagency Group's report. This report and finding aid were issued on May 7, 1997, and immediately made available at the Department of State's website and sold by the U.S. Government Printing Office. When the research widened to more countries and more subjects, and there was a great desire for an expanded finding aid to relevant records, we issued a 300-page supplemental finding aid in the fall of 1997. It was placed on the Department of State's website in November 1997. A revised and expanded finding aid, some 750 pages, was placed on the United States Holocaust Memorial Museum's website in March 1998 at *ww.ushmm.org/assets/nazigold.htm*.

NEW RECORDS

The legal bases on which national archives operate vary from country to country. Likewise the type of records maintained will vary. But for purpose of preservation and ease of access records related to Holocaust-era assets and related issues are best placed within the custody of national archives. Even NARA, which is the legal repository of the historically valuable records of the U.S. Federal Government did not have all pertinent records.

In 1996, The Clinton administration urged agencies to transfer relevant records to the National Archives. In 1997, the Central Intelligence Agency transferred Office of Strategic Services records, as well as biographical profile documentation on Thomas McKittrick, the wartime president of the Bank for International Settlements, and Emil Puhl, the Reichsbank vice-president. The National Security Agency, on the day before the report was released, transferred to NARA copies of Army Security Agency intercepts of communications between the Swiss legation in Washington, and the Swiss Foreign Ministry in Bern, Switzerland. Although their records are not federal records, the Federal Reserve Bank of New York sent to NARA two cubic feet of copies of pertinent materials. During the summer of 1997, the Department of Justice transferred to NARA a major body of Office of Alien Property Trading With the Enemy Act case files. All of the records accessioned were immediately declassified, if this had not already been done, and made available and used by researchers.

MORE RESEARCHERS

In the wake of the Eizenstat report, more researchers found their way to College Park. Not only were the researchers, including claimants, continuing to seek information about looted Nazi gold and related topics, but the boundaries of research had widened to include questions relating to looted securities, looted works of art, unclaimed and unpaid insurance policies, refugee policies, slave labor practices, and wartime trade between the neutrals and the Axis powers.

Law firms and other research teams involved in class action litigation relating to dormant accounts in Swiss banks and unpaid insurance policies of victims of Nazi persecution have found NARA's holdings critical to their research. Jewish organizations, banking organizations, and art restitution research teams have also used NARA's holdings.

Foreign researchers have found NARA an important resource to supplement the information available in the archival records in their own countries. During the past year there have been dozens of private researchers from various countries, including Austria, Sweden, the Netherlands, France, Great Britain, Germany, and Switzerland. During the summer of 1997, six researchers from Sweden made their home at Archives II for several weeks, looking at records relating to their country. In February 1998, researchers representing independent commissions from Spain, Portugal, and Argentina began their research. Representatives of foreign banks and foreign archivists, including those from Israel and Sweden have also sought information.

LEGISLATIVE INTEREST

The quest for historical accountability draws great attention from national legislative bodies. The work of national archives and independent commissions need sustained political and legislative support. The transparency of the work performed is a key element for obtaining sustained support. Fortunately for NARA our experience with Congress to date has been successful.

The Senate Banking Committee and the House Banking and Financial Services Committee have made use of NARA's holdings. Senator D'Amato, appreciative of NARA's efforts, said, "The National Archives at College Park has been nothing less that amazing...Their help was indispensable in establishing, continuing and expanding the research of the Committee."

The House committee was interested in records pertaining to heirless assets in America. Committee staff research contributed to the Holocaust Victims Redress Act being introduced in Congress during the fall of 1997 and passed and signed by President Clinton on February 13, 1998. The law authorizes $20 million for restitution and $5 million for archival research. In signing the law, the president noted that it "recognizes the need for long overdue archival research... to set the historical record straight."

In addition, Congress passed, and the President signed, legislation creating the United States Holocaust Presidential Advisory Commission, which will address American-related Holocaust assets issues.

NARA AND THE INTER AGENCY GROUP ON NAZI ASSETS

Within days of issuing its first report, the Inter Agency Group on Nazi Assets was asked by political leaders to prepare another report. Thus, in the summer of 1997, researchers from the Department of State, the Central Intelligence Agency, and the National Security Agency, representing the Interagency Group on Nazi Assets, began to do their research again with NARA's assistance. Their efforts resulted in the publication of a report, entitled *U.S. and Allied Wartime and Postwar Relations and Negotiations With Argentina, Portugal, Spain, Sweden, and Turkey on Looted Gold and German External Assets and U.S. Concerns about the Fate of the Wartime Ustasha Treasury*. This report, also authored by William Z. Slany; was issued in June 1998.

Dr. Slany and Dr. Bradsher traveled to Ascona, Switzerland, in October 1997 to attend a conference on "Nazi gold" records and research. This conference, sponsored by the Bergier Commission, was attended by representatives from Argentina, Canada, Great Britain, France, Belgium, the Netherlands, Portugal, Sweden, Switzerland, and the United States. At the conference, research methodology and archival resources were among the primary topics of discussion. Rarely, if ever, have archival records been so inextricably a part of such a major international issue. The work of all the national archives is a key to the successful conclusion of this quest for historical accountability.

THE FUTURE

Secretary of State Madeleine K. Albright, speaking to the Swiss parliament on November 15, 1997, said that "doing all we can to discover the truth about the Holocaust and events related to it, and to act on the consequence of that truth, are among the vital unfinished tasks of this century." Throughout the world, many countries, organizations, groups, and individuals share this belief. Thus, interest in the looted assets issue remains high. Commissions have been appointed in Sweden, Portugal, Argentina, France, Belgium, Norway, the Netherlands, Switzerland, the United States, and half a dozen other countries to address issues relating to victims of Nazi persecution, postwar restitution efforts, and dormant bank accounts.

In December 1997, hundreds of representatives from 41 nations met in London, England at a conference sponsored by the British Foreign Office to discuss looted gold and the disposition of the remaining gold held by the Tripartite Gold Commission. Small conferences were also held in Lisbon, Portugal, in February 1998 and in Monaco in March 1998. At the London meeting, Under Secretary of State Eizenstat announced that another international conference would be held in Washington, DC. This conference is now pushing forward into assets and restitution issues beyond that of "Nazi Gold."

If the independent commissions are to succeed in their task of clarifying the historical record and assist with the issues of accountability and compensation, they require the closest cooperation with their national archives. The national archives need to bring all relevant documentation into their custody, preserve them, and provide equal access. This is necessarily a symbiotic relationship which requires understanding the roles of each partner and providing support for their respective tasks. Both parties will succeed together or fail together. NARA certainly faces this challenge and responsibility with the soon to commence work of the American Commission of independent experts.

Undoubtedly, interest in and all aspects of the looted assets issues will continue for years, if not decades, and just as certainly archival research will accompany that interest. NARA will continue to be a critical resource for those doing "Nazi Gold" research, for contained in its holdings is what the Archivist terms "essential evidence." This evidence, with the assistance of NARA's skilled and dedicated staff, will be made available and used for a multitude of purposes. The end result of the various research efforts at NARA and elsewhere, one hopes, will

contribute to countries, including the United States, being more capable of addressing their pasts and accepting their current responsibilities.
Thank you.

Dr. Siegfried Büttner

VICE PRESIDENT, GERMAN FEDERAL ARCHIVES
GERMANY

The Treatment of Enemy Archives in
the Third Reich

Plenary Session on Archives, Books and Role of Historical
Commissions

PRELIMINARY REMARK

History is, in a complex manner, information embedded in a
context. Historical facts cannot be understood in any other way.

Archives consist of recorded facts and a context which can either
be depicted openly or hidden in the structure of the documents, the
archives and the overall portrayal of events.

While, however, understanding history involves linking
historical facts and complex phenomena with present-day individual and
social awareness, archives are solely bound by the visible as well as
hidden historical origin and context from which they emerged. For they
should enable every future generation to gain access to information
which will help it understand what has been. That is the purpose of the
archival principle of provenance.

Unfortunately, my short contribution deals with a historical
situation in which archivists themselves failed to uphold this principle
and helped damage, distort and destroy records in the pursuit of goals
which they regarded as victorious and enduring.

However, the Nazis did not invent the concept of using archives
and records for one's own "superior" principles and objectives. It existed
up until recently, and indeed still exists.

What the Nazis, both organizations and individuals, did can only
be compared to a limited degree to what had previously taken place
between enemy states. Rather, they began encroachments on archival

records which, in most cases, were irreversible and could only be rectified to a certain extent. The outcome of this and subsequent measures carried out by the Allies under the conditions of the Cold War was that records and documents of German origin of all kinds, including those of Jewish communities, are today fragmented and scattered around the world.

The disaster began with the immediate confiscation in 1933 of the archives (as well as libraries and research institutions) of the Nazis' political opponents with the aim, on the one hand, of using them in the direct fight against Communists, Social Democrats, left-wing trade unionists and their organizations and, on the other, as propaganda against these groups. The archives, including those of the national executive of the German Trade Union Federation and some of its affiliated trade unions were handed over to the archives of the NSDAP and the German Labor Front, as trophies as it were.

From 1938 onwards the archives (and academic institutions) of those intellectual, religious and racial groups considered enemies by the Nazis, e.g. Jews, Freemasons, writers, artists, etc., were seized and exploited for the purposes of so-called research and propaganda with the aim of "eradicating" them from the "Volkskörper" (national community). One of the most important Jewish archives, the complete archive of German Jews, fell, without it being formally seized, into the hands of the Reichssippenamt (Reich Genealogy Office) and under the control of the Security Police (SD) of the SS, and was then used as a central agency for Jewish genealogy up to the 1940s. Although this helped to preserve the records of the Jewish community in Berlin and many others collated in this archive, it was in the end no less fragmented than other German archives.

From the outbreak of war the archives in the annexed and occupied territories were subject to many different measures aimed at protecting and securing, exploiting and seizing them, in some cases removing and destroying them, the latter most pronounced in Poland and the Soviet Union. Naturally, this included not only the archives of the state there and everywhere else but also all those of the aforementioned "enemies". Several specialized organizations were set up for this purpose in addition to the police and the SD.

The most specialized was the Archivschutz (Archive Protection) headed by Ernst Zipfel, Archivschutzbeauftragter (Commissioner for Archive Protection) in the Reich Ministry of the Interior, who was also President of the Reich Archive and Director of the Prussian Secret State Archive. In addition to his function of protecting archives he quickly gained corresponding responsibilities in Reichsleiter Rosenberg's task force (Einsatzstab Reichsleiter Rosenberg - ERR) and in the Reich Ministry for the Occupied Eastern Territories. The archivists sent out by him were set different tasks depending on the country in which they were working: in Poland it was to deprive the Polish people of its identity, in Denmark, for example, and in The Netherlands their task was to genuinely conserve buildings and records. The army (the head of the army archive) seconded archivists independent of the Commissioner for Archive Protection but with the same aims.

The ERR was established in occupied France with a view to capturing academic material and works of art, in particular those of Jewish origin. It later developed its most diverse and extensive operations in the East. The feigned academic objective of researching Jewry was used as a pretext to seize major academic libraries and collections, as well as the personal papers of academics and religious leaders.

The task of the Künsberg Special Unit (Sonderkommando Künsberg), which was answerable to the Federal Foreign Office, was to continue in Warsaw what had been started in Paris with the seizure of the documents of the Quai d'Orsay; however, the unit took advantage of being with the combat troops in Poland to extend its terms of reference to include libraries and works of art, including those in the territory of the Soviet Union and Norway.

Other organizations, such as the Reichskommissar für die Festigung deutschen Volkstums (Reich Commissioner for the Consolidation of German Traditions) and the Ahnenerbe (Ancestral Heritage) subordinate to him sometimes cooperated and sometimes competed with one another, so that loot often became a bone of contention.

The SD and the Gestapo remained predominant.

Even after the war had ended an interest in being able to identify and combat opponents under mostly humane conditions based on the rule of law but, at the same time, governed by the laws of the Cold War, determined the fate of the archives stolen by the Nazis and the files and documents of the Reich and NSDAP subsequently seized by the Allies. The Soviet occupying power acted likewise in this regard:

In general, the fate of archives and documents seized from Nazi organizations cannot be understood fully without looking at the treatment of German archives, which was quite different in East and West. But that is not on the agenda here.

In the former GDR, however, we still find fragments of archives or documents which were originally seized by the SD or Gestapo, e.g. unpublished papers of émigré writers from Paris or Amsterdam.

In the Secret State Archive of Prussian Cultural Heritage there are also some documents taken from Polish archives (e.g. the 74 medieval documents relating to the Teutonic Order).

As far as I know, the western German state archives have no material of this kind.

The documents handed over by the former Soviet Union to the state security service of the GDR also include papers seized earlier, e.g. those belonging to Office VII of the Reichssicher heitshauptamt (Reich Central Security Office) ("Ideological research and evaluation"), a large part of which is still in Moscow. They include many individual papers whose origin can no longer be established.

In general, however, the situation created by measures taken by Nazi Germany against "enemy" archives did not last long: in the western occupied territories especially the American military government collected the archival material stolen by the Nazis in the Offenbach Archival Depot in order to hand it back to the owners; in particular this included most of the material stolen by the ERR. The Red Army initially kept most material as booty. Parts of it are still in the special archive (Archive for the Preservation of Historical Documents), others were returned to Germany. Before they reached the state archives, the GDR security service (Stasi) raked through them on behalf of the Party.

After the fall of the Communist regime, the Central State Archive of the GDR began to return seized archives (the estates of émigrés, the archive of the exiled publishing house Allert and Lange in Amsterdam), and the Federal Archives continue to act in accordance with the owners' instructions. However, returns on such a small scale are out of all proportion to the magnitude of the overall damage which will have a long-term impact.

The damage was caused by the fact that parts of the written records of one and the same historical individual (a person, organization, authority, government) fell into the area of responsibility of various agencies, was used for different purposes, i.e. often reordered and opened up with differing aims, which leads to many misunderstandings, perhaps especially when all lists of documents are made available alongside each other in the Internet.

IF THE DAMAGE CANNOT BE REMEDIED WHAT LESSONS CAN AT LEAST BE LEARNED FROM THIS?

1. Archives are not like any other cultural asset which might be looted in times of war. Each archive belongs to a historical individual. He or she will have the most enduring interest in preserving an archive because it is part of their lives.

2. For this reason the confiscation or long-term disposal over the archive is an ineffective means of fostering historical truth. Even good intentions, for example the punishment of German war criminals, arise from prevailing conditions and should have as little effect as possible on the archival records themselves.

3. When it comes to dealing with the past each individual and organization has a responsibility, especially with regard to written records, to ensure that the historical truth (what has happened) remains unadulterated. Hopefully the controversial discussions of the last few years have helped to foster awareness of this responsibility, also in private organizations.

4. Individuals and peoples do not always live in harmony; they have conflicts and wage wars. If they involve their archives in this they damage more than each other. Once the conflict is over our viewpoints and attitudes change, as the ending of the Cold War showed. After that it is certainly conceivable that interests concerning written historical records can also be reconciled, thus enabling a people, for instance, to gain its own historical portrayal from the records of the occupiers during a period of foreign rule or occupation by opening them up and perhaps microfilming them. The cooperation between the National Archives, the Institute of Contemporary History and the Federal Archives at the end of the seventies in opening up and filming the files of the Office of the Military Government of Germany, U.S. Element (OMGUS) is, in my view, an example of this. I hope that the ongoing process of reconciling interests in various directions with all our eastern neighbors can be brought to a speedy conclusion.

No conflict should involve archival records; their use is liable enough as it is to provoke conflict.

Professor Jean-François Bergier

CHAIRMAN OF THE INDEPENDENT COMMISSION OF EXPERTS (ICE)
"SWITZERLAND – SECOND WORLD WAR"
SWITZERLAND

Statement translated from the original French by the
U.S. Department of State Office of Language Services, Translating Division

Plenary Session on Archives, Books and Historical Commissions

In my capacity as Chairman of the Independent Commission of Experts: Switzerland – Second World War, first of all I want to welcome all the participants at this Conference and thank those who took the initiative for it and organized it, particularly Mr. Stuart Eizenstat and Mr. Miles Lerman. My Commission highly values and attaches great importance to this meeting, inasmuch as it could be conclusive with respect to the two issues in which we are all involved: restitution of the property of the victims, and an obligation to remember. Beyond these specific requirements, knowledge about our pasts is the foundation of our national identity, as well as a condition for harmony among our countries.

It is in this spirit that our Commission was established by the Swiss Authorities in December 1996 and assigned the mission of conducting the historical and legal investigation of all questions that could shed light on the responsibility of Switzerland, its public and private institutions, or its private citizens, in the tragic events brought about by National Socialism and the Second World War. Thus, these investigations concern not only unclaimed assets, insurance policies, or stolen or missing cultural property, but also anything that may have intentionally or unintentionally caused harm to the victims and anything that may have afforded an advantage to the National Socialist regime, its allies, and its accomplices. The Commission must submit the results of its work to the Swiss Federal Council within five years, that is, by 2001. It has for this purpose a budget of 22 million francs and the legal privilege to override the secrecy of business records, subject to respect for the requirement of confidentiality.

The investigations in progress are proving more complex than anticipated owing to the myriad questions that require examination and the volume of sources to be consulted, sources which are widely scattered. In addition, we should resist the pressure of those who, either because memories are, inevitably, imprecise, or because they wish to draw a partial or one-sided picture, do not want to know about this, or think they already know everything about it.

In order to prevent any misunderstandings, it should be clearly noted here today that the primary task of the Commission I chair is not to locate every individual asset deposited in Switzerland and identify its rightful owner. We do not have the means to do this, and other institutions have been set up for this purpose, such as the Volcker Committee for unclaimed funds in banks. The Commission must, above all, reveal the networks and mechanisms of the various transactions that have caused such assets to exist. It must attempt to analyze and comprehend the context in which these transactions were conducted and the means and conditions that made them possible. It must calculate their profits or their costs. It must account for strategies, those of the Federal State and those of the individuals involved. Its approach is economic, political, and legal, but must also bear in mind the attitudes and trends of the era in question.

At the London Conference on Nazi Gold, we introduced a highly preliminary, very provisional balance sheet of the gold transactions of the National Bank of Switzerland. In it we proposed definitions of gold that were more precise and historically more useful than the political distinction customarily made between monetary and non-monetary gold. And we presented statistical data contrasting the amount of gold held by the German Reichsbank, classified by source, with the amount deposited in Switzerland on behalf of Germany or other Central Banks. This past May we submitted more complete findings, which reveal that, on the one hand, as of 1941, the National Bank of Switzerland suspected, and as of 1943, had knowledge of, the suspicious, to say the least, origin of a large part of the gold it was acquiring from the Reichsbank, but that, on the other hand, it did not know that about 120 kilograms of gold deposited in its coffers had been extracted from the victims, melted down, and recast. The National Bank continued its purchases, at reduced levels, until the end of the War, justifying them with legal and political arguments that do not stand up to examination. We have also revealed the more discreet role played by some commercial banks and other economic agents such as insurance companies.

Next year, probably in the fall, we will publish a new report focusing on refugees. A document was made available to all participants at this Conference which presents an outline of this report and the principal questions it will seek to answer. It will put the Swiss policy on refugees back in the international context; it will examine the good or not so good reasons for this restrictive policy and the reactions of the population; it will attempt, despite the shortage of sources, to count the refugees admitted or turned away at various times between 1933 and 1945, at various segments of a border that was, as of 1940, completely controlled by the Axis and, as of September 1943, exclusively by agents of the Third Reich. It will describe the material and psychological conditions of the refugees and will assess the financing of their admission (approximately 100,000 civilians) and the action of the Jewish organizations, as well as of the charitable institutions, churches, labor unions, etc., that were active in this field. It will also address the infamous issue of the "J," the Evian Conference of 1938, the ransoms demanded for the safety of certain people, and the role of those figures who dared to break the law in order to save lives, such as Police Officer Grüninger in St. Gallen in 1938 and Consul Lutz in Budapest in 1944.

The Commission is not yet ready to present here today the results of its investigations on stolen or lost cultural property. A report of the Federal Office of Culture on this subject will be published in a few days, and will serve as a basis for our own work. This work, however, can be fully accomplished only in close cooperation with the authorities of the other countries, since in this area, international networks operated, and the links must be traced. We are expecting a great deal from this Conference in terms of laying the groundwork for managing such cooperation.

Beyond these issues, our efforts are directed essentially toward learning about the behavior and activities of private Swiss companies: banks, insurance companies, business firms, and industrial corporations. We are looking at the "repossession", in Germany and the occupied countries, of Jewish-owned businesses and real estate (Aryanization), the use of forced labor, the export of weapons or any other hardware that could have contributed to the war effort of either the Germans or the Allies, movements of capital, sales of licenses, etc. From another perspective, we must take into account the Swiss need for supplies, fuel, and raw materials. Under the circumstances in which it found itself, Switzerland had to make concessions to both sides but especially to Germany, of which it was – geographically – the hostage. The issue is how much room Swiss economic policy had to maneuver and to what extent that room to maneuver was perceived by public or private leaders. That is where Switzerland's responsibilities lie.

This is a very extensive program to be achieved in a relatively short period of time, that is, by the end of the year 2001. It will have to address all items listed above with as much clarity as possible. This effort to achieve clarity is something we owe to the memory of our victims; to Switzerland and its inhabitants, whose lives it has affected and rendered unsettled; and to the international community.

Permit me to conclude with two wishes:

It is my wish that our Conference will implement the means urgently needed for international cooperation in identifying the problems and the sources, as well as in establishing an effective methodology. In particular, it is necessary to render possible and convenient access to all relevant sources and to prepare lists of such sources. I propose that an international working group be established to ensure follow-up for this Conference in terms of investigations.

It is also my wish that the sharing of our work with one another will enable us to overcome prejudices and taboos, as well as futile and costly confrontations, and will help us be sure of our history so that we can look towards the future with confidence. Mrs. Madeleine Albright recalled here yesterday the power of memory, reason, and justice. It is up to us to help restore this power.

Prof. Eric Ketelaar

LEGAL COUNSEL, NATIONAL ARCHIVES
THE NETHERLANDS

Understanding Archives of the People, by the People, and for the People

Break-out Session on Archives and Books

SUMMARY

Archival documents are more than bits and pieces of information. Assessing the evidential and research values of archives presupposes an understanding of records creation. Records are created to support and manage work, to record why, when, where, in what capacity and by whom what actions were carried out. These actions determine context and structure of an archival *fonds*, and convey meaning of the form and the content of a document. Presentation of archival information has to focus on context, structure, and form, rather than content.

Thorough research commissioned by the Netherlands commissions on Holocaust-assets has established a catalogue of actions and actors involved in the looting of assets (1940-1945), their recuperation (1945-1950), restoration of legal rights and restitution (1945-1971) and compensation (1950-1987). This catalogue will be published on December 9th. It is a 364 pages guide of 75 agencies, both public and private, Dutch and German, and their archives (ranging from one file to more than 2500 running meters of shelving). Even with this guide, searching for individual names will be difficult and time-consuming, since many institutions did not create indexes to their records, and because one individual case may have been dealt with by different agencies, each according to its mandate.

Understanding of archives contributes to enhancing their evidential and research value. Such research requires free and equal access to public archives 'of the people, by the people, and for the people'. According to Freedom of Information and archival legislation in the Netherlands, no government record or archival document from the '40s, '50s and '60s is totally closed: they are either accessible for anyone, Dutch and non-Dutch, or – if restricted e.g. to protect the privacy of living individuals – by special clearance if the interest of the applicant outweighs the interest served by the restrictions. Any decision concerning access is liable to judicial appeal.

A framework for legislation and regulations is provided by the Draft Recommendation for a Standard European Policy on Access to Archives, prepared by the Council of Europe. Archival practice is guided by the code of ethics, adopted by the International Council on Archives. It requires from archivists that they promote the widest possible access to archival material and provide an impartial service to all users.

"That this nation, under God, shall have a new birth of freedom; and that government of the people, by the people, and for the people, shall not perish from the earth."
— Abraham Lincoln, Gettysburg Address (1863)

INTRODUCTION

From these famous words I have taken the title of my paper. Archives - well preserved and accessible to the people - are as essential in a free democracy as government of the people, by the people, and for the people. Because archives are not only tools of government, not only sources for historical research: access to public archives gives the people the possibility to exercise their rights and to control their government, its successes, and its failures.

Archives of the people, by the people, and for the people. As the great American archival teacher Theodore Schellenberg affirmed: "Public records obviously define the relations of the government to the governed. They are the ultimate proof for all permanent civic rights and privileges; and the immediate proof for all temporary property and financial rights that are derived from or are connected with the citizen's relations to the government."[1] The consequence is that the public archivist is not merely a state official, but truly a public servant, who has "an implicit obligation to safeguard the integrity of the contractual relationship that exists between citizens and their government which the records document; and to intercede on behalf of record subjects in administering access to such records so as to ensure that citizens' rights are protected under the terms of that contract".[2] Concomitant is the people's right on access to public archives. A Draft Recommendation on a European Policy on Access to Archives, currently under consideration within the Council of Europe[3], identifies access to public archives as 'part of the rights of the citizen, and, by extension, in a political system that respects democratic values, part of human rights'.

Hundred years ago, 1898, Zola's 'J'accuse' started the Dreyfus affair.[4] Zola engaged chemical experts and archivists to expose the infamous *bordereau* as a forgery. Giry and other professors of the Ecole des Chartes were among the scholars who in court and in the press used their scientific methodologies in taking a stand in the political debate that had grown out of the Dreyfus affair. They made it clear that their professional ethics, based upon integrity and objectivity of the scientific method, should play a role in the public arena too. Scientific integrity and objectivity should be the instruments to restore truth and human dignity.

Today, as in 1898, archivists can be called to arms, when public affairs question their professional ethics, when archivists have to use their moral defense to defend societal values, which are at the heart of the archivist's endeavor. Archivists have to cry out and to denounce any manipulation of evidence so as to conceal or distort facts. The code of ethics, adopted in 1996 by the International Council on Archives, requires from archivists that they promote the widest possible access to archival material and provide an impartial service to all users.

---

[1] T.R. Schellenberg, *Modern archives. Principles and techniques* (Chicago 1956) p.9.

[2] H. MacNeil, *Without consent; the ethics of disclosing personal information in public archives* (Metuchen; NJ, 1992) p. 144.

[3] Council of Europe, Draft Recommendation on a European Policy on Access to Archives, cc/livre (97) 7 rev.

[4] B.Joly, L'École des chartes et l'affaire Dreyfus, in: *Bibliothèque de l'École des chartes* 147 (1989) p. 611-671; A.B. Spitzer, *Historical truth and lies about the past. Reflections on Dewey, Dreyfus, de Man and Reagan* (London 1996) p. 50.

The same year 1898 saw the publication, in The Netherlands, of the 'Manual for the arrangement and description of archives,' drawn up at the instruction of the Netherlands Society of Archivists, by Muller, Feith en Fruin. Their Manual has had a global impact: it was translated into German, Italian, French, Bulgarian, English, Portuguese, Chinese, and Estonian. The Manual was the first to formulate and disseminate coherently the basic principles of archival science and methodology. These principles are the principle of respect for archival structure and the principle of provenance: archives of the same provenance are a whole whose historically determined individual structure may not be disturbed, but on the contrary should be restored if necessary; every archival document should be part of the *fonds* to which it by nature belongs and to which it should be restored. We respect the provenance, the administrative context in which the archival document, as a component part of the *fonds*, was created or received. Archives (records) are created, received and maintained by institutions and individuals by virtue of and as a by-product of their activities and business. Archival information is intrinsically bound to a specific business process, be it managing an agency, treating a patient or looting Holocaust-assets. That origin as transaction-tied information gives archives their special value as a historical source. This contextuality gives each record its specific meaning.

Why referring to the 1898 Dutch manual for archival processing and to the role archivists played in the 1898 Dreyfus affair?

Because today, in bringing to light the sources revealing what happened in the looting, recuperation, restoration and restitution of Holocaust-era assets, archivists have to deliver the same message as in 1898. Professional integrity and objectivity are the instruments to sustain society's dignity and to restore truth. That requires the widest possible and impartial access to archival material. Archival information that must be processed, presented, used, and interpreted in the context in which the archival documents originated.

ACCESS TO ARCHIVES[5]

Access to public records and archives is realized at different levels or layers.[6]

The first layer is legislation: Freedom of Information legislation, archival legislation, legislation protecting personal data and personal privacy.[7] Dutch archival legislation states that access restrictions must be specified at the time the records are transferred to a repository. The conditions of transfer therefore constitute a second layer of regulation of access.

Legislation should specify an authority that may grant exceptional access to closed records. This 'special clearance' is the third layer of regulation of access.

In The Netherlands, the conditions of transfer for personal information often include a regulation stipulating that archives that are sensitive are only accessible to researchers who have signed an undertaking. This undertaking constitutes a fourth layer for regulating access to and publication of personal information.

The fifth layer of access regulation is formed by the physical and practical regulations that archives have in place to prevent records being examined by unauthorized persons: storage in secure repositories (sometimes, additionally, in locked cases), careful application and lending procedures, an archives control system (such as Archeion, in use in all state archives in The Netherlands) that alerts whenever a part of a record group may not be issued to a researcher etc.

---

[5] See my: 'Archives of the people, by the people, for the people', in: *S.A. Argiefblad / S.A. Archives Journal* 34 (1992) p. 5-16; 'The right to know, the right to forget ? Personal information in public archives', in: *Archives and manuscripts. The Journal of the Australian Society of Archivists* 23 (1995) p. 8-17; ' Der Archivar als Vermittler zwischen der toten Vergangenheit und dem lebenden Volk', in: *Der Archivar* 48 (1995) col. 589-596; 'Can we trust information ?', in: The International Information & Library Review 29 (1997) p. 333-338. All four have been reprinted in: Eric Ketelaar, *The Archival Image. Collected essays* (Hilversum 1997).

[6] I have derived this image of layers of protection from: H. Raaska, *Personal privacy and the archivist* (unpublished paper; NARA Professional Career Training Program; 1989).

[7] *Access to archives. Legal aspects. Proceedings of the thirty-second International Conference of the Round Table on Archives XXXII Edinburgh 1997* (Paris 1998).

The final layer is the area where professional ethics guide access to archives.

Let us consider these six layers.

1.   In The Netherlands the archives law limits the grounds to restrict access to public records transferred to a public repository. Restrictions may be imposed solely in the interests of
- the respect for personal privacy or
- the interest of the State or its allies or
- the prevention of disproportionate advantage or
- disadvantage to the persons concerned or to third parties

2.   Each restriction on access must be specified in a formal document, with reference to the legal basis and the purpose of the restriction. Restrictions should preferably apply to individual items, and not indiscriminately to whole bodies of records.

3.   In 1996 the International Council on Archives published 'Principles for archives and current records legislation', building upon an earlier set of principles and guidelines developed in an UNESCO study.[8]   One of these principles is 'Legislation should specify an authority who may grant exceptional access to closed records…This power should be exercised within a process that provides a further opportunity for citizens to appeal the decision'. Such a special clearance procedure was recommended as early as 1985 by the 23rd International Conference of the Round Table on Archives under the proviso that such procedure 'should be transparent and governed by objective criteria, so as to guarantee equal treatment of all interested parties'.[9]   The Council of Europe's Draft Recommendation on a European Policy on Access to Archives also insists on 'the possibility of seeking from the competent authority special permission for access to documents that are not freely available. Special permissions for access should be granted under the same conditions to all users who request them.'

---

[8]   See www.archives.ca/ica. The UNESCO study was: E. Ketelaar, *Archival and records management legislation and regulations; a RAMP study with guidelines* (Paris 1985).

[9]   Access to archives and privacy. Proceedings of the twenty-third International Archival Round Table Conference, Austin 1985 (Paris 1987) p. 174.

Under Dutch legislation, whenever access has been restricted, the archival authority can, having heard the transferring agency, lift the restrictions on access or set them aside in favor of a particular applicant, if the interest of the applicant's ability to consult or use the document outweighs the interest of the restrictions. Generally speaking, the interest of the citizen, seeking for his rights, outweighs other interests which may be served by access restrictions (and which were specified in the document mentioned under 2). In this way we can serve individuals researching the Holocaust-era, while still adhering to a general restriction on access.

4. Another means to give access to records, which are generally closed to protect privacy, in Dutch archival institutions, is the declaration that researchers have to sign before they are granted access to specific sensitive records. That declaration is based upon regulations that the Council of Ministers drew up in 1973 with regard to the use of Council minutes and related documents. The researcher confirms with his or her signature

- that the data obtained from the documents will be used solely for a specified purpose
- that he or she shall divulge nothing, by publication or by any other means, which might harm disproportionately the interests of living people
- that he or she shall not publish anything from the documents without written permission of the State or municipal archivist concerned
- that he or she shall use information from the documents for which no permission has been obtained to publish, for his or her own study only and that this information will not be communicated to third parties.

This arrangement was accepted in 1984 by the Society of Dutch Archivists, on the proposal of a commission consisting of both archivists and researchers. The arrangement resembles the 'contractual agreement' procedure, which is applied in the states of Michigan and New York. In Michigan it has even been codified: an act stipulates that confidential records from government agencies 'shall be kept confidential pursuant to the terms of a written agreement'.[10]   One of the main differences, however, between the Dutch and the American arrangement is that the latter includes a penalty of $ 1 000 for violating the provisions of the agreement. In The Netherlands we do not need such a penalty, because the researcher - historian or journalist - knows the issue at stake: his future research. If he fails to comply, the researcher risks exclusion by virtue of the authority of the archivist to refuse access, if in his opinion documents 'cannot be safely entrusted to the applicant'. Since this came into force in 1968 the sanction has been applied in the General State Archives in The Hague only two or three times, during the whole period, out of a hundred to two hundred applications per year to get access to confidential records. And in our Dutch permissive society, with its long tradition of a free press and unhampered scholarly research, it is the exception that it appears necessary to consult with the researcher about a change in his manuscript to prevent disproportionate harm to the interests of still living people.

5.   The Council of Europe's Draft Recommendation on a European Policy on Access to Archives rightly points to the fact that how liberal the access rules may be, 'the actual communication of archives depends primarily on the facilities and on the human and financial resources which an archives service possesses for the preservation and the processing of its holdings'. But in my opinion this should never be an argument to withhold documents from victims seeking their rights!

In providing access to sensitive records it may be necessary to involve social workers and other counselors who help people to cope with the psychological effects of a confrontation of the past. This is being done in Amsterdam at the Foundation for Jewish Social Work and at the Institute for War Documentation, as is the case in the archives of Metropolitan London with regard to patient records.

The first five forms of access regulation - legislation, conditions of transfer, special clearance, researchers' undertakings, and

---

[10] R.M. Baumann, The administration of access to confidential records in state archives: common practices and the need for a model law, in: *American Archivist* 49 (1986) p. 360-366.

physical conditions - appear sufficient enough. But not quite. The first four protective layers consist partly of flexible provisions. For example, how will, in the case of the first and second layers, 'respect for personal privacy' be substantiated, how does one weigh up the need to restrict the disclosure of personal information against the interests of the researcher who requests dispensation or special clearance, at the third layer, how does one test at the fourth layer whether the interests of living persons could be unfairly impaired?

6. At this point we reach the sixth and final layer, an area not formally and legally defined: an area where only professional ethics can provide guidance[11]. The code of ethics, adopted in 1996 by the International Council on Archives, requires from archivists that they promote the widest possible access to archival material and provide an impartial service to all users. Archivists should protect the integrity of archives and should resist pressure from any source to manipulate evidence so as to conceal or distort facts. They also have to take into account the rights and interests of owners and data subjects and they must think of the user. Archivists should discourage unreasonable restrictions on access and use. They should observe faithfully and apply impartially all agreements made at the time of acquisition, but, in the interest of liberalization of access, should renegotiate conditions in accordance with changes of circumstance.[12]

UNDERSTANDING ARCHIVES

Access to archives, in Dutch archival terminology, covers two concepts: the availability of archival documents for consultation as a

---

[11] Anne Cooke, 'A code of ethics for archivists: some points for discussion', in: *Archives and Manuscripts*, 15, no. 2 (1987), p. 8 quotes EW. Russell (1978): professional ethics being of the kind which are too particular to be controlled by law, by-law or regulation but too general to be regarded solely as a matter for the individual judgement of the archivist concerned. See G.M. Peterson -T. Huskamp Peterson, *Archives & Manuscripts: Law* (Chicago 1985), for the difference between ethical and formal legal responsibilities.

[12] *Code of ethics adopted by the General Assembly of the International Council on Archives, 6 September 1996*: www.archives.ca/ica.

result of legal authorization (*openbaarheid*) and the consultability (*toegankelijkheid*): the intellectual control of archives by arrangement and description in such a way that a user can effectively consult the archives. 'Records that are merely accumulated, and never arranged or described, are as unavailable to future users as records that have been destroyed,' Sharon Thibodeau remarks. [13] She continues by specifying the fundamental principles for arrangement and description, first articulated in the Dutch Manual of 1898. Underlying these principles mentioned in the introduction of this paper (the principle of respect for archival structure and the principle of provenance) is the premise that the arrangement and description of a body of records 'reflect a knowledge of its custodial history as well as an understanding of any previously established methods of intellectual control', to quote Thibodeau. And it is here that the archivist as well as the researcher is daunted by the documentary heritage of the Holocaust-era. Not only the sheer bulk of the archives is intimidating. Most archives have been subject to intricate adventures during and after World War II: dislocation, dispersion, confounding disarrangement, re-use of original documents in building new files, destruction of parts of an archival *fonds* and restructuring of the remainder, etc. The resulting confusion is not only bound to confuse and intimidate any researcher, but it also has made the evidential and historical value of many archives and records questionable at least, not to say void.

This complexity of the Holocaust-era archives is aggravated by the intricacies of the administrative organizations, agencies and institutions that created, processed, used and maintained the records - both during and after the war. An archival *fonds* is a fabric of relationships and context. Because we have to respect that structure and to understand that fabric, we have to study its history, to get insight in the historical process that determined the structure of the *fonds*. This contextual approach is a powerful tool for any user to find, to use and to interpret his sources properly. But this presupposes that the user is enabled by the archivist to have access to the records' contextual history. [14]

---

[13] S. Gibbs Thibodeau, Archival arrangement and description, in: J.G. Bradsher (ed.), *Managing archives and archival institutions* (Chicago 1989) p. 67
[14] E. Ketelaar, Archival Theory and the Dutch Manual, in: *Archivaria* 41 (Spring 1996) p. 31-40, reprinted in E. Ketelaar, *The Archival Image. Collected essays* (Hilversum 1997) p. 55-65; R.J. Cox, Archival anchorites. Building

Let us take as an example the fate of diamonds of Dutch Jews. In 1942 Jews had to hand in all jewelry and other valuables to Lippmann Rosenthal & Co., Sarphatistraat (Liro), who also received all or most goods confiscated by the Germans on deportation. Diamonds were used by Jews as payment to get a

'Sperr' stamp which temporarily exempted them from deportation. Diamonds deposited by Jews with the Amsterdamsche Bank were confiscated by the Devisenschutzkommando Niederlande and sent to Berlin in January 1945. To Berlin were also brought (by Seyss-Inquart personally) the diamonds 'safeguarded' by the Rijksbureau voor Diamant, locked away in bank safes in Arnhem and looted by the Germans in September 1944. A third shipment to Berlin consisted of the diamonds of Jewish diamond cutters and dealers, requisitioned by the leader of the Devisenschutzkommando and sent by him to Berlin in March 1945.

Restitution and reparations payment with regard to diamonds after the war were dealt with by different agencies and organizations: the Liquidators of Liro (LVVS), the Recuperation Bureau of the Ministry of Finance, the Foundation Jewelry-Committee (Stichting Sieraden-Comité) and the Foundation Recuperated Diamonds (Stichting Teruggevoerde Diamant), the Commissioner General for Netherlands Economic Recuperation, the Ministry of Foreign Affairs, the Netherlands Military Mission at the Allied Control Council, the Restitution Control Council OMGGUS, the Reparation, Deliveries and Restitution Division UK, the Wiedergutmachungsämter.

To discover the fate of a particular set of diamonds, one has - before actually searching the archives - to get acquainted with the different 'missions' of both looting and restituting agencies and organizations, and to check to which competency the looting, restitution and reparation of that type of diamonds might have belonged. Furthermore one has to study the administrative histories of the institutions and the vicissitudes of their archives and to ascertain where within the archival remains of an individual agency one has to search. All this pertains to the contextual and custodial history of the records.

Through this jungle the searcher is led by the archivist, cutting a path, pointing to pitfalls and peculiarities, assisting without taking over. Serving as an itinerary in The Netherlands is a guide of actions and actors involved in the looting of assets (1940-1945), their recuperation (1945-1950), restoration of legal rights and restitution (1945-1971) and

public memory in the era of the culture wars, in: *MultiCultural Review* 7/2 (June 1998) p. 57.

compensation (1950-1987).[15] This research guide - to be published on December 9th - is the fruit of thorough research commissioned by the Netherlands commissions on Holocaust-assets. It is a 364 pages guide of 75 agencies, both public and private, Dutch and German, and their archives (ranging from one file to more than 2500 running meters of shelving). The guide is the key to grasping the institutional and administrative history of the agencies, and the custodial history of the archives. It is a prerequisite for finding one's way to and into the archives and to understanding the archives.

The guide also mentions finding aids that may guide the searcher to the document level. Sometimes a particular *fonds* is enriched by lists and indexes with names, in other cases the files may be arranged physically according to names. The guide explains the meaning of the various signs, symbols, stamps, and references like ' H.R.' (presumably for Hausrat = household effects), with a number between 1 and 23015, used by Liro and, after the war, by various recuperation, restoration and restitution agencies. For indeed, German and Dutch bureaucrats maintained their files, card indexes and ledgers so meticulously that, once we understand the administrative and record keeping history, their detailed accounts can be checked as if their creators are still working at their desks.

All too often, however, the custodian of the material can only identify the boxes on the shelves, and has to leave it to the researcher to browse through the documents and to find the needle in the haystack. Searching for individual names will be difficult and time-consuming, since many institutions did not create indexes to their records, and because one individual case may have been dealt with by different agencies, each according to its mandate.

By dissecting the machinery of looting, recuperation, restoration and restitution of Holocaust-era assets, as well as making its archival vestiges contextually transparent, the guide constitutes a major instrument not only in understanding archives as a tool for research. We also plan to develop the guide into an educational instrument. To teach young people how bureaucratic control, registration and accounting during and after the war were used for good and for evil purposes. This

---

[15]   J.M.L. van Boxmeer - P.C.A. Lamboo - H.A.J. van Schie, *Onderzoekgids Archieven Joodse oorlogsgetroffenen. Overzicht van archieven met gegevens over roof, recuperatie, rechtsherstel en schadevergoeding van vermogens van Joden in Nederland in de periode 1940-1987, vervaardigd in opdracht van de Commissie van Onderzoek Liro-archieven* (Den Haag 1998).

may assist in Holocaust education and remembrance but also serve current concerns about registration of immigrants, discrimination, invasion of privacy etc. In this broader framework the guide will constitute a major instrument in understanding ARCHIVES OF THE PEOPLE, BY THE PEOPLE, AND FOR THE PEOPLE.

Rev. Fr. Marcel Chappin

PROFESSOR, GREGORIANA PONTIFICAL UNIVERSITY
THE HOLY SEE

Statement by The Holy See about the Accessibility of its Archives

Break-out Session on Archives and Books

1. The Holy See wants to call to mind the principles of International Legislation regarding State Archives, in which is stated that every State is autonomous in its exclusive right of regulating the conservation and the accessibility of its Archives. It is therefore an inherent attribute of the sovereign character of the Holy See, that it alone must be the judge of the pace, timing and scope of the process of making its Archives accessible for research.

2. Ecclesiastical Archives cannot be compared with the Archives of secular governments and institutions. Because of the primarily spiritual mission of the Church, documentation in these archives mostly include discussions and correspondence on religious and spiritual matters, which also concern the "forum internum", the realm of conscience, on which guidance and counsel are sought and offered for the spiritual life of persons. This applies to Diocesan archives and those of Religious Orders, but also to the Archives of the Holy See, since no aspect of its activity, including its diplomatic one, is really separate from its primary spiritual, religious, apostolic and pastoral mission.

The Church would be unfaithful to her mission, and indeed hindered in that same mission, if she would not maintain a scrupulous regard for the most intimate sphere of personal privacy. This respect for privacy is intrinsic and unrenounceable for the life of the Church. She has a sacrosanct duty towards the persons who entrusted her with their secrets and cannot and should not betray them, for any reason whatsoever. People have to be sure that their innermost secrets are safe with the Church.

3. This fact explains that the process of making Church Archives gradually accessible for research – as the Holy See is doing for more than a century – is necessarily a slow one. A scrupulous screening has to take place, one which can only be done by those who have enough knowledge not only of civil and ecclesiastical history, but are also experts in moral theology and canon law.

The period up until 1922 has been completed. More recent decades are being processed now.

4. However, for the Holocaust-Era is at disposal the exhaustive information in the twelve volumes of the *Actes et Documents du Saint-Siège relatifs à la Deuxième Guerre Mondiale*. Notwithstanding insinuations, the curators of this publication have in no way tried to hide documents that would incriminate the Holy See, as explained by one of them, Fr. Pierre Blet S.J., in an article in *Civiltà Cattolica*, published March 21, 1998 (*La Civiltà Cattolica* 1998 I 531-541); an English translation is available.

5. An attentive study of the 12 volumes will reveal the constant policy of the Holy See: trying to stop the outbreak of the war, to alleviate the suffering of its victims and to help to hide and to save as many persecuted people as possible. The same volumes as well as other published testimonies also reveal the motivation why there was not an explicit public protest. The Holy See judged that such a protest would not stop the persecutions, but only result in even more victims, while at the same time it would block the prudent but persistent efforts to save human lives through the means of diplomacy. Many statements of gratitude, also by Jewish persons, organizations and institutions, are found on the public record. They thank the Holy See for what it achieved by its persistent efforts.

Would an open protest have saved more lives? There is no answer to this question that is and always will be hypothetical. If there is any hint at all, the contrary seems to be true. The open protest of the Dutch bishops resulted in even more victims. In any case, the Holy See rejects all accusations that it did not do its best to save as many lives as it could in the given circumstances.

6. The Holy See is aware of the fact that the 12 volumes do not make for quick and easy reading, although is has to insist that they be taken seriously. It wants however to draw the attention to the summary prepared recently by Fr. Pierre Blet, S.J., "Pie XII et la Seconde Guerre

Mondiale d' après les archives du Vatican". An English translation is soon to be published by the Paulist Press.

7. During this Conference and the preceding one, the words "truth and justice" have been uttered many times. The Holy See wants to insist also on "trust", if a better world is to be built. No fruitful discussion and dialogue, no real understanding and reconciliation are possible without mutual respect and trust. One has to be confident that the other is not telling lies or in any other way being deceitful or following some hidden agenda. If the Holy See is not trusted about what it has said or published so far, why should it expect to be trusted afterwards?

It is essential that the respect and trust shown by the Holy See to others, are in no less measure shown by those others to the Holy See.

Dr. Yaacov Lozowick

DIRECTOR OF THE ARCHIVES
YAD VASHEM
THE HOLOCAUST MARTYRS' AND HEROES'
REMEMBRANCE AUTHORITY

The Names of the Jews

Break-out Session on Archives and Books

Yad Vashem in Jerusalem is uniquely positioned to assist in attempts to restore Holocaust era assets to their rightful owners, in two ways:

1. THE LIST OF JEWS IN THE HOLOCAUST

Since there never was a full list of Jews persecuted in the Holocaust, no archive can ever be in possession of it. In lieu of such a list, however, many thousands of local lists were created by various agencies during and after the Holocaust, and Yad Vashem has been collecting them for decades: Approximately 10,000 lists to date, with a rough estimate of 16-20,000,000 relevant names.

We have created a computerized database with information about the lists; however, only a small proportion of the names themselves have so far been computerized. The collection of additional lists is an actively pursued, ongoing project, and many hundreds of lists are added each year.

Some of the information is overlapping data about the same individuals: i.e., an attempt to cross a border in 1941, a deportation list from 1942, a list of transfers between camps in 1943, and an official post-Holocaust death notice. The amount of information on each individual varies from list to list. Only by collating all the information do we acquire a detailed profile of the individual victims. Such collating, however, is extremely complex, and hence the need for Yad Vashem's second set of capabilities:

2.   THE ORGANIZED KNOWLEDGE

In the volatile cauldron that was Europe in the first half of the 20th century, individuals often went by more than one name, cities and towns changed their names or were simultaneously referred to differently by their various ethnic inhabitants, administrative regions were in a state of constant flux, and borders often moved. Even countries were often founded only to be abolished a few years later, perhaps to be re-established later on. The lists reflect this chaos: the same individual may appear on two lists with different names, places of birth and vocation, and still be the same person; elsewhere, two individuals who seem likely to be identical, may indeed not be – and all of the information will be accurate and authentic.

In an attempt to overcome these pitfalls, Yad Vashem has created computerized tools, or thesauri, that contain libraries of knowledge about the politics, semantics and geography of Europe in the 20th century. We have collated information from contemporary lexicons, atlases, indexes, as well as executed data-mining on the documentation in our collections. For example, we can tell that Jewish men in Hungary who were called Avraham at home, called themselves Adolf outside. This custom did not apply anywhere else, and thus is useful only for identifying Adolfs and Avrahams from Hungary – a country whose borders changed frequently. These computerized thesauri contain hundreds of thousands of items, and will be essential in any attempt to integrate information on individuals in the Holocaust.

The combined significance of the lists of victims and the organized knowledge is that it is now possible to create a list, at times quite detailed, of the Jews in the Holocaust: the sic million who perished and hundreds of thousands who survived. These resources are indispensable to any effort to identify individuals, their assets, their fate, or their possible heirs.

Yad Vashem alone has both the extensive data and the know-how to cross-reference and collate them.

Description	Estimated number	Type of Persons	Digitization
Hall of Names: Pages of Testimony	1,700,000	Jews who perished	450,000 digitized without scanning
Hall of Names: Survivors	160,000	Jews who survived	Partially digitized
Yizkor books	1,000,000	Jews who perished	Non-digitized
Archival lists	15-17,000,000	People of all types, but mainly Jews	Non-digitized
Total	18-20,000,000		

Mr. Robert J. Vanni

GENERAL COUNSEL, NEW YORK PUBLIC LIBRARY
UNITED STATES

Opening Statement

Break-out Session on Archives and Books

The purpose of this session is to examine the complex issues surrounding various types of assets seized, looted, plundered, captured and confiscated during the Holocaust-era, and in particular, the matter of archives and books. Being associated with one of the world's great research libraries, it is an honor to be included on this session to make some comments which, I hope, will serve as a departure point for discussion, though I point out that the opinions I offer are strictly my own.

For purposes of analysis, I would like to separate the materials we are discussing into two main categories. The first is book and library materials, seized, looted and confiscated during the Nazi era that originated in national, local, private and other collections, which, due to their great historical significance, rarity, value or uniqueness, can be considered cultural objects or "collectibles." Such "collectibles" might include antique or unique manuscripts, fine bindings and first editions. The second category is records and archives of individuals, organizations (religious, fraternal, charitable or commercial), and governmental or quasi-governmental entities such as towns and municipalities. It is my opinion that the first category of "collectibles", are more in the nature of precious museum or art-type assets, and should be treated as such for the purposes of restitution, repatriation and compensation. Further, much of these precious materials have been carefully handled by their current custodians, catalogued and preserved and to a degree are accessible for study and research. It is the second category, more routine in nature, of archives and records of individuals, organizations and governmental entities that I would like to direct my comments. I would submit that for the following reasons these materials are unique among the Holocaust-era assets being discussed and hence should be dealt with differently. Unlike other assets, they may have little intrinsic monetary value in comparison to precious books and manuscripts, art, gold or bank accounts.   Their <u>great</u> value, however, lies in the information and intellectual content preserved on their pages. It is this information that gives witness to lives, communities and organizations that no longer exist. It is this information that may perhaps offer the very proof needed by those seeking restitution of all the other types of Holocaust-era assets. And it is this information that will add to the history of each nation represented here, since as a result of the war time diaspora, population movements across national boundaries and continental divides, all our national histories are revealed, in part, in these records and archives.

Archives and records are also unique and different from art and cultural objects in that their value can be exploited separate and apart from the original artifact or document through the use of what librarians refer to as "surrogates", that is, research copies created by use of xerography, microfilming techniques or newer technologies.   The original artifacts should, to the extent possible, be preserved, but the minimum to be done is to capture for posterity the intellectual content they contain.   Let me also state at the very outset, that the great artifactual, and associational value of the <u>original</u> documents must not be lost sight of. In this regard there need be a two-pronged discussion as to these materials.   First, how to preserve and make accessible their intellectual content; and second, once accomplished, where should the original artifact reside.   This second question is very much one for diplomatic negotiation or private claims, since many countries and organizations have legitimate claim to be custodians of artifactual original materials, should restitution to their rightful owners not be possible.   It would be unjust and immoral to delay access to the intellectual content of such material while solutions to the complex questions of reparation and return of the original documents to rightful claimants is completed.

Returning to the first question of preservation and access, I would suggest there are three steps to be taken:
1. The troves of records and archives need to be identified and catalogued, at least into broad categories, including location and physical condition.   Such information should be integrated into existing catalogues, perhaps being made accessible via the internet.

2. A triage effort must be undertaken to identify those collections of greatest research and historic value and/or at greatest risk of physical deterioration, so as to establish a reasoned priority order in which to expend limited resources available for preservation and preparation.
3. A useable surrogate (using xerography, microfilming and newer electronic technologies) needs to be created to both preserve the intellectual content of such material and make it broadly available for access by claimants, researchers and scholars.

Though these three steps are a major task, already many nations have commenced the work of cataloguing, preserving and making such materials accessible over the past decades.

How then, might this work be organized and undertaken? As a departure point for discussion, I would suggest the formation of an international commission of interested governments, institutions and organizations that would serve as a coordinator and liaison with existing and to be established national efforts to:

a) Set standards for the cataloging and collection of information on extant collections of historical Holocaust-era documents, as well as the establishment of standardized protocols for preservation techniques;
b) Upon the recommendation of scholars and specialists, assist in the triage of those materials establishing which categories should be acted upon first;
c) Coordinate and cooperate with and/or assist in establishing national projects for the cataloguing, preservation and accessibility of these materials;
d) Assist in raising funds in support of national projects, (which might include government and international organization grants, private sector donations or perhaps using a small percentage of cash equivalent Holocaust-era assets that cannot otherwise be restituted to their rightful owners).
e) Serve as a facilitator or forum for the consideration of where the original artifacts, documents, records and archives might best reside, and as a conduit for claims;
f) Assist in educating professionals in whose care these materials reside, as well as informing researchers, scholars and claimants of the availability of such materials, by making use, among other things, of the internet and world wide web.

As for the establishment of country or locally-based projects for cataloguing and preservation, grants can serve to equip preservation and microfilming laboratories, assist in creation of electronic catalogues and databases, train personnel and, to a limited extent, assist in meeting local costs.

My fear is that unless swift action is taken in regard to the preservation and accessibility of Holocaust-era records and archives, those individuals and institutions seeking information upon which to base claims will continue to be frustrated in their efforts, while the slow fires of deteriorating acid based papers made worse by inadequate environmental storage will result in the loss to the world forever, not only of these unique original archives and records, but, more significantly, the intellectual content and the national, organizational and personal histories they contain.

Dr. Abby Smith

DIRECTOR OF PROGRAMS,
COUNCIL ON LIBRARY AND INFORMATION RESOURCES
UNITED STATES

Recovering the Past: How Books and Archives Matter

Break-out Session on Archives and Books

It has often been said at this conference that the present attempt to locate and restore Holocaust-era assets to their rightful owners or heirs is not about money, but about memory. Be that as it may, it is certainly about *assets*, about things that are of value to people, past and present, things that mattered greatly to those who suffered and who perished, as well as things of value for those who remember the dead today. If the current endeavor is indeed about justice and not retribution, if it is about memory and not money, then books and archives play special roles as agents of justice in our efforts.

Books matter because few things are more dear in purchase than knowledge. At the same time, few things are more freely shared than books, because they are such efficient and civilized carriers of knowledge. It is paradoxical that, in the context of this conference, focusing as it is on artworks, insurance claims, and property disputes, books and manuscripts appear to be cheap. True, most books have little financial value -- rare books that are, in fact, of some monetary value are treated as works of art, along with paintings, furniture, jewels, and other objects prized by connoisseurs. Most books are not usually assigned this value because they are not rare or unique, at least not books printed within the last 150 years. Moreover, the contents of books are easily replicated without substantial loss of value in most cases and, in fact, are designed to be easily affordable, readily shared, and inexpensively copied.

But beyond any value that a book might or might not have as an aesthetic object, there are other, one might even say higher, levels of value for the recorded word. How we approach the matter of the rightful place and ownership of these words, and of the books and manuscripts that contained them and that have been displaced, depredated, or orphaned by the war, depends largely on why we value them.

THE PAST

There are essentially three ways in which print and manuscript materials are of value in the context of the task at hand:

    * As *keys to the past:* Books and manuscripts provide information about the past that can unlock for us different types of consciousness and cultural sensibility. The recorded words that are valuable for the information that they contain -- cultural history and memory found in newspapers, novels, journals -- are important sources for understanding the way people lived and thought. Daily newspapers from the Vilna ghetto in the 1930s that tell us what the community ate and wore; socialist tracts that reveal how some political activists understood the revolutions of Russia and how they conceived the ideal relationship between state and individual; novels published in Tallinn that bear witness to how the Estonian literary language evolved in the inter-war period -- these constitute important sources for historians of language, culture, music, art, politics, and so on. These sources are important for the information they contain, and should be copied and made available internationally, especially because they were often printed on acidic paper now aged and fragile.

    * As *records of the past:* Archival records, both official and unofficial, can provide important evidence for locating relatives, lost assets, and so forth, because they testify to the whereabouts of people and things before, during, and after the war. Many of these records are in government archives and repositories and should be made accessible to researchers without restrictions and to the best of any given repository's ability to process and make available their records.

    * As *relics of the past:* There are books and papers that are important as objects themselves because of their associational value. While they may not be valuable because of their intellectual content, nor be particularly rare, they were once the personal property of someone. This is, in my view, the only category of book in which the object itself should be returned to legitimate claimants in order to achieve restitution.

To the extent that books and manuscripts are valuable for the information they contain, we need to distinguish between the ownership of the physical objects themselves and access to the information that they contain. One does not speak of possession of information the way one does of, say, an art object. Is information per se property? Can it be privately owned? This is a question of more than passing interest, because the copyright regimes in effect in each nation represented here today, designed to protect intellectual property at the same time they promote its dissemination, are challenged by a new digital environment in which ownership of and access to information are no longer synonymous. There are well-established traditions in libraries and archives of making information widely accessible, traditions that are observed in the breach in totalitarian countries where information, like intelligence, is considered to be the property of the state. There are no countries here that espouse that ethic today. Ten years ago we could not have said that, and ten years ago we could not have had such a colloquy.

It is important to note that we are not talking just about Jewish materials. The Nazis were fighting an ideological war, and ideas were the most powerful tools of engagement. There were certain ideas that were considered, in and of themselves, to be pernicious. Books that were written by Freemasons, by anti-fascist writers, by devotional and patriotic writers in Catholic and Orthodox Slavic countries, by homosexuals, socialists, communists, and other so-called degenerates – these works were seized and disposed of, destroyed or hidden. And those books and manuscripts that after the war came within the pale of the Red Army were twice seized and repressed. All these books together bear witness to the past. Those books that managed to survive after the communities they belonged to were entirely wiped out, especially the communities or individuals who were dissenters of conscience and who left no heirs or relatives, should be located and restored so that their reality can now become part of history as told in their own, now silent, voices.

THE PRESENT

The important tasks for us today are *identification, preservation,* and *access.* We must identify library and archival materials that are missing, we must preserve those that we can, and we must make them accessible to those who need to consult them. As I said, books of associational value should, when possible, be returned to rightful claimants in order to achieve restitution. Given the physical state of much that remains, this is often a daunting challenge and demands major expenditures of time and money.

For materials that contain valuable cultural information, copies can be made and widely shared. Physical restitution may or may not be desirable, but it is at times simply impractical. These items are often severely damaged due to poor storage conditions and improper handling; they are also frequently very fragile because they were printed on poor-quality, high-acid paper. It is important to make these materials accessible, even when we cannot preserve them, and preservation microfilming is an efficient and relatively inexpensive way to maximize universal access to remote and fragile resources. For those records that are of value to current and future researchers trying to determine the fate of people and their possessions, we must press for open access to archives, a principle endorsed both by the International Council on Archives (ICA) and the International Federation of Library Associations and Institutions (IFLA).

For purposes of access, digital technology offers an unparalleled opportunity to share not only databases of information about people, places, and things, but also the historic documents themselves. I must caution the enthusiastic, though, that digital conversion is very labor intensive and expensive. It can range anywhere from $5 to $30 an image, with yet more expense for creating all the access points that make digital information retrievable. Access to digital materials depends upon computer hardware and software, both of which are expensive and prone to obsolescence. Materials scanned and made available in one file format today may well be obsolete and unreadable 20 or 30 years hence. We have not yet developed practical solutions to the problem posed by the impermanence of digital information.

Given the expense of digital conversion, especially for archival materials that may be infrequently consulted, we are better off putting our limited resources into creating inventories of and finding aids to collections. This route offers the best way to share information – by making known that it exists and where it can be found.

Libraries and archives seldom, if ever, have enough funds to provide the kind of services they want to. As the national archives in America and the Netherlands know quite well, researchers gaining access to Holocaust-era records represent a new constituency and added workload. And in Eastern Europe, where many of the most valuable materials are found, we are talking about libraries and archives that are opening up to public use for the first time in our lives, at exactly the moment in history when they are losing – have already lost -- their core funding. They are forced to close reading rooms because they cannot pay utility bills, and more often than readers know, the small staff that remain on the job to serve them are not merely underpaid. They are often unpaid for months at a time.

Frankly, of the three actions that we must undertake now – identification, preservation, and access -- the first is the by far the hardest. It is not uncommon that libraries and archives, even those that are well funded and staffed, do not know precisely what they have and where it is. There may well be books and manuscripts that lie unidentified in libraries and archives. Gaining control over those backlogs involves physical processing of items that are often in precarious states of preservation. To make those items accessible, catalogers and archivists must grapple with name authority problems, the use of multiple names for people and places in Eastern Europe. Certainly some libraries that took possession of book collections that had been confiscated received them with no record of their provenance and, if they were not known to be rare or from an important collection, these collections would have been broken up and shelved according to the usual library scheme rather than kept together as a coherent collection. To reassemble collections would involve physical examination of whole library collections shelf by shelf, book by book.

THE FUTURE

Restitution as such is a troubling and difficult concept when it comes to books. Who are the rightful heirs of the books in stranded in book depots in such cities as Vilnius and Kaunus, books that belonged to communities that have been effaced from the earth? To some extent, books belong to anyone who cares about them, anyone who finds value in them, anyone who uses them. Without readers, books lose their meaning as well as their value. We all know that history is written by the survivors, and we, as survivors, must take some responsibility for the way that the history of the Holocaust era is written. All books and manuscripts, claimed and unclaimed, are keys to the past, and I would encourage all who seek to recover the truth about the past to declare their interest in the fate of the information about the past that these resources carry.

Dr. Shimon Samuels

DIRECTOR FOR INTERNATIONAL LIAISON,
THE SIMON WIESENTHAL CENTER, PARIS

Break-out Session on Archives and Books

I am grateful to Under Secretary Eizenstat for his invitation, extended to me at last week's Buenos Aires meeting of the CEANA (Argentine Commission on Nazi Activities) of which we are both members.

As Paris-based Director of the Simon Wiesenthal Center for both Europe and Latin America, I have long focussed on the trans-Atlantic triangulation of war criminals, gold, art and other assets, flowing from Germany, through the Iberian Peninsula to the Southern Cone.

As this jigsaw required the Argentine Commission to have access to Spanish and Portuguese archives, so too the porous borders show the need for a regional approach to what are now called the Mercosur countries. In this context, I have had meetings with government and Central Bank officials in Brazil, Chile and Uruguay.

A massive lacuna has been the absence of access to the Stroessner period archives in Paraguay. Last week, I met in Asuncion with Foreign Minister Dido Florentin and the Paraguayan Central Bank Director Dr. Jorge Schreiner, to propose an Argentine-style commission.

Our Center was requested to present models of national commissions for Paraguay's consideration, especially in view of a current investigation by the Central Bank's Controller into the 1989 disappearance of Argentine-origin gold ingots, allegedly bearing Reichsbank markings.

Moreover, in Buenos Aires, I proposed to President Carlos Menem, the establishment of a Mercosur-level commission, especially to track the intra-regional traffic in assets through the Latin American network of such Nazi banks as the Banco Aleman Transatlantico and the Banco Germanico.

Menem charged Interior Minister Carlos Corach with discussing this proposal with his Mercosur counterparts.

I believe that with the end of this conference a phase will be closing, i.e. that of **defining** the problem through the work of the national archival research commissions.

We now enter phase two – that of enforcing settlement, the closure of commitments, the fulfillment of promises. In the spirit of the Biblical injunction of Leviticus, Chapter 25, verse 10: "In the fiftieth year…thou shalt restitute to each…his property…"

From my perspective in Paris, I wish to mention the following examples:

- An ironic paradox, in some cases, is that the creation of a national archival commission has cut off access to formerly available archives, e.g. the Bercy French Finance Ministry, where I was able to research the Tripartite Gold Commission reports, until these were closed for the use of the Matteoli Commission.
- The Spanish Central Bank archives were open to me and others until Lord Janner called for the creation of a Spanish Commission. Henceforth, the researcher of the Argentine CEANA has been denied access.

Other obstacles to transparency are:

- Delay in granting access to the Tripartite Gold Commission archives recently moved to Paris.
- Refusal of the Portuguese Central Bank to permit research on gold flow to Latin America and Asia.
- Access to the Austrian Finance Ministry archives relating to pre-Anschluss bank accounts, especially of the State-owned PSK.
- The opening by the Holy See of its World War Two-era archives relating to Croatian-looted gold and other Holocaust issues.
- Immediate implementation of restitution by the British government of property and accounts confiscated from "enemy aliens", including thousands of Nazi victims. *To attempt archival reconstruction, the Simon Wiesenthal Center posted a questionnaire on its Internet site to seek potential claimants. We have since been mandated by some 130 account holders.*
- The fulfillment of the promise to transfer several looted art objects, currently in French State museums, to the newly-opened Paris Museum of Jewish Art and Tradition.

I am reminded of a bitter historical coincidence. In August 1944, with the Allies about to liberate Paris, the Resistance stopped a train of looted art that was on its way to the German frontier. On the same day, the last train of deportees left Drancy for Auschwitz – it was never stopped. *Ars longa, vita brevis.*

In conclusion, restitution is not charity, nor of concern exclusively to Jewish claimants. The work here is a contribution to an evolving jurisprudence on the war crime of looting. CNN's financial analyst, Myron Kandell, emphasized this during Kabila's march on Kinshasa, when he said, "It took a Holocaust bank scandal to open Mobutu's Swiss accounts..."

We are also refining an expanding moral pedagogy on human rights with significance for the treatment of refugees, the professional responsibility of insurance companies towards beneficiaries, an exercise in prudence for art dealers and museum curators, and a reminder of client-first good practice for the banking industry. Above all, exposure of the truth lances a long-festering boil, allowing the pus to drain. The cleansing of this wound can be an act of catharsis for the collaborator, added armament against Holocaust denial and a final accounting for the victim – both Jewish and Gentile – and for their heirs.

Thank you.

Prof. Peter W. Klein

SECRETARY OF THE SCHOLTEN COMMISSION
THE NETHERLANDS

Report on Dutch Historical Research on Financial Restitution for War Victims

Break-out Session on the role of Historical Commissions

Let me say first that the following short survey of Dutch committees engaged in research on restitution for Dutch war victims will be as factual as possible. I will try to avoid any value judgements. Of course this in no way implies that there are no moral issues at stake. The organized, systematic persecution and robbery, by the German national socialist civil authorities, to which the Netherlands, and its Jewish population of 135,000 in particular, were subjected, was, of course, absolutely reprehensible from a moral point of view. Contrary to the pretence of the German occupying forces it was, moreover, completely criminal and illegal. The small and rather helpless Dutch nation of about ten million people, that for more than a century had taken great pride in its pacifist principles of neutrality, was in no way prepared to cope with the national socialist reign of terror - either mentally or physically. Its reaction was not unambiguous. It consisted partly of passive, unheroic accommodation and partly of active and courageous resistance. It also took the form of collaboration with the enemy, either indirectly and unwillingly, or directly and with full intent. The variety of reactions of course also raises many moral issues, but they are not the subject of this report.

The Dutch government in exile in London carried on fighting the war, in particular at sea, where the substantial Dutch merchant navy succeeded in contributing significantly to the Allied success. While contending with serious shortages of qualified manpower, the government also took the legal steps required to undo the harm done at home as far as possible.

Repairing the war damage and reconstructing postwar Dutch society was naturally one of the major issues concerning the Dutch government in exile. The preparation of emergency legislation for the restitution of Dutch Nazi war victims' legal rights had begun as early as June 1940, one month after the occupation. Drawn up meticulously by one of the most distinguished representatives of the Dutch legal profession, this extensive and extremely complicated legislation was not completed until 17th September 1944, on the very day Allied paratroopers landed a bridge too far in the Netherlands, and lost the Battle of Arnhem.

At the time nobody could have predicted that the fighting in the Netherlands would rage on for yet another 8 months, throughout the terrible, bitter winter of 1944 - 1945. Nobody could have predicted that at the end of the war the most damaged economy in Western Europe would be that of the Netherlands. The extent of the damage is comparable only with the destruction of the most heavily hit industrialized areas of Germany itself. Nobody could have predicted that the liberation would not be followed immediately by the restoration of the traditionally tolerant Dutch regime of parliamentary democracy. Instead, the government retained its military status until well after the war. Nobody could have foreseen the absolutely overwhelming number of complex problems, some new and some extremely urgent, confronting postwar Dutch society. They included purging society of traitors and collaborators; restoring public health, which had suffered badly; guaranteeing a food supply; repairing war damage; reconstructing the economy; bringing order to chaotic public finances; reviewing traditional foreign policies; coping with the decolonization of the Dutch East Indies, and so on.

There was also of course the problem of rehabilitating war victims. Amidst all these worries few Dutchmen realized that in the end only about 5,000 of their Jewish fellow countrymen were to return from the death camps. Let me repeat: only 5,000 of the 107,000 who were deported ever returned. Who could have realized it then? Who can even now? Half a century after the war, Dutch society - now prosperous and content - has been confronted almost out of the blue by a terrible question: is it possible that the state, insurance companies, banks and other sectors of the Dutch business community systematically profited - illegally or improperly - from large-scale looting, amounting to an unknown and now undoubtedly large sum of money? The next question is, of course: if this is the case, what can we do about it?

The Dutch tribe, being Dutch, followed its tried and tested, traditional way of doing things - particularly where there is something to be investigated. It sets up committees - not just one, but preferably as many as possible, each recruited from its own specific sector of society and well-stocked with professional expertise. Apart from the separate ministerial committee of five or six members, headed by the prime minister himself, and instructed by the Dutch government to supervise and coordinate the research, there are now another five committees. Each of them works according to its own rules, methods and research techniques, and each has its own job description and its own perspective. There are also of course a number of sub-committees, each with its own job description and perspective. Needless to say, there is some overlap and duplication. It would appear that we have major coordination problems and that efficiency is suffering somewhat. But the advantage of this rather cumbersome approach is evident: the chance that anything will be overlooked is less than minimal.

The first committee to be appointed by the Minister of Finance was intended to monitor international research in order to learn from it. Headed by an eminent representative of the body politic, it consists of distinguished civil servants, members of the business community, scholars, lawyers, economists and persons who have close relations with the Dutch Jewish community. It has also instigated academic research into the matter of looting and restitution, and the financial and demographic background. Its report is expected in the middle of next year. This committee established a second committee, headed by the former vice president of the Council of State, to guide independent and autonomous academic research on financial restitution. It first of all focused on the controversial matter of dormant accounts with banks and insurance companies. The research was soon extended, however, to include other financial assets such as shares and securities, social insurance, patents, royalties, copyrights, mortgages and so on. The research is being carried out by historians, lawyers and economists under my direction. The committee will publish its first report on 16th December. It will publish its final report in the spring of next year. A third committee, headed by the former Auditor General, concerns itself mainly with the problem of restitution of material property. Its final report will be published on 9th December. Each of the three committees will present its results to the Minister of Finance. This is not the case with the committee established to trace works of art looted by the

Germans. When the time comes it will report its findings to the Minister of Education, Culture and Science. A separate committee has been set up by the Minister of Health, Welfare and Sport. It is looking into the matter of financial damages in the Far East resulting from unlawful Japanese war activities. It has already published its first report showing that there is no evidence of such activities. The committee will continue its research until the end of next year.

Leiden, 26th November 1998

Ambassador Krister Wahlbäck

SWEDISH FOREIGN MINISTRY
AND MEMBER OF THE SWEDISH COMMISSION ON JEWISH ASSETS
SWEDEN

Break-out Session on the Role of Historical Commissions

Madam Chairman,

Before I left Stockholm for Washington, I was told that our American hosts wanted me to address at this session <u>problems with regard to source material</u> faced by the Swedish Commission on Jewish Assets. Thus the focus of my presentation will be a bit different than that of some of the previous speakers.

I am not going to discuss the results or the conclusions of the Swedish Commission except to say that we are not empowered to investigate or pass judgement on Sweden's foreign and trade policies in general during the war. Our terms of reference as laid down by the Government are not remotely as wide in their scope as those given to Commissions in some other countries, for instance the Bergier Commission in Switzerland. The task assigned to us is a fairly precise one: to establish to what extent Jewish property, in whatever form, came into Swedish hands as a result of Nazi persecution.

In fact, even this limited task is quite extensive and complicated, considering that we are looking for transactions which took place more than fifty years ago, and that we want to identify all kinds of transactions, whether they concern arts and antiques, bank accounts and safe deposits, patents and licenses, shares and looted gold. However, the Government has decided that our final report should be presented before the end of February 1999, i.e. after less than two years' work.

Now, which are the difficulties with regard to source material that we have run into? First, <u>access</u> has not been a problem. With regard to official record in <u>public</u> authorities, they are in principle always available even to ordinary citizens in Sweden, according to a constitutional law which has been in force for more than two hundred years. There are some exceptions, however, one of them covering documents dealing with Sweden's relations to foreign powers during the last forty years. But this, of course, does not now apply to any documents relevant to our investigations.

As for the records of our security services, restrictions apply for reasons of safeguarding the personal integrity of people under surveillance. While the Commission's access to these records has not been restricted, we have had to deal carefully, in a somewhat time-consuming way, with a lot of quite interesting documents about illegal German business-related activities in Sweden.

Concerning private archives, or documents in the possession of individual political or business leaders and their families, they are of course private, i.e. researchers depend upon the good will of their keepers to be granted access. However, while the Commission has not been given any special investigative powers by legislation, we have never been denied access to the records of banks, companies or private persons that we have approached. On the contrary, in most cases we have encountered a quite helpful attitude. This applies not least to the Wallenberg bank, Stockholms Enskilda Bank, which has by far the best kept records of any Swedish bank, dating all the way back to 1856. Of course, these cooperative attitudes are not unrelated to the Commission's official status, and I would certainly not wish to give you the impression that they can be taken for granted when other researchers come knocking on the door.

If access has not been a problem, paucity or scantiness certainly have. It is a regrettable fact that traditionally, in the Swedish political and administrative system, only formal minutes are kept of discussions preceding decisions. This is true even for cabinet meetings. The formal sessions with the King on Friday morning were meticulously documented, but not the real, informal debates in the course of the preceding week. These may be recorded in the private diaries kept by five or six cabinet members; but as issues concerning gold transactions or other possible transferal of Jewish property were not considered high politics, very little of interest to us has been found in these diaries.

The Foreign Ministry, which handled all foreign trade matters, was a quite small outfit in the 1940's. Most decisions were taken by informal consultation among half a dozen of top officials, with no records whatsoever. Further, we have got nothing comparable to the British tradition at this time of circulating important documents inside a folded four-sided sheet of foolscap on which different layers of the hierarchy could scribble their comments, and even remark upon previous comments by their colleagues. Thus, the reasoning of the Foreign Ministry and the Government often has to be inferred from decisions, unfortunately in a somewhat speculative way.

Happily, the culture was a bit different in the Bank of Sweden. Fairly good records were kept at their Board meetings, and above all, the President of the Bank in the 1929-1948 period, Mr. Ivar Rooth, was a painstaking diarist, or perhaps I should say compulsive diarist. Not at all in the sense of registering his private life or private thoughts. But he always kept a pen in hand when receiving visitors or taking phone calls, and he was exceptionally able in jotting down what was said in a legible handwriting. These daily notes, thousands of pages each year, have been a most important source to us. And they are now of course freely available to any serious researcher.

Paucity of source material may occur not only by poor note-taking at decision-making gatherings, but also by records being destroyed, or weeded out because of their presumed routine nature. As for official records, this is a rigorously regulated process, but in one or two instances it has in fact happened that investigations contemplated by us, involving very extensive perusal of records covering routine transactions, have proved impossible to carry out because of such weeding many years ago.

In the private and business sector, this problem is much worse. It is costly to keep and maintain archives, and there are no legal obligations in Sweden for private companies or banks to safeguard records more than ten years old. And unfortunately, few of them do. It is primarily in companies run by the same family for a long time that a sense of history may emerge. Again, the Wallenberg bank is the prime example. As I said, the Commission has full access to their archives, including the private correspondence of the two brothers who were running the bank at the time, Jacob and Marcus. Marcus Wallenberg's private diary, which he kept in the 1938-43 years and to which no researcher has been granted access before, is available to the Commission as well.

Madam Chairman,

As indicated at the outset, I have not told you anything at all about the results or conclusions of the Commission. We are right now in the process of drafting these parts of the Commission's Report, which is scheduled for publication in early March 1999. An Interim Report, covering only the gold transactions of the Bank of Sweden with Nazi Germany, was published in July 1998 and is now available in English translation.

Ambassador Sevinc Dalyanoglu

GENERAL DIRECTOR FOR MULTILATERAL ECONOMIC AFFAIRS,
MINISTRY OF FOREIGN AFFAIRS
TURKEY

Notes on Archival Research Undertaken by the Turkish Commission to Determine the Actual Position of Turkey Before, During and After the Second World War

Break-out Session on the Role of Historical Commissions

At the very outset, we did not expect to be involved in this issue at all. We had been surprised when we learned that we would be involved, but we are used to being surprised and therefore we reacted swiftly by forming a Commission under the leadership of a Minister of State, compromising three scholars, two ambassadors, two Deputy Directors-General, two representatives of the Turkish Jewish community, and the necessary staff, and moved on to work.

Following the publication of the first report by the US State Department in May 1997 on the subject of "Nazi gold", The Turkish Commissions Response, reflected in several papers, has been included in the "Nazi Gold Report Of The London Conference" published by the British Foreign And Commonwealth Office in 1998.

In the papers presented by Turkey to the London Conference Secretariat, either copy of related Turkish and foreign documents and of the relevant paragraphs of historical books and memoirs have been annexed or referred to in the footnotes. In addition, bibliographies and further reading lists have been added to these papers, when and where deemed useful for the interested reader.

As for the Turkish Research concerning the second report published by the State Department in June 1998, two press statements expressing Turkey's initial reactions were issued in that very same month by the head of commission, Minister of State Professor Sukru Gurel. Relevant Turkish documents were attached to these two press statements as annexes. Foreign documents on the same subjects were later submitted to Dr. William Slany, the Historian of the U.S. State Department, during his visit to Ankara in November 1998.

For such encompassing research on several topics of 50 and 60 years ago, some of which persisted until the late 1950s, our main objective was to be as scholarly and objective in our endeavors and to compile data from as many different sources as possible. Naturally books on history and memoirs of prominent political figures such as Roosevelt, Churchill and Inonu were of foremost importance as starting points of our research. References and footnotes in those books helped us locate other archival sources such as articles published in Turkish newspapers 55 years ago or the texts of the laws adopted by and speeches delivered the Grand National Assembly Of The Republic Of Turkey on the chromium issue. Our point of departure for this subject was Edward Weisband's book entitled "Turkish Foreign Policy (1943-1945)."

The archives of The Turkish Central Bank and The Ministry of foreign affairs were complementing each other especially on the gold issue. The Turkish Central Bank, which is well known for the perfection and the impeccability of its archives, provided the commission with all the documentation needed to finalize the research. The Archives and records on gold transactions of the Central Bank of Turkey are open and accessible to all interested parties for research. However, nobody had previously asked to look into them. We were happy to brief Dr. Slany on the Gold Transactions of the bank from 1934 to 1952 during his visit to Turkey in November 1998. Copies of all the related documents and records were handed to him. Laborious research carried out in the archives of the Ministry Of Foreign Affairs of Turkey yielded fruitful results as well, although the ministry moved to another location some ten years ago and its archives reminded in its former building for the preliminary archival research, a retired ambassador, who has served in the past as the Deputy Director General for the ministry's Archival and Communication Department, was commissioned for this task. After a month of through research, his file contained not only the necessary Turkish documents but also some allied notes, which were not present even in the first report of May 1997.

For prospective researchers, it became easier to find the documents in the ministry's archives as the pathways led us to explore other related matters. At a later stage documents compiled as the outcome of the dedicated archival research effort by Turkish missions abroad, primarily the Turkish Embassies in Paris and London as well as the Turkish Consulates in Paris, Marseilles and Rhodes, were brought in and utilized as further sources in the commission's historical work. These endeavors subsequently led us to another source that is, the International Committee of the Red Cross (ICRC) In Geneva. A Turkish Diplomat who was assigned the task of conducting research in the archives of the ICRC returned with a huge pile of documents testifying to Turkey's role in saving thousands of Jews fleeing from the Nazi persecution in severs European countries during the last year of the war. As to the documents -- or three thick files-- we received from our Embassy in Paris we were happy to find out that every single document concerning the protection of the properties of the Turkish Jewish Citizens was kept in the archives of the Turkish Embassy in Paris. As a matter of fact, these documents were explored upon the advice of retired Ambassador Mr. Name Yolga, who is one of the more than twenty Turkish Diplomats Personally saved many Jews and their properties during the war. Unfortunately, besides Ambassador Yolga, only two others of those diplomatic are still alive.

As stated above the primary goal and principle in our research was to be as objective and honest as possible so as to confront our history with a clean conscience, without prejudice.

As the founding father of our Republic, Ataturk said very wisely: "it is more difficult to write history than to make history."

Therefore, at the outset of our studies we decided to play the "devils advocate" against us and started with two books, which directly targeted Turkey. These two books, entitled "Methoden Der Deutsch-Faschistischen Propagandataetigkeit in Der Turkei Vor Und Waehrend Des Zweiten Weltkrieges" and "Turkei Im Deutsch-Angloamerikanischen Spannungsfeld," and published in 1966 and 1968 respectively, were written by a citizen of the former German Democratic Republic, Mr. Johannes Glasneck.

Although these two books tried to dissect Turkey's position more harshly than the two recent reports of the U.S. State Department, they summarized Turkey's actual position from the mouth of the late American President, Franklin D. Roosevelt who evaluated Turkey's position more accurately and positively than Winston Churchill. President Roosevelt's son, Elliott Roosevelt has drawn the most appropriate picture of history from his father's perspective in his book, "as he saw it." To find a copy of this book, we had to refer to the Library of Congress, as original copies of it were no longer available, except for the Turkish translation of the book, which we readily found at the Library of the Turkish War Academies.

The Book, "As He Saw It," was later complemented by other American and British books and documents the official documents of the State Department concerning the Second World War, particularly those relating to the Cairo Conference, were easy to find at the Library of the Turkish Ministry of Foreign Affairs.

The Footnotes in Mr. Stanford Shaw's book "Turkey and the Holocaust," Copies of which have been distributed to the valuable participants of this conference, also gave us some clues in discovering more facts on the Turkish role in saving the Jews from Nazi persecution throughout the European Continent, as documented in the American Archives.

For the documents of other countries, we are grateful to the Polish Embassy in Ankara, which furnished US with their documents on the 70 tons of Polish Gold that Turkey saved during the first month of the war in September 1939. We are also obliged to Ms. Bennett of the British archives for the British documents to complement ours on the chromium issue. However, we are still expecting the documents from our German Colleagues on the Gratis Return of the German assets in Turkey during the late 1950s. When we recall the remarks of the distinguished German delegate at the London Conference last year about the opening of the Turkish archives, we are now pleased that we have responded to his wish positively we think that it is now our turn to ask the same from our German colleagues.

Dr. Ignacio Klich

ACADEMIC COORDINATOR
COMMISSION OF ENQUIRY INTO THE ACTIVITIES OF NAZISM IN
ARGENTINA (CEANA)
ARGENTINA

Argentine Documents on the Nazi Era

Break-out Session on Historical Commissions

No inventory of Argentine sources on the country's performance during the Nazi era can ignore the fact that the culture of secrecy has long been prevalent here. This, and the low priority ascribed to archives and their organization, have conspired against historical research. Unsurprisingly, Argentina's diplomatic history of the period under consideration only began to be the subject of detailed academic research as U.S. and British papers entered the public domain in the 1970s, with some Argentine records only growing increasingly accessible since the latter years of the military regime that ruled the country until 1983.

Such access had little to do with decreed policy. As is the case in other Latin American and European countries, official documents were meant to be declassified half a century after the events. In practice, though, various institutions have shied away from the release of papers fifty years later, while the authorities of others have shown themselves informally prepared to lift such a restriction earlier. Against the background of such discretionary powers, Buenos Aires University Press (Eudeba) published the first annotated collection of documents on Argentina during World War II in 1988, including, among others, a host of Argentine papers post-1938.[1]

Since the 1980s, the study of the subject has been facilitated by three quantum leaps in access to Argentine documents. The first took place in 1992 when the then interior minister announced that he was

---

[1] Mario Rapoport, comp., *¿Allados o neutrales?* (Buenos Aires, 1988).

opening the so-called Nazi archives. While Argentina has no Nazi archives as such, only materials on various aspects of the country's record during the Nazi era scattered throughout a host of repositories, the announcement resulted in the release into the public domain of some ten Federal Police files on a number of Nazi war criminals. Disappointing as these were to historians and other interested parties because of their number and the large proportion of press cuttings in such files, their release set in train developments that since then have steadily increased the body of available Argentine documents.

The second quantum leap occurred during 1993-96, when records became generally easier to consult. Access to diplomatic documents at the Foreign Ministry Archive (AMRECIC) was facilitated in 1993. All bars were removed to studying judiciary papers on the extradition of Nazi war criminals, thereby allowing researchers to access documents regardless of the date when such extradition requested were lodged or of their result. A useful selection of these has now seen the light of day as part of a documentary project sponsored by Argentina's Jewish representative body (DAIA).[2] In line with its housing of presidential papers, the National Archives (AGN) received records of Juan Perón's presidency, in particular those of his Ministry of Technical Affairs, which shed light on the role played by the presidential information secretariat in the arrival in the country of former Third Reich scientists, technicians and other so-called useful Europeans. By 1996, the Central Bank (BCRA) released documents on gold transactions with neutral and other countries during the Nazi era and early postwar period.

The third leap dates back to 1997 and was initiated by researchers working for the Commission of Enquiry into the Activities of Nazism in Argentina (CEANA), created that year. CEANA's wide-ranging research agenda has three major aims: (i) reaching an informed estimate of the number of Nazi war criminals that settled in Argentina and analyzing the conditions that made this influx possible; (ii) determining whether Nazi loot may have been stashed away in Argentina or used the country as a transit point; (iii) assessing Nazism's impact on Argentine society, government and culture. Included among the records consulted by CEANA that were not previously seen by others are diplomatic papers that for one or another reason have not been transferred hitherto to AMRECIC by Argentine embassies and

---

[2] Paul Warszawski, comp., *Respuesta del Estado argentino ante los pedidos de extradición de criminales de guerra y reos del delito contra la humanidad bajo el III Reich* (Buenos Aires, 1998).

consulates; papers belonging to the various branches of the military, in particular those pertaining to army and air force personnel on the one hand, and to naval operations on the other hand; papers of the Directorate of Military Industries (DGFM), nowadays under the aegis of the Economy Ministry; Federal Police files on Argentine identity documents sought by German and other newcomers (these accessed via the Ministry of Interior); other Central Bank records; Ministry of Justice papers of the vice presidential commission that investigated Perón administration irregularities.

In summary, the corpus of Argentine papers bearing on the Nazi era and early postwar period is no longer one that would impel researchers to study one or another aspect of the country's performance on the sole basis of non-Argentine papers. This said, there are limitations to what can be gained from these important documentary sources, some such hurdles making it all the more necessary to exchanging information with researcher for CEANA and other commissions at foreign repositories. Moreover, there are still Argentine papers to be seen: to name but three groups that have been requested by CEANA, there are papers of Argentina's Ministry of Defense, intelligence secretariat (SIDE) and provincial police forces.

By the end of 1999 a CEANA final report is expected. Among other things, this will include a detailed inventory of Argentine and other records consulted by each of the 23 research units that have been launched so far. For the time being, three interim CEANA reports have been issued; these can be seen at the U.S. Holocaust Memorial Museum, as well as on the Internet at www.ceana.org.ar. In this way, CEANA hopes to play its part in Argentina's lengthy transition from a culture of secrecy to one of greater transparency, a transition that should hopefully make possible other self-introspective exercises such as that in which CEANA has been involved.

Holocaust Education, Remembrance and Research

Mr. Miles Lerman

CHAIRMAN, UNITED STATES MEMORIAL HOLOCAUST COUNCIL
UNITED STATES

Overview of the Importance of Holocaust Education, Remembrance and Research

Break-out Session: Overview of the Importance of Holocaust Education, Remembrance and Research

In the Hall of Remembrance of the Holocaust Memorial Museum, the Eternal Flame is surrounded by the prophetic inscription of the Holy Scriptures of Deuteronomy, chapter 4. It reads:

"Only guard yourself and guard your soul carefully, lest you forget the things your eyes saw, and lest these things depart your heart all the days of your life, and you shall make them known to your children, and to your children's children."

What a fitting quote to inspire remembrance.

Our session today is dedicated to Holocaust education, remembrance and research.

How remarkable and how wonderful it is that in the midst of discussions of financial assets, of what to do to bring some modicum of justice after the biggest theft in human history, that we decided to discuss future plans for Holocaust education.

It is a mark of great foresight to understand how important it is that this century not end with assets, not end with a business deal, but with consideration of the hearts and minds of future generations. I am very pleased that so many dignitaries, scholars and specialists from several countries have seen fit to address the need to shape the future through Holocaust education, and I look forward to the exciting presentation of the Task Force for International Cooperation on Holocaust Education.

Dr. Beate Kosmala

CENTER FOR THE STUDY OF ANTI-SEMITISM
TECHNICAL UNIVERSITY BERLIN
GERMANY

Holocaust Education - Research - Remembrance in Germany

Break-out Session: Overview of the Importance of Holocaust Education, Remembrance and Research

"Those who run away from their past will be caught up by it. We Germans face up to the past for the sake of the future." This conviction was expressed by German President Roman Herzog during the visit of Israel's President Ezer Weizmann to Bonn in early 1996.

With the exception of Israel, probably no nation has placed a greater emphasis on Holocaust education than Germany in the last decades. Since the early 60s, the conference of ministers of education and culture in the German states has provided explicit guidelines for teaching about National Socialism and the Holocaust. All official schoolbooks published since the mid-1980s have dealt with the Holocaust. Libraries for teachers and for students contain extensive literature in the German language on National Socialism and the Holocaust. Many German schools include a visit to a concentration camp memorial, meetings with survivors and eyewitnesses, and the use of related resources in Holocaust education. Outside the school setting, the subjects of World War II, the Holocaust and Jewish issues are very often featured in print media, television and radio, as well as in the world of the arts.

So it seems the younger generation have received a comprehensive education about this terrible chapter of German history. Unfortunately, one sometimes hears German students - and even teachers - say, "I've heard enough already." This reaction does not necessarily follow an intensive confrontation with the theme. Instead, it has to do with, on one hand, weariness with the many media programs in these issues, and on the other hand it involves a defense-mechanism and resistance to these themes. Clearly, what are needed are not just more hours, more material and more media coverage, but new pedagogical-psychological concepts. It raises questions not about the quantity of information but rather the quality of educational developments in Holocaust education.

What are the unique conditions of Holocaust education in Germany, regarding the destruction of European Jewry? Youth are confronted with the fact that the map of terror bears German names; that Germans ordered and planned the murder of European Jewry, and were the majority of perpetrators. This raises issues - for Germans most of all - of guilt, collective guilt and responsibility. Even though the educational target is by now the third or fourth post-war generation, with fewer direct family ties to National Socialism, the Holocaust theme draws sometimes resistance, characterized by a diffuse guilt-complex. Youth often feel as if they have been held collectively responsible, on an international stage. To reach this generation, to prepare them for intensive confrontations with this chapter of history, concepts must be developed that take into account this feeling, and that tie in to the lifestyles and thought patterns of youth.

Another situation unique to Germany is that until 1989 there were two German nations, in which the Holocaust and National Socialism were handled quite differently. The official antifascist policy of East Germany was like a political religion, built on concepts of guilt and pardon. With National Socialism subsumed under Fascism and with the new economic system allowing a distancing from the past, questions about German guilt and complicity faded out of the picture. In the last history schoolbook of GDR, published in 1988, the problem was explained away as yet another imperialistic crime, while antifascist resistance became increasingly important in educational material.

Both parts of Germany now have to learn together how to handle the tragic inheritance of our history from 1933 to 1945.

In 1995, when youth in the former East German state of Brandenburg were asked their position in Jews and Israel, researchers noted "a remarkable lack of feeling and paucity of words regarding the persecution and murder of Jews." In fact, teachers are confronted more often with disinterest, declarations of irrelevance - such as "history doesn't interest me" - and ignorance among students than with aggressive prejudice or denial. And disinterest is certainly not only a problem in former East Germany or even in unified Germany. To combat disinterest and indifference regarding recent history - and therefore regarding the suffering of millions - is the greatest challenge for Holocaust pedagogy.

In universities, on the research level, the confrontation with the murder of European Jewry had a slow start, both in West and East Germany. In its first phase, primarily in the 50's, research focused on the SS, who were made out to be the lone group responsible for Germany's massive crimes. This supposedly all-powerful character of the SS and security police helped explain the lack of resistance among the populace.

In the second phase of the research, as more urgent questions were raised in West Germany about the massive crimes of National Socialism - brought on by the Eichmann trial in Jerusalem and the Auschwitz trial in Frankfurt am Main and other war-crimes trials - studies were begun on the persecution and murder of Jews; the concentration camp system; the SS and police; which influenced and determined the level of knowledge regarding the National Socialist politics of extermination for decades.

In comprehensive German-language collections and debates of that time, research focused on the events leading up to the Nazi seizure of power.

Not until the mid-80's did the Holocaust itself become a prime topic for German historians. The 70's and early 80's can be seen as a second phase of repression. Perpetrators and crime scenes, accomplices and those who profited from the crimes - and most importantly the victims themselves - remained anonymous. One symptom is that it took 20 years for Raul Hilberg's ground-breaking work of 1962 "The destruction of European Jews," to come out in German, and then only through a relatively unknown publisher. Only in 1990 was it republished by a prominent house.

True, since the 1980s the Holocaust has been increasingly a topic of public discussion in Germany - receiving a major push from the 1979 broadcast of the American TV series, "Holocaust" - but it was usually discussed as metaphor for genocide in general rather than as a concrete expression of genocide.

The German contribution of empirical research on the persecution and murder of the Jews in Europe was minuscule, compared to that of the United States and Israel.

Since the early 80's, researchers shifted from discussion of "Fascism and totalitarism" to a discussion about the decisions leading to the so-called "Final Solution." This debate, too, concentrated not on the murders themselves - it was assumed that one was already informed - but rather on the interpretation and result of genocide.

The mid 80's brought new initiatives related to concrete, empirical questions; this in turn drew the attention of the international research community. It is worth mentioning in that context the research project of Munich's Institute for Contemporary History ("Dimensions of Genocide," published in 1991), aimed at establishing the number of Jews who were murdered in all occupied countries and in Germany.

Since the mid-90's, younger German historians have made important contributions to Holocaust research, based on empirical data, investigating the actions of the German occupiers in specific locations in Middle and Eastern Europe. Such research makes it clear that the National Socialist politics of extermination was no secret, but rather a clear part of the conquest and occupation plan in Europe. It is not seen today as an isolated issue but as an essential part of the occupation policy in the East.

Clearly, the number of those who participated directly or indirectly in the National Socialist murders extends far beyond the circle of those who fired weapons or shut the gas chambers doors. This conclusion can be drawn from studies by Goetz Aly on the murder of Jews in the Warthegau in Western Poland ("Endlösung: The Displacement and Murder of European Jewry," 1995); by historian Christoph Dieckman on the mass murder of Jews of Lithuania; Christian Gerlach on the occupation politics and murder of the Jews of White Russia, and the works of Dieter Pohl and Thomas Sandkühler on the so-called "Final Solution" in Galicia (1996), all of which describe the circumstances, perpetrators and victims of the murders.

Clearly, the racist attitudes - anti-Semitism - had a decisive effect in preparing the individual to commit murder. Racism and anti-Semitism designated a hierarchy of human worthiness, of the right to live, and imposed a moral imperative toward extermination by brute force, in direct opposition to the Humanistic or Christian ideals.

Just as the goal of research should be a clearer perception of the experience of perpetrators and victims, so should it be a central goal for Holocaust education that those whose lives were devalued should not be nameless and undefined, not simply referred to as the "victims," but rather as individuals with their own history and identity.

At this point I want to mention still another project. I myself am involved in research at the Center for the Study of Anti-Semitism in Berlin, regarding the phenomenon of help and rescue for Jews in Germany in the face of the Holocaust. Such systematic research has not yet been done. We will now try to determine how many rescuers there were in Germany, who they were, under what circumstances they lived, what religious and political orientations they had, in which situations they became rescuers, what their relationships were to the persecuted, and what motivated them. This raises questions about the possibilities for contact between Jews and non-Jews during the war and about the actual dangers to those helping Jews in Germany. It is known that in Berlin 1,400 Jews were able to survive. When one looks at individual cases, it's clear that most of them involved a long chain of rescuers. From that we can conclude that several thousand Berliners helped to rescue Jews from deportation. This is an important area of resistance history that still needs to be explored.

The goal of this project is to produce a social history of solidarity under dictatorship and a contribution toward an understanding of the mentality of Germans under National Socialism. It is clear from the start that this won't result in an "anti-Goldhagen" image of the German people as a nation of rescuers and helpers. Even if a few thousand found the courage to help, how much more meaningful it is then to point out the millions who looked away, who stood by, or who helped carry out delusional racist policies. The meritorious behavior of a minority does not outweigh the culpability of the majority.

Nevertheless, this research may have its own value to Holocaust education. It shows that, despite dictatorship, there was a way for people to help, to confront the reality of persecution and fear of death for Jews, to retain their own humanity. Such people stand out from the sea of indifference. Through discussion of such examples, German students today may be confronted with their own indifference, and forced to come to terms with it. In the beginnings of 1996, German President Roman Herzog declared the 27th of January - the anniversary of the arrival of Soviet troops in Auschwitz - as a national day of remembrance for the victims of National Socialism. Though the day is marked by public discussion on the Shoah, on racism and anti-Semitism, the average German calendar still does not note this day. The future importance of this day will depend on how involved students and young people can become in the discussions and debates taking place. Their involvement would break through the usual, state-sponsored mechanical rituals of remembrance, creating a direct connection to the younger generation's spheres of experience. But an appropriate education must come first.

Mrs. T.J. Blankert-van Veen

HEAD OF THE DEPARTMENT FOR RESISTANCE MEMBERS, VICTIMS
OF PERSECUTION AND CIVILIAN VICTIMS OF WAR,
MINISTRY OF HEALTH, WELFARE AND SPORT
THE NETHERLANDS

Break-out Session: Overview of the Importance of Holocaust
Education, Remembrance and Research

First of all I will thank the organizers of this special so-called break-out session in this unique Museum to give me, on behalf of the Dutch government, the opportunity to tell something not only about our efforts to support Dutch victims of the Second World War, but how to keep the memory alive of one of the darkest periods in human history and to inform young people.

Of my present compatriots one in three lived through the Second World War. Roughly speaking, everyone born before 1942 has conscious memories of that period. Even those who are too young to remember the war have been deeply affected by it. Of course the country suffered as a whole during the occupation but certain groups were singled out for a particularly tragic fate. Most prominent among them were the Dutch Jews, but also gypsies, Jehovah's Witnesses, homosexuals, political prisoners and those returning from Japanese internment in the Dutch East Indies. The Dutch people who had not spent the war in Polish, German or Japanese camps were unable to conceive of what their compatriots had been through in captivity. And I am sorry to say that it took some years for Dutch society to realize this.

Notwithstanding this lack of understanding the Netherlands has always seen it as its duty and responsibility to give material and non-material support to the victims of the Second World War. Over the years a unique system of legislation has been created to meet the needs of different categories of Dutch war victims: those who were prosecuted; those who were active in resistance groups and civilian victims of war.

The most important act came into force in 1973: the "Victims of Persecution 1940-1945 Benefits Act". The act is primarily aimed at groups whom the Nazis threatened with annihilations but also at victims of the Japanese occupation. In terms of its scope the act is unique. It still provides benefits and facilities for about 30,000 people. Most of them live in the Netherlands, but the rest are scattered across the globe, in countries such as Israel, Canada, Australia or here in the United States, where approximately still 1,400 people are eligible for benefits under this scheme. In addition to providing material assistance, the Dutch government funds a number of organizations that specialize in non-material assistance for war victims, for example psycho-social help.

But as all of us here today are aware, we seem not to have learnt our lesson from the Second World War. People still oppress others and people are still forced to flee their homes or live in hiding, terrified that they will be killed or beaten or locked up because of their race, religion or their beliefs. Knowing what happened during the Second World War and understanding the background of what made such a chain of events possible, enables one to follow present developments critically, to reflect on one's own behavior and if necessary to change it. For the main thing for all of us, young and old, is to remain alert. That is why the Dutch government encourages and supports projects that inform young people about the Second World War. We fund information campaigns and have made them standard policy. Over the years a variety of activities have been organized to tell young people about the events that took place during the war and the lessons that can be drawn from them.

Memorial centers and museums have been set up at various sites in the Netherlands which have a special significance relating to the Second World War. They provide information on the Second World War in general, and on the events that took place especially on that site, providing a direct link for present-day visitors to the history of the Second World War. The centers receive government funding to maintain their facilities for the public at large. They may use this grants for maintenance, conservation and so forth, but a substantial share must be spent on educational activities focusing on the Second World War and the events leading up to it in relation to contemporary human rights violations and instances of discrimination. I shall briefly mention a few of the many activities organized by museums and schools.

-One project has been set up whereby people tell school children about their wartime experiences. The guest lecturer's account is then used as a starting point for a discussion on discrimination, racism and intolerance.

-Another project centers on monuments. Classes at about 1,000 schools have "adopted" over 650 war and resistance monuments. The aim is to tell the children about the event that "their" monument commemorates, and to make them understand its relevance today.

-Yet another project encourages schools to arrange museum outings for their pupils. Since the project started, an average of 10,000 pupils visit a war or resistance museum each year.

And of course we have our yearly Day of Remembrance on the fourth of May. And I am happy to say that young people take part in the commemoration programs that day, all over the country. Many of them feel such a special day of remembrance makes people think about current events, racism today, and developments in other parts of the world, and therefore highlights the importance of the Dutch Constitution and a democratic political system.

War museums in the Netherlands work hand in hand with similar organizations abroad. The government encourages these partnerships not simply because they are intrinsically valuable, but also to extend the scope of Dutch policy on information campaigns. Because the Netherlands -like many other countries- is becoming increasingly multicultural, the Ministry of Health, Welfare and Sport has recently chosen to broaden its approach to youth education on the Second World War to include present day forms of discrimination. This principle and practice are probably also familiar to other countries. We are particular interested in the way authorities and organizations in your countries have developed your information campaigns, the methods you use, the targets you have set and the results you have managed to achieve. Recent study in France, Germany, Belgium and Denmark has taught us the value of changing ideas on this subject.

Ladies and gentlemen,

Let us never forget the victims. A time may come when they will be a part of world history, but we must never allow them simply to be consigned to the past. We are morally obliged to keep their memory alive and to keep reflecting upon the moral questions raised by the Holocaust and upon our responsibilities as citizens of democratic nations. The session of today will provide us a unique forum in which we can exchange ideas as to what should happen to achieve these goals. Hopefully it's start of working together as countries to keep the memory alive and to educate our youngsters.

Dr. Adolphe Steg

DEPUTY CHAIRMAN,
FACT-FINDING MISSION ON THE LOOTING OF JEWISH ASSETS
(MATTÉOLI COMMISSION)
FRANCE

Remembrance and Education

Break-out Session: Overview of the Importance of Holocaust
Education, Remembrance and Research

I would like to describe how France is assuming the double responsibility of memory and of transmission. Today, in France, teaching about the Holocaust is largely organized and overseen by the government. This has not always been the case, however. Initially, the decimated, ravaged, and exsanguine Jewish community itself was able to put memory to use. In April 1943 in Grenoble, occupied at the time by Italian troops, Isaac Scheerson and some friends established the Center for Contemporary Jewish Documentation (CDJC) in order to collect the documents of persecution.

At the Liberation, Leon Poliakov and George Wellers, the directors of the CDJC at the time, established substantial archives, particularly those of the SS and of the Gestapo in France. In 1946, the CDJC published *The Jewish World,* the first journal in the world entirely devoted to the Shoah.

The Center's documentation was a major source for Leon Poliakov *Breviary of Hatred* which was translated worldwide, as well as for Joseph Billig's monumental work on the *Central Commissariat for Jewish Questions.*

In 1958, the Memorial to the Unknown Jewish Martyr (MMIJ) was unveiled, the first and long, the only building in the world which included in a single setting a memorial, an archival center, a library and a permanent exhibit. From 1956 on, the Memorial and the CDJC were the principal sources for research and teaching about the Holocaust.

The CDJC is not the sole commemorative site. Nearly 76,000 Jews were deported in France and only 2500 returned. At the war's end, the survivors were determined to set the memory of those who had been massacred in stone. The numbers of plaques, steles, and monuments erected to the memory of survivors on buildings, schools and children's homes from which Jews had been wrenched, as well as on the internment camps where they had been grouped before being deported, are too numerous to be individually cited here.

In 1978, Serge Klarsfeld published *his Memorial of the Deportation*, a major work on the Shoah. This work not only carefully inventories the names of deportees, but also serves as a tomb for all those who have disappeared, often without a trace. As early as 1954, a "National Day of Deportation " to the memory of political, resistance, and racial deportees was established. But it was only in 1990, that an essential step was taken: The French Government acknowledged the genocide and Vichy's responsibility for the persecution of Jews in France. A National Day of Commemoration of racist and anti-Semitic persecutions was decreed on February 3, 1993, and set for the anniversary of the Winter Velodrome round-up, on the Sunday following July 16. On this day, an official ceremony was organized in Paris as well as in cities all over France that were also requested to set commemorative plates to the racial and anti-Semitic persecutions of 1940 and 1944. The State thus initiated a deliberate policy of placing commemorative plates and erecting monuments.

Here we might mention the sites of the principal monuments.

- The camp at Drancy, just outside of Paris.
- The Winter Velodrome, inaugurated by President Francois Mitterand and Prime Minister Edouard Balladur.
- The more recent monument at Izieu, in the Ain Department, where 44 children, their school director, and their teachers were rounded up by Klaus Barbie's Gestapo.

Last, the historic speech made by President Jacques Chirac on July 16 is a major part of this process. He emphasized his concern to see France make its contribution to memory and to history and to accept responsibility for the Vichy Government's role in carrying out the anti-Jewish measures adopted during the German Occupation. Finally, with respect to those Jews who did not return, the President declared, "We have an imprescriptible debt. To acknowledge past errors, and the errors committed by the Government, to hide nothing of the somber hours of our history is quite simply to defend the idea of humanity, of human liberty and of human dignity."

As we can see, the Government's creation of these memorials throughout France and these moments punctuating the calendar year mark the memory of the Holocaust.

The transmission of memory, however, is first and foremost based on teaching in the schools. For the last 20 years or so, teaching about the genocide of the Jews and of the role and responsibility of the Vichy Government for the persecution of the Jews are part of the mandatory national school program. These subjects are taught at two different points in the national curriculum: First, in the 9th grade, when students are 14-15 years old and then in the senior year of high school, when students are 16-19 years old. In this way, every young French person knows something about the Holocaust, from an historical point of view. While we can, therefore, say that in France, we have the means to reach the Holocaust, we have not yet resolved the very difficult question of "how" to teach it, and more specifically, how to teach it to children. How can we describe an altogether singular phenomenon that is at once inexpressible, incomprehensible, and unthinkable?

First, this is a phenomenon for which there are no words. Manes Sperber illustrates this in his paraphrase of a traditional text in the liturgy of Whitsun:

> "Even if the firmament were made of parchment,
> And all the trees were pens,
> All of the seas filled with ink,
> > And every dweller on the earth a scribe
> > Writing day in and day out,
> > Never could the Holocaust be described,
> > This Jewish tragedy of our era and of times to come."

Shouldn't this eloquent text be set in exegue to every work that deals with genocide?

Second, the Holocaust is, by its nature, inconceivable. What can we tell children, when what was done goes beyond human understanding and cannot be grasped by the imagination? What can we tell them without making their blood run cold? These questions take on an even more painful acuity when we are talking to Jewish children. Children, to whom, for more than 3000 years on the eve of Passover, we have recounted the story of the Jews' suffering under Pharaoh and the miraculous flight from Egypt. But what shall we tell them when no miracle has occurred? The Red Sea. The red sea of Jewish blood did not open up to save the Jews and its waves did not come down to drown Jewish persecutors.

Third, teaching the Holocaust is incomprehensible. Every teacher is faced with a question that is asked over and over again: Why? Why the Jews? Why the Germans? Why God? Yes, why did God let this happen?

We do not emphasize these difficulties in order to diminish the importance of teaching the Holocaust, but rather because these particularities make this a subject unlike any other, which, in order to be taught, requires a specific pedagogy. Indeed, as teachers gain experience in teaching the Holocaust, their pedagogy will evolve.

I would like to offer some recommendations made by our teachers, based on their own experience. First of all, they consider that this teaching should not in preference be based on images. Children are stuffed with images on a daily basis; on television, they constantly see images of murders, blood, and bodies. The issue is not to speak to their eyes but to their hearts and to their minds.

Paradoxically, Claude Lanzmann's monumental and definitive work, *Shoah,* is often used in this context because this film shows neither blood nor cries, nor tears nor bodies. It shows only witnesses and through their testimony, we see what no image can show.

Isn't it enough, on occasion, to simply read a page of Serge Klarsfeld's *Memorial.* Take, for example, the Holz family, page 590. The parents were deported. Their children were sheltered in a children's home, but two years later were arrested and deported. Listen:

> Holz, David, 13 years old
> Holz, Joseph, 12 years old
> Holz, Jacques, 10 years old
> Holz, Myriam, 8 years old
> Holz, Paul, 6 years old
> Holz, Emmanuel, Barely 4 years old.

When were they deported? On July 31, 1944.

The Allies were about to enter Paris. The German Army used every means possible to resist their advance and despite this, even though there were not enough trains to carry German troops to the Western Front, the Germans did not hesitate to send one train eastwards, to Auschwitz.

Isn't this example the best illustration for the children of this unbelievable phenomenon; for the Germans, the destruction of the Jews took priority over everything else, even over victory. Doesn't this example lead to a consideration of the hundreds and hundreds, the thousands of children murdered by these beings bearing human faces without flagging or being revolted by their acts? Doesn't this example lead, at least for the oldest high school students, to thinking about these children, the young Holz children and their cohort of poor little Jewish children, denuded, terrorized, walking quickly towards the sites of their murder? And yet, they had children's eyes and cried children's tears.

Next recommendation this teaching should not be taking place solely in history classes. It should cut across disciplines and be referred to in literature classes, in geography classes, in classes on civic education, and on philosophy so that this expression of Andre Neher; in particular, might be dwelled upon: "The millenary adventure of the human spirit underwent a complete failure at Auschwitz."

Last, and this is the final particularity of this teaching, the goal is not simply to acquire a knowledge but to bear a moral message based on values, on the absolute value of human life and on the absolute value of human dignity. For, and with this we shall conclude, in the words of Jean-Louis Forges:

"After Auschwitz, it is not enough to teach about Auschwitz, we must teach against Auschwitz."

Rev. Dr. Remi E. Hoeckman, O.P.

SECRETARY, COMMISSION FOR RELIGIOUS RELATIONS WITH THE JEWS
THE HOLY SEE

Break-out Session: Overview of the Importance of Holocaust
Education, Remembrance and Research

The Holy See published on 16 March of this year a document
entitled *We Remember: A Reflection on the Shoah*. This document is
addressed to Catholics throughout the world, especially in countries far
removed, by geography and history, from the scene where the Shoah
took place. It invites everybody else to join them in remembering this
horrendous crime perpetuated by the Nazis against the Jews in Europe.

On the occasion of its publication, His Holiness Pope John Paul
II expressed his fervent hope that this document would enable memory to
play its necessary part in the process of shaping a future in which such a
tragedy will never again be possible.

On several occasions prior to the publication of this document,
Pope John Paul II was already very strong and clear on this point, but
especially on the occasion of a concert in commemoration of the Shoah
which took place in the Vatican on 7 April 1994. "We remember", His
Holiness affirmed, "but it is not enough that we remember", "we have a
commitment".

Part of this commitment is the Catholic Church's engagement in
a process of consciousness-raising and reflection on the Shoah, in
opposing attempts to deny the reality of the Shoah or to trivialize its
significance for the Jews, and in combating anti-Semitism. Hence the
publication by the Holy See of the document *We Remember*.

The Catholic Church wishes to remember, but it wishes to
remember with a purpose. The purpose of this document, therefore, is
primarily educational in that it helps people to reflect on the past in order
to draw from it the appropriate lessons for the present and for the future.
"For", as His Holiness has put it, "in our own day, regrettably, there are
many new manifestations of the anti-Semitism, xenophobia and racial
hatred which were the seeds of those unspeakable crimes. Humanity can
not permit all that to happen again" (7 April 1994).

With regard to "Holocaust Education" specifically, the Holy See
would like to point out that a great deal of work is being done in Catholic

education through the publication and distribution of relevant texts including the official documents of the Church [e.g. the Second Vatican Council's Declaration Nostra Aetate; the Guidelines and Notes published by the Holy See's Commission for Religious Relations with the Jews; the teaching of Pope John Paul II on the Shoah and anti-Semitism; statements made by the national Catholic hierarchies of many of the nations most deeply affected by the events of the Shoah], the revision of textbooks [cf. the content analysis studies of Catholic textbooks and manuals by Dr. Rose Thering O.P. (1960), Dr. Eugene J. Fisher (1976), Dr Philip A. Cunningham (1992), and update reports]; pertinent educational programs and the circulation of appropriate educational materials [for instance Notre Dame College in Manchester (New Hampshire) offers several undergraduate courses on the Shoah; resource materials such as "Facing History and Ourselves: Holocaust and Human Behaviour", developed by Margot Stern Storm and William S. Parsons, are used in the Catholic school system in the USA; the Sister Rose Thering Foundation at Seton Hall University each semester mails out 3,500 brochures on Holocaust Education to Catholic high schools and grade school principals; also the Sisters of Our Lady of Sion and their SIDIC Centers are doing a great deal of work in this field], and many other events, efforts and initiatives.

Most Catholic high school textbook series in this country include units on the Shoah. On a higher level, just to speak of institutions, there are many examples: The Institute for Jewish-Christian Studies at Seton Hall University (New Jersey) has been offering courses on the Shoah for decades; The National Catholic Center for Holocaust Education at Seton Hill College (Pennsylvania) was started over a decade ago; The Center for Christian-Jewish Understanding at Sacred Heart University in Fairfield (Connecticut); The joint Archdiocese of Washington–Anti-Defamation League–US Holocaust Memorial Museum project develops curricula for Holocaust Education in Catholic schools and religious education programs. Moreover, in many places Catholic communities join Jewish communities to remember the Shoah on Yom Hashoah each year, or organize special services or study sessions on this occasion. In this country, for instance, the Catholic Bishops' Conference in 1988 urged all parishes to include prayer for the victims of the Holocaust on the Sunday closest to Yom Hashoah.

Also in other countries serious efforts are being made in this regard, for example in Canada, Australia, Italy, Germany, Poland, France, the United Kingdom. In Italy, for instance, the SIDIC Center in Rome develops educational programs; initiatives taken by bodies such as

FIDAE (organization of Catholic teachers) touch schools in various parts of the country. In Poland, relevant materials are being translated into the Polish language and distributed. The Catholic "Center for Information, Meeting, Dialogue, Education and Prayer" in Auschwitz/Oswiecim assumes an important role in Holocaust Education, also internationally. In Germany, the Catholic Church has created a wide-spread network of adult education in which Christian-Jewish programs occupy a prominent place.

Nonetheless the efforts need to continue and the necessary "reception process", especially on the "grass roots" level, needs to be furthered, for an in-depth reflection on the Shoah reveals its fundamental cause, namely the fact that when society is stripped of respect for God it is also stripped of respect for man.

Prof. Yehuda Bauer

PROFESSOR, YAD VASHEM INSTITUTE
ISRAEL

On Holocaust Education

Break-out Session: Overview of the Importance of Holocaust
Education, Remembrance and Research

The basic question we face when we deal with Holocaust
education is - why deal with this particular Genocide rather than with any
other of a host of similar events in this or the previous centuries? The
answer of course is not that one should not deal with the other Genocides
- on the contrary, anyone dealing with the Holocaust must compare, and
must deal with the other tragedies as much as possible. But the basic
response to the challenge must be to understand that the Holocaust has
increasingly become, for the democratic world at least, a symbol of all
the other Genocides, for racism, anti-Semitism, hatred of foreigners,
ethnic cleansing, and mass destruction of humans by humans generally.
The reason for this is, possibly, that a vague realization is taking hold of
people that the Holocaust, the planned total annihilation of the Jewish
people at the hands of the Nazi regime, is both a Genocide like other
Genocides, and also an unprecedented event in human history, which
should serve as a warning to all of us.

The unprecedentedness of the Holocaust consists in the fact that
there are elements in it that are not found in other Genocides, whereas
there are no elements in all the other Genocides that cannot be found in
parallel events of this sort. For the sake of our argument, we are using the
definition of Genocide as it appears in the UN Convention of 1948,
although that definition may be subject to legitimate criticism. The
elements that are <u>not</u> unprecedented in the Holocaust are first and
foremost the suffering and pain endured by its victims. There can be no
gradation of suffering as between Jews, Roma ("Gypsies"), Russians,
Poles, or others who suffered under the Nazi regime. Individual suffering

is equal as between victims of torture, humiliation, deprivation, and death. But there are elements in the Holocaust that do not appear in the other cases, such as Rwanda, or the Genocide of the Armenians, or the auto-Genocide in Kampuchea, or with Native Americans, or others. First, there is the totality of the planned murder: every single individual defined by the Nazis as Jewish was to be murdered. Second, the globality: ultimately, every such individual all over the world was to be found, registered, dispossessed, humiliated, marked, arrested, concentrated, transported and killed. Third, whereas all other Genocides were committed with some kind of ideological rationalization and excuse, they all had a pragmatic basis of sorts. Ethnic groups were murdered because they were thought to be in the way of political programs, or military plans, or economic and social ideologies aimed at reorganizing society. With the Holocaust, the ideology was based on pure fantasy: an imagined world Jewish conspiracy to control the globe; the idea of Jewish "blood" contaminating and corrupting cultures, ritual murder accusations, and the like. One only needs to think of the fact that the German authorities in February 1943 took trained Jewish armament workers from their factories in the Berlin area, put them on trains and shipped them to Auschwitz to be killed - after the German defeat at Stalingrad, when they needed every pair of trained hands to produce arms. Fourth, the fact that the Jews were a very special group of people in Europe, the only non-Christian group at the time, who occupied a unique position in relation to Christianity. Christian civilization depended on their Scriptures on the one hand, and rejected them because of their refusal to accept the Christian Messiah on the other hand. Nineteen hundred years after the appearance of the Christian Savior, His people were murdered in Central Europe by baptized heathens. This creates a major problem for what is known as Christendom, even when most Christians never go to church; it parallels the unsolved problem for Jews, who consider their relation to the Deity to be a special one, and who have to ask why this tragedy was visited upon them, and what is its meaning, if any.

Yet on the other hand, as I said before, the Holocaust is a Genocide similar to others, and therefore can and must be dealt with in both its aspects: it's Jewish specificity - it happened to a specific people, for specific reasons, at a specific time; and in its universality - it symbolizes the mass evils we are all capable of. It can serve as a warning, so it should not become a precedent. Ultimately, the Holocaust challenges us to work towards a world in which these evils are dammed in, and perhaps, hopefully, possibly, prevented altogether. Anyone who wishes to project a pessimistic prognosis for the future will have an easy time of it; we have not learned much from the Holocaust, or any other similar tragedies; we have not established an international community that is capable of dealing with it, and so on. But there is an imperative for all of us: we must try and change that situation. Today, at least, governments and groups of governments are ashamed of what humans do, and one can see stirrings of international conscience. That is where we come in: we must engage in the most basic activity directed towards such a change: education, on all levels.

That in deed is what the Task Force for Remembrance, Education and Research is all about. It was established at the initiative of the Swedish government, in order to spread efforts at Holocaust Education worldwide. The governments of the United States and the United Kingdom responded, and then those of Germany and Israel. At this conference, the governments of Poland, the Netherlands and France also joined. The purpose of the Task Force is to design practical ways to teach young and old, to spread the knowledge that the example of the Holocaust shows the danger we all face because we are all of us capable of extreme evil; but we are also capable of preventing it, and behave in a way that is the exact opposite of what happened then. It is indeed absolutely essential that we emphasize the behavior of those few - pitifully few, to be sure, but yet there were many thousands of them - who saved and rescued at the risk of their own lives. They show that we can be different, and that it is a matter of environment, and most importantly, education, how we will act. For the first time in the history of mankind politicians, governments, got together to advance a specific educational project. We are all determined to do all we can to have this project continue as a permanent fixture: to provide a political umbrella to international educational efforts based on true cooperation. One should give full credit to the Swedish initiators of this project, who themselves are engaging in a massive educational effort in their own country, and provide a model that might well be imitated by others.

A historian is someone who not only analyzes history, which of course is his/her primary task, but also tells stories. So let me conclude by telling a true story. His name is Yankele Skorochod, and he is a carpenter in Tel-Aviv. He was born in a place called Novogrudek in what today is Belarus, and became a carpenter's apprentice. He then moved to a ghetto in a town called Baranovichi, and joined a group that planned an armed uprising. The uprising failed, it never took place. Yankele fled to a Belorussian graveyard in the town, where he was saved by a local gravedigger, who also showed him the way to the forest (that person is one of the about 16.000 people recognized by Yad Vashem as a Righteous Among the Nations). He followed the advice of his rescuer and wandered through the Belorussian forests in search of Soviet partisans. Luckily, he found a group that had been sent from Soviet-held territory through the lines, of some one hundred men. He made friends there with a Belorussian youth of his own age, whom he remembers as Ivan. The two friends were sent out, together with three others, to recover a machine-gun far in the enemy rear. They were told not to take food from the peasants, for fear the peasants would turn against the partisans. The young men-boys became very, very hungry. Ivan saw a tree with some fruit - they did not know what that fruit was. The others told him not to eat it, but Ivan was so famished that he disregarded the advice, climbed the tree, and ate the fruit. A few hours afterwards he came down with dysentery. Yankele, his best friend, took care of him. They hid in a barn in a small village, and tried to cure Ivan. They failed, and Ivan died in Yankele's arms, saying that Yankele had taken care of him more lovingly than Ivan's own mother had.

They had to bury Ivan. Yankele went into the village, and at gun-point he forced two candles and an old Russian Orthodox Bible (in Old Slavonic - Yankele could make out the letters) out from the reluctant peasants. Yankele, the carpenter, then fashioned a crude casket, and put an Orthodox type of cross on it. They put the body in, and lowered it into the ground. Then Yankele, the Jewish carpenter, lit the candles and read out from the Bible what he thought an Orthodox priest would have read. Then, silently, they started in their way back to their unit. They never found the machine-gun.

You must understand - Yankele was telling this story at Hebrew University, to my seminar. He is a heavy-set man, with large hands. He told his story haltingly, and we sat around in complete and stunned silence. When he finished, there was an oppressive silence in the room, and he was resting on his elbows staring at the table in front of him. Someone had to break the silence, and I was the teacher. So I asked him the most stupid question I could possibly have asked: Yankele, I said, why did you do it?

He stared at me, uncomprehendingly, and after a while he stammered: but...but...he would have done the same for me, had it been the other way round.

Ever since then, I have always considered myself a pupil of Yankele Skorochod. So, I think, should all of us who are venturing on this path of Holocaust education.

Stuart E. Eizenstat

UNDER SECRETARY OF STATE FOR ECONOMIC, BUSINESS AND
AGRICULTURAL AFFAIRS
UNITED STATES

Task Force on Holocaust Education, Remembrance and Research

Break-out Session: Goals of the Task Force for International
Cooperation on Holocaust Education, Remembrance, and Research

At the initiative of Swedish Prime Minister Goran Persson, the
Swedish, UK and U.S. governments, together with experts from our
countries, gathered in Stockholm last May to launch an unprecedented
initiative – The Task Force for International Cooperation on Holocaust
Education, Remembrance and Research. Our countries and many others-
– Germany among the first and most consistent-- have engaged in
Holocaust education efforts at home for many years. But this is the first
time that heads of government have agreed to cooperate directly with
others countries, through diplomatic and other channels, to strengthen
Holocaust education efforts on both sides of the Atlantic and beyond.

As Prime Minister Persson said so eloquently in May, and as did
our speakers on the first panel here at the Museum this morning,
Holocaust education and remembrance can help ensure that the crimes of
the Holocaust are never forgotten nor repeated. As this century comes to
a close and we enter the new millennium, our international cooperation
can encourage and reinforce work in many nations to strengthen
Holocaust education efforts, to create new ones and to finally begin such
efforts where they have been overlooked.

Sweden served commendably as Task Force Chairman from
May until September 25, when the U.S. assumed the Task Force
Chairmanship, which will pass to the UK in January 1999. On

September 25, Israel and Germany became members of the Task Force, and have already made valuable contributions.

On behalf of the Task Force, I would like to give special recognition to the Prime Minister of Sweden and his representatives on the Task Force, State Secretary Pär Nuder and Foreign Ministry Political Director Ulf Hjertonsson.   I wold also like to thank my Task Force colleagues from Germany, Israel, and the UK for the hard work they have put into this initiative these past months. Finally, I would also like to commend Professor Yehuda Bauer of Yad Vashem, one of the great Holocaust scholars and educators in the world, for his intellectual guidance as Personal Advisor to the Task Force.

During the U.S. tenure as Task Force Chairman, we have focused the initiative on a number of priority areas initially agreed in May.   These projects, some of which are work in progress to be completed in the first half of next year, are highlighted in the Task Force report that I present to you today.   Our hope is to give maximum exposure to this unique and innovative work before the many distinguished participants with us at this Conference.

Let me now present a very brief summary of each project that the Task Force has undertake to date.

First, Swedish Task Force representative have been leading an effort to assemble a catalog of Holocaust-related institutions and a survey to efforts currently underway in the field of Holocaust education around the world. This challenging task has begun in earnest, but is still in its early stages.   In the Task Force report you will find a brief paper introducing a preliminary directory of organizations engaged in Holocaust education and remembrance activities in a large number of countries. We expect that the directory of organizations engaged in Holocaust education and remembrance activities in a large number of countries.   We expect that the directory, itself a gold mine of information, will become the basis of a much more comprehensive survey of such efforts to be completed next year and to be made available internationally.

Second, as part of the Swedish government's Living History Initiative, Holocaust historian Paul Levine and Stephane Bruchfeld prepared a test on the Holocaust that could be made available to every family with high school children in Sweden. Their product, "Tell Ye Your Children," has been so well received in Sweden as to exceed all expectations.   There are now almost 800,000 copies of the book in circulation in that country of approximately 9 million people, making it the second most-widely owned book in Sweden after the Bible.   The book has been translated into the most common immigrant languages in Sweden to increase its accessibility to non-native Swedish speakers. At the request of the Task Force, the book's authors have created an insert demonstrating how an international version and individual national versions of the book can be prepared, should other counties choose to consider adapting it for their own use. Sweden has also completed a series of videotapes for use in their school system.

Third, the Chief Historians of the U.S. Department of State and the British Foreign and Commonwealth Office will produce, at the request of the Task Force, a guide to finding and using Holocaust-related archives with the intention that it be employed as a tool by researchers and educators. The recent opening of archives bearing on the Holocaust, and in particular those related to Nazi gold and other looted assets, have made accessible millions of pages of material recent years and have had an important impact on our collective knowledge about the Holocaust. Making these archives more accessible is a central goal of the Task Force. Contained in this report is a brief proposal as to how activities in this area should proceed over the next year – highlighting in particular a website which is becoming a nexus of information for research in virtually every dimension of the Holocaust-era assets issues discussed at the London and Washington Conferences.

Fourth, in close consultation with Yad Vashem and U.S. Holocaust Memorial Museum, the UK has led the effort to develop a set of internationally applicable guidelines, or best practices, for use in teaching about the Holocaust. In crafting the guidelines, the Task Force looked to those institutions with the most extensive experience in navigating the difficult waters of teaching this emotionally charged and intellectually taxing subject. The guidelines are intended to facilitate the work of educators both in places where programs exist and in those where they are yet to be developed. They are based on the experiences, both positive and negative, of two generations of Holocaust educators.

Fifth, the Task Force has considered and accepted a British proposal to encourage each of our nations to designate a Day of Remembrance for Holocaust Victims. In Israel and the United States, Yom HaShoa serves this purpose. In Germany, January 27, the day of the liberation of Auschwitz, is recognized. Other Task Force member countries will designate a day of their choosing on which to honor the memory of those who perished, and we will all make a concerted effort to ensure that our government employees and societies as a whole are aware of the day and recognize it appropriately. We hope other nations will designate their own Day of Remembrance as well. These acts of remembrance will reinforce awareness of the event of the Holocaust and reach a large audience, while demonstrating solidarity in the fight against anti-Semitism, racism, prejudice, persecution, and hatred.

In addition to the projects I have already listed, the Task Force has made commitments in the form of two declarations: one concerning archival openness and the other the promotion of Holocaust education efforts. We invite all Washington Conference governments to join us in endorsing these goals. The Task Force Declaration on the opening of Holocaust-relevant archives presents as our aim the opening of "all public and private bearing on the Holocaust and the fate of Nazi-confiscated assets by December 31, 1999." We call on all who posses such material to open it to as many researchers as possible on an urgent basis and commit ourselves a governments to do everything possible to ensure that this important target is met.

The second declaration and final element of the Task Force to the Conference emphasizes our common conviction that urgent international attention to paid to Holocaust education, remembrance and research to reinforce and spread the historic meaning and enduring lessons of that tragic event. In the declaration we commit our governments to "reinforce Holocaust education, remembrance and research in our own countries, with a special focus on our own countries' histories." We also pledge to strengthen existing programs or launch new ones, and encourage other countries to do likewise.

We have pledged our governments' commitment to this endeavor, and to our intergovernmental cooperation to advance its objectives, principally to ensure that the lessons of the Holocaust are not forgotten and its horrors never repeated. We have full confidence that when the U.S. chairmanship concludes at the end of the month, the UK will serve the Task Force admirably in the role of Chairman. We furthermore hope that Conference participants will find the report of the Task Force a valuable and useful contribution to the cause of Holocaust education, remembrance and research.

Most important, whether by working with us through the Task Force or through other mechanisms, we hope that all countries represented at the Washington Conference will choose to embrace our goals and strengthen their Holocaust education and remembrance efforts. Because our effort is an inclusive one, we also urge other countries to consider working directly with us in the Task Force. Nothing could be more important than to honor the many victims and to prevent such tragedies in the future.

Mr. Pär Nuder

STATE SECRETARY, PRIME'S MINISTER'S OFFICE
SWEDEN

Break-out Session: Goals of the Task Force for International Cooperation on Holocaust Education, Remembrance, and Research

Mr. Chairman, Ladies and Gentlemen:

The book that you have in front of you, *Tell ye your children...* forms the core of the Swedish information campaign about the Holocaust. On page 50 you will find two pictures.

One shows a group of naked women huddled close together as they line up. Some are holding children in their arms. Although the Pietum is indistinct, you can see, you can sense, the fear in their eyes.

The other picture shows the same group of women. this time lying dead in a heap. Among the dead bodies a small head is sticking out. One child remains alive. His executioner stands close by, rifle raised.

This child, perhaps aged two or three, could have been your child or grandchild.

These terrible events, which took place fifty years ago on the continent of Europe, must never ever be repeated. The Nazi crimes against humanity must never ever happen again.

Motivated by this conviction, the Swedish Government, supported by broad political consensus, initiated the information campaign known as *Living History.*

So far more than 500,000 households have ordered the book *Tell ye your children..* to help adult members of the family pass on knowledge about the Holocaust to the younger generation. 800,000 copies of the book have been distributed. Extrapolated to an equivalent number of families in Great Britain, this equals 2.5 million books. In the US this would be 10 million copies. 100,000 people have visited the Living History Web site. 1000 schools have shown movies offered as part of the information campaign.

By choosing active dialogue instead of passive silence, we decided to initiate a discussion of ways to develop democracy, strengthening its powers of resistance, and increasing our understanding of the challenges to it. We wanted to make everyone aware of the negative forces behind the Holocaust.

The Nobel Laureate Elie Wiesel once said that it is necessary to remember, because if we forget the crimes of the past we are doomed to repeat them. He meant that if one group of people can be killed, any group of people can be killed.

He was right of course, democracy gives life its moral purpose. It is built an understanding and, awareness, It rests on the tacit agreement that we all try to live by the set of values which it represents.

To cite the words of British Prime Minister, Tony Blair, in another context. Our society, he said, rests on,

"A set of values- A belief in society. In co-operation. In achieving what we are unable to achieve alone. It is how I try to live my life. The simple truths. I am worth no more than anyone else. I am my brother's keeper. I will not walk by on the other side. We aren't simply people set in isolation from each other, face to face with eternity, but members of the same family, community, the same human race."

Mr. Chairman,

These simple truths - so simple, so difficult to live up to.

Democracy is vulnerable if we forget.

We must fight ignorance with facts and knowledge.

We must tell its story, We must repudiate without compromise every new manifestation that violates democracy and human dignity. We must summon the courage to be clear and resolute.

This responsibility lies with each and everyone of us who has children. Our parents know and have told us. If we don't remember, if we don't have the strength, if we don't have the courage - then we have failed those who died and those who survived. Then we will fail coming generations.

The Swedish *Living History* project used the exhortation in the Old Testament as the title of the book which has become the symbol of the project: "Tell ye your children of it, and let your children tell their children, and their children another generation."

In response to the immensely positive reaction to Prime Minister Persson's initiative on Holocaust education the Task Force for International Cooperation on Holocaust Education, Remembrance and Research was established in Stockholm in May of this year. It is a platform for international cooperation to spread knowledge about the Holocaust. This group will continue its work, in particular this conference has acted as an important stimulus for further action.

Mr. Chairman,

In a year's time, mankind will enter a new millennium. We are leaving the 20th century and entering the 21st.

What can we learn from the past?

What should we leave behind us 'in the old millennium?

What fundamental values should we take with us into the new age?

We need to discuss these issues – as individuals, as human beings, as parents.

We live in an age of rapid transition, Information hurtles around the globe at the speed of light. In an age such as this we all need basic values: founded upon simple truths. Simple truths such as, I am worth no more than anyone else.

No single event can never replace the need for a constant dialogue about values and ideas, about right and wrong. But as the present millennium, which gave us the darkest event in the history of mankind, the Holocaust, draws to an end we should let the new millennium begin with an event that contains a bright and hopeful message of humanism. We need an event that deals with the past in a way that will prevent us from repeating its horrors.

Mr. Chairman,

On behalf of Prime Minister Persson and the Swedish Government I would like to extend an invitation to governments, institutions, NGOs and experts dedicated to Holocaust education to attend an international conference in Stockholm on Holocaust Education, Remembrance and Research at the turn of the millennium.

This conference will be held under the auspices of high-ranking political, civic and religious leaders and be devoted to all aspects of Holocaust Education, Remembrance and Research. Politicians, historians, educators, curators, artists, authors and other experts shall meet in work-shops and seminars to discuss how they can contribution to Holocaust education, and to share their experiences. I propose that the Task Force serve as a kind of preparatory committee for this conference on Holocaust Education in Stockholm,

The aim of the Stockholm Conference will be to manifest our common commitment to teaching our children that there is always a choice, there is always an alternative. It is our responsibility to endow them with the ability to distinguish between good and evil.

I would like to conclude by quoting one of the finest educators of young children - Swedish author Astrid Lindgren, "mother" of Pippi

Longstocking and Karlsson on the Roof. Through her characters, she has untiringly taught children about the right choices in the complex world of adults, adults who sometimes fail to fulfill a child's expectations of care and guidance.

"Sometimes we have to do things, even though we don't really dare. Otherwise we aren't human, just a speck of dirt."

Thank you.

Dr. Avner Shalev

CHAIRMAN OF THE DIRECTORATE, YAD VASHEM
ISRAEL

Break-out Session: Goals of the Task Force for International
Cooperation on Holocaust Education, Remembrance, and Research

The International Task Force on Holocaust Education, Remembrance and Research, was established at the initiative of the Swedish Government. It is an exciting new undertaking which the Delegation of Israel, a member of the Task Force, enthusiastically supports.

Yad Vashem, in co-ordination with other Israeli institutions dealing with the legacy of the Holocaust, looks forward to sharing with other countries the experience it has gained over several decades and agrees to coordinate future international meetings of educational experts, with the Task Force.

Yad Vashem will cooperate with the Task Force in its efforts to spread programs on Holocaust education through the Internet and other media and will put the educational principles developed in Israel, (including those achieved at its international teacher training courses) at the Task Force's disposal.

We welcome the idea put forward by the United Kingdom to establish a national day in every country to commemorate the Shoah.

We add our voice to those who believe that the Holocaust, because of its Jewish specificity, should serve as a model in the global fight against the dangers of racism, anti-Semitism, ethnic hatred and genocide.

Together with our fellow Task Force members, Israel will do its utmost to advance our common goals in this important and promising endeavor.

Dr. Albert Spiegel
DEPUTY HEAD, CULTURAL SECTION, FOREIGN OFFICE
GERMANY

Break-out Session: Goals of the Task Force for International
Cooperation on Holocaust Education, Remembrance, and Research

This conference deals with the most terrible chapter of German history: the Holocaust, the persecution and extermination of European Jews by the National Socialists. I welcome the fact that this task force has been set up within this conference to deal with the important problem of how the Holocaust can be portrayed above all to young people more than 50 years after the end of National Socialism.

Today's democratic Germany admits full responsibility for the guilt which Germans burdened themselves with during the years of National Socialist control of large parts of Europe and their own country. Hence, imparting knowledge of the terrible events of this period to today's and future young generations is an indispensable task of the education system.

Today's Germans cannot draw a line under the past. We can only learn from it and thereby ensure that such a crime does not happen again.

We gladly accepted the invitation for Germany to participate in establishing international cooperation in imparting knowledge of the Holocaust. In Germany, we also see this as significant recognition of our long-standing efforts to make teaching about the Holocaust a focal point of the educational work on the agendas of the German federal states responsible for education as well as the related areas of general youth work, adult education, teaching about memorials and educational research.

1. What could be the aim and object of increased international cooperation over and above the initial steps which have already been taken in this area?

The imparting of knowledge of the Holocaust is a topic which each country must approach in a particular way. Israel, as the country built up by survivors of the Holocaust, and Germany, as the country where the Holocaust started and which today bears responsibility for it, inevitably have to tackle this question differently from countries which were less or only indirectly involved. In Germany, we face the challenge of teaching young people about crimes of which their forefathers were either perpetrators or passive observers.

The Holocaust raises questions which are crucial for every civilization and every culture. Why did civilized, often educated people become murderers? How did an effective and modern state machinery come to be abused as an almost perfect instrument of state mass murder? Why did a whole country, and to a certain extent neighboring countries, turn a blind eye?

An important task for all of us today is to find answers to such questions and draw conclusions for our future together.

The differing situations of countries as they approach the issue of Holocaust education are reason enough for fruitful international cooperation. It would be important to devise joint programs for young people from different countries who, on meeting others, would have the opportunity to exchange their various national viewpoints. What possibilities would be opened up by organizing teacher training in this field at international level? If Holocaust education is viewed as a truly international task, then we must learn from one another and with one another.

The original scenes of the Holocaust, in Germany and the neighboring countries to the east, are to be included directly in teaching. More intensive use should be made of teaching about memorials within the framework of international cooperation. As well as imparting knowledge, carefully prepared bilateral or multilateral events at the places themselves could be useful for portraying the essential emotional elements of the Holocaust subject.

Vast opportunities are contained in the initiative to make Holocaust education an international issue. International cooperation should aim to complement national programs and add to them what can only evolve from different countries comparing views. I am thinking here, for example, of jointly devising and coordinating curricula and programs which reflect the various national perceptions.

Much has already been done to this end in Germany, for example in the development of new schoolbooks in cooperation with experts form Israel and Poland. During bilateral German-Israeli talks on schoolbooks, the Georg Eckert Institute for International Textbook Research in Braunschweig, whose first series was completed in 1985, aimed to develop guidelines for the portrayal of "the other side" in schoolbooks. Events following the Holocaust, in particular German-Israeli relations as a whole, are also outlined. The aim is to make it possible for today's children and young people in both countries to have the same unprejudiced knowledge of the Holocaust, as well as of other aspects of their common history.

2. As we deal with the Holocaust, we also have to ask ourselves what we want to achieve amongst the people of today who are living more than fifty years after the crimes of National Socialism and who are quite often more interested in other things.

I would like to focus briefly on Germany in particular with its specific situation. In Germany today, we have a generation which no longer feels directly involved with the crimes which took place in their grandparents' and great-grandparents' time. Nowadays, young Germans want to be regarded for the most part as normal Europeans but see over and over again that the word "German" triggers associations with National Socialism. Holocaust education has been a part of all school curricula for decades, just as visits to memorial sites have been. The Day to commemorate the victims of National Socialism on January 27 (the liberation of Auschwitz) and the night of the pogrom on November 9 are dates of remembrance all over Germany.

And yet in Germany today, just as in other European countries, there are some young people who feel attracted by extreme right sometimes anti-Semitic ideas, and believe they provide the answers to today's problems.

In teaching about the Holocaust, it is not a question of bare facts; it is a question of imparting to people the fathomlessness of a crime planned at state level, a crime that few teachers are able to understand properly nowadays. It is also a question of drawing upon the personal experience of the students. In Germany this now includes contact with fellow citizens of foreign origin as well as the experience of a globalized culture and economy.

It must also be remembered that in one part of our country, the former GDR, the biased analysis of the National Socialism period centered for forty years on the persecution of political, and above all communist, opponents of National Socialism. The collapse of communism has left a particular void of values there.

3.   When speaking of the possibilities of international cooperation on the question of Holocaust education, we must also consider the qualitative aspect. Imparting knowledge of such a unique crime must not be ticked off as material for lessons, or a burdensome duty. Education about the Holocaust remains ineffective unless teachers manage to portray the deep emotional side of the Holocaust as well as the feeling for the unwarranted, dreadful suffering of millions of victims. And of course it also depends on the environment for teaching about the

Holocaust. What do parents say and think of the problem, what influences have youth culture trends? How does it happen that many young people feel it is somehow "cool" to express ideas on the far right of the political spectrum? These trends can be seen the world over, and I believe this to be an obvious starting point for international cooperation on teaching about the Holocaust. Because it is not just lack of knowledge of the facts of the Holocaust which leads to people's indifferent attitude to events. Now and then, there is also the view that the Holocaust is history while we ourselves live in the present. This is a point for our efforts to start.

It also must not be forgotten that teaching about the Holocaust cannot be better than general standards of education and of imparting knowledge and values in a particular country. We have all heard the discussions on the quality of education which have been going on in many countries for years. It is important that general education furthers the aims of the rule of law, human rights and tolerance.

We ought to try to make a valuable contribution to this general discussion through international cooperation on Holocaust education.

Today in Germany there is a whole array of projects, initiated by schools and young people to increase understanding of the Holocaust and show its repercussions up to the present day. Many of these projects are transmitted all over the world via the Internet. Schoolchildren in Berlin have tackled the topic of the synagogue destroyed in 1938. Students in East Frisia are carefully examining how the often difficult and yet periodically positive coexistence of Jews and Christians in their town has evolved over the centuries. Other young people erect or maintain memorials in their local area. The Action Reconciliation Service for Peace which has been working closely for many years with Israeli partners organizes many encounters for young people from both countries.

There is a common element in all these examples: they link the portrayal of the local area, of the attachment to the town or area in which the children or young people grow up, with the portrayal of the negative events that belong to the area. I know that many people who otherwise show little interest in the Holocaust are very upset when they realize that such crimes did not take place just anywhere but rather in their town, in their street or perhaps even in their own house. In Berlin, schoolchildren have put up names of murdered Jewish citizens on the houses where they once lived. That is both education and remembrance which touches many. And it also shows that Jewish life and Jewish culture was not out of place in Germany as the National Socialists maintained, rather an integral part of our own German history and culture; but at the same time, also an autonomous cultural world, to which Germany owed a great deal. I believe that anyone who grasps and accepts this has drawn one of the most important lessons from the Holocaust: Christian and Jewish people have lived side by side in Germany for centuries. Viewing the historical roots of the incomprehensible can also help explain on the one hand why the Holocaust was able to happen in Germany and on the other hand why it is so difficult to understand.

Such projects carried out in Germany offer a range of possibilities for cooperation with other countries. Examples can already be identified. In the large Jewish graveyard in Berlin-Weißensee, German, Israeli and Polish young people work together on the upkeep of graves. Particularly in the field of German-Polish relations, there is a whole array of similar programs.

We have already done a lot in Germany. But I also know that the issue of the Holocaust will persist for a long time. Holocaust education also has a topical dimension. Children and young people should be brought up to cope responsibly with freedom, to be tolerant, to have a peaceful attitude towards other people and respect others in a spirit of international understanding. Only such an attitude guarantees that a crime such as the Holocaust can never be repeated.

This conference could help us to find new ways of doing this.

4. The basis of all education about the Holocaust is the existence of scientifically supported, high-quality materials. In Germany, our vast range of documentation and teaching material is constantly expanded also using modern methods of communication. The discoveries made by extensive Holocaust research carried out at universities, institutes and other research centers in Germany influence the further development of the curricula directly through teacher training and new editions of textbooks.

Perhaps our long experience and the discoveries made from teaching the children and grandchildren of the generation in whose younger days the atrocities actually took place could serve as an example and a stimulus for education in your country.

On behalf of Germany, I can assure you that we are keen to work actively in the task force and in so doing hope to make a further contribution to strengthening tolerance and human rights for the future.

Ms. Regina Wyrwoll
HEAD OF MEDIA DIVISION, GOETHE-INSTITUT, MUNICH
GERMANY

Learning from History: The Nazi Era and the Holocaust in German Education
A CD-ROM edited by Annette Brinkmann, Annegret Ehmann, Sybil Milton, Hanns.Fred Rathenow, and Regina Wyrwoll

Break-out Session: Best Practices and Future Projects in Holocaust Education, Remembrance and Research: Remembrance

The CD-ROM "Learning from History" presents (both in English and in German) 50 projects that show the varieties of ways that the Holocaust is taught in Germany's sixteen states since 1990. The fifty projects were selected from an extensive survey of Holocaust education activities in Germany. These projects originated in primary and secondary schools, special classes for the learning-disabled, in programs for apprentices in trade and commercial schools, at memorial sites and foundations.

The CD-ROM, unique in the world, provides insights into best practices in classrooms and independent programs for youth in contemporary Germany.

The CD-ROM provides a significant view of how the history of the Holocaust is taught in contemporary Germany. It thus offers North American teachers a rich range of ideas and strategies for helping young people understand the historical facts and continuing significance of Holocaust education in the world of today and tomorrow.

This survey is especially important because it allows North American teachers to enter into direct dialogue with their German counterparts.

Most projects focus on the fate of the Jews in Germany. Nevertheless, there are also projects about the fate of the disabled, Gypsies (Roma/Sinti), the White Rose resistance movement, perpetrator biographies, and postwar trials. The projects include children's music at Theresienstadt ("Brundibar"), songs of the political resistance written in the early concentration amps ("The Peat Bog Soldiers"), student literary texts after a visit to the memorial at Natzweiler-Struthof, plays about Janusz Korczak and deportation to Auschwitz performed by students, and materials about the treasury and tax departments' role in the persecution of Jews. There are also projects about archeological digs by students at the Bergen-Belsen, Buchenwald, and Sachsenhausen memorials, as well as apprentice stonemasons and construction workers assisting in the repair and restoration of buildings at the Sachsenhausen memorial.

The projects are interdisciplinary, combining history, German language and literature, social studies, music, art, law, and ethics, originating in formal classroom instruction and students activities in independent projects in non-school settings. The CD-ROM includes the teacher's lesson plan and reports as well as student products (artwork, literary and historical texts, theater and musical pieces, videos made by students), extracts from memoirs written by victims and survivors, as well as interrogations from postwar trials.

The CD-ROM contains extensive supplementary materials, including maps, a list of memorials, a glossary of historical terms, addresses of all institutions in Germany that deal with Holocaust education, lists of media available for teachers for use in schools, and a bilingual booklet with background about the German educational system and how to use the CD-ROM.

A complementary website will be launched by Spring 1999 with information about significant new projects, activities, current and planned exhibitions in Germany, as well as links to existing websites at German and foreign institutions that provide or produce significant material for Holocaust education.

Scholarly advisory groups from both Germany and the United States have overseen the projects, including Annegret Ehmann (House of the Wannsee Conference), Professor Hanns-Fred Rathenow (Institute for Didactics, Technical University Berlin), Sybil Milton (former Senior Historian at the United States Holocaust Memorial Museum). The CD-ROM was tested by North American teachers and benefited greatly from scholarly expertise provided by the Association of Holocaust Organizations and the U.S. Holocaust Memorial Museum in Washington D.C.

The CD-ROM has been produced with the support from the Archive for Cultural Policy, Bonn, The Fund for Cultural Education, Bonn, The Goethe-Institut, Munich, The Robert Bosch Foundation, Stuttgart, and the Press and Information Office of the German Federal Government, Bonn.

Mr. Kenneth Jacobson

ASSISTANT NATIONAL DIRECTOR, ANTI-DEFAMATION LEAGUE
UNITED STATES

ADL's Holocaust Programming: Education, Reconciliation, Atonement

Break-out Session: Best Practices and Future Projects in Holocaust Education, Remembrance and Research: Remembrance

In a society and Jewish community where there is a large amount of activity concerning the Holocaust, ADL tries to focus its work on those areas which are consistent with the mission of the organization and which reflect and intermesh with our programmatic strengths in other areas.

ADL's mission for 85 years has been to fight anti-Semitism and to combat other forms of hatred. Our Holocaust programs serve to meet those challenges, educating how the history of anti-Semitism culminated in the Shoah and how this tragic history has relevance to broader issues of bias and intolerance in today's world.

ADL's Holocaust programming is filtered through our **Braun Holocaust Institute**. Education, remembrance and research are the three major facets of the Institute, and they are carried out in conjunction with and strengthened by a unique range of institutional programs including ADL's Youth Services, our Interfaith Affairs and our Civil Rights work.

The work of the **Braun Holocaust Institute** utilizes the professional and lay leadership services of its 31 Regional Offices across the U.S. and in Austria and Israel. Thus, the Holocaust Institute is able to outreach and effectively channel its centralized services and programs to serve the needs and interests of a particular community.

Programmatically, the work of the **Braun Holocaust Institute** takes several approaches emphasizing the strengths of ADL.

EDUCATION OF YOUNG STUDENTS

The ADL's Youth Programs including A World of Difference and Children of the Dream (which brings Ethiopian Jews from Israel to meet with inner city youngsters) target high school age youth. Across the U.S., thousands of teachers and students (through peer training) and teachers through (Train the Trainer Programs) incorporate Holocaust Education as a significant component in lessons on anti-bias. Through one chapter in the Anti-Bias Curriculum, through supplementary holocaust discussion and curriculum guides, films, and first hand survivor testimony, the Braun Holocaust augments the work of these programs by demonstrating the lessons of the Holocaust as one extreme manifestation of hate.

Particularly successful is the National Youth Mission to Washington, D.C. This program combines the work of community service, civil rights, Holocaust education and diversity anti-bias programs by bringing together 80 students from around the U.S., students of a diverse ethnic and racial background to the USHMM in Washington, D.C. For four days they not only learn about the Holocaust, but they learn about its lessons and relevance to contemporary society.

INTERFAITH

ADL's interfaith programs, both in the U.S. and abroad, have particular strength in training Christian teachers and seminarians about the way to educate about Judaism in order to reduce and eliminate religious anti-Semitism. Our Holocaust programming takes advantage of these strengths by developing services, commemorations and symposiums stressing atonement, reconciliation, and coalition building.

While acknowledging the silence of most of the world, rare acts of courage on the part of individuals and nations are remembered through programs from **The Jewish Foundation for Christian Rescuers**. For example, the National Holocaust commemoration program "From Shoah to New Life: Honoring Italian Rescuers" (Last year, honored Albanian Rescuers.) Each year this program, along with "Courage to Care" commemoration will look at the rare and noble Christians and Moslems who assisted Jews during the Holocaust...individuals who made a difference.

A particularly impressive interfaith effort regarding the Holocaust is ADL's 'Bearing Witness Program.' This program targets

Catholic School educators and works in conjunction with the USHMM, The National Conference of Bishops, and The National Catholic Education Association. For five days Catholic teachers from all over the U.S. came to D.C. to learn about ways they can implement Holocaust education in their schools and community. In addition to providing overall instruction on the Holocaust, the content of this program is geared specifically to the needs and interests of parochial school teachers and students. It sees the Holocaust in the context of Christian anti-Semitism and other biases. It is a program which reflects the vast improvement in Catholic-Jewish relations (such a program could not have happened decades ago), and fosters continued openness.

EDUCATION OF COLLEGE STUDENTS

ADL has extensive programs around the country to help students, faculty, and administrators deal with anti-Semitism and bias. Our Holocaust programming directs itself to editors of campus newspapers who are repeatedly confronted by efforts of Holocaust deniers to get their hateful message to the students. While being a staunch defender of free speech, ADL makes clear to editors that they are under no First Amendment obligation to publish advertisements advocating denial of the Holocaust, which are intrinsically hateful and inaccurate. In our further effort to educate editors, we sponsor an annual Mission to Israel, which includes a stop in Poland to experience first-hand the camps where Jews were murdered.

CIVIL RIGHTS AND HOLOCAUST DENIAL

A major task of ADL's civil rights programs is to prevent extremist, anti-Semitic groups from gaining credibility and legitimacy. We recognize that a major obstacle to the resurgence of Nazism and Fascism over the past 50 years has been the taint of the Holocaust. Extremist groups see Holocaust denial as a key ingredient for their goal of renewed respectability; convince enough people that the Holocaust didn't happen and the road is open to winning renewed respectability. That is why we take seriously our work to combat Holocaust denial, including reports and investigations on the movement and the groups that foster it, as well as monitoring and countering such activity on the Internet.

THE JEWISH FOUNDATION FOR CHRISTIAN RESCUERS AND THE HIDDEN CHILD FOUNDATION

While keeping the focus of the Holocaust on its evil and the absence of enough courageous people to stand against the Nazis, we also try to impart the lessons of what happened when individuals acted to save Jews. We give a Courage to Care Award to highlight those who rescued. We have established a Sugihara Essay Writing contest, first in the New York City Publish School System, now in San Francisco and Japan, which looks at the example of the rescuer Chiume Sugihara and asks the students to look at their own lives and depict an occasion where they made a difference.

The Hidden Child Foundation brings together those survivors who had been hidden as children from the Nazis. Through the ADL Braun Institute, a National Speakers bureau has been formed and a Hidden Child Discussion Guide developed. The Foundation works with educators at Teacher Training and Student Workshops on the Holocaust and organized conferences and gatherings for Survivors and Second Generations.

PUBLICATIONS AND MATERIALS

Consistent with our broader educational effort, the Institute provides and develops a number of educational materials on the Holocaust including discussion guides, curriculums, and background primers. Dimensions: A Journal of Holocaust Studies reaches out to a broad community in providing a forum for debate on topics that are both controversial and extremely relevant to contemporary society. Each issue focuses on one aspect of the Holocaust – the churches, rescuing science, culture, historiography, etc. – and provides wide-ranging perspectives from top scholars and thinkers, which make for excellent educational tools in and out of the classroom.

A new vehicle to educate, is "The Lasting Impact of the Holocaust on the Arts," a series that seeks to spur a new public awareness of the Holocaust through presenting creative and artistic works of survivors, second generation, and others who are profoundly impacted by the Holocaust.

Educating about the Holocaust will be a continuous challenge as we move further and further away from that great tragedy. As one thoughtful political leader in Germany has recently said, we must find new and creative ways to teach each new generation as the years make for greater distance. We are committed to using the many strengths of ADL to participate in this challenging mission in the years ahead.

Kenneth Jacobson
Assistant National Director
Anti-Defamation League
823 United Nations Plaza
New York, NY 10017

Mrs. Vladka Meed
AMERICAN GATHERING OF JEWISH HOLOCAUST SURVIVORS

Life and Resistance during the Holocaust

Break-out Session: Best Practices and Future Projects in Holocaust Education, Remembrance and Research: Curricular Education

There is a growing awareness in our country, as well as in other countries, of the need to transmit the events and the lessons of the Holocaust to coming generations. More and more studies about our shattering past are making their way into the American public school system. And we, the survivors, the last eyewitnesses, are concerned. How will our people be remembered? Will history do them justice? Will myths and half-truths prevail? Or will the young only learn the frightening numbers of deaths, the clinical aspects of planned destruction? Or will they be able to see beyond the numbers of mass murders the victims as people -- as individuals who struggled to remain human in a world which was so inhuman? Will they be able to understand the life of the individual who was ground to dust in the gigantic murder machine and is still waiting to be raised out of the abyss of death, to be seen in full light?

For the last 14 years I have been privileged to lead an educational program – a three-week Summer Seminar on the Holocaust and Jewish Resistance for American high school teachers, who implement Holocaust studies in their schools. The program embraces all aspects of the Holocaust era with special emphases on Jewish resistance in all its forms. We travel to Israel, with a stop in Poland. The teachers go to the former death camps. In Auschwitz they see the heaps of hair, eyeglasses, valises with the names of the victims, the blown up crematoria in Birkenau. And in Majdanek, they see the mountain of shoes. In Treblinka they walk on the road which lead to the gas chambers. They touch history. Everything around them speaks of torture of death I walk with them and want so much to show them a glimpse of the Jewish life which once existed -- and is no more.

Splinters of memory -- I see again and again my home in the Warsaw Ghetto; my worn-out mother, with eyes puffy from starvation, hiding a piece of bread from us hungry children - the payment for the old tutor who was preparing my brother for his Bar Mitzvah, which he never lived to see. I see our neighbor selling saccharine and watching for approaching Germans, while upstairs her daughter holds illegal classes. I see Jews, with faces covered to hide their beards, rushing to secret synagogues. I see the faces of friends, both young and old, whom I met at secret meetings -- the organizers of illegal cultural, social and political activities in the ghetto - until they all were caught up in the Nazi vise and sent to the gas chambers of Treblinka. Yes, this was resistance -- to survive as a people and a spirit that refused to be crushed. This was the soil in which the seeds of armed resistance took hold.

Now after 50 years, historical facts connected with organized, armed resistance, mostly carried out by the idealistic Jewish youth from various political groups, are more or less known. And it seems to me that a primary task today should be to individualize the young fighters, to elaborate more about their lives, their homes, their thoughts and beliefs which shaped their personalities and their actions in decisive times and which helped shape our history.

Despite the vast body of Holocaust literature, still little is known of the remarkable life that was destroyed. Yes, beyond starvation, terror, fear and killing, there was life -- life filled with meaning, with loyalty, with sacrifice, with hope. Documenting this aspect of Jewish life in Europe, before and during the era of Nazi horrors, is a fundamental challenge facing scholars, writers and educators today.

The teachers in the program on "Holocaust and Jewish Resistance" learn about this remarkable world. They learn as well about all forms of Jewish resistance through lectures by prominent scholars at the renowned Holocaust Center at Yad Vashem in Jerusalem and at the Study Center of Lohamei Haghetaot; through testimonies by survivors, through workshops and trips to historic sites. We try to give them a deeper understanding of the life before and during the Holocaust. And this chapter of history should not only be written by historians basing their knowledge on documents and books, but they should include more about the experiences of the survivors who lived this history with their own flesh and blood.

Yes, teachers have a special warm relationship with survivors whom they meet at the conferences or in their classrooms when they give testimony. They respect them and our survivors leave a deep impression on their students.

The experiences which our teachers share during the intensive 3-week seminar, forge deep and lasting bonds. An alumni family was formed by our program. Alumni Conferences, co-sponsored by the U.S. Holocaust Memorial Museum, are being organized featuring lectures and workshops. An alumni Newsletter is being regularly published. Our teachers maintain contact with each other as well as with the program leaders. They are recognized in their communities and states as respected advisors on Holocaust education. They serve on Holocaust commissions, organize seminar, write curricula. It is impossible to list all their work and achievements.

Permit me, finally, to share with you a few lines from John Iiori, a teacher from Jacksonville, FL. He wrote to us: "The unique program in which I participated in 1990 changed the way I look at every day life. For 3 years I checked boxcars as an employee for a railroad company. Today, as a teacher, I cannot see a railroad track without seeing Treblinka and the gate at Birkenau. The bond we teachers now have will not break. We will continue to teach, to bear witness, long after the survivors are gone. This is the mission we educators have accepted."

Yes, these teachers are the link between our past and present. They can transmit our memories, our warnings, our fears and our hope for the future.

Dr. Robert Sigel

JOSEF EFFNER HIGH SCHOOL, DACHAU
GERMANY

Holocaust Education in Germany

Break-out Session: Best Practices and Future Projects in Holocaust Education, Remembrance and Research: Curricular Education

Ladies and Gentlemen,

As a teacher of a German High School in Dachau and as a historian who works on the educational guidelines as a part of the reconceptualization of the Dachau concentration camp memorial site I will present a short survey on the subject.

In the international guidelines on Holocaust Education - a British draft for the Task Force declaration - one can read in point 4 concerning the age of the students:

"Teachers tend to favor age 10-14 as the best time to introduce the subject, in terms of the students' educational and emotional development."

In the Internet you were able to find the outline on the curriculum of the New Jersey Commission on Holocaust Education. This outline covers the age group Kindergarten up to 12th grade students.

The Holocaust Human Rights Center of Maine has developed a guide titled, "Teaching about diversity, Prejudice, Human Rights and the Holocaust. For Grades Kindergarten through Four."

If you ask teachers in Germany if it was reasonable to teach children in Kindergarten or ten-year-old students about the Holocaust, most teachers would reject the idea.

Considering these different attitudes, one should ask oneself what is understood by Holocaust Education.

- Is Holocaust Education moral education in general?
- Is it teaching tolerance?
- Is it a kind of peace education?

- Is it imparting values to the students?
- Is it instilling a sense of understanding for diversity?

If you understand all of these by Holocaust Education, there is no reason why you should not start as early as Kindergarten.

In Germany of course all these values are part of education, of any kind of education, but Holocaust Education in Germany means something different. Holocaust Education in our country is mainly "teaching about the Holocaust." It means teaching and studying the historical period of National Socialism in Germany and Europe and the persecution and extermination of European Jewry.

In Germany as a federal state it is the 16 Länder that are responsible for education, schooling and research. The curricula on this subject however are not very different from each other.

Holocaust Education in Germany takes place mainly and primarily in the history lessons. At the age of about 15 years the students learn the history of the 20th century and the period of National Socialism and in this context the Holocaust is given ample space. The fact that this subject is taught again on the secondary level shows what emphasis is laid on teaching about the Holocaust.

The main focus of these lessons is on cognitive studies. We believe that the accurate and detailed knowledge of what happened and how it happened is the indispensable basis.

- The basis for a lasting emotional empathy.
- The basis to immunize against all attempts to deny the Holocaust.
- The basis to resist racism and neonazism.

Being the country of the perpetrators Germany has a great number of memorial sites, the former concentration camps Dachau, Bergen-Belsen, Buchenwald, Sachsenhausen etc.

A guided tour of these authentic places, where the traces of persecution and terror can still be seen, has a powerful impact on visitors.

Such a visit is strongly recommended to school classes by the ministries of education. During these visits the guide and the teacher have the opportunity to show individual biographies of prisoners, to show how they were humiliated, tortured and often murdered, to visualize the prisoners living conditions in a concentration camp, at the roll call place, in front of the barracks, inside the crematorium.

Whenever it is possible to include former concentration camp prisoners, eyewitnesses, and survivors of the Holocaust in the guided tours, in a conversation with the students, in a workshop, this opportunity is certainly taken. Apart from the history lessons and the visits to a memorial site the Holocaust is also a topic in lessons of religious education, literature and civics.

Since the founding of the German Federal Republic the Holocaust has always been part of the curriculum. It goes without saying that the treatment of this topic has been different and more intensive since the late seventies.

The results of scientific research have found their way into schools; new aspects have been introduced: rescuers, conditions in concentration camps, perpetrators.

My synopsis would therefore be:

- The Holocaust is an important topic in curricula, lessons, schoolbooks and other teaching materials on all levels.
- Holocaust Education in Germany means teaching the Holocaust as a specific historical event, the consequences of which have an impact in the present and will have one in the future.
- We do, of course, expect that studying the Holocaust leads to attitudes and perceptions which are important for a democratic society and prevent similar events from happening in the future.
- Holocaust Education in the wider sense as defined at the start of my talk does not exist as a term or as a curriculum in itself in Germany, but it contents are of course taught.
- International cooperation will be useful and helpful in the following areas:
- Exchange of teaching materials and teaching approaches.
- Exchange of experience between educators and teachers of different countries and international teacher training.
- Student exchange programs with joined workshops and projects on the topic.

German educators, teachers and institutions are certainly prepared to share their experience and knowledge with colleagues abroad and are eager to learn and profit from the experience of their colleagues.

Margot Stern Strom

EXECUTIVE DIRECTOR,
FACING HISTORY AND OURSELVES NATIONAL FOUNDATION
UNITED STATES

Break-out Session: Best Practices and Future Projects in Holocaust
Education, Remembrance and Research: Curricular Education

Thank you so much for inviting Facing History and Ourselves to
participate in the Washington Conference on Holocaust-Era Assets. I am
honored to be among such a distinguished group of panelists and
participants. I would like to assure you that Facing History and Ourselves
is eager to be involved in this innovative, precedent-setting international
approach to Holocaust education. It would be a great honor to work with
the committee and such scholars as Yehuda Bauer.

Facing History and Ourselves provides a nationally and
internationally-recognized educational program that focuses on the
events that led to the Holocaust as well as the Holocaust itself. In so
doing, we explore the universal themes that connect that history to the
moral choices young people confront each day. We are positioned to
reinforce and strengthen our outreach in Holocaust education, both in
communities we already serve and in those where this vital education has
been overlooked. Our core work builds public awareness of the
Holocaust through professional development for with middle and high
school educators – both in the US and in Europe. Our work is informed
by our experience in adapting our materials and approaches to the needs
of particular nations.

Facing History and Ourselves is a non-profit educational
organization whose mission is to promote democratic citizenship through
curriculum and strategies for teachers, students and communities.
Through workshops, institutes and public events, educators learn to
engage students in a study of history and ethics.

With a national office in Brookline, Massachusetts and regional
offices in New York, Memphis, Chicago, Los Angeles, and San
Francisco, Facing History annually conducts more than twenty 5-day
institutes, over two dozen advanced seminars and workshops, and
ongoing, technical assistance to teachers. Our Resource Center makes
available to educators books, films, slides, articles and videotapes that

are integrated into classroom instruction. Founded in 1976, Facing History serves a growing network of over 10,000 educators in the US who reach one million students each year.

Facing History and Ourselves has written and published *Facing History and Ourselves: Holocaust and Human Behavior* (now in its second edition), which is the key resource book for the program. In cooperation with the Fortunoff Video Archive for Holocaust Testimonies at Yale University, we developed videos for classroom use and an accompanying resource guide, *Elements of Time*. We have also published the writings of a member of our survivor network, *I Promised I Would Tell* by Sonia Schreiber Weitz. Our latest resource book is *The Jews of Poland*, which describes the rich life of the Jewish community in Poland before World War II and leads young people to an examination of their own personal identities.

Facing History and Ourselves produces materials that support multi-media projects in classrooms including a study guide to Steven Spielberg's *Schindler's List*, and educational materials for the Survivors of the Shoah Visual History Foundation's recent CD-ROM *Survivors: Testimonies of the Holocaust*. This summer, Facing History and Ourselves was selected by Public Affairs Television, Inc. to produce and disseminate a study guide to accompany Bill Moyers' upcoming PBS broadcast, *Facing the Truth*, which documents the work of South Africa's Truth and Reconciliation Commission.

Facing History brings Holocaust survivors into classrooms to tell their stories and to inspire young people to learn from history. We are actively involved with survivor networks in the Boston area and in our regions as well as with One Generation After. We work closely with leading Holocaust scholars, including Dr. Lawrence Langer and Dr. Michael Berenbaum, to ensure the accuracy and timeliness of our materials. Each year, members of Facing History's program staff undertake an intensive month-long study of the Holocaust at Yad Vashem.

For nearly 15 years, Facing History has explored the efforts of individuals and nations to respond to collective violence and heal the wounds of widespread atrocities. Our first Human Rights and Justice conference in 1985 was on the Nuremberg trials. Our most recent Annual Human Rights and Justice Conference in 1997, entitled *Collective Violence and Memory: Judgment, Reconciliation, Education*, was co-sponsored by the Harvard/Facing History Project and the Graduate Program at Harvard Law School. These conferences have been an important vehicle for promoting awareness of these issues not only to educators but also the greater community.

At this most recent public forum, Dullah Omar, Minister of Justice of South Africa and Pumla Gobodo-Madikizela, member of the Human Rights Violation Committee of South Africa's Truth and Reconciliation Commission, joined fellow panelists in an examination of the judicial, religious, psychological and political themes inherent in the varied responses to collective violence. As a result of the conference, Harvard Law School Professor Martha Minow's book, *Between Vengeance and Forgiveness: Facing History after Genocide and Mass Violence*, was released this fall from Beacon Press. Next week, we will host *Choosing to Participate: A Global Perspective*, a symposium which introduced Justice Richard Goldstone, the first chief prosecutor of the United Nations International Criminal Tribunals for the former Yugoslavia and Rwanda, to 400 community members in an examination of our role as citizens in an increasingly global society.

The Facing History and Ourselves program has repeatedly demonstrated its effectiveness. Since its inception, the program has undergone continuous external and internal evaluation. As a member of the National Diffusion Network, evaluation research was regularly submitted to an independent panel convened by the US Department of Education for validation. A current study sponsored by the Carnegie Corporation of New York followed 400 students in Facing History and Ourselves classrooms as well as in comparison classes and found that students in our programs achieved greater gains in relationship maturity while reported violence decreased. The thinking of Facing History students moved towards more differentiated, complex, and reflective perspectives, while reported incidents of fighting went down.

In 1996, Facing History launched a new program to aid law enforcement personnel in connecting the Holocaust to the moral choices they face on the job daily. The project is designed to help officers better meet the diverse needs of the neighborhoods they serve and the goals of community policing. In a Department of Justice-funded project, the Boston Police Department and Facing History are partners with other local institutions in conducting regional community policing training institutes designed to advance community policing nationally. Facing History is also providing programs for other law enforcement agencies based on its educational model, including immigration officers, housing and school police forces. Recently, Senior Associate for Police and Community Programming Bill Johnston received the first-ever Civil Rights Award from the International Association of Chiefs of Police.

For the past twenty years, members of the Facing History program staff have traveled abroad to conduct workshops, deliver presentations at conferences, and study with scholars and local organizations at the site of the history about which we teach. In addition, educators from all over Europe continue to attend Facing History's professional development programs—both in the United States and in Europe—and meet with program staff and other scholars. To enrich this professional development, Facing History maintains strong connections to European educators, scholars and other experts who both learn from us and teach us about democracy and civic participation.

Facing History's full-time representative based in Switzerland, August Zemo, who is also in attendance at this conference today, develops and oversees our European activities. Beginning in 1992, Facing History's materials and methodologies have been adapted for use in schools in Western, Central and Eastern Europe. In those eight years we have held a series of teacher training seminars in Europe; held seminars on tolerance for students from state and international schools in Europe; participated in three study tours in Eastern Europe (a fourth is upcoming in spring, 1999); established working relationships with major research institutes in Europe including the Memorial House of the Wannsee Conference (Berlin), the Fritz Bauer Institute (Frankfurt am Main), Stichting Sintiwerk Best (the Netherlands), Auschwitz-Birkenau State Museum (Oswiecim), the Center for Human Rights Education (Prague), and the Musee memorial des enfants d'izieu (France). We have also established ties with the International Romani Union and the Landelijke Siniti Organisatie. Our resource book has been translated for adoption into Hungarian state schools and we have recently been approached by the Slovak Republic to develop school textbooks and the Ministry of Education in Romania to integrate Facing History system-wide.

In Sweden, Facing History has recently conducted an institute in collaboration with Hedi Fried, a psychologist and Auschwitz survivor who is also in attendance today. The institute was sponsored by the Teachers College in Stockholm and the Teachers for Peace organization. Plans are underway for a similar institute in Norway.

Facing History has promoted public awareness of the Holocaust in the national and international media including NBC's *Today Show*, ABC's *American Agenda*, CNN and many local television outlets. Articles about Facing History have appeared in *The Boston Globe*, *The Los Angeles Times*, *The Chicago Tribune*, *The London Times*, and *Le Monde*, as well as in a number of educational journals, including

Columbia Teachers College Record, Harvard Education Review, Education Week, Educational Leadership, and *English Journal.* Internationally, we have been cited in UNESCO's Human Rights journal, and educational journals in Germany and Hungary. Currently, Facing History is working with a *Today Show* producer on a new segment about our work, tentatively scheduled for an April broadcast.

The work of Facing History and Ourselves has been supported by the Charles A. Dana Foundation, the John D. and Catherine T. MacArthur Foundation, the Ford Foundation, the Carnegie Corporation of New York, the Charles H. Revson Foundation, the Surdna Foundation, the Crown Family Foundation, the Covenant Foundation, state and federal government agencies, other major foundations and corporations, as well as individual donors. In 1994, we were awarded a National Endowment for the Humanities Challenge Grant, which helped to build our endowment, which totals approximately $2 million. The Facing History budget for fiscal 1998-99 totals $7.9 million to support its programs and operation. Our current staff totals 74, both at the national office and in our regions.

Facing History and Ourselves was selected as a model program by the U.S. Department of Education's National Diffusion Network and for sixteen years received funding for national dissemination. Harvard University has recognized Facing History's expertise and joined with us in a multi-year project to address intolerance and violence among young people through research and the development of new curricular materials.

In 1997, I received the 12th Annual Charles A. Dana Award for Pioneering Achievement in Education for Facing History's "role in creating an innovative curriculum on moral development." The Foundation recently awarded Facing History a two-year grant for its work in the area of academic standards in K-12 education. A recent citation from Northeastern University recognized that Facing History has "enable(d) millions of students to study the Holocaust; investigate the root causes of racism, anti-Semitism and violence and realize their obligations and capabilities as citizens in a democracy."

Facing History and Ourselves was selected by the President's Initiative on Race to appear on the White House web site under the heading, *Promising Practices.* Last year, First Lady Hillary Rodham Clinton spoke with Facing History and Ourselves students at Orchestra Hall in Chicago where she had heard Martin Luther King, Jr. speak in 1962. We have also been invited to serve on the National Advisory

Board of The Television Race Initiative, which is bringing national attention to issues of race in America.

As a non-profit organization with a proven capacity for dissemination nationally and internationally, Facing History and Ourselves would be happy to collaborate with or assist those who are working on Holocaust education issues. We stand ready to share what we know about developing and supporting teachers so that they can effectively address the critical issues raised by this history.

Dr. Marcia Sachs Littell

DIRECTOR, NATIONAL ACADEMY FOR HOLOCAUST AND GENOCIDE
TEACHER TRAINING
RICHARD STOCKTON COLLEGE, NEW JERSEY
UNITED STATES

Holocaust Education in the 21st Century: Breaking the Silence in 1945, Avoiding Premature Closure in 1999

Break-out Session: Best Practices and Future Projects in Holocaust
Education, Remembrance and Research: Curricular Education

In the years directly following liberation - there was silence --
stunning silence. From the Jewish Community, from the churches, from
government agencies. During this time, the majority of Americans were
comfortable with the silence. Even the word "Holocaust" did not come
into current use until the 1960's.

The growing awareness in America of the significance of the
Holocaust can be marked with the date 1960, with the publication and
wide sale of the English edition of Elie Wiesel's classic: Night, which
after four decades remains one of the most influential publications about
the Holocaust.

Complementing this literary work was the first edition of Raoul
Hilberg's scholarly work: The Destruction of the European Jews. This
landmark work, using sources then available, carefully recorded the mass
Nazi genocide of the Jews.

The trial of Adolf Eichmann and his execution on June 1, 1962
aroused intense interest all over the world. The trial was a major
landmark of Holocaust awareness and education, although in different
contexts for Americans than for Israelis. A major public and political
breakthrough was delayed in the USA.

Americans received their first real jolt of awareness at the time of the Six Day War (1967) in Israel, when "a Second Holocaust" seemed threatened. With the realization that Jews might be destroyed in their homeland, not only Jews in the Diaspora were aroused: Christians friendly to Jewish survival were also moved to act.

Within three years, three important organizations resulted from Christian initiative in the United States: the National Christian Leadership Conference for Israel, the Christian Study Group on Israel and the Jewish People, and the Annual Scholars' Conference on the Holocaust and the Churches. Of greatest outreach among the three was the Annual Scholars' Conference on the Holocaust and the Churches. The Annual Scholars' Conference - interdisciplinary, interfaith and international - brought together for the first time Christian and Jewish Scholars to examine issues raised by the Holocaust and the response of the Churches - before, during and after the tragedy.

In March of 1999, in its 29th consecutive year, the conference will bring together c600 registrants from c25 countries. In recent years the Conference has also expanded to embrace teachers, clergy, survivors, community leaders and graduate students. It has each year rotated geographic location and academic co-sponsorship around the United States. At first the Annual Scholars' Conference was small, with a few dozen professors. Attendance doubled in the late 1970s with an influx of primary and secondary school teachers. Since 1990 participation has numbered in the hundreds, and the 29th Annual Conference will bring in another major constituency - the Community Colleges, increasingly important in American higher education. The university, college and community college campuses have become centers of Holocaust awareness.

If the 1967 war paved the way for changed attitudes towards the Holocaust and the formation of a major interfaith conference, the 1973 Yom Kippur War served to shake loose the last reservations held by the American Jewish communities. Initially, the Jewish defense agencies had stood aloof from the Scholars' Conference and intense Holocaust education, counting such work counter-productive to amicable Christian-Jewish relations. But the Yom Kippur War propelled them to a greater readiness to clearly and directly confront the Holocaust and its lessons.

In 1975 community Holocaust Resource Centers were launched - the first by Professor Yaffa Eliach in Brooklyn. Six weeks later the Philadelphia Center was started by Professor Franklin Littell on the campus of Temple University. The growth of local Holocaust Resource Centers has flourished in recent years. Holocaust education is now a major commitment of Jewish communal education programs, in all major cities. There are now 122 centers in North America.

The Gathering of Jewish Holocaust Survivors and the United States Holocaust Memorial Museum have added powerful dimensions to the education of the public.

In spite of large numbers of individual courses on the campuses, programs toward the M.A. and Ph.D. degrees have been slow to emerge. For high quality Ph.D. work in the Holocaust, American students have for years made the trek to study in Hebrew University with the group around Yehuda Bauer and Yisrael Gutman. There was a short spring in 1975 at Temple University, with a doctoral program of which Dr. Mordecai Paldiel - now of Yad Vashem - was the first Ph.D., but it did not outlast its relegation to a section of the Jewish Studies program.

Since the 1970's teacher interest in presenting the Holocaust in the middle and high schools has flourished. The growing interest in America in ethnic and minority studies has helped. So too has the work of Lawrence Kohlberg at Harvard in creating the "moral education and values clarification movement." The major media event during the 1970's was the 1978 television production "Holocaust." It was an antiseptic, soap opera type presentation of genocide, dramatic with love on the run and a happy ending. It received high ratings from the American public if not from the critics. Some specialists found it set their teeth on edge, even though it was useful in exposing millions of viewers to the basic facts of the Holocaust. With all its flaws, it played a major part in opening the door to the public-at-large and in stimulating public support for Holocaust education in the United States.

President Jimmy Carter's interest in memorializing the Holocaust led to the establishing of the President's Commission on the Holocaust. By 1980, through an act of Congress Yom HaShoah became a regular calendar day in America. The President of the United States, the governor of every state and the mayor of every major American City now declares it an official Day of Remembrance.

Documentary films flourished in the 1980s. Among the most notable was Sister Carol Rittner's documentary based on rescuers, "The Courage To Care." Pierre Sauvage's "Weapons of the Spirit" told the story of the Trocmés and Le Chambon, the latter the village of rescuers where he had been an infant. Claude Lanzmann's nine and one-half hour "SHOAH" was widely viewed in America, and is still used in schools.

In the 1990s Schindler's List, Jon Blair's Academy Award-winning Anne Frank Remembered, and Gerda Klein's All But My Life have brought major attention to the Holocaust. As we prepare to enter a new millennium a new genre of film is appearing on the scene, beginning with Roberto Benigni's remarkable, sensitive "Life is Beautiful."

Monuments, memorials and Holocaust centers continue to abound. The Holocaust Centers provide varied services, including museums, resource centers, archival facilities, family memorials, research facilities, libraries and depositories of oral and video testimony.

Numerous states have established Commissions on the Holocaust and recommendations to teach. Five states have mandated Holocaust Education in the schools[1]. More have vigorously recommended that teachers deal with the subject[2]. There are estimated to be several hundred courses at the college and university level, although no recent or precise study of them throughout the entire USA has been conducted. Dr. Margaret Crouch's study, which covered "The Holocaust in Undergraduate Education in the Middle Atlantic Region,"[3] discovered a continuing growth of course offerings in the region.

The U.S. Holocaust Memorial Museum presents the story for all Americans of conscience – Jew and non-Jew, young or old. The opening of the Museum encouraged public discussion of the Holocaust. It has been responsible for an avalanche of events, one-time conferences and new courses on the campuses, with a rush to include Holocaust Education in the secondary and college curricula.

We now have a dual set of problems to deal with, one on the secondary school level and another at the college and university level.

At both levels of instruction we lack properly trained master teachers and professors. This problem now has become acute in the secondary school arena, where more and more states are mandating or recommending the teaching.

In both cases there is a funding problem. Still lacking are the endowments to create interfaith chairs of Holocaust studies in the universities. Currently there are chairs in the U.S. at the University of California: Los Angeles, at Santa Cruz, Yeshiva University, Emory, Clark, Florida Atlantic University, and at the Richard Stockton College

---

[1]   The States mandating Holocaust Studies are California (grades 7-9 & 10-12), Florida, Illinois, New Jersey (grades k-12), New York.

[2]   The states recommending Holocaust instruction are Connecticut, Indiana, Nevada, North Carolina, Pennsylvania, South Carolina, Tennessee, Virginia, and Washington. Beginning in September of 1997, Wisconsin has recommended Holocaust Education in secondary schools.

[3]   Unpublished Ph.D. dissertation at Wilmington College; Dr. Crouch's address is 604 Norman's Lane, Newark DE 19711.

of New Jersey. The first endowed chairs in a community colleges have been announced, at Monroe Community College, Rochester NY. and Brookdale Community College (New Jersey). Only at The Richard Stockton College of New Jersey however, is there a deliberate effort to assure that the study and the teaching remains truly interfaith. The endowed chair for a Visiting Distinguished Scholar rotates between a Christian and a Jewish Scholar year by year.

A problem of recent years in the United States has been a marked tendency to place Holocaust Studies, and now the new chairs, in Departments of Jewish Studies. This insulates the topic from having any general impact.

Training teachers at the secondary and primary school level points up an additional set of problems. Grass roots support is important, as is individual teacher initiative. However, we have passed the point in the development of Holocaust Education where the training of teachers can any longer be delegated to the "ad hoc" method - occasional in-service workshops, voluntary summer institutes or faculty development seminars.

In order to achieve sustainability and quality control in the curriculum and meet the needs of a pluralistic society, we need degree programs for teachers within colleges and universities. These programs must be closely linked - on an interdisciplinary basis - with content departments. Teachers need to receive college credit - with concrete consequences in salary increments - for their advanced work in Holocaust Studies. In order to accomplish this, a top level commitment is required with appropriate funds for resources and graduate training for teachers.

With the emphasis in some K-12 programs on diversity, tolerance, and prejudice reduction we must be very clear about the goals and objectives of Holocaust Education. One of the problems is that presently we have so many curricula that teachers find it difficult to know what and how to select units to use in their classrooms. Sometimes the factual information is not dependable. We need active cooperation between the historians and the professors of methodology to achieve a better integration of pedagogical and content expertise. In the United States, however, we have a decentralized educational system that leaves requirements to the individual states. There is no one standard, no national curriculum for the Holocaust. This leaves Holocaust Education vulnerable to parochial interests.

On the university level we now face the danger of premature Closure, of an administrative solution that slides Holocaust Studies into

Jewish Studies, rather than maintaining it as a discrete field or an inter-disciplinary program.   This is as dangerous as the widespread indifference or denial of earlier years. In fact Franklin Littell refers to this administrative solution as "soft" denial. Merging Holocaust Studies into Jewish Studies is the wrong approach. It simply sends the wrong message. That the Holocaust is the most traumatic event in the death and life of the Jewish people since the destruction of the Second Temple goes without saying. But study of the Holocaust is also to study the pathology of Western civilization and its flawed structures. It must not be hidden away by false bracketing of courses.

For university administrators, attuned to public opinion, the solution of subsuming "Holocaust" under Jewish Studies is attractive. It keeps the subject under control. In the several disciplines, we academics all face the same temptation to render antiseptic the story and lessons of the Holocaust. Sociologists are tempted to put the message in the box of "racism." Political Scientists are tempted to put the message in the box of "war and dictatorship." Psychologists find it congenial to talk about the special cases of survivors and perpetrators. Theologians find the Holocaust a neat illustration of the Problem of Evil: "theodicy." Sectarians - both Jew and gentile - pigeon-hole it as "a Jewish affair."

Within recent months - and here I shall conclude - major breakthroughs have occurred at Clark University and the Richard Stockton College of New Jersey. In the former, with Professor Deborah Dwork taking the lead, a Ph.D. program of study, research and dissertation defense has been initiated. In the latter, a Master of Arts program at Richard Stockton College of New Jersey has been started, primarily to help school teachers. Among the more than fifty who applied for admission to the program there are a few who expect to go on for the Ph.D. The large majority, however, are teachers of various subjects who under the New Jersey mandate are directed to teach a topic on which they need help in building lessons, locating videos and books, and in attaining a general competence in the subject.

These school teachers, flocking to a degree program in Holocaust studies at Stockton College, remind us that the dialogue with the past is alive. And we are reminded that, above all else, we must strive to avert premature closure in Holocaust Studies. The big questions are still open, and they are vital to the mind and spirit of every student whatever his or her "major." For some time to come, the Holocaust will require the vigorous attention of minds and consciences for whom history is not the dead past, but rather a part of our present awareness, and above all a topic where careful study and teaching are an arrow pointing in the direction of a future without genocide.

Dr. David Singer

DIRECTOR OF RESEARCH, AMERICAN JEWISH COMMITTEE
UNITED STATES

Knowledge and Remembrance of the Holocaust in Different Countries: Data from American Jewish Committee-Sponsored Surveys

Break-out Session: Best Practices and Future Projects in Holocaust Education, Remembrance and Research: Curricular Education

INTRODUCTION

Beginning in June 1992, the American Jewish Committee launched a series of public opinion surveys in various countries probing issues related to knowledge and remembrance of the Holocaust. The countries covered in this research effort include the United States (1992; 1994), Great Britain (1993), France (1993), Slovakia (1993), Australia (1994), Germany (1994), Austria (1995), Poland (1995), and Russia (1996). A number of key questions were asked in all of the countries, providing a wealth of comparative data. Other questions explored in detail Holocaust related concerns specific to individual countries.

The tables which follow present the full set of findings from the American Jewish Committee-sponsored surveys. For those engaged in Holocaust education the data are of immediate relevance in that they make clear the base line of knowledge that exists at present. Clearly, much work needs to be done to overcome the knowledge gap that prevails in many countries with regard to the Holocaust, including the United States.

In the year 2,000, the American Jewish Committee will conduct follow up surveys in all of the countries included in the initial effort, plus others. This follow-up round will make available, for the first time, trend line data on knowledge and remembrance of the Holocaust. The information generated should serve as a valuable yardstick for measuring progress in the area of Holocaust education.

Questions Asked in Multiple Countries

1.   "As far as you know, what does the term `the Holocaust' refer to?" (in percents) (OPEN-ENDED)

Country	Extermination/ murder/ persecution/ treatment of Jews by Hitler/ Nazis/ Germans	Extermination murder/ persecution of Jews	Other relevant responses	Others	DK/NA
Germany (1994)	59	23	5	3	10
W.Germans (1994)	59	27	5	3	6
E.Germans (1994)	58	11	4	2	25
France (1993)	35	21	12	12	20
Great Britain (1993)	33	18	5	35	18
Australia (1994)	39	17	17	15	12
United States (1992)	24	30	7	10	28
United States (1994)	24	35	9	12	19
Poland (1995)	3	32	6	11	48
Austria (1995)	10	49	23	2	20
Russia (1996)	3	3	1	2	91

Note: In the French and American surveys, if an incorrect response was given, respondents were told, "To be precise, the Holocaust was the Nazi extermination of Jews during the Second World War." In the Australian survey, all respondents were so informed. In the British survey, multiple answers were allowed.

"Other relevant responses" may include: concentration camps, German death camps, Hitler, Nazis, Germans, World War II, and the 1940s. "Others" may include: death/murder/slaughter, destruction/ disaster/tragedy, war/nuclear war, cataclysm, the end of the world, starvation, or other answers.

The low figures in Poland and Russia for correct/partially correct responses reflect lack of usage of the English term "the Holocaust."

2. "From what you know or have heard, what were Auschwitz, Dachau, and Treblinka?" (in percents)

Country	Concentration camps	Other responses	DK/NA
Germany (1994)	92	3	5
W.Germans (1994)	91	4	5
E. Germans (1994)	95	3	2
France (1993)	90	4	6
Great Britain (1993)	76	4	20
Australia (1994)	85	4	13
United States (1992)	62	11	27
United States (1994)	67	4	28
Poland (1995)	91	8	1
Austria (1995)	91	4	6
Russia (1996)	50	2	49

Note: This question was closed-ended in the French, Australian, and American surveys, and open-ended with codes in the British, German, Polish, Austrian, and Russian surveys. Australian respondents were not given the option of answering "other."

3. "Approximately how many Jews were killed in the Holocaust?" (in percents)

Country	25,000	100,000	1 million	2 million	6 million	20 million	DK/NA
Germany (1994)	2	5	13	15	36	8	21
W. Germans (1994)	1	5	12	14	36	9	23
E. Germans (1994)	3	5	16	19	36	6	16
France (1993)	2	4	11	14	45	12	12
Great Britain (1993)	2	4	5	9	41	13	26
Australia (1994)	2	9	12	10	47	6	14
United States (1992)	1	4	7	13	35	10	30
United States (1994)	1	5	6	9	44	7	28
Poland (1995)*	1	2	10	25	34	6	22
Austria (1995)	1	3	12	19	31	8	26
Russia (1996)*	1	2	8	12	21	5	52

* Respondents in Poland were asked, "Approximately how many Jews were killed by the Nazis during the Second World War?" Respondents in Russia were asked, "Approximately how many Jews in all of Europe were killed by the Nazis during the Second World War?"

4.   "Many Jews in Europe were forced to wear a symbol on their clothes during the Second World War. What was it?" (in percents)

Country	Yellow star/ Jewish star*/ star of David*	Other responses	DK/NA
Germany (1994)**	91	1	8
W. Germans (1994)	90	1	9
E. Germans (1994)	98	1	1
France (1993)	88	9	3
Great Britain (1993)	56	9	34
Australia (1994)	72	17	12
United States (1992)	42	30	29
United States (1994)	42	24	33
Poland (1995)	74	8	18
Austria (1995)	84	1	17
Russia (1996)	34	7	59

Note: This question was closed-ended in the French, Australian, and American surveys, and open-ended with codes in the British, German, Polish, Austrian, and Russian surveys.

* This response was not included in the Australian, French, and American questionnaires.

** In Germany, Poland, Russia, and Austria, "yellow star," "Jewish star," and "star of David" were accepted as responses.

5.   "In addition to the Jews, which of the following groups, if any, were persecuted by the Nazis?" (in percents)

Country	Gypsies	Poles	Homo- sexuals	Aryans	Other	DK/NA
Germany (1994)	74	43	68	7	24	14
W. Ger. (1994)	75	40	66	6	21	15
E. Ger. (1994)	70	55	78	8	37	8
France (1993)	57	52	33	8	4	7
Great Britain (1993)	51	63	51	9	14	20
Australia (1994)	49	75	47	9	--	--
United States (1992)	26	50	25	7	10	30
United States (1994)	27	47	26	4	9	34
Austria (1995)	75	41	61	5	14	17

Note: Australian respondents were not given the option of answering "other," and they were asked to answer "yes" or "no" for each response; respondents from the other countries were asked to specify their responses from the list.

6. "Some people claim that the Nazi extermination of the Jews never happened. Have you ever heard this claim, or not?" (in percents)

Country	Heard this claim	Have not heard this claim	DK/NA
Germany(1994)	60	30	9
W. Germans(1994)	62	29	9
E. Germans(1994)	56	34	10
France(1993)	67	33	0
Great Britain(1993)	50	46	4
Australia (1994)	70	28	3
United States(1992)	38	54	8
United States(1994)	49	44	7
Poland (1995)	29	70	2
Austria (1995)	59	21	20
Russia (1996)	13	81	6

7a. "Does it seem possible or does it seem impossible to you that the Nazi extermination of the Jews never happened?" (in percents)

Country	It seems possible	It seems impossible	DK/NA
Germany (1994)	8	80	13
West Germans (1994)	7	79	14
East Germans (1994)	10	82	8
France (1993)	5	94	1
Great Britain (1993)	7	84	9

7b. "Does it seem possible to you that the Nazi extermination of the Jews never happened, or do you feel certain that it happened?" (in percents)

Country	It seems possible it never happened	Feel certain it happened	DK/NA
United States (1994)	1	91	8
Australia (1994)	4	93	3
Poland (1995)	1	96	2
Austria (1995)	7	88	6
Russia (1996)	2	90	8

Note: In Australia, the question was asked of a half-sample.

8. "Please tell me whether you strongly agree, mostly agree, mostly disagree, or strongly disagree: `The Holocaust is not relevant today because it happened almost 50 years ago.'" (in percents)

Country	Strongly agree	Mostly agree	Mostly disagree	Strongly disagree	DK/NA
Germany (1994)	11	26	33	20	10
W. Germans (1994)	12	28	32	17	10
E. Germans (1994)	5	17	37	31	11
France (1993)	8	12	15	64	1
Great Britain (1993)	5	13	20	53	9
Australia (1994)	7	9	23	57	4
United States (1992)	8	13	17	46	15
United States (1994)	8	13	17	48	14
Poland (1995)*	6	22	43	25	4
Austria (1995)	10	18	26	29	18

*Respondents in Poland were asked about "the Nazi extermination of the Jews."

9.   "In your view, how important is it for Germans [for the French/for the British/for Australians/for all Americans/for all Austrians/for all citizens of Russia] to know about and understand the Holocaust--is it essential, very important, only somewhat important, or not important?" (in percents)

Country	Essential	Very important	Only somewhat important	Not important	DK/ NA
Germany (1994)	18	50	19	7	7
W. Germans (1994)	17	48	20	7	8
E. Germans (1994)	20	55	14	6	5
France(1993)	45	43	11	1	0
Great Britain (1993)	33	39	20	4	4
Australia (1994)	29	43	23	3	2
United States (1992)	33	39	13	2	13
United States (1994)	39	37	12	2	11
Poland (1995)*	17	69	11	1	3
Austria (1995)	20	42	17	5	16
Russia (1996)*	31	31	22	8	8

*Respondents in Poland and Russia were asked about "the Nazi extermination of the Jews during the Second World War."

10.   "Please tell me whether you strongly agree, mostly agree, mostly disagree, or strongly disagree: `The Holocaust makes clear the need for the State of Israel as a place of refuge for Jews in times of persecution.'" (in percents)

Country	Strongly agree	Mostly agree	Mostly disagree	Strongly disagree	DK/NA
France (1993)	19	32	19	23	7
Great Britain (1993)	24	33	14	6	23
Australia (1994)	17	42	17	10	15
United States (1992)	28	32	8	5	27
United States (1994)	25	33	11	6	25

11a. "For each of the following, please tell me if you think it is a lesson to be learned from the Holocaust or not: (a) Firm steps need to be taken to protect the rights of minorities." (in percents)

Country	Is	Is not	DK/NA
France (1993)	87	10	3
Great Britain (1993)	89	3	8
United States (1992)	83	6	11
United States (1994)	76	13	10

11b. "For each of the following, please tell me if you think it is a lesson to be learned from the Holocaust or not: (b) There is no hope for the human race." (in percents)

Country	Is	Is not	DK/NA
France (1993)	38	57	5
Great Britain (1993)	34	51	15
United States (1992)	21	67	13
United States (1994)	18	73	9

11c. "For each of the following, please tell me if you think it is a lesson to be learned from the Holocaust or not: (c) People must speak out against oppression so that another Holocaust will not happen." (in percents)

Country	Is	Is not	DK/NA
France (1993)	92	6	2
Great Britain (1993)	92	2	6
United States (1992)	84	4	12
United States (1994)	81	9	10

11d. "For each of the following, please tell me if you think it is a lesson to be learned from the Holocaust or not: (d) In relations between people and countries, what counts is power and not morality." (in percents)

Country	Is	Is not	DK/NA
France (1993)	57	35	8
Great Britain (1993)	29	48	23
United States (1992)	29	55	16
United States (1994)	22	66	13

11e. "For each of the following, please tell me if you think it is a lesson to be learned from the Holocaust or not: (e) It is important to stand by what you think is right instead of going along with everyone else." (in percents)

Country	Is	Is not	DK/NA
France (1993)	76	18	6
Great Britain (1993)	94	1	5
United States (1992)	85	4	11
United States (1994)	84	7	9

12. "In your view, how likely is it that the Jewish people could be subject to another Holocaust somewhere in the world in coming years - - very likely, somewhat likely, or not very likely?" (in percents)

Country	Very likely	Somewhat likely	Not very likely	DK/NA
France (1993)	7	31	59	3
Great Britain (1993)	16	31	40	13
Australia (1994)	15	34	48	4
United States (1992)	13	28	43	17
United States (1994)	13	29	41	17

13.   "Are there any situations similar in nature to the Holocaust going on in the world today?" (in percents)

Country	Yes	No	DK/NA
France (1993)	86	10	4
Great Britain (1993)	77	9	14
Australia (1994)	77	16	7
United States (1992)	47	26	27
United States (1994)	52	25	23

14a.   "Some people say that 45 years [50 years] after the end of World War II, it is time to put the memory of the Holocaust, Hitler's extermination of the Jews, behind us. Others say that we should keep the remembrance of the Holocaust strong even after the passage of time. Which opinion comes closer to your opinion?" (in percents)

Country	Behind	Remember	DK/NA
Hungary (1991)	28	61	10
Czechoslovakia (1991)	21	71	9
Poland (1991)	13	81	6
Poland (1995)	10	85	5
Russia (1996)	6	78	16

14b.   "With the opening of a new chapter in German history, 45 years after the end of the Second World War, it is time to put the memory of the Holocaust behind us." (in percents)

Country	Agree strongly	Agree somewhat	Disagree somewhat	Disagree strongly	DK/NA
Germany (1990)30	28	20	14	8	
W. Ger (1990)	34	31	18	9	8
E. Ger (1990)	21	23	26	21	9

14c. "Recently someone said: "Today, in the aftermath of German unification, we should not talk so much about the Holocaust, but should rather draw a line under the past." Would you say this is correct or incorrect?" (in percents)

Country	Correct	Incorrect	DK/NA
Germany (1994)	52	34	14
West Germans (1994)	56	29	15
East Germans (1994)	36	54	10

14d. "Now, 45 years [50 years] after the end of the Second World War, it is time to put the memory of the Holocaust behind us." (in percents)

Country	Agree strongly	Agree somewhat	Disagree somewhat	Disagree strongly	DK/NA
Austria (1991)	34	19	15	13	20
Austria (1995)	13	20	26	24	16

14e. "Some people say that 48 years after the end of World War II, it is time to put the memory of the Holocaust, the deportations and extermination of Jews, behind us. Others say that we should preserve these remembrances. Which opinion comes closer to your attitude?" (in percents)

Country	To stop remembering deportations and extermination of Jews	To preserve the remembrance	DK/NA
Slovakia (1993)	38	42	20

15.   "Jews are exploiting the National Socialist Holocaust for their own purposes." (in percents)

Country	Agree strongly	Agree somewhat	Disagree somewhat	Disagree strongly	DK/NA
Germany (1990)	11	28	27	15	20
W. Ger (1990)	13	32	25	11	19
E. Ger (1990)	4	16	34	21	25
Germany (1994)	15	24	27	14	20
W. Ger (1994)	18	26	25	13	18
E. Ger (1994)	4	15	36	20	24
Austria (1991)	13	19	21	15	32
Austria (1995)	8	20	24	20	28

16a. "What is your opinion about `revisionist' statements which assert that there was no such thing as gas chambers and the Nazi extermination of the Jews? (a) We must forbid these statements and penalize those who spread them. (b) We must allow these statements and writings to be freely expressed." (in percents)

Country	Forbid	Allow	DK/NA
France (1993)	54	43	3

16b. "If people say that there were no such things as gas chambers and Nazi extermination camps, do you think we should forbid these statements and penalize those who spread them or allow these statements and writings to be freely expressed?" (in percents)

Country	Forbid	Allow	DK/NA
Australia (1994)	12	81	7

17. "From which of these sources, if any, have you learned about the Holocaust?"* (MULTIPLE ANSWERS ALLOWED) (in percents)

Response	Poland 1995	Australia 1994	United States 1994	United States 1992
Books	75	68	43	42
Television	-	82	58	50
The movies-	-	62	33	24
Newspaper and magazine articles	-	73	35	31
Mass media: TV, radio, newspapers, magazines, movies	92	-	-	-
School	67	44	48	37
Churches/synagogues	-	9	15	10
Church	29	-	-	-
People I know	-	43	26	20
Your own experience, that of a family member, or people you know	47	-	-	-
Other (SPECIFY)	-	-	4	5
This is the first I've heard of the Holocaust	1	1	4	6
DK/NA	-	-	4	5

Note: Australian and Polish respondents were asked to answer "yes" or "no" for each response; American respondents were asked to specify their responses from the list.

*In Poland, respondents were asked where they had heard of "the Nazi extermination of the Jews."

18.   "Who was the leader of Nazi Germany?" (in percents)

Response	Australia 1994	United States 1994	United States 1992
Joseph Stalin	1	1	2
Adolf Hitler	96	89	87
Hirohito	1	0	1
Winston Churchill	0	0	0
DK/NA	3	10	10

Questions Asked in Individual Countries

Germany (1990)

1.   "Do you think that the German government should, after the unification of the two German states, teach about the Nazi period in history lessons in the schools?" (in percents)

Country	Yes	No	DK/NA
Germany (1990)	73	16	11
West Germans (1990)	69	20	12
East Germans (1990)	84	7	9

2.   "Do you think that the German government should, after the unification of the two German states, prosecute Nazi war criminals?" (in percents)

Country	Yes	No	DK/NA
Germany (1990)	55	36	9
West Germans (1990)	48	43	10
East Germans (1990)	74	20	6

3. "Do you think that the German government should, after the unification of the two German states, pay reparations to Jews?" (in percents)

Country	Yes	No	DK/NA
Germany (1990)	22	66	12
West Germans (1990)	15	75	11
East Germans (1990)	40	44	16

Germany (1994)

1. "A proposal has been put forward to establish a national Holocaust memorial museum in Germany. Do you approve or disapprove of this idea?" (in percents)

Country	Approve	Disapprove	DK/NA
Germany (1994)	37	37	26
West Germans (1994)	33	42	25
East Germans (1994)	52	20	28

Soviet Union (1990)

1. "Have you heard or not heard about the mass extermination of Jews during the Second World War?" (in percents)

Country	Yes, I have	No, I haven't
Soviet Union (1990)	89	11

2.   "How many Jews do you think were exterminated by the Nazis in those years?" (OPEN-ENDED) (in percents)

Response	Percent
1,000,000 or less	10
1-3,000,000 (including 3)	7
3-4,000,000 (including 4)	1
4-5,000,000 (including 5)	2
6,000,000 (or about)	2
7-8,000,000 (including 7 or 8)	1
8-10,000,000 (including 10)	1
greater than 10,000,000	0
no response	73

Commonwealth of Independent States (1992)

1.   "Do you think history classes should talk about the mass extermination of Jews during WWII?" (in percents)

Country	They should	They shouldn't	Difficult to say
Russia (1992)	66	15	19
Ukraine (1992)	78	8	14
Belarus (1992)	60	24	16
Estonia (1992)	78	9	13
Latvia (1992)	75	6	22
Lithuania (1992)	69	15	16
Moldova (1992)	88	5	7
Azerbaijan (1992)	38	30	32
Kazakhstan (1992)	65	10	25
Uzbekistan (1992)	51	25	24

Austria (1991, 1995)

1.   "With which of the following statements do you agree? `We Austrians, too, lost the war in 1945.' `We Austrians were liberated by the Allies in 1945.'" (in percents)

Country	Lost	Liberated	DK/NA
Austria (1991)	48	43	10
Austria (1995)	42	49	9

2.   "Was Austria in 1938 the first victim of Hitler's Germany or also responsible, as a participant, for the events up to 1945?" (in percents)

Country	Victim	Responsible	DK/NA
Austria (1991)	34	39	33
Austria (1995)	28	29	43

3.   "It is often asserted that Austrians must especially stick up for the Jews, because Austrians participated in the crimes against the Jews during the Hitler era." (in percents)

Country	Agree	Agree partly	Undecided	Disagree	DK/NA
Austria (1991)	4	19	30	41	6
Austria (1995)	5	28	33	31	3

4.   "Do you think that the Austrian government should prosecute Nazi war criminals?" (in percents)

Country	Yes	No	DK/NA
Austria (1991)	38	56	7

United States (1992 and 1994)

1.   "In which country did the Nazis first come to power?" (in percents)

Response	United States 1994	United States 1992
Belgium	1	1
France	1	1
Germany	81	78
Russia	2	3
Other (SPECIFY)	1	1
DK/NA	14	16

2.   "Where did you hear this?" (MULTIPLE ANSWERS ALLOWED) (in percents of respondents who have heard the claim that the Nazi extermination of the Jews never happened)

Response	United States 1994	United States 1992
Books	9	14
Television	71	59
The movies	5	5
Newspaper and magazine articles	35	37
School	6	4
Churches/synagogues	2	2
People I know	15	14
From neo-Nazi groups	10	12
Other (SPECIFY)	1	4
DK/NA	4	5

Slovakia (1993)

1. "The atrocities committed against Jews during World War II must be condemned." (in percents)

Country	I absolutely agree	I rather agree	I rather disagree	I absolutely disagree	DK/NA
Slovakia (1993)	71	20	2	1	6

2. "Slovak political representatives also take their share of responsibility for the extermination of the Jews." (in percents)

Country	I absolutely agree	I rather agree	I rather disagree	I absolutely disagree	DK/NA
Slovakia (1993)	19	28	14	8	32

3. "President Tiso saved the lives of thousands of Jews and the Jewish people should therefore be grateful to him." (in percents)

Country	I absolutely agree	I rather agree	I rather disagree	I absolutely disagree	DK/NA
Slovakia (1993)	8	16	17	16	43

4.   "What do you think of the sharing of responsibility and guilt of the ordinary Slovak population for the fate of the Jews?" (in percents)

Response	Percent
Everybody was trying to save the Jews to the best of their possibilities; nothing more could have been done	35
More could have been done to save the Jews	26
Don't know	39

France (1993)

1.   "Would you say that the French state led by Marshal Pétain between 1940 and 1944 was responsible for the deportation of Jews to the extermination camps, or not responsible?" (in percents)

Country	Yes, it was responsible	No, it was not responsible	DK/NA
France (1993)	57	29	14

2.   "In your view, is the remembrance of the Holocaust necessary so that it doesn't happen again, or dangerous because it risks a revival of anti-Semitism?" (in percents)

Country	Necessary	Dangerous	DK/NA
France (1993)	74	23	3

Australia (1994)

1. "And in your view how likely is it that any other people could be subject to an event similar to the Holocaust somewhere in the world in coming years? Would you say it was ...? (in percents)

Country	Very likely	Somewhat likely	Not very likely	Not likely at all	DK/NA
Australia (1994)	41	40	13	4	2

2. "Do you think that the topic of the Holocaust is sufficiently important to warrant it being taught as a special subject in Australian secondary schools?" (in percents)

Country	Yes	No	DK/NA
Australia (1994)	41	55	4

Poland (1995)

1. "In your view, who was the main victim of the Nazis during the Second World War?" (OPEN-ENDED) (in percents)

Response	Percent
Poles/Poland	26
Jews	28
Poles/Poland and Jews	28
Russians/Russia	1
Europeans/several nations	2
Everyone/every country suffered about the same	5
Other	7
Don't know	3

2.   "What percent of Poland's population before the Second World War was Jewish?" (in percents)

Response	Percent
Less than 2 percent	1
2-9 percent	10
10-19 percent	26
20-29 percent	29
30-49 percent	17
50+ percent	3
Don't know	15

Note: Historians agree that Jews constituted 10 percent of Poland's population prior to the Second World War.

3.   "What happened to most Polish Jews during the Second World War?" (OPEN-ENDED) (in percents)

Response	Percent
Killed	77
Emigrated	3
Some were killed, some emigrated	13
Survived	1
Other	4
Don't know	2

4.   "Which group suffered more from Nazi persecution during the Second World War: Poles or Jews?" (in percents)

Response	Percent
Poles	28
Jews	29
Both groups suffered about the same (volunteered)	40
Other responses (volunteered)	1
Don't know	3

5. "What percent of Polish Jews were killed by the Nazis during the Second World War?" (in percents)

Response	Percent
Less than 10 percent	3
10-49 percent	31
50-79 percent	38
80+ percent	13
Don't know	15

6. "There are now many fewer Jews in Poland than there were before the Second World War. Is this good for the country, bad for the country, or neither?" (in percents)

Response	Percent
Good	35
Bad	5
Neither	51
Other	1
Don't know	8

7. "Were there any Poles who participated in rescuing Jews during the Second World War, or not?" (in percents)

Response	Percent
There were many such Poles	67
There were few such Poles	28
There were no such Poles	0
Don't know	5

8.   "Were there any Poles who participated in the persecution of Jews during the Second World War, or not?" (in percents)

Response	Percent
There were many such Poles	11
There were few such Poles	62
There were no such Poles	14
Don't know	13

9.   "Did Poles do enough to help Jews during the Second World War, or not?" (in percents)

Response	Percent
Did enough	49
Did not do enough	15
Did as much as they could under the circumstances (volunteered)	26
Other (volunteered)	1
Don't know	8

ADDENDUM

The data appearing in this document are taken from the following American Jewish Committee-sponsored surveys:

Bashkirova, Elena. *Current Russian Attitudes Toward Jews and the Holocaust*. New York: American Jewish Committee, 1996.

Bútorová, Zora, and Martin Bútora. *Attitudes Toward Jews and the Holocaust in Independent Slovakia.* New York: American Jewish Committee, 1995.

Cohen, Renae, and Jennifer L. Golub. *Attitudes Toward Jews in Poland, Hungary, and Czechoslovakia: A Comparative Survey.* New York: American Jewish Committee, 1991.

Cohen, Renae, and Jennifer Golub. *Current Austrian Attitudes Toward Jews and the Holocaust.* New York: American Jewish Committee, 1995.

Golub, Jennifer. *Current German Attitudes Toward Jews and Other Minorities.* New York: American Jewish Committee, 1994.

Golub, Jennifer, and Renae Cohen. *Knowledge and Remembrance of the Holocaust in Poland.* New York: American Jewish Committee, 1995.

Golub, Jennifer, and Renae Cohen. *What Do Americans Know About the Holocaust?* New York: American Jewish Committee, 1993.

Golub, Jennifer, and Renae Cohen. *What Do Australians Know About the Holocaust?* New York: American Jewish Committee, 1994.

Golub, Jennifer, and Renae Cohen. *What Do the British Know About the Holocaust?* New York: American Jewish Committee, 1993.

Golub, Jennifer, and Renae Cohen. *What Do the French Know About the Holocaust?* New York: American Jewish Committee, 1994.

Gudkov, Lev, and Alex Levinson. *Attitudes Toward Jews in the Commonwealth of Independent States.* New York: American Jewish Committee, 1994.

Gudkov, Lev, and Alex Levinson. *Attitudes Toward Jews in the Soviet Union: Public Opinion in Ten Republics.* New York: American Jewish Committee, 1992.

Jodie, David A. *United Germany and Jewish Concerns: Attitudes Toward Jews, Israel, and the Holocaust.* New York: American Jewish Committee, 1991.

Charmin, Fritz. *Austrian Attitudes Toward Jews, Israel, and the Holocaust.* New York: American Jewish Committee, 1992.

Smith, Tom W. *Holocaust Denial: What the Survey Data Reveal.* New York: American Jewish Committee, 1995.

Stuart E. Eizenstat

UNDER SECRETARY OF STATE FOR ECONOMIC, BUSINESS AND
AGRICULTURAL AFFAIRS
UNITED STATES

Report of the Task Force on Holocaust Education, Remembrance and Research

Plenary Session: Holocaust Education, Remembrance and Research

At the initiative of Swedish Prime Minister Goran Persson, the Swedish, UK and U.S. governments, together with experts from our countries, gathered in Stockholm last May to launch an unprecedented international initiative -- the Task Force for International Cooperation on Holocaust Education, Remembrance and Research. Our countries and many others -- Germany among the first and most consistent-- have engaged in Holocaust education efforts at home for many years. But for the first time, heads of government agreed to cooperate directly with other countries, through diplomatic and other channels, to strengthen Holocaust education efforts on both sides of the Atlantic and beyond. On September 25, Israel and Germany joined the Task Force, and have since contributed very substantially to its work.

On behalf of the Task Force, I would like to give special recognition to the Prime Minister of Sweden, Goran Persson, for developing and giving life to the idea of international, intergovernmental cooperation to promote Holocaust education. I would also like to commend Professor Yehuda Bauer of Yad Vashem, one of the great Holocaust scholars and educators in the world, for his intellectual guidance as Personal Advisor to the Task Force.

As Prime Minister Persson said so eloquently in May, and as did so many speakers at the remarkable half-day breakout session held at the Museum yesterday, Holocaust education and remembrance can help ensure that the crimes of the Holocaust are never forgotten nor repeated. As this century comes to a close and we enter the new millennium, our international cooperation can encourage and reinforce work in many nations to strengthen Holocaust education efforts, to create new ones and to finally begin such efforts where they have been overlooked.

During the U.S. tenure as Task Force Chairman, we have built on Sweden's excellent work in focusing the initiative on a number of priority areas agreed to at the May 7 meeting in Stockholm. These projects, some of which are works in progress to be completed in the first half of next year, are highlighted in the Report that the Task Force is presenting to the Washington Conference.

Let me now summarize very briefly the projects that the Task Force has undertaken to date.

First, an effort is underway to assemble a directory of organizations engaged in Holocaust education and remembrance and a survey of current efforts in the field of Holocaust education worldwide. We expect that the directory, itself a gold mine of information, will become the basis of a much more comprehensive survey of such efforts that can be helpful to countries seeking advice and assistance as they consider ways to improve their own efforts. Sweden has also just completed a series of videotapes for use in their school system.

Second, as part of a domestic initiative, Sweden produced a book on the Holocaust that was made available to every family with high school children. At the request of the Task Force, the book's authors have created an insert demonstrating how an international version and individual national versions of the book can be prepared, should other countries wish to draw on it as part of their own Holocaust education efforts.

Third, the Chief Historians of the U.S. Department of State and the British Foreign and Commonwealth Office will produce a guide to finding and using Holocaust-related archives with the intention that it be employed as a tool by researchers and educators. Making these archives more accessible is a key Task Force goal. Contained in the Task Force Report is a brief proposal as to how activities in this area should proceed over the next year. We highlight in particular a website which is becoming a nexus of information for research in virtually every dimension of the Holocaust-era assets issues discussed at the London and Washington Conferences.

Fourth, in close consultation with Yad Vashem and the U.S. Holocaust Memorial Museum, the UK has led the development of a set of internationally applicable guidelines, or best practices, for use in teaching about the Holocaust. The guidelines are intended to serve as a starting point to facilitate the work of educators both in places where programs exist and in those where they are yet to be developed. They are based on the experiences -- both positive and negative -- of two generations of Holocaust educators.

Fifth, the Task Force has considered and accepted a British proposal to encourage each of our nations to designate a Day of Remembrance for Holocaust victims. In Israel and in the U.S., Yom HaShoa serves this purpose. In Germany, January 27, the day of the liberation of Auschwitz, is recognized. We hope other nations will designate their own Day of Remembrance as well. These acts of remembrance will reinforce awareness of the events of the Holocaust and reach a large audience, while demonstrating solidarity in the fight against anti-Semitism, racism, prejudice, persecution, and hatred.

In addition to these projects, the Task Force has made commitments in the form of two declarations: one concerning archival openness and the other the promotion of Holocaust education efforts. We invite all Washington Conference governments to join us in endorsing these goals.

The Task Force Declaration on the opening of Holocaust-relevant archives presents as our aim the opening of "all public and private archives bearing on the Holocaust and the fate of Nazi-confiscated assets by December 31, 1999." We call on all that possess such material to open it to as many researchers as possible on an urgent basis and commit ourselves as governments to do everything possible to ensure that this important target is met.

The second declaration and final element of the Task Force Report to the Conference emphasizes our common conviction that urgent international attention be paid to Holocaust education, remembrance and research to reinforce and spread the historic meaning and enduring lessons of that tragic event. In the declaration we commit our governments to "reinforce Holocaust education, remembrance and research in our own countries, with a special focus on our own countries' histories." We also pledge to strengthen existing programs or launch new ones, and encourage other countries to do likewise.

We have pledged our governments' commitment to this endeavor, and to our diplomatic cooperation to advance its objectives, principally to ensure that the lessons of the Holocaust are not forgotten and its horrors never repeated. We have full confidence that when the U.S. chairmanship concludes at the end of the month, the UK will serve the Task Force admirably in the role of Chairman. We furthermore hope that Conference participants will find the report of the Task Force a valuable and useful contribution to the cause of Holocaust education, remembrance and research.

Most important, whether by working with us through the Task Force or through other mechanisms, we hope that all countries represented at the Washington Conference will choose to embrace our goals and strengthen their Holocaust education and remembrance efforts. We are delighted that France and the Netherlands have just indicated their interest in joining. Because our effort is an inclusive one, we also urge other countries to consider working directly with us in the Task Force. Nothing could be more important than to honor the many victims and to prevent such tragedies in the future. Thank you.

Appendices

Conference Preparations

Appendix A:
SUMMARY OF THE ORGANIZING SEMINAR FOR THE WASHINGTON CONFERENCE ON HOLOCAUST-ERA ASSETS

TUESDAY, JUNE 30, 1998
WASHINGTON, DC

EXECUTIVE SUMMARY

On June 30, 1998, the U.S. Department of State and the United States Holocaust Memorial Museum co-hosted an Organizing Seminar in preparation for the Washington Conference on Holocaust-Era Assets, which took place from November 30, 1998-December 3, 1998 at the Department of State.

This day-long international organizing seminar, presided over by Under Secretary Stuart E. Eizenstat, reviewed progress on gold issues and helped fashion the agenda for the Washington Conference, scheduled to take place later in the year. The Washington Conference on Holocaust-Era Assets will address issues of Nazi-confiscated art, insurance, other assets such as communal property, archives and libraries and Holocaust education, remembrance and research. The goals of the Washington Conference on Holocaust-Era Assets are to provide a forum in which the international community can seek a consensus on means of addressing Nazi-era injustices as they related to specific asset categories. The organizing seminar was attended by delegations from 38 countries and from eleven Non-Governmental Organizations.

The seminar opened with a reception at the U.S. Holocaust Memorial Museum. Remarks by Miles Lerman, Chairman of the U.S. Holocaust Memorial Council, and by Under Secretary Eizenstat emphasized the need to complete the historical record, to examine what nations have already done to seek to redress injustice, to see what more could and should be done, and to keep the memory of the Holocaust and the victims alive.

GOLD

The Organizing seminar reviewed progress since the December 1997 London Conference on Nazi Gold, and announced the close-down of the Tripartite Gold Commission. The formal close-out ceremony was scheduled for Paris in September 1998.

ART

Speakers on the panel on Nazi-confiscated art discussed the historical background, efforts made to protect cultural treasures, and current issues. Due to the massive theft of artworks by the Nazis, over half of the 220,000 works remain lost to their original owners or their heirs, according to one panelist. Panelists cited examples of efforts and treaties in place during World War II, which were designed to protect and retrieve stolen art objects in Europe. The panelists highlighted the guidelines created by the Association of Art Museum Directors (AAMD) as an example of recent efforts on behalf of museums to provide guidelines and principles to address issues of unclear provenance. Furthermore, open access to museum records and the creation of a central database were cited as means of closing gaps of unclear ownership.

INSURANCE

The complexity of issues surrounding the investigation and restitution of Nazi-era insurance policies was highlighted by seminar participants. Based on growing public and anecdotal evidence, it appears that some insurance companies either never paid claims or paid them to third parties. In addition, insurance policies were nationalized in some instances, thereby allowing nations to avoid payment. Records have been lost or destroyed. However, panelists pointed out that insurance companies are initiating efforts to investigate their internal records and wartime policies. Panelists from leading insurance companies pointed to the need for a commission to address future claims on Nazi-era insurance.

OTHER ASSETS

In the area of other assets, encompassing assets such as archives and libraries, bonds, securities, gems, and communal property, delegates stressed the need for increased research. However, delegates pointed out that the lack of a systematic exchange of information hinders a comprehensive study of the fate of these areas of assets and called for further research on these subjects.

HOLOCAUST EDUCATION, REMEMBRANCE AND RESEARCH

Delegates agreed that Holocaust education should be emphasized, in order to act as a warning against future injustices. Panelists observed that positive examples of heroism should be highlighted in addition to the destruction and horror of the Holocaust. Panelists from educational institutions around the world discussed their views on current efforts underway, citing as an example the educational projects implemented both in Sweden and in Germany.

SUMMARY OF THE PROCEEDINGS OF THE ORGANIZING SEMINAR

Under Secretary Eizenstat provided a brief record of the following main points at the conclusion of the Organizing Seminar for the Washington Conference on Holocaust-Era Assets.

Gold
- Italy announced the establishment of a new commission to investigate Italian wartime banking activities.
- Greece announced its willingness to open the archives of its Finance Ministry.
- Several delegations called for an opening of Vatican archives.
- A call for attention to the Romani community was made, who had suffered Nazi persecution and genocide.
- Norway announced a decision to designate $60 million towards a Holocaust victims restitution program.
- A call was made for the synthesis of the Swiss Bergier Commission and the US gold reports, in order to create an accurate account.
- The creation of a central web site on archives was suggested, which would act as a link between the sites of individual countries.

Art

- Less than half of the 220, 000 works of art stolen during World War II were recovered and restituted.
- The Association of Art Museum Directors (AAMD) announced the creation of guidelines for Nazi-confiscated art.
- Lithuania called upon the Council of Europe to create similar guidelines.
- Delegates discussed the London Declaration of 1943, in which the Allies nullified commercial art transactions in occupied Europe.
- Questions of provenance and sovereignty still are of issue to the art world as a result of Nazi looting and postwar restitution policies.

Insurance

- Representatives from the National Association of Insurance Commissioners discussed the complexity of issues surrounding the investigation and restitution of insurance policies purchased before the war.
- German representatives outlined its investigations of wartime and postwar insurance activities.
- Representatives from Allianz insurance company discussed internal records investigations.
- Delegates recognized that a structure is being created in order to achieve results with minimal confrontation.

Other Assets

- Gems are being investigated by Belgium.
- Delegates made a call for the investigation of communal property.
- Research on and restitution of savings of slave laborers brought to Germany was requested.
- An investigation of the theft and sales of victims clothing and other personal belongings was suggested.

Education

- Delegates recognized the importance of Holocaust education, beyond restitution of assets.
- Positive examples of heroism should be taught in addition to the destruction and horror of the Holocaust.
- Education, research and remembrance are key, becoming an enduring legacy for future generations.

Appendix B:
SUMMARY OF THE ROUNDTABLE DISCUSSION ON NAZI-LOOTED ART

TUESDAY, JUNE 9, 1998
WASHINGTON, DC

On June 9, 1998, the U.S. Department of State and the United States Holocaust Memorial Museum co-hosted a **Roundtable Discussion on Nazi-Looted Art** at the Museum. This roundtable was one of a series of events in preparation for the Washington Conference on Holocaust-Era Assets. This event brought together government officials, scholars, and representatives of interested and affected institutions, in order to provide an educational opportunity for all parties involved as well as to gain a better understanding of the numerous complex issues associated with restitution of Nazi-confiscated art. In order to structure the discussion effectively, the roundtable was divided into three sections that focused on separate elements of the issue.

NAZI LOOTING OF ARTWORKS: HISTORY AND SOURCES

The history session discussed the gaps in our knowledge of the history of Nazi-looted art, needed archival sources, and concerns related to such archival sources. The implications of issues surrounding Holocaust era confiscated art extend beyond individual cases to affect the entire process of art collection, whether by individuals or institutions, such as museum or galleries. The question of restitution of works of art to individual victims of the Holocaust is complex. There is a large body of *unclaimed* and *unidentified* works. In addition, there are works that are unaccounted for, which came to their current owners through a variety of reasons. These works may have been sold under duress, sent to Nazi leaders from occupied countries, lesser known works by minor artists, so-called "degenerate" artworks that were stolen and fed to the art trade, works taken to the Soviet Union, or art considered "war loot". Many of these unrecovered works are in private collections and therefore virtually untraceable. *Heirless* works, for which no claimants remain living, compose another difficult category of relevant art works.   Art restitution efforts by Allies after WWII were sometimes incomplete and some artworks, handed over to their country of origin, were not returned to their pre-war owners.   National efforts during the post-war period were largely completed by the late 1960s.

Large-scale restitution measures could possibly affect the art market in the areas of purchasing, exhibiting and borrowing. Three areas of difficulty were identified that may contribute to the enormity of the problem of art restitution: determining what is missing, determining locations and owners, and devising an equitable method of restitution for past and present owners.

The need to create a comprehensive inventory of international, freely accessible archival holdings of materials related to restitution issues was considered one of the most important steps.   Sources are presently dispersed in archives, government repositories, and private collections, as well as among personal papers belonging to organizations and individuals.   Archives in many countries continue to hamper and restrict research efforts by being inaccessible, maintaining prohibitive classification systems or by using local privacy laws as the basis for blacking out references to specific individuals. A lack of funding for the support of scholars further limits research efforts in this area.

Many participants called upon archives to extend their identification of relevant source material to include the war and post-war period.   Although numerous restitution claims were made during the 1960s, they were unsuccessful in part because the claimants, rather than the current owners, were required to produce documentation of ownership rights.   In order to help families to properly identify their missing works of art, relevant documents should be made available to them to allow for a complete research effort. This is important because many families are unable to fully identify their lost assets, since inventories of collections were often taken at the time that the works of art were taken. Proposals included making Nazi documents available for those not aware of specific losses.   Similarly, insurance companies should be asked to audit policies with art schedules in order to help individuals and families close gaps in provenance and to provide victims with full appraisals, locations and names to be checked against published sources.

In order to be able to effectively research and resolve claims, the creation of a database of private and state claims, as well as the creation of a framework for research guidelines was suggested. The framework should address both the practical concerns of claimants as well as the moral implications of research into Holocaust era assets. The creation of a board of experts, tasked with the assessment of historical record regarding individual works of art, was also suggested as a means of contributing to a more structured approach in restitution measures. Underlying the discussion was the need to research both for historical momentum and for the benefit of individual Holocaust victims.

The most often repeated theme was that researchers should have free access to relevant archives worldwide. A lively debate ensued over the possibility of a time limit on the validity on claims in order to encourage active current investigation into Holocaust era assets. All agreed with the need for an ongoing discussion among nations, organizations and individuals.

LEGAL, MORAL, AND POLICY PERSPECTIVES

The London Declaration of 1943 was one of the defining policy and legal tenants regarding art transactions within Nazi-occupied territories. This Declaration gave the signatory countries the right to declare invalid the transfer of goods situated in occupied lands, including sales under duress. It was proposed that a necessary point of discussion during the Washington Conference should be the validity of the London Declaration. A further 1946 accord that signed away all rights to German assets held by Switzerland or Sweden was also sighted as problematic in the establishment of ownership rights. It was suggested that claims to art works which were sold by museums in Germany before the war, including so-called "degenerate" art, should be considered acts of state and therefore to be invalid.

Legal differences from country to country, from state to state, on the issues of property rights, good faith purchases, statutes of limitations, adjudication means, and costs and methods, complicate action that has been and may be taken by claimants. Since many restitution laws do not apply internationally, one suggestion was that US courts be the ones to judge restitution cases in order to avoid incurring vast costs in unsuccessful attempts by Holocaust survivors to reclaim property in numerous countries. Many of these victims are now reaching the end of their lives. Claimants face varying statutes of limitations. It was recognized that the codification of statutes of limitations on the basis of moral issues is extremely problematic. One participant suggested that if Nazi confiscation of art is considered a war crime, no such specific statute applies.   Despite the ethical ramifications, present-day owners have, in some claims cases, used statutes of limitations as a trump card in order to retain Nazi-confiscated art.

In discussing broader implications of this debate on cultural property, all agreed that the Washington Conference define its art issue to deal only with Nazi confiscated art or forced sales of art. Unlike gold, insurance, or bank accounts, art is now primarily owned by good-faith purchasers who have no knowledge of the questionable history of their objects. Many participants, concerned about the dilemma created by such good-faith purchasers, suggested that some form of non-binding mediation be made available to reach agreements. The practicality of reaching international consensus on restitution issues was questioned. Instead, it was felt that international pressure should be applied to those possessing looted art. In cases where claimants had found that museums regarded restitution cases as closed and were not interested in dealing with survivors, some means of resolving disputes morally was needed. Similarly, claimants had found it difficult or impossible to lodge claims in some countries in which art returned at the end of the war had been nationalized.

Concern was raised that many claimants to Nazi-looted art simply cannot afford to fight current owners; legal fees alone can run very high. In many cases, current owners possess greater means and may not be willing to go to arbitration to settle disputes. Alternative methods of resolution, such as mediation, were suggested as a means of creating non-binding agreements aimed to solve individual cases.   Specifically, participants proposed the formation of a comprehensive, searchable list of claims (as in the first session), called for an inventory of all national and international laws concerning restitution of art works, suggested alternative, non-binding forms of resolution to individual cases, asked for an exploration of assistance measures for claimants without the means to pursue law suits, and called for tax breaks or other incentives for good faith purchasers of paintings with a tainted provenance.

PRINCIPLES, PROCESSES AND PRACTICAL STEPS

This session examined the possibility of establishing guiding principles for claims processes, as well as practical steps necessary for such procedures. There is strong and urgent public interest in seeing that Holocaust victims recover lost assets. Stabilizing the international art market and cultural exchange are also major concerns. Museums and galleries are fearful of purchasing any work of art with even the slightest question of provenance. This is hindering the availability of works of art for public knowledge, research, and display. Participants noted that the art world craves certainties, especially when considering a purchase. U.S. museums must play a proactive role, serving as leaders in the restitution and research process. The guidelines recently created by the Association of Art Museum Directors were included, as an example of an effort to clarify and establish needed measures to ensure consistency of action among an affected group.

Participants saw the immediate creation of a complete, user friendly database as the single most important measure for claims research. The Art Loss Registry has announced a new endeavor to locate and identify looted art. Working with museums, galleries, dealers, and collectors, the ALR will attempt to return stability to the art market. The ALR will offer its services free-of-charge to Holocaust survivors.

While participants recognized that some questions of provenance will never be answered, they found it vital to call upon buyers and sellers of works of art to investigate gaps in provenance, alerting affected parties of possible tainted histories. Possible regulatory mechanisms for claims cases could be found in non-binding third-party intervention. Increased availability of archives and documentation, the expanded publication and display of art objects, and international consensus can contribute to an open environment.

Momentum created by the London Conference on Nazi Gold will be expanded to focus on previously excluded categories of assets. Inevitably, participants addressed the inclusion of claims that extend beyond the realm of the Holocaust period. There was a recognition, however, that while principles and processes discussed in relation to the restitution of Holocaust era art relate to art restitution claims in general, this particular forum should focus itself exclusively on addressing the immediate concerns of victims of this period.

Appendix C:
SUMMARY OF THE SEMINAR ON HOLOCAUST-ERA INSURANCE CLAIMS

SEPTEMBER 4, 1998
PRAGUE, CZECH REPUBLIC

On September 4, 1998, the Department of State hosted an international Seminar on Holocaust era insurance claims in Prague, Czech Republic. This seminar was one of a series of events in preparation for the Washington Conference on Holocaust-Era Assets, which took place at the Department of State from November 30 to December 3, 1998.

This event brought together government officials, scholars and representatives of private institutions, in a non-confrontational atmosphere to discuss the complex historical issues associated with Holocaust era insurance claims, as well as to support the international claims resolution and humanitarian process initiated by the National Association of Insurance Commissioners (NAIC).

BACKGROUND

Holocaust era insurance claims are complex and difficult issues. The painful history of Nazi persecution was address, as well as the ensuing totalitarian governments during the Cold War, left unresolved compensation for Holocaust era insurance claims due to nationalization of claims and the liquidation of insurance company assets. Representatives from Poland, Hungary, Czech Republic and Slovakia described how assets belonging to insurance companies were seized first by the Nazis during World War II and, following the War, by the Communists. Foreign insurance company assets, mostly in the form of real estate, were taken by Communists to cover any liabilities companies may have had. German insurance companies, specifically, were said not have had any assets from which claims could have been paid.

The government of Poland signed an agreement with the United Kingdom to transfer 500,000 pounds to Great Britain, in order to allow British to pay claims from policies issues in Poland. Agreement between Poland and Italy for Italian insurance companies, Generali and RAS, was not achieved. Both companies suffered extensive losses of real property assets during the War and were unable to pay claims from their pre-War holdings. Potential claimants were referred to Generali's headquarters in Trieste, in order to collect on unpaid insurance policies, but many remain unresolved.

A compensation program initiated by the German government did not benefit East European victims of the Holocaust because the German Hallstein Doctrine prevented Germany from supplying compensation to states recognizing the Communist East German regime. However, following the collapse of communism, some of the East European governments liquidated assets belonging to Western insurance companies and created national compensation programs. Both the Czech Republic and Hungary argue that the funds received from the liquidation of these assets have begun to assist needy Holocaust victims.

Claimants applying for compensation for insurance policies previously held in Poland were experiencing difficulty settling their claims due to disagreements among the current government of Poland and Italian insurance companies that conducted business in Poland before WWII. The claims adjudication procedures in place, according to some participants, were inadequate and did not allow for resolution of the claims. Further disagreement, according to another seminar participant, arose from the modest amounts allotted to Holocaust victims through compensation programs. Hungary's program was cited as an example. Since the contention over unpaid claims and seized assets still hampers the compensation process, affected countries considered meeting again in October 1998 to attempt to resolve their differences.

NATIONAL ASSOCIATION OF INSURANCE COMMISSIONERS (NAIC) PROCESS

The Chairman and Vice Chairman of the National Association of Insurance Commissioners outlined at the seminar their proposal for the resolution of outstanding Holocaust era insurance claims. They reported the task force, designed to create an international commission. The commission would be made up of European and U.S. insurance regulators, insurance company representatives and members of Jewish organizations representing Holocaust survivors. The U.S. Department of State, as well as the European Commission would be granted an observer seat. The proposed commission would have a balanced membership, six European and six U.S. representatives, and would be head by a Chairman acceptable to all commission members. Decisions would be made by consensus. The commission would establish a claims adjudication process, as well as distribution procedures designed to quickly resolve outstanding individual claims. They would also establish a humanitarian fund designed to provide prompt assistance to needy Holocaust survivors.

Commission membership would be voluntary and all members could withdraw from the process at any time. The procedures are meant to substitute for the class action lawsuit filed against sixteen European insurance companies. Five European insurance companies, AXA, Allianz, Zürich, Winterthur and Basler, had signed the Memorandum of Understanding for the International Commission. Others, such as Generali, were still reviewing it. However, the general reaction from representatives of Italian insurance companies, as well as from government representatives seemed to be in support of the process suggested by the NAIC.

FUTURE EFFORTS

NAIC representatives advocated an international commission process that would seek early result through its empowerment to negotiate settlements of Holocaust era insurance claims with individual insurance companies. They also hoped that the momentum created by support for the MOU and international commission will extend to those insurance companies outside the process.

Appendix D:
SUMMARY OF THE ROUNDTABLE DISCUSSION ON NAZI-CONFISCATED LIBRARIES AND ARCHIVES

SEPTEMBER 11, 1998
WASHINGTON, DC

On September 11, 1998, the US Department of State and the United States Holocaust Memorial Museum co-hosted a Roundtable Discussion on Nazi-Confiscated Libraries and Archives at the Museum. This roundtable was one of a series of events in preparation for the Washington Conference on Holocaust-Era Assets. The program for this roundtable discussion was modeled after an earlier roundtable discussion on Nazi-confiscated art.

This event brought together government officials, scholars, and representatives of interested and affected institutions, in order to provide an educational opportunity for all parties involved as well as to gain a better understanding of the numerous complex issues associated with the restitution of Nazi-confiscated libraries and archives. In order to structure the discussion effectively, the roundtable was divided into three sections that focused on separate elements of the issue.

NAZI CONFISCATION OF LIBRARIES AND ARCHIVES: HISTORY AND SOURCES

Participants discussed the history and found the gaps in our knowledge of the history of Nazi-confiscated libraries and archives. The discussion focused on known archival sources for research on this topic. An historical discussion of wartime looting and plundering provided insight to the Nazi policy of progressive cultural theft, which included the systematic confiscation of the libraries and archives of nations, communities, religious and political organizations.

Unlike artworks, there were no Nazi collectors of archives. No comprehensive list or census of all archives existing at the beginning of World War II exists. The MFA & A did compile catalogues of targeted libraries and archives, which it used to pinpoint and aid in the post-war restitution process.

Outstanding issues concerning confiscated libraries and archives are primarily intergovernmental and not particularly financial in nature. With the exception of the YIVO and Telshe Yeshiva Collections currently held in the National Library of Lithuania, there do not appear to be major conflicts in the library world concerning restitution of Nazi-confiscated library and archival collections to US institutions.

Library collections held at the Offenbach Archival Depot were generally restituted successfully; monthly reports of post-war activities at Offenbach are available at the National Archives and Records Administration. Records of the materials collected at Offenbach also exist. Materials not initially recovered in 1945 and 1946 remain a problem, as identifying missing archives is difficult. The post-war military government was interested in recording collected materials, not investigating privately held materials. The Allies had a policy of not returning Jewish materials to the Soviet Union. Some of these can now be found in Israel, and others were sold at auction.

Many important Nazi-confiscated archives have been hidden in Central and Eastern Europe for over half a century. Originally appropriated by the National Socialist regime, these libraries and archives were claimed by the Soviet Union at the end of the Second World War. Two major collecting points were identified in the East – one operating under Rosenberg and another operating under RSHA. A total of approximately 11 million books were taken from Germany to the Soviet Union at the end of World War II. These were distributed to libraries throughout the USSR, but only 4.7 million books from Germany had been identified as of 1996. In 1992 approximately 600 books were restituted to the Bibliotheca Rosenthaliana in Amsterdam from the Rudomino Library of Foreign Literature in Moscow. The Russian-German Library Commission on Restitution has agreed on unlimited access to library collections for both sides.

Confiscated materials found in the former Soviet Union are not catalogued, and many collections were not discovered until recently. Many unrestituted archives are being held by the Osobyi Archive in Moscow. These archives are available to scholars on a very limited basis due to lack of funds for resources such as electricity, heat and security. Full-scale finding aids to these collections are not available. These archives and libraries include unique documents, which relate the histories of destroyed communities for which no other records exist. In some cases, administrators of Jewish and Hebrew archives in Eastern

Europe do not possess the means to organize, archive or even read archival materials.

Information on confiscated libraries and archives, including lists of missing materials, can be found in the appendices of the *Jewish Social Studies Journal* and the *Spoils of War* Newsletter. Some individual countries have compiled lists of missing archives; additional lists are needed to identify other lost collections and to develop an international inventory of libraries and archives. Roundtable participants noted a number of web sited dedicated to "trophy" materials, some of which present inaccurate information.

LEGAL, MORAL, AND POLICY PERSPECTIVES

Participants discussed the international legal basis and precedents for restitution of unique official records of state and private agencies and concluded they are even stronger than for works of art. By 1976, reinforcing the Hague Conventions of 1907 and 1954, UNESCO had adopted the position that military occupation does not authorize a right to retain archives acquired through occupation. The Council of Europe has issued a resolution and publication, outlawing the term "trophy" as well as calling on the international community to return archives to their place of origin. Such resolutions, however, do not have legal effect.

Conflicting laws and legal principles of Anglo-American and Continental-European law create tensions regarding issues of restitution claims. For example, European statutes of limitation expired 25 to 30 years after World War II. Unlike the US and the UK, Europe does not recognize a "discovery rule". The Anglo-American "discovery rule" extends claims a further 2 to 6 years following the "discovery" of a missing or hidden work. A consensus is needed to define the terms "booty" and "confiscation" consistently on an international basis.

In some cases of confiscated libraries and archives, the identification of the rightful heirs has been contested. For example, YIVO archives could be seen as belonging to the present-day Jewish community in Lithuania, or to the YIVO Institute in New York, which considers itself the direct descendent of the pre-War community library. Also, the United States National Archives holds many items from businesses seized as enemy property during the Second World War. Restitution of these materials and corporate archives could be seen as morally obligated.

The Washington Conference aims to encourage good will, not to institute legal procedures. It was suggested by one participant that microfilm copies of collections be considered as a form of restitution, promoting international accessibility for researchers. Other participants resisted this proposal, as such restitution measures do not address basic questions of original theft and rightful ownership.

It was agreed that original materials should be returned to the country of origin and made available in accessible locations. Also agreed was that law courts would likely not effectively resolve issues. Accordingly, professional archivists should work together to resolve standing issues. To this end, resolutions may be more easily reached on a bilateral basis.

PRINCIPLES, PROCESSES, AND PRACTICAL STEPS

In this session participants examined the possibility of establishing guiding principles for claims processes, as well as practical steps necessary for such procedures. The group unanimously agreed that documentation of events of this period is of great importance. Although countries are encouraged to examine the entirety of their archives, such measures are impractical. Alternatively, countries are encouraged to identify missing materials. All existing information needs to be discussed, not only the active heirs of one group. Private archives and the records of Jewish communities which were completely annihilated during the Holocaust should also be investigated in the attempt to gain a clear picture of historical events.

There is no equivalent for archives and libraries to the guidelines set forth earlier this year by the American Association of Museum Directors for artwork. Several models for restitution were suggested, including the Art Loss Registry. Another example was the Jewish Cultural Reconstruction, as heirs would appreciate recognition of previous ownership as well be consulted regarding archival losses. It was suggested that heirless archives be sent to Israel, where they could be placed in the Central Jewish Library. Such an action would make records available for research in addition to ensuring their documentation and preservation.

In general, it appears that an open exchange of information concerning library collections and continuing discussions and consultations should help resolve outstanding issues.

Conference Documents

Appendix E:
CONFERENCE SCHEDULE

MONDAY, NOVEMBER 30, 1998

19:00-20:00   **Opening Ceremony**
Hall of Witness, United States Holocaust Memorial
    Museum
100 Raoul Wallenberg Place, S.W.
(15th Street entrance – Raoul Wallenberg Place)
Followed by a Reception, Wall of Remembrance,
    Concourse Level

Speakers:
Miles Lerman, Chairman, United States Holocaust
    Memorial Council
Stuart E. Eizenstat, Under Secretary of State for
    Economic, Business and Agricultural Affairs
Abner J. Mikva, Conference Chairman
Elie Wiesel, Founding Chairman, United States
    Holocaust Memorial Council and Nobel Peace
    Laureate

20:00-22:00   Reception guests are invited to visit the Museum
    exhibitions

TUESDAY, DECEMBER 1, 1998

08:30   Registration at U.S. Department of State
    2201 "C" Street, N.W.
    ("C" Street entrance)

The Washington Conference on Holocaust-Era Assets, co-hosted by the U.S. Department of State and the United States Holocaust Memorial Museum, is a government-organized, international meeting of forty-four governments and a limited number of non-governmental organizations seeking to address Nazi-confiscated assets, specifically art and insurance, and to conclude any remaining gold issues, as well as communal property, archives, books, the role of historical commissions, and Holocaust education, remembrance and research.

09:15 Delegates proceed to the Loy Henderson Auditorium

09:30 **Conference Begins in Plenary Session**
Open to Press via live transmission into Dean Acheson Auditorium

Miles Lerman, Chairman, U.S. Holocaust Memorial Council
  Welcome and Introduction of the Conference Chairman

Abner J. Mikva, Conference Chairman
  Opening Remarks

09:50 Stuart E. Eizenstat, Under Secretary of State for Economic, Business, and Agricultural Affairs
  Welcome and Introduction of the Secretary of State

Madeleine K. Albright, Secretary of State of the United States of America
  Keynote Address

10:15 Anthony Layden, Head of Delegation of the United Kingdom
  Greetings from Robin Cook, Foreign Secretary, United Kingdom

Stuart E. Eizenstat, Under Secretary of State for Economic, Business, and Agricultural Affairs
  Opening Remarks on behalf of U.S. Delegation

Avraham Hirchson, Head of Delegation of Israel
  Opening Remarks

Dr. Rajko Djuric, Head of Delegation, International Romani Union
  Opening Remarks

10:45

Plenary Session *Closed to Press*
REVIEW OF GOLD ISSUES, RESEARCH AND RESOLUTION
CHAIRED BY WILLIAM J. MCDONOUGH, PRESIDENT AND CHIEF EXECUTIVE OFFICER, FEDERAL RESERVE BANK OF NEW YORK

Presenters:
Stuart E. Eizenstat, Under Secretary of State for Economic, Business and Agricultural Affairs/United States
Ambassador Louis Amigues, Director of Archives and Documentation, Ministry of Foreign Affairs/France
Anthony Layden, Head, Western European Department, Foreign and Commonwealth Office/United Kingdom

Followed by discussion

11:45

Plenary session on gold ends; delegates proceed to lunch

12:00-13:45

Lunch at the State Department
Benjamin Franklin Room, 8th Floor

Speakers:
Edgar Bronfman, President, World Jewish Congress and World Jewish Restitution Organization
Lord Janner of Braunstone, Chairman, Holocaust Educational Trust

14:00

Plenary Session *Closed to Press*
OVERVIEW OF HOLOCAUST-ERA INSURANCE CLAIMS
CHAIRED BY AMBASSADOR LYNDON OLSON, U.S. AMBASSADOR TO SWEDEN AND FORMER TEXAS INSURANCE COMMISSIONER

Presenters:
Gerald Feldman, Professor of History, University of California, Berkeley and Fellow, American Academy in Berlin/United States
Israel Singer, Secretary General, World Jewish Congress

Glenn Pomeroy, North Dakota Insurance Commissioner
and President, National Association of Insurance
Commissioners (NAIC)/United States
Neil Levin, Superintendent, New York State Insurance
Department, and Vice Chair, NAIC International
Holocaust Commission Task Force/United States
Herbert Hansmeyer, Member of the Board of
Management, Allianz AG

Followed by discussion

15:30   **Break**

15:45   **Plenary Session**   *Closed to Press*
OVERVIEW OF NAZI-CONFISCATED ART ISSUES
CHAIRED BY REPRESENTATIVE JAMES A. LEACH,
    CHAIRMAN, COMMITTEE ON BANKING AND
    FINANCIAL SERVICES, U.S. HOUSE OF
    REPRESENTATIVES

Presenters:
Jonathan Petropoulos, Professor, Department of History,
    Loyola College in Maryland/United States
Lynn Nicholas, Independent Scholar/United States
Ernst Bacher, Chairman, Austrian Art
    Commission/Austria
Valeriy Kulishov, Restitution Expert, Ministry of
    Culture/Russia
Ronald S. Lauder, Chairman of the Board, Museum of
    Modern Art/United States
Earl Powell III, Director, National Gallery of Art/United
    States

Followed by discussion

17:30   Plenary session on art ends

17:30   *Press briefing on gold, insurance and art plenaries*
                    Dean Acheson Auditorium

18:00-19:30   **Reception**
Hosted by His Excellency Sir Christopher Meyer, British Ambassador
British Embassy
Ambassador's Residence
3100 Massachusetts Avenue, N.W.
Delegation members and by invitation only

WEDNESDAY, DECEMBER 2

09:00   **Plenary Session**   *Closed to Press*
SEPARATE OVERVIEWS OF NAZI-CONFISCATED
   COMMUNAL PROPERTY AND
ARCHIVES, BOOKS AND HISTORICAL COMMISSIONS

COMMUNAL PROPERTY
CHAIRED BY REPRESENTATIVE BENJAMIN A. GILMAN,
   CHAIRMAN, COMMITTEE ON INTERNATIONAL
   RELATIONS, U.S. HOUSE OF REPRESENTATIVES

Presenters:
Stuart E. Eizenstat, Under Secretary of State for
   Economic, Business and Agricultural Affairs
Ignatz Bubis, President, European Jewish Congress
Erzsébet Pék, Second Secretary, Ministry of Foreign
   Affairs/Hungary
Saul Kagan, Executive Vice President, Conference on
   Jewish Material Claims Against Germany
Andrew Baker, Director, European Section, American
   Jewish Committee

ARCHIVES, BOOKS AND HISTORICAL COMMISSIONS
CHAIRED BY AMBASSADOR LOUIS AMIGUES, DIRECTOR
   OF ARCHIVES AND DOCUMENTATION, MINISTRY OF
   FOREIGN AFFAIRS/FRANCE

Presenters:
Gill Bennett, Head Historian, Foreign and
   Commonwealth Office/United Kingdom

Michael Kurtz, Assistant Archivist, National Archives
and Records Administration/United States
Siegfried Büttner, Vice President, German Federal
Archives/Germany
Jean-Francois Bergier, Chairman, Bergier
Commission/Switzerland
John Van Oudenaren, Head, European Division, Library
of Congress/United States

10:45   Plenary session on other assets ends

11:00-12:45   **Delegates proceed to concurrent break-out
sessions on art, insurance and other assets, as
well as education, remembrance and research
(off-site)**

WEDNESDAY, DECEMBER 2

BREAK-OUT SESSION: NAZI-CONFISCATED ART
Loy Henderson Auditorium   *Closed to Press*

CHAIRED BY REPRESENTATIVE JAMES A. LEACH, CHAIRMAN,
    COMMITTEE ON BANKING AND FINANCIAL SERVICES, U.S. HOUSE OF
    REPRESENTATIVES

11:00-12:45   Government Restitution Policies, Postwar to Present

Presenters:
Wojciech Kowalski, Head, Dept. of Intellectual and
    Cultural Property Law, University of Silesia/Poland
Oliver Rathkolb, Kreisky Archives and Institute for
    Contemporary History, University of Vienna/Austria
Hector Feliciano, Independent Scholar/United States
Richard Bevins, Historian, Library and Records
    Department, Foreign and Commonwealth
    Office/United Kingdom
Nikolai Gubenko, Deputy Chairman of the Committee
    on Culture, State Duma/Russia
C.E. van Rappard-Boon, Head Inspector, Ministry of
    Education, Culture, and Science/The Netherlands

13:00-14:30   **Lunch at the State Department**
              Benjamin Franklin Room, 8th Floor

Speaker: Representative Charles E. Schumer, U.S.
    House of Representatives

14:45-15:30   Identification of Art, Archives and Databases

Presenters:
Seymour Pomrenze, First Director, Offenbach Archival
    Depot/United States
Connie Lowenthal, Director, Commission for Art
    Recovery, WJC/WJRO
Ronald Tauber, Chairman, The Art Loss Register
Gilbert Edelson, Administrative Vice President and
    Counsel, Art Dealers Association of America

Konstantin Akinsha, Research Director, Project of
Documentation of Wartime Losses
Ori Soltes, former Director, Klutznick National Jewish
Museum

15:30-17:00   Principles to Address Nazi-Confiscated Art

Presenters:
Philippe de Montebello, Director, Metropolitan Museum
of Art, U.S. Association of Art Museum Directors
Task Force/United States
Francoise Cachin, Director, Museums of France and
Ambassador Louis Amigues, Director of Archives and
Documentation, Ministry of Foreign Affairs/France
Sharon Page, Tate Gallery and Chair of Working Group
on Nazi Spoliation of Art, National Museums and
Galleries' Directors Conference/United Kingdom
Carla Schulz-Hoffmann, Deputy Director General,
Bavarian State Paintings Collection/Germany

WEDNESDAY, DECEMBER 2

BREAK-OUT SESSION: HOLOCAUST-ERA INSURANCE CLAIMS
Room 1107 (Overflow Room 1207 with Audio)   *Closed to Press*

CHAIRED BY AMBASSADOR LYNDON OLSON, U.S. AMBASSADOR TO
SWEDEN AND FORMER TEXAS INSURANCE COMMISSIONER

11:00-11:40   Historical Overview: Nazi Confiscation of Insurance
Policy Assets

Presenters:
Gerald Feldman, Professor of History, University of
California, Berkeley, and Fellow, American Academy
in Berlin/U.S.
Tomas Jelinek, Office of the President of the Czech
Republic

11:40 – 12:45 Postwar Government Compensation Programs and
Nationalizations

Presenters:
Rudolph Gerlach, Department Chief, German Federal
Regulatory Agency for Insurance Practices
Gideon Taylor, Vice President Elect, Conference on
Jewish Material Claims Against Germany
Tamás Földi, Public Policy Institute/Hungary
Vojtech Mastny, Senior Research Scholar, Woodrow
Wilson International Center
Elzbieta Turkowska-Tyrluk, Vice President, Powsechny
Zaklad Ubezpieczen (PZU)/Poland

13:00-14:30   **Lunch at the State Department**
Benjamin Franklin Room, 8th Floor

Speaker: Representative Charles E. Schumer, U.S.
House of Representatives

14:45-15:30   <u>Unpaid Claims</u>

Presenters:

Gerald Feldman, Professor of History, University of
California, Berkeley, and Fellow, American Academy
in Berlin/United States

Alan Hevesi, Comptroller of the City of New
York/United States

Catherine Lillie, Director, Holocaust Claims Processing
Office, New York State Banking Department/United
States

Bobby Brown, Adviser to the Prime Minister for
Diaspora Affairs, Prime Minister's Office/Israel

15:30-17:00   <u>Solutions: Addressing Claims and Providing
Humanitarian Relief</u>

Presenters from the International Commission on
Holocaust-Era Insurance Claims:

Neil Levin, Superintendent, New York State Insurance
Department, and Vice Chair, NAIC International
Holocaust Commission Task Force

Bill Nelson, Commissioner, Florida Department of
Insurance

Israel Singer, Secretary General, World Jewish Congress

Alberto Tiberini, Assistant General Manager,
Assicurazioni Generali S.p.A.

Lawrence S. Eagleburger, Chairman, International
Commission

WEDNESDAY, DECEMBER 2

BREAK-OUT SESSION: OTHER NAZI-CONFISCATED ASSETS AND THE ROLE OF HISTORICAL COMMISSIONS
Room 1105 (Overflow Room 1205 with Audio)   *Closed to Press*

11:00-12:45   Communal Property: Progress and Challenges

CHAIRED BY REPRESENTATIVE BENJAMIN A. GILMAN, CHAIRMAN, COMMITTEE ON INTERNATIONAL RELATIONS, U.S. HOUSE OF REPRESENTATIVES

> Presenters:
> Ambassador Naphtali Lavie, Vice Chairman, World Jewish Restitution Organization
> Jerzy Kichler, President, Union of Jewish Congregations in Poland
> Michael Lewan, Chairman, U.S. Commission for the Preservation of America's Heritage Abroad

13:00-14:30   **Lunch at the State Department**
Benjamin Franklin Room, 8th Floor

> Speaker: Representative Charles E. Schumer, U.S. House of Representatives

14:45-16:00   Archives and Books

CHAIRED BY AVNER SHALEV, CHAIRMAN OF THE DIRECTORATE, YAD VASHEM/ISRAEL

> Presenters:
> Eric Ketelaar, Legal Counsel, National Archives/The Netherlands
> Rev. Fr. Marcel Chappin, Professor, Gregoriana Pontifical University/The Holy See
> Yaacov Lozowick, Director of the Archives, Yad Vashem Institute/Israel
> Robert Vanni, General Counsel, NY Public Library/United States

Abby Smith, Program Officer, Council on Library and
Information Resources/United States

Robert Waite, Historian, Office of Special
Investigations, Department of Justice/United States

Shimon Samuels, Director for International Liaison,
Simon Wiesenthal Center, Paris

16:00-17:30   The Role of Historical Commissions

CHAIRED BY GILL BENNETT, HEAD HISTORIAN, FOREIGN AND
COMMONWEALTH OFFICE/UNITED KINGDOM

Presenters:

Peter Klein, Professor, and Secretary of the Scholten
Commission/The Netherlands

Pablo Martin-Aceña, Fundacion Empresa Publica/Spain

Ambassador Krister Wahlbäck, Swedish Foreign
Ministry and Member, Swedish Commission on
Jewish Assets

Ambassador Sevinc Dalyanoglu, General Director for
Multilateral Economic Affairs, Turkish Ministry of
Foreign Affairs

Ignacio Klich, Academic Coordinator, Commission of
Enquiry into the Activities of Nazism in Argentina
(CEANA)

WEDNESDAY, DECEMBER 2

BREAK-OUT SESSION: HOLOCAUST EDUCATION, REMEMBRANCE AND RESEARCH

Held offsite at the U.S. Holocaust Memorial Museum   *Open to Press*

11:15-12:30   Overview of the Importance of Holocaust Education, Remembrance, and Research
Joseph and Rebecca Meyerhoff Theater

CHAIRED BY MILES LERMAN, CHAIRMAN, UNITED STATES HOLOCAUST MEMORIAL COUNCIL

Presenters:
Lord Janner, Chairman, Holocaust Educational Trust/United Kingdom
Representative Tom Lantos, House of Representatives/United States
Avraham Burg, Chairman of the Executive, The Jewish Agency for Israel
Beate Kosmala, Center for Anti-Semitism Research, Technical University, Berlin/Germany
T.J. Blankert-van Veen, Head of Department, Ministry of Health, Welfare and Sport/The Netherlands
Adolphe Steg, Vice President, Mattéoli Commission, and Professor of Medicine, University of Paris/France
Rev. Dr. Remi Hoeckman, Secretary of the Holy See's Commission for Religious Relations with the Jews, O.P.
Yehuda Bauer, Professor, Yad Vashem Institute/Israel

12:30-13:15   Goals of the Task Force for International Cooperation on Holocaust Education, Remembrance, and Research

CHAIRED BY BENNETT FREEMAN, SENIOR ADVISOR TO THE UNDER SECRETARY FOR ECONOMIC, BUSINESS AND AGRICULTURAL AFFAIRS

Presenters:

Stuart E. Eizenstat, Under Secretary of State for
Economic, Business and Agricultural Affairs/United
States

Pär Nuder, State Secretary, Prime Minister's
Office/Sweden

Anthony Layden, Head, Western European Department,
Foreign and Commonwealth Office/United Kingdom

Avner Shalev, Chairman of the Directorate, Yad
Vashem/Israel

Albert Spiegel, Deputy Head, Cultural Section of the
Foreign Office/Germany

**13:15-14:45   Lunch at U.S. Holocaust Memorial Museum
(Museum Café)**

14:45-16:00   Best Practices and Future Projects in Holocaust
Education, Remembrance and Research

A.   Concurrent Panel Session
(Meyerhoff Theater, with emphasis on remembrance)

CHAIRED BY SARA BLOOMFIELD, ACTING DIRECTOR, UNITED STATES
HOLOCAUST MEMORIAL MUSEUM

Presenters:

Teresa Swiebocka, Senior Curator, Auschwitz-Birkenau
State Museum/Poland

Yehuda Bauer, Professor, Yad Vashem Institute/Israel

Stephen Smith, Beth Shalom Holocaust Memorial and
Education Centre/United Kingdom

Regina Wyrwoll, Head of the Media Section, Munich
Head Office, Goethe-Institute/Germany

William Shulman, President, Association of Holocaust
Organizations/United States

Mark Weitzman, Director, National Task Force Against
Hate, Simon Wiesenthal Center/United States

Kenneth Jacobson, Assistant National Director, Anti-
Defamation League/United States

Daisy Miller, Survivors of the Shoah Visual History
Foundation/United States

B. <u>Concurrent Panel Session</u>
(Rubinstein Auditorium, with emphasis on curricular education)

CHAIRED BY WILLIAM PARSONS, CHIEF OF STAFF, UNITED STATES HOLOCAUST MEMORIAL MUSEUM

Presenters:
Vladka Meed, American Gathering of Jewish Holocaust Survivors/United States
Shulamit Imber, Pedagogical Director, Yad Vashem/Israel
Trudy Gold, Spiro Institute/United Kingdom
Robert Sigel, Josef Effner High School, Dachau/Germany
Paul Levine, Prime Minister's Living History Project/Sweden
Margot Stern Strom, Director, Facing History and Ourselves National Foundation/United States
Marcia Sachs Littell, Director, National Academy for Holocaust & Genocide Teacher Training, The Richard Stockton College of New Jersey/United States
David Singer, Director of Research, American Jewish Committee/United States

C. <u>Exhibits of Holocaust resources and curricula by individual governments and NGOs involved in Holocaust education, remembrance, and research</u>
(Concourse Area – on view all day)

17:30   Break-out Sessions Close

17:30   Press briefings on other assets plenary and on art, insurance, other assets and education break-out sessions
U.S. Department of State
Dean Acheson Auditorium

19:00-21:00   Reception at the National Archives Rotunda
Host: John W. Carlin, Archivist of the United States
Delegates by invitation only

Speakers:
John W. Carlin, Archivist of the United States
Nili Arad, Director General, Justice Ministry/Israel

THURSDAY, DECEMBER 3

08:45   Delegates arrive at U.S. Department of State and proceed to Loy Henderson Auditorium

09:00   **Conference Sessions Resume**
Open to Press via live transmission into Dean Acheson Auditorium

Task Force for International Cooperation on Holocaust Education, Remembrance, and Research

Statement by representatives from the United States, Sweden, the United Kingdom, Germany, and Israel

09:30   **Closing Plenary Session**

Presenters:

Miles Lerman, Chairman, United States Holocaust Memorial Council

Benjamin Meed, President, American Gathering of Jewish Holocaust Survivors

10:00   Concluding Statements by Country Delegations

Austria
Hans Winkler, Head of Delegation

Belarus
Vladimir Adamushko, Head of Delegation

Bulgaria
Ambassador Philip Dimitrov, Head of Delegation

Canada
Howard Strauss, Head of Delegation

Czech Republic
Jiri Sitler, Head of Delegation

France
Ambassador Louis Amigues, Head of Delegation

Germany
Ambassador Antonius Eitel, Head of Delegation

Greece
Ambassador Alexander Philon, Head of Delegation

Israel
Yaakov Levy, Deputy Director General, Ministry of
   Foreign Affairs

Italy
Minister Franco Tempesta, Head of Delegation

Macedonia
Vladimir Naumovski, Head of Delegation

Netherlands
Ambassador Jan d'Ansembourg, Head of Delegation

Poland
Agnieszka Magdziak-Miszewska, Advisor to the Prime
   Minister

Switzerland
Ambassador Thomas Bohrer, Head of Delegation

Ukraine
Igor Lushnikov, Head of Delegation

United Kingdom
Anthony Layden, Head of Delegation
Lord Janner of Braunstone

United States
Under Secretary Stuart E. Eizenstat, Head of Delegation

11:15   Delegation Statements Conclude

11:45   Abner J. Mikva
                       Concluding Remarks by Conference Chairman

12:30-13:30   **Lunch at the State Department**
                   Benjamin Franklin Room, 8ᵗʰ Floor

13:00   **Press Conference**   *Dean Acheson Auditorium*

14:00   **Washington Conference on Holocaust-Era Assets**
                   Concludes

*The U.S. Department of State and the United States Holocaust
Memorial Museum gratefully acknowledge the support of The Blanche and
Irving Laurie Foundation, the British Embassy, and the National Archives and
Records Administration.*

Appendix F:
WASHINGTON CONFERENCE ON HOLOCAUST-ERA ASSETS PARTICIPANTS

CONFERENCE CHAIRMAN

The Honorable Abner J. Mikva

HOSTS

Stuart E. Eizenstat, Under Secretary of State for Economic, Business and Agricultural Affairs
Miles Lerman, Chairman, United States Holocaust Memorial Council

CONFERENCE DIRECTORATE

J.D. Bindenagel, Conference Director
Stanley Turesky, Conference Working Group Director
Richard A. Smith, Jr., Conference Deputy Director
Wesley A. Fisher, Conference Working Group Deputy Director

CONFERENCE STAFF

United States Department of State
Ambassador Henry Clarke, Communal Property
Judy Osborn, Art
Milton Gwirtzman, Art
Basil Scarlis, Insurance
John Becker, Communal Property
Steve Dubrow, Press Officer

Bennett Freeman, Senior Advisor
Ananta Hans, Program Assistant
Jody L. Manning, Program Assistant
Eric Kneedler, Special Assistant
Holly Waeger, Intern

United States Holocaust Memorial Museum
Sara Bloomfield, Acting Museum Director
William Parsons, Chief of Staff
Ralph Grunewald, Director of External Affairs
Mary Morrison, Director of Communications
Shana Penn, Director of Media Relations
Linda S. Lazar, Director of Special Events
Sylvia Kay, Museum Conference Planning
Susanne Brose, Intern
Nicolas Gauvin, Intern
Sarah Lueer, Intern

National Archives and Records Administration
Greg Bradsher, Director, Holocaust-Era Assets Records Project

DELEGATIONS

Albania
Ambassador Petrit Bushati, Ambassador
Mrs. Zhaneta Mansaku, Second Secretary

American Gathering of Jewish Holocaust Survivors
Mr. Benjamin Meed, President *(Presenter)*
Mr. Sam Bloch, Senior Vice President
Mr. Roman Kent, Chairman of the Board
Mr. Max Liebmann, Treasurer
Mrs. Vladka Meed, Educational Committee Chairperson *(Presenter)*
Mrs. Lidia Budgor
Mr. Freddy Diament, Former President of Ernst Strauss, Inc.
Mr. Leon Stabinsky, President, California Association of Holocaust
   Child Survivors

Gene Korf, Executive Director, The Blanche and Irving Laurie
  Foundation .
Mr. Albert Rich
Laura Master
Adelaide Zagoren

American Jewish Committee
Mr. David Harris, Executive Director
Rabbi Andrew Baker, Director of European Affairs *(Presenter)*
Dr. David Singer, Director of Research *(Presenter)*
Ms. Dottie Bennett, President, Washington Chapter
Mr. Nicholas Lane, Chairman, International Relations Commission
Mr. Eric Fusfield, Assistant Director of European Affairs

American Jewish Joint Distribution Committee
Mr. Eliyahu Shashua, Legal Counsel, International AJJDC
Mrs. Caryn Wechsler
Mrs. Anja Heuss
Mr. Peter Heuss

Anti-Defamation League
Mr. Kenneth Jacobson, Assistant National Director *(Presenter)*
Stacy Burdett, Assistant Director, D.C. Office
Mr. Irving Shapiro, Vice-Chairman
Mr. Irving Geszel
Ms. Susan Heller, Director, Middle East Affairs and International
  Analysis
Ms. Margery Russell, Co-Chair, Brown Holocaust Institute
Mr. Herman Ziering

Argentina
Ambassador Diego Guelar
Ambassador Daniel Castruccio
Mr. Jose Gutierrez Maxwell, Minister
Dr. Ignacio Klich, Academic Coordinator, Commission of Enquiry into
  the Activities of Nazism in Argentina (CEANA) *(Presenter)*
Manuel Mora y Araujo, President, Commission of Enquiry into the
  Activities of Nazism in Argentina (CEANA)
Minister Alberto de Nunez, Deputy Chief of Mission
Mr. Pablo Beltramino, Secretary of Embassy

Mr. Rodolfo Blachowicz, Counselor, Embassy of Argentina
Mr. Marcelo Massoni, Secretary of Embassy

Australia
Mr. Andrew Todd, Counselor
Ms. Elizabeth McKenna, Congressional Liaison Office

Austria
Mr. Hans Winkler, Director for the Americas, Ministry of Foreign
    Affairs
Professor Ernst Bacher, Chairman, Austrian Art Commission *(Presenter)*
Mrs. Hannah Lessing, Secretary General, National Fund of the Republic
    of Austria for Victims of National Socialism
Mr. Ariel Muzikant, President, Federation of Jewish Communities
Mr. Bertrand Perz, Historian, Member of the Austrian Historical
    Commission
Mr. Martin Weiss, Counselor (Political and Congressional), Embassy of
    Austria
Dr. Gerlinde Manz-Christ, Consul, Consulate General, New York

Belarus
Dr. Vladimir Adamushko, Deputy Chairman, State Committee on
    Archives
Mr. Valtantsin Herasimav, Chairman, Mutual Understanding and
    Recognition Fund
Professor Olga Nekhai, Professor, Minsk State Linguistic University;
    President, Belarussian Association of Former Nazi Prisoners "Lyos"
Mr. Leonid Sennikov, Counselor
Mr. Leonid Levin, Chief of the Workshop, Project Enterprise; President,
    Belarussian Association of Jewish Communities
Arkady Cherepansky, Charge d'Affairs, Embassy of Belarus

Belgium
Mr. Walter Lion, Minister Plenipotentiary, Deputy Director General
Mr. Nicolas Vanhove, Conseiller Adjoint, Mission Restitution of Spoiled
    Goods, Ministry of Economic Affairs
Mr. Philippe Dartois, Minister Plenipotentiary
Professor Georges Schnek, President, Consistoire of Belgium
Mr. Walter Stevens, First Secretary (Economic), Embassy of Belgium

B'nai B'rith International
Mr. Richard D. Heideman, Esq., International President
Dr. Sidney Clearfield, Executive Vice President
Mr. Donald Sussis, International Chairman, B'nai B'rith Center for Public Policy
Mr. Michael Hausfeld, International Chairman, B'nai B'rith Lawyers Network
Mr. Daniel Mariaschin, Director, B'nai B'rith Center for Public Policy

Bosnia and Herzegovina
Ambassador Sven Alkalaj, Ambassador to the United States
Mr. Sead Tikvina, First Secretary
Ms. Meliha Basic, Political Attache

Brazil
Mr. Marcos Vinicius Pinta Gama, Counselor (Human Rights and Social Affairs), Embassy of Brazil

Bulgaria
Ambassador Philip Dimitrov, Ambassador to the United States
Professor Nikola Toholakov, Deputy Chief of Mission
Mrs. Nedyalka Chakalova, Second Secretary

Canada
Mr. Howard Strauss, Director, Oceans, Environment and Economic Law Division, Department of Foreign Affairs and International Trade
Mr. Irving Abella, Professor, York University and Glendon College
Mr. Paul Marsden, Archivist, State, Military and Justice National Archives of Canada
Ms. Susan Murdock, Manager, Government Action and Institutional Development, Department of Canadian Heritage
Mr. Charles Black, Senior Advisor, Insurance Operation Canadian Life and Health Insurance Association
Mr. David Walden, Director, Moveable Cultural Property Program, Department of Canadian Heritage
Ms. Rochelle Wilner, Senior Vice President B'nai B'rith Canada

Conference on Jewish Material Claims Against Germany
Dr. Israel Miller, President
Mr. Saul Kagan, Executive Vice President *(Presenter)*
Mr. Gideon Taylor, Executive Vice President Elect *(Presenter)*

Mr. Karl Brozik, Representative in Germany
Mr. Moshe Jahoda, Associate Executive Vice President

Croatia
Ms. Snjezana Bagic, Deputy Minister of Justice
Mrs. Ljerka Alajbeg, Chief Legal Advisor to the Ministry of Foreign
    Affairs
Ms. Branka Sulc, Assistant Minister of Culture
Mrs. Branka Grabovac, Head of Department for Public Debt

Cyprus
Dr. Erato Kozakou-Marcoullis, Ambassador of Cyprus to the United
    States
Mr. Andreas Kakouris, Deputy Chief of Mission
Mr. George Chacallt, Counselor

Czech Republic
Mr. Jirí Sitler, Director, Department of Central European Affairs,
    Ministry of Foreign Affairs
Mr. Karel Holomek, Chairman of the Association of Friends and Experts
    of the Museum of Roma Culture
Mr. Tomás Kraus, Executive Director, Federation of Jewish
    Communities
Mr. Tomás Jelínek, Counselor of Political Affairs, Office of the
    President *(Presenter)*
Mr. Vít Vlnas, Director of Archives, National Gallery
Ambassador Alexandr Vondra, Ambassador to the United States
Mr. Antonin Hradilek, Deputy Chief of Mission

Denmark
Mr. Svend Olling, Secretary of Embassy
Mr. Jeffrey Cohen, Director, Member of the Jewish Community,
    Denmark
Professor Therkel Straede, Professor

Estonia
Ambassador Kalev Stoicescu, Ambassador to the United States
Jaan Salulaid, First Secretary

European Council of Jewish Communities
Mr. David J. Lewis, President

Mr. Michael May, Executive Director
Mrs. Hannah Lewis
Mr. J. Zissels, Chairman, Association of Jewish Organizations and
  Communities of Ukraine

European Jewish Congress
Mr. Ignatz Bubis, President, European Jewish Congress, and President,
  Zentralrat der Juden in Germany *(Presenter)*
Mr. Eldred Tabachnik, Q.C., President of the Board of Deputies of
  British Jews, and Honorary President, European Jewish Congress
Mr. Henri Hajdenberg, Vice President, EJC; President of the Counseil
  Representatif des Institutions Juives de France
Rabbi Yaakov Bleich, Chief Rabbi of Kiev and the Ukraine
Mr. Serge Cwajgenbaum, General Secretary
Mr. Joop Sanders, Director, Federation of Dutch Jewish Communities
Mr. David Susskind, Member, Directing Committee of the Comitee de
  Corrdination des Organizations Juives de Belgique
Mr. Ben Helfgott, Chairman, Yad Vashem Committee of the Board of
  Deputies

Finland
Ambassador Esko Kiuru, Ambassador
Mr. Teemu Tanner, Deputy Chief of Mission
Heikki Hämäläinen, Secretary to the Board, Bank of Finland
Mr. Jukka Hartikainen, Editor, Otava Publishing Company
Ms. Kirsti Kauppi, First Secretary

France
Ambassador Louis Amigues, Director, Archives and Documentation,
  Ministry of Foreign Affairs *(Chair, Archives, Books and Historical
  Commissions Plenary session, and Presenter)*
Fact-Finding Mission on the Looting of Jewish Assets (Mattéoli
  Commission):
Professor Adolphe Steg, Deputy Chairman of the Commission
  (Presenter)
Mr. Serge Klarsfeld, Esq., President of the Association of Sons and
  Daughters of Deportees; Member of the Commission
Mr. Alain Pierret, Member of the Commission
Mrs. Annette Wieviorka, Member of the Commission
Mrs. Claire Andrieu, Member of the Commission
Mr. André Larquié, Director of the Mission

Mr. Jean Saint-Geours, Inspector General of Finance, Chairman of the Committee, Bank Oversight Committee accredited to the Fact-Finding Mission on the Looting of Jewish Assets

Mr. Jacques-Henri Gougenheim, Representative of the Committee, Insurance Oversight Committee accredited to the Fact-Finding Mission on the Looting of Jewish Assets

Mr. Claude Lanzman, Film Director, Eminent Person

Mr. Pierre Gisserot, Inspector General of Finance, Chief of Mission, Ministry of Economy, Finance, and Industry: Coordinating Mission on Looting and Restitution

Mr. Patrice Dreiski, Special Assistant, Ministry of Economy, Finance, and Industry: Coordinating Mission on Looting and Restitution

Mrs. Myriam Constantin, Special Assistant, Ministry of Economy, Finance, and Industry: Coordinating Mission on Looting and Restitution

Mrs. Françoise Cachin, Director of the Museums of France, Ministry of Culture and Communication, *(Presenter)*

Mr. Norbert Engel, Inspector General, Ministry of Culture and Communication

Mr. Philippe Lefort, Second Counselor, Embassy of France in Washington

Germany

Prof. Dr. Tono Eitel, Ambassador, Ministry of Foreign Affairs

Prof. Dr. Dr. Rudolf Dolzer, Professor, Legal Consultant, Bonn University

Hagen Graf Lambsdorff, Ministerial Director, Press and Information Office

Dr. Albert Spiegel, Deputy Director, Cultural Affairs, Ministry of Foreign Affairs *(Presenter)*

Mr. Michael Geier, Head of Division, Ministry of Foreign Affairs

Mr. Otto Loeffler, Director, Ministry of Finance

Mr. Richard Wiemer, Counselor, Ministry of Foreign Affairs

Mr. Enrico Brandt, Attache, Ministry of Foreign Affairs

Ambassador Juergen Chrobog, Ambassador to the United States

Mr. Harald Braun, Minister (Political) Embassy of the Federal Republic of Germany

Mr. Volker Schlegel, Minister (Economic), Embassy of the Federal Republic of Germany

Mr. Claus Wunderlich, First Political Counselor, Embassy of the Federal Republic of Germany

Mr. Thomas Terstegen, Counselor, Embassy of the Federal Republic of
Germany

Mr. Claudius Fischbach, First Secretary, Embassy of the Federal
Republic of Germany

Mr. Jens Hanefeld, Second Secretary, Embassy of the Federal Republic
of Germany

Greece

Ambassador Alexander Philon, Ambassador to the United States
(Presenter)

Dr. George Dertilis, Professor of History, Athens University

Mrs. Photini Constantopoulou, Expert Counselor, Director of the Service
of Historical Archives, Ministry of Foreign Affairs

Dr. Hagen Fleischer, Professor of History, Athens University

Mr. Albert Hagoul, Secretary General, Jewish Community of
Thessoloniki

Dr. Gabrielle Etmektsoglou, Historian - Visiting Fellow, Princeton
University

The Holy See (Observer Delegation)

Rev. Dr. Remi Hoeckman, Secretary of the Holy See's Commission for
Religious Relations with the Jews, O.P. *(Presenter)*

Rev. Fr. Marcel Chappin, Professor, Gregoriana Pontifical University
(Presenter)

Hungary

Dr. Zsolt Visy, Deputy State Secretary of the Ministry of National
Cultural Heritage

Dr László Asztalos, President, State Insurance Supervision Agency

Dr. Erzsébet Pék, Senior Legal Advisor, International Law Department,
Ministry of Foreign Affairs *(Presenter)*

Dr. György Boytha, Ambassador, Associate Professor of Law, ELTE
University

Dr. Zoltán Bányász, Counselor, Embassy of Hungary

Dr. Zsuzsanna Bóna, Legal Assistant, State Insurance Supervision
Agency

Ms. Zsófia Trombitás, First Secretary, Cultural Attache

International Romani Union

Dr. Rajko Djuric, President, International Romani Union *(Presenter)*

Mr. Marcel Courthiades, Rromani Baxt

Zoran Dimov, TV BTR Nacional
Mr. Victor Famulson, Vice President
Fredi Reinhard-Hoffmann, Representative to the United Nations
Alija Mesic
Josef Muscha Muller
Jovan Nicolic, Vice President
Stefan Pailson
Rita Prigmore
Zivadin Radosavljevic
Dr. Emil Scuka, Secretary General
Milorad Vujicic
Mr. Barry Fisher, Legal Counsel

Israel
Ambassador Zalman Shoval, Ambassador to the United States
Mr. Avraham Hirchson, Member of Knesset *(Presenter)*
Ms. Nili Arad, Director General, Ministry of Justice
Mr. Ya'akov Levy, Deputy Director General, Ministry of Foreign Affairs
Mr. Bobby Brown, Advisor to the Prime Minister on Diaspora Affairs
    (Presenter)
Mr. Levi Ben-David, Minister, Deputy Chief of Mission
Mr. Avi Granot, Minister, Public and Interreligious Affairs
Dr. Avner Shalev, Chairman, Yad Vashem *(Chair, Archives and Books
    Break-out session, and Presenter)*
Mr. Mattityahu Droblas, Chairman, World Jewish Congress
Ms. Talya Lador-Fresher, Counselor, Ministry of Foreign Affairs
Mr. Zvi Barak, Co-Chair, World Jewish Congress
Mr. Aharon Mor, Coordinator, Israel Committee on Restitution of Jewish
    Property
Ms. Zigora Samet, Commissioner of Capital Market, Insurance, and
    Saving
Ms. Yehodit Ben-Susan
Mr. Itamar Levin, Globes INC
Mr. Gideon Koren, Aid to Delegation Chairman

Italy
Mr. Franco Tempesta, Minister Plenipotentiary - Deputy Director
    General for Economic Affairs, Ministry of Foreign Affairs
Mr. Mario Bondioli-Osio, Chair, Commission on Stolen Italian Art
    during WWII

Mr. Vittorio Tedeschi, Minister, Economic & Commercial Affairs, Embassy of Italy
Mr. Giuseppe Perrone, First Secretary

Latvia
Dr. Armands Gutmanis, Foreign Policy Advisor to the President
Ambassador Ojars Kalnins, Ambassador to the United States and Mexico
Dr. Einars Semanis, Deputy Chief of Mission, Embassy of Latvia
Mr. Gregory Krupnikovs, Co-chair, Riga Jewish Community

Lithuania
Mr. Emanuelis Zingeris, Member of Seimas (Parliament); Chairman, Committee on Human and Civil Rights and Ethnic Affairs; Chairman, The Genocide Investigation
Ambassador Stasys Sakalauskas, Ambassador to the United States
Mrs. Ausra Semaskiene, Second Secretary

Luxembourg
Ambassador Arlette Conzemius, Ambassador to the United States
Dr. Paul Dostert, Director, Centre National de la Resistance; Historian, Charge de Direction
Mr. Carlo Krieger, Deputy Chief of Mission

Macedonia
Mr. Vladimir Naumovski, Minister
Ambassador Ljubica Acevska, Ambassador to the United States
Mr. Ivan Dejanov, Macedonian Academy of Sciences and Arts
Mr. Vangel Panovski, Head of US Department, Ministry of Foreign Affairs

National Association of Insurance Commissioners
International Holocaust Commission Task Force
Mr. Glenn Pomeroy, NAIC President and North Dakota Insurance Commissioner *(Presenter)*
Mr. Neil Levin, Superintendent, New York State Insurance Department *(Presenter)*
Ms. Diane Koken, Commissioner, Pennsylvania Department of Insurance
Mr. Bill Nelson, Commissioner, Florida Department of Insurance *(Presenter)*
Ms. Deborah Senn, Commissioner, Washington State Insurance Department

Mr. James Brown, Jr., Commissioner, Louisiana Department of
Insurance
Ms. Charlotte M. Acquaviva, Principle Attorney, Connecticut Insurance
Department
Mr. Paul DeAngelo, Assistant Commissioner, New Jersey Insurance
Department
Mr. William Palmer, Deputy Commissioner, California Department of
Insurance
Mr. Timothy Knapp, Chief of Staff, Pennsylvania Department of
Insurance
Ms. Audrey Samers, Deputy General Counsel, New York State Insurance
Department
Mr. George Brady, International Policy Analyst, NAIC
Mr. Daniel Kadden, Special Projects Manager, Washington State
Insurance Department

Netherlands
Count Jan d'Ansembourg, Ambassador
Drs. C.J. Ruppert, Secretary, Working Party WWII Assets, Ministry of
Finance
Mrs. A.C.M. Proost, Project Manager, Ministry of Health, Welfare and
Sport
Mr. Bob Lodder, Deputy Director Cultural Heritage, Ministry of
Education, Culture and Science
Mr. Ronny Naftaniel, Central Jewish Committee
Drs. Erik de Feijter, Desk Officer, Ministry of Foreign Affairs
Mrs. Thea Blankert-van Veen, Director of Department Resistance
Members, Victims of Persecution and Civilian Victims of War,
Ministry of Health, Welfare and Sport *(Presenter)*
Professor Eric Ketelaar, Legal Counsel *(Presenter)*
Professor Dr. Peter Klein, National Archives *(Presenter)*
Mrs. Charlotte van Rappard-Boon, Ch.E., Head Inspector, Ministry of
Education, Culture, and Science *(Presenter)*

Norway
Ambassador Wegger Strømmen, Special Advisor to the Minister,
Ministry of Foreign Affairs
Dr. Mrs. Berit Reisel, Representative, Norwegian Jewish Society
Ms. Hilde Svartdal, First Secretary, Royal Norwegian Embassy

Poland

Mrs. Joanna Wnuk-Nazarowa, Minister of Culture and Art
Mr. Marek Siwiec, Secretary of State, National Security Advisor
Mrs. Agnieszka Magdziak-Miszewska, Advisor to the Prime Minister
Mr. Jan Jagielski, Jewish Historical Institute
Prof. Wojciech Kowalski, Professor, University of Silesia, Department of
    Intellectual and Cultural Property Laws *(Presenter)*
Mr. Jerzy Kranz, Director, Legal Department, Ministry of Foreign
    Affairs
Ms. Teresa Swiebocka, Senior Curator, Auschwitz-Birkenau State
    Museum *(Presenter)*
Ms. Elzbieta Turkowska-Tyrluk, Vice President, Powsechny Zaklad
    Ubezpieczen (PZU) *(Presenter)*
Mr. Jerzy Kichler, President, Union of Jewish Congregations in Poland
    (Presenter)
Mr. Zygmunt Rakowiecki, Counselor, Ministry of State Treasury
Ambassador Jerzy Kozminski, Ambassador to the United States
Mr. Piotr Ogrodzinski, Deputy Chief of Mission
Mr. Tomasz Michalak, Director of the Department for Political Strategy,
    Chancellery of the President of the Republic of Poland
Mr. Mariusz Handzlik, Political Counselor, Embassy of Poland

Portugal

Professor Joaquim da Costa Leite, Researcher and Historian
Mr. Nuno Mathias, First Secretary

Romani Representative

Mr. John Nickels

Romania

Ambassador Mircea Geoana, Ambassador of Romania to the United
    States
Dr. Elena Zamfirescu, State Secretary, Ministry of Foreign Affairs
Mr. Dorel Dorian, Member of Parliament (Chamber of Deputies),
    Member of the Board of Federation of Jewish Communities of
    Romania
Mrs. Ecaterina Vrinceanu, Deputy General Secretary of the Justice
    Ministry
Mrs. Felicia Waldman, Head of Division, Ministry of National Education
Mrs. Maria Calangiu, Legal Advisor, Ministry of Finance
Mrs. Daniela Bleoanca, Third Secretary, Ministry of Foreign Affairs

Mrs. Raduta Matache, First Secretary, Embassy of Romania

Russia
Ambassador Valentin Kopteltsev, Chief Advisor, 4th European
    Department, Ministry of Foreign Affairs
Mr. Victor Petrakov, Deputy Director, Department of Cultural Heritage,
    Ministry of Culture
Mr. Valery Kulishov, Chief of Restitution Section, Ministry of Culture
    (Presenter)
Mrs. Tatiana Zanina, Chief of Research Section, Federal Archive Service
Mr. Anatoliy Oreshin, Counselor, Department of Economic Cooperation,
    Ministry of Foreign Affairs
Mr. Nikolay Makhutov, Vice President of the Board, Fund of
    Understanding and Reconciliation

Slovak Republic
Dr. Peter Burian, General Director, Ministry of Foreign Affairs
Dr. Robert Fico, Member of Parliament, National Council
Dr. Peter Alexander, Executive Chairman, Central Union of Jewish
    Religious Communities
Dr. Jan Gabor, Charge d'Affairs
Dr. Miroslav Musil, Counselor, Embassy of the Slovak Republic

Slovenia
Ambassador Dimitri Rupel, Ambassador to the United States
Dr. Dusan Biber, Vice President of the International Committee on the
    History of World War II
Mr. Marjan Smonig, Counselor, Embassy of Slovenia

Spain
Mr. Enrique Múgica-Herzog, Member of the Spanish Parliament and
    Chairman of the Spanish Historical Commission on Holocaust Assets
Mr. Francisco de Cáceres, Member of the Spanish Parliament and the
    Spanish Historical Commission
Mr. Fernando de Galainena, Deputy Director General for International
    Economic Affairs (Ministry of Foreign Affairs) and Secretary to the
    Spanish Historical Commision
Mr. Pablo Martín-Aceña, Professor of Economic History (University of
    Alcalá de Henares, Madrid) and Director of the Research Team of the
    Spanish Historical Commission *(Presenter)*
Mr. Mauricio Hatchwell, Member of the Spanish Historical Commission

Mr. Agustín Núñez, Minister for Political Affairs, Embassy of Spain in Washington

Sweden
Mr. Pär Nuder, State Secretary, Prime Minister's Office *(Presenter)*
Ms. Ann-Christin Nykvist, State Secretary
Mr. Ulf Hjertonsson, Director General for Political Affairs
Mr. Krister Wahlbäck, Ambassador *(Presenter)*
Mrs. Veronika Bard-Bringéus, Deputy Director for International Affairs
Ms. Anna-Karin Johansson, Head of Section
Ms. Maria Martinsson, Information Officer
Mr. Stéphane Bruchfeld, Historian
Dr. Paul Levine, Ph.D - Research Fellow *(Presenter)*
Ms. Hédi Fried, Psychologist
Mr. Christer Mattsson, Doctorial Candidate
Mr. Bertil Ahnborg, Deputy Director
Mr. Salomo Berlinger, Special Advisor to the Commission
Mrs. Ingrid Lomfors, Commission Secretary
Ms. Nina Ersman, Press Counselor
Mr. Peter Tejler, Minister, Deputy Chief of Mission

Switzerland
Ambassador Thomas G. Borer, Ambassador, Head of Task Force, "Switzerland - Second World War"
Mr. Lukas Beglinger, Minister, Deputy Head of Task Force "Switzerland - Second World War"
Mr. Andreas Kellerhals, Vice Director of the Swiss Federal Archives
Mr. Peter Streit, Vice Director of the Federal Office of Private Insurance
Mr. Andrea Rascher, Head of Service for Cultural Objects Transfer in the Federal Office for Cultural Affairs
Mr. Christoph Bubb, Counselor - Legal Advisor, Embassy of Switzerland
  Independent Delegation Members representing only the Independent Commission of Experts "Switzerland – Second World War":
Professor Jean-Francois Bergier, Chairman, Independent Commission of Experts, "Switzerland - Second World War" *(Presenter)*
Ms. Sybil Milton, Deputy Chairperson, Independent Commission of Experts, "Switzerland, Second World War"
Christian Graf-Zumsteg, Expert mandated by the Education Director's Conference of the Swiss Cantons
Thomas Buomberger, Historian

Turkey

Ambassador Sevinc Dalyanoglu, Ambassador, Director General for Multilateral Economic Affairs *(Presenter)*

Ambassador M. Nuri Yildirim, Special Advisor to the Minister of State

Professor Dr. Ilber Ortayli, Professor of History, University of Ankara

Professor Dr. Hasan Unal, Professor of Political Science, University of Ankara

Professor Dr. Bahri Yilmaz, Professor, Bilkent University and Senior Advisor to Minister of State

Mr. Ethem Seckin, Deputy Director General, Turkish Central Bank

Mr. Ahmet Alpman, Head of Department, Multilateral Economic Affairs, Ministry of Foreign Affairs

Mr. Avraam Alkas, Vice President, Jewish Community of Turkey

Mr. Danyal Navaro, Deputy Vice President, Jewish Community of Turkey

Ukraine

Mr. Igor Lushnikov, Head, Ukrainian National Foundation "Mutual Understanding and Reconciliation"

Mr. Volodymyr Lytvynov, Director, All-Ukrainian Union of the Nazi's Minor Prisoners

Mr. Volodymyr Repryntsev, Assistant of the Vice Prime Minister on Humanitarian Issues

Professor Gennady Boriak, Professor, Leader of the Scientific and Analytical Group of the UNF

Mr. Danylo Kurdelchuk, President, Ukrainian Bar Association for Foreign Affairs

Natalia Zarudna, Deputy Chief of Mission

United Kingdom

Mr. Anthony Layden, Head, Western European Department, Foreign and Commonwealth Office *(Presenter)*

Sir Christopher Meyer, Ambassador to the United States

Ms. Gill Bennett, Chief Historian, FCO *(Chair, Historical Commissions Break-out session, and Presenter)*

Ms. Julia Painting, Desk Officer, Western European Department, FCO

Mr. Richard Bevins, Senior Historian, FCO *(Presenter)*

Mr. Steven Chandler, Western European Department, FCO

Lord Janner of Braunstone, Chairman, Holocaust Educational Trust *(Presenter)*

Ms. Janice Lopatkin, Director, Holocaust Educational Trust

Mr. Stephen Ward, Associate Director, Holocaust Educational Trust
Ms. Sharon Page, Secretary, Tate Gallery and Chair of Working Group
  on Nazi Spoliation of Art, National Museum Directors' Conference
  (Presenter)
Mr. Michael Helston, Head, Cultural Property Section, Department for
  Cultural Media and Sport
Mr. John Cooke, Head of External Relations, Association of British
  Insurers
Ms. Trudy Gold, Director of Education, Spiro Institute *(Presenter)*
Professor David Cesarani, Professor, Wiener Library
Mr. Paul Salmons, Holocaust Education Coordinator, Imperial War
  Museum
Mr. Stephen Smith, Holocaust Education Expert, Beth Shalom
  (Presenter)
Mr. William Shapcott, First Secretary

United States
Stuart E. Eizenstat, Under Secretary of State for Economic, Business and
  Agricultural Affairs, U.S. Department of State *(Presenter)*
Mr. Bennett Freeman, Senior Advisor to the Under Secretary of State for
  Economic, Business and Agricultural Affairs, U.S. Department of State
  (Chair, Education Break-out section)
Ambassador Henry Clarke, Senior Advisor for Restitution Issues, U.S.
  Department of State
Mr. E. Anthony Wayne, Principal Deputy Assistant Secretary, Bureau of
  European and Canadian Affairs, U.S. Department of State
Dr. William Slany, The Historian, U.S. Department of State
Representative Sidney Yates, U.S. House of Representatives
Representative Sam Gejdenson, U.S. House of Representatives
Representative Tom Lantos, U.S. House of Representatives *(Presenter)*
Mr. Greg Rickman, Legislative Director, Office of Senator Alfonse M.
  D'Amato
Mr. Miles Lerman, Chairman, United States Holocaust Memorial
  Council *(Chair, Education Break-out section and Presenter)*
Mr. Jim Robinson, Assistant Attorney General, Criminal Division, U.S.
  Department of Justice, and Justice designee to the Presidential
  Advisory Commission on Holocaust Assets in the United States
Mr. Eli Rosenbaum, Director, Office of Special Investigations,
  Department of Justice
Mr. Earl A. Powell III, Director, National Gallery of Art *(Presenter)*

Ms. Nancy Weiss, Deputy General Counsel of the National Foundation on the Arts and Humanities

Ms. Maria Papageorge Kouroupas, Executive Director, Cultural Property Advisory Committee, United States Information Agency

Dr. Michael Kurtz, Assistant Archivist, National Archives and Records Administration *(Presenter)*

Dr. Greg Bradsher, Director, Holocaust-Era Assets Records Project, National Archives and Records Administration

Ambassador Donald Blinken, Former U.S. Ambassador to Hungary

Uruguay
Mr. Nelson Chaben, Minister Counselor, Political and Cultural Affairs

World Jewish Congress
Mr. Israel Singer, Secretary General *(Presenter)*
Mr. Edgar Bronfman, President *(Presenter)*
Mr. Elan Steinberg, Executive Director
Ambassador Ronald Lauder, Chairman of the Board, Museum of Modern Art *(Presenter)*
Dr. Avi Beker, Director
Douglas Bloomfield
Prof. Irwin Cotler, Faculty of Law, McGill University
Mr. Hector Feliciano, Independent Scholar *(Presenter)*
Mr. Benjamin Fishoff
Mr. Curtis Hoxter, Advisor
Dr. Connie Lowenthal, Director, Commission for Art Recovery *(Presenter)*
Dr. Laurence Weinbaum, Senior Research & Editorial Officer
Sidney Zabludoff, Adviser

World Jewish Restitution Organization
Mr. Avraham Burg, Chairman of the Jewish Agency for Israel *(Presenter)*
Ambassador Naphtali Lavie, Vice Chairman of the WJRO *(Presenter)*
Mr. Noach Flug, Secretary-General of WJRO
Mr. Eliyahu Spanic, Director-General of WJRO
Mr. Zvi Ramot, member of the Executive of the Jewish Agency
Rabbi Chaskel Besser, Chairman for Poland and Ukraine
Mr. Yoram Dori, Spokesman
Mr. Dan Eldar, Senior Advisor to the Chairman

Mr. David Zwiebel, Director for Government Affairs/General Counsel, Agudath Israel of America

Yad Vashem
Dr. Yaacov Lozowick, Director of the Archives *(Presenter)*
Mrs. Shulamit Imber, Pedagogical Director *(Presenter)*
Mr. Eli Zborowski, Chairman, American Society for Yad Vashem
Ms. Caroline Arfa

PRESENTERS

Dr. Konstantin Akinsha, Research Director, Project of Documentation of Wartime Losses
The Honorable Madeleine K. Albright, Secretary of State, the United States of America
Mr. Giulio Baseggio, Riunione Adriatica di Sicurta
Professor Yehuda Bauer, Yad Vashem Institute
Sara Bloomfield, Acting Director, United States Holocaust Memorial Museum *(Chair, Education Break-out section)*
Dr. Siegfried Büttner, Vice President, German Federal Archives
Mr. Philippe de Montebello, Director, Metropolitan Museum of Art
The Honorable Lawrence S. Eagleburger, Chairman, International Commission on Holocaust-Era Insurance Claims, and former U.S. Secretary of State
Mr. Gilbert Edelson, Administrative Vice President and Counsel, Art Dealers Association of America
Prof. Gerald Feldman, Fellow, and Professor of History, American Academy in Berlin
Dr. Tamás Földi, Public Policy Institute, Budapest
Mr. Rudolph Gerlach, Department Chief, German Federal Regulatory Agency for Insurance Practices
Representative Benjamin A. Gilman, Chairman, Committee on International Relations, U.S. House of Representatives *(Chair, Communal Property Plenary and Break-out sessions)*
Mr. Nikolai Gubenko, Deputy Chairman of the Committee on Culture, State Duma, Russian Federation
Mr. Herbert Hansmeyer, Member of the Board, Allianz AG
Mr. Alan Hevesi, Comptroller, City of New York

Dr. Beate Kosmala, Center for Anti-Semitism Research, Technical University in Berlin

Representative James A. Leach, Chairman, Committee on Banking and Financial Services, U.S. House of Representatives *(Chair, Nazi-confiscated Art Plenary and Break-out sessions)*

Mr. Michael Lewan, Chairman, U.S. Commission for the Preservation of America' s Heritage Abroad

Ms. Catherine Lillie, Director, Holocaust Claims Processing Office, New York State Banking Department

Prof. Vojtech Mastny, Senior Research Scholar, Woodrow Wilson International Center

Mr. William McDonough, President & Chief Executive Officer, Federal Reserve Bank of New York *(Chair, Gold Plenary session)*

Ms. Daisy Miller, Survivors of the Shoah Visual History Foundation

Ms. Lynn Nicholas, Independent Scholar

Ambassador Lyndon Olson, U.S. Ambassador to Sweden and former Texas Insurance Commissioner *(Chair, Holocaust-Era Insurance Issues Plenary and Break-out sessions)*

William Parsons, Chief of Staff, United States Holocaust Memorial Museum *(Chair, Education Break-out section)*

Dr. Jonathan Petropoulos, Professor, Department of History, Loyola College

Col. Seymour Pomrenze, First Director, Offenbach Archival Depot

Dr. Oliver Rathkolb, Univ. Doz. DDr., Kreisky Archives and Institute for Contemporary History, University of Vienna

Dr. Marcia Sachs Littell, Director, National Academy for Holocaust and Genocide Teacher Training, The Richard Stockton College of New Jersey

Dr. Shimon Samuels, Director for International Liaison, Simon Wiesenthal Center, Paris

Dr. Carla Schulz-Hoffmann, Deputy General Director, Bavarian State Paintings Collection

Representative Charles E. Schumer, U.S. House of Representatives

Mr. William Shulman, President, Association of Holocaust Organizations

Mr. Robert Sigel, Josef Effner High School, Dachau

Dr. Abby Smith, Director of Programs, Council on Library and Information Resources

Mr. Ori Soltes, former Director, Klutznick National Jewish Museum

Ms. Margot Stern Strom, Director, Facing History and Ourselves

Mr. Ronald Tauber, Chairman, The Art Loss Register

Mr. Alberto Tiberini, Assistant General Manager, Assicurazioni Generali S.p.A. ·

Mr. John Van Oudenaren, Head, European Division, Library of Congress

Mr. Robert Vanni, General Counsel, New York Public Library; Astor, Lenox and Tilden Foundation

Dr. Robert Waite, Historian, Office of Special Investigations, U.S. Department of Justice

Mr. Mark Weitzman, Director, National Task Force Against Hate, Simon Wiesenthal Center

Mr. Elie Wiesel, Founding Chairman, United States Holocaust Memorial Council, and Nobel Peace Laureate

Ms. Regina Wyrwoll, Goethe-Institut

OBSERVERS

Dr. Gerard Aalders, Netherlands State Institute for War Documentation

Mr. Mario Adler, Congregacao Israelita Paulista

Mr. Wayne Berman, Generali

Ms. Susan Boren, Congressional Research Service

Ms. Virginia Canter, National Endowment for the Humanities

Mr. Christopher Carnicall, Generali

Rabbi Abraham Cooper, Simon Wiesenthal Center

Ms. Anita DiFanis, Association of American Art Museum Directors

Mrs. Frances Eizenstat

Mr. Michael Feldstein, Pink Triangle Coalition

Mr. Andrew Frank, Allianz AG

Rabbi Hertz Frankel, World Council of Orthodox Jewish Communities, Inc.

Ms. Guila Franklin, Jewish Council on Public Affairs

Ms. Ladeen Fremuth, Office of Representative Frank Pallone, Jr., United States House of Representatives

Mr. Stuart Goldman, Congressional Research Service

Mr. Michael Hausfeld

Rabbi Marvin Hier, Simon Wiesenthal Center

Ms. Elaine Johnston, Smithsonian Institution

Ms. Helen Junz

Ms. Rositta Kenisberg, United States Holocaust Memorial Council

Mr. Rawle King, Congressional Research Service

Mrs. Ruth Knox, Kindertransport Association

Ms. Ruth Laibson, Jewish Council for Public Affairs
Ms. Rosalind Lazarus, U.S. Department of Transportation
Mr. Peter Lefkin, Fireman's Fund Insurance Company
Ms. Rosalie Lerman, United States Holocaust Memorial Council
Ms. Sophia Miskiewicz, Polish American Congress
Mr. William Nagel
Mrs. Carla Nicolini
Mr. Riccardo Nicolini, Generali
Mr. Jonathan Olsoff, Sotheby's
Mr. Alexander Osovtsov
Mr. Marc Porter, Christie's Inc.
Ms. Anita Ramasastry, Claims Resolution Tribunal for Dormant
    Accounts in Switzerland
Mr. Timothy Reif, Office of Representative Charles B. Rangel, U.S.
    House of Representatives
Ms. Jean Rosensaft, United States Holocaust Memorial Council
Mr. Menachem Rosensaft, United States Holocaust Memorial Council
Mr. Jim Schrieber
Mr. Lucian Simmons, Sotheby's
Rabbi Henry Sobel, Congregacao Israelita Paulista
Mr. Michael Steiner
Mr. Mark Talisman
Ms. Irit Tamir, Jewish Community Relations Council
Mr. Michael Traison, Miller, Canfield, Paddock, and Stone PLC
Mr. Melvyn Urbach, World Council of Orthodox Jewish Communities
Mr. David B. Vogt
Ms. Maureen Walsh, Helsinki Commission
Mr. Douglas Weimer, Congressional Research Service
Ms. Alice Whelihan, Federal Council on the Arts and Humanities
Mr. Christopher Worthley, Allianz AG

Appendix G
WASHINGTON CONFERENCE PRINCIPLES ON NAZI-CONFISCATED ART

In developing a consensus on non-binding principles to assist in resolving issues relating to Nazi-confiscated art, the Conference recognizes that among participating nations there are differing legal systems and that countries act within the context of their own laws.

I.   Art that had been confiscated by the Nazis and not subsequently restituted should be identified.

II.   Relevant records and archives should be open and accessible to researchers, in accordance with the guidelines of the International Council on Archives.

III.   Resources and personnel should be made available to facilitate the identification of all art that had been confiscated by the Nazis and not subsequently restituted.

IV.   In establishing that a work of art had been confiscated by the Nazis and not subsequently restituted, consideration should be given to unavoidable gaps or ambiguities in the provenance in light of the passage of time and the circumstances of the Holocaust era.

V.   Every effort should be made to publicize art that is found to have been confiscated by the Nazis and not subsequently restituted in order to locate its pre-War owners or their heirs.

VI.   Efforts should be made to establish a central registry of such information.

VII.   Pre-War owners and their heirs should be encouraged to come forward and make known their claims to art that was confiscated by the Nazis and not subsequently restituted.

VIII.   If the pre-War owners of art that is found to have been confiscated by the Nazis and not subsequently restituted, or their heirs, can be identified, steps should be taken expeditiously to achieve a just and fair solution, recognizing this may vary according to the facts and circumstances surrounding a specific case.

IX.   If the pre-War owners of art that is found to have been confiscated by the Nazis, or their heirs, can not be identified, steps should be taken expeditiously to achieve a just and fair solution.

X.   Commissions or other bodies established to identify art that was confiscated by the Nazis and to assist in addressing ownership issues should have a balanced membership.

XI.   Nations are encouraged to develop national processes to implement these principles, particularly as they relate to alternative dispute resolution mechanisms for resolving ownership issues.

Appendix H:
Task Force for International Cooperation on Holocaust Education, Remembrance, and Research

Report to the Washington Conference on Holocaust-Era Assets

Work in Progress, May – November 1998

CONTENTS

b) Proposal for International Version of the Book *Tell Ye Your Children...*
Stéphane Bruchfeld, Levande Historia, and Paul A. Levine, Research Fellow, Centre for Multiethnic Research, Uppsala University, Sweden

c) Elements of Guidelines for Holocaust Education
Anthony Layden, Head, Western European Department, Foreign and Commonwealth Office of the United Kingdom

d) Update on Archival Initiatives
Gill Bennett, Head of Historians, Library and Records Department, Foreign and Commonwealth Office of the United Kingdom

e) Proposal for International Commemoration of the Holocaust
Stephen D. Smith, Director, Beth Shalom Holocaust Memorial and Education Centre, United Kingdom

I. OVERVIEW OF THE TASK FORCE FOR INTERNATIONAL COOPERATION ON HOLOCAUST EDUCATION, REMEMBRANCE, AND RESEARCH

a) Introduction

Stuart E. Eizenstat, Under Secretary of State for Economic, Business, and Agricultural Affairs, United States Department of State; Chairman of the Task Force for International Cooperation on Holocaust Education, Remembrance, and Research

It gives me great pleasure to report on the progress of the recently formed Task Force for International Cooperation on Holocaust Education, Remembrance, and Research, which I have had the privilege to chair on behalf of the United States from September to December 1998.

No one can question how important and how tragically overdue is the international community's focus on Holocaust-era assets. Equally clear is the importance of a fresh focus on Holocaust education, remembrance, and research. As we come to the close of this century and enter the new millennium, it is memory - memory of the most tragic events of this century - that must endure so that such horrors are not repeated. It is therefore critical for us all to intensify and improve our efforts in the realm of Holocaust education. Swedish Prime Minister Persson recognized this imperative and launched a Holocaust education initiative first at home and then abroad in the spring of 1998 by inviting the cooperation of Prime Minister Blair and President Clinton. Israel and Germany have now joined Sweden, the United Kingdom, and the United States in the Task Force.

We, of course, recognize and salute the efforts over many years of non-governmental organizations and individuals in the Holocaust education domain. This initiative nonetheless embodies real innovation. There is no precedent for heads of state and government, as they have in this case, to work through diplomatic channels to foster international cooperation in Holocaust education.

Represented here are five governments, each of which brings to the table notable strengths; each has much to contribute. Sweden originated the concept of the Task Force and has offered for consideration its own Holocaust educational effort, which reaches deeply and comprehensively into Swedish homes and schools. In the United Kingdom, we have the example of long-time public and private sector institutions cooperating in Holocaust education as well as the leadership the British government has provided in meeting head-on Holocaust-assets issues – leadership highlighted by last year's London Nazi Gold Conference. In the United States, we see Holocaust education woven through the nations social fabric in the work of NGOs; in school curricula determined at national, state, and local levels; and in the United States Holocaust Memorial Museum, which has established itself as a solemn treasure for our nation and the world. Israel is, of course, the home to a large number of Holocaust survivors as well as great institutions of learning and remembrance like Yad Vashem. Germany's efforts can also serve as a model in our discussions because of its particularly pertinent lessons from over 50 years of thorough and cathartic Holocaust education practices.

To date, representatives of these five governments have been reviewing efforts under way in these priority areas: a survey of international Holocaust education, remembrance, and research; an adaptation of a Swedish Holocaust education booklet for international use; a draft report on Holocaust education guidelines; and progress on archival access. Further descriptions of our work in progress may be found in the pages that follow.

The work of the Task Force has already provided heartening proof of a new international consensus to put Holocaust education at the forefront of our collective consciousness. Our five governments have begun to develop the substantive and diplomatic frameworks to move forward together and with other countries to advance our common Holocaust education goals in the months and years ahead.

b) Discussion Paper Agreed Upon by the Working Group of the Task Force on International Cooperation on Holocaust Education, Remembrance, and Research

United States Holocaust Memorial Museum
September 25, 1998

Since the end of the Second World War, the world has struggled to come to terms with the history and legacy of the Holocaust. Many countries have made great strides in this regard, while others are only now taking steps. The recent focus on the long-neglected assets dimension of the Holocaust is serving as a catalyst for countries that have not concentrated as intensely on the Holocaust in a broad context, including their own roles and responses to its events.

Holocaust education and remembrance will help us recall the importance of *fighting intolerance,* racism, and other challenges to basic human values. As we enter the new millennium, we should encourage and reinforce work in many nations to strengthen Holocaust education efforts, to create new ones, and to finally begin such efforts where they have been overlooked. Through education and remembrance we shall do all we can to ensure that the crimes of the Holocaust are neither forgotten nor repeated.

It is and will remain the shared responsibility of parents and teachers, as well as of political, religious, and civic leaders, to teach our children that moral choices exist. Countless wrong and evil choices accompanied by mass indifference made the Holocaust possible. Holocaust education efforts undertaken by many countries for a number of years have been encouraging.

The unique importance of the Holocaust and its lessons for contemporary society, however, require that the peoples of all our countries engage in teaching about the Holocaust and their countries' relationship to these events. International exchange and cooperation can greatly facilitate this work.

Recognizing its history, Sweden launched its own initiative in 1997 on Holocaust education, and in early 1998, Swedish Prime Minister Goran Persson invited U.S. President Bill Clinton and U.K. Prime Minister Tony Blair to join in developing on an international basis an initiative to promote Holocaust education. To this end the Swedish, British, and US. Governments decided on May 7, 1998, in Stockholm to establish a Task Force to spread knowledge about the Holocaust by promoting international cooperation in a variety of fields related to Holocaust education, remembrance, and research.

The Task Force consists of personal representatives of the heads of state or government and the independent advisor Professor Yehuda Bauer of the Yad Vashem Institute. It will collaborate closely with NGOs and others active in disseminating knowledge about the Holocaust.

The Task Force will work to increase public awareness of the Holocaust. It will focus international cooperation on educational activities, specifically with respect to education in middle and high schools as well as at institutions of higher education. The Task Force will encourage international commemoration of the Holocaust.

It is furthermore making available, among other resources, an international adaptation of the Swedish book *Holocaust in Europe 1933-1945,* as well as further research-related collection and documentation of testimonies by survivors, perpetrators, and bystanders. An international survey will be initiated to identify needs and priorities of Holocaust education and research. A set of guidelines will be developed and distributed internationally that can be used by countries seeking to strengthen or expand efforts in Holocaust education, remembrance, and research. It is furthermore of high priority to find proper ways to reach out to young people, for example, through organized visits to concentration camps and memorial institutions. The use of Internet, CDs, and publications for international projects will be investigated.

To support the broadest possible national educational efforts, the Task Force will provide expertise for educational projects, also drawing on information from all relevant archives. The Task Force will moreover encourage the opening of relevant archives.

The Task Force will seek a commitment from participating governments to promote Holocaust education in accordance with the above stated aims. Some form of financial support may be needed.

The initial priorities agreed to by the Task Force for work through 1998 and extending into 1999 include:

1) developing a catalogue of Holocaust education, remembrance, and research efforts currently underway;

2) making available existing or new written material for Holocaust education, remembrance, and research (possibly drawing on the Swedish book *Tell Ye Your Children ...*);

3) showcasing the initiative and highlighting efforts underway in Holocaust education, remembrance, and research at the Washington Conference on Holocaust-Era Assets;

4) promoting openness and accessibility of public and private archives bearing on the history of the Holocaust including Holocaust-era asset issues;

5) giving further impetus to international efforts in Holocaust education, remembrance, and research.

c) Summary of the Meeting of the Working Group of the Task Force held May 7, 1998, in Stockholm

REGERINGSKANSLIET
Prime Minister's Office

The evil that is the Holocaust constitutes a fundamental challenge to our ability to learn lessons from the past. Remaining indifferent and not trying to understand the "why" of the Holocaust could threaten our common future.

It is thus always the responsibility of parents, teachers, politicians, and all adults to teach our children that the right choice exists equal to the wrong one. To accomplish this task in a complex world, people and countries need to share experiences.

International cooperation should be directed toward highlighting the Holocaust and making an inventory of those aspects that merely have been touched upon and those that have been neglected.

Joint international actions and projects should aim at long-term changes and effects of attitudes. Knowledge about the Holocaust should be woven into existing structures, for example, the educational system, research, and training of teachers and journalists.

Preserving the narratives of Holocaust survivors is a key issue since the time left to document the memories is running out.

Young people are a key group, likewise their parents. In fact, it was an opinion poll revealing young people's lack of historical knowledge that gave rise to the Swedish project. One way to influence young people is to organize and give support to visits to the concentration camps.

Another suitable area for cooperation is the use of the Internet as an instrument for spreading information about the Holocaust. This would include discussions of the most effective ways to utilize this channel, and how to deal with the proliferation of Nazi and racist material on the Internet.

Further training for teachers and expanded research are two suitable areas for international efforts. By giving the key figures in the education of children and young people - that is to say, the teachers - a sound grounding, knowledge about the Holocaust will spread like rings on the water.

Cooperation might also entail support for the compilation and production of information as well as various types of cultural events.

Conclusion

At the Stockholm meeting on the Holocaust, it was decided by participating representatives of the British, Swedish, and US. Governments to establish a task force for international cooperation to spread knowledge about the Holocaust. The group should consist of personal representatives to the heads of state or governments. Professor Yehuda Bauer of the Yad Vashem Institute will work as an independent advisor to the group.

The group has agreed to follow up on issues and projects discussed and proposed at the Stockholm meeting. It will collaborate closely with NGOs and others active in disseminating knowledge about the Holocaust.

It was agreed that the group will have a meeting in Washington in September this year in order to present progress reports on the projects listed below. It was agreed upon to elaborate an action-oriented report to be presented by high representatives of the heads of state or governments to the Washington Conference on Holocaust-Era Assets on November 9,1998.

The Swedish representative is willing to act as coordinator until the first meeting in Washington in September 1998.

It was agreed upon to focus international cooperation on Holocaust educational activities, public activities, testimonies of survivors, proper ways to reach out to young people, a global survey on Holocaust education to be presented in national reports, and cooperation on how to use the Internet in connection with these activities.

d) Summary of the Meeting of the Working Group of the Task Force held September 25, 1998, in Washington, D.C.

Summary

Chairmanship of the Task Force was passed from Sweden to the United States, and the Task Force welcomed Germany and Israel as members. Agreement was reached on a discussion paper outlining the purpose and goals of the overall initiative, and the paper was released to the public at a press conference following the morning session. The Working Group agreed on a set of concrete projects, some of which would be works in progress, to be presented to the Washington Conference on Holocaust-Era Assets. They would include:

1) a directory of organizations involved in Holocaust education as a preliminary step toward completing a comprehensive survey/catalogue of Holocaust education efforts underway worldwide, to be prepared by Sweden and the United States;

2) an insert to the Swedish book *Tell Ye Your Children...,* demonstrating how an international version and individual national versions of the book can be created, to be prepared by Sweden;

3) a guide to finding and using archival material, to be prepared by the UK and the U.S.;

4) a set of suggested Holocaust education guidelines, to be prepared by the UK;

5) a proposal for an International Day of Remembrance, to be prepared by the UK;

6) Task Force declaration on archival openness, to be drafted jointly by the U.S. and the UK;

7) Task Force declaration on promoting Holocaust education, to be drafted by the U.S.

Each respective lead nation will work with relevant NGOs and other participating governments to prepare material for the Washington Conference. Subject to final agreement among the five governments, those projects and other supporting materials will constitute the report of the Task Force to the Conference.

Opening Remarks

The second meeting of the Working Group was opened by United States Holocaust Memorial Museum (USHMM) Acting Director

Sara Bloomfield. Swedish MFA Political Director Ulf Hjertonsson highlighted the important progress made by the Task Force since Sweden last proposed the initiative. Senior Advisor to the US Under Secretary of State for Economic, Business and Agricultural Affairs Bennett Freeman praised Hjertonsson and the other Swedes for extraordinary work as chair since the project's inception and emphasized that a high standard had been set that the US. would work hard to maintain. The UK's FCO Western European Department Head Anthony Layden told the group that the UK has one of the highest levels of knowledge about the Holocaust and hoped it could apply the lessons it has learned in its work with the Task Force. Israel's Ambassador to Sweden Gideon Ben Ami told the group that Prime Minister Netanyahu warmly welcomed international cooperation on Holocaust education. Germany's Ambassador to the U.S. Jürgen Chrobog said that we can never be finished with the past, but can and must learn from it. Director of Yad Vashem's International Center for Holocaust Studies (and personal advisor to the Task Force) Yehuda Bauer called the Working Group meeting "very unusual," saying never before have governments come together to support such an education initiative.

Concept Paper

A Swedish-initiated "discussion paper" on the work of the Task Force was adopted by the Task Force governments. Progress reports were given by each of the lead nations on projects for which they are responsible.

Washington Conference Plans

After the press conference and luncheon remarks by Chairman of the United States Holocaust Memorial Council Miles Lerman and Under Secretary of State for Economic, Business and Agricultural Affairs and incoming Task Force Chairman Stuart Eizenstat, Bennett Freeman briefed the group on plans for the Washington Conference on Holocaust-Era Assets. Museum officials described the showcase idea, explaining that Task Force materials and other educational material would be displayed at the Museums tile wall, while sessions on different aspects of Holocaust education would take place in the classrooms. They said the aims were to demonstrate the topic's importance, to persuade attendees that they could implement Holocaust education programs, and to make lasting contacts that lay a foundation for future cooperation.

Declarations on Promoting Holocaust Education and Archival Openness

The Task Force decided to produce working drafts of declarations on promoting Holocaust education and archival openness. While the Conference is not a governmental decision-making event, it would be useful to put before the Conference serious non-binding declarations on these subjects.

Closing/Conclusions

The meeting closed with the U.S. chair thanking the participants and circulating a draft list of Washington Conference deliverables. The Working Group meeting was adjourned.

II. TASK FORCE DECLARATIONS PRESENTED TO THE WASHINGTON CONFERENCE ON HOLOCAUST-ERA ASSETS

a) Task Force Declaration on Promoting Holocaust Education, Remembrance, and Research
(Germany, Israel, Sweden, United Kingdom, United States)

The international community's recent attention to the long-neglected issues of Holocaust-era assets has prompted a number of countries to look more closely at both their own roles and the broader history of this tragic period. While differing enormously in content and intensity, these developments are encouraging, useful, and necessary. Holocaust education, remembrance, and research strengthen humanity's ability to absorb and learn from the dark lessons of the past, so that we can ensure that similar horrors are never again repeated.

As the international community continues to focus on the Holocaust-era assets issues at the 1998 Washington Conference and beyond, the priority and urgency for international attention must also encompass Holocaust education' remembrance, and research. Efforts and resources in this direction should be expanded to reinforce the historic meaning and enduring lessons of the Holocaust ("Shoah") and to combat its denial.

To address this imperative, we are committing our countries to encourage parents, teachers, and civic, political, and religious leaders to undertake with renewed vigor and attention Holocaust education, remembrance, and research, with a special focus on our own countries' histories. We will strengthen our existing programs or launch new ones to advance this common objective.

We pledge our commitment to this endeavor and have joined together to develop an unprecedented diplomatic cooperation in this field, in a spirit of partnership, humanity, and justice. We call on the other nations participating in the Washington Conference on Holocaust-Era Assets to also take steps to strengthen existing Holocaust education, remembrance, and research efforts, and to undertake new ones where necessary. We invite nations to work with the Task Force for International Cooperation on Holocaust Education, Remembrance, and Research to pursue these common goals.

As this century comes to a close, our determination never to forget is a key to realizing progress for mankind. The healing of the world (in Hebrew, tikun olam) is a solemn duty of all who cherish freedom and human dignity. We hope our efforts to deepen Holocaust education, remembrance, and research will help to fulfill that responsibility as we begin a new millennium.

b) Task Force Declaration on Archival Openness and Access
(Germany, Israel, Sweden, United Kingdom, United States)

The recent opening of archives bearing on the Holocaust ("Shoah"), in particular those related to Nazi-looted gold and other confiscated assets, has made possible important new historical research on these complex issues. As a result, the international community's understanding of this tragic period in the history of the twentieth century is being strengthened substantially as scholars gain access to millions of pages of documents for the first time.

The presentations made to the December 1997 London Nazi Gold Conference and subsequent work on the part of historical commissions in many nations demonstrate that although much progress has been made, there is still more work to be done in bringing the full historical record to light. The governments ˙comprising the International Task Force on Holocaust Education, Remembrance, and Research agree on the importance of encouraging all archives, both public and private, to make their holdings more widely accessible. This will facilitate further research and encourage greater understanding of the Holocaust and its historical context.

The Washington Conference on Holocaust-Era Assets provides an ideal opportunity for all participating governments to join us in endorsing the importance of full archival openness, and in undertaking to work toward the goal of making all documentation bearing on the Holocaust and the fate of Nazi-confiscated assets available to researchers. The adoption of December 31, 1999, as a target date to meet this goal will reinforce the commitment of humanity to· learn from the history of this century as we enter a new millennium.

III. TASK FORCE PROJECTS

a) **Introduction to the *International Directory of Organizations in Holocaust Education, Remembrance, and Research***
Stéphane Bruchfeld, Office of the Prime Minister of Sweden
Wesley A. Fisher, United States Holocaust Memorial Museum
Nicolas Gauvin, United States Holocaust Memorial Museum

At the initiative of the government of Sweden, the Task Force for International Cooperation on Holocaust Education, Remembrance, and Research was established at a meeting in Stockholm in May 1998. Consisting of personal representatives of heads of state or government, the Task Force cooperates closely with both governmental and non-governmental organizations active in disseminating knowledge about the Holocaust as well as in commemoration and research. As of this writing, personal representatives of the heads of state or governments of Germany, Israel, Sweden, the United Kingdom, and the United States are members of the Task Force, as is the independent advisor Professor Yehuda Bauer of the Yad Vashem Institute.

The Task Force has identified as one of its first priorities the development of a catalog or survey of Holocaust education, remembrance, and research efforts currently underway worldwide. This *International Directory* is a first step toward that goal. It provides basic information on the approximately 900 institutions throughout the world concerned with Holocaust education, broadly defined. The listings incorporate and supplement those of the Association of Holocaust Organizations, Yad Vashem, the United States Holocaust Memorial Museum, the Goethe-Institut, the Council of Europe, and others. To our knowledge, this *International Directory* is the most comprehensive guide to organizations concerned with the Holocaust ever compiled.

It is far from a perfect directory, however. Given the very limited time in which the listings were assembled, there are omissions and undoubtedly errors, despite our best efforts to ensure that the information is complete and correct. Please send all additions and corrections to Dr. Wesley A. Fisher, United States Holocaust Memorial Museum, 100 Raoul Wallenberg Place, SW, Washington, DC 20024-2126; telephone (202) 479-9732; fax (202) 488-2693; e-mail <wfisher@ushmm.org>. An electronic searchable version is being made available on the website of the United States Holocaust Memorial Museum that will be updated on a regular basis. The home page of the Museum's website may be found at <www.ushmm.org>. In the current printed version, organizations are listed alphabetically within the listings for each country. International organizations can be found both under "International" and under the country of location.

Such an international compilation would be impossible without the generous assistance of many organizations and individuals in many countries. In particular, we are most grateful to Dr. William Shulman, President of the Association of Holocaust Organizations (AHO), for permission to include the current (1999) listings for the organizational members of the AHO. Institutions that are members of the AHO are marked with an asterisk (*). Shulamit Imber, Pedagogical Director, and Richelle Budd-Caplan of Yad Vashem, kindly provided us with Yad Vashem's list of relevant institutions in Israel and abroad. Regina Wyrwoll, Head of Media Division, Goethe-Institut, Munich, and Annette Brinkmann generously provided the address list of German institutions resulting from the project Learning From History: The Nazi Era and the Holocaust in German Education. Also useful was information collected by Katherine Klinger for the Council of Europe's publication *The Holocaust in the School Curriculum.- A European Perspective.*

Veronika Bard-Bringéus, Deputy Director International Affairs, and Mia Löwengart of the Office of the Prime Minister of Sweden, and Swedish embassies in Europe and Israel helped collect and verify information. Many staff members of the United States Holocaust Memorial Museum assisted, in particular Joan Ringelheim, Sara Greenberg, Stephen Feinberg, Jacek Nowakowski, Radu Ioanid, Klaus Mueller, Michael Haley Goldman, Andres Abril, Alberto Rios, Arnold Kramer, Harry Lee, Susanne Brose, Sarah Lueer, Solomon Danzig, Monica Schaeffer, Robert Price, Carmen Marrero, and Jessica Marrero. Support for the dissemination of this *International Directory* was provided to the Museum by The Blanche and Irving Laurie Foundation in connection with the Washington Conference on Holocaust-Era Assets. In addition, we thank the numerous organizations worldwide that provided us with information on their activities. We hope this directory will prove useful to the Task Force and to a plethora of future cooperative international projects involving a multitude of countries in Holocaust education, remembrance, and research.

b) Proposal for International Version of the Book
Tell Ye Your Children...
Stéphane Bruchfeld, Levande Historia, and Paul A. Levine, Research Fellow, Centre for Multiethnic Research, Uppsala University, Sweden

When the original Swedish edition of *Tell Ye Your Children. . .* (Om detta må ni berätta; en bok om Förintelsen I Europa 1933 - 1945) was published in January 1998, no one expected the reaction it received. Not least has the Swedish public, one with little previous exposure to Holocaust history, warmly responded to our mediation of our understanding of the history of the Holocaust. Since the formation of the Task Force on International Cooperation, the response outside of Sweden to the form and content of the book has also been most positive.

The following "insert" is our initial response to both criticisms and suggestions received, and one realization of our ideas about how a book about the Holocaust originally written with a Swedish public in mind can be internationalized. We believe the insert demonstrates the inherent flexibility of the original, showing that the book can be adapted and expanded without losing the qualities that elicited such positive comments. The insert seeks to retain the stylistic and textual integrity of the original, yet address some issues and problems, which the original could not. There remain, of course, many issues to be discussed and individual stories to be told.

A primary point we have made in Task Force discussions is that individual nations interested in their own adaptations could add several pages treating their own specific histories for the existing publication. We reiterate here our conviction that the book remain essentially unchanged if it is to retain its unique character. In conceptualizing what has been described as an international version, we have stressed that the original is a book about the Holocaust at large, albeit with specific pages treating the Swedish and Scandinavian response. While a truly international version is desirable, it appears most likely that individual nations will seek to create their own national versions. These adaptations would expand and deepen the discussion on one or more issues specific to a particular nation, such as Germany, Poland, or Israel (prewar Palestine), or a category of Holocaust history, such as "bystander" (i.e. the U.S. or UK), but such changes would not necessarily internationalize the book by any significant meaning of the word. The Holocaust was, as we know, an international event of the first order.

Interestingly, we received from Task Force colleagues suggestions not to diminish the Swedish element, but rather to maintain or even enhance it. From the U.S. came this suggestion, "Education about the Holocaust requires... unvarnished truth... in expanded section on Sweden's role (both negative and positive)... could serve as an extremely powerful example to other nations. It would in our view help them to treat their histories...with as much candor as Sweden." An Israeli colleague verbally made a similar comment, adding that the Swedish sections highlighted the issue of choice by a "bystander," showing that small nations and individuals are not powerless, even in extreme circumstances.

Many of the delegates to the Washington Conference will be first time readers of the book. It is therefore important to point out first that the English book in hand is a second, revised edition incorporating many textual suggestions made by Professor Yehuda Bauer. Secondly, it is essential to stress that, in general, the book avoids comment and reflection on present day issues. It is a book on the history of the Holocaust. And reactions to the book and independent pedagogic experience confirm that readers, adults and students alike make an almost inevitable linkage between the history they read and the problems they face in contemporary society. We feel confident this will be the case for all readers, regardless of which society they hail from.

c) Elements of Guidelines for Holocaust Education
Anthony Layden, Head, Western European Department, Foreign and Commonwealth Office of the United Kingdom

1. Rationale: The Need for Holocaust Education
1.1 The episodes of mass murder that took place in the course of the twentieth century were among the most profoundly tragic and evil aspects of that century's history. They were the worst crimes against humanity yet committed. The most striking example of these was the Holocaust. It represented a huge and grievous loss not only to the Jewish people, but to all mankind. No one can properly understand twentieth century history without knowing something of the Holocaust.

1.2 The Holocaust was in many ways a unique event. But unfortunately, other acts of mass murder have occurred since World War II, and continue to occur. Professor Yehuda Bauer of the Yad Vashem Institute in Jerusalem has observed: "The Holocaust will either be a warning or a precedent." All peoples share a vital interest in ensuring that it is seen as a warning for the future, and that everything possible is done to prevent such tragedies from happening again. Learning about the Holocaust, and trying to understand the behavior involved in it in various ways, is an essential part of this endeavor.

1.3 The message of the Holocaust, and the relevance of its warning, are worldwide. It was carried out by a well-educated and technically advanced country: the Nazi regime utilized all the apparatus of a sophisticated modem state to plan and execute this crime. But mass murder has occurred also in far less developed societies. No country is immune. And education, unless accompanied by a sound structure of morality, provides no protection.

1.4 Study of the Holocaust can help students in considering the moral questions arising from racism and other forms of prejudice in any society. It helps them to develop an awareness of the value of pluralism and of diversity, and increases their maturity as future citizens.

1.5 Sensitive and appropriate education about the Holocaust has proved extremely effective in schools in, for example, the UK in reducing social and racial tensions and bullying. Schools have described the effect in this area of visits by Holocaust survivors as little short of miraculous. Holocaust education can make a significant contribution to the healing of many kinds of divisions in society.

1.6 It is important that everyone should accept that the Holocaust actually happened. There is a tendency in many quarters to avoid recognizing this, partly because of the sheer horror of the event, and partly because of the guilt of those who perpetrated it, or with others who were associated in varying degrees with it. A few people actively try to deny that it happened at all, or to minimize its scale.

1.7 Finally, the world community owes it to the memory of those who died in the Holocaust, to those who suffered in it and survived, and those who lost relatives and friends, to try to turn understanding of that horrific episode into 'a potent force to benefit humankind in the future.

2. The Role of Governments
2.1 The commitment and active support of governments is essential if Holocaust education is to be established worldwide. The specific role of governments in this will vary.

2.2 In countries where the government, central or local, specifies a curriculum to be taught in schools, this subject should be included in the set curriculum. In the UK, for example, the National Curriculum requires all students at age 13 - 14 to be taught about the Holocaust as part of their modern history course, in a section dealing with the Second World War.

2.3 Where no compulsory curriculum is specified, governments can still make it clear that they favor systematic education about the Holocaust. In Germany, for example, this has been done by a series of Resolutions of the Standing Conference of the Ministers of Education and Cultural Affairs of the Länder (States).

2.4 In countries where the Government, central or local, provides funds for education, it should ensure that adequate funds are available for teaching about the Holocaust, including teacher training and the development and provision of teaching resources. The 'Living History" project undertaken by the Swedish Government is an example of this.

2.5 Governments can also help by providing, or supporting the provision of, museums or departments in existing museums, dealing with the Holocaust. Such institutions can make an enormous impact on public awareness. Yad Vashem in Jerusalem and the United States Holocaust Memorial Museum in Washington are examples, as is the large permanent Holocaust display now planned at the Imperial War Museum in London. In Germany, the state authorities arrange and finance visits by school students to the sites of concentration camps and to Holocaust memorial sites.

3. The Role of Non-Governmental Organizations
3.1 Partnership between governments and NGOs in this field is essential. It is non-governmental bodies that have hitherto acquired most of the knowledge and experience needed for successful Holocaust education programs. Their advice and assistance to governments and academic authorities on the methods and approaches that will be most successful in particular countries and regions is invaluable.

3.2 The preparation of suitable and effective teaching materials is one area where NGOs have been responsible for most of the work done until now, The "Lessons of the Holocaust" package produced in the UK by the Holocaust Educational Trust and the Spiro Institute is an example of this.

In the US and Sweden also, close cooperation between governments and NGOs have been a striking feature of the progress that has been made.

4. General Principles for Holocaust Education

4.1 Experience in a number of countries over many years of teaching about the Holocaust shows that it is a subject that must be approached with extreme care. Teaching will always be based on a central collection of facts, among them the resource book "Teaching About the Holocaust" produced by the United States Holocaust Memorial Museum in Washington, and the Swedish book *Tell Ye Your Children*.... But the way these are presented must be carefully calculated if they are to have the desired effects: realization and acceptance of what happened, a desire to know more, a perception that similar events could happen again, and a determination to try to prevent this. injudicious approaches to the subject can alienate those receiving teaching, and provoke reactions to it.

4.2 Among the factors to be taken into account are:

- The age of the students; teachers tend to favor ages 13 -14 as the best time to introduce the subject, in terms of the students' educational and emotional development,

- The extent of students' previous knowledge of the history of the 1930s and 1940s;

- The history of the country concerned - in particular, its own experiences in World War II, and current perceptions of its role;

- The traditions of each country as regards the freedom of information, the openness with which events past and present are discussed, and the way in which information is usually presented there - how direct and frank, or how guarded and circumlocutory, is the usual level of discourse, especially about sensitive subjects.

4.3 Against this background, it is clear that materials prepared for, and approaches successful in, one country will not necessarily be effective in others. It will be vital to involve existing organizations in each country with an interest in, or experiences of, Holocaust studies in preparing or adapting both materials and methods. The cooperation of governmental authorities in this process will often be crucial, so will that of the

academic   communities: historians,   educators,   and   teachers'
organizations.

4.4 The precise aim or purpose of Holocaust studies may also differ from
country to country: have there been local episodes to which students
there can relate that would help engage their commitment to Holocaust
studies as a contribution to efforts to avoid the repetition of such
episodes? Are there local divisions with the potential to promote
violence? Again, the participation of local people in the whole endeavor
will be essential in ensuring that not only the methods adopted, but the
ends to be served, are as effective and relevant as possible.

5. Some Specific Educational Guidelines

5.1 These guidelines are derived from practical experience gained by
teachers in the five countries that currently form the International Task
Force on Holocaust Education: Germany, Israel, Sweden, the United
Kingdom, and the United States. They are not intended to be exhaustive:
it is important for those undertaking teaching on this sensitive subject to
prepare themselves as thoroughly as possible, ideally with the help of
institutions with experience in the field.

5.2 In addressing the history of the Holocaust, it is advantageous to study
the period immediately before the events in question, and introduce
students to the lives of those who were to become Victims in pre-Nazi
Europe. There are two reasons for this. It avoids having students
encounter the victims purely as victims – this can lead to the perception
that the Holocaust was inevitable. It also helps students in considering
the choices made at various points by those who participated in various
ways: as perpetrators, bystanders, victims, rescuers and survivors.
Concepts such as fairness, justice, individual identity, peer pressure,
conformity, indifference, and obedience are ones that adolescents
encounter in their daily lives. Considering the actions of Holocaust
participants in these terms makes them more comprehensible, and helps
students to derive appropriate lessons from them.

5.3 Similarly, addressing these choices helps students to derive the lesson
that tragedies similar to the Holocaust could happen again. Those who
took the choices were not inhuman, but were reacting to a number of
influences in their society and its immediate history. The moral
dimensions of these choices, and the lesson that societies must be on
their guard against similar events, will emerge from such study.

5.4 It is a mistake to employ trivial activities such as word games in the study of this subject, as well as wasting time, it detracts from the seriousness of approach that is essential if the right lessons are to be derived from the study. Also, simulating Holocaust experiences has been found not to be a useful technique. It can mislead students into believing that they know what it must have been like to be involved.

5.5 Teachers must be extremely careful about exposing students to the horrific images that have been preserved from the Holocaust period. This can constitute an unjustified assault on students' sensitivities, and an abuse of the teacher/student relationship. Faced too suddenly with horrific images, some students will react by feeling that they do not wish to know any more about the subject; some may feel cynicism about human nature in general; a few may derive a perverse enjoyment from the experience. In general, teachers should set themselves clear aims as regards the factual and moral objectives they wish to achieve from each lesson, and include in the materials used only such images as are necessary for these objectives.

5.6 It is difficult for students to come to terms with the numbers of victims involved. It is usually helpful to include stories and images of individual people in lesson material. At the same time, teachers should take care to avoid unwarranted generalizations from individual episodes to categories of participants. It should be made clear, for example, that not all perpetrators had the same degree of guilt for what happened.

5.7 When showing how the panoply of the state – Nazi uniforms, banners, etc., -- were used to rationalize and justify criminal activity by the Nazi regime, teachers should remember that these images can have a seductive appeal to students. At the same time, it is important not to undermine the images that modern democratic states use to interpret their own authority to their peoples. A balance should be struck between the imagery itself and the nature of the power behind it.

5.8 Holocaust studies are often most effective when they are multidisciplinary; they can usefully form part of the curricula for language studies, history, religious education, philosophy, ethics, and human rights.

d) Update on Archival Initiatives
Gill Bennett, Head of Historians, Library and Records Department, Foreign and Commonwealth Office of the United Kingdom

In view of the importance of access to the full archival record of the Holocaust and its historical context for understanding this tragic period of history, the Task Force wishes to draw attention to the work already underway and planned in this area.

Archives relevant to the study of the Holocaust are scattered in many public and private institutions in a great many countries around the globe. In recent years both the United States Holocaust Memorial Museum and Yad Vashem have implemented wide-ranging global programs to microfilm these records and make them available to researchers. In this way, invaluable data banks are being created that provide essential reference material for those researching or teaching Holocaust-related issues.

On the specific issue of Holocaust-era assets, an Internet-based international guide to archival sources is at present being created, following discussions held at the London Conference on Nazi Gold in November 1997 and the subsequent proposal made by the United Kingdom in June 1998 at the planning seminar for the Washington Conference. An encouraging number of countries and institutions have already made details of their archival holdings and access arrangements available on dedicated websites, linked by a central information site managed by the United States Holocaust Memorial Museum (www.ushmm.gov/assets).

In order to maximize the effectiveness of these developments in the field of Holocaust education, remembrance, and research, the Task Force encourages all governments and archival institutions to give further cooperation and support to the microfilming projects run by the United States Holocaust Memorial Museum and Yad Vashem; and to extend their contributions to the international guide to archives on Holocaust-era assets to include details of all Holocaust-related archival material. The goal must be the widest possible dissemination of information for the benefit of all those who wish to learn more about the Holocaust.

e) Proposal for International Commemoration of the Holocaust
Stephen D. Smith, Director, Beth Shalom Holocaust Memorial and Education Centre, United Kingdom

- It is widely accepted that among the many episodes of mass murder that have disfigured 20th century history, the most profoundly tragic was the Holocaust: the attempt by the Nazi regime in Germany to annihilate the Jews of Europe. The deaths of six million victims who perished in the Holocaust represented a catastrophic loss for the Jewish people, and an atrocity committed against humanity as a whole.

- The countries participating in the International Task Force on Holocaust Education, Remembrance, and Research (currently Germany, Israel, Sweden, the United Kingdom, and the United States) have considered the question of the introduction internationally of the practice of observing a Holocaust Remembrance Day. Such a practice would have the following objectives:

    Commemoration: Task Force participants consider that it would be appropriate for countries to set aside a day each year on which the victims of the Holocaust were formally remembered;

    Awareness: the lessons of the Holocaust for the way all peoples conduct their affairs in the future must be regularly recalled and recognized, so that future tragedies of the same kind can be avoided;

    Solidarity: by observing a Remembrance Day, the peoples of the world, present and future, would express their opposition to anti-Semitism, racism, and other forms of discrimination, and their support for those subjected to them;

    Education: a Holocaust Remembrance Day would provide a focal point for activities and projects in the field of Holocaust Education.

Possible Dates for Holocaust Remembrance Day
Task Force participants do not consider it necessary or desirable that all countries that decide to institute a Holocaust Remembrance Day should

hold it on the same date. A number of different dates are already regarded as significant in this area in different countries. Some of these are mentioned below. Countries may wish to consider them, or other dates with more significance for them, should they decide to adopt a Remembrance Day.

27 January

This is the anniversary of the liberation of the Auschwitz concentration camp complex by the Soviet forces in 1945. It was officially designated in the German Parliament in 1996 by Federal President Roman Herzog as a Day of Commemoration for the Victims of National Socialism. This date was also chosen by the Swedish Government in 1998 for a memorial ceremony in the Riksdag, and for the launch of the Swedish Holocaust Education Initiative by Prime Minister Goran Persson.

12 June

This is the birthday of the Holocaust victim and diarist Anne Frank. It is observed by many people, particularly younger people in her native country, the Netherlands, and other Western European countries.

Yom Ha Sho'ah

This is the Day of Holocaust Remembrance in the Jewish calendar. It is widely and actively observed by Jewish communities internationally as a day of remembrance for victims. It has been observed in the United States as an occasion for public, religious, and servicemen's commemoration. The fact that it occurs on a different date each year in the Christian calendar might, however, be a practical obstacle to its widespread adoption.

Possible Ways of Observing a Holocaust Remembrance Day
The following are some of the ideas and activities that have been employed or suggested for a Remembrance Day:

> The observation of a period of silence in parliaments, government offices, and elsewhere;

> Ceremonial events with the participation of leading figures in public life;

> Special religious services, or the inclusion of references to the Holocaust in services;

> The inclusion of the Remembrance Day in educational calendars: reference to the Holocaust in school assemblies and similar ceremonies or activities;

> Readings in schools and other educational institutions from the literature of the Holocaust, including poetry;

> The dedication of memorials, such as gardens, trees, or art projects;

> The wearing of symbolic badges or emblems.

Additional Conference Statements

Appendix I:
APPEAL BY THE REPRESENTATIVES OF FORMER PRISONERS OF FASCISM FROM BELARUS, RUSSIA, AND UKRAINE TO THE PARTICIPANTS IN THE WASHINGTON CONFERENCE ON HOLOCAUST-ERA ASSETS

Statement translated from the original Russian by the
U.S. Department of State Office of Language Services, Translating Division

To: The Honorable Abner J. Mikva,
Chairman of the Washington Conference on Holocaust-Era Assets:

We, the representatives of 1.2 million former child and adult prisoners of fascism, 350,000 of whom have joined in the International and National Unions [of Former Prisoners of Fascism] of Belarus, Russia, Ukraine, and other member states of the CIS [Commonwealth of Independent States] and the Baltic states, are taking part in the Washington Conference with high hopes that, more than half a century after the end of the Second World War, the international community will be able to produce a complete and objective assessment of the tragedy of the victims of Nazism.

The elements of this tragedy were as follows:

- the death of tens of millions of innocent people in combat zones, in fascist torture chambers, in German industry, and in occupied territories;
- the premature death of millions of victims of Nazism in the post-War years;
- the painful fates of many hundreds of thousands of surviving inmates of concentration camps, ghettos, and prisons;

-   the irreparable loss of health incurred by millions of people whom the fascists rounded up and herded to Germany and other countries for slave labor;
-   the destruction of hundreds of thousands of dwellings, schools, hospitals, and religious structures;
-   the looting of cultural and material assets belonging to the victims of Nazism.

This tragedy was experienced by the victims of nazism in 40 countries of the world. Particularly heavy losses were inflicted on the USSR (up to 40%) and the countries of Eastern Europe.

The plans of fascist Germany called for the displacement and extermination of entire peoples: Belarussians, Jews, Poles, Russians, Slovaks, Ukrainians, and Gypsies.

To us who lived through the horrors of concentration camps, ghettos, prisons, and backbreaking toil it is clear that genuine humanitarianism and fairness in regard to the victims of nazism will prevail only when the international community finds ways to overcome all the above-mentioned consequences of the tragedy.

These ways might be:

-   perpetuation of the memory of the victims of nazism who died during the Nazi era and thereafter;
-   elimination of the disturbing 5- to 8-fold difference in material support for the victims of Nazism based on national and ethnic affiliation;
-   fair compensation to all victims of Nazism, taking into account the severity of their sufferings and loss of health, regardless of their country of residence;
-   establishment of an agreed-upon system of international and national funding organizations to assist all the victims of Nazism, making use of "Nazi gold," unclaimed insurance monies, cultural and material assets, and humanitarian contributions by governments and international organizations.

Every year, tens of thousands of victims of Nazism depart this life. But we hope that the Washington Conference, having resolved the very important issues relating only to a fraction of the victims of Nazism, will succeed in mapping out new procedures and new goals to make a reality out of our dream-we want to be the last mass victims, not only in the outgoing twentieth century, but also in the twenty-first century that is commencing. Inhuman sufferings befell us, but we have faith in human memory and in human kindness toward us.

President of the International Union of Former Child Prisoners of Fascism	[signature]	N. Makhutov (Russia)
President of the Pan-Ukrainian Union of Prisoners of Fascism	[signature]	V. Litvinov (Ukraine)
President of the Belarussian Association of Former Prisoners of Nazism	[signature]	0. Nekhay (Belarus)
President of the of Belarussian Association Jewish Communities	[signature]	L. Levin (Belarus)

December 03, 1998, Washington

Appendix J:
REPORT OF THE GOVERNMENT OF THE RUSSIAN FEDERATION COOPERATION AND CONCILIATION FUND

PROFESSOR NIKOLAY ANDREYEVICH MAKHUTOV
CORRESPONDING MEMBER, THE RUSSIAN ACADEMY OF SCIENCES
AND DEPUTY CHAIRMAN OF THE BOARD, THE COOPERATION AND
CONCILIATION FUND

*Statement translated from the original Russian by the
U.S. Department of State Office of Language Services, Translating Division*

Mr. Chairman, Ladies and Gentlemen, Friends:

We are addressing a problem that is rooted in the most horrible tragedy the human race has known in the century that is now drawing to a close. Whether for its scale, the level of tensions, the combat forces and material involved, the tremendous number of casualties, or its social consequences, the Second World War is without equal in human history.

That terrible war also had a direct affect on the fate of my family. The Bryansk area, where I was born, was occupied by German fascist forces in the early months of the war in 1941. I was forced to endure personally both a fascist concentration camp and the hardships of the occupation right down to the liberation in 1944. So what we are discussing here is especially close and comprehensible to me. I would like to tell you about the activities of the Russian and International Unions of Former Child Prisoners of Fascism[1] and about the activities of the Russian Fund for Cooperation and Conciliation, works hands-on with victims of nazism.

Translator's note(s):
[1] Formal titles of these organizations in English could not be confirmed.

Recall that armed conflict encompassed the greater part of the globe, covering a territory of 22 million square kilometers. There were active hostilities on the European continent, a significant portion of Asia, Eastern and Central Africa, and on the Atlantic, Pacific, and Arctic Oceans. **Forty countries became theaters of combat. A total of 61 countries, with a population of 1,700,000,000 people, became involved in hostilities, *i.e.* about 80% of all the inhabitants of our planet were forced into that bloody war. Troops numbering in the millions fought on the battlefields: about 110 million people were mobilized to wage war.**

In this auditorium, before so many well-read individuals, it would be superfluous to recall that it was the peoples of the Soviet Union who suffered enormous human and material losses in the vast conflict with fascism. After all, the war crossed the Soviet Union twice: once with the Soviet forces in a defensive posture, and again when they expelled the invaders. I'd like to take the liberty of citing a few figures. 1,710 cities and towns lay in ruins. The USSR lost 30% of its national wealth. Material damage is estimated at $127 billion (in 1945 dollars), which is about half the amount of damage inflicted on all of the other European countries. Adding in military expenditures, the war cost the Soviet Union $485 billion, far more than it cost the U.S., England, and France combined.

The Soviet Union also suffered the greatest numbers of human losses: more than 27 million people died on battlefields, in the ruins of towns and villages, shot on occupied territory, worked to death in concentration camps and taxed beyond their strength in Hitler's Germany. This is more than 40% of all the deaths in the Second World War.

Hitler did to a considerable extent what he described in his book *Mein Kampf:* "... first and foremost, we should expel and annihilate the Slavic peoples - the Russians, Poles, Czechs, Slovaks, Bulgarians, Ukrainians, and Belorussians. There is no reason not to do so."[2]

And so they did. In the occupied territories of the Soviet Union, the fascists deliberately took steps to weaken biologically the Russian, Ukrainian, Belorussian, and other peoples. They premeditatedly created intolerable living conditions for the local inhabitants. Forced labor was

---

Translator's note(s):
[2] Neither the original German nor any existing English translation of this quotation could be confirmed.

instituted even for nine-year-old children, and the workday was set at 14 to 16 hours. No wages were paid. Rural inhabitants were taxed on their land, homes, windows, doors, cats, and dogs. A significant portion of the healthy, able-bodied population was deported to Germany by the occupation forces. An absolute majority of those people were held in locked camps and had the right to leave them only to do their jobs.

It is generally known, for example, that 2.3 million Soviet citizens of Jewish nationality suffered a tortured death at the hands of the occupation forces.

The famous Nuremberg judgement against the nazi criminals related that **"in the East, the mass murders and cruelties were not committed solely for the purpose of stamping out opposition or resistance to the German occupying forces. In Poland and the Soviet Union these crimes were part of a plan to get rid of whole native populations by expulsion and annihilation in order that their [thus liberated][3] territory could be used for colonization by Germans."** Various methods were used to destroy civilians: mass shootings, poison gas, hanging, killing of hostages, death by hard labor, and hunger.

There were more than 14,000 concentration camps, Gestapo prisons, and ghettoes in Germany and the countries it occupied. By admission of SS officers themselves, one prisoner - whose life expectancy on the whole was less than one year - brought in 1,430 Reichsmarks of pure profit.   When prisoners were transferred from concentration camps to German companies, the SS charged a fee of six Reichsmarks per day for a skilled laborer, and four per day for an unskilled laborer. Furthermore, all property (including money and valuables) was confiscated. A prisoner brought in revenue even after death: gold crowns were removed from the corpse, soap was manufactured from the remains, and ashes became fertilizer. For example, surviving members of "death squads" testify that in Lvov, after corpses from civilian mass grave sites were burned, 110 kg of gold was "winnowed" and sent to Germany in the course of only five months. And how many such sites were there in Minsk, Kiev, Novgorod, Simferopol, and elsewhere in the former USSR! In 1944 alone, the Reich's concentration camps transferred more than two tons of gold to the treasury. There were even special companies in Germany that processed

_____

Translator's note(s):
[3] The bracketed phrase is missing from the original English-language text of the judgements

precious metals "extracted" at locations where free citizens of Europe were held in captivity.

Such are the historical facts. That is the ocean of human blood with which "nazi gold" is commingled. And would it not be more humane if part of this "nazi gold" were to be devoted to providing supplemental financial assistance to the victims of nazism in various countries, primarily people who were in the western territories of the USSR, including Russia? Then, in our opinion, people who were subjected to nazi persecutions could be embraced by the spirit of justice while they still live. Who can give them a decent life, if not we? Who must, if not we? Why let things go so far that feelings of discontent and injustice endure in the hearts of their children and grandchildren? By ignoring human morality and the lessons of history, are not German companies, German banks, and their subsidiary institutions committing yet another indecency?

I speak on behalf of people whose destinies are shattered. It turns out that, for reasons we all know, neither the victor nor the vanquished cared about their fate. But today there is a chance to help these people. Let us ask ourselves what is preventing us from displaying historical justice toward them? Nothing prevents it now. This is a matter of conscience, a matter of specific actions. Only we must hasten, hasten to help, while these people are still alive. The international community, whose word is so influential, must also speak up about this.

Nor must we separate people by ethnic affiliation. We must not permit our national approach to the former victims of nazism to contain any discrimination. To do so would be unacceptable. All of us were and remain people, inhabitants of our beautiful planet.

On June 22, 1998, the most recent, and the grimmest, anniversary in the lives of the peoples of the Soviet Union, the anniversary of the attack by Hitler's Germany against the USSR, 350 delegates to the conference of the International Union of Former Child Prisoners of Fascism, in Kiev, adopted an appeal. They represented the interests of 1.2 million surviving victims of nazi persecutions, citizens of the new independent states, and addressed themselves to the heads of state, parliamentary leaders, and heads of government of Belarus, Kazakhstan, Latvia, Lithuania, Moldova, Russia, Uzbekistan, Ukraine, and Estonia to call for just compensation payments by Germany to those who suffered from nazi enslavement. A separate statement addressed to the Secretary General of the Council of Europe and the Chancellor of the Federal Republic of Germany was also adopted. These documents have been distributed here in the hall, and you may acquaint yourselves with their texts in full.

What do we really have today? The true victims of nazism have been discriminated against, while nazi accomplices receive compensation, pensions, and other material benefits. And let's be self-critical: this didn't happen without the connivance of public and state organizations within the international community.

In its statement to the participants in the Washington Conference on the disposition of "nazi gold," the International Union of Former Child Prisoners of Fascism rightly notes that a discriminatory approach to the distribution of this wealth can only heighten tensions among countries and peoples on the threshold of the new millennium.

Fifty-three years after the end of the Second World War, justice has not triumphed for the former victims of nazism. Yet they were in practically all countries, and left a trail still raw, not yet scarred over. Attendees at a conference in the Greek city of Delphi have also issued a reminder of this. In their appeal, which was printed in the newspaper *Frankfurter Rundschau* on November 7, 1998, the conference participants ask the government of the Federal Republic of Germany to enter into negotiations with the Greek government to clarify the issues of compensation payments to victims of nazism and their next of kin. The appeal says, "Admission of guilt also includes a sincere and serious attempt to expiate some small part of that guilt through commensurate material payments. Fifty-three years since the end of the war is rather late to do so, but it is not too late."

The media in most countries have recently carried a lot of information about how industrialists, businessmen, and banks in other countries grew fat off the sufferings of nazism's victims. For example, Switzerland kept, in its banks and their branches (including branches in the U.S.) the nazis' gold ingots melted from plundered gold. Turkey, Sweden, Portugal, and Spain took wealth plundered by the nazis, and supplied Germany with goods and raw materials that were in short supply, including strategic materials such as Portuguese tungsten and Swedish [iron] ore. Argentina and Brazil concealed nazi criminals after the fall of the Third Reich. Switzerland also hoarded diamonds secretly brought in from Germany by submarine along with diplomatic mail, and sold high-quality steel for money obtained from the sale of the gemstones the nazis took from their victims before sending them to the gas chambers. Even the Vatican helped the nazis move to Spain and

Latin America after the fall of the Third Reich, and received gold in exchange for those services.

Russian prisoners feel it would be just if a Fund - in which the aforementioned countries and their capital would participate - were created to assist former victims of nazism.

In our view, even the notion of compensation requires elaboration.

Compensation is complete restitution of damages for physical and moral suffering and for forced labor. The amount of compensation for physical and moral damages is determined based on established international practice. Compensation for forced labor must be made according to contemporary standards applicable to the German population during the war years. Any other payments are humanitarian aid.

If victims of nazism living in Russia received lump-sum material assistance today thanks to the Government of Germany and Russia, they cannot consider it full compensation. More than half a century after the end of the Second World War, the victims of nazism. cannot demand compensation for forced labor, nor for the gold and other wealth appropriated by the nazis and sent to various banks in other countries.

On the international level, the problem of compensation for nazi persecution was raised immediately after the end of a war whose logical conclusion was the Nuremberg trial. The judgment of the International Tribunal became the basis "for the confirmation of new first principles moral norms of intercourse among individuals and peoples"[4] One of the acts that ratified these first principles was the decision that Germany would pay damages to victims of the national-socialist regime.

A January 16, 1986, Resolution by the European Parliament (Official Bulletin of the European Community, No C 36/129, February 17,1986, document B-2-1475/85/geu[5]) recognizes a **"moral and legal obligation on the part of companies using slave labor to pay compensation."**[6] The second paragraph in this Resolution contains a direct demand that companies which have not done so make payments **immediately**. In a separate paragraph (paragraph 4), the European

---

Translator's note(s):

[4] Neither the source nor wording of the quotation can be confirmed.

[5] The text of the Resolution was unavailable; translation given here follows the Russian of the present document.

[6] The Russian term here connotes damages, not "compensation" in the sense of remuneration or wages.

Parliament **"demands that all German entrepreneurs who used slave labor organize a Fund to Compensate Individuals Formerly Subjected to Forced Labor."** Certain public organizations in Stuttgart, Köln, and Berlin are preparing materials to substantiate and present the claims in a suit by former *Ostarbeiter* [Eastern workers] and former nazi concentration camp prisoners against German corporations and government agencies; the suit asks for damages for the physical and emotional harm inflicted on them and also calls for withholding of certain sums of windfall profits those corporations received from the unpaid labor of those persons.

Many people understand the impoverished condition in which the former republics of the USSR, including Russia, find themselves today. There are no funds in state budgets for decent assistance to the victims of nazism. Every day takes away a little more life from people whose fate it was to bear the brunt of the worst trials of the World War 11 years. It is their slave labor, it is the blood and sweat of their fellow captives from many countries that smelted the "nazi gold."

There is as yet no reliable information on the number of accounts in Western banks that were opened by the nazis or their surrogates during the Second World War. But one thing is without a doubt: the sums of money stored in those accounts may turn out to be very large.

It would be highly undesirable that the glitter of "nazi gold" eclipse any of the real victims of fascism. It would be unjust even to think that this gold belongs only to one people or ethnic organization. I welcome the active efforts of international public and ethnic organizations, including Jewish ones, that have been crowned with success in the case of the Swiss banks. We are anxious that other victims of the Holocaust - citizens of the former Soviet Union - receive material assistance from the monies set aside for the victims of nazism. And this assistance must be adequate, regardless of what country an individual may live in. There must be no distinctions according to ethnic identity. And there are no such differences within our Russian and International Unions of Former Child Prisoners of Fascism; there are no such differences in the activities of the Russian Fund for Cooperation and Conciliation. And we hope that our international forum here today will make it possible to see the tragedy of World War 11 victims as a truly international tragedy.

The victims of nazi persecution in the Soviet Union can be divided into various groups, namely:

- **adult and child prisoners of nazi concentration camps, ghettoes, and prisons;**

- involuntary laborers, *i.e.,* people who were forcibly deported to nazi Germany and its allied countries to work in businesses there;
- people who were exploited in temporarily occupied territories, etc.

As we discuss this problem, we must clearly view all of these groups as having suffered.

My dear colleagues, we know of the attempts by German companies to create a fund to assist people who worked as involuntary labor. We know the position of the current government of the Federal Republic of Germany headed by its new chancellor, Mr. Schröder, which has announced its readiness to resolve this problem without delay. We are very hopeful that a **single, unified German fund for the payment of compensation for involuntary labor under the nazi regime** will be created, a fund into which the companies that used such labor during the war years can pay their monies. This would also apply to certain large banks, insurance companies, etc.

We know that such megacompanies as Volkswagen and Siemens have created humanitarian assistance funds for former involuntary laborers, and that they are in no hurry to split up their activities. Given the current situation in Russia, it is asserted that money, shall we say, disappears irrevocably and with no hope of finding it again. Yes, there are criminal organizations in Russia, just as there are in any other country. But, you see, we have a well-refined[7] system for distributing such funds among the former prisoners of nazism. It has been operating for five years now. Citizens personally receive such assistance in marks or rubles, as they desire. This work proceeds in close contact with public social service committees. The Russian government, the German Embassy in the Russian Federation, and organizations of former nazi victim organizations are kept apprised of the progress of this work on a regular basis.

To put it bluntly, such assertions lack substance. There is a distribution mechanism, criteria, and controls. All self-contained within a single organization. On November 4, 1993, the Russian Federation Government created a special agency, the Russian Fund for Cooperation and Conciliation. It operates under a Russian-German agreement to assist persons persecuted under nazism during the war years. The Fund

---

Translator's note(s):
[7] The Russian term is unclear.

operates in Russia and in other republics of the former USSR (except Ukraine, Belarus, Moldova, and Estonia).

For the Fund to operate normally, a number of organizational and legal issues had to be resolved. An organizational plan for the Fund and its regional field offices was devised, and a constitution and by-laws were drafted and approved. These specify the criteria by which individuals persecuted under nazism are defined as individuals who were deported to Germany and its allies. All of these are classified into categories depending on their age (minors, adults) and the place where they were held in captivity (concentration camp, ghetto, etc.).

Thanks to a well-organized data collection system, a database has been created that includes both information on the places - located almost everywhere in Europe - where *Ostarbeiter* were held captive (concentration camps, ghettoes, etc.), and on the identities of former Eastern workers living in Russia. Naturally, information on the majority of former *Ostarbeiter* did not appear in the database immediately. As compensation claim applications have been received and are carefully reviewed, appropriate payments are made and the Fund has gathered information on the *Ostarbeiter* who have survived to the present day.

At present, the majority of the individuals persecuted by the nazis have received compensation payments that naturally only to a small degree compensate them for the physical and mental traumas they endured under fascist slavery. And after all, is it really possible at all to measure in money a life lived, the experiences of a lifetime?

Once it received the money allocated to it, the Fund decided to pay compensation first of all to those persons who had become invalids and to individuals aged 80 and older, since they represented the highest-risk group. After that, once the number of victims of nazism was ascertained, the Fund was able to increase the size of the payments and to perform the necessary recalculations on the compensation. The average payment was about 1,200 German marks. It should be noted that some of these people died before they ever received their compensation. In such cases, the Fund assists the relatives by paying for funeral services.

Friends, **out of about 7.7 million citizens of various countries who were forcibly deported to fascist Germany, the majority were citizens of the USSR (4,978,000).** During the nazi years, these people were subjected to inhuman physical and moral humiliations. But their torture did not end, even after the war did. In fact, down to the present day these people live considerably worse off than the rest of the population. They live on the brink of poverty and on the brink of extinction. Their lot today is one of loneliness, penury, and lack of medications.

Under these conditions, the 400 million German marks allocated by Germany that we continue to distribute to date have played a positive role. **The victims of nazism view this material assistance as penance by those Germans who were implicated in their sufferings and their shattered destinies. This material assistance consists of a one-time payment. It cannot compensate them for all the slave labor, the torture and the suffering that fell to these innocent victims as their lot. Furthermore, the payments to their fellow unfortunates in Germany itself are ten times greater, and in Western Europe seven times greater, than in Russia. It causes consternation and bitterness that an unjust distinction is drawn along ethnic lines between people who were in the very same camps. For example, Jews who were nazi prisoners and who now live in the West receive higher lump-sum payments and a larger monthly pension. It would be reasonable to make adequate provision for prisoners of other nationalities as well.**

Attempts to evade a fair resolution of this problem frequently cite a 1950's statement by the Soviet Government that it had resolved all the issues, or so it said. If only it were possible in this life to heal the wounds of human memory so simply, just with one statement! But there are people walking this earth who found themselves in a tragic situation, and it was not their fault, but their misfortune, that for a very long time (and for understandable reasons) they were not in a position to appeal directly to those Germans that had exploited their labor, thereby earning enormous incomes. "Only with the fall of the Iron Curtain," observes the popular German magazine *Stern* (August 28, 1998), "did a risk arise for German companies that former 'foreign workers' would demand compensation for the wages withheld from them and for their mental and physical sufferings."

Can it be that these companies bear no moral guilt or responsibility for the fate of involuntary laborers, the innocent victims of nazism? I do not know who is taking care of the image of these internationally known German companies these days, but I know one thing for sure: there is not, and cannot be, any better advertising than a humanitarian, human attitude toward the former involuntary workers, the victims of nazism. This is Christian love for one's neighbor; it is penance; it is a last, definitive act of conciliation. Why push the matter to the point of court proceedings, which the German firms have lost from the moral standpoint even before they really begin? There is more than enough documentation and evidence. To count on these people to depart this life before their contemporaries would be the antithesis of humanity.

I would like to bring up one other serious question, which is obviously on the minds of many of those present in this room. Is it possible to estimate how much money is needed to pay for the forced labor? Yes, it is possible.

To come up with a total compensation figure, we would have to figure in slave labor plus physical and moral damages. However, a full quantitative assessment of the latter two factors is impossible at the present time. Therefore, we shall merely proceed on the basis that, because of the damage done to health, we shall omit from our calculations that portion of wages that was withheld by the owner of the company for beggarly housing and food. This will compensate in some way for the loss of health.

We can make a quantitative estimate of unpaid labor from comparative data on wages paid for the labor of eastern workers versus that paid to German workers, drawing on an official Reich document - the Bulletin of Imperial Laws of June 30, 1992 (paragraphs 3 and 10) - from which we can see that payment per laborer was set at 7.1% to 25% of what a German worker received.

Based on a six-day work week, unpaid slave labor comes out to DM 150 per month in 1941-1944 prices; over the average period worked by Russian citizens (two years), that comes to DM 3,600. With devaluation of the mark by a factor of three over the ensuing half-century, the minimum compensation in today's prices comes to DM 10,800.

Based on the anticipated number of claimants in Russia at the time of the first disbursements (350,000 people), the total amount of funds needed is:

- in 1941-1945 prices: DM 1.2 billion
- in 1997 prices: about DM 3.5 billion.

So DM 3.5 billion is the minimum sum we can currently estimate for the unpaid labor of prisoners of nazism still alive in Russia, and that is just for one category of victims. This year alone, however, 30,000 victims of nazism departed this life. This figure is terrible in itself. We must not wait to do good.

Friends, in the late 1980's and early 1990's, changes took place in our world that are global in their scale and consequences. First of all, the Cold War ended, which cleared a path for the establishment of civilized relations between states that played different roles both during a bloody war and during the long years of an arms race, mutual suspicion, and hostility.

The altered political climate in our world-first and foremost in Europe-has paved the way for better mutual understanding among the peoples of the former Soviet Union, on the one hand, and Germany, on the other hand. The leaders of these countries, political and public figures, and broad strata of society have realized that the greater part of the present-day population of Germany-and certainly all the post-war generations-is not guilty of everything that happened to the peoples of the USSR as a result of nazi aggression.

So let us all turn over the last tragic page of the bygone world war, and put into practice our humanitarian, human attitude toward those who were victims of nazism. It is not proper that we should classify them by ethnic labels, and not proper to fan the flames of anti-Semitism on our territory or that of any other country.

We appeal to government officials, commercial and banking executives, businessmen's associations, and civic organizations in Russia, Germany, and other countries to do everything in their power to alleviate the fate of the victims of nazism. If we succeed in doing this, we shall convince these innocent victims - and not them alone - that a spirit of fairness, compassion, and love prevails in our day.

Supplemental Information

Appendix K:
NAZI PERSECUTEE RELIEF FUND DOCUMENTS

December 1, 1997

- Account Agreement
  An agreement between the Bank and the Account Holder to establish an Account for the Fund.

- Annex A -- Terms of Reference Governing the establishment and operation of the Fund

- Annex B -- List of NGOs

- Annex C -- Form of Contribution Instruction Used by Donor Countries to accompany their Contribution and to accept the Terms of Reference

- Annex D -- Form of Allocation Instruction Used by Donor Countries to allocate their Contribution

- Annex E -- Form of Amended Allocation Instruction Used by Donor Countries. to reallocate specific Allocations in the event that they determine the initial grant recipient did not comply with Fund Terms

- Annex F -- Form of Accelerated Allocation Instruction Used by Donor Countries to accelerate the disbursement of their allocated Contributions

- Annex G -- Form of Agreement between Account Holder and NGO Used by NGOs on Annex B to acknowledge their obligations pursuant to the Terms of Reference

Account Agreement between the Federal Reserve Bank of New York and the Government of the United Kingdom of Great Britain and Northern Ireland

1. ACCOUNT

a. The Federal Reserve Bank of New York ("Bank") and the Government of the United Kingdom of Great Britain and Northern Ireland ("Account Holder") agree that the Bank shall establish on its books a special account in the name of the Account Holder, designated as the "Nazi Persecutee Relief Fund Account," which shall consist of cash, securities custody and/or gold custody accounts, and sub-accounts thereto, as necessary (together, the "Account").

     b. The Account shall be operated in accordance with the Bank's standard terms and conditions, operating procedures, and applicable Operating Circulars, as amended from time to time, except as provided in this Account Agreement and Annexes thereto (together, the "Fund Documents").

     c. Any undefined terms used herein shall have the meaning defined in the Terms of Reference (Annex A).

2. CONTRIBUTIONS

     a. Contributions shall be received into the Account in accordance with the Terms of Reference.

     b. Contributions shall be subject to the sole control of the Account Holder in accordance with the Fund Documents.

     c. Contributions in gold shall be delivered to the Bank for deposit into the gold custody account. Donor Countries wishing to contribute gold located outside of New York City should arrange to engage in a location swap with a party able to make delivery of a like amount of gold in New York City on their behalf. Upon receipt of gold in New York from a Donor County, the Bank will deposit such gold into the gold custody account established in the name of the Account. Such deposits should be accompanied by a "weight list" specifying, for each of the bars individually (or, if U.S. Assay bars in "melt form", each melt) the refiner and bar number, gross troy ounces, fineness and fine troy ounces. Upon receipt, the gold will be verified against the weight list, with any discrepancies notified to the Donor Country and the Account Holder. Such verification will be completed as soon as possible after deposit. Acting as agent for the Account Holder, the Bank will endeavor to sell the gold so deposited to a reputable gold dealer in New York City, in the following manner:

i. After the verification of the gold deposit has been completed, the Bank will contact various gold dealers and solicit bids to purchase the gold, disclosing that the Bank is acting as agent for the Account Holder. Dealers will be asked to proffer bids in written form, and such bids will be communicated via authenticated telecommunication to the Account Holder.

ii. The Account Holder will accept the highest bid from among those proffered and notify the Bank via authenticated telecommunication of the accepted bid, and the Bank will arrange for the delivery of gold in New York City to the gold dealer whose bid was accepted, against payment in electronic funds. These funds will be deposited into the cash account.

3. INVESTMENT OF FUNDS

Until drawn down, the funds shall be invested by the Bank in United States Government securities with maturities of one year or less from the date of such investments and in the Bank's repurchase agreement pool, subject to the Bank's standard terms and conditions. Earnings on such investments shall be credited by the Bank to the Contributions on a pari passu basis in proportion to the amounts of such Contributions and shall be deemed a part of such Contributions. The Bank may commingle funds as it deems necessary for investment purposes.

4. DISBURSEMENTS

Contributions shall be disbursed in accordance with the Terms of Reference.

5. TERMINATION

The Account shall automatically close and this Account Agreement terminate upon the first of the following events to happen: (a) the instruction of the Account Holder; (b) the occurrence of a zero balance in the Account for a period of more than 365 days; (c) the resignation of the Bank as depository of the Account pursuant to Paragraph 13 below; or (d) five years after the entry into effect of this Account Agreement. Any funds remaining in the Account upon termination shall be distributed in accordance with the instructions of the Account Holder pursuant to the Terms of Reference.

6. REPORTS

a. The Bank shall provide the Account Holder and Donor Countries with a monthly statement detailing the receipt, investment, earnings thereon, and disbursement of all Contributions.

b. The Bank shall provide a status report on the Account at the annual meeting in accordance with the Terms of Reference.

7. EXPENSES

No fee shall be due from the Account Holder to the Bank for services rendered by the Bank under the Account Agreement; provided, however, that the Bank shall be reimbursed for all out-of-pocket expenses incurred by the Bank in connection with the Account. All such expenses shall be deducted from the Account's investment proceeds on a pari passu basis.

8. AMENDMENT OF FUND DOCUMENTS

The Fund Documents shall not be subject to revocation, modification or amendment except by a document signed by the Bank and the Account Holder. Any amendment of the Terms of Reference (Annex A) shall be made in accordance with Paragraph 9 of the Terms of Reference.

9. AMENDMENT OF NGO LIST

The NGO List (Annex B) shall be amended in accordance with the Terms of Reference.

10. NO THIRD PARTY RIGHTS OR OBLIGATIONS

a. The Fund Documents are not intended and shall not be construed to create any rights in favor of any person or any entity other than the Bank or the Account Holder.

b. The responsibilities of the Bank and the Account Holder are strictly limited to those specifically set forth in this Account Agreement, and no unstated functions, responsibilities, duties, obligations or liabilities shall be read into the Fund Documents or otherwise exist against the Bank or the Account Holder. The Bank shall not be deemed to be acting as a trustee or-fiduciary for the Account Holder, Donor Countries, or NGOs and shall not be an agent for any of them (other than the United States), except as otherwise expressly provided in the Fund Documents.

c. The Bank or the Account Holder shall in no event be required to initiate any suit, action, or proceeding arising out of or in connection with the Fund Documents, on behalf of each other, any Donor Country, or any NGO.

11. COMMUNICATIONS

a. The Account Holder authorizes the Bank to act on Contribution Instructions (Annex Q, Allocation Instructions (Annex D), Amended Allocation Instructions (Annex E) and Accelerated Allocation Instructions (Annex F) received from Donor Countries in accordance with the Terms of Reference.

b. Any authorization, instruction, notification or other communication made under this Account Agreement shall be made by authenticated telecommunication in a form acceptable to the Bank, or in such other manner as the Bank and the Account Holder may agree.

c. The Bank shall have the authority to interpret and act under the authorizations, instructions, notifications or other communications received by it in such a manner as the Bank in its sole judgment deems reasonable.

d. The Bank shall be authorized to make calculations and rounding adjustments as necessary.

12. STANDARD OF CARE AND LIABILITY

The Bank shall use reasonable care in the performance of its duties under this Account Agreement but shall incur no liability for any acts, arrangements, or agreements entered into or performed in connection with the Account by the Account Holder, except for the Bank's own gross negligence, bad faith or willful misconduct.

13. RESIGNATION OF BANK

The Bank may at any time resign as the depository of the Account upon 90 days written notice to the Account Holder. Such resignation shall take effect upon transfer by the Bank of any Contributions and any earnings thereon then remaining in the Account to the successor depository.

14. GOVERNING LAW

The Fund Documents and all amendments thereto shall be construed and enforced in accordance with the Federal law of the United States and, in the absence of controlling Federal law, the laws of the State of New York.

15. ENTRY INTO EFFECT

This Account Agreement shall become effective when both the Bank and the Account Holder have executed the Account Agreement by their duly authorized representatives.

16. OTHER FUND DOCUMENTS

The following documents are attached to this Account Agreement and form a part of it:
Annex A. Terms of Reference
Annex B. NGO List
Annex C. Form of Contribution Instruction
Annex D. Form of Allocation Instruction
Annex E. Form of Amended Allocation Instruction
Annex F. Form of Accelerated Allocation Instruction
Annex G. Form of Agreement between Account Holder and NGO

17. SIGNATURES

Federal Reserve Bank of New York

Name: William J. McDonough
Title: President
Date: November 26,1997

Government of the United
Kingdom of Great Britain and
Northern Ireland
Name: Robin Cook
Title: Secretary of State
Date: 1 December 1997
(for Foreign & Commonwealth
Affairs)

Annex A:
Terms of Reference

1. <u>INTRODUCTION</u>

    a.   These terms of reference (the "Terms") set forth the understandings that will govern the establishment and operation of the Nazi Persecutee Relief Fund (the "Fund"). The Fund will consist of an account at the Federal Reserve Bank of New York under the name of the Government of the United Kingdom of Great Britain and Northern Ireland (the "Account Holder") established pursuant to the Account Agreement dated December 1, 1997 (the "Account"). The Fund will be funded by contributions ("Contributions") made by donor countries ("Donor Countries") acting through their authorized institutions. Any undefined terms used herein shall have the meaning defined in the Account Agreement.

    b.   The primary purpose of the Fund is to provide resources for the relief of needy victims of Nazi persecution who to date have received very little or no compensation for their persecution, and its subsidiary purpose is to provide resources for other related projects, in particular projects aimed at benefiting the communities most severely affected by Nazi persecution or at preventing similar injustices in the future.

    c.   Fund grants will be channeled through established non-governmental organizations that already have in place the administrative and organizational infrastructures necessary to fulfill Fund purposes. An initial list of eligible non-governmental organizations, developed through consultation among interested potential donor countries and persecutee communities, is provided in Annex B.

2. <u>GUIDELINES FOR USE OF FUND MONEYS</u>

    a.   All moneys and gold contributed to the Fund, except those amounts required for certain bank expenses as provided in the Account Agreement, shall be disbursed in accordance with Paragraph 4 below to one or more non-governmental organizations listed on Annex B (the "NGOs"). The Account Holder will perform its functions specified in the Fund Documents without charge to the Fund.

b. NGOs will be limited to organizations that (i) provide direct assistance, services or other benefits to victims of Nazi persecution who currently live in difficult financial circumstances; or (ii) engage in related activities, in particular projects aimed at benefiting the communities most severely affected by Nazi persecution or at preventing similar injustices in the future.

c. "Victims of Nazi persecution" means those who suffered damage to health or loss of liberty, property, or income as a result of Nazi persecution directly against them.

d. "Living in difficult financial circumstances" means living with an income level or standard of living at or below the official poverty line in the country in which the individual permanently resides.

e. An NGO may make onward grants to other non-governmental organizations, provided that such onward grantee organizations fit the eligibility criteria set forth in subparagraph (b) of this Paragraph and have been identified in advance on the NGO prospectus described in Paragraph 6(a)(i) below. The NGO shall obtain in writing the agreement of the Donor Country or Donor Countries concerned prior to making such onward grants.

3. CONTRIBUTIONS

a.   Each Donor Country shall make its Contribution by transferring its Contribution to the Account in U.S. dollars or gold. Submission of a Contribution and a Contribution Instruction (Annex C) shall constitute a Donor Country's acceptance of these Terms and an acknowledgment that its Contribution will be handled. in accordance with the Account Agreement. Any Contribution that is received into the Account without a complete and accurate Contribution Instruction shall be returned to the Donor Country by the Bank.

b.   Each Donor Country shall also submit an Allocation Instruction (Annex D), specifying the manner in which it desires its Contribution to be allocated among one or more of the NGOs listed on Annex B (the "Allocations"). Only an NGO listed in Annex B is eligible to receive an Allocation. A Donor Country may specify that its Allocations may only be used by an NGO for a specific project:

                    i. listed in the prospectus described in Paragraph 6(a)(ii)
below; or

                    ii. determined by mutual consent between the NGO and
the Donor Country subsequent to the submission of the Contribution. In
this event, the prospectus described in Paragraph 6(a)(ii) shall be revised
to list that project.

          c. A Donor Country may submit its Allocation Instruction with
its Contribution or separately from and subsequent to its Contribution. A
Donor Country must submit the Allocation Instruction within 12 months
after its Contribution, or the entire Contribution and any earnings thereon
shall be returned to the Donor Country. The Account Holder shall notify
all other Donor Countries in the event that a Contribution is returned to a
Donor Country for failure to specify an Allocation.

          d.   All Contributions transferred to the Account shall be
irrevocable and shall become part of the Account.

          e. A Contribution Instruction, Allocation Instruction, Amended
Allocation Instruction, and Accelerated Allocation Instruction shall be
submitted directly to the Bank, and a copy shall be submitted to the
Account Holder.

4. DISBURSEMENTS AND OVERSIGHT

          a. In accordance with the Allocations specified in the Allocation
Instruction, the Bank shall disburse an amount equal to 25 percent of
each Allocation within ten New York business days of the receipt of the
Allocation Instruction.

          b.   An Oversight Period with respect to each Allocation shall
commence on the date a Donor Country submits its Allocation
Instruction. The Oversight Period shall be 6 months. The Bank will
disburse the remaining portion of each Allocation, including any
earnings thereon, within 10 New York business days after the conclusion
of the Oversight Period.

          c.   Prior to the conclusion of the Oversight Period, the Donor
Country may submit to the Bank (i) an Amended Allocation Instruction
pursuant to Paragraph 4(d) below; or (ii) an Accelerated Allocation

Instruction (Annex F). Upon receipt of an Accelerated Allocation Instruction from a Donor Country, the Bank shall disburse the remainder of the relevant Allocations within ten New York business days.

      d. Each Donor Country shall ensure that each of its Allocations is used by the selected NGO in accordance with these Terms. If, prior to the conclusion of the Oversight Period provided for in Paragraph 4(b) above, the Donor Country determines that an NGO has failed to comply materially with these Terms, the Donor Country may submit an Amended Allocation Instruction (Annex E). The Bank shall reallocate the undisbursed portion of each affected Allocation accordingly, and disburse it in the same manner as an initial Allocation under this Paragraph, meaning that 25 percent shall be disbursed initially to the NGO specified on the Amended Allocation Instruction, followed by a new Oversight Period and subsequent disbursement. The Account Holder shall also notify all other Donor Countries upon receipt of any Amended Allocation Instruction.

5. ANNUAL MEETING

Until the termination of the Account, the Account Holder shall organize and hold an annual meeting to review the Fund's activities. Each Donor Country may send a representative. Each NGO shall report at the meeting on its use of Fund grants. The Bank shall report on the status of the Account. The first meeting shall be held one year after the first disbursement from the Account. The Account Holder shall circulate among Donor Countries information where this is provided for under these Terms.

6. NGOs AND ANNEX B

      a.   Obligations of NGOs. Each NGO, as a condition of its eligibility to receive Allocations, shall agree in Annex G to:

          i. use Allocations in strict compliance with these Terms;

          ii. make available to the Account Holder, to each Donor Country, and to each country that has demonstrated to the Account Holder a serious interest in becoming a Donor Country, a prospectus which identifies the specific projects that would be funded by any Allocation, which states the maximum percentage of each Allocation that will be used for administrative, auditing, and overhead expenses, which shall be revised in the event that an NGO and a Donor Country agree by mutual consent on a specific project not listed on the NGO's original prospectus to list that project, and which identifies in advance any other non-governmental organization it may utilize -as an onward grantee pursuant to Paragraph 2(e) of the Terms of Reference;

iii. maintain records pertaining to the use of any Allocation in accordance with international accounting standards and make such records available for review by any Donor Country;

iv. make available to each Donor Country the results of an annual audit, conducted by an independent auditor, of its handling of all Allocations. The first audit must occur between 3 and 6 months after the initial disbursement to the NGO as provided in Paragraph 4(a) above;

v. be liable to the Donor Country concerned for the misuse of any allocations; and

vi. report at the Fund's annual meeting on the use of Allocations.

b.   Adding NGOs to Annex B. Any Donor Country or country that has demonstrated to the Account Holder a serious interest in be coming a Donor Country may propose the addition of a non-governmental organization to Annex B by notifying the Account Holder of such a proposal. The Account Holder shall circulate the proposed amendment to each Donor Country. If the Account Holder has not received objections to it from more than 50 percent of the Donor Countries within 30 days, the proposed amendment is deemed accepted. The Account Holder shall notify the Bank, each Donor Country, and any prospective Donor Country of each amendment to Annex B.

7. IMMUNITY, STANDARD OF CARE, AND LIABILITY

a.   Nothing in these Terms or related documents shall be considered to constitute, in whole or in part, a waiver of any immunity to which the Account Holder, Bank, or Donor Countries may be entitled in any jurisdiction.

b. Nothing in these Terms or related documents shall require the Account Holder to verify that an Allocation has been used by an NGO in accordance with the Allocation Instruction, whether or not the Allocation Instruction has been subsequently varied by the submission of an Amended Allocation Instruction and/or an Accelerated Allocation Instruction.

C. The Account Holder shall use reasonable care in the performance of its duties under the Fund Documents, including these Terms, but shall incur no liability toward Donor Countries or NGOs for any acts, arrangements, or agreements entered into or performed in connection with the Account.

8. NO THIRD PARTY RIGHTS OR OBLIGATIONS

a. The Fund Documents are not intended and shall not be construed to create any rights in favor of any person or any entity other than the Bank or the Account Holder.

b. The responsibilities of the Bank and the Account Holder are strictly limited to those specifically set forth in the Fund Documents, and no unstated functions, responsibilities, duties, obligations or liabilities shall be read into the Fund Documents or otherwise exist against the Bank or the Account Holder. The Bank shall not be deemed to be acting as a trustee or fiduciary for the Donor Countries or NGOs, and shall not be an agent for any of them (other than the United States), except as otherwise expressly provided in the Fund. Documents. The Account Holder shall not be deemed to be acting as a trustee or fiduciary for the Donor Countries or NGOs, and shall not be an agent for any of them.

c. The Bank or the Account Holder shall in no event be required to initiate any suit, action, or proceeding arising out of or in connection with the Fund Documents, on behalf of any Donor Country, or any NGO.

9. AMENDMENTS

The Account Holder shall circulate any proposed amendment to the Terms to each Donor Country. If the Account Holder has not received objections to it from more. than 50 percent of the Donor Countries within 30 days, the proposed amendment is deemed accepted. The Terms shall be amended in accordance with the Account Agreement.

10. TERMINATION

The Fund shall be terminated when the Account is closed and the Account Agreement is terminated pursuant to the Account Agreement. Any funds remaining in the Account upon termination shall be returned to Donor Countries in proportion to the amount of each Donor's Contribution that remains undisbursed. The Account Holder shall notify each Donor Country in the event of termination.

Annex B
List of NG0s

American Jewish Joint Distribution Committee(AJJDC)
Association of Former Political Prisoners of Concentration Camps
Board of Deputies of British Jews
Center of Organizations of Holocaust Survivors in Israel
Conference on Jewish Material Claims against Germany (CJMC)
Consultative Council of Jewish Organizations
European Council of Jewish Communities
European Jewish Congress (EJC)
International Romani Union (IRU)
Jewish Central Committee of Sweden
National Fund of the Republic of Austria for Victims of National
   Socialism
Pink Cross
Swedish Red Cross
World Jewish Congress (WJC)
World Jewish Restitution Organization (WJRO)

Annex C:
Form of Contribution Instruction

[Note: The following instruction should be sent to the Bank via authenticated S.W.I.F.T. message or tested telex, with a copy sent to the Account Holder.]

1 . We refer to the Account Agreement between the Federal Reserve Bank of New York and the Government of the United Kingdom of Great Britain and Northern Ireland dated December 1, 1997 ("Account Agreement), the Terms of Reference (Annex A) of the Account Agreement, and the NGO List (Annex B) of the Account Agreement.

2. The (Donor] hereby irrevocably contributes [USD amount] [gold fine troy ounces] ("Contribution") to the Nazi Persecutee Relief Fund Account on your books.

3. The [Donor] hereby accepts the Terms of Reference, as may be amended from time to time, and acknowledges that the Contribution will be handled in accordance with the Account Agreement.

Annex D:
Form of Allocation Instruction

[Note: The following instruction should be sent to the Bank via authenticated S.W.I.F.T. message or tested telex, with a copy sent to the Account Holder.]

1. We refer to the Account Agreement between the Federal Reserve Bank of New York and the Government of the United Kingdom of Great Britain and Northern Ireland dated December 1, 1997 ("Account Agreement), the Terms of Reference (Annex A) of the Account Agreement, the NGO List (Annex B) of the Account Agreement, and our Contribution Instruction dated [date] ("Contribution Instruction").

2. The Contribution and any earnings thereon shall be allocated in accordance with the Terms of Reference as follows:

    a. Funds:

[NGO on Annex B]	[USD amount]	
[NGO project]		[USD amount]
[NGO project]		[USD amount]
[NGO on Annex B]	[USD amount]	
[NGO project]		[USD amount]
[NGO project]		[USD amount]
Total	[USD amount]	

    b.   Gold:

[NGO on Annex B]	[fine troy ounces]	
[NGO project]		[fine troy ounces]
[NGO project]		[fine troy ounces]
[NGO on Annex B]	[fine troy ounces]	
[NGO project]		[fine troy ounces]
[NGO project]		[fine troy ounces]
Total	[fine troy ounces]	

Annex E:
Form of Amended Allocation Instruction

[Note: The following instruction should be sent to the Bank via authenticated S.W.I.F.T. instruction or tested telex, with a copy sent to the Account Holder.]

1 . We refer to the Account Agreement between the Federal Reserve Bank of New York and the Government of the United Kingdom of Great Britain and Northern Ireland dated December 1, 1997 ("Account Agreement), the Terms of Reference (Annex A) of the Account Agreement, the NGO List (Annex B) of the Account Agreement, and our Allocation Instruction dated [date] ("Allocation Instruction").

2. The [Donor] hereby notifies the Federal Reserve Bank of New York and the Government of the United Kingdom of Great Britain and Northern Ireland that it wishes to amend the Allocation Instruction as follows: [original NGO from Annex B] should be deleted from the Allocation Instruction and replaced with [new NGO from Annex B], and [new NGO from Annex B] should receive the undisbursed portion of [original NGO from Annex B]'s allocation pursuant to Paragraph 4(d) of the Terms of Reference.

Annex F:
Form of Accelerated Allocation Instruction

[Note: The following instruction should be sent to the Bank via authenticated S.W.I.F.T. instruction or tested telex,, with a copy sent to the Account Holder.]

1.   We refer to the Account Agreement between the Federal Reserve Bank of New York and the Government of the United Kingdom of Great Britain and Northern Ireland dated December 1, 1997 ("Account Agreement), the Terms of Reference (Annex A) of the Account Agreement, the NGO List (Annex B) of the Account Agreement, and our Allocation Instruction dated [date].

2.   The [Donor] hereby notifies the Federal Reserve Bank of New York and the Government of the United Kingdom of Great Britain and Northern Ireland that it wishes to accelerate the disbursement of its Contribution pursuant to Paragraph 4(c) of the Terms of Reference, with respect to the following NGOs:

        [NGO or NGO project on Annex B]
        [NGO or NGO project on Annex B]

Annex G:
Form of Agreement between Account Holder and NGO

[Note: The following agreement should be sent to the Account Holder, with a copy to the Federal Reserve Bank of New York.]

1 . We refer to the Account Agreement between the Federal Reserve Bank of New York and the Government of the United Kingdom of Great Britain and Northern Ireland (the "Account Holder") dated December 1, 1997 ("Account Agreement), the Terms of Reference (Annex A) of the Account Agreement, and the NGO List (Annex B) of the Account Agreement.

2. In accordance with Paragraph 6 of the Terms, we agree, as a condition of our eligibility to receive Allocations from the Fund referred to in those documents,
to:

   i. use Allocations in strict compliance with the Terms of Reference;

   ii. make available to the Account Holder, each Donor Country, and each country that has demonstrated to the Account Holder a serious interest in becoming a Donor Country, a prospectus which identifies the specific projects that would be funded by any Allocation, which states the maximum percentage of each Allocation that will be used for administrative, auditing, and overhead expenses, which shall be revised in the event that an NGO and a Donor Country agree by mutual consent on a specific project not listed on the NGO's original prospectus to list that project, and which identifies in advance any other non-governmental organization it may utilize as an onward grantee pursuant to Paragraph 2(e) of the Terms of Reference;

   iii. maintain records pertaining to the use of any Allocation in accordance with international accounting standards and make such records available for review by any Donor Country;

   iv. make available to each Donor Country the results of an annual audit, conducted by an independent auditor, of its handling of all Allocations. The first audit must occur between 3 and 6 months after the initial disbursement to the NGO as provided in Paragraph 4(a) above;

v. be liable to the Donor Country concerned for the misuse of any allocations; and

vi. report at the Fund's annual meeting on the use of Allocations.

3. We specifically accept the provisions in Paragraph 7 of the Terms of Reference on immunity, standard of care, and liability. We also accept that, pursuant to Paragraph 8 of the Terms of Reference, the Fund Documents do not create any rights in favor of any person or any entity other than the Bank or the Account Holder; the responsibilities of the Bank and the Account Holder are strictly limited to those specifically set forth in the Fund Documents, and no unstated functions, responsibilities, duties, obligations or liabilities shall be read into the Fund Documents or otherwise exist against the Bank or the Account Holder; the Bank or Account Holder shall not be deemed to be acting as a trustee or fiduciary for the NGOs, and shall not be an agent for any of them; and the Bank or the Account Holder shall in no event be required to initiate any suit, action, or proceeding arising out of or in connection with the Fund Documents on behalf of any NGO.

4. All allocations disbursed to us should be sent to [name of U.S. correspondent bank] for credit to [name of NGO's local bank) account number [account number].

Appendix L:
MEMORANDUM OF UNDERSTANDING REGARDING HOLOCAUST-ERA INSURANCE CLAIMS

1. It is agreed by the undersigned European insurance companies, United States insurance regulatory authorities, and Jewish and survivor organizations that a just process shall be established that will expeditiously address the issue of unpaid insurance policies issued to victims of the Holocaust.

2. It is agreed by the undersigned that an International Commission ("IC") will be established. The parties to this Memorandum of Understanding ("MOU") agree to actively and voluntarily pursue the goal of resolving insurance claims of Holocaust victims through the IC. The IC will be composed of twelve persons or their alternates: six persons designated by the United States regulators and the World Jewish Restitution Organization, together with the Conference of Jewish Material Claims Against Germany, and the State of Israel, and six persons designated by the undersigned European insurance companies and European regulators. Each group above that is a member of the IC will designate two alternates to attend in observer status. In addition, there will be three additional observers designated by the World Jewish Restitution Organization, together with the Conference of Jewish Material Claims Against Germany, and the State of Israel, one observer designated by the European Economic Commission and one observer designated by the United States Department of State. The twelve representatives will appoint an additional member who shall serve as the Chairperson. The Chairperson shall be independent and not affiliated with any of the persons or groups represented on the IC. Members of the IC shall serve on a volunteer basis and without remuneration. The

IC shall attempt to resolve all issues within two years from its formation.

3.   Following the creation of the IC, insurance companies or their successors that issued policies to persons who were subsequently victims of the Holocaust and were not original signatories to this MOU will be given the opportunity to become signatories to this MOU and participate in the IC process. The IC process, at the discretion of the signatory companies, can be extended to affiliates of the signatories.

4.   The IC shall initiate and conduct an investigatory process to determine the current status of those insurance policies issued to Holocaust victims during the period of 1920 to 1945 for which claims are filed with the IC. To assess the remaining unpaid insurance policies of Holocaust victims, a reasonable review will be made of the participating companies' files, in conjunction with information concerning Holocaust victims from Yad Vashem and the United States Holocaust Memorial Museum and other relevant sources of data. The IC or its participating companies shall retain one or more internationally recognized auditing firms that operate in those countries where the above-referenced insurance companies are based and other experts as needed.

        a.   The IC shall promulgate an audit mandate implementing the goal of this MOU. This mandate shall outline a work program for the audit firm(s). In addition to establishing a framework for an overall work plan, the mandate shall also establish a mechanism whereby any investigatory or audit work already performed by the various insurance companies in this area is reviewed to determine whether it is consistent with the standards and goals of the mandate and if so, shall be incorporated into the work plan of the IC auditors. The insurance companies and insurance regulators that are parties to this MOU shall ensure that the respective auditing firm(s) and other experts have complete and unfettered access to any and all of their relevant books, records and file archives as is necessary to their audit activities. Such access shall be in cooperation with and in accordance with local insurance authorities and laws. Any documents reviewed or received by the IC will be maintained as strictly confidential.

b.   As part of the audit mandate, the IC will address the issue of a full accounting by the insurance companies and publication of the names of Holocaust victims who held unpaid insurance policies. In addition, the IC shall establish a toll free mechanism to aid survivors, beneficiaries and heirs of Holocaust victims in the submission of claims and inquiries.

5.   The IC shall establish a claims and valuation process to settle and pay individual claims that will be of no cost to claimants. The initial responsibility for resolving claims rests with the individual insurance companies, in accordance with guidelines to be promulgated by the IC. The signatory companies shall submit to the IC all claims received directly by the company within 30 days of receipt. The IC shall endeavor to integrate data already collected by the various U.S. states into the overall process. Such process shall include the establishment of relaxed standards of proof that acknowledge the passage of time and the practical difficulties of the survivors, their beneficiaries and heirs in locating relevant documents, while providing protection to the insurance companies against unfounded claims.

6.   Such claims process shall also include the valuation of policies, including, but not limited to, the establishment of standards and formulae to account for currency reforms, currency conversions and interest. In the case of insurance claims that were previously submitted for resolution through a post-war governmental restitution program, the IC shall examine the program, payments and payment calculations to determine if they were equitable and adequate. To the extent an insurance policy was subject to a post-war governmental restitution program, the insurance company will receive credit for the amount paid out for the insurance policy against the value of the policy as determined by the IC. The IC process shall constitute an exclusive remedy. Claim awards shall be compensatory only.

7.   Each insurance company that has agreed to voluntarily submit to this process shall establish its own dedicated account, sufficiently funded, to be used exclusively for the immediate payment of Holocaust related insurance claims which have been submitted to the IC and which are determined by the IC to be valid and attributable to each specific insurance company. No signatory insurance company shall be required to pay any claim that the IC determines to be attributable to an existing insurance company that has not signed this MOU.

8.   The IC shall establish and administer a Special Fund consisting of two sections. Each signatory company will make an initial contribution to the two Specific Humanitarian Sections.

A. Specific Humanitarian Section:

(1)   This section shall provide relief to claimants who seek relief under policies that cannot be attributed to a particular insurance company as well as to claimants who seek relief under policies issued by companies no longer in existence. These funds shall be separately maintained.

(a)   If the audit process develops additional claims and if additional claims are received that fall into the category of paragraph (8)(A)(1) of this section and there are insufficient funds remaining in the segregated (8)(A)(1) account, each signatory company shall make additional contributions as the IC deems necessary to be assessed on an equitable basis taking into account both historic and current involvement.

(2)   In addition, each signatory company agrees to make an equitable contribution to this section, to be used to satisfy claims on any of its policies that were nationalized or any of its policies that were paid, as required by local law, to a governmental authority that was not the named

beneficiary of the policy.   The monies contributed by each signatory company shall be used to satisfy claims awards only against that company.   These funds shall be separately maintained.

(a)   In the event the audit process develops additional claims and if additional claims are received that fall into paragraph (8)(A)(2) and there are insufficient funds remaining in the segregated (8)(A)(2) account, each signatory company shall contribute an additional amount to pay any monies awarded by the IC on that signatory company's paragraph (8)(A)(2) policies.

B.   General Humanitarian Section:
This section shall be used for the benefit of needy victims of the Holocaust and for other Holocaust-related humanitarian purposes. It is understood that the contributions made under this section give due consideration to the category of "heirless claims," i.e., unpaid policies issued by the signatory companies to Holocaust victims as to which there is no living beneficiary or other living person entitled to receive the proceeds. Each signatory company shall make an initial contribution to this fund, with subsequent contributions to be determined by the IC to be assessed on an equitable basis taking into account both historic and current involvement.

9.   Upon execution of this MOU, the insurance companies will establish a fund to cover the expenses of the IC. Each signatory company shall make an initial contribution of $250,000.00. Thereafter, as the IC deems necessary, subsequent contributions will be assessed based on an equitable basis.   The cost of auditing an individual company's books and records and any expenses relating to the processing or investigation of claims against an individual insurance company shall be borne by that insurance company. There shall be an annual budget for the

operation of the IC administered by the Chairperson and an annual audit of the IC's expenses.

10.   The IC signatories will work to achieve exemptions from related pending and future legislation and will work to resolve all pending litigation for those insurers that become signatories to this MOU and which fully cooperate with the processes and funding of the IC.

11.   Upon agreement to the terms of this MOU, the respective parties shall announce the members of the IC and the Chairperson.

August __, 1998
Signed and agreed:

Insurer Signatories:

Appendix M:
FEDERAL LAW NO. 64-FZ OF APRIL 15, 1998 ON CULTURAL TREASURES TRANSFERRED TO THE UNION OF SOVIET SOCIALIST REPUBLICS AS A RESULT OF WORLD WAR II AND LOCATED IN THE TERRITORY OF THE RUSSIAN FEDERATION

Adopted
by the State Duma   on February 5, 1997

Approved
by the Federation Council   on March 5, 1997

This Federal Law regulates relationships connected with cultural treasures transferred to tile Union of Soviet Socialist Republics as a result of the World War II and located on the, territory of tile Russian Federation.

The main purposes of the Federal Law are:

the defense of the said cultural treasures from plunder, preventing their illegal export out of the Russian Federation, as well as the illegal transfer to, whomever it may be;

the creation of necessary legal conditions for the practical return of the said cultural treasures for partial compensation of the damage caused to the cultural property of the Russian Federation as a result of the plunder and destruction of its cultural treasure by Germany and her military allies during World War II;

the protection of the interest of the Russian Federation when settling with foreign states controversial issues concerning the said cultural treasures on the basis of consistent observation of the principle at reciprocity;

the granting of the possibility of the acquaintance with the said cultural treasure by citizens of the Russian Federation and foreign citizens including specialists in the field of education, science and culture;

the creation of favorable conditions for further development of international partnerships in the sphere of education, science and culture.

CHAPTER I. GENERAL PROVISIONS

Article 1. Legislation of the Russian Federation on Cultural Treasures transferred to the Union of Soviet Socialist Republics as a Result of World War II and Located in the Territory of the Russian Federation

Legislation of the Russian Federation on cultural treasures transferred to the Union of Soviet Socialist Republics as a result of World War II and located in the territory of the Russian Federation consists of this Federal Law and other legislative acts promulgated in accordance with the Constitution of the Russian Federation and this Federal Law.

Article 2. International-Legal and Other Acts Upon Which This Federal Law Is Based

This Federal Law in based an international legal and other acts, which were adopted in the period of and after World War II and have remained in effect for property relationships arising by virtue of these acts:

Peace Agreements of 1947, acts adopted on the basis of rights and the command of the occupying forces in Germany in 1945-1949, the State Treaty an the Restoration of Independence and Democracy to Austria of May 15, 1955, the Treaty on the End of the Final Settlement in Respect to Germany of September 12, 1990 as well as regulations of Article 107 of the Charter of the United Nations Organization and the Declaration of the United Nations of January 5, 1943.

Article 3. The Effect of This Federal Law in Regards to Actual Possession of Cultural Treasures Transported to the Union of Soviet Socialist Republics as a Result of World War II and Located in the Territory of the Russian Federation

This Federal Law is effective in regards to all cultural treasures transported to the Union of Soviet socialist Republics as a result of World War II and which are located in the territory of the Russian Federation irrespective of whose actual possession they am in as well as the circumstances of the arising of this actual possession.

Article 4. Fundamental Concepts Used in This Federal Law

For the purpose of this Federal Law the following fundamental concepts are used:

restitution - form of material international legal responsibility of the states having committed acts of aggression or other internationally illegal deed containing the obligation of a given state to eliminate or reduce the material harm caused to another state by means of the restoration of a former condition in part by means of the return of property plundered and illegally taken by it through its forces occupying another state:

compensatory restitution - form of material international legal responsibility of an aggressor state applied in cases if the implementation of responsibility of the given state the form of typical restitution is not possible and consists in the obligation of the given state to compensate another state for resulting material harm or by means of removal by the state suffering harm for its benefit; items of the same type that were stolen and illegally taken by the aggressor-state from the territory of the suffering state;

cultural treasures - valuable property of religious or secular character having historical, artistic, scholarly or other cultural significance, such works of art, books, manuscripts, incunabula, archival materials, component parts and fragments of architectural, historical, artistic statutes, as well as statues of monumental art and other categories items defined in <u>Article 7</u> of the Law of the Russian Federation on Exporting and Importing Cultural Treasures;

transferred cultural treasures - cultural treasures transferred in implementation of compensatory restitution from the territory of Germany and her farmer Military allies - Bulgaria, Hungary, Italy, Romania, and Finland to territory of the Union of the Soviet Socialist Republic in accordance with orders of the military command of the Soviet Army, the Soviet Military Administration in Germany, and orders of other competent organs of the Union of the Soviet Socialist Republics and located at this time in the territory of the Russian Federation;

formerly hostile states - Germany and allied status during the period of World War II - Bulgaria, Hungary, Italy, Romania and Finland;

property of formerly hostile states - property of state, private, municipal, social and other organizations and societies in formerly hostile states,

interested states - states (with the exception of The Russian Federation and states given in Article 7 of the Federal Law) whose territories fully or partially were occupied by armies of former enemy states;

property of interested states - property of state, private, municipal, social and other organizations and societies in interested states;

cultural institutions - Russian state (including departmental) and municipal museums, archives, libraries and other scientific, educational, entertainment and instructional institutions and organizations implementing its work in the sphere of education, science and culture.

Article 5. Composition of Transferred Cultural Treasures
From the point of view of their former state affiliation, transferred state treasures include:

cultural treasures which were property of former enemy states;

cultural treasures, which within the meaning given in Article 4 of this Federal Law, were property interested states that have lost the right of ownership to these cultural treasures as a consequence of failing to call for their restitution within the period that was established by legal acts stated in Article 9 of this Federal Law;

cultural treasures whose state ownership has not been established (ownerless things).

CHAPTER II TRANSFERRED CULTURAL TREASURES AND
PROPERTY RIGHTS TO THEM

Article 6. On the Right of Ownership of the Russian Federation
to the Transferred Cultural Treasures
All transferred cultural treasures taken, into the Union, of Soviet Socialist Republics in the implementation of its right to compensatory restitution and located in the territory of the Russian Federation with the exception stipulated by Articles 7 and 8 of this Federal law are property of the Russian Federation and are federal property

Article 7. On the Guarantee of the Rights of Ownership of the
Belarus Republic, Latvian Republic, Lithuanian

Republic, Moldavian Republic, Ukraine and the
Estonian Republic to Transported Cultural Treasures

1. The provisions of <u>Article 6</u> of this Federal Law does not affect
the tight of ownership of the Belarus Republic, Latvian Republic,
Lithuanian Republic, Moldavian Republic, Ukraine and Estonian
Republic to cultural objects that can be proven to be a part of transported
cultural treasures but were plundered and taken during World War II by
Germany and (or) her military allies not from the territory of the Russian
Soviet Federated Socialist Republic, but from the territories of the
Belorussian Soviet Socialist Republic, the Latvian Soviet Socialist
Republic, the Lithuanian Soviet Socialist Republic, the Moldavian Soviet
Socialist Republic, the Ukrainian Soviet Socialist Republic and the
Estonian Soviet Socialist Republic and constituted the national property
of the given, but not the other union republics, coming within the borders
of the Union of the Soviet Socialist Republics an February 1,1950.

2. Cultural items given in <u>Item 1</u> of this Article can be given to
the Belarus Republic, Latvian Republic, Lithuanian Republic, Moldavian
Republic, Ukraine and Estonian Republic according to their ownership
when they observe the conditions stipulated by <u>Item 4 of Article 18</u> of
this Federal law as well as by their agreement to ensure on the basis of
the principle of reciprocity the same such approach to for cultural
treasures of the Russian Federation transported from <u>former enemy states</u>
to the Union of Soviet Socialist Republics and located on their territories.

Article 8. Transported Cultural Treasures Not Falling Under the
Effect of Articles 6 and 7 of This Federal Law

The following transferred cultural treasures do not fall under the
effect of <u>Articles 6 and 7</u>:

1) Cultural treasures in respect to which and <u>interested state</u>
shall present proof of the fact that it made the demand for their <u>restitution</u>
before the expiration of the periods established by the legal acts given
below, namely:

before March 15, 1949 in regards to Bulgaria (Item 7 at Article
22 of the Peace Treaty with Bulgaria). Hungary (Item 7 of Article 24 of
the Peace Treaty with Hungary). Italy (Item 6 of Article 75 of the Peace:
Treaty with Italy). Romania (Item 7 of Article 23 of the Peace Treaty
with Romania);

before September 15, 1948; in regards to Finland (Item 2 of
Article 23 of the Peace Treaty with Finland):

before February 1, 1950 in regards to Germany in the manner established by the Council of Ministers of the Union of Soviet Socialist Republics;

2) cultural treasures that are the Property of religious organizations or private charitable institutions used exclusively for religious or charitable purposes and did not serve the interests of militarism, (or) Nazism (fascism);

3) cultural treasures that belong to persons deprived of these treasures in connection with their active fight against the Nazism (fascism), including in connection with their participation in the national resistance to the occupying regimes of former enemy states and collaborationist regimes, and (or) in connection with their racial, religious, or national affiliation.

Article 9. The Conditions of Transfer of Interested States of Cultural Treasures Falling Under the Effect of Article 8 of this Federal Law

1. Cultural treasures, which were given in the subitems 1, 2, and 3 of Article 8 of this Federal Law and in respect to which interested states in the course of 18 months from the day of coming into force of this Federal Law shall make a claim for their return as well as present proof of the fact that these treasures fall under the effect of the corresponding subitem (subitems) of Article 8 of this Federal Law, and in doing so officially confirm that it did not receive for these treasures lumpsum compensation from Germany or another formerly hostile state, are subject to be handed over to an interested state and on conditions stipulated by Article 18 of this Federal Law.

The powers stipulated by the firm paragraph of Item 1 of this Article can be used by any interested state that presents to the Russian Federation on the basis of the principle of reciprocity no less favorable legal conditions for the return of that part of cultural treasures plundered by former enemy states and that are located or turn up in the future in the territory of the stated interested state and in respect to which the Union of Soviet Socialist Republics have announced a claim for restitution.

2. All transferred cultural treasures which were given in subitem 1, 2 and 3 of Article 8 of this Federal law and in respect to which interested states in the course of 18 months from the day of coming into effect this Federal Law did not declare a claim for their return and did not present the proof required in accordance with the mentioned subitem of Article 8 of this Federal Law, become federal property.

Article 10. Conditions of Transfer to Former Enemy States
Cultural Treasures Given in subitems 2 and 3 of
Article 8 of This Federal Law

1. Cultural treasures, which were given in <u>subitem 2</u> and <u>3</u> of Article 9 of this Federal law and in regards to which a <u>former enemy state</u> announces a claim for their return and presents proof of the fact that treasures fall under the effect of subitem 2 and (or) subitem 3 of Article 8 of this Federal Law, can be handed over to the proper quarter of the government making the claim on the conditions stipulated by <u>Article 18</u> of this Federal Law.

The powers, established by the first paragraph of Item 1 of this Article, can be used by a state from former enemy states that bring together special legislative measures for ensuring the fulfillment of its obligations for uncompensated return to the Russian Federation of its cultural treasures that were plundered and illegally taken by former enemy states and are located or can be found in the figure in the territory of the said former enemy states.

2. All <u>transferred cultural treasures</u> that have been pointed out in <u>Subitem 2</u> and <u>3</u> of Article 8 of this Federal Law and in respect to which a corresponding former enemy state has not announced a claim in the course of 18 months from the day that this Federal Law <u>comes into force</u> and not presented the required proof in accordance with the mentioned subitem of Article.8 of this Federal law shall become federal property.

Article 11. The Transferred Cultural Treasures Not Subject to Be Handed Over to Foreign States, International Organizations and (or) Taken from the Russian Federation

Transferred cultural treasures (archives and other materials, relics and other valuables), which by their content or character can serve in revive the spirit of militarism and (or) Nazism (fascism) cannot he handed over to foreign states, international organizations and (or) taken from the Russian Federation.

Article 12. The Transfer of Cultural Treasures That Are Family Relics

1. Transferring cultural treasures that art family relics, family archives, photographs, letters, medals and awards, portraits of family members and their ancestors becoming federal property in accordance with <u>Article 6</u> of this Federal law, based on humanitarian considerations can be handed over properly authorized to representatives of families that

that earlier owned these treasures (relics) on conditions stipulated by Article 10 of this Federal law.

2. The effect of Item 1 of this article does not extend to family relics of active figures of militaristic and (or) Nazi (fascist) regimes.

Article 13. The Rights of Cultural Institutions in Respect to Transferred Cultural Treasures

1. A <u>cultural institution</u> to which has been assigned the right to manage in accordance with regulations of the <u>Civil Code</u> of the Russian Federation transferred cultural treasures that are Federal property in accordance with Article 6 of this Federal law, shall implement the right of management, use and direction of the said cultural treasures in accordance with the goals of their activities and purposes of their treasures. However, the alienation of the said cultural treasures and (or) their transfer, with the exception stipulated in Item 2 at this Article, can be implemented only on the basis of a federal law and on conditions established by this Federal law.

2. Duplicates of transferred cultural treasures in the operative management of an institution of culture: books, lithographs, and other printed publications can be the object of a cultural exchange with foreign institutions and organizations in cases where these duplicates do not represent interests of other cultural institutions of the Russian Federation

CHAPTER III. INTERNATIONAL COOPERATION ON ISSUES OF EXPOSING AND RETURNING CULTURAL TREASURES TO THE RUSSIAN FEDERATION

Article 14. Cultural Treasures Illegally Taken from the Territory of the Russian Federation by Occupying Forces of Germany and Its Military Allies During World War II

The Russian Federation will cooperate with states implement jointly with the Union of Soviet Socialist Republics supreme power in Germany during its occupation of Great Britain and Northern Ireland, the United State of America and the Republic of France for the purpose of exposing and returning to the ownership of the Russian Federation its cultural treasures which were transferred to these states from corresponding occupation zones of Germany.

The Russian Federation will cooperate in those same goals with other states in which can be found Its cultural treasures and which have signed the Declaration of the United Nations of January 5, 1943 or joined it in supporting the concluded International treaties stipulated by <u>Article 22</u> of this Federal Law.

Article 15. The Conditions of Exchange of the Cultural Treasures for Cultural Treasures of the Russian Federation Found Beyond the Borders of the Russian Federation

Exchange of the <u>transferred cultural treasures</u> for cultural treasures of the Russian Federation that are found beyond the borders of the Russian Federation and in regards to which the Russian Federation has not announced a demand for restitution shall be allowed only with the equivalence of the said exchange determined by the justified conclusion of the authorized federal organ for the preservation of cultural treasures. The said exchange shall be formalized by an international agreement of the Russian Federation with account of the regulations of <u>Chapter V</u> of this Federal law.

CHAPTER IV. THE PROCEDURE FOR REALIZING THIS FEDERAL LAW

Article 16. The Authorized Federal Organ for Preserving Cultural Treasures

1. Control for the preservation of transferred cultural treasures and preparation of the decisions on issues concerning rights of ownership of these treasures shall be entrusted to the authorized federal organ for preservation of cultural treasures (hereinafter - federal body).

2. To the federal body is also entrusted the following functions:

consideration of the claims of foreign states and petitions of foreign citizens established respectively by <u>Article 18</u> and <u>Article 19</u> of this Federal law, preparation of the decisions on these claims. and deciding them petitions;

distribution of the transferred cultural treasure between the cultural institutions for the purpose of the practicable use of these treasures for compensation of damage undergone by these <u>cultural institutions</u> as a result of plunder and destruction of their property by forces of former enemy states;

the decision of controversial issues between cultural institutions concerning the distribution between them of transferred cultural treasures;

the determination of categories of transferred cultural treasures not subject to being handed over to foreign states, international organizations and (or) taken from the Russian Federation as well as the method of their preservation;

the issuing to cultural institutions permission for implementation of the rights stipulated by Article 13 of this Federal Law for the use of duplicates of transferred cultural treasures for a cultural exchange with foreign institutions and organizations;

the implementation of control over the observation of the rules at foreign economic activities concerning transferred cultural treasures;

the granting together with the Ministry of Foreign Affairs of the Russian Federation or on agreement with it, proposals to the Government of the Russian Federation on conducting negotiation concerning cultural treasures;

implementing control over the observation of this Federal Law.

3. The decisions of the federal organ adopted in accordance with its functions and authorities, as determined by this Article, are mandatory. The decisions of the federal organ can be appealed in a judicial procedure in accordance with the legislation of the Russian Federation. A decision not appealed in the time established by legislation of the Russian Federation shall be considered entered into force and can be changed or rescinded only by a new decision of the federal organ.

4. The Inter-Departmental Council for Issues of Cultural Treasures Transferred as a Result of World War II shall be created as a collegiate, deliberative organ. The head of the federal organ shall be the Chairman of the Inter-Departmental Council for Issues on Cultural Treasures Transferred as a result of World War II.

Article 17. The Petitions and Claims of Cultural Institutions Regarding Transferred Cultural Treasures and Regarding the Return of Their Property

Cultural institutions can turn to the federal body with a petition for the discharge to them of definite cultural treasures from those transferred as compensation of damages undergone by these cultural institutions as the result of plundering and or destruction of its property by forces of former enemy states and in the same manner make a petition disagreeing with the distribution of such property. The procedure for consideration of the said petitions and claims shall be determined by the regulation confirmed by the Government of the Russian Federation.

Cultural institutions can also turn to the federal body with claims for the return of cultural treasures belonging to them and groundlessly handed to other cultural institutions.

Article 18. Claims of Foreign States for Transferred, Cultural Treasures

1 - Claims for transferred cultural treasures given in subitem 1, 2, and 3 of Article 8 of this Federal law cm be declared by the government of a state, which has declared a claim to these treasures, only to the Government of the Russian Federation; claims of natural and legal persons, municipal organs, social organizations, and other organizations and societies are not accepted for consideration.

2. The handing over to the state that made a claim for transferred cultural treasures shall be implemented on the basis of a Federal law. The federal law on the handing over of transferred cultural treasures shall be approved on the of a draft law introduced by the Government of the Russian Federation with the approval of the organ of state power of the entity of the Russian Federation on the territory of which is located the cultural institution implementing the operative management of the given cultural treasure.

3. Without adopting the corresponding federal law the transferred cultural treasure cannot be the subject of a transfer, gift, exchange or any other alienation for the benefit of any state, organization or separate individual.

4. The handing over of a cultural treasure that is the object of a claim to a state that made the claim shall be implemented with the compensation by the given state of expenditures for its identification, expert examination, storage, restoration as well as expenditures for its handing over (transportation and so forth).

5. On the basis of the federal law an the handing over of transferred cultural treasures, the federal law shall give instructions to the cultural institution in the operative management of which is located the transferred cultural treasure that is an object of a claim to, conclude an agreement with the organization (institution or separate individual) authorized by that government of the state making a claim in accordance with which shall be carried out the compensation of expenditures stipulated by Item 4 of this Article and the actual handing over of the treasure (relic).

The original of the deed of transfer of the transferred cultural treasure shall be registered and kept at the federal organ and a copy kept at the cultural institution and with the interested parties.

Article 19. Petitions Concerning Family Relics

1. Petitions concerning transferred cultural treasures which are family relics as defined in Article 12 of this Federal law can be submitted to the federal organ by properly authorized representatives of the family earlier owned thew treasures (relies).

2. In the case of the acknowledgment of a petition as subject to satisfaction the federal organ shall decide whether the family relic that is the object of the petition shall be handed over to the family that formerly owned it under the condition of the payment of its costs as well as compensation for the expenses of its identification, examination by experts storage, restoration and expenditures for its transfer (transportation and so on).

3. The cultural institution in the operative management of which is located the transferred cultural treasury that is the object of the transfer shall conclude an agreement on the basis of an order of the federal organ with a properly authorized representative of the family that previously owned this cultural treasure (relic) in accordance with which shall be carried out the payment of its cost, compensation of expenditures stipulated by Item 2 of this Article and the actual handing over of the treasure (relic).

Originals of the deed of transfer of the transferred cultural treasures (relics) shall be registered and kept at the federal organ, and a copy of the deed shall be keep at the cultural institution and with the interested parties.

Article 20. The Transferred Cultural Treasures at the Cultural Institutions of the Entities of the Russian Federation and Municipal Cultural Institutions

Henceforth, before the expiration of the period for taking into consideration of claims of foreign states for transferred cultural treasures determined by Articles 9 and 10 of this Federal Law, those of the said treasures that are located in cultural institutions of entities of the Russian Federation or municipal cultural institutions in accordance with Article 6 of this Federal Law shall be considered to be federal property. The redistribution of the transferred cultural treasures between federal cultural institutions, cultural institutions of the entities of the Russian

Federation or municipal cultural institutions before the expiration of the said period is not allowed.

Article 21. Responsibility for Violations of This Federal Law
Persons guilty of violating this Federal Law shall bear administrative civil-legal and criminal responsibility in accordance with the legislation of the Russian Federation.

CHAPTER V. THIS FEDERAL LAW AND INTERNATIONAL TREATIES OF THE RUSSIAN FEDERATION

Article 22. International Treaties of the Russian Federation Being Concluded for Achievement of the Goals of This Federal Law
The Russian Federation shall conclude international treaties that promote the achievement of the goals of this Federal Law, including international treaties:

on settling issues connected with compensation of expenditures of the Russian Federation and its cultural institutions for preserving and restoration of transferred cultural treasures that were handed over to foreign states outside the agreed procedure or according to international treaties that did not establish such compensation and were concluded by the Government of the Union of Soviet Socialist Republics or the Government of the Russia Federation with governments of other states before the coming into force of this Federal Law;

an equal valued exchanges of transferred cultural treasures for cultural treasures of the Russian Federation located beyond the borders of the Russian Federation;

an assistance to cultural institutions of the Russian Federation in implementation of collaboration with cultural institutions of other states for exchanges of transferred cultural treasures for cultural treasures taken from the territory of the Russian Federation at different times on legal grounds as well as the reacquisition of such treasures;

on state guarantees of assurances by the accepting state of safety and the inviolability of the transferred cultural treasures during their showing in artistic salons, at foreign shows and at other expositions;

on the return tot he Russian Federation of its cultural treasures plundered and illegally taken from the territory of the Union of Soviet Socialist Republics by occupying forces of formerly enemy states.

Article 23. Ratification of International Treaties of the Russian
Federation Concerning Cultural Treasures of the
Russian Federation

International treaties of the Russian Federation concerning
transferred cultural treasures, as well as any other international treaties of
the Russian Federation concerning its cultural treasures, shall subject to
be ratified.

CHAPTER VI. FINAL PROVISIONS

Article 24. The Coming into Force of This Federal Law

This Federal Law shall come into force from the day of its
official publication.

Article 25. Introduction of Regulatory Legal Acts in Accordance
with This Federal Law

It is proposed to the President of the Russian Federation and
entrusted to the Government of the Russia Federation to bring regulatory
legal acts in accord with this Federal Law.

President of the Russian Federation   B. Yeltsin

Appendix N:
PROJECT FOR THE DOCUMENTATION OF WARTIME CULTURAL LOSSES

The **Project for the Documentation of Wartime Cultural Losses (The Documentation Project)** has been initiated to gather and make available information relating to works of art, archives, and other types of cultural property displaced as a consequence of war. The main focus of our research is the period of World War II, although other conflicts are also considered relevant. The Project is administrated under the auspices of the Cultural Property Research Foundation, Inc., a not-for-profit foundation incorporated in 1998 in New York.

Our primary aim is to publish the results of our research and, where appropriate, to disseminate information in a more abbreviated format on the World Wide Web (http://docproj.loyola.edu). Several research projects are now in progress and can be accessed at our website, including "The Jeu de Paume and the Looting of France" and **"Trophy Art and Archives Removed to the USSR."** Among the documents posted in facsimile is the complete **"Art Looting Investigation Unit Final Report."** In the future, we hope to sponsor lectures and symposia, provide student internships, and promote scholarly research projects in the United States and abroad.

The Documentation Project is non-sectarian and non-partisan and will operate a manner that is unbiased and impartial regarding special interests, whether of nations, organizations, religious groups, or individuals. In this respect, we differ from the World Jewish Congress's Commission for Art Recovery (CAR) and the Holocaust Art Restitution Project (HARP), two other private research organizations formed recently to conduct research on property displaced as a result of World War II. While these two organizations will focus on claims of Holocaust victims and the provenance of artworks relating to such claims, The Documentation Project aims to widen the discourse and promote the subject as a field of scholarship. At the same time, we welcome collaborative efforts involving our colleagues at CAR, HARP, and other organizations.

The Documentation Project is administrated by three highly respected scholars. Konstantin Akinsha (Research Director) is a Ukrainian art historian and prize-winning journalist who, with his colleague, Grigorii Kozlov, discovered the existence of the Soviet secret repositories. Dr. Akinsha is co-author of *Beautiful Loot - The Soviet Plunder of Europe's Art Treasures* (New York: Random House, 1995). Jonathan Petropoulos (Administrative Director) is a professor at Loyola College in Baltimore and a prominent historian of Nazi Germany, specializing in the art and cultural policies of the Nazi regime. Dr. Petropoulos is the author of *Art as Politics in the Third Reich* (Chapel Hill: University of North Carolina Press, 1996). Elizabeth Simpson (Chairman) is a professor at The Bard Graduate Center for Studies in the Decorative Arts in New York, specializing in the protection of cultural property and the arts and archaeology of the ancient world. Dr. Simpson was the organizer of the internationally acclaimed symposium *The Spoils of War -- World War II and Its Aftermath: The Loss, Reappearance, and Recovery of Cultural Property* and is the editor of the published proceedings (New York: Harry N. Abrams, Inc., 1997).

The Documentation Project also includes a group of affiliated scholars who hold the position of Research Associate. These scholars contribute their expertise toward the projects we undertake and in certain cases conduct their own research under the auspices of **The Documentation Project.** Fund raising for the Project is coordinated by Andrea Lowenthal, Treasurer of the Board of Directors of the Cultural Property Research Foundation. Ms. Lowenthal is a prominent New York lawyer with a Fortune 50 corporation who has an interest in cultural property issues and art law. Legal counsel is provided to the Foundation by the law firm of Herrick, Feinstein in New York. Resumes of the officers of the Project and the Foundation are available on request.

More than ten research projects are now in preparation. **"The Jeu de Paume and the Looting of France,"** is in progress and can be accessed at *http://docproj.loyola.edu.* The on-line version of this project provides a virtual tour of the Jeu de Paume Museum in Paris during the German occupation. The museum was used by the Einsaustab Roichsleitor Rosenberg (ERR) as a repository and exhibition area for Nazi-confiscated artworks from French Jewish collections. Currently available at our site are eleven views of galleries in the Jeu de Paume, hung with artworks from plundered collections. Most of thew views have never been seen before, and many of the individual objects exhibited have now been identified by **The Documentation Project.** High-resolution images of these objects ran be accessed, along with their identifications and the names of the collectors from whom they were stolen. When completed, this reconstruction of the exhibitions at the Jeu de Paume will constitute a valuable resource that will aid in the identification of works that passed through the museum and were then dispersed, never to be returned to their former owners.

"Trophy Art and Archives Removed to the USSR" can also be accessed at our website. This project explores the vast quantity of documentation relating to the removal of cultural property to the countries of the former Soviet Union during and at the end of the Second World War. According to one estimate, the Soviet "trophy brigades" confiscated and transported 2½ million art objects and books seized in the Soviet-occupied countries of Europe. Objects and archives removed from the Soviet zone of occupied Germany included not only German property but also property the Nazis themselves had confiscated from other countries, including France, Belgium, Luxembourg, the Netherlands, Austria, Poland, and Hungary. Objects were removed to the USSR from museums, religious organizations, and private collections, many of them Jewish. Thousands of these objects are still stored in Russian repositories, their provenance, in some cases, unknown even to their custodians. Research will be directed toward the accumulation and dissemination of documents from Russian and Ukrainian archives relating to the Soviet removals, as well as an assessment of the 1998 Russian law nationalizing the property now in Russia. The collection and publication of this data will be important to an understanding of the methods and scale of the Soviet operations and will help in attempts to trace and claim lost works.

Other projects now in progress include a catalogue of the collection of Hermann Goering, which comprised more than a thousand paintings as well as numerous sculptures and works of applied arts. Goering had planned to house his collection in a museum in his country estate Karinhall, scheduled to open in 1953 in celebration of his 60th birthday. The defeat of Germany put an end to Goering and his collection, the major part of which was recovered at the end of the war in Bavaria by Allied troops. However, hundreds of objects, including paintings and all types of decorative arts, disappeared without a trace. The project will reconstruct the Goering collection, providing an important resource for provenance inquiries, and will detail the taste and activities of Goering as a collector.

Also in preparation is a project that will result in the first systematic catalogue of the objects acquired by the Sonderauftrag Linz for the Führermuseum in Linz, Austria. Over a period of five years,

Hitler acquired approximately 8,000 paintings, according to one estimate, and many other objects including sculpture, furniture, armor, coins, and books.   These were acquired by confiscation or purchase, which often took the form of forced sale.   Included were works from famous state and private collections, such as 527 drawings from the Franz Koenigs collection in Rotterdam. Many of the works acquired for the Linz museum were recovered at the end of the war, but others remain at large. Of the 527 drawings from the Koenigs collection, for instance, 39 have been returned to the Netherlands, 307 are known to be in the Pushkin State Museum of Fine Arts, Moscow, but 182 remain unaccounted for. The catalogue of the Linz collection will thus be an invaluable resource for investigations into the provenance of works of art, it will provide insight into the artistic tastes of the Nazi elite, and will reveal much about the mechanism of the systematic Nazi confiscations of art and property during the war.

Further information on the Project for the Documentation of Wartime Cultural Losses can be obtained from the officers of the Project and the Foundation:

Prof. Elizabeth Simpson
The Bard Graduate Center
18 West 86th Street
New York, NY 10024
Tel: 212-501-3081; Fax: 212-501-3045

Dr. Konstantin Akinsha
1526 Corcoran Street
Washington, D.C. 20009, N.W., Apt. 1
Tel: 202-986-1249

Prof. Jonathan Petropoulos
Department of History
Loyola College
4501 N. Charles Street
Baltimore, MD 21210-2699
Tel: 410-617-2019; Fax: 410-617-2832

Andrea Lowenthal, Esq.
250 West 94th Street, 5G
New York, NY 10025
Tel: 212-670-0185; Fax: 212-670-4519

Appendix O:
THE MYTH IN THE LIGHT OF THE ARCHIVES: THE RECURRING ACCUSATIONS AGAINST POPE PIUS XII

LA CIVILTÀ CATTOLICA, MARCH 21, 1998

PIERRE BLET, S. J.
THE HOLY SEE

When he died on 9 October 1958, Pius XII was the object of unanimous tributes of admiration and gratitude: "The world," declared President Eisenhower, "is now poorer since the death of Pius XII." Golda Meir, the Foreign Minister of the State of Israel: "The life of our times was enriched by a voice speaking out about great moral truths above the tumult of daily conflict. We mourn a great servant of peace."[1] A few years later however, beginning in 1963, he had become the subject of a black legend: during the War, it was claimed, due to political calculation or faintheartedness, he remained impassive and silent in the face of crimes against humanity, which would have been prevented had he intervened.

When accusations are based on documents, it is possible to discuss the interpretation of texts, verify whether they have been misunderstood, received in a non-critical way, misrepresented or chosen selectively. But when a legend is created from unrelated elements and with the aid of imagination, discussion is meaningless. The only thing possible is to counter the myth with the historical reality proved by incontestable documentation. For this reason, Pope Paul VI, who as Substitute of the Secretariat of State had been one of the closest collaborators of Pius XII, as early as 1964 authorized the publication of the documents of the Holy See relating to the Second World War.

---

[1] *L'Osservalore Romano, 9 October* 1958.

THE LAY-OUT OF "ACTES ET DOCUMENTS"

The Archives of the Secretariat of State preserve the files in which it is often possible to follow day by day, sometimes hour by hour, the activity of the Pope and his offices. Here are found the messages and addresses of Pius XII, the letters exchanged between the Pope and civil and ecclesiastical authorities, notes of the Secretariat of State, service notes from junior officials to their superiors to communicate information and suggestions and, in addition, private notes (in particular, those of Monsignor Domenico Tardini, who had the habit, most fortunate for historians, of thinking with pen in hand), the correspondence of the Secretariat of State with the Holy See's representatives abroad (Apostolic Nuncios, Internuncios and Delegates) and the Diplomatic Notes exchanged between the Secretariat of State and Ambassadors or Ministers accredited to the Holy See. These documents are for the most part sent with the name and signature of the Secretary of State or the Secretary of the First Section of the Secretariat of State: this does not detract from their expressing the intentions of the Pope.

On the basis of these documents it would have been possible to write a work describing the attitude and policy of the Pope during the Second World War. Or an official report could have been produced to demonstrate the groundlessness of the accusations against Pius XII. Since the main charge was that of silence, it would have been particularly easy to use the documents to illustrate the Holy See's activity on behalf of war victims and particularly on behalf of the victims of racist persecutions. It was considered more suitable to undertake a complete publication of the documents relating to the War. Various collections of diplomatic documents already existed, many volumes of which dealt with the Second World War: *Documenti diplomatici italiani; Documents on British Foreign Policy: 1919-1939; Foreign Relations of the United States, Diplomatic Papers; Akten zur deutschen auswärtgen Politik 1918-1945*. Given the existence of these collections and on the lines of such models, it seemed useful to allow historians to study from the documents the role and activity of the Holy See during the War. With this perspective the publication of the collection entitled *Actes et documents du Saint-Siège relatifs à la seconde guerre mondiale* was begun.[2]

---

[2] *Actes et documents du Saint-Siège relatifs à la seconde guerre mondiale*, edited by P. Blet, A. Martini, R. A. Graham, B. Schneider, Città del Vatcano,

The difficulty lay in the fact that for this period the archives both of the Vatican and of other States - were closed to the public and also to historians. The particular interest in the events of the Second World War, the desire to write its history on the basis of the documents, and not only from more or less direct accounts or testimonies, had led the States involved in the conflict to publish the documents still inaccessible to the public. Trustworthy persons charged with such a task are subject to certain rules: not to publish documents which would call into question people still living or which, if revealed, would hamper current negotiations. On the basis of these criteria the volumes of the *Foreign Relations of the United States* relating to the Forties were published, and the same criteria were followed in the publications of the documents of the Holy See.

The task of publishing the documents of the Holy See relating to the War was entrusted to three Jesuit priests: Angelo Martini, editor of *La Civiltà Cattolica,* who had already access to the secret archives of the Vatican, Burkhart Schneider and the author of the present article, both professors in the Church History Faculty of the Pontifical Gregorian University. The work began in the first days of January 1965, in an office near the storeroom containing the archives of the then Congregation for Extraordinary Ecclesiastical Affairs and First Section of the Secretariat of State; documents relating to the War were normally kept there.

In such conditions, the work was both easy and difficult. The difficulty was that since the archives were not open to the public there were no systematic inventories geared to research, documents were not classified, either in chronological or strictly geographical order. Those of a political nature, and hence relating to the War, were sometimes stored with documents of a religious, canonical or even personal nature, placed in fairly manageable boxes but sometimes with widely differing contents. Information relating to Great Britain could be found in files on France, if the information had been sent through the Nuncio in France, and naturally interventions on behalf of Belgian hostages were in the boxes of the Nuncio in Berlin. It was therefore necessary to examine every box and go through the entire contents in order to identify the documents relating to the War. The research was simplified, however, thanks to an old rule of the Secretariat of State in force since the time of Urban VIII: Nuncios were to deal with only one subject in each letter.

Libreria Editrice Vaticana, 11 Volumes in 12 parts (two parts for volume 3), 1963-81.

Despite such difficulties, certain circumstances made our task easier. Since we were working in an office of the Secretariat of State and as members of the Commission, we were not bound by the conditions placed on researchers given access to the public storerooms in the consultation areas; one of us would take the boxes of documentation directly from the storeroom shelves. Our task was also made considerably easier by the fact that the documentation was for the most part typewritten and had been stored as separate letters (except for manuscripts to be typed for the printing office). Thus when a particular document was recognized ad pertaining to the War it could simply by removed and photocopied, and the photocopy together with explanatory notes - as scholarly work requires - given to the printing office.

Although in the winter of 1965 the work was proceeding quickly enough, we decided to ask the help of Father Robert Leiber, who had retired to the German College after serving for more than thirty years as private secretary of Pacelli, first when the latter was Nuncio, then Secretary of State and finally Pope Pius XII. Leiber had followed the situation in Germany very closely, and it was he who had told us of the existence of drafts of Pius XII's letters to the German Bishops. These became the material of the second volume of the series and are the documents that best reveal the thoughts of the Pope.

THE INDIVIDUAL VOLUMES

The first volume, which covers the first seventeen months of the Pontificate (March 1939 - July 1940) and which reveal Plus XII's efforts to stave off war, was published in December 1965 and was given a generally positive reception. In 1966, while Father Schneider was busy preparing the volume of the letters to the German Bishops, Father Robert A. Graham, an American Jesuit of the magazine *America* who had already published a work on the diplomacy of the Holy See *(Vatican Diplomacy)*, asked for information covering the period on which we were working. In reply to his request, he was invited to join our group, especially as we had learned of the ever more frequent contacts of Pius XII with Roosevelt and since we were coming across documents in English fairly frequently. He worked directly on the preparation of the third volume, which was devoted to Poland and modeled on the second volume, concerning the relationships of the Holy See with the Bishops. But the direct exchange of letter with other Bishops proved much less intense, with the result that volumes two and three (in two parts) remained the only ones of their kind. Thus we decided to divide the documents into two sections: one was to be a continuation of the first volume, for questions primarily diplomatic in nature, as indicated by their title *Le Saint-Siège et la guerre en Europe, Le Saint-Siège et la guerre mondiale.* These were volumes 4, 5, 7 and 11. Volumes 6, 8, 9 and 10, entitled *Le Saint-Siège et les victimes de la guerre,* present in chronological order documents pertaining to the efforts of the Holy See to help all suffering in body or spirit because of the War, prisoners separated from their families and exiled far from their loved ones, peoples subjected to the devastation of the War, and victims of racial persecution.

The work lasted more than fifteen years; the group divided the workload according to the planned volumes and the time that each member could give. Father Leiber, whose help had been so valuable to us, was taken from us by death on '18 February 1967. Father Schneider, after the publication of the letters to the German Bishops and while continuing to teach Modern History at the Gregorian University, had devoted himself to the section on the victims of the War. With the help of Father Graham he prepared volumes 6, 8 and 9, which were completed at Christmas 1975. But in the summer of that same year he had been stricken by the illness from which he would die the following May. Father Martini, who had devoted himself full-time to this work and had in some way worked on every volume, did not have the satisfaction of seeing the work completed in its entirety: he was only able to see the proofs of the last volume, at the beginning of the summer of 1981, before he himself passed away. Volume 11 (the last of the series) came out towards the end of 1981, under the auspices of Father Graham and myself. Thus Father Graham, although the oldest among us, was able to work until the project was brought to completion. During those fifteen years he was also able to work on related research and publications, which mainly came out as articles in *La Civiltà Cattoli*ca, and which themselves also constitute a source of information which historians of the Second World War can profitably consult. He left Rome on 24 July 1996 to return to his native California, where he ended his days on 11 February 1997.

Since the beginning of 1982, I had resumed my own research on seventeenth century France and papal diplomacy. But seeing that after fifteen years our volumes remained unknown even to many historians, I devoted the years of 1996-1997 to putting the essence and conclusions of that work into a single column of modest size, but as complete as possible.[3]   A dispassionate reading of this documentation clearly brings to light in its concrete reality the attitude and conduct of Pius XII during the World War and, consequently, the unfoundedness of the accusations made against him. The documentation clearly shows that he did everything he possibly could in the area of diplomacy to avoid the War, to dissuade Germany from attacking Poland, to convince Mussolini's Italy to dissociate itself from Hitler. There is no trace of the alleged pro-German partiality that he is purported to have developed while he was at the Nunciature in Germany. His efforts, joined with those of Roosevelt, to keep Italy out of the conflict, the solidarity telegrams of 10 May 1940 to the Sovereigns of Belgium, the Netherlands and Luxembourg after the invasion of the Wehrmacht, his courageous admonition to Mussolini and to King Victor Emanuel calling for a separate peace certainly do not point in that direction. It would be unrealistic to think that with the halberds of the Swiss Guard, or even with the threat of excommunication, he would have been able to stop the tanks of the Wehrmacht.

But the accusation which is often repeated is that he remained silent about the racial persecution aimed at the Jews, even when this was carried to its ultimate consequences, and that he thus left the way open for the Nazi atrocities. The documentation, however, shows the Pope's unfailing and constant efforts to oppose the deportations, the outcome of which was the subject of ever increasing suspicion. The apparent silence hid a clandestine activity on the part of the Nunciatures and Bishops to circumvent, or at least limit, the deportations, the violence, and the persecutions. The rationale behind this caution is clearly explained by the Pope himself in different speeches, in the letters to the German Bishops, and in consultations within the Secretariat of State. Public declarations would have been of no use: they would have only served to make the fate of the victims worse and to increase their actual number.

RECURRING ACCUSATIONS

In an effort to obscure this evidence, the detractors of Pius XII have cast doubts upon the seriousness of our publication.   Quite remarkable in this regard is an article published in a Paris evening newspaper On 3 December 1997: "Those four Jesuits have produced [!]

---

[3] Crf P. Blet, *Pie XII et la seconde guerre mondiale d'après les archives du Vatican*, Paris, Perrin, 1997.

in the *Actes et documents* texts which have absolved Pius XII of the omissions with which he is charged [.]. But those *Actes et documents* are far from being complete." It is insinuated that we had omitted documents that might prejudice the memory of Pius XII and the Holy See.

First, it is not clear how the omission of certain documents would help to clear Pius XII of the failures of which he has been accused. On the other hand, to state peremptorily that our publication is not complete is to state something impossible to prove: to do so, one would have to compare our publication with the archival material and indicate documents present in the archives but missing in our publication. Even though the pertinent archival material is still closed to the public, some people have gone so far as to furnish alleged proofs of such gaps in the *Actes et Documents.* In doing so they have shown their scanty knowledge of research into archival collections, the opening of some of which they are demanding.

Repeating an identical statement in a Roman daily newspaper on 11 September 1997, the 3 December article states that the correspondence between Pius XII and Hitler is missing from our publication. Let us first note that the letter in which the Pope informed the Head of State of the Reich of his election is the last document published in the second volume of the *Actes et documents. As* for the rest, if we did not publish any correspondence between Pius XII and Hitler it is because such correspondence exists solely in the imagination of the journalist. The latter mentions contacts between Pacelli, then Nuncio in Germany, and Hitler, but he should have checked his dates: Hitler came to power in 1933 and thus would only have been able to meet the Apostolic Nuncio after that late. But Archbishop Pacelli had returned to Rome in December 1929; Pius XI had created him a Cardinal on 16 December 1929 and Secretary of State on 16 January 1930. Most importantly, had such correspondence ever existed, the Pope's letters would have been preserved in the German archives and it would be natural for some trace of them to be found in the archives of the Foreign Ministry of the Reich. Hitler's letters would have ended up in the Vatican, but some mention of them would be found in the instructions given to the German Ambassadors, Bergen and then Weitzäcker, who were charged with delivering them, and in the reports filed by these diplomats confirming that they had in fact transmitted them to the Pope or the Secretary of State. There is no trace of any of this. In the absence of such references, it must be said that the seriousness of our publication has been impugned without a shred of evidence.

These observations about the alleged correspondence between the Pope and the Fiffirer are also applicable to other documents, ones which actually existed. Very frequently documents from the Vatican, e.g. notes exchanged with ambassadors, are attested to by other archives. One can presume that many telegrams from the Vatican were intercepted and deciphered by the information services of the warring powers, and that copies can be found in their archives. Consequently, had we in fact attempted to hide certain documents it would be possible to establish their existence and thus have a basis for casting doubt on the seriousness of our work. The same article in the Paris newspaper, after imagining relations between Hitler and the Nuncio Pacelli, refers to an article in the Sunday *Telegraph* in July 1997, which accuses the Holy See of having used Nazi gold to help war criminals flee to Latin America, and in particular the Croat Ante Pavelic: "Some studies support this thesis (!)." One is amazed at the casualness with which journalists can content themselves with documenting statements. Historians, who often labor for hours in order to verify their references, will envy them. One can understand that a journalist will trust a colleague, especially when the English name of the paper gives him an air of respectability. But there are two other statements which deserve to be studied separately, namely the arrival in the Vatican coffers of Nazi gold, or more exactly the gold belonging to Jews and stolen by the Nazis, and its use to facilitate the flight of Nazi war criminals to Latin America.

Some American dailies had in fact produced a document from the U.S. Treasury Department in which the Department was informed that the Vatican had received, through Croatia, Nazi gold of Jewish origin. The fact that the document was "from the Treasury Department" might appear impressive, but one has to read what is printed beneath the headline and one discovers that it is a note based on the "report of a trustworthy Roman informant." Those who take such statements for gospel truth should read Father Graham's article on the exploits of the informant V. Scattolini, who made a living out of "information" concocted in his own imagination which he then passed on to all the Embassies, including the American Embassy, which dutifully forwarded it to the State Department.[4] In our search of the archives of the Secretariat of State, we found no mention of the alleged entrance into Vatican coffers of gold stolen from Jews. Obviously those who make such statements have a responsibility to furnish documented proof, for

---

[4] Crf R. A. Graham, "Il vaticanista falsario." L'incrediblile successo di Vittorio Scattolini, in *La Civiltà Cattolica* 1973 III 467-478.

example a receipt, not kept in the Vatican archives, as in the case of the alleged letters of Pius XII to Hitler. In the archives themselves, one finds only the prompt response of Pius XII when the Jewish communities of Rome were subjected to extortion by the SS, which demanded that they hand over fifty kilograms of gold. At that time the Chief Rabbi turned to the Pope to ask him for the fifteen kilograms needed to make up the amount, and Pius XII immediately ordered his offices to make the necessary arrangements.[5] Recent checks of the archives have discovered nothing further.

Nor is the report about Nazi criminals fleeing to Latin America with the alleged help of the Vatican something new. Obviously we cannot exclude the naivete' of some Roman cleric who may have used his position to facilitate the escape of a Nazi. The sympathies of Bishop Hudal, Rector of the German national church in Rome, for the Great Reich are well-known; but on these grounds to imagine that the Vatican organized a large-scale escape of Nazis to Latin America would be to attribute heroic charity to the Roman clergy, as the Nazi plans for the Church and the Holy See were well-known in Rome. Pius XII referred to them in his Consistorial Address of 2 June 1945, recalling that the persecution by the regime of the Church had been intensified by the War, "when its adherents still entertained the illusion that, following a military victory, they would eliminate the Church once and for all."[6] The authors referred to by our journalist have a rather lofty idea of the forgiveness of wrongs practiced in papal circles, if they imagine that a number of Nazis were sheltered in the Vatican and thence taken to Argentina, under the protection of the Per6n dictatorship, and then on to Brazil, Chile and Paraguay, as a way of salvaging whatever could be salvaged of the Third Reich: thus a "Fourth Reich" would have been created in the pampas.

In these reports it is hard to differentiate fact and fiction. For those who like to read fiction we can recommend Ladislas Farago's *Aftermath: Martin Bormann and the Fourth Reich.* The phrase "the Fourth Reich" says it all. The author takes us from Rome and the Vatican to Argentina, Paraguay and Chile on the trail of the Reichsleiter and other fleeing Nazi leaders. With the attention to detail of an Agatha Christie, he describes the exact position of each character at the moment of the crime, indicates the numbers of the hotel rooms occupied by the fleeing Nazis and the Nazi hunters hot on their trail and paints a picture

---

[5] Cfr *Actes et documents*, vol.9, 491 and 494.
[6] Pius XII, "Consistorial Address" (2 June 1945), in *Acta Apostolicae Sedis* (1945) 159-168.

of the green Volkswagen which transported them. One is struck by the modesty of the author, who presents his book as "a typically French investigative report, a study that is serious yet without pretensions to pure scholarship" (!).

CONCLUSION

The reader will understand that the Vatican archives may contain nothing of all that, even if it actually happened. If Bishop Hudal did help some prominent Nazis to escape, he certainly would not have gone seeking the Pope's permission. And if he had later confided to him what had happened, we would know nothing of it now. Among the things which the archives will never reveal we must mention the conversations between the Pope and his visitors, with the exception of the ambassadors who reported on them to their governments, or de Gaulle who speaks of them in his Memoirs.

This does not mean that when serious historians wish personally to check the archives from which published documents have been drawn their desire is not legitimate and praiseworthy. Even after a publication carried out as accurately as possible, consultation of the archives and direct contact with the documents makes for historical understanding. It is one thing to cast doubt on the seriousness of our research, and another altogether to wonder if something perhaps escaped us. We have not deliberately ignored any significant document on the grounds that it seemed to us to damage the image of the Pope and the reputation of the Holy See. But in an undertaking such as this the person doing the work is the first to wonder whether he has forgotten something. Without Father Leiber, the existence of the drafts of Pius XII's letter to the German Bishops would have gone unnoticed, and the collection would have been deprived of the text which are perhaps the most valuable of all for an understanding of the Pope's thinking.[7] Yet those letters do not contradict in any way what we had learnt from the notes and diplomatic correspondence. In them, we see more of Pius XII's concern to depend

---

[7] Thus when we prepared the first volume, it was not, known who edited Pius XII's appeal for peace on 24 August 1939, opportunely corrected and approved by the Pope. Only later research allowed us to discover that the editor had been Monsignor Montini (cfr B.Schneider, "Der Friedensappell Papst Pius XII. Vom 24 August 1939," in *Archivum Historiae Pontificiae* 6 [1968] 415-424), although it is difficult to attribute particular sections to the two authors.

upon the teaching of the Bishops in order to put German Catholics on their guard against the perverse seductions of National Socialism, more dangerous than ever in time of war. This correspondence, published in the second volume of the *Actes et Documents,* therefore confirms the tenacious opposition of the Church to National Socialism, though we knew already of the first warnings of German Bishops like Faulhaber and von Galen, of many religious and priests, and finally the Encyclical Letter *Mit brennender Sorge,* read in all the churches of Germany on Palm Sunday 1937, despite the Gestapo.

We can therefore only consider as a pure and simple lie the claim that the Church supported Nazism, as a Milan newspaper wrote on 6 January 1998. Moreover, the texts published in the fifth volume of the *Actes et Documents* deny outright the idea that the Holy See supported the Third Reich because it was afraid of Soviet Russia. When Roosevelt sought the Vatican's help to over come the opposition of American Catholics to his plan to extend to Russia at war against the Reich the support already granted to Great Britain, he was listened to. The Secretariat of State charged the Apostolic Delegate in Washington to entrust to American Bishops the task of explaining that the Encyclical *Divini Redemptoris* - which enjoined Catholics to refuse the hand held out by the Communist parties - did not apply to the current situation and did not forbid the USA to help Soviet Russia's war effort against the Third Reich. These are unassailable conclusions.

Therefore, without wishing to discourage future researchers, I very much doubt whether the opening of the Vatican archives of the War years will change our understanding of the period. In the archives, as we have explained earlier, the diplomatic and administrative documents are mixed with documents of a strictly personal character; and this demands a longer closure than in the archives of the Foreign Ministries of the various States. Those who do not want to wait but wish to study in depth the history of that convulsed period can work fruitfully in the archives of the Foreign Office, the Quai d'Orsay, the State Department, and in the archives of the other States which had representatives accredited to the Holy See. Better than the notes of the Vatican's Secretariat of State, the dispatches of the British Minister Osborne evoke the situation of the Holy See, surrounded by Fascist Rome which then fell under the control of the German army and police.[8]   It is by devoting themselves to such

---

[8] Cfr. O. Chadwick, *Britain and the Vatican during the Second World War*, Cambridge, 1986.

research, without asking for a premature opening of the Vatican archives, that they will show that are really seeking the truth.

Appendix P:
Nazi Documents from the Russian Archives Made Public by the Russian Delegation at the Conference, December 3, 1998

Kunstwerke aus dem beschlagnahmten

Wiener Besitz

Für das Gaumuseum N i e d e r d o n a u

bezw. Museen in K r e m s und St. P ö l t e n .

Krug mit blasenden Hirten   Bo 1028

Vexierkrug   1033

Krug mit Blumen   1035

Zwiebelschüssel   1044

gelbe Fayenceschüssel mit Hirsch   1045

Elfenbeinstab   1144

Perückenmacher   1173

Bildnis d. Kremser Schmidt, Stiich   1191

Schreibtafel   1220

Pokerlspiel   1221

24 Fliesen aus dem Passauerhof in Krems   1228

Weißkrügel mit reichem Figurensschmuck   1272

mährischer Plutzer   1275

Fayenceschüssel   1276

Kremser Schmidt, Martyrium eines Apostels   1315

Kremser Schmidt, Kreuzigung   1316

Pettenkofen, Studienkopf   1335

Stickerei, Mustertuch   1397

Weste   1543

Wandbehang   1545

Leinenbehang   1547

Kremser Schmidt, Märtyrerszene   LR   51

Kremser Schmidt, Opfer der Jphigenie, Zeichnung LR 763

Kunstwerke aus dem beschlagnahmten

Wiener Besitz

Für das Museum in S a l z b u r g .

Salzburgerofen	Bo	44
Kachel mit Reiter		67
2 Eckkacheln, die zu 67 gehörenn		71
Wasserblase mit Bergpredigt		87
Obermillnerkrug		97
Obermillner Puppenkrüglein		98b
Salzburger Hanswurst		123
Obermillner Krug		148
Alabastergruppe, Vesperbild, ennglisch		208
Buchsgruppe, spielende Putten		209
Blumentopf grünglasiert		216
Kleines Weihwasserbecken		219
Dreifarbiges Terracottarelief		220
Pokalglas mit Hausorchester		242
Wandwaschbecken, glasierter Ton1, grün		256
Geschnitzter Buchsbaumlöffel		261
Goldfutteral		264
Pfeifenbehälter		266
Geschnitzter Löffel		273
Schlüssel mit 3 Zinken		284
Schlüssel aus Bronze		285

Bronzemörser	Bo 986
Ostensorium	1000
Jaspisgefäß	1005
Krug mit Brautpaar	1021
Süddeutsche Fayenceschale	1042
Süddeutsche Fayenceschale	1043
Minnekästchen	1064
Kästchen	1069
Holskasette	1070
Holzdudelsackpfeifer	1095
Zupfinstrument	1128
Geigenkasten	1158
Puppenkommode	1162
Stickerei	1164
Stickerei	1165
Musikantenfigürchen	1174
Kleiner Krug mit Hirsch	1273
Kachelmatritze	1295
Kutschenmodell	1432
Bauernsessel	1444
Bauernsessel	1446
Bauernsessel	1447
Reich geschnitzter Sessel	1448
Sessel	1449
Bauernsessel	1452
Bauernsessel	1453
Lehnsessel	1454
Bauernsessel	1479
Runder Tisch	1512

Steinbockhorn   AR 2945

Rundschild, salzburgisch   LR 673

Kunstwerke aus dem beschlagnahmten

Wiener Besitz

Für das Tiroler Landesmuseum Ferrdinandeum in I n n s b r u c k .

I. Gemälde

Werkstatt des Friedrich Pacsher, Abschied Christi von Petrus	Bo 16a
" " " "' , Enthauptung eines Heiligen	Bo 16b
Deutsch, Ende 15.Jhdt, Darstellung eines Bergwerks	Bo 167
Cranach, Das ungleiche Paar·	Bo 1302
Florentinisch Mitte 15.Jhdt;, Cassone	AR 3
Magnasco, Korbflechtende Nonnen	Goldm. 14
Guardi, Landschaft mit römischer Ruine	Haas 14
Guardi, Venezianische Vedutse	AR 421
Nachfolger des Adrian Isenbsrandt, Kreuzigung	Bo 1333
Rembrandt (?), Bildnis seiner Mutter	Bo 1301
Rembrandt-Nachfolger, Maleratelier	Bo 1375
Aert de Gelder, Weibliches IBildnis	AR 872
Frans Hals, Weibliches Bildrnis	AR 705
Jacob Backer, Weibliches Billdnis	AR 871
Holländisch Mitte 17.Jhdt, IBildnis einer alten IDame mit weißer Haube	Bo 1317
Jan van Goyen, Flußlandschafft mit Turm	Bo 1321
Jacob von Ruisdael, Landscheaft mit Ziehbrunnen	Haas 21
Salomon van Ruisdael (?), Flußlandschaft	LR 49
P. Bout, Stadtbild	AR 17
G. van Tilboroh, Ein Maler vor der Staffelei mit ...	Thorsch 2(

Jan Mytens, Englischer Edellmann mit zwei Damen	Thorsch 2;
Teniers, In der Schenke	LR 85!
Teniers, Polnische Edelloutte in einem Pferde-stall	Bo 1332;
Theobald Michau, Landschafft mit Windmühle	Kornfeld
Jan Weenix, Jagdstilleben nmit Geflügel	AR 42;
Jan Weenix, Jagdstilleben nmit Hasen	AR 876
Niederländisch 17.Jhdt, Grcoßes Stilleben	Thorsch 2;
Hondecoeter, Geflügel	AR 8
Nattier, Marie-Louise de Laamoignon	AR 461
Hogarth, Tischgesellschaft (des Malers Familie)	Bo 1314(
Lampi, Gräfin Potocka	AR 326
Boecklin, Toteninsel	Thorsch 11
Pettenkofen, Rastendes Zigeeunerfuhrwerk	LR 78
Pettenkofen, Zigeunerjunge mit Pferd	AR 380
Egger-Lienz, Ave Maria nachh der Schlacht am Berge Isel (Entwurf zu dem großen Gemälde im Ferdinandeuum)	B.Altman

zusammen 35 Bilder:

II. Kunstgewerbe und Möbel

Haller Passglas	Bo 108
Stangenglas mit Deckel	109
1 Krautstrunk	111c
gerippter spätgotischer Becbher	112
Kindersessel	130
Eisernes Augenvotiv	138
Blauer Venezianerpokal	160
Antikes Glas	176
Kanne aus grünlichem Glas	181
Rote Glasflasche	182

Vierzehnender   AR 951

Kleine Bronzegruppe   AR 2799

Kunstwerke aus dem beschlagnahmten

Wiener Besitz

Für das Museum K l a g e n f u r t

Geschenkmedaillon der steyrischen Stände, 1578	AR 3289
Muttergottesstatuette	Bo 10
Steinzeugkrug in Form einer Pilgerflasche	89
Krautstrunk	111b
Blumenvase, Wiener Porzellan	198
Miniaturschale	206
~~Birnholzfigur, Juno~~	~~210~~
Kleine Steinzeug-Schraubflasche	218
Kleine Weihwasserbecken	223
Gegenstück zu 198	227
Kakaotasse mit Untertasse, Meißen	233
Porzellanteller, Meißen	236
Porzellandeckelschüssel zu 236 gehörig	237
Schraubflasche aus Glas, dat. 1703	243
Steinzeughumpen um 1675	252
Steinzeugdeckelkrug	253
Fliese mit Handwerkzeug	254
Dolch in Scheide mit Liebespaar	262
Brautbecher, Silber	276
Hochzeitskachel	279
Blauer Steinzeugkrug	281
Doppelkleiderhaken, Gamsgehörn u. weibliche Halbfigur	282

Kinderrassel	Bo 756
Holzgerät	762
Calendarium perpeteum	807
Italienischer Majolikateller	833
Zinnlavabo	834
Majolikakrug mit Adler	847
Fayenceplatte	848
Apothekergefäß	851
Majolikagefäß	853
Hafnerschüssel	854
Kachel mit wildem Mann	856
Kachel mit Männerprofil	857
Urbinoschüssel	858
Kachel mit Landsknecht	878
Kachelfragment mit Sündenfall	881
Majolikateller mit jungen Mann	885
Urbinoteller mit Mythologie	886
Majolikaschale mit bärtigem Mann	887
Krippenfigur, Muttergottes mit Kind	906
2 Engelsköpfe	907
weiblicher Kopf einer Krippenfigur	909
Krippenfigur, Reiter	922
Pieta	928
Hafnerkrug mit Madonna	929
Urbinoteller mit Orpheus	930
Majolikateller 1545	932
Majolikateller mit Schiff	933
Majolikateller mit Herakles	935
Majolikateller mit Leda	936

Kachel	Bo 1056
Tintenzeug	1060
Minnekästchen	1062
Minnekästchen	1063
Minnekästchen	1066
Minnekästohen	1067
Minnekästchen	1068
Minnekästchen	1074
Minnekästchen	1075
Leuchterengel aus Holz	1088
Gegenstück dazu	1089
Immaculata, Tonbozzetto	1096
Mörser	1100
Kupfergefäß	1102
Standuhr J.F. Schuch	1115
Schachspiel	1139
Tonrelief, Enthauptung Johannes	1182
Holz, schwebender Engel	1183
Kleiner schwebender Engel	1184
Kleiner schwebender Engel	1185
Engel um 1500	1188
2 Leuchterträger, Halbfiguren	1189a,b
Teil einer gotischen Stuhlwange	1190
Handtuchhalter	1200
Messingschüssel	1211
Messingschüssel	1213
Messingschüssel	1214
Messingschüssel	1215
Messingschüssel	1216

Messingschüssel	Bo	1217
Messingschüssel		1218
Messingschüssel		1219
Brotschneider		1229
3 Türklopfer		1241
Holzkamm		1243
Holzkamm		1244
Holzkamm		1245
Holzkamm		1246
Holzkamm		1248
Türklopfer		1253
Türklopfer		1255
Tintenfaß		1280
Tintenfaß		1281
Tintenfaß		1282
Tintenfaß		1283
Tintenfaß		1285
Tintenfaß		1286
Tintenfaß		1287
Tintenfaß		1288
Großer grüner Krug		1289
Eckkachel mit Pax		1292
Eckkachel mit Justizia		1293
Art des Canaletto, Venezianische Landschaft		1331
Gotische Truhe		1352
Bäuerlicher Schrank		1353
Kleine Zunfttruhe		1354
Holz, Mönch mit Geldtruhe		1415
Holz, Mann mit Kind		1420

Porzellanschale	Bo 1433
Porzellanteller	1434
Schokoladebecher	1436
3 Alt-Wiener Porzellanteller	1439
Porzellanteller, Meißen	1440
Drehsessel	1443
Bauernsessel	1451
1 türiger Schrank	1480
Truhe mit Kerbschnitt	1485
Leuchterweibchen	1505
Hirschkopf als Leuchter montiert	1519
Stickerei, Mustertuch	1541
Egger-Lienz, Tote Krieger, sign.	unbek. Besitz
" ", Bauernfrauen und Kruzifix	" "
" ", Vorbeimarsch von Tiroler Bauern mit Kruzifix, sign.	" "
" ", Vier aufständige Bauern mit Tod, sign. 1916	" "
" ", Bauernmahlzeit, sign.	" "
" ", Mäher, sign.	" "
" ", Fries mit ritterlicher Szene	" "
" ", "Nach dem Friedensschluß 1809"	" "
" ", Waldinneres, sign., 1899 (?)	" "
" ", Kopf (Toter Christus ?)	" "
" ", Jäger beim Gebet, Brustbild, sign. 1896	" "
" ", Alter Bauer, Brustbild	" "
" ", Sturmangriff, Zeichnung	" "
" ", Verwundete, Zeichnung	" "
" ", Brustbild eines Bauern, Zeichnung	" "

Kunstwerke aus dem beschhlagnahmten

Wiener Besitz:

Für die Landesbildergalerile in G r a z

Jacopo Tintoretto, Bildnis des lDogen Grimani	Bo 1374
Frans Hals, Knabe mit Hund	LR 1
Jacob van Ruisdael, Landschaft	LR 14
Englisch (?), Damenbildnis	AR 846
Nattier, Damenbildnis	AR 701
Ranftl, Steirischer Bauer mit Kiindern	Go 28

zusammen 6 Bilder.

Kunstwerke aus dem beschlagnahmten

Wiener Besitz

Für das Kunstgewerbemuseum in G r a z

Venezianisch um 1510: Madonna mit Heiligen	Bo 1337
Bunte Kachel mit Frauenfigur	68
Gläserner Humpen	157
Gläserner Humpen mit Jagd	158
Ofenkachel, " Das Geher "	217
Wasserblase	226
Ofenkachel, grün glasiert	248
Silberlöffel	268
Silberlöffel	269
Silberlüffel	270
Silberlöffel	271
Silberlöffel	272
Kirchenschlüssel	287
Schlüssel	288
Schlüssol	290-99
Bronzeschlüssel	300
Stangenglas, Schützenszenen	303
Ofenkachel	326
Schmiedeeiserner Wandarm	327
Herrngrunder Schale	333
Kleiner Rahmen	342

Eckkachel mit Landsknecht	Bo 863
Kachel mit Verkündigung	864
Kachel mit weiblichem Brustbild	865
Nischenkachel	867
Kachelfragment mit Läufer	868
Bunte Kachel mit Frau	869
Bunte Kachel mit Frauenakt	875
Bunte Kachel mit allegorischer Figur	876
Bunte Kachel mit Verkündigungsengel	877
Bunte Kachel mit Nikolaus	879
Frieskachel mit Jagd	880
Emailschale mit hl. König	899
Emailschale mit Falkner	900
Goldschmiedehammer	916
Bohrer	917
Eiseninstrument	918
Bronzemörser	984
Metallkästchen mit Badeszene	991
Emailplakette mit Diana	996
Elfenbein Minnekästchen	1009
Elfenbeintafel mit Christi Geburt	1010
Elfenbeintafel mit Christi Geburt	1011
Falkenhaube	1012
Eiserner Wandhaken	1015
Kachel	1053
Eckkachel	1057
Eckkachel	1058
Ziegel mit Hubertus	1059
Kasette	1061

Kachel mit Fabelwesen	Bo 1076
Bronzemörser	1101
Kienspanhalter	1103
2 Wandarme	1109
Spazierstock	1147
Eisengitter	1161
Radschloß	1168
Messingschüssel	1210
Messingschüssel	1212
Wandarm	1224
Zunftzeichen der Bogner	1225
Türklopfer	1230
Türklopfer	1231
Türgriff	1232
Türgriff	1233
Türring	1234
Beschlag	1235
Türgriff	1236
Türklopfer	1237
Wandleuchter	1239
Aufsatz aus Eisen	1240
2 Kachelfragmente	1250
Baderzeichen	1251
Schlosserzeichen	1252
Türgriff	1254
Eiserner Arm	1256
Schlüssel	1257
Weihbrunnkessel	1260
Türklopfer	1266

Türklopfer	Bo 1267
Kachel mit Doppeladler	1291
Kachel mit Bärenjagd	1296
Kachel mit Johannes	1297
Eckkachel mit Engel	1298
Kachel mit Ranken	1299
Zeichnung, Kopf eines Mannes	1308
Standuhr des Weinhardt in Graz	1384
Holz, Apostelfigürchen, A. 16.Jhdt	1412
Holzskulptur, Wunder des Hl.Eligius	1431
Wiege	1481
Eiserner Arm	1521
Wirtshauszeichen	1522
Römisches Architekturbild i.d. Art des Canaletto	1564
Hl. Familie, Gemälde um 1510	1572
Schlüssel	286
Kirchenschlüssel	·289
Strauß, Kredenzgefäß, schreitender Strauß mit Hufeisen im Schnabel, das Wappentier von Leoben; auf dem eiförmigen Körper ein Adelswappen; stammt aus der Ratsstube Leoben; Ende 16.Jhdt.	AR 3307

Kunstwerke aus dem beschlagnahmten

Wiener Besitz

Für das M u s e u m   B r e g e n z

Holz, Kreuzabnahme   Bo 1413

Restbestände der Sammluung Oskar Bondy, Wien.

Vorschlag zur Zuteilung aan folgende Sammlungen:

Landesmuseum iin Bregenz.

Nr.

195	Komödiant
197	Porzellanfigur Gärtner
200	Porzellankrug mit Silbesrdeckel
231	Flakon
724	Große Deckelvase

Johanneum in Gïraz.

232	Raufendes Paar
512	Tasse mit Untertasse
515	Majolikateller
540	Van Dyk (?) Zeichnung
541	Fayenceschüssel
590	Schlüsselbrett
709	Lichtputzschere
750	Tonfigur Prophet
770	Rahmen
890	Alabaster Madonna
917	Bohrer
1085	Taufe Christi
1122	Kl.Klappaltärohen
1131	Geigenmodell mit Mohrenkopf
1132	Geigenmodell mit Fächerr
1134	Pochette (Tanzmeistergeige) mit bebrillter Fratze
1148	Dolch mit Elfenbeingrifff
1157	Armbrust
1192	Albumblatt
1201	Schlittenkopf
1206	Hausaltärohen
1238	Türklopfer
1265	Holzkästohen,Bucheinbanod
1362	Faltstuhl
1382	Ovaler Tisch
1419	Holzskulptur des hl.Vittus
1426	Holzskulptur,Bischof
1501	Gr.Lübecker Schrank
1503	Holztruhe
1548	Alter Sammt
1553	Stoff gold mit Rot,itall.
1561	Sammt, große Phantasiebblumen
1587	Elle
1595	Silberne Schliesse
ohne Nr.	6 Stück Polstermöbell

Museum Ferdinandeum Innsbruck.

Nr.

1558   Loschitzer Becher

Volkskundemuseum Inssbruck.

1494   Kl.Lederkoffer mit Beschlägen
1577   Kl.Hirschkopf

Museum Klagenfurt.

1001   Kokospokal

Landesmuseum Linz.

420   Doppelkrug
542   Steinrelief Gastmahl
548   Tonbüste
578   Brieföffner (?)
785   4 St.kleine Puppengeschirre
794   Kleiner Kupfereimer
866   Kachel mit Falkner
993   Schliesse mit Verkündigung
1084   Kindergruppe
1098   Gruppe Beweinung
1123   Bacchus
1170   Kleine Frauenbüste
1181   Relief Geburt Christi, 14.Jh.
1186   Heilige
1338   Groteskes Holzrelief
1423   Madonna Holz
1457   Kinderstuhl
1484   Postament
1506   Tartsche
1538   Kleiner Wandbehang
1584   Eiserne Wage
1581   Kl.Hirschkopf
1590   Miniatur-Schnitzbank

Museum Salzburg.

119   Kleine Kommode
143   Große Obermillner Schüssel
356   kleines Goldrähmchen mit Lautenspielerin
575   Barockrahmen mit Engel
576   kleines Barockrähmchen
674a/b 2 Miniatur-Engel,knieend,Holz
678   Barockrahmen,vergoldet mit Hermen
774   kleiner Rahmen
1361   Kl.Klappsessel von 1650
3183   Tisch,Spätbarock
1575   Großer Hirschkopf
1586   Vergoldter Flacon
1604   Großer Bauerntisch

Kunsthistorisches Museum Wien.

943   Terrakottabüste v.Minelli

Kunsthistorisches Museum Wien, Sammlung der Musikinstrumente.

Nr.	
1133	Taschengeige (Pochette)(Schildpat u.Elfenbein) mit Schreibzettel
1376	Viola d'amore mit Druckzettel: Mathias Thier in Wien anno 1764
ohne Nr.	Bratsche mit dem Druckzettel: Johann Georg Thir Lauten- und Geigenmacher in Wien/anno 1762

Kunstgewerbemuseum Wien.

1395	Schweizer Stickerei
1588	Koptische Stickerei

Städtische Sammlungen Wien.

33	R.v.Alt, Wien, Neuer Markt
613	R.v.Alt, Stephanskirche,Inneres

Volkskundemuseum Wien.

1290	Krug mit Zinndeckel
1582	Eisernes Instrument

Uhrenmuseum Wien.

817	Große Telleruhr,Reich getrieben,vergoldet,Ranken,Festoms, Vogel, 2 Delphine

Institut für Denkmalspflege,Wien.

613	R.v.Alt, Vorti'sches Kaffeehaus im Volksgarten
618	R.v.Alt, Wien,Neuer Markt
1379	Großer eingelegter Schrank um 1600
1380	Tabernokelschrank
1385	Barocktisch
1386	Barocktisch
1387	Moderne Vitrine
1388	Moderne Vitrine
1465	Barockstuhl
1487	Garderobenbrett (italien.)
1490	Barocktisch mit gewürfelter Platte
1498	Tabernokelschrank
1523	Gelber Teppich
1524	Gebetsteppich mit neuer Mitte
1530	Orientteppich
1525	Friedhofsteppich
1528	Niederländische Tapisserie E.17.Jh.
1529	Kleinasiat.Teppich
1532	Schirasbmteppich
1533	Niederländische Tapisserie E.17.Jh.
1534	" " " " " "
1535	Persischer Nomadenteppich
1602	Altwiener Pläne (v.Vasquez)
ohne Nr.	1 großer italien.Tisch
" "	2 moderne Postamente (Werkstatt)
" "	2 Kachelöfen (von geringem Wert).

Waffensammlung W i e n

Gruppe A

Morion, einteilig, mit Bandwerk und Streumuster geätzt, italienisch, um 1600 (Pompeo della Chiesa)	A R 95 ·
Trabantenkuse Kaiser Rudolfs II. 1570	A R 101 ‹
Trabantenkuse Kaiser Ferdinands III. um 1620	A R 104 ‹
Trabantenkuse Kaiser Maximilians II. um 1563	L R 358 ‹
Ganze Roßstirne mit geätzten und vergoldeten Streifen an den Rändern verziert , Augsburg, Mathäus Frauenpreis, um 1549	A R 993 ‹
Trabantenhellebarde Kaiser Matthias mit geätzter Klinge, 1617	A R 1002
Zusammenlegbare Trabantenhellebarde mit reichtauschierter Klinge, Mitte des 16. Jhdts.	A R 1007
Armbrustwinde, Eisen, geschnittem, datiert 1563	A R 2854
Pferdemaulkorb aus Eisen, durchbrochene Arbeit mit dem österreichischen Wappen und der Jahreszahl 1565	A R 289
Pferdemaulkorb aus Eisen, durchbrochene Arbeit mit dem säschischen Wappen und der Jahreszahl 1604	A R 289
Paradedegen in grüner Samtscheide, mit zwei Beisteckmessern, Gefäß mit Silberinkrustationen und geschnitten. Am Knauf Doppeladler. Anfang des 17. Jhdts.	A R 337
Zwei Trabantenseitenwaffen in grüner Samtscheide, reich vergoldete Gefäße mit Adler-bezw.Löwenkopf als Knauf, in der Klinge eingebaute Pistolen .	A R 338 A R 338

Gruppe B

Ein Paar Radschloßpistolen, Eisen, geschnitten und vergoldet. Französisch 17. Jhdt.   L R 340

Eine Radschloßpistole, Schaft verbeint und in Eisen geschnitten. Französisch, Ende 16., Jhdt.   L R 341

Eine Pistole mit Radschloß, Kolben verbeint, mit tau-
schierten und   geschnittenen Metalleinlagen, Ende 16.
Jhdt.   L R 349

Eine Pistole mit Radschloß, im Kolben Perlmuttereinla-
gen und Drahtfadenmosaik; französisch 2.Hälfte 16.Jhdt.   L R 675

Pistole, Lauf in Eisenschnitt, Rollwerkgrotesken mit
Tier und Menschenfiguren, Bandwerk mit Emblemen, Schaft
mit Beinauflagen, am Knaufende Relieffigur in Eisen-
schnitt, Krieger; französisch, Ende 16. Jhdt.   A R 2302

Ein Paar Pistolen, einläufig, Steinschloß, Schaft
Tuya mit Reliefauflagen aus geschnittenem Eisen,
Ranken mit Tieren, signiert Lazzaro Lazzarino Comi-
nazzo, Ladstock mit Affe als Kappe. Ende 17.Jhdt.   A R 2290

Gezogene Pirschbüchse, geschäftet, von Hans Maucher.
Um 1680.   A R 351

Trabantenhellebarde Erzherzog Ernst, 1593   L R 355

Jagdbesteck, teilweise vergoldet, bestehend aus einem
Vorlegemesser, zwei Tranchiermessern, einem großen
Messern und zwei großen Gabeln; auf dem Vorlegmesser
das englische Wappen und die Inschrift Anna Königin
von England, geborene Herzogin zu Gyllich und Clefe
1559, mit dazugehörigem Lederfutteral. Deutsche Ar-
beit.   A R 3032

Musketengabel. Die Beschläge geschnitten von Daniel
Sadeler, die Schäftung von Adam Fischer. Um 1620.   A R 3385

gebend gewesen, sich nur auf jene zu beschränken, welche hin -
sichtlich ihrer geschichtlichen Herkunft auf die Wiener Sammlungen zurückgehen oder aber solche, durch deren Zuteilung eine
empfindliche Lücke in den Wiener Beständen geschlossen werden
könnte.

Für die Waffensammlung des Kunsthistorischen Museums in Wien erbeutete Stücke:

Gruppe A   Herkunft nach aus Raubzug gegen Wiener Zeughaus:

A R 993 ✓ Ganze Roßstirn Kaiser Ferdinand I.   *Beilage*

A R 95 ✓ Morion Ende 16. Jahrhundert

A R 2892 Zwei Pferdemaulkörbe.
A R 2893 ✓

A R 1007 Zusammenlegbare Trabantenhellebarde
       Mitte 16. Jahrhundert, (vgl. die Stücke
       der Wiener Sammlung)

A R 2894 ✓ Armbrustwinde, eisengeschnitten, 1565
       (Parallele zur Garnitur Maximilians II.)
       aus dem Wiener Zeughaus.

A R 101 ✓
A R 104 ✓ Trabantensttangenwaffen deutscher Kaiser
A R 398 ✓ aus dem Wiener Zeughaus
A R 1002 ✓

A R 3358 ✓ Prunkdegen mit Emblemen, wahrscheinlich
       Wiener Zeughaus

A R 3381 ✓ Zwei Trabantenwaffen, breite Prunkhieb-
a,b, ✓ waffe mit eingebautem Feuerrohr, 2.Hälfte
       16. Jahrhundert. (Wahrscheinlich Wiener
       Zeughaus.

Gruppe B   Gegenstände, welche erbeten werden, um Lücken der

Wiener Sammlung zu füllen.

A R 2290 ✓ Ein Paar Pistolen, Lazzarino Cominazzo,
       italienische Eisenschnittarbeit, Ende
       17. Jahrhundert.

L R 340 ✓
L R 2303 ✓   Französische Pistolengarnituren
L R ohne Nr.347 aus der Wende des 16.und 17. Jahr-
L R 341 ✓   hunderts. Diese Art von Pistolen
       ist in der Wiener Sammlung überhaupt
       nicht vertreten.

L R 351 ✓ Gezogene Pirschbüchse, geschäftet von
            Hans Maucher; dieser berühmte süddeutsche
            Büchenschäfter ist mit keiner Arbeit in
            der Wiener Sammlung vertreten

A R 3032 ✓ Weidbesteck, 2. Hälfte 16. Jahrhundert
            (Weidbesteoke dieser Zeit besitzt die
            Sammlung keines).

A R 3385: Musketengabel, eisengeschnitten,   zu
            den Wiener Gewehren gehörig.

DER LEITER DER WAFFENSAMMLUNG :

Sammlung Fürst.

Anlage 1

V e r z e i c h n i s
der für das Führer-Museum bestimmten Stücke.

1. Kaiser Friedrich II., Augustalis.
2. Ludwig IV. von Bayern, Chaise d'or.
3. Albrecht II. von Österreich, Goldgulden Judenburg, Florentiner Typus.
4. Ferdinand II., Goldabschlag vom Taler, St. Veit 1628 (6Dukaten)
5.   "   5 Dukaten, Breslau 1628.
6.   "   5 Dukaten, Kremnitz 1632.
7. Ferdinand III., Goldabschlag vom Halbtaler, Prag 1638. (5 Duka-
8. Leopold I., Goldabschlag vom Taler, Graz 1669 (5 Dukaten).
9. Franz Josef I., 4 Dukaten, Wien 1856.
10.   "   100 Kronen, Wien Jubiläum 1908.
11.   "   100 Kronen, Wien 1909.
12.   "   100 Kronen, Kremnitz 1907, Krönungsjubiläum.
13.   "   100 Kronen, Kremnitz 1908.
14. Ungarn, Maria von Anjou, Dukat.
15. Hamburg, Goldgulden (Kaiser Sigismund).
16. England, Georg IV., 5 Pfund 1826.
17. Rumänien, Carol I., 50 Leo 1906, Reg.Jub.
18. Mexiko, Kaiser Max, 20 Pesos 1866.

Sammlung Fürst.

V e r z e i c h n i s
für das   in Wien befindlichen
der dem Münzkabinett fehlenden Stücke.

1. Sigmund von Tirol, Goldgulden o.J.
2. Rudolf II., Dukat Prag 1594.
3. Mathias, 5 Dukaten Prag 1613 (Talerabschlag).
4.   "   Dukat, Nagybanya 1615.
5. Ferdinand II. 10 Dukaten, Prag 1631.
6.   "   Dukat, Kremnitz 1626.
7.   "   10 Dukaten, Nagybanya 1631 (Talerabschlag).
8.   "   Dukat, Nagybanya 1631.
9. Ferdinand III., 10 Dukaten, Wien 1645.
10.   "   5 Dukaten, Prag 1644. (Halbtalerabschlag).
11.   "   Dukat, Breslau 1638.
12. Leopold I., 1/3 Dukat, Breslau 1694.
13.   "   1/6 Dukat, Breslau 1677.
14.   "   1/12 Dukat, Breslau 1694.
15.   "   Dukat, Kremnitz 1661.
16.   "   Dukat, Kremnitz 1689.
17. Karl VI., Dukat Siebenbürgen 1733.
18. Maria Theresia, Doppeldukat, Kremnitz 1765.
19. Karlsburg=   Dukat, Karlsburg 1743.
20. Franz I., Dukat, Nagybanya 1757.
21. Josef II., Dukat, Hall 1786.
22.   "   Dukat, Nagybanya. 1776.
23. Franz II.(I.), Sovrano, Wien 1831.
24. Franz Josef I., 4 Dukaten, Wien 1865.
25.   · "   Dukat, Wien 1872 (ohne Münzbuchstaben).
26. Ungarn, Ladislaus II., Dukat, 1507.
27. Siebenbürgen, Johann II. Sigismund Zapolya, Dukat 1566.
28.   "   Sigismund Bathory, Dukat 1585.
29.   "   Stephan Bocskai, Dukat 1606.
30. Ebtm. Salzburg, Leonhard v.Keutschach, Goldgulden 1508.
31.   "   Ernst von Bayern, Dukat 1551.
32.   "   Johann Jakob v.Khuen-Belasi, Doppeldukat 1563
33.   "   "   "   Doppeldukat 1583
34.   "   "   "   Dukat 1582.

35. Augsburg, Dukat 1647.
36.   "   Dukat 1708.
37. Köln, Dukat 1724.
38.   "   Dukat 1750.
39. Lübeck, Dukat 1793.
40.   "   Goldabschlag von Dreiling, 1698.
41.   "   Vierteldukat 1679.
42. Nürnberg, Dukat 1790.
43. Regensburg, Vierteldukat o.J. (Franz I.)
44. Schwäbisch-Hall, Dukat 1746.
45. Brabant, Karl V., Real d'or, Antwerpen.
46.   "   "   Couronne d'or au soleil, 1554.
47. Frankreich, Doppellouis d'or, 1789 AA.
48.   "   40 Francs 1818, Lille.
49. England, Karl II., 5 Guineas, 1682.
50. Jugoslawien, Alexander I., Dukat 1932.
51. Neapel-Sizilien, Ferdinand II., 30 Ducati 1833.
52.   "   "   30 Ducati 1852.
53. Portugal, Maria I., Peça 1791 R.
54. Sardinien, Karl Albert, 100 Lire 1834.
55. Spanien, Karl III., Onza (8 Escudos) 1784.
56. Toskana, Ruspone 1754.
57.   "   Ruspone 1772.
58.   "   Dukat 1789.
59. U.S.A. 3 Dollars 1856.
60.   "   1 Dollar 1852.
61. Kalifornien, 1/4 Dollar 1860, achteckig.
62. Peru, 1/5 Libra 1910.
63. Byzanz, Justinian I., Solidus, Konstantinopel.
64. Josef II., Jeton a.d.Huldigung von Brabant 1781. (Dukat).
65. Franz I., Krönungsjeton o.J. (1745). (Vierteldukat).
66. Franz Josef I., Schützenpreis des Jubiläumsschießens des
             Wiener Schützenvereins 1873 (4 Dukaten).
67. Hamburg, Bankportugalöser zu 5 Dukaten auf das 25jährige
         Stiftungsfest der Assekuranzkompagnie 1821.

Sammlung Fürst.

V e r z e i c h n i s
der für die Gau-Museen bestimmten Stücke.

Steiermark.

1. Leopold I., Doppeldukat 1682, Graz.
2. Josef I., Dukat 1706, Graz.
3. Karl VI., Dukat 1740, Graz.

Kärnten.

1. Ferdinand I.,Dukat 1556, Klagenfurt.
2. Ferdinand III., Doppeldukat 1653 (1655?), St. Veit.
3. Leopold I., Goldabschlag vom Taler 1683 (10 Dukaten), St. Veit.

Tirol.

1. Karl VI., Dukat 1734, Hall.
2. Josef II., Dukat 1788, Hall.
3.   "   Souverain d'or, 1786, Hall.
4.   "   Halber Souverain d'or, 1786, Hall.

Salzburg.

1. Matthäus Lang, Dukat 1538. (B.R. 621)
2. Leopold Anton von Firmian, Dukat 1740 (B.R.3985).
3. Jakob Ernst von Liechtenstein, Dukat 1745 (B.R.4084).
4. Andreas Jakob von Dietrichstein, Dukat 1749 (B.R.4124).

Sammlung Fürst.

Duplikat.
das Original dem
Schreiben an R. B.
beigelegt.
Hiervon kein
weiterer Durchschl.
vorhanden!

V e r z e i c h n i s
der nicht designierten Stücke.

1. Ferdinand I., Türkenbelagerungsnotklippe 1529.
2.   "   Dukat, Wien 1534.
3.   "   Dukat, Wien 1554.
4.   "   Dukat, Kremnitz, 1537.
5.   "   Dukat, Kremnitz, 1564.
6.   "   Dukat, Hermamnstadt, 1529.
7. Maximilian II. Dukat, Kremnitz, 1569.
8. Karl v.Steiermark, Dukat Klagenfurt, 1575.
9.   "   Dukat Klagenfurt, 1583.
10.   "   Dukat Klagenfurt, 1590.
11. Rudolf II., Dukat Wien, 1593.
12.   "   Dukat Prag, 1586.
13.   "   Dukat Kremnitz, 1581.
14.   "   Dukat Kremnitz, 1582.
15.   "   Dukat Nagybanya, 1599.
16.   "   Dukat Nagybanya, 1600.
17. Mathias, Doppeldukat, Wien 1616.
18.   "   Doppeldukat, Kremnitz 1614.
19.   "   Dukat, Kremnitz 1610.
20. Ferdinand II., Doppeldukat Wien 1630.
21.   "   Doppeldukat Kremnitz 1636.
22. Ferdinand III., Goldabschlag vom Talver (10 Dukaten), Wien 1657.
23.   "   Doppeldukatt, Wien 1647.
24.   "   Dukat, Graz 1645.
25.   "   Doppeldukatt, Breslau 1641.
26.   "   Dukat, Breslau 1655.
27.   "   Dukat,Kremnitz 1640.
28. Leopold I., 5 Dukaten, Wiem 1669.
29.   "   Doppeldukat, Wiien 1669.
30.   "   Dukat, Wien 1685.
31.   "   Vierteldukat, Wien 1694.
32.   "   Doppeldukat, Stt. Veit 1681.
33.   "   Goldabschlag vom Taler (10 Dukaten), Kremnitz 1666.
34.   "   Dukat Kremnitz 1692.

35. Leopold I., Goldabschlag vom Denár, Kremnitz 1662.
36.   "   Goldabschlag vom Taler (10 Dukaten), Nagybanya 1703.
37.   "   Goldabschlag vom Taler (5 Dukaten), Nagybanya 1695.
38.   "   Einsechstel-Dukat, Nagybanya 1698.
39.   "   10 Dukaten, Klausenburg 1696.
40.   "   Dukat, Klausenburg 1699.
41. Ungarische Malkontenten, Dukat, Kremnitz 1704.
42. Josef I., Vierteldukat, Preßburg 1711.
43.   "   Dukat, Hermannstadit 1711.
44. Karl VI., Dukat, Wien 1740.
45.   "   Vierteldukat, Wiem 1733.
46.   "   Halbdukat, Graz, 1728.
47.   "   Vierteldukat, Grazz 1729.
48.   "   Einachtel-Dukat, Giras 1729.
49.   "   Dukat, Prag 1740.
50.   "   Dukat, Kremnitz 1726.
51.   "   Dukat, Kremnitz 1735.
52.   "   Dukat, Kremnitz 1737.
53.   "   Dukat, Nagyabanya 1740.
54.   "   Viertel-Dukat, Nagybanya 1735.
55.   "   Einsechstel-Dukat,, Nagybanya 1728.
56.   "   Dukat, Siebenbürgen 1715.
57.   "   Dukat, Siebenbürgen 1723.
58.   "   Viertel-Dukat, Siebenbürgen o.J.
59. Maria Theresia, 6 Dukaten, Wien 1765.
60.   "   Dukat, Wien 1765.
61.   "   Dukat, Wien 1778.
62.   "   Doppel-Souverain d'or, Wien 1772.
63.   "   Doppeldukat,, Kremnitz 1765.
64.   "   Doppeldukat,, Kremnitz 1765 (Var.).
65.   "   Dukat, Kremnitz 1755.
66.   "   Dukat, Kremnitz 1763.
67.   "   Dukat, Nagybanya 1765.
68.   "   Dukat, Nagybanya 1770.
69.   "   Doppeldukat,, Karlsburg 1764.
70.   "   Doppeldukat,, Karlsburg 1780.
71.   "   Dukat, Karlsburg 1762.
72.   "   Halbdukat, Karlsburg 1780.

73. Maria Theresia, Viertel-Dukat, Karlsburg 1749.
74.   "   Viertel-Dukat, Karlsburg 1749 (Var.).
75.   "   Achtel-Dulkat, Karlsburg 1778.
76.   "   1/16 Dukat, Karlsburg 1778.
77.   "   Zecchino, Mailand 1778.
78.   "   Doppel-Souverain d'or, Antwerpen 1750.
79.   "   Souverain. d'or, Antwerpen 1755.
80.   "   Souverain. d'or, Brügge 1750.
81.   "   Doppel-Souverain d'or, Brüssel 1761.
82. Franz I., Dukat, Wien 1765 F = 1771.
83.   "   Dukat, Wien 1765 M = 1777.
84.   "   Viertel-Dukat, Nagyabanya 1764.
85.   "   Viertel-Dukat, Nagyabanya 1765.
86.   "   Dukat, Karlsburg 1755.
87. Josef II., Doppeldukat, Wien 1786.
88.   "   Dukat, Wien 1786.
89.   "   Dukat, Wien 1787.
90.   "   Halber Souverain d'or, Wien 1786.
91.   "   Doppeldukat, Kremnitz 1782.
92.   "   Doppeldukat, Kremnitz 1786.
93.   "   Dukat, Kremnitz 1784.
94.   "   Dukat, Kremnitz 1789.
95.   "   Doppeldukat, Karlsburg 1772.
96.   "   Doppeldukat, Karlsburg 1782.
97.   "   Dukat, Karlsburg, 1782.
98.   "   Sovrano, Mailand 1789.
99.   "   Zecchino, Mailand 1784.
100. Leopold II., Dukat, Wien 1790.
101.   "   Dukat, Kremnitz 1790.
102.   "   Dukat, Kremnitz 1791.
103.   "   Dukat, Kremnitz 1792.
104.   "   Dukat, Karlsburg 1792.
105.   "   Halbsovrano, Mailand 1791.
106. Franz II. (I.), 4 Dukaten, Wien 1806.
107.   "   4 Dukaten, Wien 1811.
108.   "   4 Dukaten, Wien 1828.
109.   "   Doppeldukat, Wien 1799.

110.	Franz II. (I.),	Dukat, Wien 1792.	(König v.Ungarn und Böhmen).
111.	"	Dukat, Wien 1792	(Kaisertitel).
112.	"	Dukat, Wien 1806.	
113.	"	Dukat, Wien 1815.	
114.	"	Dukat, Wien 1833.	
115.	"	Souverain d'or, Wien 1793.	
116.	"	Dukat, Salzburg 1809.	
117.	"	Souverain d'or, Günzburg 1793.	
118.	"	Halber Souverain d'or, Günzburg 1793.	
119.	"	Dukat, Kremnitz 1794.	
120.	"	Dukat, Kremnitz 1815.	
121.	"	Dukat, Kremnitz 1821.	
122.	"	Dukat, Kremnitz 1830. (österr. Typ).	
123.	"	Dukat, Kremnitz 1830 (ungar. Typ).	
124.	"	Dukat, Kremnitz 1835.	
125.	"	Souverain d'or, Kremnitz 1795.	
126.	"	Halber Souverain d'or, Kremnitz 1795.	
127.	"	Dukat, Nagybanya 1795.	
128.	"	Dukat, Nagybanya 1799.	
129.	"	Dukat, Karlsburg 1797.	
130.	"	Dukat, Karlsburg 1804.	
131.	"	Dukat, Karlsburg 1827.	
132.	"	Dukat, Karlsburg 1835.	
133.	"	Sovrano, Mailand 1800.	
134.	"	Sovrano, Mailand 1829.	
135.	"	Halb-Sovrano, Mailand 1831.	
136.	"	Sovrano, Venedig 1793.	
137.	"	Dukat, Venedig 1824.	
138.	Ferdinand I.,	4 Dukaten, Wien 1846.	
139.	"	Dukat, Wien 1836.	
140.	"	Dukat, Wien 1837.	
141.	"	Dukat, Wien 1841.	
142.	"	Dukat, Wien 1848.	
143.	"	Dukat, Kremnitz 1841.	
144.	"	Dukat, Kremnitz 1848.(Kopf-Adler)	
145.	"	Dukat, Kremnitz 1848 (Rückseite Patrona,ung.Text	
146.	"	Dukat, Kremnitz 1848 (Rückseite Patrona,lat.Text	

147. Ferdinand I., Dukat, Karlsburg 1836.
148.   "   Dukat, Karlsburg 1838.
149.   "   Dukat, Karlsburg 1845.
150.   "   Sovrano, Mailand 1840.
151.   "   Halbsovrano, Mailand 1849.
152.   "   Dukat, Venedig 1845.
153.   "   40 Lire, Mailand 1848, Governo provvisorio.
154.   "   20 Lire, Venedig 1848, Governo provvisorio.
155. Franz Josef I., 4 Dukaten, Wien 1867.
156.   "   4 Dukaten, Wien 1910.
157.   "   4 Dukaten, Wien 1915.
158.   "   4 Dukaten, 1905, bulgarische Nachahmung.
159.   "   Dukat, Wien 1848. (Nachprägung 1898).
160.   "   Dukat, Wien 1849. (Nachprägung 1898).
161.   "   Dukat, Wien 1850. (Nachprägung 1898).
162.   "   Dukat, Wien 1851. (Nachprägung 1898).
163.   "   Dukat, Wien 1852.
164.   "   Dukat, Wien 1854.
165.   "   Dukat, Wien 1855.
166.   "   Dukat, Wien 1856.
167.   "   Dukat, Wien 1863.
168.   "   Dukat, Wien 1866.
169.   "   Dukat, Wien 1867.
170.   "   Dukat, Wien 1870.
171.   "   Dukat, Wien 1871.
172.   "   Dukat, Wien 1872.
173.   "   Dukat, Wien 1878.
174.   "   Dukat, Wien 1880.
175.   "   Dukat, Wien 1891.
176.   "   Dukat, Wien 1914.
177.   "   Vereinskrone, Wien 1858.
178.   "   Vereinskrone, Wien 1863.
179.   "   Vereinskrone, Wien 1866.
180.   "   Halbe Vereinskrone, Wien 1858.
181.   "   Halbe Vereinskrone, Wien 1859.
182.   "   Halbe Vereinskrone, Wien 1866.
183.   "   8 Fl.= 20 Francs, Wien 1886.
184.   "   8 Fl.= 20 Francs, Wien 1887.
185.   "   4 Fl.= 10 Francs, Wien 1890.

186. Franz Josef I., 20 Kronen, Wien 1905.
187.   "   20 Kronen, Wien 1908 (Reg.Jub.).
188.   "   20 Kronen, Wien 1909.
189.   "   20 Kronen, Wien 1916.
190.   "   10 Kronen, Wien 1906.
191.   "   10 Kronen, Wien 1908 (Reg.Jub.).
192.   "   10 Kronen, Wien 1909.
193.   "   10 Kronen, Wien 1910.
194.   "   Dukat, Kremnitz 1854.
195.   "   Dukat, Kremnitz 1865.
196.   "   Dukat, Kremnitz 1867.
197.   "   Dukat, Kremnitz 1868.
198.   "   Dukat, Kremnitz 1869.
199.   "   Dukat, Kremnitz 1881.
200.   "   8 Fl.= 20 Francs, Kremnitz 1877.
201.   "   8 Fl.= 20 Francs, Kremnitz 1887.
202.   "   8 Fl.= 20 Francs, Kremnitz 1890.
203.   "   8 Fl.= 20 Francs, Kremnitz 1891.
204.   "   4 Fl.= 10 Francs, Kremnitz 1871.
205.   "   4 Fl.= 10 Francs, Kremnitz 1884.
206.   "   4 Fl.= 10 Francs, Kremnitz 1885.
207.   "   4 Fl.= 10 Francs, Kremnitz 1891.
208.   "   100 Kronen, Kremnitz 1907. (Reg.Jub.)
209.   "   20 Kronen, Kremnitz 1893.
210.   "   20 Kronen, Kremnitz 1916.
211.   "   10 Kronen, Kremnitz 1911.
212.   "   Dukat, Karlsburg 1854.
213.   "   Dukat, Karlsburg 1860.
214.   "   Dukat, Karlsburg 1865.
215.   "   Dukat, Karlsburg 1866.
216.   "   Dukat, Karlsburg 1867.
217.   "   Dukat, Karlsburg 1868.
218.   "   Dukat, Karlsburg 1869.
219.   "   Vereinskrone, Karlsburg 1858.
220.   "   Halbe Vereinskrone, Karlsburg 1858.
221.   "   8 Fl.= 20 Francs, Karlsburg 1871.
222.   "   4 Fl.= 10 Francs, Karlsburg 1870.

223. Franz Josef I., Dukat, Vemedig 1865.
224. Republik Österreich, 100 Kronen 1924.
225.   "   20 Kronen 1923.
226.   "   20 Kronen 1924.
227. Ungarn, Karl Robert v.Anjou, Goldgulden.
228.   "   Ludwig I.v.Anjou, Goldgulden.
229.   "   Sigismund, Dukat (Wappen von Ungarn und Luxenburg).
230.   "   "   Dukat (Wappen von Ungarn und Böhmen).
231.   "   Albrecht II., Dukat.
232.   "   Ladislaus Postumus, Dukat (K-h).
233.   "   Wladislaw I., Dukat.
234.   "   Johann Hunyadi, Dukat.
235.   "   Ladislaus Postumus, Dukat (N-e)
236.   "   Mathias Corvinus, Dukat. (Ladislaus-Wappen).
237.   "   "   "   Dukat (Ladislaus-Maria mit Kind).
238.   "   Wladislaus II., Dukat (K-h).
239.   "   Ludwig II., Dukat 1520.
240. Siebenbürgen, Johann I. Zapolya, Dukat 1540 (hl.Ladislaus-
                                    Maria mit Kind).
241.   "   Johann I. Zapolya, Dukat 1540 (hl. Ladilaus-
                                    Wappen).
242.   "   Johann II. Sigismund Zapolya und der Isabella,
                                    Dukat 1558.
243.   "   Stephan Bathory, Dukat 1573.
244.   "   Christoph Bathory, Dukat 1579.
245.   "   Sigismund Bathory, Dukat 1595, Nagybanya.
246.   "   Gabriel Bathory, Dukat 1611, Klausenburg.
247.   "   "   "   Dukat 1612, Nagybanya.
248.   "   Gabriel Bethlen, Dukat 1621, Kremnitz.
249.   "   "   "   Dukat 1622, Nagybanya.
250.   "   Stephan Bethlen, Dukat 1630.
251.   "   Georg Rakoezy, Dukat 1646.
252.   "   Achatius Barcsi, Dukat 1659.
253.   "   Michael Apafi, Dukat 1684.
254. Ebtm. Salzburg, Wolf Dietrich, Doppeldukat 1591.
255.   "   Paris, Halbdukat 1651.
256.   "   Guidobald, Vierteldukat 1659.
257.   "   Max Gandolf, Dukat 1678.
258.   "   "   Halbdukat 1668.
259.   "   "   Vierteldukat 1672.

260. Ebtm.Salzburg, Johann Ernst, 4 Dukaten 1687.
261.   "   "   Halbdukat 1705.
262.   "   "   Vierteldukat 1707.
263.   "   Franz Antoni, Vierteldukat 1725.
264.   "   Leopold Antion, Dukat 1743.
265.   "   "   Vierteldukat 1728.
266.   "   Jakob Ernst, Dukat 1746.
267.   "   Andreas Jakob, Vierteldukat 1751.
268.   ?   Sigismund, Doppeldukat 1766.
269.   "   "   Vierteldukat 1755.
270.   "   Hieronymus, Dukat 1778.
271.   "   "   Dukat 1788.
272.   "   "   Dukat 1801.
273.   "   "   Vierteldukat 1782.
274. Salzburg, Erzherzog Ferdinand Dukat 1803.
275.   "   "   Dukat 1806.
276. Deutscher Orden, Erzherzog Maximilian v.Österreich,Dukat.o..J
277. Augsburg, Dukat 1687.
278.   "   Dukat 1738.
279.   "   Dukat 1767.
280. Breslau, Doppeldukatenklippe 1617.
281.   "   Dukat 1630.
282. Regensburg, Dukat o.J. (Franz I.).
283. Schwäbisch-Hall, Dukat 1777.
284. Venedig, Franz II., Zecchino o.J.
285. U.S.A. Vierteldollar o.J.

                    Medaillem und Jetons.

286. Mathias II. Vermählung 1611 (5 Dukaten).
287. Franz I., Krönungsdukat 1745.
288. Franz I. und Maria Therosia, Jeton auf den Besuch der oberu
         Bergstädte 1751. (Dukat)
289. Josef II., Dukat 1764 (Krömungsdukat).
290. Josef II. und Erzherzog Leopold, Jeton a.d.Besuch der ung.
         Bergstädte 1764 (Dukat).
291. Leopold II. Med.a.d.belgisohe Huldigung 1791 (22½ Gramm).
292.   "   Krönungsjeton 1790. (4.4 Gramm).
293.   "   Krönungsjeton 1790 (2.6 Gramm).

294. Franz II. Jeton auf die Königswahl 1792. (2 Dukaten)

295. Ferdinand I., Jeton auf die Krönung in Preßburg 1830 (Dukat).

296.   "   Jeton auf die Krönung in Mailand 1838. (5.3 g).

297. Franz Josef I., Jeton auf die ungarische Königskrönung 1867 ((

298. Kaiserin Elisabeth, Jeton auf die ungarische Krönung 1867,
                           lateinischer Text (Dukat).

299.   "   Jeton auf die ungarische Krönung 1867,
                           ungarischer Text (Dukat).

300. Franz Josef I., Medaille auf das 2.österr. Bundesschießen,
                           Innsbruck 1885 (14 g).

301.   "   Porträtjetom zum Jubiläum 1898, junges und
                           altes Brustbild (4 Dukaten).

302. Prager Judenmedaille, Maximilian I. und Maria von Burgund
                           (25 g.).

V e r z e i c h n i s

der für das Führer-Museum bestimmten Stücke.

1. Maximilian I., Vermählungstaler 1479.(Maria v.Burgund mit Hauu·
2.　　　"　　　　Antwerpener Vermählungstaler 1479.
3.　　　"　　　　Breiter Reitertaler 1509.
4.　　　"　　　　Schautaler o.J. (Brustbild-Reiter). AR, 39mm..
5. Karl V., Porträtmedaille 1521. Rückseite Doppeladler. AR,71 ı m
6.　　"　　Porträtmedaille 1537. Rückseite Deoppeladler mit
　　　　　　großem Brustschild. Silberguß
　　　　　　65 mm.
7.
7.　　"　　Geburtstagsmedaille 1500/1550. (Christus - Kaiser)
　　　　　　verg. Silberguß, 47 mm.
8.　　"　　und Philipp I., Medaillon o.J. Silberguß, 99 mm.
9. Leopold I. und Kaiserin Eleonora, Porträtmedaille o.J. (16766)
　　　　　　AR, 53 mm.
10.　"　　Türkenbelagerung Wiens 1683. AR, 59 mm.
11.　"　　und die Alliierten von 1684 (hl. Liga). Silberguß,
　　　　　　81 mm.
12.　"　　Johann Sobiesky und der Doge von Venedig, auf dies
　　　　　　Liga von 1684. AR, 56 mm.
13.　"　　Sieg bei Gran und Einnahme von Neuhäusl, 1685.
　　　　　　AR, 61 mm.
14. Karl VI. und Ludwig XIV. Friede von Baden, 1714. AR, 48 mm.
15. Maria die Katholische von England, Porträtmedaille o.J.(1555?)
　　　　　　Rückseite Allegorie.Silberguß
　　　　　　64 mm.
15a.Elisabeth von England, politische Medaille auf die Unter-
　　　　　　stützung der bedrängten Niederländer :1
　　　　　　AR 52 mm.
16. Karl II. von England, Reise von Schevenningen nach England,116
　　　　　. Silberguß, 70 mm.
17. Heinrich IV. von Frankreich, ovale Porträtmedaille 1623, einn-
　　　　　　seitiger Silberguß, 88 x 68 mm.
18. Philipp IV. von Spanien, Porträtmedaille o.J., Rückseite Phööb
　　　　　　Silberguß, 52 mm.
19. Gustav II. Adolf von Schweden, Medaille auf seinen Tod 1634..
　　　　　　AR, 79 mm.
20. Gustav II. Adolf von Schweden, Porträtmedaille o.J., Rückseiit
　　　　　　gravierter Text, verg.Silberguß,51 x :·
21. Schweiz, Medaille auf den Rütli-Schwur in der Art des Bundees·
　　　　　　talers, Silber vergoldet, 50 mm.
22. Friedrich I. von Preußen, Bau des königl. Schlosses in Berliı
　　　　　　1704. AR, 63 mm.

23. Friedrich der Weise von Sachsen, Statthaltertaler 1519. AR,49m

24. Johann Friedrich von Sachsem, Porträtmedaille 1535. Rückseite
Wappen. Verg. Silberguß, 66 mm.

25. Ernst der Fromme von Sachsem und Elisabeth Sophie, ovale
Porträtmedaille o.J. Verg.Silberhohlguß,
45 x 35 mm.

26. Alexander Farnese, einseitige Porträtmedaille o.J. (1565),
Silberguß, 45 mm.

27. Moriz von Nassau-Oranien, Porträtmedaille 1624, Rückseite
Wappen. AR, 68 mm.

28. Wilhelm II. von Nassau-Oranien, Vermählung mit Maria von
England, 1641. AR, 72 mm.

29. Cosmos II. von Medici und Ehgn. Maria Magdalena, Porträtmedaille 1613. Silberguß, 89 mm.

30. Adolf von Burgund, Herr von Bevern, einseitige Porträtmedaill
1528. Silberguß, 54 mm.

31. Ferdinand Gonzaga-Guastalla, Porträtmedaille o.J., Rückseite
Aurora. Silberguß, 71 mm.

32. Kardinal Richelieu, Porträtmedaille 1630, Rückseite Triumph-
wagen. Silberguß, 77 mm.

33. Diana von Poitiers, Porträtmedaille o.J., Rückseite Allegorie
AR vergoldet, 53 mm.

34. Albrecht Dürer, Porträtmedaille 1526, Rückseite Wappen. Silberguß, 38 mm.

35. Lazarus Harstörfer, ovale Porträtmedaille o.J. (1588), Rückseite Wappen. Verg. Silberguß, 55 x 43 mm.

36. Andreas Imhoff, einseitige Porträtmedaille 1593. Silberguß,
53 mm.

37. Paul Paumgartner, Porträtmedaille 1592, Rückseite Wappen.
Silberhohlguß, 49 mm.

38. Porträtmedaillon eines unbekannten (niederländischen) Theolo
Einseitiger Silberguß, hohl, 97 mm.

39. Einnahme von Breda durch Friedrich Heinrich von Oranien 1637
AR, 70 mm.

40. Leo X., Klippe mit Text auf Luthers Opposition gegen den
Ablaßhandel. AR, 40 x 40 mm.

41. Albrecht von Brandenburg, Erzbischof von Mainz, Porträtmedaille 1537. Silberguß, 42 mm.

42. Prager Judenmedaille (Maximilian und Maria von Burgund).Gold

43Stück.

Verzeichnis
der dem Wiener Münzkabinett fehlenden Stücke.

1. Friedrich III. und Maximilian I., Medaille 1531 auf das Haus
   Österreich. Silber vergoldet, 48 mm.

2. Maximilian I., rautenförmige Klippe 1502, Brustbild-Schrift,
   Silberguß, 36 x 32 mm (gelötetes Dickstück.

3. Karl V., Porträtmedaille 1537, Rückseite Wappen. Silberguß.
   44 mm.

4. Karl V. und Ferdinand I., Medaille 1547 auf die Schlacht bei
   Mühlberg. Verg. Silberguß, 57 mm.

5. Ferdinand I., Schautaler 1529. Silber, 44 mm.

6. Ferdinand I., Max II. und Maria, Porträtmedaille 1563. Silberguß, 33 mm.

7. Maximilian II., einseitige Porträtmedaille o.J. (1575), Silberguß, 57 mm.

8. Maximilian II., Reitermedaille 1562, Rückseite Wappenadler.
   Silberguß, 52? mm.

9. Mathias II. und Anna, Krönung in Frankfurt 1612. Silber verg..,
   40 mm.

10. Margaretha von Österreich, Statthalter der Niederlande,
    Porträtmedaille o.J. (1567), Rückseite Allegorie
    AR, 58 mm.

11. Heinrich VIII. von England, Medaille auf seine kirchliche
    Suprematie. AR, 51 mm.

12. Eduard VI. von England, Medaille auf seine Krönung 1547.
    AR, 63 mm.

13.   Porträtmedaille o.J., Rückseite Allegorie.
    Silberguß, 49? x 41 mm. Dekorativer Henkel.

14. Elisabeth von England, ovale Porträtmedaille o.J., Rückseite
    Allegorie. AR, 55 x 47 mm.

15. Elisabeth von England, einseitige ovale Porträtmedaille o.J.,,
    AR, 44 x 38 mm.

16. Elisabeth von England, Porträt in durchbrochenem Blumenrahmem,
    Rückseite Phönix. Silberagraffe, 49 x 46 mm, ova

17. Jakob I. von England und Schottland, ovale Porträtmedaille o..J
    Rückseite Schiff auf dem Meer. AR, 57 x 47 mm..

18. Karl I. von England, Porträtmedaille o.J. (1630), Brustbild
    mit Halskrause, Rückseite Schiff. AR, 60 mm,
    gerahmt.

19. Karl I. von England und Schottland, wie vorher, aber Brustbild
    mit umgelegtem Kragen. AR, 60 mm.

20. Karl I. von England und Schottland, ovales Porträtmedaillon, in Laubrahmung, Rückseite graviertes Wappe AR, 48 x 41 mm.

21. Karl I. von England und Schottland, einseitiges Porträt in durchbrochener und gekrönter Rahmung (Agraffe oder Auflage). Silber.

22. Karl I. von England und Schottland, einseitiges Porträtstück (ausgeschnitten) aus Silber.

23. Katharina von Medici, Porträtmedaille o.J., Rückseite gebrochene Lanze. AR, 52 mm.

24.   "   und Heinrich III. von Frankreich, Schautaler o.J.; AR, 43 mm.

25. Heinrich III. von Frankreich und Ludovika von Lothringen, Porträtmedaille o.J. AR, 48 mm.

26. Heinrich IV. von Frankreich, Porträtmedaille o.J., Rückseite Pflügender. AR, 37 mm.

27. Ludwig XIII. und Maria von Medici, Porträtmedaille 1614. AR, 44 mm.

28. Ludwig XIII. von Frankreich, Porträtmedaille 1629, Rückseite Herkules. AR, 41 mm.

29. Ludwig XVI. von Frankreich, gravierte hohle Anhängekapsel, Silber, teilweise vergoldet, 42 mm.

30. Gustav II. Adolf von Schweden, Brustbild als Agraffe (ausgeschnitten). Gold emailliert.

31. Gustav II. Adolf von Schweden, Porträt-Jeton in Zierfassung mit Perlen, Rückseite Monogramm. Gold, 20 x 14 mm.

32. Philipp II. von Spanien und Maria von England, Porträtmedaille nach Jacopo da Trezzo. Silberguß, 40 mm, gravierter Text.

33. Philipp II. und Alexander Farnese, Porträtmedaille o.J. Verg. Silberguß, 39 mm.

34. Philipp II. von Spanien, Geusenpfennig 1566. Silberguß,30x24 m vierfacher Henkel.

35. Eberhard Ludwig und Johanna Elisabeth von Württemberg, Porträt medaille 1705, Rückseite Allegorie. AR, 60 mm.

36. Karl Theodor von der Pfalz, Genesung und Huldigung Mannheims, 1743 und 44. AR, 49 mm.

37. Georg der Bärtige von Sachsen, Schautaler 1527. AR verg.,44 mm

38. Wilhelm von Oranien und Charlotte von Bourbon, Porträtmedaille 1581. Silberguß, 39 mm.

39. Wilhelm von Oranien und Charlotte von Bourbon, Porträtmedaille 1580. Silberguß, 30 mm.

40. Philipp Wilhelm von Nassau-Oranien, Porträtmedaille 1607. Rückseite graviertes Wappen. Silberguß, 42 mm, gehenkelt.

41. Moriz von Nassau-Oranien, Porträtmedaille 1613 (?), Rückseite Wappen. AR, 55 x 45 mm, oval.

42. Graf Ernst von Mansfeld, Porträtmedaille o.J., Rückseite Wappen Silberguß, 49 x 42 mm, oval.

43. Herzog Alba, Porträtmedaille 1571, Rückseite Schrift. Silberguß 40) mm.

44. Alexander Fürst Chimay, Porträtmedaille o.J., Rückseite Adler. Silberguß, 42 mm.

45. Karl Philipp von Croy, Porträtmedaille 1600, Rückseite Wappen. Silberguß, 43 mm.

46. Prinz Eugen und Matlborough,, Medaille auf die Schlacht von Blenheim 1704. AR, 57 mm.

47. Graf Egmont, Porträtmedaillée 1568, Rückseite gravierter Text:. AR,, 66 mm, hohl.

48. Kardinal Granvella, ovale Pcorträtmedaille o.J., Rückseite Schiff. Silberguß, 34 x 28 mm.

49. Philipp Graf Horn, Porträtmeedaille 1568, Rückseite gravierterr Texxt. AR, 66 mm, hohl.

50. Graf Philipp Horn und Gemahllin, Porträtmedaille 1566. Silber-guß, 59 mm.

51. Graf Georg Ernst von Hohnenbberg, rautenförmige Porträtmedaillle, 15772, Rückseite gravierter Text. Verg. Silberguß, 35 x 29 mm.

52. Jean Louis de Lavalette, Porrträtmedaille 1607, Rückseite Allee-gorrie. Bronzeguß, 54 mm.

53. Johann Graf Tserclas von Tilly, Porträtmedaille 1628, Rückseiite Wappen. Silberguß, 40 mm.

54. Nicolas Brularé de Sillery, einseitiges ovales Porträtmedailllon o.JJ. AR, 65 x 52 mm.

55. Albrecht Dürer, postume Porträtmedaille 1561 nach Schwartz. Silberguß, 66 mm, gerahmt.

56. Getrennte Rückseite von Nr. 55 mit Erinnerungstext. AR, 69 mm, in Ätzung und Email ausgeführt.

57. Erzbischof Wilhelm Laud von Canterbury, Porträtmedaille o.J.,, Rückseite Allegorie. AR, 58 mm.

58. Jan Lautens, Porträtmedaillee 1598, Rückseite 3 Ringe. Silber--guß, 45 mm.

59. Martin Luther, Porträtmedaillle zum 200jährigen Reformations-jubbiläum 1717. AR, 44 mm.

60. Andreas Janus Ortho, ov les Porträtmedaillon in Zierrahmen,1669! Einseitiger Silberguß, 96 x 80 mm.

61. Johann Siemerl d.Ä. und Johaann Siemerl d.J., Porträtmedaille 1! Silberguß, 44 mm.

62. Georg Schrötl und Frau, dickke Porträtklippe 1582, Rückseite Wappen. Silber, 41 x 41 mm.

63. Margarethe Vogler, Taufmedaiille 1697, Vorderseite thronender Chrristus (wie Geburtstagsmedaille Karrls V.1550), Rückseite gravierter Texxt. Verg. Silberguß, 44 mm.

64. Einseitiges Porträtmedaillonn eines (niederländischen?) Arztess. Silberguuß, 95 mm, Blattruhmung.

65. Belagerung Amsterdams durch Wilhelm II, 1650, Rückseite gravierter Text. AR, 66 mm.

66. Bergen ob Zoom, Entsatz durcch Wilhelm von Oranien 1622. AR,6ll

67. Papst Pius V., Medaille annoo IV/1570, auf einen Sieg über diee Hugenotttten. AR, 41 mm.

68. Papst Sixtus V.. Medaille annno VI. Rückseite Rossebändiger vom Quirrinal. AR, 37 mm.

69. Anselm Franz von Ingelheim, Erzbischof von Mainz, Porträtmedda: 1695, Rückseite Wappen. AR, 49 mm.

70. Bistum Würzburg, Medaille 17706, Vorderseite Insignien, Rücksee: Stadtanssicht. AR, 76 mm.

71. Religiöses Medaillon Jakobsttraum von der Himmelsleiter. Verg:. Silberguuß, 75 mm.

72. Religiöse Medaille, Anbetungg der Könige und Opferung Isaaks. Verg. Siilburguß, 43 x 35 mm, oval, Schmuacl fassung..

73. Erzgebirgische religiöse Meddaille (1566?), Pilatus - Auferstee- hung Chrristi. Silberguß, 40 mm.

74. Benedictus-Pfennig 1677, Rücckseite Thomas von Aquino. AR, 24 x 20mm, oval.

75. Allegorische Medaille auf diie Vergänglichkeit, junges Weib -- ! Ovaler Silberguß, 59 x 48 mm.

76. Allegorische Medaille 1626, Vorderseite Zimon und Tochter, Rückseitte Störche über Dresden. AR, 45 mm

77. Prager Judenmedaille, Rudolif von Habsburg und seine Tochter Clementiia von Neapel. Gold, 56 mm.

78. Ferdinand und Isabella von Spanien, 20 Excelentes.

79. Ferdinand III., Breslauer Haalbdukat 1641, gehenkelt.

80. Bistum Münster, Heinrich II.. Graf von Mörs, Goldgulden (vor 1

81. Friedrich von Braunschweig-Lüneburg, Löser 1647 zu 3 Taler, AR, 80 mm.

82. Breda, Belagerungsnotklippe: 1625 zu 60 Sols. AR,32 x 32 mm.

83. Newark, rautenförmige Notkliippe 1646. AR, 39 x 34 mm.

84. Frauenkloster Rotenmünster :in Schwaben, Typar aus dem 15.Jahhr hundert; (Falsum?). AR, 42 mm.

V e r z e i c h n i s
der nicht ~~designiierten~~ Stücke.
erbeteiuuen

1. Karl V., Schautaler o.J., Brrustbild - Wappen. AR, 45 mm.

2. Karl V., Geburtstagsmedaillee 1500/1550. Silberguß, 46 mm.

3. Ferdinand I., Porträtjeton oo.J. Rückseite Wappen. AR, 29 mm..

4. Maximilian II., Porträtmedaiille o.J.; Rückseite Merkur, Silberguß, 67 mm.

5. Mathias II. als Erhzerzog, PPorträtmedaille 1579, Rückseite Perseus und Andromeda. Silberguß, 35 mm.

6. Josef I., Frankfurter Königskrönung 1690. AR, 48 mm.

7. Infantin Isabella Eugenia voon Spanien, Regentin der Niederlannde Porträtmedaille ö.J., Rückseite Fama. Silberguß, 41 mm.

8. Don Juan d'Austria, Porträtmedaille 1573, Rückseite Allegoriee auf die Eroberung von Tunis. Silberguß, 41 mm.

9. Karl I. von England, Porträtmedaille o.J., Rückseite Schiff. AR, 57 mm.

10. Karl I. von England, Jeton 11633 auf seine Krönung. AR, 28 mm..

11. Karl II. von England, Medaillle auf den Seekrieg mit Holland, AR, 52 mm.

12. Karl II. von England, Krönungsjeton 1661. AR, 30 mm.

13. Heinrich IV. von Frankreich,, Porträtmedaille 1598, Rückseite Embleme.. Silberguß, 43 mm.

14. Anna von Österreich und Ludwig XIV., Grundsteinlegung von Val de Grâce 1638. Silberguß, 96 mm.

15. Gustav II. Adolf von Schwedesn, Porträtmedaille 1631, Rückseitte der Könilg als Triumphator. AR, 57 mm.

16. Gustav II. Adolf von Schwedesn, Medaille wie vorher.

17. Gustav II. Adolf von Schwedesn, ovaler Porträtjeton o.J. auf die Überrfahrt nach Deutschland. AR, 33 x 3C

18. Mariaol. und Peter III. von lPortugal, Errichtung der Kirche zum hl. lHerz Jesu in Lissabon, 1779. AR, 51 mm.

19. Johann III. Sobiesky von Pollen, Porträtmedaille o.J., Rückseite Landschaift. AR, 49 mm.

20. Peter der Große von Rußland,, auf die Schlacht bei Poltawa 1709. AR, 65 mm.

21. Friedrich der Weise von Sachsen, Schautaler 1522. AR, 43 mm.

22. Johann Friedrich von Sachsen, Erzgebirger Porträtmedaille 15773, Rückseitce Reiterkampf. Verg. Silberguß,500mm

23. Philipp Reinhart Graf von Hanau, Vermählung mit Charlotte .... Sachsen-Saalfeld. AR, 53mm..

24. Ankunft der englischen Prinzessin Maria in Holland zur Vermählung mit Wilhelm von Nassau-Oranien.
AR, 73 mm.

25. Ippolita Gonzaga, Porträtmedaille o.J., Rückseite Aurora.
Silberguß, 69 mm.

26. Alexander Farnese von Parma, Porträtmedaille 1585, Rückseite
Allegorie, Silberguß, 46 mm.

27. Admiral Andrea Doria von Genua, Porträtmedaille o.J., Rücksei
Schiff. Silberguß, 40 mm.

28. Kardinal Granvella, Porträtmedaille o.J., Rückseite mythologi
sche Seeschlacht. Silberguß, 52 mm.

29. Kardinal Granvella, ähnliche Porträtmedaille mit Brustbild vo
rechts und datiert 1550. Silberguß, 59 mm

30. Kardinal Granvella, Porträtmedaille o.J., Rückseite Granvella
übergibt dem Don Juan d'Austria die Fahne
zum Türkenkrieg. Silberguß, 43 mm.

31. Viglius de Zuichem, Porträtmedaille 1568, Rückseite Tisch mit
Geräten. Silberguß, 53 mm.

32. Karl Borromäus, Porträtmedaille o.J.Rückseite Altar mit Lamm
Silberguß, 51 mm.

33. Prinzessin Ludovika Karoline Radziwill, Porträtmedaille 1675,
mit Allegorie auf den Tod ihrer Eltern.
AR, 42 mm.

34. Johann Banner, schwedischer Feldherr, Porträtmedaille o.J.
Rückseite Allegorie. AR, 45 mm.

35. Paul Beresteyn, und Frau, Medaille zur goldenen Hochzeit 1624
AR, 54 mm.

36. Jan Hus, Guß nach der erzgebirgischen Prägemedaille. Silber
vergoldet, 42 mm.

37. Philipp Melanchton, Porträtmedaille 1543, Rückseite Schrift.
Silberguß, 38 mm.

38. Abraham Ortelius, Porträtmedaille 1578, Rückseite Embleme,
Silberguß, 37 mm.

39. S.M.Freiherr von Rothschild, Porträtmedaille zum 70. Geburts
1844. AR, 49 mm.

40. Medaille auf das neue Rathaus in Amsterdam 1655. AR, 70 mm.

41. Papst Hadrian VI., einseitige Porträtmedaille o.J. Silberguß
82 mm.

42. Papst Gregor XIII., Medaille 1575 auf die Öffnung der Porta
Sancta. AR, 39 mm.

43. Papst Innocenz X., Medaille auf die Öffnung der Porta Sancta
1650. AR, 38 mm.

44. Papst Clemens X., Medaille auf die Öffnung der Porta Sancta
1675. AR, 33 mm.

45. Papst Alexander VIII., Porträtmedaille o.J., Rückseite hl.
Laurentius Justinianus. AR, 37 mm.

46. Daniel Brendl,von Homburg, Erzbischof von Mainz, Porträtmedaille o.J., Rückseite Wappen, ovaler
Silberguß, 32 x 29 mm.

47. Erzbistum Salzburg, Sedisvakanzmedaille 1772. AR, 56 mm.

48. Bistum Regensburg, Sedisvakaanzmedaille 1763, AR, 56 mm.
49. Prager Judenmedaille, Konstaantin der Große. Gold 49 mm.
50. Antipäpstliche Spottmedailles. Silberguß, 36 mm.
51. Anhänger einer St. Michaels Erzbruderschaft. AR, 32 x 28 mm, ooval
       teilweisse emailliert.
52. Kaiser Ludwig IV. der Bayer,, ein Chaise d'or o.J.
53. Johann Georg II. von Sachsen, Vikariatsdukat 1657.
54. August von Sachsen, Dresdeneer Taler 1566.
55. Graf Philipp Ernst von Mansffeld, Taler 1625.
56. Erzbistum Mainz, Johann II. Höchster Goldgulden (um 1400).
57. Karl VI. von Frankreich, Ecu1 d'or (um 1400).
58. Christian IV. von Dänemark, 1Dukat 1645.
59. Sigismund August von Polen, 1Nottaler 1564.
60. Ercole I. von Ferrara-Modena, Testone (um 1500).
61. Münster, Notklippe 1660. AR,, 29 x 31 mm.
62. Frankfurt, Schautaler 1696. AR, 51 mm.

Beilage 8.

~~Herrn Direktor Posse,~~

Münze aus Sammlung Hauser (Zdaril), für das Führer-Museum, anzukaufen.

1. Persien, Dareikos.	RM	75
2. Makedonien, Philipp II. Goldsstater	"	50
3./4. Makedonien, Alexander d.GGr.,Goldstater (2 Varianten)		100
5. Rom, Nero Aureus (Jupiter CCustos)	"	40
6. Römisch-deutsches Reich, Golldabschlag vom Dreikaiser-taler zu 10 Dukaten (Max I., Karl V., Ferdinand-Mathias) Prag o.J. (um 1612))	"	400
7. Ferdinand II., Goldabschlag des Talers zu 10 Dukaten Prag 1637	"	350
8. Ferdinand III., Goldabschlagg des Talers zu 10 Dukaten Wien 1656	"	350
9. " Goldabschlagg des Talers zu 6½ Du-katen, St. VVeit (Kärnten) 1638	"	200
10. Leopold I., Goldabschlag dess Talers zu 10 Dukaten, Nagybanya	"	35
11. " Goldabschlag vomm Halbtaler zu 6 Dukaten, Graz 1694	"	30
12. Franz I., Goldabschlag vom DDukaton zu 16 Dukaten, Antwerpen 1751	"	70
13. Maria Theresia, Goldabschlagg vom Taler zu 10 Dukaten, Wien 1754	"	35
14. Josef II., Souverain d'or, WWien 1786	"	100
15. Franz II., Vier-Dukaten, Wiezn 1806	"	15
16. Ferdinand I., Vier-Dukaten, Wien 1843	"	15
17. Tirol, Erzherzog Sigismund, Goldabschlag vom Guldiner (7 Dukaten) Hall 1486	"	40

Medaillen..

18. Maximilian I., Goldabschlag zu 4 Dukaten vom Halb-taler (Schausstück) 1518	"	30
19. Ferdinand I.- Max II. und Maaria, Goldmedaille 1563/77	"	30
20. Erzherzog Mathias, Einnahme von Gran 1601/1595, Gold-medaille von M S	"	50
21. Josef I., Wahlspruchmedailles von Philipp Becker	"	3
22. Karl VI., Wahlspruchmedailles von Ph. Becker	"	7
23. Maria Theresia, Wahlspruchmeedaille von Giov. Toda	"	3
24. Josef II., Medaille auf seinae Geburt, 1741, von D. Becker	"	4
25. Ferdinand I., Wahlspruchmedaaille von J.D.Boehm	"	5
26. Franz Josef I. und Elisabeth, Vermählung 1854, Gold-medaille von Konrad Lange	"	7

27. Erzherzog Leopold und Claudia von Tirol, Vermäh-
    lungsmedaille (5 Dukaten)   RM 200.·

...

Erzbistum Salzburg.

28. Leonhard von Keutschach, Goldabschlag zu 4 Du-
    katen vom Vierteltaler, in Klippen-
    form 1513   " 200.

29. Mathäus Lang von Wellenburg, Doppeldukatenklippe
    auf den Bürgeraufstand 1523   " 100.

30. Wolf Dietrich von Raitenau, Goldabschlag vom
    Turmschautaler 1594, zu 10 Dukaten   " 400

31. Marcus Sitticus von Hohenems, Bildnisschaumünze 1615 "150

32. Paris von Lodron, Goldabschlag vom Domweih-Taler
    zu 16 Dukaten, 1628   " 500

33. Franz Anton von Harrach, Wahlspruchmedaille von
    Ph. Müller 1711   " 300

34. Leopold von Firmian, Wahlspruchmedaille 1727 von
    Franz Matzenkopf   " 25C

35. Hieronymus von Colloredo, Medaille auf seine
    Wahl 1772 von F. Matzenkopf   " 20C

                                                       ~~RM 11.29.~~

Städte.

36. Nürnberg, 6 Dukaten 1698   " 25

37. Regensburg (Josef II.), 5 Dukaten o.J.   " 25

38. Hildesheim, Wappenverleihung durch Karl V. 1528   " 8

39. Hamburg, Bismarck-Medaille zz.80.Geburtstag
    (Georgstaller)   " 2C

                                        RM 12 0.

DER GENERALKULTURREFERENT

DES

GAULEITERS VON NIEDERSCHLESIEN

BRESLAU 2, den 26.September 1942.
Landeshaus
Fernruf Sammel-Nr. 52131

Dr.Fu.-M./Go.

Herrn

Direktor Dr. P o s s e
Staatliche Gemäldegalerie

D r e s d e n
=============
Zwinger.

Sehr verehrter Herr Direktor!

Unter Bezugnahme auf meinen Besuch am Montag, den 21.9.
fixiere ich wunschgemäss kurz noch einmal schriftlich die drei von
mir besprochenen Punkte:

1.) <u>Sichergestellte Kunstwerke im Generalgouver-
nement.</u>

In dieser Angelegenheit haben schon verschiedentlich Ver-
handlungen sowohl zwischen Gauleiter Hanke und dem Oberbürgermei-
ster der Stadt Breslau einerseits und dem Reichsminister Dr.Lammers
andererseits stattgefunden. Das damalige Ergebnis war, dass unter
den nicht in der Führerauswahl befindlichen Kunstschätzen eine Rei-
he von Werken sich befinden, die zum Teil schlesischen Ursprungs
sind, zum Teil in unmittelbarer Beziehung zu Schlesien und seiner
Geschichte stehen. Museumsdirektor Dr.Barthel in Breslau hatte sei-
nerzeit eine Aufstellung eingereicht, die sich auch bei den dorti-
gen Akten befindet, aus der hervorgeht, welche Werke für uns beson-
deres Interesse haben. An sich sollen die gesamten sichergestellten
Kunstschätze ausserhalb der Führerauswahl nach Kriegsende nach dem
Wunsch des Führers der Stadt Königsberg zugewiesen werden, doch ist
es denkbar, dass über das eine oder andere Stück noch anderweitig
verfügt werden könnte. Zweck meiner Vorsprache war der, zu wissen,
dass bei einer evtl. früheren und anderweitigen Aufteilung der in

Frage kommenden Kunstwerke der Gau Niederschlesien bezw. die
Gauhauptstadt Breslau auf Grund ihrer berechtigten Interessen
bevorzugt berücksichtigt werden.

2.) Sammlung Manheimer.

Hierfür gilt im allgemeinen das gleiche wie zu
Punkt 1 mit dem Unterschied, dass nach dem derzeitigen Stand
der Dinge die Aufteilung und Zuweisung der Sammlung ausserhalb
der Führerauswahl an die Stadt Linz erfolgen sollen. Auch hier
bitte ich im Auftrage des Gauleiters zu gegebener Zeit um bevor-
zugte Berücksichtigung unserer niederschlesischen Interessen.

3.) Schlackenwerther Handschrift.

Mit dieser Schlackenwerther Hedwigslegende hat es
folgende Bewandnis:

Die lateinische Legende umfasst die Vita maior, die
Vita minor und die Genealogia. Sie ist i.J.1300 geschrieben.

Die Legenda maior und minor liess Ludwig I., 1352-
1398 Herzog von Schlesien und Liegnitz, i.J.1353 foris ciritatem
Lubyn, im Südosten von Lüben im Schles., wo er 1349 eine der Hedwig geweihte Burgkapelle erbaut hatte, abschreiben. Der Schreiber
nennt sich Nicolaus Pruzie (aus Preussen). Er wird auch der Schöp-
fer der Illustrationen (1 ganzseitige und 60 halbseitige) sein,
die sich auf die Tatarenschlacht und das Leben Hedwigs beziehen.
Sie sind zart entworfen, die Innenflächen leicht ausgetuscht, der
Gesichtsausdruck der wenig kraftvollen Gestalten ist ohne Abwechs-
lung, die Perspektive fehlerhaft. Trotzdem sind diese Miniaturen
höchst wertvoll, nicht als Kunstwerke, aber für die Kulturgeschichte. Die Hs.enthält Bl.202 von etwas jüngerer Hand eine Zusammen-
fassung der Legende in Briefform mit der Schlusschrift von unge-
übter Hand: Hanc epistolam compilavit dominus Nycolaus de Posemaw
(= Nicol.Henrici) prothonotarius Reverendi in Christo patris domini